Social Change
Globalization from the Stone Age to the Present

Christopher Chase-Dunn
Bruce Lerro

Paradigm Publishers
Boulder • London

Published in the United States by Paradigm Publishers, 5589 Arapahoe Avenue, Boulder, Colorado 80303 USA.

Paradigm Publishers is the trade name of Birkenkamp & Company, LLC, Dean Birkenkamp, President and Publisher.

Library of Congress Cataloging-in-Publication Data

Chase-Dunn, Christopher K.
Social change : globalization from the stone age to the present / Christopher Chase-Dunn and Bruce Lerro.
pages cm
Includes bibliographical references and index.
ISBN 978-1-61205-328-8 (pbk. : alk. paper)
1. Social history. 2. Civilization—History. 3. Social change. 4. Social evolution.
I. Lerro, Bruce, 1948– II. Title.
HN13.C43 2013
306.09—dc23

2013011372

Printed and bound in the United States of America on acid-free paper that meets the standards of the American National Standard for Permanence of Paper for Printed Library Materials.

18 17 16 15 14   5 4 3 2 1

We would like to dedicate this book to the emerging generation of world citizens who will rise to solve the problems humanity has created for itself in the twenty-first century.

Brief Contents

Contents

List of Figures and Tables

Figures

Tables

Preface

The purpose of this book is to tell a story and to provide a framework for understanding this story and its implications for the human future. The story is about how the people of the earth have gone from living in small nomadic bands to the urbanized global political economy of the present over the past 12,000 years. The framework is the social geography of human settlements and interaction networks. By tracing the growth of settlement systems and interaction networks we can explain the processes of institutional transformation—the development of technology, information systems, moral orders, markets, and political structures—that have made it possible for us to live in large and complex societies.

The story and the framework make it possible for us to see the relevance of world history in our own everyday lives and to respond intelligently to the challenges that shape the world in which we live. The story we tell is based on the knowledge of the human past that has been produced by historians and social scientists (sociologists, ethnographers, archaeologists, political scientists, geographers, psychologists, and economists). The theoretical framework is based on the comparative world-systems perspective, a macrosociological approach to world history that examines groups of interacting societies rather than individual societies as if they were in isolation from other societies.

Social change is usually understood to be mainly a matter of recent trends. New technologies and less expensive transportation and communications make it possible for people to interact easily and frequently with distant others. Migrants can easily stay in contact with the communities they have left. Air transportation makes it possible for people in the Northern Hemisphere to eat fresh fruit in the winter that has been grown in the summer months of the Southern Hemisphere. And news events are often portrayed as dramatizing the existence of social change. The tragedies of September 11, 2001, are claimed by many commentators to have "changed everything." But trends and recent events need to be understood in their world-historical context if we are to know their implications for action. Technology, transportation, and communication costs have been changing for a very long time, and angry young men have been attacking symbols of power for thousands of years. The framework presented in this book allows us to see the trends and events of the recent past in terms of the patterns of social change that have been occurring for decades, centuries, and millennia.

Globalization Past and "Presentism"

Globalization is a set of processes that have affected everyone in the contemporary world. The processes of global integration and the political ideologies that have been widely trumpeted as interpretations of this integration have changed the lives of everyone in recent decades. But the rapid increase of global economic integration since World War II is only the most recent wave of the expansion of international trade and foreign investment. In the last half of the nineteenth century there was a rapid and huge expansion of international trade and investment that was similar in many respects to the wave that occurred after World War II. The nineteenth-century wave was followed by a massive backlash against the kind of global integration that had occurred—a backlash that involved the Bolshevik Revolution in Russia, World War I, the Great Depression of the 1930s, and World War II. The lessons we can learn from studying the earlier waves of global integration and disintegration are entirely relevant for understanding the problems of the twenty-first century.

The rapid technological changes of recent decades have contributed to an extreme "presentism" in which the past is seen as largely irrelevant to the present because things seem to have changed so much. The popular expression "It's history" means that something is of no importance and can be forgotten. We contend that this "presentism" is a kind of fog that prevents people from seeing the important continuities from the past that powerfully exist in the present. Another barrier to understanding is the focus of much popular and expert culture on single societies, as opposed to seeing national societies as subsystems in a larger world-system of societies. Presentism and the focus on single societies prevent us from seeing the cyclical patterns of world history that have huge implications for the human future. It is only systematic comparisons with the past and a focus on the whole world-system that allow us to know what is truly unique in the present. The assumption that everything that is important has changed is a smoke screen that must be cleared away.

This book combines our concern to provide students with the conceptual tools they will need to make intelligent decisions as world citizens with an appreciation of the human past in its own terms and for its own sake. The true understanding of the struggles of our ancestors is its own reward, as well as the raw material that can make it possible for us to do good in the future.

If we speed the camera up and use a perspective on time that comes from studying rocks (a geological time perspective), the changes in human societies over the past 12,000 years can be understood as constituting a single complicated earth-wide event of spiraling globalization. This complex event was unevenly distributed in space and time. The rise of social complexity, the increases in the size of politically organized groups (polities), the rises in degree of social inequality (the height of hierarchy), and the growing spatial scale and intensity of interaction networks were not smooth upward trends. But the overall process of social evolution, though uneven in time and space, can be thought of as a spiral of increasing complexity, hierarchy, and size as local systems became integrated into larger regional systems, which then were incorporated into a single global system. This image of the bumpy and fuzzy spiral, a combination of trends and cycles, can represent the main outcomes of human sociocultural evolution.

Our very identities, as well as our activities, are shaped by the actions and inventions of humans who lived in the past. The patterns and causal processes by which people have created institutions and societies continue to operate in the present and will continue in the future. It is important for each of us to understand how social change works so that we may comprehend our own history and participate intelligently in shaping the human future.

Our perspective does not treat nation-states or societies as separate entities whose fate is determined by what goes on within their national borders. Both the internal features of societies and the nexus of connections among societies evolve. Today the whole world is present as a force impacting the policies and collective activities of any single national state. Intersocial connections have always constrained what any society in history could or could not do.

Social change is the reorganization of relationships among individuals and groups of people. It is a process that shapes the way we live. It influences who we are and the possibilities for what we do as individuals and what we can accomplish when we work together with others.

For instance, let us take an example of keeping a calendar and a date book. In the 1960s and 1970s most teens and young adults did not carry a calendar or date book. Pocket calendars were used by businesspeople or professionals. But by the 1980s and 1990s many more young people began to carry date books, not just to use at work but to organize their lives. Why is this? If we interpreted these changes psychologically or culturally we might say that teenagers today are more organized and that people in the sixties were more dreamers and less capable of being practical. We think differently.

The average standard of living in the United States has been declining since the 1970s. In part, in order to continue to derive a profit, the pace of life has increased. People work at least ten more hours each week than they did thirty years ago, while the cost of living has increased. Services that used to be provided have been cut back. People have to use their leisure time to run errands. We think the reason young people carry date books today is so they can keep up with a declining economy and an increased pace of life. This is just one example of how a comparative world-systems analysis can make sense of the relationship between world history and individual life.

Paradoxically, in order to understand why things change in the way that they do, we need to see how existing relationships and social structures are reproduced, how they are stabilized, and how social order is accomplished. Change cannot be studied without also studying the sources of continuity. Social change is only partly random or accidental. A great deal of it is patterned and caused by powerful processes (biological, social, and cultural) that structure the relationships between people and the natural environment.

Patterns of Social Change

It is fashionable to notice that human societies are complex systems that share certain features with other natural systems that are also complex. The patterns of complex systems are the result of many small events and processes that come together and are interconnected. But the main point of this book is to show how the patterns of social change can be comprehended by focusing on a few important processes—the most powerful factors that structure human institutions and populations.

We think that social change is neither random nor designed. It would be foolhardy to deny the significant element of accident and randomness in human social change, but it would likewise be wrong to see human events as completely chaotic and accidental. It would also be a mistake to portray human history as the realization of some inherent purpose or intention or as the outcome of rationality or intelligence that makes us continually improve. The idea of progress is often a glib assumption or a crude justification for the exploitation and domination of some people by others. The main purpose of this book is to explain how social change works. We will examine the ways in which social change has produced human history and the contemporary social world. In the last chapter we will explain our position on the notion of progress and take a stand on what we see as good and what we see as bad.

Understanding social change in the past may also help us create a more humane and sustainable future world society—one that is democratic, peaceful, fair, and ecologically sustainable. Many of the dynamics of the past repeat themselves in the present. Second, comprehending the past of human history exposes the relativity of our institutions—institutions we might otherwise take as eternal. At the same time, understanding world history gives us a greater appreciation for the uniqueness of the communication, transportation, and medical systems that are truly specific to our historical period. This gives us a sense that some processes are trans-generational and transnational and that others are novel and located primarily in a particular pocket of the world.

Understanding all types of human societies is important because it gives us a broad and deep perspective on our own society and ourselves. The fact that people have lived in very different kinds of societies shows how adaptable humanity is and how human nature is capable of much more than we commonly assume. Each society legitimates its institutions and tries to control individuals by constructing a vision of human nature that emphasizes some features and excludes others. Knowledge of very different kinds of societies frees us by showing that human nature is able to take on a wide variety of aspects and vastly different types of selves playing very different roles depending on the social situation and its demands.

Comprehending long-term processes of social evolution helps us see that many of the features of modern societies that we take for granted as "natural" are in fact human inventions. Many of the justifications of existing institutions are based on claims about naturalness, inevitability, or necessity. Thus, it is useful to be able to evaluate these claims with true knowledge of the human past and of the great variation that has existed in human societies. The following are two examples.

The Information Age is not the sole product of the twentieth century. Technological change, such an important aspect of our contemporary world, began (slowly) about 2 million years ago when hominids commenced to fashion stone tools. The Information Age began in earnest when people started living inside their languages and using social abstractions such as "ancestor" and "cousin" to order their lives. Human culture is a kind of virtual reality in which consciousness is constructed out of language and socially produced images. Culture mediates our relationship with nature and with one another, so that the world in which we live is actually built out of symbols and socially created information.

The original Information Age was one in which small groups of people shared symbolic systems. However, language also made it possible for people to pass information from group to group about the availability of food, and so small bands of nomadic foragers formed networks with other such groups. Human consciousness was constructed around socially shared language, and each person lived in a virtual reality that he or she also participated in shaping and in passing to the young. Storytelling and oral histories constructed the cocoon of meaning within which individuals and groups lived their lives. The costs of communication and transportation over great distances have greatly decreased, and we now live in a global network of instantaneous information flows. But the Information Age, in the sense of humans constructing a world out of collectively defined and shared words and images, is as old as language and kinship.

While we take the sedentary life as normal and see nomadic peoples as unusual, until as recently as 12,000 years ago, all the people of the earth were nomadic for a long period of each year. The hunter-gatherers of the ancient Eastern Mediterranean (whom archaeologists call the Natufians) invented village living—the precursor of city living. This occurred about 10,000 BCE.[1] These first sedentary peoples probably were the inventors of fixed territorial boundaries and collective property, institutions that are fundamental (in their contemporary forms) to the operation of today's global political economy.

The terms "social change" and "sociocultural evolution" are largely synonymous, though there are some important differences. Both involve changes in the behavior of people. Social change traditionally includes phenomena such as fads, fashion cycles, architectural and literary styles, the diffusion of cultural traits and innovations, social movements, and revolutions. While these phenomena are often involved, sociocultural evolution refers to the fundamental reorganization of institutional structures such as the economy and the polity, and the ways in which resources are acquired, produced, distributed, and accumulated. Social change refers to any change in social processes or the behavior of people, while sociocultural evolution refers to certain kinds of directional changes in the structures of societies and intersocietal systems. This book will mainly examine those forms of social change that are relevant for understanding sociocultural evolution.

But what do we need to know about specific historical events and particular people? How are they connected to sociocultural evolution? In addition to telling the big story in structural terms, we will occasionally peek into the lives of people who contributed to social evolution or whose efforts show why some systems were not ready for structural change. These case studies can help us see how particular people, events, and places are related to the general patterns of social change and evolution. Historians are fond of pointing to the fortuitous or accidental complications of events. The idea of **conjuncture** refers to an unlikely coming together of factors that make social change possible.

---

[1] World historians now use a way of designating time that is slightly less Eurocentric than the traditional BC and AD. In this text "BCE" means "before the Common Era" and "CE" means "of the Common Era."

Anthropologist Marshall Sahlins (1985) has employed the notion of the *structure of the conjuncture*—how cultural institutions of different groups collide in historical events and create new outcomes. The case studies presented here use the structure of the conjuncture to show how particular events led (or in some cases did not lead) to the reorganization of institutions.

Sociocultural evolution is neither smooth, inevitable, nor housed in a single location. The reorganization of institutions occurred in uneven bursts that were usually followed by declines or collapses. They leapfrogged across wide spaces. The leading edge of the development of new institutions moved. Regions that were once the most complex were later eclipsed by other regions. In many places there were devolutions and evolutionary blind alleys that led back to smaller scale and simpler social structures.

On the other hand, parallel evolution (the development of similar institutions in different places) transpired in regions that were either unconnected with one another or only very weakly connected. This shows that some parts of social evolution have a deep structure that shows itself across social spaces. But *seen as a whole*, the overall pattern was one of increasing complexity, size, hierarchy, and spatial scale. This book examines these changes in more or less chronological order, except that the New World societies attained state formation much later than the Old World societies. Thus comparisons between ancient Mexico (Mesoamerica) and ancient Western Asia (Mesopotamia) require a chronological adjustment. This exception aside, chronology and complexity proceeded in the same order.

Lastly, we will examine the macro-micro links between large social structures and the microprocesses of individuals. How is society imported into the psychology of individuals? How are the results of this importation fed back into the largest social structures? While sociologists describe this process as "socialization," they mostly discuss it as it occurs within a single type of society at a given point in time. We will discuss how socialization occurs over time. For example, we will examine how there is a basic movement in the concept of the self from a **collectivist self** to an individualist self as a result of changes in technology, economics, and politics. We will also study how the human reasoning processes evolved over time as a result of the invention of coined money, the alphabet, the printing press, and the computer.

Organization of this Text

Part I provides a conceptual framework for the rest of the story. Chapter 1 explains how sociocultural evolution is different from biological evolution and discusses the nature of institutional structures and the important differences between normative, coercive, and market-like forms of social integration. It provides an overview of different theoretical approaches to social evolution, its methods, and types of evidence.

Chapter 2 introduces the comparative world-systems perspective used in this book. This includes the nature of world-systems, the definition of polities, and the different types of networks that exist within systems and how systems expand and contract. In addition we will examine the leading edges of change within world-systems and the forces that drive societies to change.

Chapter 3 discusses how biological evolution produced a form of life, the human species, that was capable of engaging in sociocultural evolution.

Chapter 4 introduces the micro-level of sociological analysis—the basic ingredients in building a social self. These include constructing a sense of subjectivity and objectivity as well as an examination of the process of abstraction and its social and historical nature.

Part II is about stateless world-systems. States are institutional inventions. Many human societies and many whole world-systems have existed in which there were no states. Indeed, up until about 5,000 years ago there were no states on the earth. Chapter 5 describes the peopling of the earth and examines world-systems composed solely of nomadic foragers. We discuss the emergence of language and culture, the gender division of labor, adaptation to the disappearance of large game animals (megafauna), and the emergence of socially structured territoriality. The chapter also examines the origins of sedentary living, the reduction of seasonal migration patterns, and the spending of more time in settled hamlets and villages. These were small scale and very egalitarian societies of hunter-gatherers (foragers). There were many different kinds of foraging societies, but we will examine their attributes in the context of our knowledge of larger-scale societies. We consider the ways in which equality was institutionally structured and how people resisted the emergence of hierarchy. We will make some educated guesses about the nature of the "**horizontal collectivist self**" that went with these social institutions as well as the nature of "concrete abstraction."

Chapter 6 describes world-systems in which some of the societies were engaged in simple farming—horticulture. It discusses the variable nature of farmer-forager interactions and the emergence of big-man political organization in which inequalities within societies were increasing. The relationship between aggressive masculinity and warfare is discussed, as are the problems of population pressure, depletion of natural resources, and conflict. A chapter available on the website for this textbook discusses the similarities and differences among Native American societies in different regions of North America before the emergence of complex chiefdoms. Chapter 7 focuses on systems of complex chiefdoms, much larger and more hierarchical societies in which a class of chiefs ruled over a class of commoners. The problems of organizing hierarchy in the face of resistance are discussed with a consideration of human sacrifice, sacred chiefs, and elite brother-sister marriage. The nature of intersocietal relations in chiefdom-based world-systems is described, as are the processes of rise and fall (centralization and decentralization) and the phenomenon of semiperipheral marcher chiefdoms that attacked older core chiefdoms to construct larger polities. We examine prestige goods systems in which chiefs monopolized luxury imports in order to control the labor of commoners. The rise of patriarchy and the control of marriage by elites are also considered.

Part III examines world-systems that are far more similar to our own in that states became the fundamental organizations that produced order. Chapter 8 explains the emergence of the first cities and states in systems in which there were none, as well as the phenomenon of secondary state formation—the formation of a state structure in a society that already interacts with other states. The focus is on the nature of early states and interstate systems, as well as the role of theocracy in the original emergence of states. The interaction between the temple and the palace (religious and political-military leaders) is an interesting aspect that reveals the nature of early state societies. We will have a close look at Mesopotamia, the locus of the earliest cities and states, but will also consider other regions in which parallel evolution led to the emergence of pristine states: Egypt, Indus River valley (Pakistan), China, Mesoamerica, and the Andes. These early states were the first to develop irrigated agriculture, systems of writing, mass production industries, and codified law. The story is one of the earliest instances of empire formation—the Akkadian Empire of Sargon of Agade. We will examine the nature of core/periphery relations in early state systems, the spread of states and agriculture, the earliest forms of commercialization, and the earliest semiperipheral capitalist city-states.

At the micro-level we will discuss the emergence of a "**vertical collectivist self**" and how this type of self was better suited to the class relationships of early states. Chapter 9 discusses how the impact of writing systems, both picture writing and the alphabet, affected people's reasoning processes. In addition, the invention of coined money forced people, at least the middle and upper classes, to reason more abstractly.

Chapter 10 surveys the continuing spread of states and the formation of the early conquest empires. Important topics are the expansion of trade networks, the commercialization of production and trade, and the rise of ever-larger empires by means of semiperipheral marcher state conquest. It was the merger of the Mesopotamian and Egyptian world-systems that produced the beginning of the Central System that eventually engulfed all others to form the contemporary global political economy. Chapter 11 compares the Central System with other large systems of empires, capitalist city-states, and peripheral peoples in Afroeurasia and the Americas and the emergence of a multicore Afroeurasian system with synchronous processes of empire expansion and city growth and decline. The important role of the steppe nomads of Central Asia in the formation of the Central System is discussed.

Part IV continues the story of the long rise of capitalism from the beginnings of the invention of money and commodities to the contemporary global capitalist political economy. Chapter 12 casts the rise of European **hegemony** in the context of the larger Afroeurasian system. Europe had long been a peripheral area to the more developed civilizations of the Near East (Western Asia). European hegemony and the transformation to a fully capitalist system could not have occurred without the prior development of the institutions of capitalism and the networks of commodified trade in the larger system. Indeed, Europe was another instance of semiperipheral upward mobility, but this time of a whole region. We will consider the question of European uniqueness and the "rise of the West" from a humanocentric perspective and as an instance of continuing sociocultural evolution.

How did the rise of capitalism affect people's psychology? While the "vertical" individualist self seems to have had its roots in the Late Iron Age (after 600 BCE), this form of identity really came into its own with the development of capitalism in Europe. The emergence of a completely secular science and the invention of the printing press paved the way for a still higher level of abstract thinking for those classes who worked in the sciences and were able to buy books and were taught how to read and write.

Chapter 13 focuses on the modern world-system in which we now live. Its basic structures and processes are described, and an overview of its structural history is provided. The developmental trends and cyclical processes of the modern system are explained. The hegemonies of the Dutch, the British, and the United States are compared, and both the British and American stories are told in more detail. The incorporation of the remaining regions of the earth by European expansion is described, as is the changing nature of core/periphery relations in the modern world-system.

Chapter 14 examines the emergence of institutional leadership by the Dutch Republic in the seventeenth century in some detail as the key development that led to a fully developed capitalism in Europe. The Dutch Republic was not the first capitalist state, but it was the first capitalist state that was not a city-state. It was the emergence of a strongly capitalist political economy and associated military technology that allowed Europe to become hegemonic over the other core and peripheral areas of the world-system, though Europe did not outperform China until the late eighteenth century.

Chapter 15 analyzes the great wave of capitalist globalization that occurred under British hegemony in the nineteenth century. The rapid acceleration of communications and transportation technology, the growth of international trade and investment, the further marketization of agriculture and mining in the less developed countries, and the last wave of European colonialism were all important features of the nineteenth-century wave of globalization. The chapter also examines the rise of the United States from the periphery to the core.

Chapter 16 examines the psychological consequences of the further institutionalization of markets, commodified property, and complex technologies since the eighteenth century. In what ways have these rapid technological changes impacted the individualist self and the forms of abstract reasoning? Is there a significant difference between the individualist self during the industrial age and the electronic age? How have the automobile and the development of cities after World War II affected personal identity? How has the impact of the computer affected how we reason?

Chapter 17 discusses the twentieth-century "Age of Extremes" as globalization backlash and hegemonic rivalry rent the fabric of the nineteenth-century global civilization with deglobalization that included the world revolution of 1917 and two world wars. The emergence of the hegemony of the United States and a "global New Deal" led to another great wave of integration after World War II. And this was followed by the "globalization project," a renewed (neoliberal) glorification of markets and attacks on the welfare state that was a response to increasing competition in the generative sectors that had been the basis of US economic hegemony. Both economic and political forms of globalization are examined, and we consider the victory of neoliberal capitalist ideology following the demise of the Soviet Union.

Chapter 18 further examines the most recent wave of globalization, the crisis of neoliberalism, the emergence of neoconservatism and a globalized version of neo-Keynesianism, and new counter-hegemonic transnational social movements and initiatives from the semiperipheral states. It also describes important institutional changes that have occurred in recent decades and places them in a long-run and comparative perspective. For instance, technological styles have been radically transformed in a series of industrial revolutions produced by capitalist development. This is a speeded-up continuation of the technological evolution that has occurred in spurts of uneven development for tens of thousands of years.

But the rate at which capitalism revolutionizes technology is unique. We will discuss the pros and cons of rapid technological change. Similarly, population growth is neither a new phenomenon nor is it newly important. But the rapid rate of demographic growth and the global limits of resources once again bring the problem of population pressure to the fore. We will discuss the factors that influence birth and death rates in the modern system in preparation for a consideration in the following chapter of different possible solutions to future global overpopulation.

Chapter 18 further discusses social movements and revolutions, as well as waves of democratization that have occurred in the modern world-system. It also examines the expansion of education, changes in family structures and gender relations, and the problems of race relations, nationalism, and ethnic strife.

Part V discusses the institutional changes that have been occurring recently in the modern world-system and applies the comparative evolutionary world-systems approach to the question of probable and possible futures.

Chapter 19 discusses events and trends that have occurred in the first decade of the twenty-first century and outlines the major challenges that humans will have to face in the next several decades. Chapter 20 contemplates the future of the contemporary world-system using the comparative and evolutionary approach. The situation of US hegemonic decline is carefully compared with the period at the end of the nineteenth and in the early twentieth centuries when the British hegemony was in decline. We reckon the problem of the environmental limits to growth and possible solutions, as well as the problem of increasing inequalities and potential new struggles between the rich and the poor. And we consider the possibility of transforming the existing world-system into a future global commonwealth that is democratic and collectively rational.

Nearly all the people of the earth have been involved in a single global system since the end of the nineteenth century. This fact has become taken-for-granted consciousness with the latest wave of global economic integration. Everyone now either celebrates or derides the existence of a single global political economy. This means that citizenship, though it is now defined nationally, should be global because the relevant political arena for changing or for resisting change is the global arena. The world polity is in formation, and all citizens will eventually be world citizens. Some already are.

Citizens of the world need to understand human history in order to appreciate the glories and tribulations of the past and to intelligently shape the future. Most of the challenges that our species faces in the next century are only unique in their dimensions. Many of the smaller world-systems that were engulfed by the expanding Central System were annihilated. But for the first time our whole species faces at least two rather probable dooms that could be total in the sense that human beings might not survive: (1) a possible future war among core states in which weapons of mass destruction are used or (2) a global ecological catastrophe that makes human life on earth impossible.

The array of possible solutions involves creative recombination of the elements of past solutions that will be appropriate to the particular nature of the coming problems. Dooms of the past and processes of social evolution are the raw materials for creating solutions for the future. This is the subject of the final chapter.

Features of the Text

- Designed for undergraduate and graduate social science classes on social change and globalization topics in sociology, world history, cultural geography, anthropology, and international studies.

- Describes the evolution of the modern capitalist world-system since the fourteenth century BCE, with coverage of the rise and fall of system leaders: the Dutch in the seventeenth century, the British in the nineteenth century, and the United States in the twentieth century.
- Provides a framework for analyzing patterns of social change.
- Includes numerous tables, figures, and illustrations throughout the text
- Supplemented by framing part introductions, suggested readings at the end of each chapter, an end of text glossary, and a comprehensive bibliography. Terms in the glossary are in **bold text** when they are first introduced.
- Offers a web-based auxiliary chapter on Indigenous North American World-Systems and a companion website with excel data sets and additional web links for students. See:
  http://www.paradigmpublishers.com/Books/BookDetail.aspx?productID=364458
  http://www.irows.ucr.edu/cd/appendices/socchangeapp/socchangeapp.htm

This book is addressed to the general reader, and it is also an introduction to advanced studies for those students who choose social science as a vocation. Social science is a calling that can help us get through the major challenges of the twenty-first century and on to less stressful times. We do not pretend to have all the answers. Rather, the point is to provide a helpful framework for finding good answers based on further theorizing, research, and political practice.

Acknowledgments

Christopher Chase-Dunn

This book could not have been written without the help of Thomas D. Hall, my coauthor of *Rise and Demise: Comparing World-Systems*. We worked for over ten years to develop the comparative evolutionary world-systems perspective that is the organizing framework of this text. I also want to recognize the stimulation, critique, and encouragement provided by the World Historical Systems working group of the International Political Economy section of the International Studies Association. William Thompson, George Modelski, Robert Denemark, Jonathan Friedman, Kasja Ekholm, David Wilkinson, Andre Gunder Frank, Barry Gills, Claudio Cioffi-Revilla, Andrew Sherratt, William McNeill, Joachim Rennstich, and Kristian Kristiansen have all influenced our thinking. We also thank the members of the Political Economy of World-Systems section of the American Sociological Association for their support and encouragement.

My research on the very small precontact world-system in Northern California was greatly helped by Kelly M. Mann, coauthor of *The Wintu and Their Neighbors*, as well as by Elaine Sundahl and Ed Clewett (formerly of the Shasta College Archaeological Laboratory). Anthropologists Marvin Harris, Robert Carneiro, Patrick Kirch, E. N. Anderson, and Jonathan Friedman have had major impacts on our thinking. I also want to thank archaeologists Gary Feinman, Peter Peregrine, P. Nick Kardulias, Guillermo Algaze, and Richard Blanton, who helped develop the comparative evolutionary world-systems perspective. Immanuel Wallerstein, Giovanni Arrighi, Beverly Silver, Charles Tilly, Stephen Bunker, Paul Cicantell, and Ho-fung Hung have helped us comprehend the evolution of the modern world-system. Terry Boswell, my coauthor on *The Spiral of Capitalism and Socialism*, contributed greatly to the ideas about past and future possibilities for transforming the modern world-system. Volker Bornschier, coeditor of *The Future of Global Conflict*, has helped penetrate the fog of globalization, as have Jeffrey Kentor, Ellen Reese, Susan Manning, Yukio Kawano, Ben Brewer, Andrew Jorgenson, Rebecca Alvarez, Gary Coyne, and Roy Kwon.

My research on the growth/decline phases of cities and empires has been carried out at the Institute for Research on World-Systems at the University of California–Riverside with the valuable help of E. N. Anderson, Daniel Pasciuti, Alexis Alvarez, Hiroko Inoue, Kirk Lawrence, Anthony Roberts, Joseph Genoa, Oswin Chan, Richard Neimeyer, Andrew Owen, and Christian Jaworski. E. N. Anderson carefully read and critiqued the manuscript for this textbook.

I would also like to thank those undergraduate students at Johns Hopkins University, Towson State University, and the University of California–Riverside who provided helpful correctives that have aided the effort to communicate with students. And I want to thank my wife, Carolyn Hock, and my daughters, Mae and Frances Chase-Dunn, for allowing me to retreat to isolated places to work on this book. Removing one's self from the modern world-system (temporarily) is a good way to think and write about that complex and long-standing "event" by which hunter-gatherer bands mushroomed to become the megacities and anthropomorphized landscapes that are now home to 7.5 billion human beings.

Bruce Lerro

Like the god Hermes, whose job is to navigate between material and spiritual worlds, a sociohistorical psychologist moves between the worlds of political economy, macro-sociology, and world history—a job that is not for the faint of heart. I would like to thank the following scholar-minstrels whose wanderings evolved similar patterns. First of all, the Russian school of sociohistorical psychology of Vygotsky, Luria, and Leontiev, who asked and answered the question of what a Marxian psychology would look like. Jack Goody and Robert Logan posed and answered provocative questions about what technologies such as writing and coined money do to reasoning processes, sense ratios, and memory. The French school of the History of Mentalities helped me bridge the gap between spiritual culture and psychology in the last five hundred years of Western history. Sociologist Richard Sennett revealed that social psychology indeed has its own history.

I would like to thank my students in Cross-Cultural Psychology at Chapman University for their curiosity, feedback, and reservations between 1991 and 2003. I would also like to thank the students in my Personality Theory, History and Systems courses at Dominican University since 2002. They never ceased to inform me and they got a lot more history than they bargained for!

Special thanks to Gene (E. N.) Anderson for his incisive criticism of my ideas about cognitive evolution and for lively e-mail discussions. Finally, thanks to my partner, Barbara Mac Lean, who has mostly loved to hear about the connections I am making between coined money and abstract thinking and the impact of the printing press and parenting styles, whether over dinner, on hiking trails, or at the beach.

PART

I

The Framework

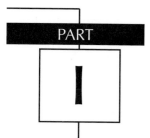

In order to understand the story of human social change we will need a skeleton on which to hang the muscles, sinews, and organs of the narrative. The story is about structures and institutions, and how they have changed. We will compare small, medium-sized, and large structures to one another, and in order to do this we need some abstractions—concepts—that will allow us to see the architecture of societies and intersocietal systems.

The first chapter is about social evolution in general and its relationship with human history. It is also about social science and its relationship with humanism and values. The idea of **institutions** is introduced and the problems of free will and determinism are discussed. A spectrum of different theoretical approaches to social change and evolution is reviewed and the synthetic approach of institutional materialism is presented.

Chapter 2 introduces the concepts of the comparative world-systems perspective—the spatial boundaries of intersocietal systems, the idea of modes of accumulation, two basic dimensions of core/periphery relations, and some characteristic features of world-systems—the rise and fall of intersocietal hierarchies and the pulsation (expansion and contraction) of trade networks. The key notion of semiperipheral development is also presented. While these abstractions are illustrated with examples, they will require grasping as analytical categories and dimensions in order that we may use them to understand the processes of human social evolution.

Chapter 3 discusses the changes that were necessary in the primate brain in order to produce a critter that could take up the game of social evolution, and how these changes may have come about.

Chapter 4 introduces key ideas about the social self as an institution, an invention that is produced by the world historical action of individuals and the possibilities and constraints that larger social structures provide. As social structures evolve so does the social self. The understanding of social psychology is important for explaining social change.

1

History and Social Evolution

This chapter explains the philosophical and scientific principles that will be the basis of our study of social change. It provides an overview of different theoretical approaches and the basic concepts of institutional materialism, the sociological perspective on social change that is employed in the rest of the book.

Science and Objectivity

The scientific study of social change is not as straightforward as studying rocks or frogs. If we were extraterrestrials sitting on the moon observing earthlings through a telescope, it would not be hard to attain a high level of objectivity. But each of us is a human speaker of a particular language living in a specific place with a head full of a particular cultural heritage and standing in a certain relationship with the rest of the occupants of our planet. We are men or women, American or Chinese, from New York or Bombay, Catholic or Moslem, Republican or Green, hunt club or bowling league. Objectivity is a key requirement of science, but we are trying to be objective about our own history and ourselves. This is a difficult task.

Because absolute objectivity is impossible, some people retreat to what we would call "extreme relativism." Some think that the enormity of this problem means that social science is impossible, and so we should just surrender to subjectivity and enjoy it. We support another path, that is, relative objectivity. Relative objectivity does not strive for absolute certainty, but probability. We try to attain a sufficient degree of objectivity by becoming aware of the sources and strengths of our prejudices for occasions when these prejudices might be getting in the way. To do this we need to understand how science itself is a cultural product and how social processes influence scientists. We need to place ourselves in historical perspective and then use that understanding as a basis for examining our own biases. We also need to be clear about what the goals of social science are, even if they are unreachable in any absolute sense.

It has been said that science should be value-free in the sense that scientists should try to ascertain the objective truth without allowing their beliefs about good and evil to influence their judgments about what is true. We will maintain this distinction in what follows. But science also has its own values. It is a philosophical venture that has its own goals, which are themselves taken on faith or, at the least, are provisionally accepted. When we play chess or basketball we agree to operate on the basis of the rules of the game. It is likewise with science. The philosophical presuppositions of science are not themselves provable by means of science. Instead, they are values that we may choose to affirm and defend.

The main goals of the scientific study of social change are to understand the truth about what happened in the human past and to build explanations of the patterns of human behavior and social institutions. These explanations should be objectively testable, meaning that empirical evidence must be relevant to proving or disproving them. Ideally, our explanations should be as simple as they can be while still accounting for the patterns of social change. Causal propositions—assertions that *A* causes *X*—can be evaluated using the comparative method (see below). Explanations will probably never be perfect, but scientific progress means better and better approximations of the way social change actually works.

Ideally, this enterprise should approach social change from an earth-wide perspective rather than from the point of view of any particular society or civilization. Modern science emerged from the European Enlightenment's encounter with the rest of the world during the rise of European hegemony. This historical fact must be acknowledged and examined in order for it to be transcended by a truly earth-wide science of social change.

Social science should also be objective with respect to the focus on human beings in relationship to other forms of life. Humanism is a fine ethical point of view, but social science should not presume that the human species is superior to other life forms. As social scientists we should focus on the human species without making any presumptions about the value of that species for good or ill. Some scientists study amphibians and others study humans.

Humanism and Values

But that is not all. In addition to being scientists we are citizens, as well as members of families and communities. The idea here is that each of us plays more than one game and has more than one role, and we need to be clear about which rules are which. Take, for example, the woman who is a social scientist during the day and a parent and citizen by night—she wears more than one hat. But the operations of one game may have implications for another. Good social science can be helpful for pursuing the goals associated with these other roles as well.

The main focus of this book is to present the best current practices of the science of social change, but in the final chapter we go beyond social science to suggest how what we know might be used to bring about a more humane and sustainable world society. As citizens we are humanists, so we will affirm that survival of the human species is a desirable goal. This does not contradict what we said above about our scientific goals. Our political and social values are choices and commitments that we have made, and we recognize that these cannot be proved by science. But science may provide useful information for realizing political and philosophical goals. Indeed, almost all modern political philosophies make appeals to science for support of their views of human nature and the possibilities for human society. The important thing here is to not put the cart before the horse. In this text the science is first.

Science need not claim to be the only valid perspective on ultimate reality. In asserting the value of the scientific approach against religious systems of thought, early scientists often took an arrogant stance that belittled other approaches to reality. Now that science itself is an important component of the emerging global culture, a more agnostic and tolerant philosophical stance is desirable, though this need not go to the extremes of cultural relativism and subjectivism advocated by many postmodernists. Science can be modest and useful without the arrogance of scientism.

We think the scientific method is best because it has the most self-correcting devices for weeding out previous errors and because it has the most built-in protective mechanisms against faulty reasoning and sloppy thinking. We agree that literature, art, and religion can also be used for inspiration and for discovering better ways to live. But we think science is the most reliable for discovering relative truths and distinguishing our subjective states—our wishes, needs, interests, fears, and past experiences—from the way the world works.

The Comparative Method

All science is based on the comparative method in the sense that causal connections are established by comparing sequences of events. When it is possible to manipulate the processes under study, scientists do true experiments because isolating and simplifying the operation of variables can more reliably test for causality. If we want to know whether *A* causes *X*, we can experimentally manipulate *A* and see what happens to *X* and isolate *X* from other influences to make sure that they are not falsely making it appear that *A* influences *X* (see Figure 1.1). If we wiggle *A*, then *X* should wiggle if *A* really causes *X*. In most of social science it is not feasible to carry out true experiments because we cannot actually manipulate *A*, but we can still employ the logic of the experimental method in order to examine causality. Thus, we design our research as if we were manipulating variables, and we look for opportunities in nature in which processes seem to be simplified and isolated. We measure variables *A* and *X* and see whether, in the course of events, a change in *A* seems to regularly correspond with a change in *X*. Or we observe a number of comparable cases and see whether there is a patterned relationship between *A* and *X* that might indicate causality. We can also measure variation in other variables to try to infer how they may be involved in the relationship between *A* and *X*.

So, for example, it is reasonable to posit that increasing the temperature causes ice to melt. This hypothesis can be tested experimentally by putting a pot with some ice on the stove. But if we were unable to manipulate temperature, we could simply measure the temperature of the pot and also measure the speed at which an ice cube melts. We would then observe that ice melts more rapidly on a warm day than it does on a cold day. By comparing the rate of ice melting on warm and cold days, we could establish that heat causes ice to melt, even without manipulating the causal variable. This is the quasi-experimental comparative method.

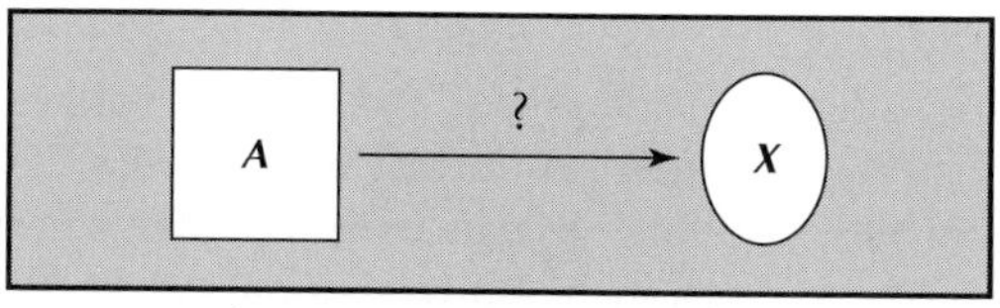

Figure 1.1 Does *A* cause *X*?

The comparative method allows us to establish causality, albeit less certainly than the experimental method. We choose comparable cases or instances of the processes of social change we care about, measure the variables that we think are causing the effect of interest, and test causal propositions by studying variation over space or time (or both). Whether we study one case over time or several comparable cases at the same time, we are employing a method that is fundamentally based on the logic of experiments.

We use probabilistic logic rather than deterministic logic in our models of social change. A probabilistic statement says that *A* is likely to cause *X* a certain percentage of the time. There is an explicit element of randomness or indeterminacy. A deterministic statement says that *A* always causes *X*. We use probabilistic logic for two reasons:

1. There is usually error in our measurements of variables
2. Social action is itself probabilistic rather than deterministic

Thus we do not speak of "laws" of social change, but rather of causal tendencies.

Probabilistic logic is also used in much of natural science, but it is even more important to use it in social science because we are trying to predict and explain the behavior of intelligent beings. The amount of indeterminacy in the behavior of a billiard ball is considerably less than the amount of indeterminacy in the behavior of a person. If you tell a billiard ball your prediction of the path it will take after bouncing off the side of the pool table, your statement cannot affect the behavior of the ball. But if you tell a voter that she is likely to vote for the Bull Moose Party, your prediction may influence her decision. Intelligent beings are difficult subjects of scientific study. We need to take these special problems into account in our efforts to explain and predict what humans do. So we use probabilistic theories and we try to understand the ways in which our subjects interpret their own worlds.

Types of Evidence

The evidence that we use to study social change over the long run is of several different kinds. For studying people who lived before the invention of writing we use archaeological evidence—the remains of peoples' lives as found in artifacts, evidence of what they ate, how they constructed their habitations, the sizes of their settlements, and so on. The accurate dating of archaeological evidence is important for understanding sequences of development and what was going on at the same time in different regions. We can often tell a great deal about patterns of trade and interaction from the locations of artifacts made of raw material for which we know the original site of procurement. For example, volcanic glass (obsidian) can be chemically "fingerprinted" so that it is possible to know that a particular obsidian arrowhead originally came from a quarry far from where the arrowhead was found. It is also possible to estimate the amount of time that has passed since the arrowhead was made. This is done by measuring the thickness of the "hydration rim," which indicates how long a surface of obsidian has been exposed. By studying the composition of arrowheads found at the site of an ancient village we can see how trade and procurement patterns have changed over time. Archaeological evidence cannot tell us directly what people thought or felt, but it does allow us to make educated guesses about their social organization based on the remnants left by human occupation.

Ethnographic evidence is information that has been gathered by anthropologists who have studied people who live in less complex societies that survived until the nineteenth and twentieth centuries. The ethnographers moved in with the remaining hunter-gatherers and tribal peoples of the nineteenth and twentieth centuries to study their languages and their material and ideological cultures. The greatest use of this corpus of evidence for the study of social evolution is the light that it sheds on the lives of people who lived thousands of years ago. But it is important to realize that hunter-gatherers who managed to survive until recently may not accurately represent those hunter-gatherers who lived long ago. Obviously those who have long been in contact with more complex societies are likely to have adapted to these interactions in important ways that change the nature of their institutions. Secondly, even if these societies had no contact with more complex societies, they still have their own internal histories that are not identical to other pre-state societies of the past (Robert Kelly 1995). Thus, regarding this problem, one must be cautious when using ethnographic evidence to supplement archaeological evidence.

It is often possible to use the written observations and records made by the first literate observers of preliterate peoples (e.g., missionaries and explorers), though the civilizational perspectives of the observers usually bias these sources of information. Once societies have developed writing we can often decipher their own written records and documents as sources of evidence about social institutions and practices. The first written languages emerged along with the original invention of states in Mesopotamia about 5,000 years ago. Records and documents were written on clay tablets that preserve rather well under dry conditions. Ironically, the development of paper documents in later millennia created a larger hole in the evidence because paper is more fragile than clay tablets. Our documentary knowledge of the great Persian Empire of the Achaemenid dynasty is largely confined to epigraphs—inscriptions on stone monuments—because the paper (papyrus) documents have decayed. We use documentary evidence in conjunction with archaeological evidence to gain an understanding of the early civilizations. We also see the development of formal systems of money and can infer much about ancient economies and polities by studying coinage.

Ancient states began to gather systematic evidence about their own finances and the populations under their control. This evolved into the modern system of statistics, censuses, and national accounts that we use as evidence of social change. Sample surveys and systematic studies of large populations allow us to be much more thorough and precise about social changes that have occurred in the last half century. We can now use satellite data to study large-scale social processes such as urbanization and global deforestation.

Sociocultural Evolution

Sociocultural evolution is most simply the idea that social change is patterned and directional—that human societies have evolved from small and simple affairs to large and complex ones. The idea of social evolution has had a rough career in social science, and it is still in disrepute in some circles. Much of the problem has been that earlier formulations of the idea embodied certain assumptions that are unscientific in nature. The idea of progress means that some human societies are superior to others because they are "more advanced." The theory of progress has been used as a justification by some people for dominating and exploiting others. The social evolutionism of the British anthropologists of the nineteenth century presented London society as the highest form of human civilization and depicted colonized peoples as savages and barbarians. Evolutionary ideas were used to support a philosophy of social Darwinism in which the current winners were depicted as better adapted and losers were portrayed as on the way to extinction because of genetic and/or cultural deficiencies. Talcott Parsons' (1966) version of structural/functional evolution presented the United States in a similar light. We consider the theory of progress in more detail below.

In reaction to these problems, some social scientists have embraced a radical cultural relativism in which each society is to be understood in its own terms as a unique constellation of institutional practices. It was assumed that there were no inherently superior social structures, but rather that all human cultures were equal, though different from one another. The ethnographer Franz Boas was the greatest proponent of this approach, and modern anthropology was heavily influenced by his stress on careful fieldwork that recorded the linguistic, spiritual, and material attributes of human societies. The body of knowledge produced by following Boas's approach is a vast resource for our understanding of ways of life different from our own, despite the cultural biases and problems of objectivity of the ethnographers who have "tented with the natives."

Beginning in the 1930s there developed dissatisfaction with cultural relativism because of its lack of concern for developing a science of social change and its refusal to make comparisons between societies. Anthropologists like Leslie White, Julian Steward, Marshall Sahlins, Elman Service, and Marvin Harris began to develop a new evolutionary anthropology that corrected the problematic aspects of earlier efforts, such as the confusion of evolution with progress. Consequently, the rejection of social evolutionism has ebbed as the elements that made it unscientific have been separated from the more basic notions of patterned and directional change (Sanderson 1990).

There were three main problems with social evolutionary thinking that needed to be rectified:

1. Social evolution is easily confused with biological evolution, and yet these are largely distinct and different processes
2. Evolutionary thinking has tended to involve teleological assumptions in which the purposes of things have been asserted to be their cause
3. Evolution has been confused with the idea of progress—the notion that things are getting better

Sociocultural Evolution versus Biological Evolution

Much confusion is generated by the failure to clearly distinguish between sociocultural evolution and biological evolution. Sociocultural evolution and biological evolution are different processes, though they share some similar characteristics. Failure to recognize the important differences often leads to theoretical reductionism in which social science is subsumed as a sub-branch of biology, and human behavior is seen as mainly determined by genetic inheritance. While biological evolution is based on the inheritance of genetic material, sociocultural evolution is based on the development of cultural inventions. Both genes and cultural codes are information storage devices by which the experiences and outcomes of one generation are passed on to future generations. Sociocultural evolution did not exist before the emergence of language. Animals that do not have the biological ability to manipulate symbols and to communicate them do not experience the processes of sociocultural evolution. The human animal is uniquely equipped to evolve socioculturally because of the presence of the relatively large unpreprogrammed cortex of the human brain. This unusual piece of biological equipment makes possible the learning of complex linguistic codes and their infinite recombination.

Humans have a lot of RAM (random access memory) relative to ROM (read-only memory), whereas nonhuman animals have more ROM than RAM. In computers, RAM can contain changeable software, whereas ROM is permanently programmed at birth. This is another way of saying that humans are less instinctual than nonhumans. Ants and termites live in large and complex societies, but their behavior in these is largely instinctive. Their social structures are hardwired, and the architecture of their mounds is rigidly bound by the instinctive behaviors of mound building. Humans learn the cultural software that enables them to build large and complex societies, but the plans are coded in language and symbolic maps that may be modified without having to wait for the evolution of new instinctive behaviors. Language itself has a genetic basis, and this is why speakers of all natural languages share a somewhat similar grammatical structure. But this biological ability makes possible the great variation that we see in meaning systems and sociocultural institutions.

When early humans developed stone tools they did not need to genetically select for carnivorous teeth in order to become hunters. Thus, cultural evolution allowed humans to occupy new niches and to adapt in new ways without waiting for biological evolution. It has been thought that the advent of sociocultural evolution slowed down the rate of biological evolution of human genes, but there is some recent evidence that some aspects of the human genome may have changed rapidly under the influence of sociocultural evolution (e.g., Cochran and Harpending 2009).

There are other rather large and important differences between biological and sociocultural evolution: In biological evolution the source of innovations is mainly the random process of genetic mutation, while in sociocultural evolution recombinations and innovations occur both accidentally and intentionally as people try to solve problems. This is not to say that sociocultural evolution is entirely rational or even intentional, because many social changes occur as the unintended consequences of the actions of many individuals and groups. But the important point here is that, compared with genetic mutation, social innovation contains an important element of intentionality.

Another big difference is in the rate of change. Biological evolution of large species takes a long time, while sociocultural evolution is much faster and is accelerating. Biological evolution occurs slowly because it is dependent on mating and reproduction and on those few unusual genetic mutations that are adaptive. Sociocultural evolution is accomplished by means of cultural inventions, and these can more easily spread from group to group. Societies can "mate" and exchange cultural code, whereas (complex) species cannot naturally exchange genetic information. Of course, advantageous genetic mutations can spread within a species and there may have been important interactions between biological and sociocultural evolution in the last ten millennia. But these are still rather different processes.

Another difference between biological and sociocultural evolution is in the relationship between simpler forms and more complex forms. In biological evolution, simple one-celled forms of life coevolve and thrive along with more complex multicelled organisms. Viruses and bacteria are doing just fine. In sociocultural evolution the situation is somewhat different. Larger and more complex societies tend to destroy or radically alter the cultures of small-scale societies. States and **empires** conquer and subjugate stateless societies (e.g., hunter-gatherer bands and horticultural villagers) by killing off their members and assimilating survivors into state-based societies. The plight of indigenous Americans since their incorporation into the Europe-centered world-system is an obvious example. Anthropologists have termed this the "law of cultural dominance." It is not a natural law in the sense that it is impossible for more powerful cultures to allow less powerful ones to survive. This said, there has been a good degree of coevolution as indigenous peoples have learned to cope with subordination in complex and hierarchical societies. Indigenes have recovered demographically and are reconstituting their cultures but as distinctive parts of a larger global culture.

Despite these contrasts, sociocultural evolution is not completely different from biological evolution: Both rely on information storage to pass the experiences of one generation on to another, both are mechanisms whereby individuals and groups adapt to changing environments or exploit new environments, and, in both, more adaptive changes drive out less adaptive characteristics through competition. And there is one more similarity. In both biological and sociocultural evolution, more complex systems can develop out of simpler systems (see Figure 1.2).

So sociocultural evolution and biological evolution are quite different processes, and it is important to understand this distinction because the word "evolution" is often used in ways that cause confusion. Many of the claims of sociobiology and evolutionary psychology are exaggerations of the extent to which human actions are instinctive and based on biological evolution. While there is undoubtedly a biological basis of human behavior (as discussed above and in Chapter 3), the idea of human nature is itself a culturally constructed notion that has powerful effects in legitimating social institutions. And yet, to argue that human behavior is less instinctive than the behavior of other animals does not require that we deny the biological basis of human actions. There are clearly constraints, as well as possibilities, that emanate from our bowels and our brain stems. Sociocultural evolution has radically reconstructed the possibilities, and we are now entering a new age of recombinant DNA in which human decisions are radically altering the biological makeup of plants, animals, and ourselves. This is the culturalization of biology.

Regarding the relationship between biological evolution and social evolution, it is obvious that there would have been no cultural evolution if the human species had not developed the ability to speak and a brain capable of storing and reconfiguring complex codes and symbols. These were the key developments that allowed culture to emerge. Once culture emerged, it acted back upon biological evolution. Social structure has taken over as the main determinant of the ability of humans and other life forms to survive and prevail. Domestication and selective breeding of animals and plants as well as the cultural and social control of human reproduction have greatly affected biological evolution, and now the emergence of biotechnology (genetic surgery, cloning, and genetic engineering by means of gene-splicing) will transform a goodly portion of biological change into cultural evolution by adding intention and by allowing the radical diffusion of genetic material across different forms of life.

Teleology and Unilinear Evolution

Teleology is a form of explanation in which the purpose of a thing is alleged to be its cause. The most famous teleological explanation is that order in the universe is a consequence of the will of God. Aristotle contended that all of nature reflects the purposes of an immanent final cause. Regarding teleology and history, we think there is a structure to history and there are definite trends, but we do not claim there is an underlying purpose to history that is separate from the many

Similarities

Information transfer across generations
Adaptation to environments
Competition drives out less adapted forms
More complex forms may emerge out of simpler forms

Differences

Biological evolution	Sociocultural evolution
Genetic inheritance	Cultural inheritance
Change through genetic mutation	Change through cultural inventions
Propagation of innovations by means of mating	Propagation of innovations by diffusion of information
Slower rate of change	Faster rate of change
Coevolution of simple and complex forms	Complex forms may drive out simple forms

Figure 1.2 Summary of similarities and differences between sociocultural evolution and biological evolution

purposes of the human historical actors. In the last chapter we argue that it will be possible in the future for the human species to take conscious control of its own collective evolution, but this is only a possibility.

The problem is that general purposes of the universe or of history cannot be scientifically demonstrated to exist. Science is limited to knowledge of proximate causation. The causes of an effect must be demonstrably present or absent in conjunction with the presence or absence of the thing to be causally explained. Proving causality requires temporal or spatial variation. General statements about characteristics of the universe that are invariably present cannot serve as scientifically knowable causes, because they do not vary. A scientific approach to sociocultural evolution cannot assert final causes or ultimate purposes. It proposes causal explanations that are empirically testable and falsifiable with evidence about human history and social change.

Another unscientific characterization of historical processes is inevitabilism, or the idea that history is the result of an unfolding process in which stages follow one from another in a necessary order, like the pages of a book. Another term for this kind of theory is "unilinear evolution." Much of the rhetorical power of Marxism came from the stage theory of history that alleged that socialism and communism would inevitably supersede capitalism. Thus, hardworking revolutionaries could claim to have history on their side. Now, ironically, Marxism itself has been thrown into the dustbin of history, and the ideologues of neoliberal capitalism claim that socialism is an outdated and flawed ideology produced by the strains of the transition from traditional to modern society. All stage theories need to be treated with skepticism, but this does not mean we should abandon the effort to see the patterns of social change.

The probabilistic approach to social change adopted above disputes the scientific validity of inevitabilism. This is not the same as arguing that there are no directional patterns of social change or that all outcomes are equally probable. But it is important to know that scientific social change theory is about probabilities, not inevitabilities. Sociocultural evolution has not been a process in which a single society goes through a set of stages to arrive at the most developed point. It has been very uneven in space and time.

For example, when some hunter-gatherers (foragers)[1] began to practice horticulture, all foraging societies did not automatically switch over to horticulture. Hunters and farmers existed side by side, changing each other. So, too, when agrarian states emerged, all hunter-gatherers and village horticulturalists did not cease to exist. Agrarian empires and nomadic societies continued to interact and to mutually affect each other for thousands of years. Further, societies that were at the highest level of complexity at one point often collapsed in a later period, and the emergence of larger, more hierarchical, and more complex societies occurred elsewhere. This uneven pattern of development is one of the most important aspects of the evolution of world-systems.

In denying that social evolution is inevitable we argue for relative, rather than absolute, contingency. While conjunctural contingency and unexpected events can fundamentally alter the course of human history, they are not completely unconstrained. For instance, the fact that Karl Marx and Friedrich Engels were born in Europe at roughly the same time was an historical accident. But even if these friends and coworkers in the critique of capitalism had never known each other, the constraints of industrial capitalism on workers and the possibilities that capitalism creates for working-class opposition (e.g., being able to meet at the same place at the same time in factories) would very likely have generated a socialist movement.

[1] Hunter-gatherers are also called foragers because they scour natural territories to harvest the products of nature rather than modifying nature to increase its productivity. This is very land-intensive because it takes a lot of unmodified nature to support each person. Some hunter-gatherers, especially those who are relatively sedentary and live in permanently established seasonal villages, engage in "proto-agriculture"—the modification of natural landscapes either to increase their productivity through the use of fire in a way that encourages edible plants to grow or to increase grazing areas for deer populations. We use the terms "hunter-gatherer" and "forager" interchangeably.

The fate of the dinosaurs, destroyed by the impact of a large asteroid on the Yucatan Peninsula, powerfully reminds us of the potential importance of unexpected events. But what appears to us as a totally random and exogenous event on a human scale may be more systemic on a larger scale. In the case of asteroids, some astronomers claim that comets and their debris (asteroids) periodically cross the path of the earth, causing catastrophes that have repeatedly affected the evolution of life. Acknowledging contingency does not prevent us from searching out the more likely patterns of development in both the past and the future, or the trajectories that social change is likely to take in the absence of catastrophic random events.

Progress and Sociocultural Evolution

The "progress" theory of evolution that came out of the European Enlightenment claimed that whichever society came later in time must be better. Also, beginning in the 1960s, there developed a kind of reverse theory of progress that grew out of the Romantic Movement in Europe that we call "degeneration theory." This theory, whose major advocates are Paul Radin and Stanley Diamond, contends that earlier societies are superior to later societies. Many ecologists, anarchists, and neo-pagan feminists are advocates of degeneration theory.

Progress is not a scientific idea in itself, because it involves evaluations of the human condition that are necessarily matters of values and ethics. The idea that a world populated by humans is better than a world in which they are absent is an aesthetic or philosophical matter of choice. Even the ideas that warm and well-fed humans are better off than cold and hungry ones, and that long, healthy life is better than short disease-ridden existence are value choices, albeit ones that would be widely agreed upon by most people. When we turn to matters of religion, family form, cuisine, or the ideal degree of social equality, it is more obvious that we have entered the world of value decisions. One of the biggest problems with many theories of social evolution is that they have tended to be permeated with assumptions about what is better and worse, and many have simply assumed that evolution itself is a movement from worse to better. And with this powerful element embedded in them, evolutionary theories have served as potent justifications of conquest, domination, and exploitation. We have already pointed out that this was the main problem that led the second generation of anthropologists to reject social evolutionism in favor of a strong dose of cultural relativism.

The collapse of an agricultural state into a tribal village is often seen as a catastrophe. According to Tainter (1988, 193), "A complex society that has collapsed is suddenly smaller, simpler, less stratified and less socially differentiated. Specialization decreases and there is less social control. The flow of information drops, people trade and interact less . . . population levels tend to drop." But how catastrophic this is must be determined on a case-by-case basis. Tainter argues that a popular version of this scenario is a war of all against all: The weak are victimized, physical strength determines who will rule, and survival is the only aim of those who are left. The notion that collapse is catastrophic is prominent among archaeologists, classicists, and historians as well.

The collapse of complex societies, Tainter (1988) claims, is often instigated by the lower classes. As a complex society continually deteriorates, some social sectors sense that the benefits of withdrawal or passive resistance outweigh the benefits of continued support. Collapse is more likely to be understood as catastrophic by those groups who are not primary food producers and who extract land, labor, and goods from the lower classes.

Theories of progress are still important ideological elements in the world of politics, and so ideas about social evolution are still susceptible to being used badly. But so are other products of science and humanistic endeavor. Physicists are painfully aware of how the knowledge they have produced has been turned into the threat of nuclear holocaust. Historians, even those who studiously avoid making generalizations about the human predicament, may find their interpretations of historical events turned to uses of which they disapprove. Neither scientists nor humanists can control the use to which their works are put.

This said, if we agree on a list of desirable ends that constitute our notion of human progress, then it can be a scientific question as to whether things have improved with respect to this list, or which kind of society does better at producing the designated valuables. The list is one of preferences, not scientifically determinable but philosophically chosen. This list may be one's personal preferences or some collectively agreed-upon set of preferences. This approach to the problem of progress will be considered near the end of this book when we ask about the implications of our study of social change for world citizens.

The notion that it is plausible to formulate general theories of social evolution is given credence by the observation that many instances of parallel evolution have occurred. Parallel evolution means that similar developments have emerged under similar circumstances, but largely independently of one another. If horticulture (planting) had been invented only once and then had diffused from its single place of invention, it might be argued that this was merely a fortuitous accident. But horticulture was invented independently several times in regions far from one another. Similarly, states and empires emerged in both the Eastern and Western Hemispheres with little interaction between the two despite that the emergence of states in the Western Hemisphere occurred some three millennia later than in the Eastern Hemisphere. It is also quite likely that the emergence of states in East Asia, near the bend of the Yellow River in what is now China, occurred largely independently of the earlier emergence of states in Southwestern Asia, in the region that we call Mesopotamia (now Iraq). The significance of important instances of parallel social evolution is that they imply that general forces of social change are operating. Our task is to determine with evidence which conditions and tendencies were the most important causes of these developments.

Theories of Social Change

Theories of long-term social change differ from one another in two basic ways. One is the extent to which they posit qualitative as opposed to merely quantitative change. And the other is the extent to which they emphasize a single master variable that is allegedly the main cause of change.

Some theories posit a single logic of social change that is thought to adequately describe the important processes in all types of human societies and in all periods of time. Others argue that the logic of social change has itself altered qualitatively, and so a model that explains, for example, the emergence of horticulture is not adequate for explaining the emergence of capitalism. Those who see long-run continuities of developmental logic are called "continuationists," while those who posit the existence of fundamental reorganizations of the logic of social change are called "transformationists." Continuationists contend that similar processes of social change have operated for millennia, while transformationists see qualitative reorganizations of the processes of change as having occurred. The content of the models within each of these categories is quite variable depending on what sorts of social change are seen as most central or powerful—the master variables. It is also possible to combine these two alternatives, as we do below.

The master variables can be broadly categorized as either cultural or material, but within each of these two boxes there are several significant subtypes. Culturalists often emphasize the importance of the ways in which values are constructed in human societies, and so they focus on religion or the most central institutions that indicate the consensual and most powerful value commitments of a society. From this point of view the most important kind of social change involves redefinition of what is alleged to exist (ontology[2]) and changes in ideas about good and evil. Culturalists understand social evolution as the reorganization of socially institutionalized beliefs. For example, the important changes in social evolution are understood to have been the transitions from the animistic philosophy of the hunter-gatherer band to the radical separation of the natural and supernatural realms in early states, to the rise of the "world religions,"[3] followed by the emergence of formal rationality and science. Culturalists see other social changes as consequences that follow from these

[2] Ontology is the philosophy of being, or the assumptions that are made about existence or reality. All cultures contain beliefs about what exists.

most fundamental transformations of ideational culture.

Materialists focus primarily on the tangible problems that all human societies face and the inventions that people employ to solve these problems. They stress the fact that humans must eat and that in order for human groups to survive, they must provide enough food and shelter to allow babies to be born and to grow up. Thus, all human societies have demographic and economic needs, and the ways in which these requirements are met are important determinants of other aspects of social life. Materialists assert that human societies need to adapt to the natural environment and to the larger social environment in which they compete and cooperate with other human societies. They stress the importance of local and regional environmental and geographical factors in structuring human societies.

Materialists often differ as to which material problem is seen as most crucial and determinant. Some emphasize demographic and ecological constraints, while others focus on technologies of production or of power. Technologies of production are those techniques and practices by which resources are acquired or produced from the natural environment. Technologies of power are those institutions that create and sustain hierarchies within human societies and that allow some societies to conquer and dominate other societies.

Institutional Materialism

The theoretical approach that we employ is termed "institutional materialism," a synthetic combination of culturalist and materialist approaches. Institutional materialism explains human sociocultural evolution as an adaptive response to demographic, ecological, and economic forces in which people devise institutional inventions to solve emergent problems and to overcome constraints. Institutional inventions include ideological constructions such as religion as well as technologies of production and power. Technologies of production are such things as bows and arrows, the potter's wheel, and hydroelectric dams. Technologies of power are such things as secret societies, special bodies of armed men, and record-keeping methods of who has paid taxes, tithes, or tribute, as well as intercontinental ballistic missiles.

Solving problems at one level usually leads to the emergence of new problems, and so the basic constraints of societies are never permanently overcome, at least as of yet. Institutional materialism sees a geographical widening of the scale of ecological and social problems created by social evolution rather than a transcendence of material constraints. It also acknowledges the importance of environmental and geographical factors in both constraining and facilitating social change. This is what allows us to construct a single basic model (see Chapter 2) that represents the major material forces that have shaped social evolution over the last twelve millennia.

As mentioned above, institutions are inventions by people for solving problems. Many of the taken-for-granted aspects of our world are social institutions that have been constructed by people in the past. The most basic social institution of all is language. We all learn a language when we are children, a particular language with particular meanings and connotations. Our "mother tongues" are social constructions invented by people who spoke and made meaning in the past, including those who raised us and those who taught them. Our particular languages are central institutions that heavily influence our understanding of what exists, what is possible, what is good, and what is evil. Other basic institutions that are historical inventions are money, the family (kinship), and productive technology.

Institutions in the sociological sense are more than just hospitals or schools. They include less tangible processes like verbal language and nonverbal codes such as gestures, styles of clothing, and the customs that govern everyday life. Institutional materialism analyzes the interactions between the material aspects and necessities of human life and the invention of culturally constructed institutions.

[3] **World religions** are those in which the moral community of believers is constituted as individuals who have chosen and affirmed their belief in the deity, for example, Christianity and Islam. In principle you are not born into the religion, as with ethnically based religions. This separates membership from kinship or ethnicity and makes possible a transethnic community of believers.

It is common to believe that whatever power social institutions have over us, they stop at the doorstep of our psyche (the personality or the self). After all, the psyche is our private business and ours to determine. At best, most of us will grant that our social institutions may interact with our psyche, but basically we have free will to make up our own minds and to form whatever identities we choose.

How do we imagine the relationship between social institutions and our psychological states—beliefs, memories, emotions, thinking processes, perceptions? It is tempting to imagine that we wear a mask to fulfill our social obligations. Our selves play the role of a good worker on the job, a good parent (or child) at home, a good drummer in our band, but these are only superficial outer layers that clothe our "real selves," which we are when we are alone. We think this view is mistaken.

Human societies contain many socializing influences. Some of these complement each other, but often they conflict. We import various combinations of these institutional forces, like mass media, school, and sports, inside us, and in the early years of life they dominate how we form our identities and how we think. As we grow older we do not transcend these influences to become a "real" individual. We become more critical about which social institutions we allow to influence our identity and our thinking, but our psychology is never really a private matter, nor is it mainly a product of our own action. The self is born in the crossfire between society and biology. Society does not just interact with our psyche; it forms and sustains it. This occurs in two ways: socialization and certification. Socialization involves a learning process in which the individual acquires skills and attitudes appropriate to social action. Certification is a process of socially sanctioned labeling in which the linguistic categories are learned and social initiation rites are performed to move the person from one socially defined position (status[4]) into another. Certification involves learning the socially prescribed definitions of positions such as dad, mom, uncle, checkout clerk, and so on. Then social identity bestowal rituals, such as passing a test, getting married, or graduating from college, are performed that locate persons in positions. Identity is conferred in socially legitimated rituals in which both the individual and important others agree that one has become, for example, a "doctor." In simple societies, initiation rituals make a girl into a woman, and a boy into a man. In rationalized societies this is organized as a series of steps that we call grades in school, but both the ritual certification and the socialization aspects are important elements of producing the self.

The process of socialization is learning skills, manipulating tools, learning how to take on roles, understanding and dealing with status hierarchies, and properly responding to situations. Only then can we sensibly participate in families, schools, hospitals, and grocery stores. Socialization can be understood as occurring in three stages. In the first stage we are dependent on other people in a local face-to-face context. Our friends or parents hold the bicycle as we try to ride. If we want to learn to bake cookies, we may start out helping our dad in the kitchen, making them together and being assigned simple tasks. As these skills accumulate there comes a point when the cooperative social activity is mastered enough to be internalized. You can ride your bike or make cookies by yourself. The second stage involves internalization.

The third stage again involves cooperative activity with others, but now in an expanded way. You take the skills you have internalized and apply them to a wider social context than the original place you learned them. In the case of learning to bake cookies, you might be asked to participate in a neighborhood garage sale and be responsible for baking cookies for the sale. Now you must stretch your skills beyond what you originally learned. You must not only bake more cookies but consider making types of cookies that others may like even if you and your dad do not like them. This is called the global interpersonal stage.

---

[4] In sociology, the word "status" means two different things. Most commonly it is a synonym for prestige or social honor. The other meaning is a position in a social structure with associated role expectations. This second meaning is the one we are using here.

The three stages of learning are local interpersonal, internalization, and global interpersonal. These stages originate in social institutions, are imported into the psychology of an individual, and hence return to larger social institutions. In stages one and two, individuals are the product of institutions; in stage three, institutions are coproduced by the actions of these individuals as we work in these institutions. As we shall see, the self, in the sense of our idea of our individual identity and how we think—how we take in information, explain, analyze, and evaluate—is an institution, too. Though individuals, in our view, do not have free will, they do have autonomy and agency. Autonomy means we sometimes make creative choices about how the three stages of learning occur. Agency means that we have some degree of choice in how we engage the institutions that form our being. Even dissent and counter-conformity are rooted in social institutions, except that these institutions are against the dominant institutions. Choice is a matter of which institutions you draw from and how you combine these influences. Thus, the self is self-constructed to some extent, but the raw materials are mainly those provided by society.

One type of social institution, social structure, is the main focus of the study of social change. Individuals are born and die, and so all societies are composed of structures in which individuals either reproduce institutions in much the way that they have been in the past or they alter these institutions. The easiest way of conceptualizing social structure is as an organizational chart in which the various positions that constitute the organization are shown along with their relationships with one another (see Figure 1.3).

All formal organizations and bureaucracies are explicitly conceptualized as constellations of social positions (statuses) in which different individuals occupy the various positions. So a football team has a quarterback, a halfback, a center, and so on. Specific duties are assigned to these positions, and a particular player is evaluated in terms of how well or poorly he or she carries out the duties associated with the position. Sociologists point out that informal as well as formal groups may be viewed as having social structures. A group of friends having lunch may be understood as performing certain scripts appropriate to equals who care about one another, with a degree of improvisation thrown in to constitute genuineness and agency. All social groups are constituted in this way as organizations with rules and assumptions.

This structural view of human society focuses on the rules and definitions that provide the boundaries within which individuals carry out and reproduce social structures. But these structures also change, and the study of social change is, in large part, the effort to explain why structures change in the ways that they do.

Social structures are held together by three basic kinds of institutional "glue." Institutions that make human behavior somewhat predictable produce social order. In order to compete, fight, or cooperate with others, I need to be able to guess what they will do in reaction to what I do.

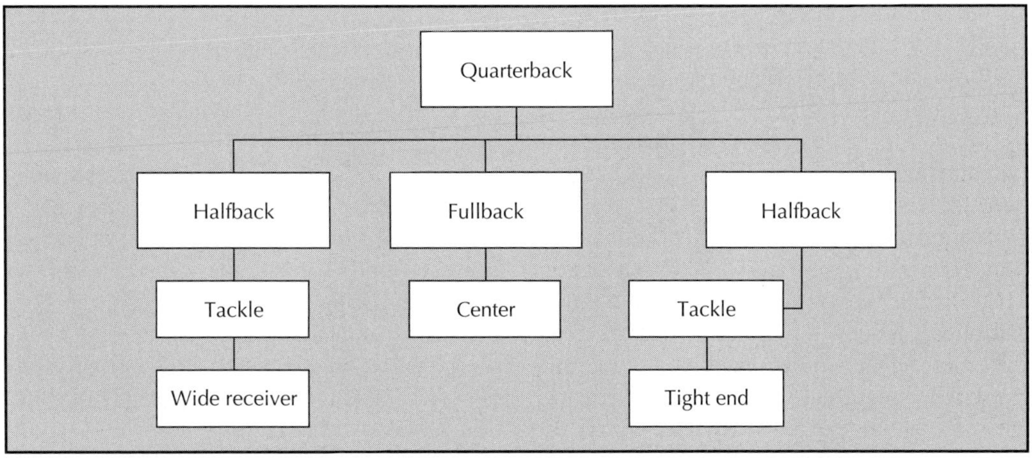

Figure 1.3 Social structure depicted as the organization chart of a football team

The three basic types of social glue that facilitate relatively stable expectations about the behavior of others are as follows:

1. Normative regulation, in which people agree about the proper kinds of behavior
2. Coercive regulation, in which institutionalized sanctions are applied to discourage behavior that is considered inappropriate
3. Market regulation, in which individuals are expected to maximize their returns in competitive buying and selling

Normative regulation based on consensus about proper behavior is the original institution of social order. It requires a shared language and a good deal of consensus about basic values and proper behavior. Individuals learn the rules and internalize them and regulate themselves and others with appeals to the moral order. This works well in small societies in which people interact with one another frequently and on a relatively egalitarian basis. It works less well (by itself) in larger societies that require that culturally different and spatially separated peoples cooperate with one another.

Coercive regulation (but not coercion) was invented with the rise of social hierarchies. Institutions such as the law do not require that each individual know or agree with the law. Thus, it works better for integrating communities that do not share common cultures and moral orders. Legal regulation is backed up by legitimate violence, the right of the lord or the king to enforce the law by means of punishment and prisons. Special bodies of armed men are used to enforce decisions made by states, as well as to engage in conflict with other societies. Courts are part of the institutionalization of coercion as an important form of social regulation.

Market regulation emerged with the invention of money and commodities. Market regulation, like institutionalized coercion, does have a basis in presumed norms, but these norms provide only the basic framework for interaction. They do not require agreement about much, except that money is useful. Markets articulate the actions of large numbers of buyers and sellers without requiring these players to identify with one another or even to agree about the general rules of legality. Markets are institutions that allow for relatively peaceful cooperation and competition among peoples who are spread over wide distances and who have rather different cultures.

Much of the sociology of roles, statuses, and social structures is based on the assumption that normative regulation is operating, but many social structures operate in the absence of much consensus because they are regulated by coercive or market institutions. The invention of these institutional forms of regulation has made organized social interaction possible on a greater and greater spatial scale, and now we have a single global network in which all three kinds of regulation play important parts. The story of how these inventions came about is the central focus of the study of sociocultural evolution.

The structuralist approach, which is an important part of institutional materialism, is not, contrary to what some critics have alleged, a necessarily deterministic approach to social life that eliminates the possibility of human freedom. Institutional structuralism allows us to understand the constraints that our own cultures have placed on us so that, to some degree, we can transcend these constraints. We see socially constructed institutions as human inventions that both empower us and constrain us in certain ways. The fact that the US government purchased, graded, and maintained a piece of property that is 3,000 miles long and 200 feet wide (I-70/I-80) makes it possible for me to drive from Baltimore to San Francisco in less than three days, while my great-grandparents took three months to make the same trip. This is technological and institutional empowerment. But the same interstate highway system means that the United States has invested a huge amount of money, energy, property, and human labor into a particular kind of transportation network that might become obsolete due to some future change in technology or in the cost of energy.

The canals of Venice and Amsterdam represent sunk costs that could not easily be reconstructed when transportation technology changed. Our religions, the ways in which we have defined male- and femaleness, the huge psychic investments in nationalistic sentiments, the expensive rituals by which we demonstrate our commitments to some people and our enmities to others—all these institutionalized aspects of our society make it possible for us to do some things, and very difficult to do others. This is both empowerment and structural alienation. The analysis of institutional structures makes it possible to understand how our history has constructed us and what we may need to do to reconstruct the future.

Institutional materialism is a synthetic theoretical focus that draws from several social science disciplines: history, anthropology, sociology, political science, economics, demography, and geography. This will be combined with social geography as it has emerged from the comparative world-systems perspective, the main topic of the next chapter. These tools will help us see the broad patterns as well as the unique aspects of different kinds of societies in the processes of social change.

Suggested Readings

Chase-Dunn, Christopher. 2005. "Global Public Social Science." *American Sociologist* 36 (3–4): 121–132. Reprinted in *Public Sociology: The Contemporary Debate*, ed. Lawrence T. Nichols (New Brunswick, NJ: Transaction Press, 2007), 179–194.

Christian, David. 2004. *Maps of Time*. Berkeley: University of California Press.

McNeill, John R., and William H. McNeill. 2003. *The Human Web*. New York: Norton.

Sanderson, Stephen K. 1990. *Social Evolutionism: A Critical History*. Cambridge, MA: Blackwell.

Tainter, Joseph A. 1988. *The Collapse of Complex Societies*. Cambridge: Cambridge University Press.

2

The Comparative World-Systems Approach

This chapter explains the main ideas that are needed to compare social systems with one another. To see the patterns of social change we need to be able to compare small networks of societies with larger regional systems and with the global system of today. This is because the spatial scale of important interactions has grown over the millennia as societies have gotten larger and long-distance transportation and communication became easier. The basic concepts of world-systems, polities, interaction networks, **modes of accumulation**, and **core/periphery relations** allow us to see and compare the architectures of rather different kinds of systems and to examine both the continuities and the important changes that have occurred with social evolution. We will also discuss the macro-micro link between these social institutions and the psychology of individuals. We will apply Lev Vygotsky's theory of learning to the formation of the social self and discuss the three phases of abstract thinking.

World-Systems

World-systems are systems of interacting polities[1] (see Figure 2.1). Systemness means that these polities interact with one another in important ways—interactions are two-way, necessary, structured, regularized, and reproductive. Systemic interconnectedness exists when interactions importantly influence the lives of people within polities,

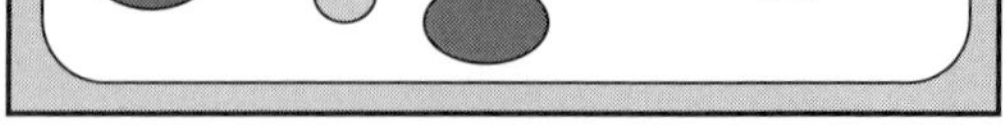

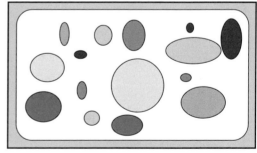

Figure 2.1 A world-system is a system of polities

[1] We use the term "polities" rather than the more commonly used "societies" because polities are usually spatially bounded realms of authority. This is an advantage in mapping relations among units. As Michael Mann (1986) has argued, the meanings included in the idea of a society are difficult to bound spatially. Polity is defined on the next page.

and they are consequential for social continuity or social change. World-systems may not cover the entire surface of the planet. Some extend over only parts of the earth. The word "world" refers to the importantly connected interaction networks in which people live, whether these are spatially small or large.

Only the modern world-system has become a global (earth-wide) system composed of national societies and their states. It is a single economy composed of international trade and capital flows, transnational corporations that produce products on several continents, and all the economic transactions that occur *within* countries and at local levels. The whole world-system is more than just international relations. It is the whole system of human interactions. The world economy is all the economic interactions of all the people on the earth, not just international trade and investment.

The modern world-system is structured politically as an **interstate system**—a system of competing and allying states. Political scientists commonly call this the international system, and it is the main focus of the field of international relations. Some of these states are much more powerful than others, but the main organizational feature of the world political system is that it is multicentric. There is no world state; rather, there is a system of states. This is a fundamentally important feature of the modern system and of many earlier regional world-systems as well.

When discussing and comparing different kinds of world-systems, it is important to use concepts that are applicable to all of them. **Polity** is a more general term that means any organization with a single authority that claims sovereign control over a territory or a group of people. Polities include bands, tribes, and chiefdoms as well as states. All world-systems are politically composed of multiple interacting polities. Thus, we can fruitfully compare the modern interstate system with earlier systems in which there were tribes or chiefdoms but no states. We will discuss the differences between tribes, chiefdoms, and states in the chapters that follow.

In the modern world-system it is important to distinguish between nations and states. **Nations** are groups of people who share a common culture and a common language. Conationals identify with one another as members of a group with a shared history, similar food preferences, and ideas of proper behavior. To a varying extent, nations constitute a community of people willing to make sacrifices for one another. **States** are formal organizations, such as bureaucracies, that exercise and control legitimate violence within a specific territory. Some states in the modern world-system are **nation-states**, in which a single nation has its own state. But others are multinational states in which more than one nation is controlled by the same state. **Ethnic groups** are subnations, usually minorities within states in which there is a larger national group. Ethnic groups and nations are sociologically similar in that they are both groups of people who identify with one another and share a common culture, but they often differ in regard to their relationship with states. Ethnic groups are minorities, whereas nations are majorities within a state. So the modern world-system is now a global economy with a global political system (the interstate system). It also includes all the cultural aspects and interaction networks of the human population of the earth. Culturally, the modern system is composed of:

- Several civilizational traditions (e.g., Islam, Christianity, and Hinduism)
- Nationally defined cultural entities—nations (and these are composed of class and functional subcultures, such as lawyers, technocrats, and bureaucrats)
- The cultures of indigenous and minority ethnic groups within states

The modern system is multicultural in the sense that important political and economic interaction networks connect people who have rather different languages, religions, and other cultural aspects. Most earlier world-systems were also multicultural.[2]

[2] One that was not multicultural was the interchiefdom system of precontact Hawaiian Islands, which was a complex world-system in which the ancestral Polynesian culture had regionally differentiated across the islands (see Chapter 7).

Interaction networks are regular and repeated interactions among individuals and groups. Interaction may involve trade, communication, threats, alliances, migration, marriage, gift giving, or participation in **information networks** such as radio, television, telephone conversations, and e-mail. Important interaction networks are those that affect peoples' everyday lives, their access to food and necessary raw materials, their conceptions of who they are, and their security from or vulnerability to threats and violence. World-systems are fundamentally composed of interaction networks.

Spatial Boundaries of World-Systems

Before we consider the nature of relations among the polities in a world-system, it is important to spatially bound the system. One big difference between the modern world-system and earlier systems is the spatial scale of different types of interaction networks. In the modern global system, most of the important interaction networks are themselves global in scale. But in earlier smaller systems, there was a significant difference in spatial scale between networks in which food and basic raw materials were exchanged and much larger networks of the exchange of prestige goods or luxuries. We call food and basic raw materials "bulk goods" because they have a low value per unit of weight. Indeed, it is uneconomical to carry food very far in the absence of cheap transportation.

Imagine that the only type of transportation available is people carrying goods on their backs or heads. This situation actually existed everywhere until the domestication of beasts of burden. Under these conditions, a person can carry, say, thirty kilograms of food. Now, imagine that the carrier is eating the food as she goes. So after a few days of walking, the carrier will have consumed all the food. This is the economic limit of food transportation under these conditions of transportation. This does not mean that food will never be transported farther than this distance, but there would have to be an important reason for moving it beyond its economic range.

A **prestige good** (e.g., jewels, bullion, or a very valuable food, such as spices) has a much larger spatial range because a small amount of such a good may be exchanged for a great deal of food. This is why **prestige goods networks** (PGNs) are normally much larger than **bulk goods networks** (BGNs). A network does not usually end, as long as there are people with whom one might trade. Indeed, most early trade was what is called **down-the-line trade**, in which goods are passed from group to group. For any particular group, the effective extent of its trade network is that point beyond which nothing that happens will affect the group of origin.

In order to bound interaction networks, we need to pick a place from which to start—a so-called place-centric approach. If we go looking for actual breaks in interaction networks, we will likely not find them, because almost all groups of people interact with their neighbors. But if we focus on a single settlement, for example, the precontact indigenous village of Onancock on the Eastern Shore of the Chesapeake Bay (near the boundary between what are now the states of Virginia and Maryland), we can determine the spatial scale of the interaction network by finding out how far food moved to and from our focal village. Food came to Onancock from some maximum distance. A bit beyond that were groups that were trading food to groups that were directly sending food to Onancock. If we allow two indirect links, we are probably far enough from Onancock so that no matter what happens (e.g., a food shortage or surplus), Onancock's food supply would not be affected. This outer limit of Onancock's indigenous BGN probably included villages at the very southern and northern ends of the Chesapeake Bay. This way of bounding interaction networks necessitates specifying a particular place and then asking how far the interaction network extends from that place. Usually the importance of interaction declines with distance from the original point. The term "**fall-off**" refers to the gradient of degradation of consequential effects over space.[3]

Onancock's PGN was much larger because prestige goods move farther distances. Indeed,

[3] Geographers also speak of "the tyranny of distance."

copper used by the indigenous peoples of the Chesapeake may have come from as far away as Lake Superior. In between BGNs and PGNs are the interaction networks in which polities make war and ally with one another. These are called **political-military networks** (PMNs).[4] In the case of the Chesapeake world-system, at the time of the arrival of the Europeans in the sixteenth century, Onancock was part of a district chiefdom in a system of multivillage chiefdoms. Across the bay on the Western Shore were at least two larger polities, the Powhatan and the Conoy paramount chiefdoms. These were core chiefdoms that were collecting tribute from a number of smaller district chiefdoms. Onancock was part of an **interchiefdom system** of allying and war-making polities. The boundaries of that network included some indirect links, just as the trade network boundaries did. Thus, the PMN of which Onancock was the focal place extended to Delaware Bay in the north and into what is now the state of North Carolina to the south.

Information, like a prestige good, is light relative to its value. Information may travel far along trade routes and beyond the range of goods. Thus, information networks (INs) are usually as large as or larger than PGNs.

A general picture of the spatial relationships between different kinds of interaction networks is presented in Figure 2.2. The actual spatial scale of important interaction needs to be determined for each world-system we study, but Figure 2.2 shows what is generally the case—that BGNs are smaller than PMNs, and PMNs in turn are smaller than PGNs and INs.

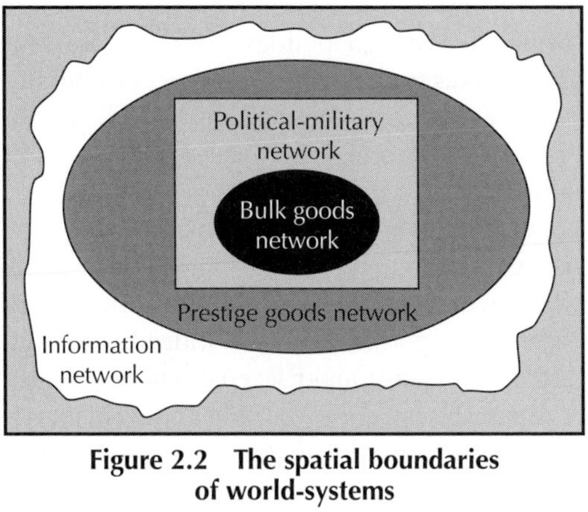

Figure 2.2 The spatial boundaries of world-systems

Defined in this way, world-systems have grown from small to large over the past twelve millennia as societies and intersocietal systems have gotten larger, more complex, and more hierarchical. This spatial growth of systems has involved the expansion of some and the incorporation of some into others. The processes of incorporation have occurred in several ways as systems distant from one another have linked their interaction networks. Because interaction networks are of different sizes, the largest ones come into contact first. Thus, information and prestige goods link distant groups long before they participate in the same PMNs or BGNs. The processes of expansion and incorporation brought different groups of people together and made the organization of larger and more hierarchical societies possible. It is in this sense that **globalization** has been going on for thousands of years. Now that we have defined the spatial boundaries of a regional world-system, we can inquire as to the nature of interpolity relations within that system.

Core/Periphery Relations

The modern world-system is also importantly structured as a core/periphery hierarchy in which some regions contain economically and militarily powerful states while other regions contain polities that are much less powerful and less developed. The countries that are called "advanced"—in the sense that they have high levels of economic development, skilled labor forces, high levels of income, and powerful, well-financed states—are the **core powers** of the modern system. The modern core includes the United States, the countries of Europe, Japan, Australia, and Canada.

In the contemporary **periphery** are relatively weak states that are not strongly supported by the populations within them and that have little power relative to other states in the system. The colonial empires of the European core states have

[4] The PMN of the contemporary global system is the international system of states studied by students of international relations.

dominated most of the modern periphery until recently. These colonial empires have undergone decolonization, and the interstate system of formally sovereign states was extended to the periphery in a series of waves of decolonization that began in the last quarter of the eighteenth century with the independence of the United States, followed by the independence of the Spanish American colonies in the early nineteenth century and by the decolonization of Asia and Africa in the twentieth century. Peripheral regions are also economically less developed in the sense that the economy is composed of subsistence producers, as well as industries that have relatively low productivity and that employ unskilled labor. Agriculture in the periphery is typically performed using simple tools, whereas agriculture in the core is capital-intensive, employing machinery and nonhuman, nonanimal forms of energy. Some industries in peripheral countries, such as oil extraction or mining, may be capital-intensive, but these sectors are often controlled by corporations based in the core.

In the past, peripheral countries were primarily exporters of agricultural and mineral raw materials. But even when they developed some industrial production, it was usually less capital-intensive and used less skilled labor than production processes in the core. The contemporary peripheral countries are most of the countries in Asia, Africa, and Latin America—for example, Bangladesh, Senegal, and Bolivia.

The **core/periphery hierarchy** in the modern world-system is a system of stratification in which socially structured inequalities are reproduced by the institutional features of the system (see Figure 2.3). The periphery is not "catching up" with the core. Rather, both core and peripheral regions are developing, but most core states are staying well ahead of most peripheral states. There is also a stratum of countries that are in between the core and the periphery that we call the **semiperiphery**. The semiperiphery in the modern system includes countries that have intermediate levels of economic development or a balanced mix of developed and less developed regions. The semiperiphery includes large countries that have political-military power as a result of their large size, and smaller countries that are relatively more developed than those in the periphery.

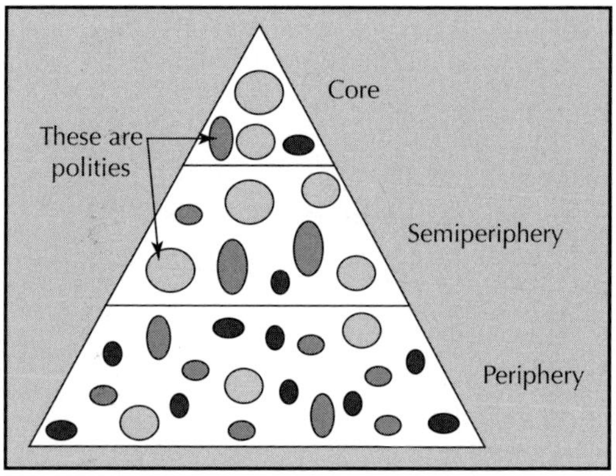

Figure 2.3 Core/periphery hierarchy

The modern semiperiphery includes Mexico, Brazil, Argentina, Venezuela, Korea, Taiwan, Singapore, Indonesia, China, India, South Africa, Russia, Israel, Ireland, Middle Eastern oil exporting countries, Hungary, Poland, and the Czech Republic. The hierarchies that exist between societies do not dissolve the class/caste hierarchies that exist within societies. The differences in absolute wealth between core and periphery, say between the United States and China, affect the comparative status and power of the classes within each society. To be upper-middle class in the core United States involves more wealth and power than being upper-middle class in semiperipheral China. So, too, a member of the skilled working class in another core country, Germany, enjoys a higher standard of living than a skilled worker in Bolivia.

In Figure 2.3 the circles and ellipses are formally sovereign polities. So there are four core polities in the figure. The exact boundaries between the core, semiperiphery, and periphery are unimportant because the main point is that there is a continuum of economic and political-military power that constitutes the core/periphery hierarchy. It does not matter exactly where we draw lines across this continuum in order to categorize countries. Indeed, we could just as well make four or seven categories instead of three. The categories are only a convenient terminology for pointing to the fact of international inequality and for indicating that the middle of this hierarchy may be an important location for processes of social change.

There have been a few cases of upward and downward mobility in the core/periphery hierarchy, though most countries simply run hard to stay in the same relative positions that they have long had. A most spectacular case of upward mobility is the United States. Over the last three hundred years the territory that became the United States has moved from outside the Europe-centered system (a separate continent containing several regional world-systems; see Chapter 7 and the Web Chapter[5]) to the periphery, to the semiperiphery, to the core, to the position of hegemonic core state (see below), and now its hegemony is slowly declining. An example of downward mobility is the United Kingdom of Great Britain, the hegemon of the nineteenth century and now just another core society.

The global stratification system is a continuum of economic and political-military power that is reproduced by the normal operations of the system. In such a hierarchy there are countries that are difficult to categorize. For example, most oil-exporting countries have very high levels of gross national product (GNP) per capita, but their economies do not produce high-technology products that are typical of core countries. They have wealth but not development. The point here is that the categories (core, periphery, and semiperiphery) are just a convenient set of terms for pointing to different locations on a continuous and multidimensional hierarchy of power. It is not necessary to have each case fit neatly into a box. The boxes are only conceptual tools for analyzing the unequal distribution of power among countries.

When we use the idea of core/periphery relations for comparing very different kinds of world-systems, we need to broaden the concept a bit and make an important distinction (see below). But the most important point is that *we should not assume that all world-systems have core/periphery hierarchies* just because the modern system does. It should be an empirical question in each case as to whether core/periphery relations exist. Not assuming that world-systems have core/periphery structures allows us to compare very different kinds of systems and to study how core/periphery hierarchies themselves emerged and evolved.

In order to do this, it is helpful to distinguish between core/periphery differentiation and core/periphery hierarchy. **Core/periphery differentiation** means that polities with different degrees of population density, polity size, and internal hierarchy are interacting with one another. As soon as we find village dwellers interacting with nomadic neighbors, we have core/periphery differentiation. Core/periphery hierarchy refers to the nature of the relationship between polities. This kind of hierarchy exists when some polities are exploiting or dominating other polities. Examples of interpolity domination and exploitation would be the British colonization and deindustrialization of India, or the conquest and subjugation of Mexico by the Spaniards. Core/periphery hierarchy is not unique to the modern Europe-centered world-system of recent centuries. Both the Roman and the Aztec empires conquered and exploited peripheral peoples as well as adjacent core states.

Distinguishing between core/periphery differentiation and core/periphery hierarchy allows us to deal with situations in which larger and more powerful polities are interacting with smaller ones but are not exploiting them. It also allows us to examine cases in which smaller, less dense polities may be exploiting or dominating larger polities. This latter situation definitely occurred in the long and consequential interaction between the nomadic horse pastoralists of Central Asia and the agrarian states and empires of China and Western Asia. The most famous case was that of the Mongol Empire of Chinggis Khan, but confederations of Central Asian steppe nomads managed to extract tribute from agrarian states long before the rise of Mongols.

One of the important systemic features of the modern system is the rise and fall of hegemonic core powers—the so-called **hegemonic sequence**. A **hegemon** is a core state that has a significantly greater amount of economic power than any other state and that takes on the political role of system leader. In the seventeenth century, the Dutch Republic performed the role of hegemon in the Europe-centered system, while Great Britain was the hegemon of the nineteenth

[5] http://www.paradigmpublishers.com/resrcs/other/1612053289_otherlink.pdf.

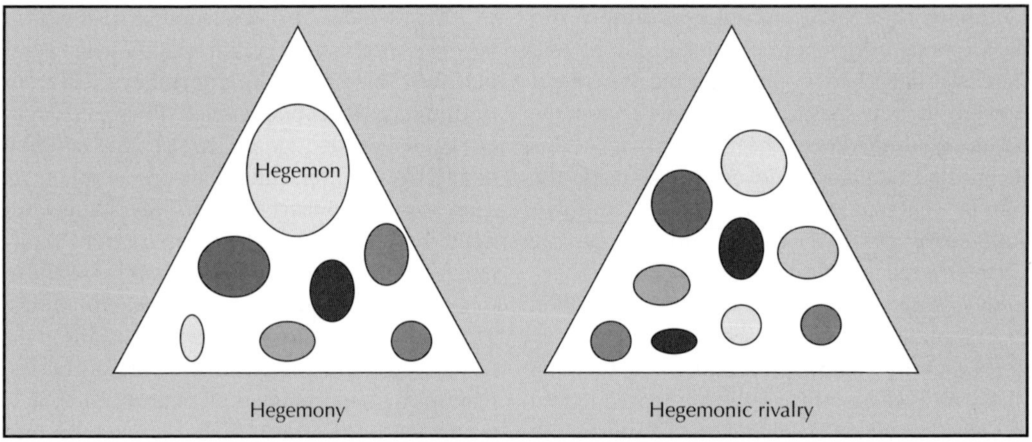

Figure 2.4 Hegemony and hegemonic rivalry

century and the United States has been the hegemon in the twentieth century. Hegemons provide leadership and order for the interstate system and the world economy. But the normal operating processes of the modern system—uneven economic development and competition among states—make it difficult for hegemons to sustain their dominant positions, and so they tend to decline. Thus, the structure of the core oscillates back and forth between hegemony and a situation in which several competing core states have a roughly similar amount of power and are contending for hegemony: **hegemonic rivalry** (see Figure 2.4).

So the modern world-system is composed of states that are linked to one another by the world economy and other interaction networks. Earlier world-systems were also composed of polities, but the interaction networks that linked these polities were not intercontinental in scale until the expansion of Europe in the fifteenth century. Before that, world-systems were smaller regional affairs. But these had been growing in size for millenia with the expansion of trade networks and long-distance military campaigns.

Modes of Accumulation

In order to comprehend the qualitative changes that have occurred with the processes of sociocultural evolution, we need to conceptualize different logics of development and the institutional modes by which socially created resources are produced and accumulated. All societies produce and distribute goods that are necessary for everyday life. But the institutional means by which human labor is mobilized are very different in different kinds of societies. Small and egalitarian societies rely primarily on normative regulation organized as commonly shared understandings about the obligations that members of families and associated groups of families have toward one another. When a hunter returns with his game, there are definite rules and understandings about who should receive shares of the meat and how much. All hunters in foraging societies want to be thought of as generous, but they must also take care of some people (those for whom they are the most responsible) before they can give to others.

The normative order defines the roles and the obligations, and the norms and values are affirmed or modified by the continual symbolic and nonsymbolic action of the people. This socially constructed consciousness is mainly about kinship, but it is also about the nature of the universe of which the human group is understood as a part. Kinship is more widely constructed than in modern societies. People may be related to bears, trees, eagles, and so on. This kind of social economy is called a **kin-based mode of production** and accumulation. People work because they need food and they have obligations to provide food for others. Accumulation mainly involves the preservation and storage of food supplies for the season in which food will become scarce. Status is based on the reputation one has as a good hunter, a good gatherer, a good family member, or a talented speaker. Group decisions are made by consensus, which means that the people keep talking until they come to an understanding of what to do. The leaders have authority that is mainly based on their ability to convince others that they are right. These features are common (but not universal) among polities and world-systems in which the kin-based modes of accumulation are the main logic of development.

As polities become larger and more hierarchical, kinship itself becomes hierarchically defined. Clans and lineages become ranked so that members of some families are defined as senior or superior to members of other families. This tendency toward hierarchical kinship resulted in the eventual emergence of class societies (complex chiefdoms) in which a noble class owned and controlled key resources and a class of commoners was separated from the control of important resources and had to rely on the nobles for access to them. Such a society existed in Hawaii before the arrival of the Europeans (see Chapter 7).

The **tributary modes of accumulation** emerged when institutional coercion became a central form of regulation for inducing people to work and for the accumulation of social resources. Hierarchical kinship functions in this way when commoners must provide labor or products to chiefs in exchange for access to resources that chiefs control by means of both normative and coercive power.

Normative power does not work well by itself as a basis for the appropriation of labor or goods by one group from another. Those who are exploited have a great motive to redefine the situation. The nobles may have elaborated a vision of the universe in which they were understood to control natural forces or to mediate interactions with the deities and so commoners were supposed to be obligated to support these sacred duties by turning over their produce to the nobles or contributing labor to sacred projects. But the commoners will have an incentive to disbelieve unless they have only worse alternatives. Thus the institutions of coercive power are invented to sustain the extraction of surplus labor and goods from direct producers. The hierarchical religions and kinship systems of complex chiefdoms became supplemented in early states by specialized organizations of regional control—groups of armed men under the command of the king and bureaucratic systems of taxation and tribute backed up by the law and by institutionalized force. The tributary modes of accumulation developed **techniques of power** that allowed resources to be extracted over great distances and from large populations. These are the institutional bases of the states and the empires.

The third mode of accumulation is based on markets. Markets can be defined as any situation in which goods are bought and sold, but we will use the term to denote what are called **price-setting markets**, in which the competitive trading by large numbers of buyers and sellers is an important determinant of the price. This is a situation in which supply and demand operate on the price because buyers and sellers are bidding against one another. There are very few instances in history or in modern reality of purely price-setting markets, because political and normative considerations quite often influence prices. But the price mechanism and resulting market pressures have become much more important. Earlier forms of exchange tend to have customary terms of trade based on notions of fairness, but these change only slowly. Once true money has emerged, prices can change much faster in response to changing availability of goods.

A **commodity** is a good that is produced for sale in a price-setting market in order to make a profit.[6] A pencil is an example of a modern commodity. It is a fairly standardized product in which the conditions of production and the cost of raw materials, labor, energy, and pencil-making machines are important forces acting on the price of the pencil. Pencils are produced for a rather competitive market, and so the socially necessary expenses given the current level of technology, plus a certain amount of profit, are included in the cost.

The idea of the commodity is an important element of the definition of the **capitalist mode of accumulation**. **Capitalism** is based on the accumulation of profits by the owners

[6] Note that this is a more restrictive definition of "commodity" than common usage. Many use the word to refer to any good that is produced for exchange. We prefer Marx's definition, which requires a price-setting market.

of major means of the production of commodities in a context in which labor and the other main elements of production are commodified. **Commodification** means that things are treated as if they are commodities, even though they may have characteristics that make this somewhat difficult. So land can be commodified—treated as if it is a commodity—even though it is a limited good that has not originally been produced for profitable sale. There is only so much land on earth. We can divide it up into sections with straight boundaries and price it based on supply and demand. But it will never be a perfect commodity. So, too, with human labor.

Commodified labor takes the form of wage labor, in which the worker sells his or her labor time to capital, or chattel slavery, in which the worker is the property of another.

The commodification of land is an historical process that began when "real property" was first legally defined and sold. The conceptualization of places as abstract, measurable, substitutable, and salable space is an institutional redefinition that took thousands of years to develop and to spread to all regions of the earth.

The capitalist modes of production also required the redefinition of wealth as money. The first storable and exchangeable valuables were prestige goods. These were used by local elites in gift exchanges with adjacent peoples, and as symbols of superior status. Trade among simple societies is primarily organized as gift giving among elites in which allegiances are created and sustained. Originally, prestige goods were used only in specific circumstances by certain elites. This "protomoney" was eventually redefined and institutionalized as the so-called universal equivalent that serves as a general measure of value for all sorts of goods and that can be used by almost anyone to buy almost anything. The institution of money has a long and complicated history, but suffice it to say here that it has been a prerequisite for the emergence of price-setting markets and capitalism as increasingly important forms of social regulation. Once markets and capital became the predominant form of accumulation, we can speak of capitalist systems.

Capital is privately owned property that is used to produce commodities and to make profits by employing commodified labor. Capital is here defined more narrowly than in many other works. It is not just wealth. Cows in a pastoralist society are not capital according to our definition.

Patterns and Causes of Social Evolution

Before the story is told, it will be helpful to have a map of the territory of world-systems evolution. This section describes a general causal model that explains the emergence of larger hierarchies and the development of productive technologies. It also points to a pattern that is noticeable only when we study world-systems rather than individual societies. The pattern is called **semiperipheral development**. This means that those innovations that transform the logic of development and allow world-systems to get larger and more hierarchical come mainly from semiperipheral societies. Some semiperipheral societies are unusually fertile locations for the invention and implementation of new institutional structures. And semiperipheral societies are not constrained to the same degree as older core societies by "lock-ins"—having invested huge resources in doing things the old way. So they are freer to implement new institutions.

It will become evident in the chapters that follow that there are several different, important kinds of semiperipheries, and that these not only transform systems but also often take over and become new core societies. We have already mentioned semiperipheral marcher chiefdoms. The societies that conquered and unified a number of smaller chiefdoms into larger paramount chiefdoms were usually from semiperipheral locations. Peripheral peoples did not usually have the institutional and material resources that would allow them to make important inventions and implement them or to take over older core regions. It was in the semiperiphery that core and peripheral social characteristics could be recombined in new ways. Sometimes this meant that new techniques of power or political legitimacy were invented and implemented in semiperipheral societies.

Much better known than semiperipheral marcher chiefdoms is the phenomenon of semiperipheral marcher states. The largest empires have been assembled by conquerors who came from semiperipheral societies. The following semiperipheral marchers are well known: the Achaemenid Persians, the Macedonians led by

Alexander the Great, the Romans, the Ottomans, the Manchus, and the Aztecs.

Some semiperipheries transform institutions but do not take over. The semiperipheral capitalist city-states operated on the edges of the tributary empires where they bought and sold goods in widely separate locations, encouraging people to produce a surplus for trade. The Phoenician cities (e.g., Tyre and Carthage), as well as Malacca, Venice, and Genoa, spread commodification by producing or assembling manufactured goods and trading them across great regions. In this way the semiperipheral capitalist city-states were agents of the development of markets and the expansion of trade networks, and so they helped transform the world of the tributary empires without becoming new core powers themselves.

We have already mentioned the process of the rise and fall of hegemonic core states that occurs in the modern world-system. All of the cases we mentioned—the Dutch, the British, and the United States—were countries that had formerly been in semiperipheral positions relative to the regional core/periphery hierarchies within which they existed. And indeed the rise of Europe within the larger Afroeurasian world-system was also a case of semiperipheral development, one in which a formerly peripheral and then semiperipheral region rose to become the new core of what had been a huge multicore world-system.

The idea of semiperipheral development does not claim that all semiperipheral societies perform transformational roles, nor does it contend that every important innovation came from the semiperiphery. Rather, the point is that semiperipheries have been unusually prolific sites for the invention of those institutions that have expanded and transformed many small systems into the particular kind of global system that we have today. This observation would not be possible without the conceptual apparatus of the comparative world-systems perspective.

But what have been the proximate causes that led semiperipheral societies to invent new institutional solutions to problems? Some of the problems that needed to be solved were new, unintended consequences of earlier inventions, but others were very old problems that emerged again and again as systems expanded—for example, population pressure and ecological degradation. It is these basic problems that make it possible for us to specify a single underlying causal model of world-systems evolution. Figure 2.5 shows what is called the "iteration model," which links demographic, ecological, and interactional processes with the emergence of new production technologies, bigger polities, and greater degrees of hierarchy.

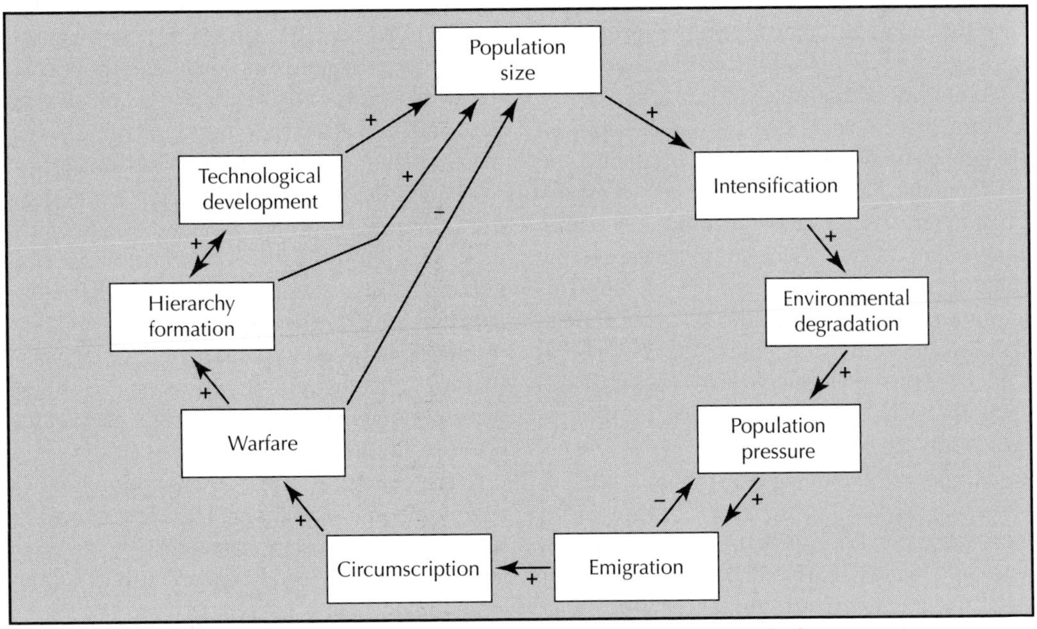

Figure 2.5 Basic iteration model of world-system evolution

It is called an iteration model because it has an important positive feedback mechanism in which the original causes are themselves consequences of the things that they cause. Thus the process goes around and around, which is what has caused the world-systems to expand to the global level. Starting at the top we see "population size." The idea here is that all human societies contain a biological impetus to grow that is based on sexuality. This impetus is both controlled and encouraged by social institutions. Some societies regulate population growth by means of infanticide, abortion, taboos on sexual relations during nursing, and prolonged nursing (lactation reduces fertility). Most of these means of regulation are costly, and when greater amounts of food are available these types of regulation tend to be eased and so the population tends to grow. Some societies encourage population growth by means of channeling sexual energy toward reproduction, pro-natalist ideologies, and support for large families. Most societies experience occasional or periodic "baby booms" when social circumstances are somewhat more propitious for reproduction, and thus, over the long run and with other things being equal (warfare, disease, resource degradation; see below), the population tends to grow.

Intensification is caused by population growth and consequent pressure on resources. This means that when the number of mouths to feed increases, greater efforts are needed to produce the food and other necessities of life, and so people exploit the resources they have been exploiting more intensively. This usually leads, in turn, to ecological degradation because all human production processes use up the natural environment. More production leads to greater environmental degradation. This occurs because more resources are extracted and because of the polluting consequences of production and consumption activities. Nomadic hunter-gatherers depleted the herds of big game, and Polynesian horticulturalists deforested many a Pacific island. Environmental degradation is not a new phenomenon. Only its global scale is new.

As Jared Diamond (1997) points out, all continents around the world did not start with the same animal and plant resources. In West Asia both plants (barley and wheat) and animals (sheep, goats, cows, and oxen) were easily domesticated. The New World peoples were able to domesticate amazing crop plants but did not have as many animal species that could be easily and usefully domesticated. Since domesticated plants and animals can more easily diffuse lattitudinally (east and west) than longitudinally (north and south), the West Asian domesticates spread more quickly to Europe and East Asia than they did to Africa. Thus original "natural capital" (the availability of zoological and botanical species that could be usefully domesticated) influenced the timing of the emergence of sociocultural complexity. And geographical conditions influenced the rate of the diffusion of domestication.

The consequences of population growth are that the economics of production change for the worse. According to Joseph Tainter (1988), after a certain point, further investment in complexity does not result in proportionate increasing returns. This occurs in the areas of agricultural production, information processing, and communication, including education and maintenance of information channels. Sociopolitical control and specialization, such as the military and the police, also develop diminishing returns.

Deer hunters first bag the deer that are close to camp. When nearby herds are depleted, hunters must go farther to find game. The combined sequence from population growth to intensification to environmental degradation leads to **population pressure**, the negative economic effects on production activities. The growing effort needed to produce enough food is a big incentive for people to migrate. And so humans populated the whole earth. If the herds in one valley were depleted, humans were often able to find a new place where herds were more abundant.

Migration eventually leads to circumscription. **Circumscription** is the condition in which no new desirable locations are available for emigration. This can be because all the alternative locations are deserts or high mountains with few resources, or because all adjacent desirable locations are already occupied by people who will resist our moving in with them or our getting resources in their territory.

The condition of social circumscription, in which adjacent locations are already occupied, is (under conditions of population pressure) likely to lead to a rise in the level of intergroup and intragroup conflict. This is because more people are competing for fewer resources. Warfare and other kinds of conflict are more prevalent under such conditions. All systems experience some warfare, but warfare can become a major focus of social endeavor that has a life of its own. Boys are trained to be warriors, and societies make decisions based on the presumption that they will be attacked or will be attacking other groups. Even in situations of seemingly endemic warfare the amount of conflict varies cyclically. Figure 2.5 shows an arrow with a negative sign going from warfare back to population pressure. This is because high levels of conflict reduce the size of the population as warriors are killed off and noncombatants die because their food supplies have been destroyed. Some systems get stuck in a vicious cycle of population pressure and warfare (e.g., Kirch 1991).

But situations such as this are also propitious for the emergence of new institutional structures. It is in these situations that semiperipheral development is likely to occur. People get tired of endemic conflict and become less resistant to hierarchy formation. The emergence of hierarchy within societies and of empire in an interpolity system reduces the average levels of conflict by regulating access to resources and creating an authority structure that can resolve disagreements without high levels of violence. The emergence of a new, larger polity usually occurs as a result of successful conquest of a number of smaller polities by a semiperipheral marcher chiefdom or state. The larger polity creates peace by means of an organized force that is greater than any force likely to be brought against it. The new polity reconstructs the institutions of control over territory and resources, often concentrating control and wealth for a new elite. And larger and more hierarchical polities often invest in new technologies of production that change the way resources are utilized. They produce more food and other valuables by using new technologies or by intensifying the use of old technologies. New technologies can expand the number of people who can be supported in the territory. But this makes population growth more likely, and so the iteration model is primed to go around again.

The iteration model keeps expanding the size of world-systems and developing new technologies and forms of regulation, but as of yet it has not permanently solved the original problems of ecological degradation and population pressure. What has happened is the emergence of institutions such as states and markets that articulate changes in the economics of production more directly with changes in political organization, cultural institutions, and technology. This allows the institutional structures to readjust without having to go through the messy Malthusian bottom end of the model (Figure 2.6).

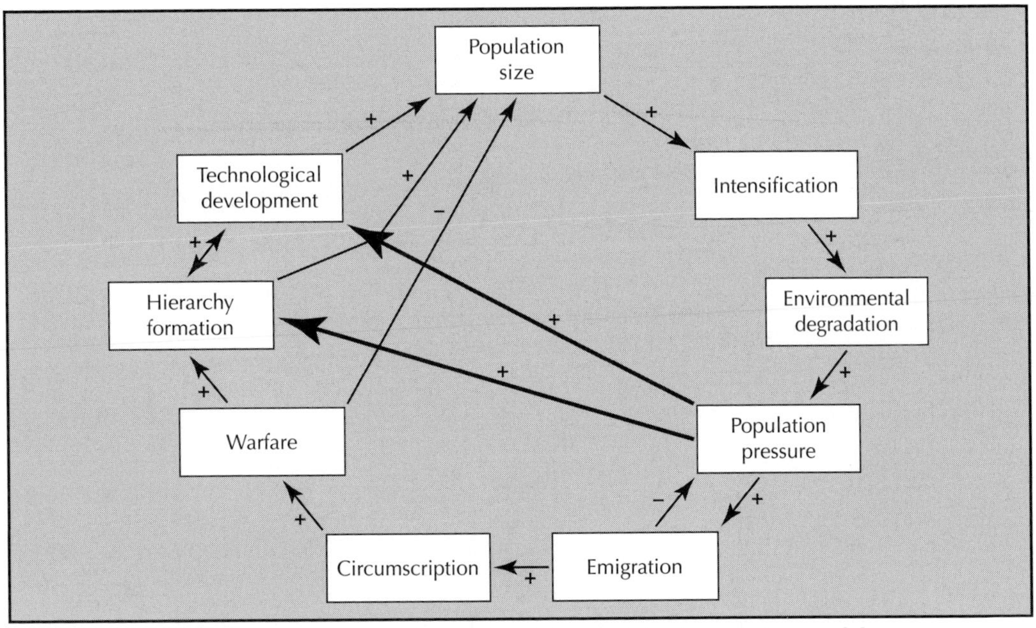

Figure 2.6 Temporary institutional shortcuts in the iteration model

Another way to say this is that political and market institutions allow for some adjustments to occur without greatly increasing the level of systemic conflict. This said, the level of conflict has remained quite high because the rate of expansion and technological change has increased. Even though institutional mechanisms of articulation have emerged, they have not permanently lowered the amount of systemic conflict, because the rates of change in the other variables have increased.

Some theorists of sociocultural evolution claim that the model described above can explain some major transformations and expansions but not others. This problem will be discussed at the point at which our story reaches the emergence of capitalism and the rise of Europe.

The basic ideas have now been described. We have a philosophical standpoint, a method, a theoretical approach (institutional materialism), and an orienting strategy (the comparative world-systems perspective). Let us now turn to the processes by which an individual learns to become a social being by developing a social self, including the ability to reason abstractly.

Now we have enough macrosociological tools from the comparative world-systems approach. With a carefully selected and thoughtfully packed bag of conceptual camping equipment, we will be ready for an excursion into the realm of stateless systems and trekking with the nomads. But before we leave on our trip we need to clarify how it was that the human species became social in the first place. Did humans produce societies by pulling themselves up by their own boot straps, or did the prehuman and protohuman ancestors also have societies?

Suggested Readings

Chase-Dunn, Christopher, and Salvatore Babones, eds. 2006. *Global Social Change*. Baltimore: Johns Hopkins University Press.

Chase-Dunn, Christopher, and Thomas D. Hall. 1997. *Rise and Demise: Comparing World-Systems*. Boulder, CO: Westview Press.

Diamond, Jared. 2005. *Collapse*. New York: Viking.

Hall, Thomas D., ed. 2000. *The World-Systems Reader.* Lanham, MD: Rowman and Littlefield.

3

Biological Bases of Social Evolution

Learning, Sociality, and Culture

There was a time in sociological discussions about, say, gender differences when the issue came down to whether tastes in erotica were more social or more biological in origin. The problem here is that if a process was social, it usually meant it was changeable, and, secondly, it had nothing to do with biology. Conversely, to admit something was biological meant that it was more or less permanent and that it was nonsocial or antisocial. One of the points we want to make in this chapter is that almost all mammalian behavior was social long before the human species came along.

Sociality for mutual benefit goes deep into organic evolution. Within the species of vertebrates, fish, birds, and mammals all have social qualities, as do insects such as ants, termites, and bees. Major activities include procuring and sharing food, defense, forming coalitions and alliances, nurturing their young, and social grooming.

"Learning" is usually defined as a relatively permanent change in behavior or behavior potential that is made through experience with the environment rather than because of genetic inheritance. While learning can take place in nonsocial species, a great deal of learning is social learning. What makes learning especially important to social species is that what can be learned can be *shared* just with family, with members of the same species, and within the same generation. Sociality beyond the family, by a mechanism called reciprocal altruism, allows experience to be pooled.

Just as it is possible for learning to take place without sociality, so, too, can sociality take place without culture. Culture is the transmission of learning across generations by nongenetic means. Not all social animals have culture. Social animals can pool their learning with other members of their species within a generation, but new learning cannot be passed on to the next generation. Learning and sociality are foundation stones for the building of culture. There is no culture without learning and sociability as its underpinnings. But, as the philosophers say, learning and sociability are "necessary but not *sufficient* conditions" for culture. Chimps learned how to make and use tools and have what might be called "simple culture," and wolves and bowerbirds are transitional cases.

The emergence of a "socio-culture" involves transmission of artifacts and symbols of what has been learned and shared within the group immediately to the next generation. Humans are the only species that does this extensively. This chapter explores what those sufficient conditions are.

We believe that there are two psychological processes that need to be in place in order to be fully sociocultural beings:

1. An expansion of the range of emotions animals can have (J. Turner 2000)
2. The development of what Pascal Boyer (2001) has called "hypothetical decoupled thinking"

Expansion of Emotional Range

Jonathan Turner (2000) argues that apes must have had three primary emotions—aggression, aversion (fear), and satisfaction. But all of these emotions are only primitively social and do not promote solidarity. They were not enough to build and sustain the type of society apes needed to survive in the open savanna when the forests receded. The range of emotions needed to be combined and elaborated on *beyond* power relations and mother-child bonds. The problem is that positive social emotions, which are the basis for group solidarity, *are not hardwired but must be built*. These new emotions had to have qualities that would allow group members to have conflicts that are not destructive and that do not promote withdrawal. Secondary and tertiary emotions must be built from a primary foundation. Over many generations, something like the following took place:

- Satisfaction must be expanded beyond biological gratification in the direction of *happiness*
- Happiness is further broken down into pride, placation, and hopefulness
- Aversion-fear is complexified to include veneration, antagonism, dismay, dejection, and depression
- Assertion is elaborated into mollification and abhorrence
- Disappointment is an emotion that is socially constructed and broken down into other social emotions such as acceptance and remorse, and being aggrieved or dissatisfied

Still more complex emotions include shame and guilt. Turner (2000) defines shame as what happens when individuals have not demonstrated competence in a situation. Guilt is generated when individuals know they have not met the expectations of others. There is disappointment with the self for having failed and sadness about that failure. This is mixed with fear about the consequences to the self and anger at oneself for having failed.

The point of developing these complex emotions is to learn to control emotional outbursts that endanger group solidarity while neither harming others nor withdrawing from society. Emotions such as sadness must be cultivated so that breaches to solidarity will not occur and the needs that are driving the sadness can be socially attended to. Without these forms of internal control, people's emotional lives would have to be constantly monitored with rewards or punishments. The larger and more complex the form of social organization, the more complex the emotional lives of its participants.

From Animal Calls to Human Language

According to Marc Hauser (2000), all animal communication can have three functions: (1) to manipulate a group of willing listeners, (2) to elicit cooperation, and (3) to evoke competition. In the process of fulfilling these functions, animals distinguish allies from enemies, males from females, conspecific from hetero-specific, old from young, and kin from non-kin.

Typically, an animal can hear a signal from another animal and specify the species and sex of the animal. The range of animal sounds varies in size from one or two distinctive signals to twenty-five or thirty. These sounds signify cooperation, competition, dominance fights over territory, discoveries of food, detection of a predator, mate attraction, playful opportunities, and group movement. Although most animals may not understand what others desire and believe, some animals have abstract representation of objects, number, space, and social relationships.

Hauser (2000) poses the following questions: To what extent can animals expand the range of meaningful utterances they produce by stringing calls together? Are they limited to labeling or naming discrete objects, or can they describe relationships and abstractions? If these enhancements are possible, do their calls fall into such abstract categories as noun, verb, and adjective? In terms of units, is the call equivalent to the word?

Hauser's answer is that calls cannot be pieced together into language for at least three reasons:

1. Animal calls are buried in the immediate present or the very immediate future. One of the extraordinary things about human language is that it refers to events in the deep past and to plans in the near and even distant future.
2. Animal calls are grounded in a species-specific environment. Animals do not abstract from it and project these calls into more general environments. The human species, on the other hand, can converge inside airplanes or underneath the water in submarines, far from our evolutionary origins.
3. While animal calls cannot be reduced to a one-to-one correspondence between a call and an event, animal calls do not have anywhere near the unpredictability of a human response to events. For example, if a five-year-old student presents an apple to the teacher, the teacher's response is reasonably predictable: "Thank you very much." There is no hidden meaning or complexity that requires a more careful response. One does not read anything more into it. But if an 18-year-old student presents a teacher with an apple, the situation is considerably more complex and the teacher will have to think very quickly and very carefully how to respond. Many responses are possible because the situation is dense with levels of meaning.

Chimps do not have the vocal apparatus required to produce most of the sounds associated with the world's languages. Human language requires a deep-set larynx, which provides a large resonating chamber at the back of the nose and mouth. We also have to possess careful control of vocal chords, which act as vibrators. When researchers tried to teach language using a computer, chimps could make requests (in this sense, the chimp is like a young child, with a "me, me" attitude). According to Hauser (2000), the structure of their calls is nothing like our concepts of noun, verb, and object.

Nonhuman Animal Minds

For Gordon Gallup (1970), the mirror test provided evidence that chimpanzees not only recognized themselves in the mirror but were self-aware. But Hauser (2000) argues that self-awareness is more than just body recognition. It involves knowledge of:

- One's beliefs
- How one's beliefs change over time
- How one's beliefs differ from the beliefs of others

Most discussions of this work concluded that great apes and human children over the age of two years have some understanding of self, but that no other species has it.

Most animals act as if they classify the world into animate versus inanimate objects. They perceive animate objects as having goals and then assign particular emotions to them. There is no evidence that animals are actually aware of their own beliefs and how they differ from those of their peers. Most animals lack the capacity to attribute mental states to others. They lack a fundamental mental tool: self-awareness.

In their book *How Monkeys See the World*, Cheney and Seyfarth (1990) conclude that monkeys do not attribute mental states to others, though their social interactions are complex.

Having a social mind means that a member of a species can imagine and anticipate what another member might be thinking based on their role and the situation. A theory of mind means knowing that others have beliefs, desires, fears, and hopes that might be different from one's own. Secondly, a member of a species calculates its next move based on another's reaction to its first move. At the same time, in using its social mind, it must remember that others will be assessing what it might be up to as well. As you can imagine, this can get very complicated very quickly. If de Waal's description of a colony of chimps at a breeding zoo in Holland is any indication, chimps definitely attribute beliefs to others. Chimps engage in power takeovers, peace negotiations, deception around food and mates, and other forms of political activities that are usually thought to be unique to humans.

Animal Minds and Group Size

Studies attempting to explain an increase in brain size in evolution are usually attributed to a more complex physical environment, stiffer competition between species, or an increasing pace of life due to an environmental crisis. Without discounting any of these factors, Robin Dunbar (1996) argues that the size of the social group is deeply connected to the size of the brain. Specifically, he says that among primates, social group size appears to be limited by the size of the neocortex of the species.

Dunbar argues that social animals walk a tightrope between two forces. On the one hand we are driven together by centripetal forces based on a fear of predation. But on the other hand, we are driven apart by centrifugal forces of diffusion to avoid overcrowding. This means that there are definite parameters to group sizes. Faced with the problem of survival and reproduction of genes, an animal may become a larger than average primate or may develop skills for living in unusually large groups.

There are many costs associated with living in large groups. The group must cover a larger area of territory each day to provide the same quality of food for each member. Since the group burns more energy traveling, they need to eat more and coordinate the processes for organizing food distribution. There is competition for sleeping sites as well as free riding.

A solution to some of these problems is coalition formation. Coalition formation allows species members to act for mutual defense, defusing competition within a species without driving members away. Alliances will be increasingly important as the group grows larger. Since the problem of free riding increases with group size, membership in a coalition must be costly, with each member expected to make a token of commitment.

Coalitions contain three properties: (1) they are voluntary involvements in which defection is possible, (2) benefits accrue with cooperation, and (3) there is a cost to continue cooperating when others defect.

Boyer (2001) defines seven conditions that need to be present for coalitions to form:

- A member behaves in such a way as to enhance the benefits gained by other members of the group but not those of nonmembers.
- A member receives enhanced benefits gained by others, but that does not require that a member receive a particular benefit for helping them.
- A member can expect similar treatments from other members but not from nonmembers.
- A member compares the benefits against the costs in interacting with *all* other members, not with each member separately.
- A member sees the behavior of members of other groups as being representative of the whole groups' behavior (stereotypes).
- A member's reaction to how a member of another group behaves is *directed at the group*, not specifically at the individual in question.
- There is great concern with other members' loyalty—whether the others in a group are reliably loyal to the group—regardless of how it affects you directly. Specifically:
  - You desire to punish those people who have defected
  - You want to punish those who failed to punish the defectors
  - You want to screen people by submitting them to ordeals so they have to incur substantial costs to demonstrate their future loyalty

But what can social primates do if they are intelligent enough to form and sustain groups but cannot verbally reassure other members?

Grooming Sustains Coalition Formation

Dunbar's (1996) answer is that *grooming sustains coalition formation*. It makes sense to invest time in grooming your allies. Grooming stimulates endorphins, but the basis goes far beyond hygiene. Grooming takes a lot of time and shows willingness to act as an ally of another. The amount of time devoted to grooming is roughly correlated to the size of the group; that is, bigger groups require individuals to spend more time building trust. But this proportion does have its limits. The more time spent grooming, the less time spent foraging for food, defending against predators, or looking for mates. According to Dunbar, no primate spends more than 20 percent of the day engaged in grooming. At what point did group size pass through the critical threshold? Around 250,000 years ago, group size was already in the region of 120–130, and grooming time would have been running at 33–35 percent of the time spent. By what means might social primates continue to reassure each other, continue to grow in size, and have plenty of energy left over for other adaptation needs?

From Grooming to Verbal Language

The solution was to develop "vocal grooming" or verbal language. There are at least four ways in which verbal language, what Dunbar (1996) calls "gossip," is more economical than grooming:

1. Verbal language allows us to reach more individuals at the same time.
2. Verbal language allows us to keep track of other people's reputations as well as our own. It is easier to keep track of who's doing what with whom.
3. Verbal language allows for self-advertising in ways that monkeys and apes cannot advertise.
4. Verbal language allows us to produce the reinforcing effects of grooming (opiate release—laughing, smiling) from a distance.

Language evolved in at least these stages, becoming progressively more complex as the demands of larger group sizes became more pressing:

1. Conventional contact calls including those of Old World monkeys and apes. Here we have grooming *at a distance*.
2. Gestures convey the same kind of information that monkeys and apes express using vocalizations. Gestures are good for making commands, drawing someone's attention, emphasizing a point, expressing anger or submission, or indicating friendship. But it is very difficult, if not impossible, to use gestures for expressing abstract concepts, indicating place or time other than the present, or making plans for the future.
3. Vocal grooming—chatter—supplemented physical grooming. Two million years ago, this would roughly correspond to *Homo erectus*.
4. Song and dance play an important part in holding together large groups. They rouse emotions and stimulate the production of opiates to bring about states of elation and euphoria. Chris Knight (1990) argues that use of ritual to coordinate human groups by synchronizing emotional states is very ancient behavior.
5. Vocalization acquires highly social meaning, what Dunbar (1996) calls "gossip." Verbal language is capable of making reference to abstract concepts. Verbal vocalization goes with a change in style, quality, and variety of stone tools.

Orders of Intentionality

Earlier we discussed how in order to be social we must put ourselves in the framework of the mind of another in order to plan our next move. Further, we said that chimps in primate societies have theories of mind. But how far can this strategic thinking go? Robin Dunbar (1996) refers to this as "orders of intentionality." He gives us five orders (see Table 3.1):

0 Zero order intentionality: A species is not aware of its own mental states. Most insects and other invertebrates fall under this category.

1 First order intentionality: A species is aware that it has mental states, but it doesn't know that others also have mental states. Furthermore, it thinks its thoughts are universally shared by others and are transparent to others. Children at a very young age fall into this category. This is why, up until about age three, children are not good liars. To lie, one has to be able to imagine what another expects and then do something different.

2 Second order intentionality: We move from self-involved thinking to one who is not only aware that others think but is able to skillfully imagine what others might be thinking with some degree of reliability. Great apes are the only species that we know of that can do this. At about four and a half years of age, children realize that other individuals can hold beliefs different from their own.

3 Third order intentionality: Here you are making a distinction between what you think someone's perception of you is and what you actually are, and you make your move based on that misconception—"I believe that you believe that I believe." Now it is starting to get complicated. Dunbar categorizes great apes under this umbrella.

4 Fourth order intentionality: This is the arid land of cognition where only humans are likely to dwell. At this point you may be wondering, why would anyone twist their mind up like a pretzel? After all, at some

point, isn't it better to simply either *act* on your thoughts or *ask* the other person what his or her intentions are?

Originally, the value of fourth order intentionality must have had a great deal to do with coalition formation. As we've already established, in order for human beings to survive, cooperation with other humans is essential. Evolutionary psychologists tell us we cooperate through kin selection and reciprocal altruism among strangers. Fourth order intentionality would come in handy in accessing the willingness or unwillingness of others to cooperate.

We are especially hardwired to detect problems of trust and ongoing commitment. In a significant number of situations we cannot know whether others will cooperate or cheat. For this reason, we are very sensitive to reading faces in order to detect sincerity and to punish cheating. If people don't stick together to make cheaters pay, then confidence in cooperating is undermined.

Because cooperation among humans is something that has to be negotiated, people *think strategically*. Simply defined, strategies are where people imagine their moves based on what they think someone else's moves will be. To be able to do a reasonable job, mind reading is a substantial asset not only in social relations but in stalking prey and avoiding predators.

Fourth order intentionality takes place in everyday life among unequals in situations where exiting the situation is not an option. Suppose revealing your intentions or asking someone else to reveal their intentions is *dangerous*? Parents facing their teenage sons or daughters over curfews or choices of boyfriends/girlfriends are the kinds of settings where no one can afford to play with an open hand. Other examples include a husband suspecting his wife of infidelity and routine engagements between guards and inmates in prisons. So, fourth order intentionality is making your moves based on what I believe that you believe that I believe that you believe.

Even though fourth order intentionality can be used in the service of strategic self-interest, it can also be used for more noble purposes. To possess fourth order intentionality means to be able to step back not just from ourselves but from other people in our vicinity and begin to look at the world objectively. At this order of thinking, long-term time and space displacement becomes possible. Fourth order intentionality is the basis of science, religion, and the arts.

Table 3.1 Orders of intentionality

Level of intentionality	Definition	Example
Zero order	A species is not aware of its own mental states.	Most insects and other invertebrates.
First order	A species is aware it has mental states but is unaware of the mental states of others.	Children up until about three years of age. Lying is not possible.
Second order	A species is aware of the mental states of others and can plan accordingly. "I believe that *you believe* something is the case."	Children by about age four and a half; great apes. Lying is possible, but not very sophisticated.
Third order	A species is aware of the distinction between how it is perceived by others and how it perceives itself. "I believe that you believe that I believe something is the case."	Children after about age five; great apes; *Homo habilius; Homo erectus; Homo neanderthalensis.* More cooperation and lying are now possible.
Fourth order	A species is capable of forming long-term strategies based on the projected moves and countermoves of humans. "I believe that you believe that I believe that you believe something is the case." Space-time displacement creates the possibility of objectivity.	*Homo sapiens.* Forming and assessing coalitions; stalking prey. Human situations of incarceration or dense, power-dominated social contexts: teenager–parents encounters; suspicions of infidelity in marriage; inmates and guards in prisons. Science, the arts, religion.

Emergence of Hypothetical Thinking

In order to think socially as humans, we have to learn to think *hypothetically*. According to Pascal Boyer (2001), a fundamental characteristic of our inference systems is that they operate in a "decoupled mode"; that is, our minds can disengage from the immediate external inputs from our biophysical world and consider various hypothetical alternative situations before deciding on a course of action. This means thinking about what could be, rather than what just happened. In humans, this happens as early as the "let's pretend" stage of play we will study in the next chapter. The hypothetical choices that present themselves over and over again to human beings have a biological foundation in our "cognitive unconscious."

The legacy of our biological heritage is built into our programmed preferences to make some choices over others. There are rules about how the mind of *Homo sapiens* can work based on what was (and is) selectively advantageous. We have control over the conscious part of our mind, but we cannot rework our hardwiring.

According to Boyer (2001), what makes our minds smart is not their content but our specialized systems of inferences, which are selectively turned on or off when we consider different kinds of situations and desired outcomes. We live in a world of physical objects, biological organisms, and social beings along with the tools and artifacts we shape as a society. Our inference systems are programmed for dealing with each of them. Therefore, we have ontological categories—very abstract concepts for "animals," "tools," and "persons"—and we have certain expectations about each.

Because we deal with physical objects we make intuitive inferences about physical causation that are not a product of learning but of our evolutionary heritage. We are also hardwired to detect the difference between inanimate objects that move only when pushed or pulled and biological organisms that move in more unpredictable ways because they are motivated by intentions. We can only *hypothesize* about what they will do. Because we are primarily social beings, it is most important that our inferences track the conditions of social interaction—Who knows what? Who is not aware of what? Who did what with whom?

Finally, part of being social means we make and use tools. In using tools we spontaneously link structure to function. If we are told that a person was accidentally hurt by a screwdriver while working on a household project, we automatically assume the tool was hard and had a sharp point at the end. We expect tools to have specific functional features that are manifested in their structure. We would be surprised to encounter a screwdriver made of rubber or cotton.

Different species come to the natural landscape with different sets of categories based on what has served them in the past. Boyer (2001, 114–115) gives the following example:

> Mary and her little lamb are resting under a tree next to a lamppost. Now imagine how this is processed in the minds of different organisms. For a human being, there are four very different categories here (human, animal, plant and artifact). Each of these objects will activate a particular set of inference systems. The human observer will automatically encode Mary's face as a distinct one but probably not the sheep's, and will consider the lamppost's function but not the tree's. If a giraffe were to see the same scene it would probably encode these differently. For a giraffe there is probably no deep difference between the sheep and Mary (assuming that the giraffe does not identify Mary as a predator). Because neither is a conspecific and the lamppost is just like a useless (leafless) tree. Now if a dog were around it would have yet another take on the scene. Because dogs are domesticated animals, they make a clear distinction between humans and other non-dog animals, so Mary and the sheep would activate different systems in the dog's brain. But the dog would not attend to the difference between the lamppost and the tree. Indeed both afford the same possibilities in terms of territorial marking.

In other words, the inference systems we use are species-specific. We have them because they provide us with solid typical solutions to problems unique to our species based on the ecological niches we inhabit.

While we have freedom to hypothesize imaginary situations in our conscious, everyday life throughout social evolution, this is undergirded by our biological legacy in our cognitive unconscious. Inferences must be plausible. Wild inferences were not adaptive.

When we can verbalize our thoughts we can separate them from the immediate present, engaging in time-space displacement. When we develop theories of mind we begin to think strategically, imagining other people's goals and planning our moves accordingly. Verbal language and theories of mind make hypothetical thinking possible. Hypothetical reasoning is one source for all our cultural institutions—collective, creative cooperation at work that produces art, religion, politics, economics, and tool improvement.

Primate Evolution: From Forests to the Savanna

The purpose of this section is to show how the growing sociality of some primates (specifically chimps) was adaptive to their survival. Approximately 60 million years ago, early proto-primates began to climb trees in dense forests. According to Maryanski and Turner (1992), this ecological condition placed selective pressure for better vision and touch among its inhabitants. This was a departure from most mammals whose sense of smell is dominant. Better vision allowed these proto-primates to move quickly across the branches of trees, and increased sensitivity of touch helped define the texture, weight, and strength of branches. Hands, fingers, toes, and wrists became more flexible, and this economized movement. A more generalized digestive system gave higher primates a more diversified diet.

Approximately 34 million years ago, Old World monkeys, New World monkeys, and great apes (orangutans, gorillas, and chimps) begin to differentiate out from the anthropoid line. Monkeys split off between 15 million and 20 million years ago, orangutans between 10 million and 16 million years ago, gorillas between 5 million and 8 million years ago, and chimps 5 million years ago. Table 3.2 gives a comparative overview of the differences between monkeys and apes.

According to Maryanski and Turner (1992), by modern standards apes are evolutionary failures compared to Old and New World monkeys. Today, there are only four species of apes remaining, while there are twenty-one species of New World monkeys and seventy-eight species of Old World monkeys. Why is this? What changing ecological conditions worked for monkeys and against apes? In the late Miocene the rain forests began to recede, meaning that an evolutionary choice had to be made between continuing to live in the forests or adapting to the woodlands of the open savanna. Approximately 16 million years ago both Old World monkeys and apes were established in Africa, but monkeys increased and apes declined. If apes were to stay in the forest, they were left to forage at the tops of trees.

One reason monkeys survived better than apes in the forest was that they had a more specialized diet. They were able to consume unripe fruit. Another reason was their densely packed and intergenerational social organization (see below). However, apes had more specialization of feet, wrists, hips, and hands and had a more developed sense of touch. Further, apes had more flexibility in whether they lived on the ground or in the trees. Apes had larger brains and a wider range of behavioral responses. These tendencies, however, were less adaptive to life in the forest. In the forests the looseness of ape social organization was somewhat adaptive because males and females could afford to move about *alone*, knowing that escape in the trees was an ever-present option. But if apes were to survive on the African savanna, selection had to make them more tightly organized socially.

Unlike monkeys, apes do not have social continuity across generations and they do not live in large groups. Like monkeys, apes have strong ties between mothers and offspring. However, unlike apes, among Old World monkeys there are strong ties among adult females and between mothers and daughters all the way into adulthood. Yet in an interesting reversal, among chimps (the most socialized type of ape) there is a *stronger* mother-son bond than in Old World monkeys, and *females* rather than males are dispersed at puberty (monkeys disperse males). Orangutans for the most part have been found in stable groups, and gorillas have stable groups of approximately ten members, but the group dissolves with the death of the male silverback unless there is another one present. Chimps do have brief groupings of between twenty-five and one hundred members, and community relations are centered on males. Ape societies have low density, low sociality, and high mobility.

Table 3.2 Comparison of monkeys and apes

Category of comparison	Monkeys	Apes: Gibbon	Orangutan	Gorilla	Chimp
Time of split	15–20 million years ago	15–20 million years ago	10–16 million years ago	5–8 million years ago	5 million years ago
Habitat		Southwest Asia, tropical rain forests Arboreal	Southeast Asia, tropical islands, Borneo/Sumatra Arboreal	Africa On ground; travel more (15 square miles)	Africa, forest belt of the tropics Ground and forest
Diet		Frugivores	Frugivores		Frugivores
Mating units	Matrifocal units; strong male dominance	Monogamous; males help with childcare/grooming	Horde	Horde/harem; male dominant (silverback)	Horde
Size of primate		20 lbs.	80 lbs. female; 150 lbs. male	185 lbs. female; 335 lbs. male	85 lbs. female; 100 lbs. male
Group continuity across generations	Large groups	Mostly solitary; no stable groups outside of mother and offspring		Stable groups (10 members); group dissolves with death of silverback (unless replaced by another one)	Brief groupings (25–100 members); community relations centered on males
Body movements and locomotion	Routinized movements	Forelimb dominance and suspensory locomotion for greater motor control; high mobility Freeing of cortical modalities from limbic control	Forelimb dominance and suspensory locomotion for greater motor control; high mobility	Forelimb dominance and suspensory locomotion for greater motor control; high mobility	Forelimb dominance and suspensory locomotion for greater motor control; high mobility
Emotional expression		Emotional sounds advantageous in trees	Emotional sounds advantageous in trees	Emotional sounds less advantageous on ground	Emotional sounds less advantageous on ground
Senses used		Tacticity important in trees	Tacticity important in trees	Tacticity less important on ground	Tacticity less important on ground
Population density		Low	Low	Low	Low
Sociality	High	Low	Low	Low	Low

Compared to apes, monkeys have more intricate social organization and are male dominant. Monkey social organization could afford the conflicts that would follow between males because there were female networks to preserve the group over time. On the other hand, given the more dangerous ecological situation that apes faced and their biological predisposition for low density, low sociality, and high mobility, male dominance would not work. Because of the weak social ties among apes, male dominance would (and does) escalate competition and fighting and/or cause other males to withdraw. The dominant male would spend a great deal of time punishing and monitoring competing males. In addition, this dominant male would try to hoard females. This is a problem because unlike female monkeys, female chimps do not easily bond. This would create more competition among females than already existed. In the absence of a female matrilineal line (as with monkeys), the group would be weakened and risk desolation. In fact, Turner (2000) suggests that many of the species of apes probably took the male dominance alternative into the open country and were unsuccessful.

The four species of great apes that survive today (excluding *Homo sapiens*) are not in the savanna but in the tops of trees, woodlands, or secondary forests. Obedience to a male dominant authority is a weak form of solidarity within a species as hardwired toward independence as apes. In order to survive in a new evolutionary niche (the savanna), apes did not need dominance to hold them together but bonding, which involved a more complex emotional life.

Chimpanzee Material Culture

In West Africa, chimpanzees use hammers and anvils to open nuts. Further, chimps have cultural traditions for using tools that vary in different parts of the world. Chimps are good at making and choosing tools that are just right for the job at hand. For example, Bill McGrew (1992) in *Chimpanzee Material Culture* reported on a rehabilitated chimpanzee in Gambia who used four tools in succession to acquire honey. All this supports the notion of the high intelligence of chimps.

However, in making tools, chimps show a certain rigidity. Chimps use the *same kinds of actions* for making tools that they use for feeding. There is little flexibility. In addition, they do not make technical advances. Each generation strives to achieve the technical level acquired by the previous generation. Lastly, chimps are not very good at thinking of new ways to use tools. Some chimps have a social division of labor, while others do not. Some chimps hunt in large groups, and there is a high degree of cooperation. Others are less cooperative. Table 3.3 compares chimp and human tool use.

Bipedalization as an Adaptive Response to Drier, More Open Climates

Creating social bonds was not the only adaptive response to living in a drier, more open environment. What advantage could an erect *bipedal* gait afford a species in adapting to more open country? Bipedalism makes it possible to carry infants and food while continuing to have the capacity to climb. Maryanski and Turner (1992) point out that erect posture would enable a species to see over tall grasses, which would enable it to discover resources and avoid predators. Another advantage, as Engels (1953) pointed out over a hundred years ago, was the freeing of the hand. This would enable the organism to design tools (rather than just use them) and carry food and weapons. Furthermore, the hand would allow an animal to throw objects, thereby warding off predators and killing prey at a distance.

An erect posture would also be more energy efficient in traveling over long distances when food became less plentiful and would reduce thermal stress by exposing less of the body to the sun. Thus, a biped could forage for longer periods before needing food or water. Erect posture would allow them to forage in environments that have less natural shade and to take advantage of niches not open to other predators. Finally, a biped could scavenge carcasses at periods of the day when their competitors would need to find shade.

Earlier we mentioned that the brains of apes were larger than the brains of monkeys. The continued increase in the size of the brain would require more fuel, and larger brains would need to be kept cool. An increase of meat in the diet that came with living in the open country would reduce the size of the gut and release more

Table 3.3 Chimp and human tool use

Category of comparison	Chimp use of tool	Human use of tool
Kind of tool	Termite stick	Fishing pole
Type of design	Simple design of parts	Specialized hooks and weights
Use of hands and movements	Uses same hand and arm movements as other behaviors	Unique gestures specific to tool use
Number of functions	Narrow range of functions (do not think of new functions for the same tool)	Tool use has many functions
Rate of diffusion	Slow	Rapid (due to imitation)

metabolic energy to the brain while maintaining a constant basal metabolic rate. The evolution of bipedalism and increased meat, seed, and fruit consumption allowed the brain to continue to expand without too high a cost in energy.

Another outcome of bipedalism concerns an increase in human communication. With bipedalism, individuals expose not just faces but full bodies to each other in most interactions. The flexibility of hands, wrists, elbows, and shoulder joints could all be used in a wide range of visual gestures. Savanna-dwelling apes could send information *visually and quietly* under conditions where noise would increase the risks of survival. Upright posture also frees the vocal tract and lowers the larynx. This would give apes greater capacity to form sounds of vowels and consonants. It also changes the pattern of breathing, which would improve the quality of sound. These mechanisms set the stage for the possibility of speech later on.

Rewiring the Brain for Social Life

An ape's brain is relatively large in proportion to the rest of its body. But how was the brain wired as apes faced the ecological crisis in the late Miocene? What brain wiring did apes bring to drier climatic conditions? As we said earlier, apes, like all primates, had a poor sense of smell, as their brains were rewired for vision and touch to dominate in the forest. There was cortical control over visual and tactile responses. However, the auditory cortex was wired into the emotional center of the brain, the limbic system. That meant that emotions were only partly under cortical control. Having loud, uncontrollable reactions in the open savanna, together with weak social organization, would not bode well for their future survival.

In order to sustain themselves in the open environment without the option of large groups, natural selection experimented with evolving a wider range of social emotions. The first step in that evolution would be to *rewire the auditory cortex from the limbic system to the neocortex and brainstem systems*, bringing the emotions under voluntary control. This option would make the ape quieter emotionally in potentially dangerous situations.

Turner (2000) goes on to say that three major changes must have occurred in the brain (see Table 3.4):

1. There were more asymmetries on significant sections of the neocortex, bringing more differentiated functions. There is specialization for language production (Broca's area), comprehension (Wernicke's area), pattern recognition (right side), and temporal recognition (left side). There was also more integration of specialization through the corpus callosum connecting both hemispheres of the brain.
2. There was an increase in the frontal lobe, where thought and long-term memories are stored. The prefrontal cortex developed significantly beyond that in any other primate. This is where the integration of emotion and cognition takes place.
3. There was significant growth in ancient limbic systems in the symmetrical subcortical

Table 3.4 Evolution of ecology, sense ratios, emotions, and communication

Category of comparison	Mammal	Proto-primate	Incipient protohuman (beyond chimps but before "Ardi")
Ecological setting		Forest	Open savanna
Senses used	Smell	Sight, touch	Sight, touch
Body posture	All fours	Semi-biped	Semi-biped
Nonverbal communication	Very limited body communication	Facial body communication	Full body communication
Brain organization		Auditory cortex of the brain wired to limbic system	Rewiring of the auditory cortex from limbic to neocortex
Organization of emotions		Loud	Quiet
Sociality	Some sociality	More sociality	Even more sociality

regions of the brain. These include the following areas:

- septum—sexuality
- amygdala—aversion and aggression
- hippocampus—linking cognition with emotions
- thalamus and hypothalamus—governing emotional responses (this means that the brain is both more intelligent *and* more emotional)

New Mating Practices

In order to survive, protohumans had to increase social bonds so that they would cooperate as they worked. One way this was done was to strengthen bonds among males, especially between brothers, making possible a stable male cooperative core. The same social emotions could be used to extend commitment in mating practices if emotions could be aroused beyond the pleasure of the sex act itself. But the solution to the problem of creating community bonds creates new problems within the microcommunity of the family.

With the exception of gibbons, apes are promiscuous and do not form stable conjugal bonds. Male and female promiscuity represents an obstacle to the formation of conjugal units. *So while the increase in social emotions might allow humans to stay together longer and form families, it does not address the problem of how to stay together longer while maintaining distance with ground rules about who within the nuclear family is fair game to mate with.* How could fathers be kept from mating with their daughters, or mothers kept from mating with their sons? How did animals whose promiscuity and mobility suddenly switched gears develop stable nuclear families and at the same time repress inbreeding? How is it possible to regulate mating practices within the family? Within those expanding social ties there had to be sexual ground rules that were not based on power but on rules that were hardwired. How could natural selection generate stronger bonds between couples while discouraging incest within the family? Incest avoidance is universal among higher animals, but it is a formally stated rule that intensifies the taboo by the attention that is drawn to it.

Maryanski and Turner (1992) identify three types of explanations for the origin of incest avoidance: biosocial theories, alliance theories, and sociological theories. Biosocial theories argue that mating among closely related individuals can lead to deleterious pairing of recessive genes that would decrease fitness. Alliance theories argue that incest avoidance forces mating options outside the local group (exogamy) while inadvertently leading to expanding societies, creating a division of labor between them, and decreasing the chances of war. Sociological theories claim that incest would disrupt the viability of the nuclear family, leading to conflicts between fathers and sons, and daughters and mothers.

Among chimps, while there were strong ties between a mother and her offspring, the ties between siblings were not equal. The bonds between the chimp mother and daughter were severed during the daughter's puberty when she migrated to another community. On the other hand, the mother's tie to her son remains through puberty (up to fifty years), and males mate with females from other groups. This is the reverse of the situation of male and female monkeys, where male monkeys leave shortly after puberty and female monkeys stay within the natal group.

While chimps are promiscuous, male chimps and their mothers rarely engage in sexual intercourse. In fact, this is uncommon among all primates as well as sexual avoidance between brothers and sisters. This means that mother-son avoidance of sex goes deep into evolutionary history and has a strong foundation. In human societies, mother-son incest and brother-sister incest are much less prevalent than father-daughter incest, which is less hardwired. Incest between stepfather and stepdaughter is the most common.

From Prehuman to Protohuman Species

With the rudiments of sociality in place, we now turn to the evolution of primates even closer to our species, from the newly discovered *Ardipithecus* to *Homo neanderthalensis*, and trace the emerging complexity of social life.

Ardipithecus

In 1994 in the Afar desert of Ethiopia a research team pieced together 45 percent of the remains of a skeleton that was dated as 4.4 million years old. According to T. D. White et al. (2009), *Ardipithecus* is the closest yet to the common ancestor. Apparently "Ardi" lived in a deeply forested flood-plain, sustaining itself as both an omnivore and a fruitivore. Ardi's brain size measured between 300 and 350 cubic centimeters, which is about the same size as a chimp's brain. Ardi was adapted to both arboreal life and bipedalism but was not likely to move on the ground over long distances. Interestingly, compared with chimps, the less pronounced size of upper canine teeth between males and females could imply that Ardi was less aggressive socially and increases the prospect of more male-female bonding and more parental investment than any primate up until now.

Australopithecines

About a million years later (3.2 million years ago), australopithecines (such as "Lucy") inhabited the forests and wooded savannas of Africa. The larger brain size (400–550 cubic centimeters) might have been driven by ecological pressures to stay in the savannas and develop bipedal locomotion. As far as we know, they were vegetarians and used no stone tools. We have no indicators of their social organization.

In anticipating future developments, Steven Mithen (1996, 95) wrote:

> [We] can see our ancestors setting off in two different evolutionary directions. The australopithecine went down a route of ever-increasing robustness as a specialized plant-grinding machine, while early Homo took a more cerebral route of increasing brain size.

Homo habilis

The oldest indicators of the first of the "Homo" lines emerged approximately 2 million years ago with the bipedal *Homo habilis*, with a brain size between 500 and 800 cubic centimeters. Here there is evidence of the use of the first Oldowan stone tools, which consisted of removing flakes from stones and sharpening the flakes to cut hides and tendons of scavenged animals. But do these tools mark a cognitive breakthrough? Steven Mithen thinks so. Mithen (1996) begins his argument by contrasting the tools made by *Homo habilis* with the tools of chimps. First, other than the difference in the materials used (stone versus sticks), *Homo habilis* used some tools to *make other tools*. Second, making these tools required precise eye-hand coordination—hitting the material in the right direction with the right pressure to be successful. Hitting the stone too softly makes no impact; hitting the stone too hard shatters it. Therefore, dexterity was required. Third, *Homo habilis* transported materials over a larger spatial scale. Fourth, whereas chimps transported stone to fixed locations (nut trees), *Homo habilis* artifacts were continually found in changed locations. Fifth, *Homo habilis* transported foodstuffs that needed processing to tools (rather than transporting tools to foodstuffs). Further, very often both tools and foodstuffs were transported from separate sources to a third location.

When we turn to social life, the issue is controversial because it involves whether *Homo habilis* lived in large or small groups, whether they had a division of labor in work, whether they had a home base or were opportunists following their prey, whether they hunted or scavenged their meat, and whether they shared meat. Glynn Isaac and Lewis Binford argue the extreme ends of the spectrum (Table 3.5; from Shreeve 1995).

Mithen (1996) believes that the answer is somewhere in the middle, with *Homo habilis* being a nonspecialized forager, sometimes hunting and sometimes scavenging.

What about verbal language? From the investigation of brain casts and social grooming and from the nature of the physical objects made, it is not realistic to think *Homo habilis* had language. A fully developed language relies on mental modules specialized for language alone (Broca's area and Wernicke's area).

Table 3.5 Isaac and Binford on *Homo habilis* behavior

Isaac	**Binford**
Ate large quantities of meat	Ate small quantities of meat (scavenger)
Lived in large social groups	Lived in small groups
Had specific places as home base	Moved along with prey
Divided up the work	
Shared food	

Source: Shreeve (1995).

Homo erectus

Homo erectus first appeared about 1.8 million years ago, leaving Africa and inhabiting East Asia, Java, the Near East, and Eastern and Southeast Asia just before the beginning of the Ice Ages 1.6 million years ago. *Homo erectus* presents us with a mystery. The "scene," as Mithen (1996) likes to call it, opens with new types of stone tools, hand axes (the Levallois method) that existed between 1.8 million and 1.4 million years ago. Then human toolmaking flattens out *in spite of* dramatic climatic changes. At least eight major glacial and interglacial cycles occurred (see Table 3.6).

In Europe the landscapes went from ice-covered tundras to thick forests to tundra again. But the tools the actors used do not match these changes. Between 1.4 million and 250,000 years ago we have only one major technical innovation, and the material culture seems very similar to *Homo habilis*. On the other hand, the brain size of *Homo erectus* is considerably larger than that of *Homo habilis*, varying between 750 and 1250 cubic centimeters.

Why did early humans not make tools designed for specific purposes? There seems to be no relationship between the form of the tool and its likely function. Hand axes were general purpose tools used for woodworking, chopping plant material, cutting animal hides, and removing meat. Why did early humans not make multi-component tools such as hafting, which involved

Table 3.6 Ice Ages, climatic cycles, and the hominid line

Pleistocene Ice Age	Climatic cycles	Species
Early Ice Age:		
1.6 million BCE	20 shorter climatic cycles	*Homo erectus*
Middle Ice Age:		
730,000 to 130,000 BCE	7 climatic cycles	*Homo erectus* (extinct 300,000 BCE)
250,000 to 180,000 BCE	Mainly temperate and cool with some glacial intervals. Large oceans, small ice caps.	*Homo neanderthalensis* (230,000 BCE)
180,000 to 130,000 BCE	Full glacial with some milder intervals. Small oceans, large ice caps.	
Late Ice Age:		
130,000 to 10,000 BCE	1 climatic cycle	
Interglacial 130,000 to 115,000 BCE	Warm conditions. Heavily forested and high lake levels. Large oceans, small ice caps.	*Homo sapiens* in Africa
Early glacial 115,000 to 75,000 BCE	Temperate, cool	*Homo neanderthalensis* in Europe Herds of grazing species of red deer and horse; decreasing temperature thinned out some of the megafauna species in northern latitudes.
Early glacial 75,000 to 30,000 BCE Cool glacial	Exposed area of continental shelf increases dramatically. In northern latitudes, tree cover reduced to refuge woodlands along well-sheltered valleys. Rapid oscillations in ice-to-ocean volume.	Cro-magnon in Europe *Homo neanderthalensis* extinct (30,000 BCE)
Full glacial 30,000 to 13,000 BCE	Rapid growth of continental and mountain ice sheets leads to worldwide drop in sea level. Last glacial maximum saw full exposure of continental shelves (18,000 BCE).	Many large mammals go extinct (13,000 BCE)

Source: Adapted from Stringer and Gamble, 1993.

making a shaft and ensuring that the end is the appropriate size and shape?

How did *Homo erectus* survive in such difficult circumstances without more complex tools? According to Mithen (1996) it was because they lived in large groups that protected them against failure in the food supply. They worked very hard together at physically demanding work. In the uncertain climatic conditions in which *Homo erectus* lived, it was adaptive to live in large groups only *sometimes*. *Homo erectus* were likely to live in larger social groups when the environment was dangerous and when food came in large parcels that were irregularly distributed around the landscape. Conversely, when the environment was less dangerous and when the food supply came in small packets and was dispersed across the landscape, there was less need for group protection. It pays under these conditions to break into small groups. So it is possible to be intelligent and live in large groups under certain conditions and small groups under other conditions. Changing climatic conditions made flexibility in social situations essential.

In terms of language, Mithen (1996) argues that while the vocalizing capacity of *Homo erectus* was advanced over any other primate, it would be overstating our case to call it language. The muscle control necessary for the refined regulation of respiration required of human speech was lacking.

Homo neanderthalensis

Homo neanderthalensis inhabited the Near East and Europe roughly between 230,000 and 30,000 years ago. *Homo neanderthalensis* occupied the northerly regions of Europe but only those places where the proximity of mountain ranges and foothills softened the climate and where there were more varieties of food.

The brain size of *Homo neanderthalensis* was considerably larger than that of *Homo erectus* (750–1250 versus 1200–1750 cubic centimeters). The tools *Homo neanderthalensis* made were limited to stone and wood. This meant they had to understand animal behavior very well, probably mastering the use of visual clues like hoofprints. Yet they hunted individual animals only opportunistically and killed prey on an encounter basis, concentrating on small or medium-sized game. There is no indication of groups organizing hunting drives in order to kill numbers of animals at one time. Lewis Binford (1983) argues that they lacked "planning depth." Apparently they didn't have the tactical means to preserve salmon and reindeer.

So far as we know, *Homo neanderthalensis* lived in small groups in spatially diverse settings. They flourished in the warm interglacial periods and survived some mild glaciations, but they disappeared at the start of the full Ice Age 30,000 years ago.

Their archaeological remains show an absence of items of personal decoration. There is also no evidence of ritualized burial. It is true that *Homo neanderthalensis* buried individuals in pits, but there are no artifacts in the pits that would indicate that a ritual was performed.

Homo neanderthalensis must have communicated with gestures, but full verbal language was not physiologically possible as discussed earlier. A single-chamber acoustical system may have restricted Neanderthals to a slow and limited form of speech.

In reaction to environmental decline, *Homo neanderthalensis* relocated to areas where resources could still support existing lifestyles at more favorable population densities rather than intensify their self-help networks. To ensure biological reproduction, there would have to be a mating network of somewhere between 175 and 500 individuals. But beyond their small groups *Homo neanderthalensis* seemingly showed little interest in establishing social ties. The distribution of their remains seemed to be *environmentally* determined. When faced with a climatic challenge, they did not intensify their networks or their tool use. With only finite resources, *Homo neanderthalensis* would have had to withdraw to more marginal areas with less sheltered ground. With inclement weather, their populations must have experienced severe stress, resulting in higher infant mortality rates and shorter lifespans. Imagine this process repeated across many parts of Europe and over many centuries or even millennia. This attrition rate would probably have caused Neanderthal populations to gradually decline toward extinction.

The fundamental differences between *Homo neanderthalensis* and *Homo sapiens* lay in society and culture, not just anatomy. *Homo sapiens* were verbal, visual, and symbolic. This affected organization of campsites, exploitation of the landscape, and colonization of new habitats.

Before we discuss *Homo sapiens*, let us look at visual and verbal communication. Jonathan Turner (2000) and others argue that visual gesture communication of the body occurred prior to verbal communication in the formation of *Homo sapiens.*

Visual Communication Predominates among Protohumans

Earlier we said that apes had a well-developed social life. A great deal of the source of this sociality was the use of bodily and facial gestures. In everyday life, apes would have to be attuned to the expectations of other apes through what they reveal visually. Turner (2000) raises the question as to why protohumans did not move immediately to a verbal language. Australopithecines were at least partly bipedal and they had gained control over their auditory sounds. Turner gives the following reasons:

- *Auditory modality was not cross-linked* among early australopithecines *with the visual and haptic (touch) modalities*, and this linkage is a precondition for spoken language.
- The *vocal tract* of protohumans up to *Homo erectus* was not yet organized in ways that would facilitate speech production.
- Higher primates had already relied on nonverbal gestures, and the conservative nature of natural selection would indicate that it builds on what has already been established.
- Spoken language depends on lateralization and integration of left-right brain functions. This could not occur until:
  - Hominids had begun to use tools in a precise way. This tool use is a precondition not only for integrated lateralization but also for muscular control of the entire vocal apparatus necessary for speech production.
  - Higher cognitive abilities based on a larger cerebral cortex.

Furthermore, with the exception of birds, which localize song in the left brain (just as we do with language), Turner (2000) argues that social bonds are more likely to develop from visual rather than auditory communication because visual communication is more compelling. In addition, the areas for speech production along the left hemisphere of the brain appear to be late additions to human neuroanatomy.

Verbal language, then, is not adaptive until the brain has been rewired for emotional control. As Turner (2000) says, language is the unselected by-product of the need to integrate sense modalities under visual dominance in order to adapt to the arboreal environment. Yet, once verbal language did emerge, it could increase fitness by complementing visual communication with precision. Verbal communication makes it possible to communicate when the body is preoccupied with other activities, such as carrying tools or goods or taking care of babies.

Turner (2000) argues that just as verbal language came after visual communication, rationality came after emotions. The foundation of decision making, weighing the consequences of alternatives, is based on the emotional value one gives to the alternative. Until a wide range of emotions could be generated so that the *impact of other members* of the group would be included in the decision, there would be little basis for rational decision making.

Homo sapiens

The origin of *Homo sapiens* begins in Africa roughly 100,000 years ago, spreads to the Near East, and then moves to Europe about 60,000 years ago. On the European side, the climate moved from cool glacial to full glaciations by 18,000 BCE. What is important for us is how differently *Homo sapiens* responded to the increasingly colder conditions compared to *Homo neanderthalensis*.

Whereas *Homo neanderthalensis* tried to diversify their food sources while avoiding other cultural groups during the increasingly cold climate, *Homo sapiens* concentrated their food resources on big game and systematically hunted by joining together with other groups, engaging in food sharing and a division of labor, including status decoration indicators. The use of symbolic activity connects with Turner's point about the use of ritual to consolidate human emotions. Ritual helped build solidarity by linking more elaborate emotions to a rhythmic recurrence in time and place. Because strong bonds do not come naturally to apes or to protohumans, the complexification of emotional life needs to be housed in a social institution that would remind them of the importance of the group's solidarity and sustain its moral codes. The exchanging of objects as part of a ritual grounds emotions in symbolic objects. When rituals are performed in large group settings, they create a sympathetic effect even among those who do not meet consistently on a face-to-face basis.

Compared to *Homo neanderthalensis*, *Homo sapiens* did more walking as they circulated seasonally from one area to another. According to Stringer and Gamble (1993), in the Upper Paleolithic 53 percent of the flint used for tools came from as far away as 75 miles. In the Middle Paleolithic the distance was only 31 miles. The raw material used for making ornaments came all the way from the Black Sea to the central Russian plain 430 miles away. *Homo sapiens* crossed oceans and colonized inhospitable interiors of continental Asia and as far away as Australia.

While the rest of the hominid line tended to become extinct during very harsh climatic conditions, *Homo sapiens* survived a full Ice Age even when large mammals went extinct by about 13,000 BCE. The artistic explosion including cave art, the first open-air burials, and the emergence of sacred practices might all be looked at as meaning-making systems designed to help survive a worsening climate.

How was this possible? Brain size gives us no answer. There is no difference between the brain size of *Homo neanderthalensis* and that of *Homo sapiens*. If anything, *Homo neanderthalensis* had bigger brains. One part of the puzzle is the changing nature of male-female relations. We know that Neanderthals were never forced to live in cold climates permanently, and so they probably never had to learn to subsist on meat exclusively. Neanderthals of the Middle Paleolithic occupied the northerly regions, but only those places where there were more kinds of food available both to hunt and to gather. James Shreeve (1995) points out that archaeological sites show two separate but contemporaneous kinds of living. One was a nest of robust females and dependent children, and the other was a site that males inhabited. There was no integration of males into ongoing family roles.

With *Homo sapiens* facing a way of life in which plant life was nonexistent and meat was the only resource, natural selection favored those groups in which males provided meat for females in exchange for regular sex. This would lead to long-term, reasonably stable sexual and economic relations. Neanderthals could not build alliances through exchange of mates, because their society was essentially mateless. *Homo sapiens* did not have to have direct confrontations with Neanderthals to survive against them. They only had to outpopulate them. Sites show that *Homo sapiens* had hearths for fires, home bases, huts made of bone, and storage pits. All this supports long-term planning. The use of words allows for space-time displacement, which opens up communication about the past and, most importantly, planning together for the future.

Primate Evolution in Review

We began this chapter by distinguishing learning, society, and culture. The main focus was to show the mechanisms by which prehuman primates and protohuman beings gradually developed social organization and culture.

Jonathan Turner (2000) argues that in order for humans to become more social, our emotions expand quantitatively and qualitatively. This means moving beyond the three primary emotions of primates and gradually expanding the emotional repertoire to include emotions that promote social bonding, solidarity, and the ability to manage conflicts without either violent deaths or withdrawal from society. Physiologically, this required the rewiring of the auditory cortex of the brain from the limbic system to the neocortex. This allowed a species not only to have more complex emotions but to be quieter about expressing them.

Marc Hauser (2000) makes some important distinctions between animal calls and verbal

Table 3.7 Comparison of primates: Apes to *Homo sapiens*

Time period (years ago)	Species	Brain size	Tools	Social organization	Ecology	Communication	Cognition/Order of intentionality
6 million	Modern apes, chimps, gorillas	250–300 cc	Use of sticks to catch termites; many tools but no replication; no specialized motion	Small groups	Africa; arboreal; frugivores		3rd order, can learn limited symbols, cannot make symbols
4.5 million	*Ardipithecus* (Ardi)	440–550 cc	No tools	Unknown	Dense forest, flood plain, frugivores	Unknown	3rd order assumed
3.2 million	*Australopithecus ramidus* (Lucy); walks semi-upright or upright	250–300 cc	No tools	Unknown	South and East Africa only; wooded environments; tree-climbing vegetarians	Unknown	3rd order assumed
2 to 1.5 million	*Homo habilis*	500–800 cc	Oldowan stone tools, flakes removed from pebbles	Small groups	South and East Africa only; woodland areas near water sources; cannot cope with dry, cold environments	Body nonverbal communication	3rd order assumed
1.8 million (Pleistocene begins, ice sheets form at high latitudes)	*Homo erectus*	750–1250 cc	Levalloisian stone tools, handaxes; hunter or scavenger?	Small groups	Left Africa and inhabited Java, Near East, and Eastern and Southeast Asia	Body nonverbal communication	3rd order assumed
230,000 to 30,000	*Homo neanderthalensis* (survived to 30,000)	1200–1750 cc	Tools made of stone and wood; hunted opportunistically on individual animals	Small groups, spatially diverse; no decoration status markers; lacked art and ritual; some burial of dead	Near East, Europe; good in interglacial settings, difficulty at beginning of full Ice Age	Body nonverbal communication, perhaps simple speech	3rd order assumed
100,000	*Homo sapiens*	1200–1700 cc (lateralization and integration of the left-right brain functions)	Use of bone, blade technology; complex technology; grinding stones for planting; boat building	Large groups with division of labor; spatially concentrated; planned systemic hunting of large game; takeoff of art, religion; decoration status markers	Africa, Near East, Europe, Southeast Asia, Australia; survived full Ice Age	Facial, body, and verbal language	4th order, hypothetical thinking

language with emphasis on time-place displacement, which verbal language allows. Robin Dunbar (1996) points out how economical verbal language is in expanding social relations and tracking reputations in managing mating and coalition formation. Dunbar also points out that there is a correlation between the size of the brain and the size of group membership. The larger the group, the more kinds of relationships we have to track.

Verbal language also changes how we think. With time-place displacement, we can develop "theories of mind" ascending to high orders of intentionality and allowing us to think strategically and, as Pascal Boyer (2001) points out, hypothetically.

The first part of the chapter dealt with the differences between the socialization practices of monkeys and apes. We discussed the difficulties of building social bonds among apes. While monkeys have a more developed social structure than apes, it is rigid and is more adaptive to forests. The social organization of a particular type of ape, a chimp, is more flexible and more likely to be adaptable to habitats beyond the forest. The shrinking of the forests and the prospect of living on the open savanna invited bipedalization on the one hand and increased socialization on the other.

The second part of the chapter dealt with the history of protohumans—*Ardipithecus*, *Australopithecus*, *Homo habilis*, *Homo erectus*, and *Homo neanderthalensis*—and their ecological settings, form of social organization, size of the brain, and use of tools. In the last section we dealt with the emergence of *Homo sapiens*. One reason for our survival was intense socialization on the one hand and our ability to collectively plan on the other. This meant building and sustaining coalitions. The biological foundations for this were the rewiring of the brain and the lateralization and integration of the left-right brain functions. However, while our ability to collectively plan must have originally had to do with coordinating social efforts in the hunt and managing political relations within the group, once unleashed, hypothetical reasoning began to be applied to imaginary and possible worlds, which resulted in improved tools, art, religion, and eventually science. Table 3.7 sums up the major changes in primate evolution.

Suggested Readings

Diamond, Jared. 1992. *The Third Chimpanzee*. New York: HarperCollins.

Donald, Merlin. 1991. *Origins of the Modern Mind*. Cambridge, MA: Harvard University Press.

Dunbar, Robin. 1996. *Grooming, Gossip and the Evolution of Language*. Cambridge, MA: Harvard University Press.

Hauser, Marc. 2000. *Wild Minds*. New York: Henry Holt.

Klein, Richard G., with Blake Edgar. 2002. *The Dawn of Human Culture*. New York: John Wiley and Sons.

Mithen, Steven. 1996. *Prehistory of the Mind*. London: Thames and Hudson.

Shreeve, James. 1995. *Neanderthal Enigma*. New York: Avon.

Stringer, Christopher, and Clive Gamble. 1993. *In Search of the Neanderthals*. New York: Thames and Hudson.

Turner, Jonathan H., and Alexandra Maranski. 2005. *Incest: Origins of the Taboo*. Boulder, CO: Paradigm Publishers.

———. 2008. *On the Origins of Human Societies by Means of Natural Selection*. Boulder, CO: Paradigm Publishers.

4

Building a Social Self: The Macro-Micro Link

The Social-Individual Dialectic

In the last chapter we saw that both societies and cultures are not unique human achievements but have an evolutionary history that includes other animals and especially primates. In this chapter we examine the processes by which societies complete the humanization of individuals by constructing social selves and how, in turn, individuals collectively through their labor produce society.

How are we to understand the relationship between society and the individual? There are two polarized positions on this. The first, which we'll call "atomist," says society is no more than an aggregate of individuals and has no special characteristics that are not already inside of individuals. Only concrete individuals think, act, and have needs and goals. To say society has these things is a reification, or giving life to something that is not real. The other position, which we'll call "holistic," argues that society is like a superorganism that is more than the sum of individuals. Individuals are aspects of this organism, and individuals have no life outside society. Societies undergo processes that are more complex than individuals.

One problem that makes this difficult to talk about is the differences in the time scale. On the one hand, concrete individuals live in industrial capitalist societies and live to be anywhere from sixty-four to seventy-five years old, while society continues to exist and the nation-state of the United States continues to exist. But on the other hand, we agree to an extent with the atomists when they say that without individuals there is no society. Without the collective labor, breeding, and child rearing of concrete individuals there is no society. At the same time, these acting individuals can do so only because they acquire the social skills they do not create from scratch.

On the one hand, throughout our lives we are limited by the tools, institutions, and beliefs passed on to us by previous generations. An individual is born into a particular type of society, within a specific social class and gender, at a particular point in history. These constraints are the parameters an individual has to operate within. In this sense, society is like a weaver while the growing individual is like the yarn.

On the other hand, while individuals are in one sense subservient (especially as children) to the agents of socialization, these tools and institutions of previous generations contain the very raw materials by which individuals can overcome these constraints. Once we learn language, learn to manipulate tools, learn roles, and go to school, we have trained ourselves to become more than yarn. We become coweavers shaping and reorganizing the parameters that constrain us.

Human Nature

In the first chapter we discussed the differences between biological and social evolution. Our next step will be to clarify how the human species fits within these systems. In what proportion are we biological creatures, and in what proportion are we sociocultural beings? Furthermore, how do biology and society interact through humanity? In other words, what is our human nature?

Ideas about human nature are important in all human societies because they define what it means to be a human being, and they provide justifications for other institutions. For example, societies in which warfare is a major preoccupation define humans as aggressive and men as fearless warriors who will naturally defend their group against attacks. When warfare is less prevalent, people are seen as more pacific, and the male *identity* is more multidimensional.

Sociobiology is the study of the societies of human and nonhuman animals, including insects. Many species exhibit social behavior such as the building of large communities and hierarchical relations among groups within communities. Nonhuman animals also exhibit interesting intergroup and interspecies relationships that are similar in some respects to the intersocietal relations and structures revealed by the social geography of human communities. Ecologists study the geographical aspects of interspecies relationships, and these studies are suggestive for analogous patterns found in human world-systems. The rising importance of the modern science of genetics and the emergence of biotechnology as a generative sector in the contemporary world-system have given old arguments about the importance of human "hardwiring" a new lease on life. The current bearers of this emphasis come mainly from the discipline known as evolutionary psychology.

Evolutionary psychologists argue that human nature is predominantly biological. They argue that our most important predispositions (formed through natural selection) have been biologically based adaptations to the hunter-gatherer environment, because during most of our existence as a species we have been hunter-gatherers.

Biological arguments have had a stormy history in both Europe and the United States because they have been used, especially from the eighteenth century through World War II, to justify racism and sexism. If some races are genetically superior to others, then slavery, subjugation, or genocide can be justified as the natural order of things. If men are genetically superior to women, then patriarchy is justified. Sociobiology has also been accused of reductionism. Reductionism means that all human tendencies, including art, religion, and even our most everyday choices, are alleged to be explained by drives, genes, or hormones. Contemporary evolutionary psychologists, however, argue that they have overcome these problems of earlier instinct-based explanations.

In his text on evolutionary psychology, Buss (1999) names five of the most common misconceptions about the field:

1. *Human behavior is genetically determined.* According to Buss, evolutionary psychologists do not argue that genes control all behavior. He acknowledges that human behavior is also affected by environmental and social feedback. Furthermore, even within the genetic realm of causation, some genes are more responsive to environmental and social conditions. Gaulin and Mc Burney (2001) distinguish between two types of genes: obligate and facultative. Obligate genes resist environmental interference, while facultative genes are more responsive. Why is this? Obligate genes have evolved for more stable circumstances, while facultative genes have evolved to respond to rapidly changing environments. Obligate genes govern processes like the body plan of a species, which will remain the same in virtually all environments. Facultative genes evolved to deal with two circumstances: (1) when the environment is variable within the lifetimes of organisms and (2) when the fittest alternative varies from one environment to the next. Facultative genes allow a species to deal effectively with rapid environmental change.

Evolutionary psychology rejects instinct theory, which assumes that instincts rigidly determine what an organism will do, regardless of time, place, and circumstance. Rather, evolutionary psychologists talk of genetic "predispositions," which are more flexible adaptations to context.

2. *If it is evolutionary, we cannot change it.* On the contrary, knowledge of our evolved adaptations, along with the social inputs they were designed to be responsive to, can have a liberating effect on changing behavior. For example, our desire for sugar and fat in foods was an adaptation to the mobile life of hunter-gatherers where neither of these was in great supply in most early evolutionary environments. However, our social institutions have modified the environment and made sugar and fat much more available. But because most people in most societies are far more sedentary than our hunter-gatherer ancestors, we do not burn off the energy provided by large amounts of sugar and fat, creating serious health problems.

   Two things are worth keeping in mind in this regard. One is that social institutions have massively changed the environments that we now adapt to. The other is that knowledge of our biological legacy can help us improve upon our habits. Buss stresses that changing behavior is not simple or easy, and that some things are easier to learn than others because they are less deeply rooted in our evolutionary history. We think this is a good counter to the old culturalist notion that *anything* can be learned. On the other hand, the history of hunter-gatherers was also a cultural history. The institutions that hunter-gatherers developed (gender division of labor, egalitarian sharing) are still an important part of the tool kit of the human heritage. So it was not only genes that were shaped by the long period in which humans were hunter-gatherers.

3. *Humans need to consciously know the rules of adaptation in order for those rules to apply.* Evolutionary psychologists claim that people can execute rules for adaptive behavior rooted in our biological past without being conscious they are operating. For example, people do not know the reasons why they are attracted to people with faces that are more symmetrical than asymmetrical. Symmetrical facial features are a sign of the absence of disease and increase the chances of healthy offspring in a prospective mate. But a mate-chooser does not need to know this functional relationship in order for it to play an important part in mate selection.

4. *Currently adaptive mechanisms are optimally designed.* Sometimes it is assumed that all evolutionary adaptive mechanisms are matched to the existing environment. Evolutionary psychologists deny this, claiming that many adaptive mechanisms are survivals from earlier environments that have since changed. Some no longer have a purpose in current environments.

5. *Evolutionary theory implies all-purpose fitness maximization.* Evolutionary psychologists claim that there is no general behavior for optimal fitness. What is fit varies depending on gender, age, and situations. There is not a general course of action that maximizes fitness for both sexes, for all ages, and for all situations.

If we weed out these misconceptions, what do we have left? What are evolutionary psychologists saying? They claim that a large part of human behavior has been genetically structured by our long exposure to hunting-gathering environments in which "human nature" was formed. Contemporary genetically structured behavior is often not consciously motivated, and, whether conscious or not, behavior varies over the course of a lifetime based on gender, age, and situation. The mechanisms of adaptation are far from optimal and are not optimally matched with the contemporary environment. It is possible to change some behavior that was rooted in our biological past, but it is far from easy.

Mc Elvaine (2001, 41) poetically summarizes the evolutionary psychology position:

> Our biological inheritance does not determine our destiny: it does restrict our choices. Our human nature is the hand that is dealt to us. What we do with that hand is still up to us. The cards we receive place certain limits on what we can do, and if we hope to do well, we had better look at the

cards. We can win at poker with almost any hand, but winning is unlikely to happen without one knowing what cards are held.

Traditionally, sociologists and cultural anthropologists have opposed biological explanations for social behavior, and though this is changing, sociologists usually claim that social institutions are a product of society and that *these institutions* more than biological hardwiring produce the desirable goals that individuals try to achieve. Sociologists often disagree with one another over which social institutions are primarily responsible, but with rare exception, sociologists are on the "nurture" side of the controversy. If biological explanations were equated with social Darwinist or sociobiological formations of the mid-1970s, sociologists would be right to claim that biological explanations are reductionist. However, evolutionary psychologists have learned from these criticisms and cannot be accused of reductionism. However, we still have our reservations.

Cross-cultural studies have shown that men are more promiscuous than women. Evolutionary psychologists argue that this is because sperm is cheap and easy to produce (as opposed to ova), and because men, unlike women, can never know for sure whether the product of their mating is carrying half their genes. This makes sense to us. However, evolutionary psychologists have to explain the mechanism by which this varies, both cross-culturally and historically. For example, in contemporary industrial capitalist societies, males have accepted the institution of monogamy, which challenges Darwinian sexual selection theory. The process by which monogamy supplanted promiscuity or polygamy was a social-historical production of the monotheistic religions, not male sexual mating strategies. In other words, evolutionary psychology makes a good prediction in saying that if promiscuity exists, males are the more likely sex to be promiscuous. However, where, when, and how this varies is a sociohistorical question.

The same problem occurs in other areas if evolutionary psychologists claim that all societies are patriarchal. By this they usually mean that men will do the work that requires upper-body strength and speed while women will do the child rearing; men's work will monopolize the public realm, including warring, politics, and economics. Lineage and residency lineage will be traced along the male line (patrilineality). It is unarguable that not only have there been more patriarchal societies than matriarchal societies, there are no known matriarchal whole societies (though there have been matriarchal subcultures). However, *the absence of matriarchy is not necessarily the presence of patriarchy*. Patriarchy is not a universal; it is a variable. Some societies are far more patriarchal than others.

Radically patriarchal societies in which men have vastly more power than women tend to be those in which warfare is a social preoccupation. Since human societies all oscillate through periods in which warfare is an important activity for survival in competition with other societies, there is an *intermittent pervasive pressure* toward patriarchy. We think the difference in patriarchal variation both cross-culturally and historically cannot be explained biologically.

Even more critically, hunting-and-gathering societies, the longest-lasting human societies of all, cannot be characterized as patriarchal. To take one piece of this, while it is true that there are some work roles that are exclusively male and female, these differences can be better understood as gender differentiation, rather than gender hierarchies. The roles of women and men can be radically different but equal, as among egalitarian hunter-gatherers. Gender differentiation is the degree of difference between the appropriate roles of women and men. For example, in many hunter-gatherer societies, women are forbidden to touch the weapons that men use for hunting, and men are not to be present at the locations where women are performing their gathering tasks. But differences are not always accompanied by different amounts of social power. Gender differentiation can exist in a situation in which women and men have approximately equal say over collective decision making, and this is the case in many hunter-gatherer societies. What evolutionary psychology can predict very well is that *if* a society has hierarchies, they will be male. But when, where, how, and even whether they exist are sociohistorical questions.

We think that evolutionary psychology is very important to understanding human behavior. But an important question is *which* aspects of genetic structures are most important for understanding human behavior. The cortex of the brain is preprogrammed for flexibility and learning at least as much as it is for specific genetic traits or behavior. As George Herbert Mead (1972) stressed, human beings are genetically structured to absorb social influence transmitted by language and by observing the behavior of parents, siblings, and playmates. It does not erase the primal needs for food, air, warmth, and sex. But it does cast these drives into a culturally ordered context in which they are strongly linked to secondary needs for approval, success, status, and autonomy that are based in normative, economic, and legal institutions. It is human nature to be cultural.

Agents of Socialization

Family

At the micro-level, the family is the primary transmitter of socio-culture to the newborn. Parents are hardwired to want their children to succeed but come into these roles either well equipped or poorly equipped depending on their class location, preparation, and personal experiences.

Ethnologist John Bowlby (1983) stressed the importance of attachment in early childhood socialization not just because of the need for a safe environment but because attachment provides support for learning new things. Bowlby identified four stages of attachment:

1. *Preattachment*—the first six weeks of life. Here the child is "happily aloof." This means the newborn does not distinguish familiar from unfamiliar people or objects.
2. *Attachment in the making*—from six weeks to six to eight months. In this period the infant begins to differentiate between familiar and unfamiliar objects and people and emotionally develops a sense of wariness when confronted with unfamiliar people and things.
3. *Clear-cut attachment*—from eight months to eighteen to twenty-four months. This is a crucial stage that Bowlby calls "separation anxiety," where the child recognizes how dependent they are on their mother.
4. *Reciprocal relationship*—from eighteen to twenty-four months and beyond. It is at this stage that the young child is not only aware of their dependence but begins to sense that they have the power to affect the interaction with their mother. The battle over toilet training during the "terrible twos" is just the beginning!

In her work with children, Mary Ainsworth became interested in Bowlby's separation anxiety stage and suspected that it was an important key to understanding childhood (and later adolescent and adult) problems in attachment. She set up experiments with children who had gone through the separation anxiety stage and was able to discover three forms of attachment: avoidant, anxious-ambivalent, and secure. Avoidant two- or three-year-olds tended to have difficulty getting close to their mothers at all. In contrast, anxious-ambivalent types tended to be needy and constantly needed reassurance. Ainsworth (1979) believed that these forms of attachment derived from parents either being unavailable or being inconsistent in their involvement with their children. Contrary to these, secure attachment forms resulted from parents who were available and consistent. Ainsworth believed that these forms of attachment, for better or worse, impacted how well individuals could attach themselves in friend formation, relations with teachers, and romance later on in life.

Being socialized into the family is not something the newborn can choose to partially accept or reject. Parents set the rules of the game. The child can play the game with enthusiasm or with sullen resistance, but at least for a while, it is the only game in town. The child does not internalize the world of her caregivers as one of a number of worlds, but as *the* world.

Parents consciously or unconsciously raise their children around morals, emotional life, and skills they think the child will need to work based on their own class location. Psychologists have identified at least three parenting styles: authoritarian, permissive, and authoritative. Authoritarian parents want a high degree of control over what their children do. They expect obedience at all costs and do not justify their decisions with reasons. "Do it because I say so!" is a most common refrain. Authoritarian parents use force as a method of discipline, and their values tend to be rigid, black and white. Research shows that children raised by authoritarian parents often grow up having difficulty in unstructured situations or in trying new things.

Permissive parenting is the exact opposite. Permissive parents believe their job as parents is to provide resources to their child and stay in the background, because they believe the child should direct their own development. They have a high degree of acceptance of their child's choices, including the child's deciding what to eat, where to play, and what time to go to bed. Permissive parents think that imposing adult standards on children will hamper the child's development and creativity. Research shows that the children of permissive parents lack impulse control later in life, especially in social situations where they cannot receive special attention (Wade and Tarvis 2004).

Authoritative parents have a moderate degree of control of their children. They set standards, but the standards are subject to change as a result of the interaction with the child. They justify their authority with reasons. Like authoritarian parents, they set standards, but authoritative parents can see things from many sides rather than from just one side. Children raised this way tend to be more self-reliant, are more willing to explore, have a greater degree of self-control, and have better school performance.

As you might suspect, there is a relationship between the social class location of the family and the parenting style. In industrial capitalist societies, authoritarian parents are most often working class, because working-class work requires obedience. Children of working-class authoritarian parents will not be rewarded for asking questions, because asking too many questions in working-class jobs will get you fired. Conversely, permissive parents give their children room to explore and be creative, because upper-middle-class work requires trial and error and innovation.

Education

At its best, education opens children up to worlds wider than the world of their parents. When textbooks are written that truly represent cross-cultural human experience in the arts, sciences, and humanities, the class texts should be a microcosm of the whole world. At the same time, texts that are truly representative of the full range of world history should take the student's breath away. At its best, education reduces prejudice, invites critical thinking, and trains students for political and economic life. Classroom settings should teach students how to cooperate in groups and invite dialogue among the students as well as with their teachers.

In actuality, textbooks in the United States have not provided an accurate account of how political and economic institutions actually work, or opened up the very dark side of US history (although the texts are getting better). The type and quality of classroom setting varies with the social class and race of the student. Working-class children are stuffed into large classrooms, receive little attention, and are taught to keep their mouths shut (just like at home). On the other hand, because investment in education has declined for at least thirty-five years, teachers are underpaid and overworked. This leads to high teacher turnover and less stable modeling for students.

Peers

Children and adolescents who go to school together are in the same social position, are the same age, and share the same problems, and thus it is natural to compare notes and form a common identity and common interests. Schools are good places to make friends and develop relationships that exist outside the school. Friendships allow children to form their own relationships unsupervised by teachers or parents. They can ask questions, talk about things their parents or teachers don't want to discuss (like sex), and try things that are forbidden (like sex and drugs). Kids may practice how to be in groups in terms of rules, roles, and systems of inclusion and exclusion without adult input. Part of the formation of social identity among peers is contrasting themselves with who they are not. This takes the form of mocking parents and teachers. But other sources of information provide powerful contexts for friendship formation and cohesion: mass media. Research shows that peers can affect each other in the way of short-term interests, but parents still hold sway in the long run, in terms of schooling.

Mass Media

Ninety-eight percent of households in the United States have a television, and eighty-eight percent have more than one television set. The average household has at least one set turned on for seven hours a day, and people spend about half their free time watching television (Eitzen and Baca Zinn 1995). What does this mean? That depends on what is being watched.

On the positive side, television makes possible our ability to track current events, provides educational programs that are less didactical, and can expose viewers to ways of life that are far from the circles they travel in. Does television actually do this? For the most part, it doesn't. But so what. Isn't entertainment innocent, socially neutral harmless, and value-free? Michael Parenti, in his book *Make Believe Media: The Politics of Entertainment*, shows the extent to which television and movies, whether consciously or not, promote the following values:

- Individual effort is preferable to collective action
- Free enterprise is the best economic system in the world
- Private monetary gain is a central and worthy objective of life
- Affluent professionals are more interesting than blue-collar or working-class white-collar service workers
- All Americans are equal, but some must prove they are worthy of equality
- Women and ethnic minorities are not really as capable, effective, or interesting as white males
- The ills of society are caused by individual malefactors
- There are some unworthy persons in our established institutions, but they usually are dealt with and eventually are deprived of their positions of responsibility

On the whole, television and movies tend to reinforce conventional socialization. In terms of what it does to individuals, social learning theorist Albert Bandura showed that watching violent programs on television impacts how violent children can become if they have a predisposition to violence and they witness violence at an age when the line between fantasy and reality is not clear in their mind (Carver and Scheier 2004).

In their text *Movies as Mass Communication*, Jowett and Linton (1989) summarize ten "articles of faith" in the movie industry. Among the articles is that in order to make a profit, entertainment is the ultimate goal. Entertainment must include diversion and escape. Why? Because the industry's assessment is that the average moviegoer is "juvenile in his needs and interests . . . including voyeurism, sadomasochism, sentimentality, levity, and excitement. These needs can be fulfilled by sex, violence, romance comedy and adventure" (32). And, "These topics must be treated in a manner that *masks* the fact that they are not noble, so that the movie goer is not embarrassed or so that his self-esteem is not diminished" (32). Because movies are in competition with free television, they must treat subjects such as sex and violence in an even more sensationalistic way than television does in order to keep up.

Religion

At its best, religion provides meaningful answers to the great mystery questions: What does it mean to be human? Where did we come from? Where are we going? Religion provides an opportunity to rise above everyday life in structured seasonal and weekly rituals in order to remember "the big picture." At its best, religion also provides moral guidelines on how to live and how to create altered, inspired states of consciousness.

In practice, at least in class societies, as a socializing institution religion generally promotes obedience, fear, and hatred. If we look at the broad view and limit our scope of the world religions to Judaism, Christianity, and Islam, it is hard to imagine any other social institution that has been as responsible for the deaths of so many human beings over the course of history. Religion is usually responsible for sexual repression. Also, as Marx pointed out, religious promises of a better life in the hereafter is an expression of the lack of confidence in humanity's ability to create heaven on earth. It is a projection onto an imaginary being of the alienated collective creativity of humanity.

The State (Nationalism)

The process by which people learned to be loyal to strangers within their own territory to the point of being willing to kill others and risking their own lives is one of the most powerful historical socialization processes in modern times. For most of human history, human loyalty was limited to family, kin group, or local city. The great agricultural empires never commanded loyalty to the state. Though there is great debate about the origins of nationalism, its modern form can be dated with the Great French Revolution.

In his book *Nation into State*, cultural geographer Wilbur Zelinsky (1988) traces the stages of American nationalism from the colonial period to the present. He groups the stages first into ethnic loyalties, national loyalty in the early nineteenth century, and, finally, after the Civil War, to state loyalty. What is important for our purposes is the means of political socialization. Zelinsky identifies five processes:

1. Language reform (Noah Webster) and mottos
2. Mythology—Uncle Sam, Horatio Alger, pioneers, frontiersmen, cowboys
3. Performances—Independence Day, Columbus Day, Thanksgiving, Olympic Games, presidential inaugurations, pilgrimages to Washington, DC, and the Pledge of Allegiance
4. Iconography and the arts
    - American flag, bald eagle
    - Literature—western novels
    - History paintings (*Washington Crossing the Delaware*); the work of Remington, Thomas Moran, and Norman Rockwell
    - Music—national anthem, "My Country 'Tis of Thee," "God Bless America"
    - Films—Frank Capra and Walt Disney
5. Landscapes
    - Pristine; the American West, rugged mountains
    - National military cemeteries
    - Monuments—Bunker Hill, Statue of Liberty, Plymouth Rock, Mount Rushmore
    - Within cities—streets named after presidents, monumental state buildings

This political socialization process has led most Americans to make the following assumptions about the state:

- There is no indoctrination to loyalty in the United States; people are spontaneously loyal
- The state does not significantly interfere in the economy
- The state exists only to maintain order and has no interests of its own
- The law is essentially neutral and applies to all groups equally
- Its wars are always just
- Unlike any other country in the world, the United States has no political prisoners
- Unlike any other great civilization, the United States has never had an empire
- The state has files only on proven subversives and terrorists

Sports

One of the benefits of *playing* sports is that it teaches a very structured and dramatic form of group cooperation, role-taking, and learning to improvise within the context of rules that everyone must abide by. These skills are amplified when the games are self-managed by kids themselves as opposed to being supervised by coaches. The pride and loyalty that can emerge from these games at least come out of actual experience and performance. The downside of participatory sports is that it creates an illusion that the chances are reasonable for poor or working-class kids to rise in social status by becoming professional athletes. For every kid who makes it to the major leagues, there are tens of thousands who do not make it and have lost many years of training for work that has more reasonable prospects.

Spectator sports have a very different socialization impact than that of playing sports. In their book *In Conflict and Order*, Eitzen and Baca Zinn (1995) argue that there is a deep relationship between loyalty to sports teams and nationalism. For example, pride in the performance of American Olympic athletes creates an "us versus them" mentality that permeates not just fans but coaches and players. The Olympic Games can be a kind of symbolic world war. Just like world wars, the suspense of the up-and-coming drama tends to create a false unity among classes, ethnicities, and regions that might otherwise have justifiable conflicts.

The convergence of sports with nationalism can be seen in the use of military metaphors to describe offensive and defensive plays, in fans standing for the national anthem, in the presentation of the colors, and in the band forming a flag or liberty bell at halftime in football games. At the level of the local professional team, sports fans engage in what seems like mindless loyalty to teams whose owners have no loyalty to their city whatsoever, and to players whose local loyalties are no different than those of the owners. Why is this? Why be loyal to a team when, for the owners and the players, the games are just business?

In his book *Social Structure and Testosterone* Theodore Kemper (1990) argues that the roles, rules, and setting for team sports resemble Adam Smith's "Garden of Eden" model of capitalism come true. First, it appears that the teams are evenly matched, so winning and losing are truly determined by hard work and sacrifice rather than by inheritance, as in actual capitalism. Second, unlike life in industrial capitalism, in sports there is a definite resolution by the end of the game: You win or you lose. Third, unlike real life in industrial capitalism, where emotional control is required on the job, for fans the full range of emotions can be expressed. Fourth, the rules are fair and transparent. There is not one set of rules for one class and another set of rules for another class (or race). Fifth, there is a direct relationship between performance and success or failure that is rare in real life. Sixth, after the game there is clear feedback about which strategies worked and which didn't work. Finally, even if your team loses, it can start from scratch in the next game. At the end of the year, even the fans of a last-place team can hope and "wait 'til next year!" Winners can't accumulate victories across seasons the way capitalists can accumulate capital across generations. This is not to say that all of these beliefs about sports (or even any of them) are true. It is only that they appear to be true to the fans, and this has a lot to do with their reasons for suspending good judgment and ignoring the truth about professional sports.

The extent to which sports fans' loyalty knows no bounds can be seen by simply performing the following thought experiment. Imagine telling a sports fan that a researcher has evidence that the political elections are fixed and that the public votes are not really counted. Now imagine telling a loyal sports fan that a sports sociologist has found evidence that baseball games and football games are fixed. For example, in football the "prevent defense" (which offensive teams usually eat alive) is really a way for the offense to catch up and keep the game from being a blowout. Our guess is that the sports fan would be far more insulted and up in arms over allegations of games being fixed than over any insinuation of political or economic conspiracies.

Socializing Mechanisms

Classical and operant learning, learning through observation, and learning through cooperation form the mediating bridge by which the messages of socializing agents get imported inside the individual. The simplest forms of learning are the kinds discovered by radical behaviorists Pavlov and Skinner. Classical conditioning, founded by Pavlov, has to do with the associations formed right before a behavior. Associations have to do with where you were, the time of day, and who you were with. These associations become linked with a behavior. If association theory has to do with what happened before a behavior, operant conditioning occurs in the immediate consequences after the behavior. Pavlov and Skinner were radical in that they denied that it was important to know what is going on in a person's mind when these associations and consequences take place.

A higher form of learning occurs when an individual learns by associations and consequences that do not happen directly to them. Observational learning occurs when individuals learn by watching others who model the behavior. Most famously, Albert Bandura wanted to know if watching violence on television could actually make children more violent. The answer, according to Bandura's research, has to do with the nature of the model (are they attractive or powerful, or do they appear to be an expert?), the behavior of the model (distinctive, clear, and simple), and the consequences of the model's behavior (whether they are rewarded or punished) (Carver and Scheier 2004).

Lev Vygotsky (1978) argued that the leading edge of new learning does not take place within the minds of individuals but between individuals in cooperative work, school, and home settings. Let's take an example of a dad teaching his son to bake cookies. At first, the dad does most of the complex activities and gives the child the simpler tasks. But gradually, the dad cedes more and more activities to the child. Vygotsky called this the "zone of proximal development" because cooperative activity is the leading edge of new learning. For our purposes we will call this the "local interpersonal." The second stage for Vygotsky is "internalization." This means that the child can do all the activities of baking cookies by himself. The third stage, which Vygotsky never articulated as far as we know (but we speculate that he would agree with), returns to the social, but on a higher level that we call the "global interpersonal." This is where the child takes the baking skills he learned in making cookies and applies them to a wider social context. In other words, suppose that the child is recruited by the neighbors to bake cookies for a community event. The child would be stretched further because he would have to learn to bake a wider variety of cookies and on a grander scale.

Building a Social Self

Layers of Identity

It is conceptually useful to divide human identity into three interacting layers. The first layer is temperament. Temperament is the biological predispositions an organism has prior to becoming socialized. These are processes such as whether a child is introverted or extroverted or displays calmness or hyperactivity. The second layer of identity is personality. Personality results from the interaction between temperament, which is innate, and personal experience, which is learned as part of being socialized into the human community. Personality is a relatively stable set of characteristics that make an individual unique compared to others. These characteristics appear to remain stable over time and to vary little across the roles that we play and the situations we find ourselves in. While personality is socialized, the focus is on the particular biography of the individual.

The third layer of identity is the self. Social institutions and local groups that make up society are relatively indifferent to people's personalities, but they have high expectations that this individual can learn roles, navigate a situation, and learn rules. The "self" is the microunit of society. The self learns through classical and operant, social, and cooperative learning to be a recipient of the agents of socialization and their dynamics and to eventually become, as an adult, co-constructor of those agencies through their work. Furthermore, in order for society to be transmitted across generations, those who develop selves must also, as parents, help build the selves of their children.

In order for an individual to develop a social self, the following "building blocks" must be mastered:

- Distinguish the inner world from the outer world
- Learn language, both verbal and nonverbal
- Manipulate tools effectively
- Suppress or relativize biological urges
- Cultivate a conscience
- Learn to play in an improvised and designed manner
- Decipher beliefs and customs of society
- Master how to role-take and role-make
- Learn the status and entitlements of people in roles
- Learn to think abstractly to draw from past experiences and plan future intentions
- Navigate across routine, mildly problematic, and crisis situations
- Learn to cooperate and produce synergy in groups
- Manage the tension between individual and social self-interest ("I-Me" dialogues)

All of these skills can be grouped into "objective" skills or "subjective" skills. Usually when we think of these words we think of subjectivity being inside us and objectivity being outside us. As we will see, both objectivity and subjectivity require cultivation, and when a baby is first born, they have neither.

What babies possess at birth is a protosocial self that is pre-subjective and pre-objective. On the one hand, babies are too lost in their own needs to see their caretakers as full beings playing roles and navigating situations that are independent of them. They have no social objectivity. Other people are used as a means to satisfy their needs. At the same time, this protosocial self does not realize that its own internal states (emotions, fantasies, and urges) are closed off and invisible to others. In order to develop subjectivity, there must be awareness that one's inner life cannot be publicly scrutinized.

Let us review the building blocks and connect them up to the cultivation of objectivity and subjectivity. A number of important skills and concepts that a child must learn as part of socialization cannot be categorized in the service of either subjectivity or objectivity, because they are both. These include learning to distinguish the inner world from the outer world, learning to use verbal language and nonverbal body language, and learning how to manipulate tools.

All beings have to earn a living in the environment. Most other biological beings are limited to their physical anatomy in earning that living—claws for raking, teeth for tearing, and beaks for pecking. Human beings craft objects—tools—that allow them to act upon other objects to meet their needs. Tools help us focus our attention, intensify our actions, and permit us to carve and shape what the world becomes. In order to become fully human and navigate through the world, we must master the most important tools—spoons and knives, hammers, nails, chisels, weaving looms, telephones, computers, and later on, cars.

Learning verbal language is vital in enabling us to live beyond the here and now. It allows us to analyze our experiences by comparing them with our past experiences and to project future plans. Language allows us to share our experiences with others. This advances the learning curve for everyone. Further, verbal language allows us to build from others' experiences in the past and share experiences with future generations.

Another foundational skill in cultivating objectivity is to develop a conscience. As all parents know, it is futile to expect a one- or two-year-old to know what is right and what is wrong. So, too, it is unrealistic to tell a child what is right and wrong and expect this moral encouragement to govern their behavior from that point forward. Tangible consequences—reinforcement or punishment—are more likely to be effective. But there is a point at which the conversations between parents and children about beliefs and morals move from interpersonal discussions to intrapersonal dialogues. In other words, the child internalizes these conversations between themselves and parents and makes them their own. Then an individual possesses a conscience.

Of course, having a conscience does not guarantee that the child will do what their parents want. But if the child does not enact the beliefs and morals of their parents, they will be aware of the difference, experience an inner conflict, and probably feel guilty about their actions. Prior to this internalization of previous conversations, guilt and remorse do not exist. Wrongdoing is merely a matter of fear of punishment, and following what the parent wants is motivated by an anticipated reward. The child is building a conscience at the same time they are learning their society's morals and beliefs as their parents pass them on.

Another skill is learning how to suppress and relativize biological functions. Biological elimination and sexual play have to be structured spatially and temporally so as not to offend social customs and laws.

One of the most important skills a self must learn is how to role-take and role-make. Roles are a predictable range of expected actions that are embedded in specific situations. Roles result from a conscious or unconscious division of labor between people as to how to negotiate situations successfully. Role-taking and role-making generally take a long time to learn. Learning to play roles in specific situations and switch roles in new situations takes even longer. Children must first learn what the roles are. They first do this through play, and then they learn to do this in earnest.

Mead's (1972) four stages of self-development or role development are as follows:

1. *Preparation.* In this first stage, the child is still mastering the language, tool manipulation, body movement, and developing a conscience. The child imitates the actions of others in roles without understanding that they are roles and without understanding their meaning.
2. *Play.* In this stage, the child begins to understand roles but can only play the roles *one at a time*. Secondly, the child cannot see themselves from the perspective of others. Play involves "let's pretend" games in which the imagination is cultivated at the expense of structure. Roles, rules, and purposes are

invented, changed, and ended quickly at the whim of the child and their friends.[1]

3. *The game.* In this stage, the child can assume the perspectives of several others *at the same time*. In addition, the individual can now see *her own self* from the perspective of others. Here, imagination is tempered by playing games that have roles, rules, and expectations built into them before the game begins, and these constraints are rarely subject to modification. "The game" teaches structure, self-discipline, and cooperation over an extended period of time.
4. *Reference groups.* In this stage, an adult begins to identify with groups beyond significant others. One's social class, ethnic/racial background, and gender become significant in understanding how one is treated and how one is supposed to treat others. A person can play different roles in each of these groups (Hewitt 1991).

Learning to play roles involves learning not only what the codes are in general but that some of the roles involve order giving and order taking. Every role has a status and a range of entitlements as to what is expected, permitted, and prohibited. This is the origin of prestige, influence, privilege, and power in adulthood.

Types of Situations

For a long time, the child does not understand that all roles are rooted in situational constraints and predicaments. This protosocial self imposes their personality over the roles and situations they stumble into, oblivious to the roles people are already playing and the type of situation they are in. Learning to identify, and navigate through, situations is a whole other skill. Children are virtually always in situations as they move across the day. Riding the bus to school requires the child to learn the role and rules of being a passenger. Being in school requires learning how to be a student, and participating in after-school drama club requires learning the role of the part they are to play.

In learning to identify a situation, at least eight dimensions need to be clarified:

1. Meaning (What is happening?)
2. Purpose/hopes (Why is it happening?)
3. Power base (Who is making it happen?)
4. Rules (How is it happening? What is expected, permitted, forbidden?)
5. Roles (How is this group organized? What is my place?)
6. Norms/customs (How am I supposed to act informally—my clothing, body language?)
7. Physical setting (Where is it happening? What is this furniture for? What are these artifacts for?)
8. Timeline (When is it happening? How long will it last?)

There are three types of situations: routine, mild-problematic, and crisis. A routine situation is one that is stable and repetitive in which most or all of the above questions are answered by everyone in more or less the same way. They are usually taken for granted and not explicitly discussed. Lack of clarity among people over a critical mass of these eight dimensions destabilizes these routine situations and leads to either a restabilization of the routine situation through discussion or a problematic or crisis situation.

Classroom dynamics is a good example of the transformation from a routine to a mild-problematic to a crisis situation. When students come into the classroom, most of them sit away from the front of the room. They understand they are in a classroom, they are in the role of students, their purpose is to get a decent grade, and they have to play by a certain set of rules. They are expected to raise questions, bring paper and pens to class, and take turns when speaking. The teacher does not have to announce that the students cannot spontaneously come to the front of the room, sit on their desks, or move furniture around.

A mildly problematic situation is one in which unexpected minor events *stretch* the boundaries dimensions but without calling them into question. However, in a mildly problematic

[1] In the comic strip *Calvin and Hobbes*, the "Calvinball" game between Calvin and Hobbes, his stuffed tiger, is a great example of this.

situation, some of the eight dimensions come to the level of group consciousness because they must be discussed and negotiated in order for the situation to be stabilized. Sometimes mildly problematic situations emerge not because of real events but because a significant number of people in the group either misunderstand some of the dimensions of situations or do understand them and are in conflict about them.

In the example of a classroom, a mildly problematic situation might arise when a number of students question the absence policy or grading criteria in front of other students. The authority of the teacher, the rules for the class, and the timeline are being tested. But the reason why everyone is present and what they are doing in the class remain stable. Whether this situation returns to routine or escalates into a crisis depends on how everyone in the room negotiates over these reservations.

A crisis situation occurs when either most of the dimensions of situations are called into question or only the most important ones are, such as the meaning, purpose, or power base of the group. A natural disaster that rocks a school can immediately turn the routine situation of a classroom into a crisis. It ends the formal educational setting and forces the same group of people to renegotiate how they are to be together in a collapsing building. Because the situation has changed, all the dimensions of the situations have to be reorganized.

Most groups cooperate. The agreement to play roles has embedded in it the assumption that if we divide up the tasks into roles, the end result will be more than anyone could achieve alone. When groups do this they produce "synergy." They produce a whole that is more than the sum of its parts. Even the most seemingly uncooperative and competitive groups have some level of cooperation at their foundation.

Roles Are Not Static

For a young child the fluidity of role-making seems self-evident. In pretend play, the child and their friends are constantly taking on and discarding roles. However, it is much harder to understand that adults switch roles as well. The child must learn (1) that their parents play many different roles in the course of a single day in addition to "mom" and "dad," (2) that roles are detachable from particular people (roles can be played by anyone, not just the people they know), and (3) that these multiple and detachable roles will change depending on whether a person is in a routine, mildly problematic, or crisis situation. Playing all these roles, of course, is preparation to play roles at work.

There is an important relationship between Mead's "play" and "the game" on the one hand and routine and crisis situations on the other. Designed play (Mead's "the game") socializes children to respect structure and perseverance in order to participate in routine actions. Improvised play (Mead's "play") teaches a child how to be imaginative when the group is faced with a crisis situation. When an individual is operating in a routine situation they are role-*taking*. They are entering a role that is already in place. When an individual is operating in a crisis situation they are role-*making*. They are creating the role (with others) on the spot. These skills are the grounds in everyday life for understanding that individuals, by their actions, are always creating order and conflict by conforming and being creative (see Table 4.1).

Improvised play, role-making, and learning how to navigate in crisis situations in everyday life are not just the skills needed to participate in normal adult life, but the skills required for participating in social movements, as we shall see.

Thus far, the tools that go with cultivating objectivity include playing roles and learning how to change roles as situations dictate. When a child begins to be able to take the role of the "generalized other," she develops an internalized sense that other people are objective realities that are independent of her own internal wishes, hopes, and fears.

Children come to realize that the domestic household, which they think is *the* world, is, in fact, a tiny slice of a world surrounded by many

Table 4.1 Order and conflict

Order	**Conflict (creativity)**
Designed play	Improvised play
Routine situations	Problematic or crisis situations
Role-taking	Role-making

other domestic households. They may learn that the roles they master are small parts of historical structures that have come into being before their individual lifetime and may remain after they die. So a teenager doing an apprenticeship in carpentry may learn that carpenters as a role have existed for thousands of years and that the tools and materials carpenters work with have changed over the centuries.

But what about an individual's "subjectivity," or what symbolic interactionists call their "biographical self"? According to Mead (1972), developing a sense of subjectivity is impossible without first understanding what it means to be objective. Once objectivity is understood, one's personal identity can be seen in perspective, as relatively small but also unique. The protosocial self is not born with subjectivity. This is because the child believes (1) that their inner world is transparent to others and (2) that the way they experience the world is the way others experience the world. Subjectivity is developed when the child realizes that their inner world is opaque and not on display to others to experience, and that others are not simply an audience for the child's personal dramas. Other people have individual lives that are unique to them, theirs to make for better or worse. This awakening of subjectivity allows the child to think about, fantasize about, and act toward themselves, not as the center of the universe but as a unique being among other unique beings.

Once an individual develops a picture of an independent objective world and a distinct subjective world, a unique problem presents itself. An understanding of the objective world means that there are stable expectations that social groups and the situation they are embedded in have for the individual. Yet at the same time, because the individual understands how to navigate these social roles and situations, they have a greater chance of transforming them in the service of what they want. The problem now is how to reconcile individual and social self-interest.

Once this conflict is recognized, internal negotiations must take place. Mead (1972) calls the part of the individual that is spontaneous and active the "I" part. This part of the self represents what the individual brings to the table of social situations. But the self is also an object about which others have expectations. As part of conscience-building, the individual develops an internalized set of expectations of what others may want. Mead calls this the individual's "Me" part of the self. Mead calls the subsequent negotiation between these two parts the "I-Me" dialogue. These two sides both cooperate and compete with each other; they haggle, trade, and plead with each other when in roles and situations. Here is an example.

Suppose an individual in a tribal society sees a member of their kin group headed toward their hut expecting to visit and be fed. The "I" part of the potential host says, "Here comes so-and-so, the loafer, expecting a handout. Let's leave quickly so we don't have to entertain him." The "Me" part says, "No, he is our kinsman and I am responsible for treating him as one of our own." The "I" part counters with, "But he is such a freeloader, he wouldn't do the same for me." The "Me" part counters with, "But the members of his family would be upset with me, and they are not loafers. I don't want to start trouble with them." The "I" part tries a compromise: "Maybe I can stay with him for a few minutes and pretend to be sick in order to send him on his way."

Learning to Think Abstractly

Abstract thinking is common to all human beings as a result of the cultivation of language, which allows us to think beyond the here and now. The process of abstraction can be broken down into three moments: extraction, deliberation, and generalization. Let's take an example.

Let us suppose someone is in the middle of an argument with their partner about how much they can afford to spend on a new car. The process of abstraction begins the moment they use their thinking about this particular problem to compare it temporally to their past and future problems in their relationship. After a bitter fight about the car they begin to extract the essential elements of this problem from its accidental properties. From analysis they realize that they spent a lot of time in the argument "spinning their wheels" in fruitless mutual accusations.

At the same time, one person notices their partner eating an orange as they watch a fly buzz around a sandwich. The orange and the fly are accidental events in this situation that are best left ignored. "Spinning our wheels" is the essential part that is extracted. They then extract this part of the argument out of the context of buying a car and deliberate about it. This means they compare their present problem with the car with how well they have fought about other issues in the past. Then they think about issues in the future that are unresolved, such as whether to have children or whether to live the rest of their lives in the United States. The last moment of abstraction comes when they generalize beyond the particular problems in their relationship and think about how they fight at work, with neighbors, or with friends. Do they also spin their wheels in mutual accusations there? Then, ultimately, it may occur to the person that maybe there is something wrong with the way they fight.

The ability to develop a generalized other and a biographical self requires living in the present with an expanded sense of time and space. In order to do this, an individual must learn to think abstractly. This means to extract the important from the unimportant properties of objects and situations from the present, to deliberate how the essential property that was extracted compares to both individual and group past experiences and to both individual and group future plans, and then to generalize how to use this essential property in situations other than the situation in which it was first found.

Conversely, a person thinking in a concrete way would not be able to distinguish essential from inessential properties of things and would be lost in the accidental properties of situations, such as a passing butterfly or the smell of food in the next room during an important staff meeting. Having little sense of how present experiences are connected to past experiences, they would be less likely to think clearly about the future. Lastly, they would not learn much from one situation to another. They would repeat the same actions regardless of where they were or whom they were with. The movement from concrete to increasingly abstract thinking is beautifully described in Jean Piaget's stages of cognitive development.

Because we have described these building blocks as first taking place in childhood, it is tempting to imagine that once this elementary socialization takes place, socialization is all over. This is not the case. Socialization and resocialization never end. Every time we enter a new occupation we must learn a new language, master a new set of tools, and learn to role-take and role-make again. The socialization described above is a kind of foundational socialization. But as we grow into adulthood, new spirals of socialized building blocks interpenetrate with this foundation, modifying it.

In addition, in our society many of the building blocks of the social self are constructed by different socializing agents, and many of them give contradictory messages. The conflicted nature of these agents may cause unique problems and opportunities for the modern self that the premodern self did not face, as we shall see.

Role Conflicts

Social life would be much easier if there was a one-to-one correspondence between roles and situations. When we are in the role of teacher during the day, we are in a routine situation, and the role ends (temporarily) at the end of the day. We are parents in the evening, and we might be in a mild problematic situation with our children, but the role ends temporarily when we go to teach. As social organizers on picket lines we may be in a crisis situation with the administration, but our role ends when the labor strike ends. But of course, social life is messier than this. What do you do when you are in the role of a waitress and your boyfriend shows up for lunch with some of his friends and expects to be served? What do you do when your football coach insists that you need to practice and this conflicts with a class presentation you must give? Suppose you are hired as a cashier at a grocery store, yet you find yourself managing the store for the same wages you are paid as a cashier? Suppose you have spent ten years of your life as a nun and decide religious life is not for you. You have been in the role of a nun for ten years and your friends have gotten used to it.

All these problems are rooted in the fact that (1) people play more than one role at a time and sometimes the roles conflict, (2) sometimes a single role is stretched beyond its normal parameters, (3) sometimes the roles are vaguely defined, and (4) sometimes people become so attached to roles that they continue in these roles even though the situation no longer requires them.

Our waitress is in what social psychologists call an "inter-role" conflict. Her problem consists of being caught in two roles, one as a waitress and one as a girlfriend, and these roles are expected to be played at the same time. Will her boyfriend respect her role and not ask for special treatment? We doubt it.

The student is caught in what is called an "intra-role" or "role strain," where the single role is stretched beyond its normal boundaries. It falls within the role of a student to participate in clubs at school. Yet the leaders of these clubs are expected to cede priority to academic studies. When the coach asks the student to participate in extra practices, he is straining the role of a student.

In both inter-role and intra-role conflicts, the expectations about how to act are clear. The problem is that they are conflicted or strained. The situation with the cashier is different. From one day to the next she doesn't know where the boundaries of the role are. When the owner of the grocery store is there, she is expected to take orders from him, just like the other cashiers. But when the owner is gone, she is given the role of manager, which places her temporarily above her fellow cashiers. This kind of role vagueness is very detrimental to work productivity. Role vagueness is where the boundaries of your role are mushy.

Roles are more than necessary evils. They provide rhythm, familiarity, identity, and, in many cases, status. These are all good reasons why the individual might want to hold on to the role long after the situation has dissolved. The nun in our example is having a problem with "role exit," or perhaps better called "role lag." Role exit problems occur when an individual formally announces the ending of a role but continues to act as if they were in that role, despite the situation. At the same time, people in this person's network do not want her to exit her role and continue to act as if she were still in the role.

The ex-nun may have difficulty wearing the same type of clothing women her age are wearing, and her friends will be shocked that she is dating. An ex-doctor may still be expected to give free medical advice to his friends long after he has left the field. Someone who has left Alcoholics Anonymous may still be treated as being in the role of an alcoholic even if he is clean and sober.

Focused and Unfocused Occasions

Focused Occasions

Sociologist Erving Goffman (1963) identified two types of occasions, focused and unfocused. Focused occasions involve groups with a jointly sustained focus of attention and involve conversations. Goffman identified three kinds of focused occasions: a common focused occasion such as a platoon on a parade ground, a jointly focused gathering such as a couple dancing, and a multifocused occasion like a party. Both the platoon and the dancing couple are what group dynamics theorists call "organic" groups. Organic groups have a single goal with a division of labor, a relatively clear beginning and ending time, and strict boundaries about entry and leaving. Cocktail parties are interesting as they are midway between focused and unfocused groups. All groups involve "emotional work." You perform emotional work when, in order to perform a role, you show feelings you don't have (which is required for the job) and hide emotions you do have. Within a focused occasion, Goffman calls the emotional work required "impressions management." Impressions management is the process of planning and staging how the other group members see you. More specifically, impressions management involves three skills:

1. Showing competency, tact, and likability
2. Avoiding embarrassing oneself or others
3. Striving to probe anything that may be beneath the role of another without being caught

In any focused occasion there are staging areas. The front stage is where the performance takes place. The back stage is where the preparation, rehearsal, and aftermath of a performance occur. Let's imagine a group of waiters at a restaurant as an example.

The front stage is where all emotional work is done; the back stage is where group members share their experiences with other group members about their performance. Back stage is where emotional expression is permitted in relation to the audience but is still controlled because of the presence of other group members. Back stage is where brooding, complaining, and telling stories occur.

Broadly speaking, the front stage is where all group members are on their best behavior. The setting is neat, with the sight of waste and garbage kept to a minimum; body and facial gestures and postures are consistent with the performance; and clothes, makeup, and hairstyling are consistent with the job. Proper grammar, tone, and volume are used, and vague responses such as "interesting" or "fine" are saved for if and when controversial issues come up.

Back stage in a restaurant is likely to be loud with cooks and waiters being playful with each other, while mocking the customers' food orders. Backstage areas are stacked with crates and trash, cooks are dressed informally, and there is a greater variety of sounds from humming, whistling, yelling, mumbling, and cursing and the use of slang.

What happens when a patron at the restaurant has to use the bathroom and has to enter the "employees only" part of the restaurant to get to the bathroom? Some of the most harrowing, provocative, and hilarious situations are Goffman's description of what happens when the public is forced to navigate into the backstage area for reasons such as this.

Unfocused Occasions

How are the occasions of pedestrians on city streets, users of a library room, people sitting on a public bench, or people waiting for an elevator to be made sense of? How do the social rules and emotional work differ from focused occasions?

Goffman (1963) categorizes all these examples as unfocused occasions, which mostly center around how people conduct themselves in public. Goffman defines an unfocused occasion as one in which individuals are pursuing parallel activities in public that do not require a joint activity to complete, but people are aware of the presence of others. Unlike in focused occasions, where groups are organic, in unfocused situations, groups are aggregates in which there is no division of labor, no definite beginning and ending times, porous boundaries about entry and exiting, and no production of synergy.

If impressions management is the kind of emotional work done in focused situations, "civil inattention" is what is required of people in public unfocused occasions. Civil inattention is the nonverbal process of at least two individuals stabilizing public ground so that each can occupy public space civilly (politely) while pursuing parallel activities.

The goals of emotional work on unfocused occasions are:

- Letting other people know you are aware of their presence
- Communicating that you accept their right to their own activities (Goffman calls this "circumspection gloss")
- Reassuring that you are engaging in normal activity and you are competent (orientation gloss)
- Indicating that you are not under duress (interplay gloss)
- Showing that you are not a threat

How are the goals of civic inattention achieved? By creating a gaze that is somewhere in between direct and averted. Two individuals glance at each other to establish a presence without conversation and mutually agree not to let their eyes meet, yet do so in such a way as to let the other know they are not afraid. Unlike focused occasions, the staging areas of unfocused occasions are front stage only (see Table 4.2 for an overview of focused and unfocused occasions).

Breaches in Public Order

There are numerous situations in which public interactions are sources of disruption and confusion—for example, someone inadvertently taking someone else's parking place, cutting in line, or unintentionally cutting someone off on the freeway. At least in the United States, waiting in line is a situation of unfocused occasion. If you stand too far to the side or too far back, questions may arise as to whether you are really in line. Someone may have to break the ice and inquire. Yet there is an unstated agreed-upon distance that is acceptable and a distance that is not. Another breach is being caught in public talking to yourself, that is, thinking out loud and then finding out someone else is there. People with stigmas such as being in a wheelchair or having epilepsy are vulnerable to transgressions of the rules of civil inattention. In asylums, in what Goffman (1963) calls "total situations," inmates may be subject to specific

Table 4.2 Types of occasions

Category of comparison	Focused occasions	Unfocused or diffused occasions
Definition	A jointly sustained focus of attention that probably involves conversations	People are pursuing parallel activities but are aware of each other's presence. No conversation—or small talk at the most—is the rule.
Type of group	Organic groups—single goal with a division of labor, relatively clear beginning and ending times, strict boundaries about entering and leaving, and production of synergy	Aggregates—many goals or a single goal that requires no division of labor, no definite beginning or ending times, porous boundaries about entering and leaving, and no production of synergy
Examples	• Game of tennis • Dancing couple • Music band • A professional sports team • Interacting tasks of workers • Group panels assembled to interview a potential new worker	• Pedestrians on a city street • Users of a library room • People waiting in a doctor's office • People sitting on a park bench • People in a public restroom • People waiting for a train • People watching a building being demolished • People standing in an elevator
Type of emotional work	Impressions management—the process of planning and managing how others see you in focused occasions	Civil inattention—the process of stabilizing public ground so that you let others know you intend to be in the space, while respecting their right to occupy the same space. Communicate this using nonverbal analogical messages. A gaze in between direct and averted—passers-by glance at each other but mutually agree not to let their eyes meet and do so in a way that lets each know that the other is not afraid.
Goals of emotional work	1) Show competence, tact, likability 2) Avoid embarrassing yourself or others 3) Analyze contradictions between the actual role performance and the role presentation	1) Let other people know you are aware of their presence 2) Communicate that you accept their right to their own activities 3) Reassure that you are engaging in normal activity and are competent 4) Indicate that you are not under duress and are under control 5) Show that you are not a threat
Staging area	Front stage—where the performance takes place Back stage—where the rehearsing, preparation, and wear and tear of a performance are downloaded	Front stage only—performance is a "one-night" stand because situations are fleeting

forms of material and symbolic degradation in which normal rules of forms of tact and respect are violated in creating an enforced infantilism.

No-Man's-Land

Breaches in public order can occur in either a focused occasion or an unfocused occasion. In a focused situation there might be misunderstandings and quibbling between people who are on the front stage or between people who are in backstage settings.

Even more provocative are situations that are problematic because they are transitioning from a focused occasion to an unfocused occasion. Around each occasion is a kind of no-man's-land, a reserve, or buffer space. People may pass through such spaces, but when they do, all bets are off!

For example, let's imagine a shopper and a salesperson have just completed a transaction. The shopper goes to another section of the store and the salesperson continues to work. But upon leaving the store and heading for the bus stop, the shopper sees the salesperson waiting for the bus. Previously they were in a focused situation. Waiting for the bus is an unfocused occasion. Yet, because they have had this previous focused transaction, they cannot quite act as if they have never met each other (although some will try). The reverse would be moving from an unfocused situation to a focused one. Let's suppose you are waiting at a bus stop for a long time with two or three people, but the bus does not come. This is not a serious enough situation to try to make it a focused occasion, like if you were on a bus and the bus broke down. However, the bus's not coming for a long time makes it significant enough for civil inattention to break down. If you begin the discussion of why the bus is not coming, you will move from civil inattention to impressions management.

Forms of Repair

In both breaches in public order and no-man's-land, repair kits are necessary. These include:

- *Accounts*—explaining why a transgression has occurred—ignorance, unusual circumstance, temporary incompetence, unmindfulness on your part
- *Apologies*—embarrassment, clarification that the proper conduct is known, disavowal and rejection of one's behavior, voluntary restitution, penance
- *Requests*—preemptive asking for license to do something that might otherwise be considered a violation of a norm

Varieties of Selves: Collectivist versus Individualist

Before discussing how different types of self get built, let us review the socializing agents and mechanisms of transmission. Earlier we named thirteen building blocks an individual in any society must master in order to become a fully social self. Various agents of socialization—the family, mass media, friends—discussed earlier provide opportunities to master these building blocks. The mechanisms or filters through which learning takes place are classical and operant conditioning, observation, and cooperative learning.

But up to now we have treated the building of a social self as if it had no historical or cross-cultural variation. While all societies have to provide children with the building blocks described, how they get built, what is emphasized, and what gets downplayed vary from society to society, depending on whether these are hunter-gatherer bands, horticultural villagers, agricultural states, or industrial capitalist societies. As world-systems change and evolve, so does the form of the social self.

Collectivist or Individualist Selves?

Just as hunting-gathering societies, horticultural societies, agricultural states, and industrial capitalist societies have very different technologies, economies, and political and sacred systems, they also possess different concepts of the self. We will see that, broadly speaking, individuals in egalitarian hunter-gatherer and horticultural societies have "horizontal collectivist selves," while people in Bronze Age agricultural states had "vertical collectivist selves." (Rank societies such as simple chiefdoms are a transition between the two.) It is only in the Late Iron Age (500 BCE) that we see the first signs of a "vertical individualist self." With the rise of capitalism in Europe roughly five hundred years ago, the vertical individualist self takes on a life of its own. Calling selves "horizontal" refers to the communal anti-hierarchical nature of the way the self interacts with others. Calling the self "vertical" refers to the stratified way in which a self relates to other selves. While a collectivist can be either horizontal or vertical, an individualist can only be vertical because, historically, individualism emerged thousands of years after social stratification emerged in agricultural states.

The division of social selves into individualists and collectivists has a history in twentieth-century writing and has recently been researched by a number of cross-cultural psychologists (Triandis 1995; Segall et al. 1999; Smith and Harris Bond 1998). We are interested in how these cross-cultural psychological studies about contemporary societies might apply historically. We will attempt this historical reconstruction throughout this text.

Secondly, we want to know how this difference is connected to the building blocks of the self on the one hand and the agents of socialization on the other. We will attempt that in this section of our chapter.

What exactly do we mean by "collectivism" and "individualism"? We will begin with how each identity orients itself in relation to society and nature. Individualism is a set of beliefs and practices that assumes that (1) the individual is separate from kin groups and the biophysical environment and identifies more easily with strangers, (2) the inner world is more a source of identity than objective actions, and (3) the individual is more important than the group. Collectivism is a set of beliefs or practices that assumes the reverse: (1) the individual is interdependent with kin groups and nature, and strangers are treated with suspicion, (2) the outer world of objective actions matters more than does inner experience, and (3) the kin group is more important than the individual.

But where do these assumptions come from? Do individuals just decide for themselves which type of self they like better? Are these identities like costumes that can be dressed and undressed as the individual sees fit? Hardly. Technological, political, and economic structures of society impact agents of socialization and learning mechanisms through which the self is built in order to train the individual to work and reproduce in these societies. However, the agents of socialization differ between social formation in their number, power of penetration, content, and diversity of messages.

The question that the socializing agents are trying to answer is, What is the individual supposed to do and how is the individual supposed to be? But what exactly are the differences in the agents of socialization that constrain people to learn the building blocks somewhat differently? A woman living in a simple horticultural society will not have the same "I-Me" dialogue as a merchant in the Late Iron Age. She will not face the problem of role-making and role-taking in the same way, nor will she feel and think the same as the merchant about dealing with crisis situations.

The first factor that impacts whether a person develops an individualist or collectivist self depends on the degree of specialization of society. When people make their living in a well-rounded way (as in hunting-gathering societies), this jack-of-all-trades does not develop the same kind of attachment to a single kind of work, because it is more important to move across work rather than develop specialized work. On the other hand, a central part of an individualist identity is the kind of work he does. The specialization of labor in industrial capitalist societies (Durkheim's organic solidarity), fed by the Protestant work ethic, feeds the individual's attachment to his work even as he is alienated politically and economically from other workers.

The second factor in promoting collectivism and individualism is the degree of political and economic tension between groups. In egalitarian nonstate societies there is less conflict between groups because there is little surplus to fight over. The tension between individual self-interest, group self-interest, and society as a whole is much less than in stratified societies. It is far easier to develop a collectivist identity when the individual's material relations with other groups actually support conceptualizing individual and social self-interest as more or less the same. In rank and stratified societies, conflicts between groups will arise, subgroup loyalties will grow, and a kind of class or caste loyalty will develop, which creates the seeds of individualism.

Another consideration is the degree of congruence between socializing agents. As we will see, the socializing influences of egalitarian societies are the family, the kin groups, and the local clans. Because there is little political and economic tension between these groups, they project the same conforming message to the individual: Group expectations are primary.

In industrial capitalist society, socializing forces vary greatly in the messages the individual receives. The family, the church, and the state may be mostly in agreement. However, conflict is likely to exist between these institutions and the individual's education, mass media (television and movies), friends, and sports. This situation produces confusion and conflict. This is exactly what happens to immigrants or refugees when settling in another country. Their country of origin might support collectivism, while the country they are migrating to supports individualism.

At the same time, the conflict between agents of socialization as to how the individual should be means there will be a *variety* of possibilities of identity. Even if *all* of the socializing forces are individualist, they are competing over the individualist's choices of identity—soldier, rock musician, pastor, or professional football player. But taken as a whole, as an ideology that underpins all institutions, they are all suggesting that *any* one of these identities is possible. As Berger and Luckmann (1967) point out, it is because a person sees a conflicting number of choices that they come to see (1) the relativity of all social institutions, (2) the individual is prior to the group, and (3) the constraints on an individual are not as great as the possibilities.

Identity crisis questions like "Who am I?" and "What is my place in society?" are unique to societies that promote individualism. All individuals in all societies do not ask these questions, because the questions would not even be raised unless a variety of answers were possible. For a variety of answers to be possible, socialization agents that give different answers to these questions would need to be in place.

Is there a relationship between social class location and individualism? Generally, at least under capitalism, wealth buys privacy. The extent to which an individual has economic resources, an education, and leisure time affects the extent to which they can experience themselves in a self-reflective way.

Another force contributing to a collectivist or individualist identity is the degree of centralization or decentralization of the society. Centralized control over resources muffles competition, and competition is the lifeblood of individualism. Conversely, when various political and economic blocs struggle for power and there is no means by which centralization can occur, individualism is more likely.

In addition, what the sources of wealth are and where these sources are located also impact identity. Broadly speaking, a society located near trade routes will have contact with many kinds of societies, and this breeds a cosmopolitan attitude—bilingualism, learning how to translate currencies, and travel. This kind of experience generally supports a relativistic attitude toward its own social institutions, and a wide-ranging but shallow set of loyalties and individualism. On the other hand, societies located in valleys far from coastal trade will be more parochial and less open cross-culturally. In these societies it is easier to control populations with long-term expectations of loyalty, obedience to the authorities, and conformity in groups.

Another geographical consideration that impacts collectivism or individualism is whether a person lives in an urban or rural area of society. Even in land-based civilizations such as ancient China or India, people living in cities are more likely to have individualist tendencies because in cities loyalties to kin groups are weakened and the presence of strangers invites more contractual relationships not governed by generalized reciprocity.

The gender of the individual also affects the self. Many factors, principally the responsibility of raising children and the lack of opportunity to work in public positions that require travel, make women much more likely to be collectivists than men.

Another factor is the presence of an explicit ideology of collectivism or individualism. Certainly, people do not need an ideology to have a practice of being individualist or collectivist, but it strengthens one's commitment to cultivating a particular kind of self if an ideology is available. The United States had the most well-developed and maniacal ideology of individualism in the world, from the cowboy to the frontiersman.

Summing up this section, in order to participate in society an individual must build a self. This is done by mastering a number of skills that take many years to develop. But whether the self becomes collectivist or individualist depends on a variety of sociological ingredients. These include the complexity of social organization and the consequent division of labor, the degree of stratification in society, the sources of wealth and the class membership of the individual within a society, whether the economic source of wealth is land or trade-based, the geographical location of the society, whether a person lives in the city or the country, whether the society is centralized or decentralized, and the gender of the individual.

Table 4.3 summarizes the differences in social conditions that support collectivism and individualism.

Table 4.3 Sociological conditions for the production of selves

Category of comparison	Collectivism	Individualism
Type of society	Hunter-gatherers, horticulturalists, agricultural states	Industrial, capitalist states
Division of labor	Well-rounded, do many things well (egalitarian tribal)	Greater specialization of labor, greater part of identity located in occupation
Degree of stratification	Egalitarian in nonstate societies; highly stratified in agricultural states	Class stratification in industry
Sources of wealth	Land based	Trade based
Social class membership	If classes exist, the lower classes	Middle and upper classes
Political stratification	Decentralized (tribal), centralized (agricultural states)	Decentralized
Uniformity in messages of agents of socialization	Homogeneous socialization produces conformity	Heterogeneous messages produce perception of confusion, conflict, and opportunity
Geography	Land-locked	Near large, open bodies of water; near trade routes
Region	Rural: kin-group bound, greater suspicion of strangers	Urban: cultivate relationships with strangers
Gender	Women and men	Mostly men

The Self and Social Movements

When we discussed the individual self in social evolution we talked about the individual essentially reacting to changes in social structures by developing collectivist or individualist selves on the one hand, and learning to think more abstractly on the other. But this presents social change as essentially an involuntary process. However, social collectivities do try to collectively change social evolution in a particular direction.

We will discuss the impact of social movements in later chapters. At this point we just want to point out that the seeds of acting in a collective manner in the service of social improvement are rooted in many of the skills the self is expected to build in the course of leading an ordinary life.

Social institutions produce both order and conflict, and this tension is expressed in the types of skills people are socialized to learn as selves. As we saw earlier, when children are socialized to play games, they are taught to follow rules and roles as well as how to exercise their creativity within social constraints. These skills translate into nonplay circumstances in everyday life.

Learning how to master routine situations means sizing up a circumstance and identifying physical and temporal settings, the power bases, and the norms for conforming or obeying. At the same time, being able to negotiate mild problematic and crisis situations involves a willingness to reorganize spatial and temporal settings and restructure power bases. Our point is that the skills required to participate in social movements are rooted in the skills learned in play and nonplay circumstances in everyday life as children, and later on in work settings as adolescents and adults. Without this understanding, the study of social movements (how people come to be involved and how they sustain their involvement) will be mystified. We will have social movements without concrete individuals.

At the beginning of this book we said that in the comparative world-systems perspective, nearly all human societies are parts of larger intersocietal systems. So, too, for the self to be truly optimal, individuals would gradually learn to see themselves as world-historical individuals acting within a larger system that is composed of multiple societies and cultures. What exactly does this mean?

Part of developing a generalized other is to learn to understand that the world is bigger than the individual in time (beyond their individual biography) and in space (beyond their domestic household). To become a world-historical individual means to push these boundaries beyond where most people normally go. Individuals would develop world-historical selves if they came to comprehend the fact that their own identity and cognition are rooted in civilizational and global institutions and that the arena of collective action occurs on the stage of world-historical evolution. The Internet and the electronic revolution are intensifying both human problems and human capacity to solve them because of the global scale in which they occur. It involves knowledge about the roles and occupations that are historically specific to the twenty-first century. It involves a sense that in world history and long-term social change, some roles and occupations emerge and others wither away.

A world-historical self understands that its location in the core, periphery, or semiperiphery of the global world-system both constrains and invites ways of living that may not be possible in other parts of the system. A world-historical individual does not privatize their individual biography as their own and dissociate themselves from world history. Rather, the biographical self, one's goals and plans, and one's actions are part of world history in the making.

To rise above the concrete situation of here and now requires a thinking process where time-space displacement is possible. But this thinking capacity is not simply acquired by a heroic voluntary, individual effort. Just as the self changes into both collectivism and individualism in social evolution as a result of technological, economic, and political revolutions, so, too, the nature of human abstraction is affected by technological and economic changes in social evolution. In future chapters we will see how the impact of hieroglyphics, the alphabet, and coined money affected the thinking processes of those social classes who used these devices. The rise of mapmaking, the printing press, double-entry bookkeeping, mathematical notation, and musical scores changed the nature of abstraction again. Furthermore, the rise of capitalism, banks, the stock market, the use of checks and credit cards, and the Internet affect our ability to think more abstractly today. The presence of these institutions forces virtually everyone to think more abstractly in order to keep up. The self that is built from social movements uses more abstract thinking skills for purposes *other than* to enhance private life and reproduce capitalism on the job.

Using the comparative world-systems perspective and institutional materialism, a world-historical individual would comprehend contemporary social movements both in space (around the world) and in time (in the historical evolution of the world-system). We will return to this subject when we discuss the future of the world-system.

The basic ideas have now been described. We have a philosophical standpoint, a method, a theoretical approach (institutional materialism), an orienting strategy (the comparative world-systems perspective), and a stance for understanding the social self as an institution. This is enough camping equipment for an excursion into the realm of stateless systems.

Suggested Readings

Berger, Peter, and Thomas Luckmann. 1967. *The Social Construction of Reality.* New York: Anchor.

Buss, David. 1999. *Evolutionary Psychology*. Boston: Allyn and Bacon.

Goffman, Erving. 1959. *Presentation of Self in Everyday Life.* New York: Anchor.

Hewitt, John. 1991. *Self and Society.* 5th ed. Boston: Allyn and Bacon.

Triandis, Harry. 1995. *Individualism and Collectivism.* Boulder, CO: Westview Press.

van der Veer, René, and Jaan Valsiner. 1991. *Understanding Vygotsky.* Cambridge, MA: Blackwell.

Wertsch, H. 1985. *Vygotsky and the Social Formation of Mind.* Cambridge, MA: Harvard University Press.

PART

II

Stateless Systems

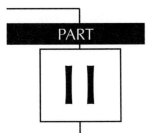

Small-scale world-systems are important to understand in their own right but also for what they tell us about larger systems as well as implications for future possibilities of human social organization. The chapters in Part II provide a feel for the lives of people in small egalitarian societies in which the main institutions are based on consensus and moral order. They also examine how ecological degradation, warfare, aggressive masculinity, and cannibalism, often resulting from growing population pressure, affected the development of sedentism and new technologies of production. The rise of early forms of hierarchy is explained, and interesting features of these systems, such as human sacrifice, sacred chiefs, and elite incest, are examined.

Chapter 5 includes a discussion of the kinds of evidence that social scientists use to make inferences about how stateless societies worked. It surveys the nomadic foraging bands of the Old Stone Age and discusses the establishment of the first permanently occupied villages of diversified foragers. An overview of settlement systems is presented. Chapter 5 also includes an overview of a regional world-system inhabited by sedentary foragers that existed in Northern California before the arrival of the Europeans. The invention and diffusion of planting is discussed in Chapter 6, and an overview of horticultural societies is presented. The effects of differences in original botanical and zoological wealth and rates of diffusion on the subsequent development of complexity and hierarchy are discussed. A chapter available on the website for this textbook (http://www.paradigmpublishers.com/resrcs/other/1612053289_otherlink.pdf) surveys the development of regional world-systems in the part of indigenous North America that eventually became the territory of the contiguous forty-eight United States. Chapter 7 discusses chiefdom formation and the process of the rise and fall of large and hierarchical polities in interchiefdom systems. It presents overviews of chiefdom systems in ancient Southwest Asia, the rise and fall of the Mississippian interaction sphere in the American Midwest, the emergence of paramount chiefs on the Chesapeake Bay, and the nearly state-like complex chiefdoms of precontact Hawaii.

5

World-Systems of Foragers

This chapter examines the lives of people in small egalitarian foraging (hunter-gatherer) societies in which the main institutions were based on peoples' agreements about what is good and the nature of reality. We begin with a further discussion of the kinds of evidence that social scientists use to understand small-scale societies. And we examine the nature of intersocietal interaction networks among small-scale societies. The chapter also discusses the migrations that peopled the earth. We describe societies of big-game hunting nomads and the eventual emergence of diversified foraging, in which people began to live in the first, more permanent hamlets and villages. And we contrast the ways in which egalitarian societies organize politics, economics, and beliefs about the world with the more familiar (to us) practices of complex and hierarchical societies.

Our scientific understanding of small-scale societies is based on three main sources: archaeological evidence, ethnographic studies, and analyses of documents written by observers of the people who lived in these societies. Foraging societies did not themselves have writing, though

California live oak
Source: M. E. Basgall and W. R. Hildebrandt. 1989. *Prehistory of the Sacramento River Canyon, Shasta County, California.* Davis, CA: Center for Archaeological Research.

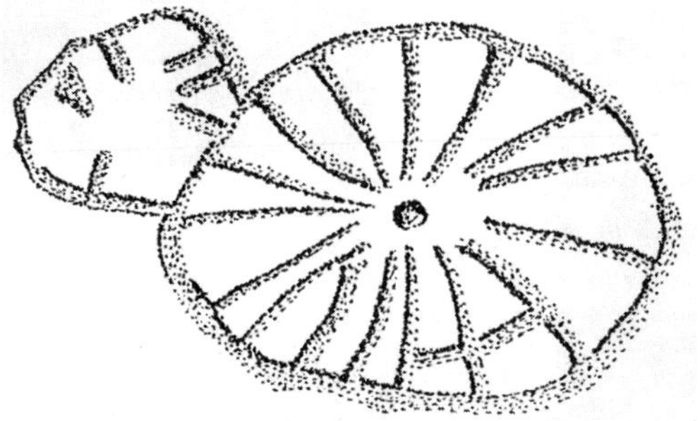

Rock art from Church Rock, Shasta County, Northern California
Source: J. Van Tilburg, F. Bock, and A. J. Bock. 1987. *The Church Rock Petroglyph Site,* Redding, CA: Redding Museum and Art Center.

many of them did produce graphical artifacts such as cave paintings and rock art that we can use to try to interpret their forms of consciousness.

Documentary evidence about foraging societies was written by literate observers or by natives who became literate during a process of assimilation into complex societies. So, for example, we can gain insights about the social customs of Native Americans by reading what early European immigrants wrote about them in journals, letters, newspapers, and court documents. Sometimes church or mission records are available that allow us to infer important things about indigenous peoples.

Ethnographic studies record information observed by dedicated professional anthropologists or untrained but systematic observers who were explicitly studying and analyzing small-scale societies. One of the main purposes of anthropology as a modern scientific discipline was to carefully and objectively study the remaining small-scale societies. Most of this ethnographic research occurred in the late nineteenth and early twentieth centuries. Ethnographers studied and recorded the languages, tools, methods of production, kinship, architecture, settlement systems, household patterns, child-rearing practices, spiritual beliefs, diets, gender relations, sexual behavior, political practices, trading activities, storytelling, celebrations, and other characteristics of people living in small-scale egalitarian societies. The corpus of work produced by the ethnographers has been summarized and systematized in the Human Relations Area File at Yale University.

Archaeology makes systematic observations of the remains of human activities, which can be found by digging in the soil or observing what is on the surface of the earth. Archaeological evidence is relevant for understanding diets, burial practices, settlement systems (the study of households, camps, hamlets, and villages), trade patterns, emerging inequalities as reflected in differential burial practices, storage facilities, procurement of lithic materials (rocks) for use as stone tools, methods of manufacturing tools, and the design and styles of tools and other artifacts (see Figure 5.1). Archaeologists have developed chemical analysis methods for dating materials (e.g., carbon-14 dating). They study skeletal remains to infer health conditions and causes of death. New methods of DNA analysis appear promising to allow archaeologists to trace the migrations of peoples and intergroup mating patterns. Archaeological information on preliterate societies has been systematized into a schema of "archaeological traditions" for all areas of the world.[1] Archaeological information is greatly affected by the conditions that allow some things to survive and other things to disappear with the passage of time. For example, pots and stone tools long remain, while wooden artifacts and foods usually are erased quickly from the archaeological record.

Figure 5.1 Obsidian knife blade from Pollard Flat, Sacramento River Canyon, Northern California

Source: M. E. Basgall and W. R. Hildebrandt. 1989. *Prehistory of the Sacramento River Canyon, Shasta County, California*. Davis, CA: Center for Archaeological Research.

Small-scale societies have been displaced or destroyed by larger and more hierarchical societies since the latter first emerged thousands of years ago. This process is now almost complete. There are very few true hunter-gatherer societies left on Earth. This process was greatly accelerated during the nineteenth century, which is why the work of the ethnographers took on a degree of haste.

[1] Human Relations Area Files (HRAF), "eHRAF World Cultures," http://www.yale.edu/hraf/collections.htm.

There are problems associated with the fact that we must rely on the above three kinds of evidence. Both archaeological and documentary evidence suffer from the fact that there is usually a large component of "selection bias" because some kinds of evidence survive but others do not. Ideally, we would like to obtain a representative sample of information about foraging societies in order to make inferences about their nature and the processes by which they evolved into more complex and hierarchical societies. The conditions of survival of human activities and the widely variable purposes of the observers who recorded documentary evidence are usually not designed to make unbiased systematic inferences about the behavior patterns and institutions of foraging societies.

Ethnographic evidence is better because observers whose purposes were close to our own gathered and recorded it systematically. Much has been written about the cultural biases of the ethnographers and the difficulties of objective study, but these problems are much smaller than those we encounter with the use of documentary and archaeological evidence. The largest problem of ethnography is that the people whom the ethnographers studied were not a representative sample of the people in whom we are most interested. We want to know how hunter-gatherers lived thousands of years ago because we are most interested in how more complex and hierarchical societies emerged out of egalitarian small-scale societies—the processes of sociocultural evolution. But ethnographers have studied hunter-gatherers who managed to survive in the context of thousands of years during the expansion of hierarchical and complex societies. The survivors were mostly peoples who had been pushed into extremely marginal environments that were of little interest to more complex societies.[2] And despite the best efforts of ethnographers to locate foragers who had not been much affected by interactions with people in more complex and hierarchical societies, the societies of many of the peoples studied had been importantly changed by such interactions. Nevertheless, we have no choice but to use the available evidence despite its problems. These difficulties need to be kept in mind as we review the evidence that is relevant to the specific questions we will be addressing.

The human species emerged from biological evolution in Africa and spread to the rest of the world—first to Eurasia and later to Australia, the Pacific, and the Americas. Early humans were nomadic foragers who slowly evolved the ability to speak and to produce tools. Hominid primates developed enhanced bipedalism (walking on two feet) and stereoscopic vision—traits that improved their ability to find food. But it was the development of language that brought forth the most important revolution of all—the emergence of cultural and social evolution from biological evolution. Once humans had language they could codify knowledge and pass it on to their young. This made technological development possible, and so new environments could be occupied without having to wait for biological evolution. Language and tools emerged over hundreds of thousands of years in interaction with one another.

Once humans had the ability to make oral symbols (words), they could develop social relations beyond the immediately present group. The word "cousin" can be used to designate a non-present person with whom we share obligations. Nomadic foraging **bands** of Paleolithic (Old Stone Age)[3] hunters developed social relations based on ideas of kinship with other foraging bands. The movements of these small groups following herds of large animals increasingly came to involve overlapping yearly circular migration routes that included seasonal camps in which several bands came together at a traditional location. These large gatherings were opportunities to exchange

---

[2] Only a few environmentally choice sites continued to be occupied by hunter-gatherers as recently as the last two centuries (e.g., on the West Coast of North America), and these were quickly displaced with the arrival of the Europeans.

[3] Archaeologists and historians have traditionally used the materials employed to make tools as a way of loosely categorizing human societies. Thus, "lithic" refers to the Stone Age, in which tools were mainly made of stones, and the terms "Bronze Age" and "Iron Age" are used for more recent societies. "Paleolithic" refers to the Old Stone Age, the long period in which nomads developed stone tools. "Mesolithic" refers to the period of diversified foraging, in which people lived in villages. And "Neolithic" refers to Stone Age gardeners who planted crops near their villages.

information, to find mates, and to develop larger group identities.

Most of the nomads of the Paleolithic (Old Stone Age) traveled in rather large yearly circuits because they were hunting large animals that were themselves nomadic. Those groups that specialized in big-game hunting may have played a role, along with climate change, in the extinction of large animal species such as the mastodon. The reduction in the availability of large animals encouraged the wider adoption of diversified foraging based on hunting smaller game and gathering more plant foods, even though it was probably more work than hunting big game, especially when herds were plentiful.

In the New World (the Americas) the shift toward smaller, yearly regional nomadic circuits and hunting smaller game can be seen in the development of regional archaeological "traditions" that are indicated by the emergence of distinctive styles for the production of stone projectile points (Fagan 1991; Nassaney and Sassaman 1995). For hundreds of years, big-game hunters all over North America used the same kinds of large spearpoints, called Clovis points. Eventually, somewhat smaller projectile points were developed to be used for smaller spears thrown in a wooden spear-throwing device that archaeologists call the *atlatl*. These smaller spearpoints display distinctive regional styles, whereas the Clovis points display substantially the same style on a continental scale. This was the archaeological signal of the development of regional identities among still-nomadic peoples who were moving toward a more diversified and territorial form of hunting and gathering.

Expansion and Incorporation

One important aspect of globalization is the expansion and intensification of interaction networks, for example, increased international trade and investment.[4] This involves an increase in the spatial scale of exchange networks and the intensification of large-scale networks relative to local ones. In this sense, globalization has been going on for thousands of years as local peoples have become increasingly connected with one another and interaction networks have gotten larger. In this sense, little world-systems have become linked into larger world-systems, and big world-systems have incorporated smaller systems into themselves.

Expansion and incorporation have long involved both trade and conquest. But trade and conquest have often provoked resistance by local people to outside influences. So the historical outcomes have been produced by the interaction of expansionist forces and efforts to resist expansion. Indeed, the creation of larger systems involved the evolution of institutional mechanisms that allowed power to be exercised over greater distances to overcome the resistance of local peoples.

An image that is helpful for envisioning the patterns of expansion, incorporation, and merger that eventually led to a single global world-system is that of a river system. Small rivulets and creeks come together to form larger streams and rivers that merge and eventually come to the ocean that is the contemporary global world-system.[5] A human hand held upright with fingers extended up can also serve as an image of how smaller sedentary world-systems merged and became incorporated into a single global system of interaction as time moves down from the fingers into the wrist.

For pre-sedentary world-systems, the river (or hand) analogy needs to be turned upside down. Before 12,000 years ago most humans lived in nomadic foraging bands that moved over large territories. As human population density became greater and more competition developed for food resources, groups modified their subsistence strategies to include the hunting of smaller game, the gathering of more vegetable resources, and fishing. This was not immediately the development of sedentism (living most of the year in a single village). Rather, it was a focusing on more intensively exploiting the resources in a relatively smaller amount of space and a more regularized round of nomadic movement through this space. This

[4] The most recent waves of globalization will be examined in Part IV, on the modern world-system.

[5] For example, see Figure 11.2 in Chapter 11 for the spatiotemporal chronograph showing the way in which small state-based systems merged or were engulfed by the growing Central System that eventually became earth-wide.

led to the development of regional archaeological traditions as indicated by the regional styles of projectile points noted above. The settlement systems of nomadic world-systems were becoming smaller in the sense that human groups were focusing more intensively on a smaller territory rather than wandering freely in pursuit of big game. Thus, a hand held with the fingers pointed downward can represent the transition pattern for nomadic world-systems. Continental-sized cultures and migration routes were replaced by regional cultures and routes, and eventually, with more population growth, the first village societies emerged in which the people spent most of the year in a single location. Regions of exceptional wealth in natural food supplies were the first to develop sedentism.

With the emergence of sedentism, the spatial size of interaction networks got smaller than they had been when nomads were ranging over very large territories. So world-systems of Paleolithic hunters were spatially larger than the world-systems that emerged once diversified foraging and sedentism were adopted. After this, the metaphor of the river system applies, because small systems of village dwellers and their nomadic neighbors became linked to one another by the development of trade networks. Thus, a system in which people moved to resources was increasingly replaced by a system in which resources were moved to people—the development of long-distance trade. The downward hand of contracting nomadic systems evolved into an upward hand of spatially growing world-systemic interaction networks.

The early village societies interacted with surrounding peoples who were still nomadic. But the consequences of interactions did not extend very far, except when sedentary groups grew so large that some number of them migrated to a distant territory. Sedentism was based in most cases on a diverse mix of foraging for vegetable materials such as roots, berries, seeds, and nuts as well as the hunting of small and medium-sized game and fishing. This diversified foraging was what enabled larger numbers of people to concentrate together in permanent villages and created the first polities in which villages and hamlets had socially structured relationships with one another—the first sedentary settlement systems.

A cyclical phenomenon that emerged with the birth of sedentism is what we can call **pulsation**.[6] The processes of network expansion were uneven in space and time—that is, trade networks and political-military interaction networks oscillated as they expanded. A wave of expansion would usually be followed by a contraction. But some of the expansion waves were so large that they created systems larger than any that had existed before. And so occasional unprecedented new levels of expansion punctuated the pulsations. This kind of unprecedented expansion and intensification of interaction is called globalization when it has occurred in recent centuries.

Settlement Systems

All human societies can be studied by examining the ways in which activities are distributed in space. In the modern world, we study cities and systems of cities—the ways in which activities and exchanges are structured and distributed among urban places. One important macrostructural feature of all sedentary societies is the size distribution of settlements. Are all the settlements about the same size, or do smaller ones surround larger settlements? Archaeologists can determine the sizes of settlements and can easily examine the distributions of settlement sizes if they systematically survey whole regions.

Once humans began living in fairly permanent hamlets and villages, it becomes possible to study the interactions of these settlements with one another. Settlements are rarely ever intelligible without knowing their relations with the rural and nomadic populations that interact with them. Archaeologists and ethnographers map out the ways in which human habitations are spread across space, and this is a fundamental window on the lives of the people in all social systems. It is the spatial aspect of population

[6] All systems, even very small and egalitarian ones, exhibit cyclical expansions and contractions in the spatial extent and intensity of exchange networks. We call this sequence of trade expansion and contraction "pulsation." Different kinds of trade (especially bulk goods trade versus prestige goods trade) usually have different spatial characteristics.

density, perhaps the most fundamental variable for understanding the constraints and possibilities of human social organization. The **settlement size distribution**—the relative population sizes of the settlements within a region—is an important and easily ascertained aspect of all sedentary social systems. And the functional differences among settlements are a fundamental aspect of the division of labor that links households and communities into larger polities and interpolity systems. The emergence of social hierarchies is often related to size hierarchies of settlements. And the monumental architecture of large settlements is related to the emergence of more hierarchical social structures—complex chiefdoms and early states. The relationship between settlements and polities is a fundamental aspect of all sedentary social systems. The political boundaries of polities are rarely coterminous with the interaction networks in which settlements are embedded, and so settlement systems must be studied "internationally" in all social systems. It is convenient to categorize settlement systems by the number of "tiers" or size categories of settlements that they have. Figure 5.2 depicts the spatial nature of single-tiered, two-tiered, three-tiered, and four-tiered settlement systems and shows how hamlets, villages, towns, and cities are often located in river valleys.

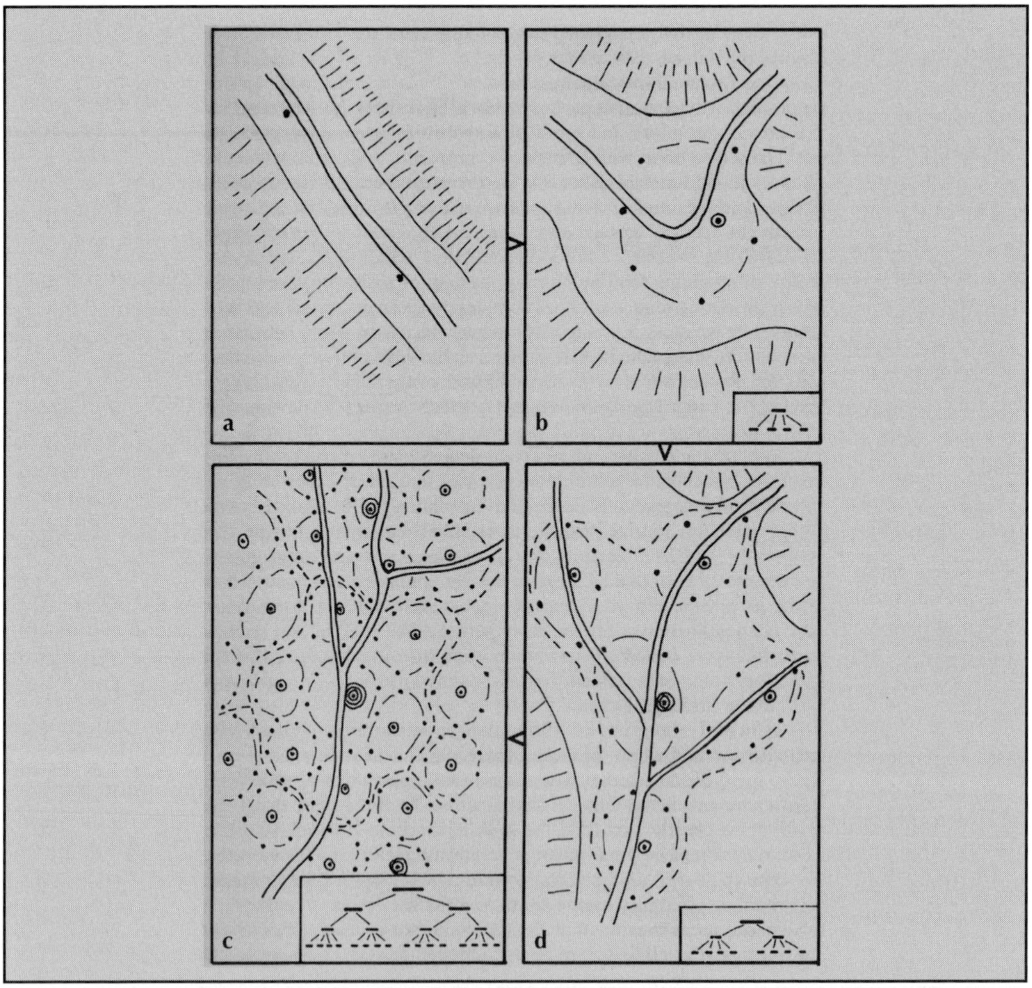

Figure 5.2 Typology of settlement systems: (a) isolated single-tiered settlements in narrow valleys, (b) simple two-tiered settlement system on a small plain, (c) three-tiered settlement system on a large plain, and (d) four-tiered settlement systems on a larger plains

Source: Nissen 1988. © University of Chicago Press.

Paleolithic Hunter-Gatherers: Cultural and Social Institutions

We begin our journey in the Upper Paleolithic Age of foraging societies in approximately 30,000 BCE. Nomadic hunting-and-gathering societies usually consisted of somewhere between fifty and one hundred people living in bands of nuclear families. There was an elementary gender division of labor, with men hunting and women gathering nuts and berries.[7] Hunter-gatherers are also called foraging societies because they harvest nature's bounty directly, without much intervention to enhance the productivity of natural processes.[8] The tools used were made of stone, wood, or bone.

While the division of labor among hunter-gatherers was partly specialized based on age and gender, specialization does not necessarily mean hierarchy or centralization. Having a special domain of activities for each group does not always imply that one group has power over another. The gathering that women did in foraging societies was highly valued, and so even though there was often a radical separation of men's and women's work, this did not usually correspond to a high degree of male domination over women.

Politics can be defined as those activities that decide who gets what and who has to do what, and the making of group decisions that affect the direction of society over time. Morton Fried (1967) has characterized the politics of foragers as "egalitarian." This means that there are only mild differences between adults and families regarding how much power, prestige, or wealth they have. Positions of leadership are open and usually temporary, so most of the people who have the talent to occupy them can achieve them. All adults have access to the occasions during which group decisions are made, and they have the right to speak and participate in the decision making. Every household has access to basic resources and the tools needed to utilize those resources.

Most hunting-and-gathering societies had no permanent leadership, and decisions were made by consensus after long discussions among the adults. What leadership existed tended to be situation-specific. This means there were no institutions of office that gave leaders coercive power over followers. When a situation emerged that required a special skill, someone took responsibility for leading. When the situation was resolved, the power of the leaders usually dissolved with it.

Perhaps it is difficult to imagine that a temporary leader would not turn into a permanent one, given that people might stop paying attention or get lazy. What must be kept in mind is that leadership in an egalitarian society was hardly an enviable position. People in these positions were not spared from working on everyday tasks just like everyone else. In fact, the leader was probably the hardest-working member of the group, gaining his or her reputation by skilled hunting and generosity. Leadership probably resembled the experience of people in volunteer groups or nonprofit organizations—lots of work and few material benefits.

Egalitarianism does not mean complete equality. Adults certainly had power over children. And some people had more influence and prestige than others, but they did not have privileges or power. Influence is the capacity to motivate people to act by persuasion or example without invoking coercion. Prestige is the degree of honor and esteem that other people grant to

[7] The cases where women were big-game hunters were few. According to Lenski, Lenski, and Nolan (1995), there were several reasons for this. Hunting with bows and spears required speed, agility, and upper-body strength, in which men excel. This difference is exaggerated for women in the later stages of pregnancy. Because of the physiological demands of pregnancy and lactation on a woman's body, women have a higher ratio of fat to muscle than men do. This provides them with nutritional reserves to draw on during food shortages. With training, women can obviously develop their muscles to a level that equals or exceeds that of the average man. But when women drop below 15 percent body fat, they often cease to ovulate and become infertile. Great muscular development in women reduces their ability to bear children. This biological fact probably produces a selection mechanism in favor of having men do the hunting.

[8] Sanderson (2001) points out that hunting was the predominant means of subsistence in roughly two-thirds of the ethnographically known foraging societies, but the balance between hunting and gathering was heavily influenced by climate and environmental characteristics. Gathering constituted a larger part of the diet in warm or hot climates, while hunting was predominant in colder climates with less vegetation.

an individual. In foraging societies, influencing others and gaining prestige are mainly the results of individual skills that are not easily passed on to sons or daughters. Leadership in egalitarian societies brought prestige and influence, but it certainly brought no entitlement to a surplus of material goods, more leisure time, or coercive power over others. The performance of the leader was subject to community input. If the leaders slacked off or were abusive, they were thrown out of the position. What compensation these leaders received was in either the intrinsic enjoyment of the work or the admiration given by others. Leaders continued to lead because it was important work and because the people recognized their contributions to the group.

To say that leadership was situation-specific does not mean that just anyone could be a leader in any situation. There were people who had greater natural talents in certain areas of life. It would have been self-defeating for a society not to use these greater skills in favor of someone with fewer skills. A band would not be likely to suffer incompetent leaders when others who could do a better job were available. The important point is that all adults had to be consulted about group decisions regarding things that would affect them.

It is an oversimplification to say that all hunting-gathering societies are nomadic and egalitarian. Their mobility patterns, size, and political organization are dependent on the nature of the geography in which they live and whether natural resources are concentrated or dispersed. Beginning in the 1980s, "optimal foraging theory" attempted to be much more specific in identifying the conditions under which certain foods would be chosen (the diet-breadth model) and when and if people would move (the patch-choice model). The diet-breadth model claims that the choices of animal or plant foods that people decide to exploit are mainly determined by the amount of work expended searching for and processing food compared to the net energy food value from the item of food. The choices people make are not solely determined by the nutrition of the resources they are pursuing. They are also influenced by the amount of effort it takes to find the resource and the time it takes to prepare the food after it has been acquired.

The patch-choice theory identifies the conditions under which hunter-gatherers stay in one area or leave for another. These include the cost of moving—the type of terrain to be crossed, how far they must travel to reach a prospective camp, and the resources they need to make the trip.

Summarizing Dyson-Hudson and Smith, Sanderson (2001) presents four possible scenarios:

- *High resource density, low resource predictability.* Here groups will be highly mobile and will share information about the state of resources, and territoriality will be low (because of constantly shifting territories).
- *High resource density, high resource predictability.* Here territoriality is prominent because the benefits of defending dense resources outweigh the costs.
- *Low resource density, low resource predictability.* Here groups are highly dispersed and highly mobile. Territoriality is absent because the costs of defending resources outweigh the benefits.
- *Low resource density, high resource predictability.* Here groups tend to remain in areas of predictable resources, and any territoriality that develops is a "passive territoriality."

Here is an example from native peoples on the West Coast of North America, according to Johnson and Earle (1987). In the spring, people from separate local groups come together for candlefish runs, harvesting them and storing their oil for themselves, and then trading the rest. In the summer, the band breaks up, and families scatter to hunt, fish, and collect roots and greens. In the winter, families band together again and spend their time building and repairing boats and designing tools and clothing. They live mainly on stored food. There is a great deal of socializing and preparing for ceremonies. They stayed together when they needed protection from the elements or had to defend themselves.

What is important here is that the degree to which people will become "territorial" is not static but depends on how concentrated the resources are and how easy it is to access them. High resource density and high resource predictability will make people more territorial because this situation will provide the most resources for the least amount of work. Low resource density and low resource predictability means people have to work harder to gain access to resources, and, because the resources are less predictable, they may come up empty-handed. Nomadic foragers will be the least territorial under these conditions because there is little worth defending.

Under conditions of high resource density and high resource predictability, members of foraging societies face an interesting problem. In these societies the population will expand and families will be vying for these resources. If competition results and conflicts break out, the groups who are part of this conflict will have to weigh the costs and benefits of staying against the costs and benefits of moving to another location. If they stay, they face conflicts and possible subordination by victorious groups, but they benefit by being well fed and not having to move. If they withdraw from the area to avoid conflict and potential subordination, they will probably have to work harder, live under more difficult geographical conditions, and subsist on less nutritious food. This description elaborates on the part of the iteration model in which population pressure causes pressures for migration and, under conditions of circumscription, raises the level of conflict. The question of whether to migrate is a matter of "push and pull" factors of many kinds.

But how could people know what the best alternatives were? We are not arguing that this decision-making process is consciously known by foragers. We are suggesting that over thousands of years of trial and error, a tendency toward cost-benefit analysis evolved that helped some hunter-gatherers survive better than the competition. The accumulated wisdom as to which resources were worth pursuing and when and under what conditions it was feasible to migrate was worked into their cultural institutions.

The economy of any society is the manner in which goods and services get produced and distributed. The economies of hunter-gatherers are one of the most interesting and difficult social processes to understand for anyone living in an industrial capitalist society. As Polanyi (1957a) has pointed out, marketless economies are inseparable from social interdependencies and obligations. While there is certainly self-interest involved, this self-interest is not separate from the group. Furthermore, there is no separate "free market" that is autonomous and independent of socialization, customs, and rituals as the economy is in modern society.

Basically, the most important goods and services were shared in a spirit of what Sahlins (1972) has called "generalized reciprocity." This meant giving among equals without explicit calculation or expectation of where or when exchanges would be reciprocated. Calculation of the labor expended or the introduction of money to mediate relations between people is taboo. In our society, relations between family members or close friends are conducted using generalized reciprocity. What boggles the imagination is that in egalitarian hunting-and-gathering societies, generalized reciprocity extended beyond intimate contacts *to the entire society*. There were no independent individuals calculating how to get ahead. In this sense, Marx and Engels were right to label these economic relations as "primitive communism."

It is important to understand that this way of life was not unduly altruistic. These economic relations served both the self-interest of the participants and the interest of the band. Individual survival was tightly wound with group self-interest. Part of this was because individuals could not afford to accumulate much wealth even if they wanted to, given their nomadic lifestyle. Possessions were limited by nomadism to what could be carried. But even sedentary foragers had only minimal inequalities among households because these societies developed institutions that actively ensured equality. Strong norms about sharing and generalized reciprocity limited the amount of wealth that an individual could accumulate. The passing of wealth from parents to children was usually limited by practices such as the burial of a person's personal property with the individual when he or she died. And there was no specialized military group to protect those who might have had the desire to accumulate wealth. The benefit of these institutions was to promote solidarity within the group.

In Chapter 2 we discussed three developmental logics by which resources are produced and accumulated. Hunter-gatherer societies mobilize the labor of people using normative regulation based ultimately on obligations that families and kin have to each other. Generalized reciprocity and sharing within the family are the main rules of normative regulation in these societies.

In generalized reciprocity, every exchange was understood in the larger context of making the world sacred. In the spiritual worldview of foragers, sacred forces are present in the everyday world (immanent) and interdependent with the individual, society, and the natural environment, including stones, mountains, rivers, and animal and plant life. Anthropologists and sociologists refer to this kind of worldview as "animism" because the people believe that even inanimate objects such as rocks and trees and mountains are alive and have will. Furthermore, the presence of immanent forces in the sacred world corresponds to egalitarian relations in the political realm. Each individual is responsible for developing a direct relationship with these sacred forces.

This egalitarianism can be seen in animistic societies in that there is no worship in the sense of submitting one's self to the superior authority of the gods. Because there is interdependence between the earth spirits and the tribes, these spirits are more like the tribe's brothers and sisters rather than a mother or father. In tribal religion there is no sense of hierarchy in the sacred world, because there is no hierarchy in the political world. As societies became more politically hierarchical, this move toward hierarchy in religion was reflected in the increasing distance of sacred presences from the earth, becoming transcendental with the rise of the universalistic religions. It is only with the coming of the universalistic world religions (e.g., Christianity, Islam) that God was worshipped, because at this point people had become alienated from natural resources and needed to petition authority for them. Just as God became a transcendental power beyond the power of human influence in the sacred world, so the upper castes came to occupy the same unapproachable position relative to the lower classes in the political world.

The first anthropologists speculated that in stateless societies the workload must have been heavier than in state-based societies. This belief was founded on the assumption that, because more complex societies have more sophisticated technology, there must have been an increase in the amount of leisure time in complex societies for the average person. Marshall Sahlins (1972) challenged this, when through cross-cultural studies he found that, on average, hunter-gatherers worked fifteen to twenty hours per week! They spent most of each day playing, sleeping, or visiting.

The studies cited by Sahlins were done during a period of history (the last two hundred years) when many hunter-gatherers had been displaced from the more lush environments by state-based societies. Hunter-gatherers in ecologically prime sites would have had even more leisure time. Hunter-gatherers worked considerably less than most people in agricultural or industrial state societies despite their simple technology.

What about property? Has individually owned private property always existed? Among hunter-gatherers there is much less in the way of individual private property than exists in state-based societies. Hunter-gatherers shared the major means of production, like land, that were needed by the whole group. There was individual personal property, but no property in land. In some sedentary forager societies, individuals had rights to particular gathering or fishing sites, but these use rights were temporary and could be reassigned by the authority of the community as needs changed.

How did men and women treat each other in foraging societies? Sociological gender theorists such as Reeves-Sanday (1981), Chafetz (1984), and Blumberg (1978) have delineated the material and social conditions under which male dominance will be minimized. These include the following:

- A warm climate where gathering is an important means of subsistence
- An abundance rather than a scarcity of natural resources
- Low population density and lack of crowding
- A low sex ratio in which there are equal numbers of women and men or a higher number of women
- A lack of environmental harshness or threat
- Little labor-intensive technology or use of tools requiring great upper-body strength
- Women's control over tools (digging sticks) and means of subsistence (gathering, horticulture)
- Production for subsistence rather than production for surplus
- Integration of work and child-rearing practices rather than segregation
- Matrilineal descent (reckoning descent in the mother's line) and matri-local residency (married couples live near the home of the mother)

Though most hunting-and-gathering societies have fairly equal gender relations, the degree to which these ten conditions are present or absent will affect how much or little influence or prestige women have in these societies. Regarding the mating patterns of hunter-gatherers, according to O'Kelly and Carney (1986) they practice serial monogamy. Divorces are not uncommon and polygamy (multiple husbands or wives) is rare. The sexuality of hunter-gatherers, compared with that of state-based societies, was not strongly subjected to social regulation. There was little of a double standard for the sexual behavior of women and men; female virginity was not a major concern and wife beating was rare. These attitudes toward sexuality were taught to children, who were allowed to explore their sexuality, provided it was not in front of the adults. Hunter-gatherers did not have large families. On average, each couple had two to four children.[9]

In sum, whether we speak of large amounts of leisure time, the expectation of generosity in economic exchanges, the lack of private property, the absence of accumulated wealth, the fluid nature of leadership, the consensual decision-making process, or the relative gender parity, all these customs point in one direction. These societies, more than any other in history, were egalitarian.

Between 13,000 and 7000 BCE, the supply of large mammals dwindled in major regions of the world. These included giant bison, horses, oxen, elephants, camels, and antelopes. In Europe, the herds of woolly mammoths, woolly rhinoceroses, steppe bison, and giant elk were greatly reduced. Archaeologists have noted a similar die-off of large animals that occurred contemporaneously with the arrival of humans in Australia about 40,000 years ago. Some believe that human hunters depleted the herds, but others think climate change may have been the culprit. It has also been surmised that humans or the dogs they brought with them may have been the carriers of diseases that reduced the megafauna populations. Whatever the cause, slowly rising human population density and growing scarcity of food resources meant that the old strategy of a group migrating to follow big game was becoming less and less of an option. A new way of living had to be invented that would feed more people and do so in a more concentrated space.

Sedentary Hunter-Gatherer World-Systems

Now that we have a sketch of the typical institutions within hunting-gathering societies, we are in a position to examine how they interacted with other adjacent hunting-gathering societies. The first world-system in which there were sedentary peoples emerged in the Levant (in what is now Lebanon and Palestine)[10] about 11,000 years ago (9000 BCE). Archaeologists refer to these early sedentary foragers as the Natufian culture (Henry 1985; Bar-Yosef and Belfer-Cohen 1991). The Natufians practiced a diversified and intensive form of hunting and gathering in a very fruitful environment. This mode of subsistence allowed for a rather high population density per land area and produced the first relatively permanent human settlements. Sedentary foragers probably invented territoriality as well as a more active intervention in the productive cycles of nature. A similar Mesolithic culture, dated to around 8650 BCE, has been found at Shanidar Cave and village sites in the Zagros Mountains on a tributary of the Tigris (Solecki and Solecki 1982). The Mesolithic invention of relatively permanent village life based on differentiated gathering of vegetable resources, as well as fishing and hunting of small game, occurred in a context in which the villagers continued to cooperate and compete with more nomadic foragers.

It is popularly believed that sedentism first emerged with the planting of gardens (horticulture). On the contrary, archaeologists have found solid evidence that proves that sedentism and social complexity preceded the first horticulture by thousands of years in the Near East and in other regions (Price and Brown 1985). Of course, the diversified and intensive foraging

[9] Lenski, Lenski, and Nolan (1995) argue that hunter-gatherer societies do not need to have many children, because hunting and gathering do not easily lend themselves to child labor. Many hunter-gatherer societies also practice strenuous population control methods such as female infanticide (Harris 1987). The need for nomadic mobility and the easy exhaustion of natural resources provide strong motives for regulating population growth.
[10] Rather than referring to the ancient Near East, we will call this region ancient Western Asia.

that formed the basis of early sedentism was a kind of proto-horticulture. In other regions, Mesolithic peoples are known to have used fire to increase the growth of useful plants and foraging areas that would attract huntable animals. These activities have been termed "protoagriculture" by Bean and Lawton (1976). It involved the management and labor-intensive usage of natural resources in a way that regulated environmental exploitation and provided reserves in case of shortages.

Territoriality, the establishment of collective use rights over particular natural resources, may have been a pivotal institutional invention of these first sedentary foragers. This claiming of places by groups as their home territories had slowly been coming into existence during the regionalization of nomadic migration routes, but it was the establishment of sedentary villages that vaulted the founding of place to a qualitatively new level. The identities of groups became tied to particular sites, and collective property, its defense and contestation, became the main focus of action. Geopolitics, the allying and contesting of adjacent polities over the control of territory, began its long history.

But what kinds of intergroup relations did these sedentary foragers have? Were these early territorial groups specialized in warfare? Did they engage in expansion by conquest? Did they engage in local or long-distance trade across cultural boundaries? Did the sedentary villagers exploit and dominate their still-nomadic neighbors? By what processes did sedentism spread, and how was it connected with the eventual emergence of horticulture?

In order to begin to answer these questions, we need to study peoples with many of the same attributes as the Natufians, who survived into the nineteenth century, and about whom we have both archaeological and ethnographic evidence. This is the most important reason for focusing on Northern California, a region that was completely isolated from state-based and even complex chiefdom-based world-systems until the 1820s.[11]

Native California had the highest precontact population density north of the Valley of Mexico, the core region of an urbanized system of states and empires. The cultures of precontact California reveal an astonishing linguistic diversity.

In the 1820s the first Euroamerican fur trappers explored the northern part of Northern California, the home of people we call the Wintu and their neighbors. It was not until 1849, the year of the California gold rush, that the lifeways of the native Californians at the northern end of the Sacramento Valley were radically altered. Before that, a very small world-system was in full operation.

The expanding Europe-centered system began to affect Northern California late in the eighteenth century. Glass beads manufactured in Europe were traded in the central California prestige goods network (PGN) and found their way to the north valley by means of down-the-line trade (goods are passed from group to group) (Ritter 1991). The Spanish missions came only as far north as Sonoma, still far from the Wintu. Spanish exploration parties never traveled farther north than the territory of the Patwin at the southern end of the Sacramento Valley (S. Cook 1960, 1962). The Euroamerican trappers who traveled through Wintu territory in the late 1820s brought malaria with them, and there was an epidemic that caused many deaths among the indigenous peoples in the 1830s (S. Cook 1955). But these factors probably had only weak effects on the lives and systemic interaction patterns of the native peoples in the north valley. It was the massive invasion of the gold rush that brought this small indigenous world-system to its end.

Unlike most ethnographically known foragers, the native Californians occupied ecologically prime sites for human habitation. Isolation allowed these societies to survive until 150 years ago in Northern California. The close study of these relatively sedentary foragers, reported fully in Chase-Dunn and Mann (1998), has important implications for our understanding of small-scale world-systems.

The native Californians lived in small but densely packed villages in a region in which nature provided great stores of food for the hunter-gatherer. They used stone tools. They did not make pots. They did not plant corn or other

[11] We are not suggesting that precontact Northern California exactly replicates the Natufians of 12,000 years ago, but rather that we can learn about the general nature of world-systems composed of sedentary foragers by studying the Wintu and their neighbors.

cultigens, though they occasionally and informally planted tobacco. They had domesticated dogs. The women made useful and stunningly beautiful baskets.

They harvested nature and managed the natural environment in order to preserve and expand its productivity. Contrary to the idea of mini-systems (self-reproducing autarchic societies), the peoples of Northern California interacted intensively with their immediate neighbors, even across huge linguistic boundaries. And all these peoples traded through long-distance networks in which valuables moved from group to group over hundreds of kilometers.

The Wintu and Their Neighbors

The primary locus of the Wintu study is Northern California, the north end of the Sacramento Valley and its surrounding foothills and mountains (see Figure 5.3). Foraging hunter-gatherers, most of whom lived in permanent villages most of the year, populated this region. Unlike most ethnographically studied hunter-gatherers, the indigenous peoples of Northern California had little or no contact with people from state-societies prior to the arrival of the Euroamericans in the early nineteenth century. Neither did they interact with any peoples who had large, complex chiefdoms with class-stratified societies. The intermarriage, bulk goods, and political-military interaction networks of the Wintu-centered world-system were quite small. The Wintu and their neighbors were part of a long-distance trading network that linked them with central California.

California is an advantageous region in which to study a small-scale world-system because there is a valuable corpus of both ethnographic and archaeological evidence. The ethnographic studies carried out in the early decades of this century by Alfred Kroeber and his colleagues and students at the University of California at Berkeley have been severely criticized by later generations, but they still represent the largest and best body of ethnographic and linguistic research on any region occupied by sedentary foragers. Northern California has also been the focus of a sustained and significant archaeological research effort since the 1930s. The combination of ethnographic and archaeological evidence provides a rich trove of evidence on the Wintu and their neighbors.

The main questions we want to answer are these: Does it make sense to apply world-systems concepts to indigenous Northern California? What were the institutional features, patterns, and spatial scales of group interaction? How were these changing over time? In what sense might there have been core/periphery differentiation and/or core/periphery hierarchy, and which groups were which?

The Wintu people are speakers of a language of the Penutian linguistic stock. At the time of the arrival of Euroamericans (referred to here as "contact"), the Wintu occupied the northern end of the Sacramento Valley near the present city of Redding and some of the surrounding foothills and mountains (see Figure 5.3). In addition to the north valley, Wintu territory included the adjacent foothills to the west and part of the Trinity River drainage. Nine other linguistic groups surrounded the Wintu linguistic group.[12]

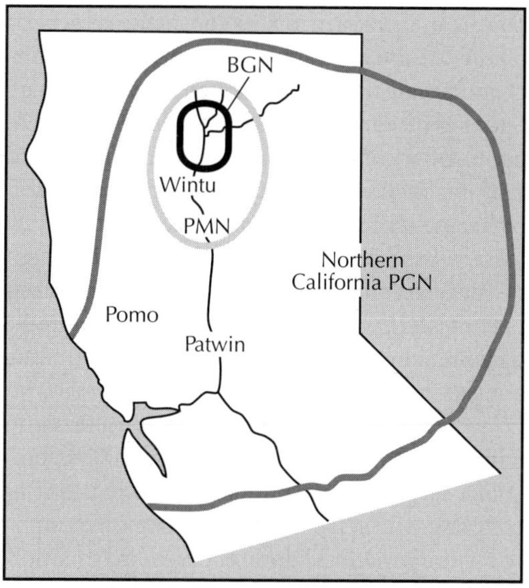

Figure 5.3 Nested interaction networks in Northern California

[12] The nine surrounding linguistic groups were the Nomlaki Wintun in the south (who spoke a language from the same Penutian language family that includes the Wintu); the Yuki, Lassik, Nongatl, Chimariko, and New River Shasta groups to the west; the Okwanuchu-Shastans to the north; the Pit River groups (e.g., Achomawi, Atsegewi) to the northwest; and the Northern and Central Yana to the east.

About 5,000 Wintu lived in villages, the largest of which had about 250 people. The villages were clustered close to each other along the rivers and creeks. They hunted both small and big game, and they gathered plants, roots, seeds, acorns, grubs, and grasshoppers. They fished, especially for the salmon that were seasonally plentiful in the rivers along which they lived. They constructed elaborate fish weirs, traps built across the streams, which enabled the harvest of great quantities of migrating fish.

Politically, the Wintu were organized as independent **tribelets** consisting of a single village led by a **headman**. The authority of the headman consisted mostly of giving speeches on important ceremonial occasions and summing up the discussions at village meetings. Temporarily appointed leaders led specialized projects, such as a large hunting or gathering expedition in concert with other tribelets. There was occasional warfare between polities, even between those that spoke the same languages. Interpolity conflicts were of two kinds: Raids were bloody affairs in which the object was to annihilate the enemy; line wars were ritualized contests organized to resolve intervillage disputes, usually involving trespass. Line wars did not usually result in serious injuries. There was considerable gender differentiation in which the productive activities of men were radically differentiated from the activities of women. Men's hunting weapons were not to be touched by women, and men did not visit the areas where groups of women did their gathering or food-preparation tasks. And yet, women were fully incorporated into the collective decision making of the tribelets, participating as equals in the discussions that required group coordination. Occasionally a woman would serve as head "man."

The Chase-Dunn and Mann (1998) study found that this hunter-gatherer world-system, unlike larger state-based systems, had no core/periphery hierarchy. There was some core/periphery differentiation (differences in population density and mode of subsistence) between the valley-dwelling Wintu and the hill-dwelling Yana. The Yana had smaller winter villages and spent more of the year in temporary camps. The Yana concentrated more on deer hunting than did the Wintu, who made great use of the immense runs of salmon to produce storable dried fishmeal. The Wintu had higher population density, more alliances linking villages and extended families with one another, and a riverine fishing technology that enabled them to harvest and store salmon flour, a source of protein that was much less susceptible to depletion than that produced by the hunting of large game animals.

The Wintu were also slowly expanding their territory at the expense of their neighbors, and there is some evidence that Wintu men were more likely to marry women from other tribes (wife-taking) than were non-Wintu men likely to marry Wintu women. These can be considered very mild forms of core/periphery hierarchy, but compared to state-based systems—in which stronger polities often extract great resources from their weaker neighbors—the degree of interpolity inequality was very slight in the Wintu-centered world-system.

The research carried out by Chase-Dunn and Mann (1998) on the Wintu and their neighbors supported the hypothesis that these groups were interacting with one another in intense and important ways despite the fact that most of the food and raw materials for everyday life were produced within households. Ceremonies, trade feasts, permissions given for procurement treks into the territories of neighbors, and intermarriages with noncontiguous villages and across linguistic boundaries support this general conclusion. And conflict data show that the regulation of resource use was partly carried out through the maintenance of, and challenges to, collective property rights. Thus, this was a world-system in the sense that important processes within polities were strongly affected by interpolity interactions.[13]

Chase-Dunn and Mann (1998) concluded that the Wintu were part of a relatively egalitarian network of intersocietal relations. The greater part of their food and raw material procurement and competition for land had a relatively small spatial scale, with most of the important interactions occurring within an eighty-kilometer radius of any starting point. More distant interactions

[13] A bibliography, a report on projectile points, and data on indigenous place-names are contained in an appendix to the Chase-Dunn and Mann study, which is accessible at http://irows.ucr.edu/cd/appendices/b6/b6append.htm.

were indirect, but some goods did move very long distances. These longer-distance interaction networks also had important consequences for local social structures. Unlike other, more hierarchical prestige goods systems, this did not operate by providing elites with a monopoly of imported goods that were used to reward their authority over local clients. Rather, the availability of clam disk beads—the main medium of wealth storage and exchange in Northern California—from the long-distance network facilitated local complementary exchange networks in which food moved from areas of abundance to areas of scarcity. This provided each community with a safety net against temporary shortages, and it facilitated trading and kinship alliances that linked local communities. This institution served as an alternative to raiding as a mechanism of making up shortages. It allowed for higher overall population densities and relatively less conflictive and destructive relations among contiguous groups. In these ways the long-distance network was an important element behind the trends of increasing population density and the intensification and diversification of foraging practices that were occurring in central and Northern California.[14]

Northern California archaeology also demonstrates the phenomenon of pulsation, mentioned earlier in this chapter. The long-distance trade network based on clamshell disk beads shown as the PGN in Figure 5.3 was only the most recent shell-based exchange network to be found in the archaeological record. An earlier long-distance exchange network based on olivella shells from the Northern California coast and extending into the Great Basin in what is now the state of Nevada had risen and disappeared in the centuries before the emergence of the clamshell-disk-based PGN referred to by King (1978) as the "Central Interaction Area." Jackson (1992) contends that archaeological evidence from other regions in California supports the existence of periods of interregional integration followed by periods of localization in which groups returned to self-sufficiency and emphasized their cultural distinctiveness from other groups. This kind of phenomenon is also thought to have occurred in the Mesolithic European context (Price 1991). This pattern of interactional expansion and contraction ("pulsation") is probably a feature of all world-systems large and small.

The multicriteria approach to spatially bounding world-systems described in Chapter 2 was supported by the case of the Wintu world-system (see Figure 5.3). The bulk goods networks (BGNs) were very small scale, yet these were linked in important ways with larger intermarriage, celebration, and conflictive networks and PGNs. In some cases, such as Wintu-Yana interaction, bulk goods exchanges were minimal despite the fact that groups were intensively interacting in other ways. This instance is a powerful argument against using the BGN criterion by itself to spatially bound world-systems.

What about the question of transformationism versus continuationism as posed in Chapter 1? We conclude that the mode of accumulation that was predominant in precontact California was qualitatively different from both state-based and capitalist world-systems. The logic of social reproduction, the nature of accumulation, and the institutional methods of mobilizing social labor were primarily organized as socially constructed kin relations. These kinship structures were modes of normative social control. They were a consensual moral order in which the rights and obligations of persons were embedded in family roles. Exchange within villages was organized entirely as sharing and generalized reciprocity. These were the main institutions that facilitated social action.

Intergroup relations in this system also functioned primarily in terms of appeals to moral order. Trade was organized primarily as gift giving, and exchangers competed with one another to establish a reputation for generosity. The standardized medium of exchange (clamshell disk beads) was used only for intergroup trade and settlements. This was not true money, because its use was quite limited to specific contexts. It was a standardized, but not a generalized, medium of exchange. Though this "protomoney" was

[14] Not all sedentary foraging societies were as egalitarian as those in indigenous California. In the Pacific Northwest, big-man leadership, ranked lineages, and reliance on imported slave labor had emerged from a foraging mode of production that harvested the rich resources of the coastal marine environment. The Pacific Northwest system and the special nature of core/periphery relations in that system are discussed in Chapter 6.

important for reproducing local structures, as explained above, it could in no way be construed as "commercialization" or market trade. Rather, it was prestige goods exchange among village heads. Though the rates of exchange among different trade items reflected scarcity and transport costs, these should not be construed as "prices," because there were no price-setting markets and the institutional nature of exchange was gift giving, not competitive buying and selling. Even some of the warfare was regulated by appeals to justice, as in the institution of the line war. Territorial expansion was largely carried out by means of kinship structures when Wintu men married into the families of adjacent villages. Such a system should not be construed as having important elements of tributary or state-based modes of accumulation.

Accumulation occurred collectively within villages. This included storage of foods, the building of fish weirs, and the burning of brushy areas to provide more grassland for game. These activities were organized by means of kinship relations and community efforts. Individual accumulation of wealth existed but was strongly constrained by leveling mechanisms. Calling this "capital" accumulation would certainly be stretching the concept of capital beyond the breaking point. Nor was it tributary accumulation.

If the mode of accumulation was neither capitalist nor tributary, this case study of precontact Northern California supports the transformationist position. The predominance of a qualitatively different logic of social reproduction in this very small world-system means that there must have been transformations in the modes of accumulation. All world-systems are not the same, at least as regards their modes of accumulation. And if the indigenous Californians represent fairly well an earlier stage of world-system evolution, then there must have been qualitative transformations from kin-based modes to tributary or capitalist modes.

It is valuable to understand egalitarian peoples because they help us comprehend what is possible for human beings. Many theories of human nature contend that our species is congenitally hierarchical. The existence of real human polities—indeed, whole systems of polities—without much hierarchy tells us that inequalities are not the inevitable outcome of a genetically determined human nature. This has implications not only for the past but also for possible futures.

Suggested Readings

Chase-Dunn, Christopher, and Kelly M. Mann. 1998. *The Wintu and Their Neighbors: A Very Small World-System in Northern California.* Tucson: University of Arizona Press.

Fagan, Brian M. 2003. *Before California.* Lanham, MD: Rowman and Littlefield.

Fletcher, Jesse B, Jacob Apkarian, Robert A. Hanneman, Hiroko Inoue, Kirk Lawrence, and Christopher Chase-Dunn. 2011. "Demographic Regulators in Small-Scale World-Systems." *Structure and Dynamics* 5 (1). http://escholarship.org/uc/item/6kb1k3zk.

Kelly, Robert L. 1995. *The Foraging Spectrum: Diversity in Hunter-Gatherer Lifeways.* Washington, DC: Smithsonian.

6

The Gardeners

The invention and spread of planting as a major method of producing food has been called the "Neolithic revolution." But we have already seen that humans had for millennia been moving away from the simple harvesting of nature toward the modification of nature to increase its productivity. Moving down the food chain from big-game hunting toward diversified foraging utilized resources that were less susceptible to depletion. This allowed greater population densities and eventually the establishment of permanent villages of sedentary foragers. As we have seen, sedentary foragers in California actively modified the natural environment to increase its productivity. Anthropologists have called this "proto-agriculture" because planting is a direct extension of the same logic. Human labor is exerted to increase the productivity of nature, and this expands the carrying capacity of the environment. Thus, the Neolithic revolution was a continuation of this trend.

The Biophysical Ecology of Egalitarian Horticulturalists

The development of horticulture[1] may have been one of the first instances of semiperipheral development.[2] Semiperipheral development may be seen in the emanation of Neolithic village communities of farmers in the context of adjacent Mesolithic villages. We know that the earliest gardening societies emerged in the same regions that had already seen the birth of village sedentism in ancient Western Asia. In the small valleys of the rain-watered hills adjacent to the prime gathering regions of the Natufian villages, naturally occurring stands of grain were less productive. It is plausible that when nomads in these neighboring regions tried to emulate the sedentary lifestyle of the Mesolithic Natufian villagers, they found those smaller natural stands were quickly eaten up, and so they experimented with planting some of the seeds that they had gathered

[1] Lenski, Lenski, and Nolan (1995) distinguish between horticultural and agricultural types of societies. Horticulture is gardening with simple tools such as digging sticks and hoes. Agriculture is larger-scale planting that uses irrigation and the plow. In practice, there are many forms of food production that fall in between these two types, but it remains a useful distinction.

[2] Recall from Chapter 2 that the hypothesis of semiperipheral development asserts that semiperipheral regions in core/periphery hierarchies are fertile sites for innovation and the implementation of new institutions that sometimes allow societies in these regions to be upwardly mobile and/or to transform the scale (and sometimes the qualitative nature) of institutional structures.

in order to augment nature's productivity. The proto-horticulture of the diversified foragers may have been transformed into true horticulture by the adjacent neighbors of the original sedentary foragers (B. Hayden 1981).

The techniques of gardening spread both east and west, raising the number of people who could be supported by a given area of land. Eventually, community sizes grew in rain-watered regions, and population growth led to migration of farmers away from the original heartland of gardening. Horticultural techniques also diffused from group to group. Thus did the Neolithic revolution spread from its first invention in ancient Western Asia.

Though the shift to planting occurred first in the Levant (Eastern Mediterranean), it also emerged independently in six other regions: East Asia, New Guinea, Africa, Mesoamerica (Mexico), South America, and North America. These independent inventions demonstrate the phenomenon of parallel social evolution in which a similar logic of development—something akin to the iteration model presented in Chapter 2—causes analogous things to emerge independently in regions that are distant and unconnected with one another. Gardening emerged independently because it was a solution to the problem of resource scarcity brought about by human population growth. As we shall see, humans tend to prefer to hunt and gather when these are good options. Farming is a lot of work.

Both the invention and the diffusion of planting were uneven in space and time. The inventions occurred much earlier in some regions (e.g., ancient Western Asia) than in others, and the paths of diffusion took much longer in some cases than in others. In ancient Western Asia, farming based on wheat, barley, sheep, and goats was well established by 8000 BCE. Farming had spread to Europe and South Asia by 6500 BCE. The independent invention of farming in the Huang Ho (Yellow) River valley of China, based on growing millet, was well established by 5000 BCE, and rice cultivation emerged in central China at about the same time. Millet and sorghum were cultivated in Africa during the third millennium BCE, and in New Guinea an independent emergence of tree and root crops began in the same period. Cultivation of squash, beans, and peppers emerged on the coast of Peru before 8000 BCE, and similar domesticated plants were being grown in Mesoamerica in the seventh millennium. Maize (corn) was domesticated in Mexico by about 5000 BCE and spread slowly north and south thereafter. These spatiotemporal differences had huge consequences for subsequent sociocultural evolution.

For example, horticulture never spread into most of California, which is why we were able to study a hunter-gatherer world-system in native California in Chapter 5. Corn (maize) planting spread north from Mexico, extending to the East Coast of what became the United States by around 400 CE. Maize planting temporarily extended into the Great Basin in what is now the state of Utah during the Fremont culture about a thousand years ago, but then the farmers retreated south during a period of drought. The Mogollon tradition in the region near what is now Phoenix, Arizona, was the first society of farmers in what is now the United States, and the Southwest experienced several waves of development of horticulture by peoples who are the ancestors of the historically known Pueblo Indians. The Yuman Indians along the Colorado River bordering the present state of California were maize gardeners, but maize never spread into the rest of California and there was no corn planting north or west of the Colorado River, with the exception of the temporary Fremont culture in Utah just mentioned. The Pacific Northwest developed rather complex and hierarchical societies based on the great productivity of coastal fishing and hunting, but they did not become planters until after the arrival of the Europeans. So why did maize horticulture not diffuse to the west of the Colorado River?

Jared Diamond (1997) has demonstrated the importance of botanical and zoological wealth for explaining the unevenness of social evolution and why some societies were able to develop the complexity, hierarchy, and technologies that enabled them to conquer and exploit other societies. Botanical and zoological wealth refer to the potential of the natural plant and animal species in a region to be domesticated by humans for use as food or in the production of food. Kent Flannery (1971) contended that the emergence of planting in ancient Western Asia was facilitated by a complementarity between humans and the grain-producing plants that were first domesticated. The availability of plants that provided good nutrition and were easy to grow in quantity was variable across regions. Some regions, such as Western Asia, had many of these human-friendly species, while others had few or none.

This also held for animals, providing the notion of unevenly distributed zoological wealth. Some animal species are easily domesticated because their genetically structured behavior patterns make it easy for humans to raise and use them, whereas others are difficult or impossible to domesticate. The key here is mainly whether the biologically set social structures of the animals are congruent with, or can easily be made congruent with, the structure of human/animal relations that facilitate breeding and raising. Horses versus zebras is a good example. It is very difficult to train zebras to do anything useful or to raise them in captivity.

The other big factor that has influenced uneven development is the pace of diffusion. Diffusion of domesticated plant and animal species is much faster and easier in an east/west dimension than in a north/south dimension because much more radical adaptation is needed to adjust to the greater climatic differences that are usually encountered in the north/south dimension. This is an important reason why domesticates and horticulture diffused rather quickly from Western Asia across the Eurasian land mass toward both Europe and South Asia, but were much slower to move south into Africa. It also helps explain the rather slow rate of diffusion of maize planting north of Mesoamerica. It was the early start and rapid spread of domesticates out of the well-endowed (with botanical and zoological wealth) West Asian part of the Old World that allowed Old World societies to develop the guns, germs, and steel that made it possible for them to conquer and exploit the societies of the Americas and Oceania.

Diamond's emphasis on the geographical factors and the importance of original zoological and biological endowments (natural capital) is important for reminding us that temporally deep features affecting cultural evolution have had important consequences that continue to shape the contemporary global world-system. Large portions of the global inequalities that plague the contemporary system are the consequence of factors that have been operating since the Neolithic. The long-run history of human social change is not just a pastime for antiquarians. It is a necessary component for understanding the world in which we now live.

Material Organization of Neolithic Simple Horticultural Societies

In hunting-and-gathering societies in which land was plentiful, groups were more likely to confront each other over misunderstandings because people knew that if the conflict was not resolved, there was not a great cost in moving. But in planting societies, the costs of direct confrontation were greater because the price of moving was higher. Simple horticulturalists lived in larger groups (one hundred to five hundred) than did most hunter-gatherers, and in more constricted areas. Because of this, people's commitments to each other grew: families bonded into kin groups, and clans formed, along with secret societies and other specialized bodies.

In hunting-and-gathering societies, the nuclear family is not obligated to share with other families, and no social institutions existed to enforce resource redistribution. Sharing among families was voluntary. One of the sources of conflict in horticultural societies was the expectation that nuclear families produce for the kin group as well as their family. As might be imagined, nuclear families must have had mixed feelings about this. Anthropologists have reported incidents in which families *hid* their food supply when a loafing kinsman appeared on the scene. On the surface, the family was cordial and observed the proper etiquette, but apparently they resented having to give to a kinsman who was not pulling his weight. Thus, obligations arising from bonds between kin were probably often regarded as onerous. On the other hand, when a harvest was bad and times were difficult, nuclear families were probably relieved to be members of a kin group.

A function of many of these groups is to lessen the conflicts likely to arise in a large group by providing structural differentiation and clear boundaries when the cost of moving is high. Specialized groups also increase solidarity in case of a famine. Excessive direct confrontation between people is a problem under conditions of interdependence; thus, community members developed ways to avoid confrontation—just as members of extended or nuclear families find ways to avoid confronting each other today. Over the course of the year, people would get lost in the mundane squabbles of daily life. They needed group rituals that would provide members with an opportunity to release these tensions, to forgive and forget. Structured in time and in space, often around the turning of the seasons, ceremonies provide such an opportunity to express hostilities through dramatization rather than direct confrontation.

At this point, it is important that we further distinguish between *horticulture* and *agriculture*, since these words are often used interchangeably. Horticulture is the form of planting that originated during the Neolithic Age, while agriculture originated in Bronze Age states. Horticulture usually involves the cultivation of small gardens of fruits and vegetables. Agriculture involves the cultivation of grains in large, permanent fields. Horticultural societies often used a slash-and-burn technique. New grounds are cleared by cutting and then burning existing vegetation, especially shrubs and small trees. Larger trees are left standing but are killed by "girdling"—cutting a circular strip of bark all the way around the trunk, thus stopping the flow of nutrients from the roots to the branches. When all the existing vegetation is burned to the ground, the resulting layer of ash provides mineral nutrients for the season's planting. In a few years, when the soil is exhausted, the people move to another location nearby. The abandoned plots are allowed to lie fallow for twenty to thirty years before the horticulturalists return to plant again.

Compared with agriculturalists, horticulturalists are more nomadic. This is because agriculturalists can cultivate the land more efficiently by the use of the plow and large draft animals. The type of technology a planting society possesses dictates how settled they really are. Why is this?

It has to do with the difference between digging sticks and hoes on the one hand and plows on the other. According to Lenski, Lenski, and Nolan (1995), a digging stick cannot penetrate very deep into the ground; thus, horticulturalists weren't able to access soil nutrients much below the surface. With a digging stick, it is also hard to get deep enough into the ground to root out weeds, and the presence of weeds undermines productivity. In addition, a certain portion of the land must remain untouched and allowed to revert to wilderness so that it recovers its nutrients. When cultivated areas are exhausted, the group must move on. All of this means that horticulturalists ran out of land quickly if there was any significant rise in population. In contrast, agriculture permitted people to stay in one place longer, because the plow exploits the nutrients in the soil more fully and raising domesticated animals produces fertilizer.

The evolution from hunting and gathering to horticulture had an important impact on the work activities of men and women. Women probably led the revolution from foraging to planting because planting is closer to gathering than it is to hunting. They took the lead in seeding, tending, and harvesting the plants. They learned about the healing properties of plants. Women also protected, fed, and cared for many of the small animals brought back alive, eventually leading to animal domestication. Men did the unskilled labor of clearing the brush and preparing the ground while doing occasional hunting.

This division of labor resulted in an increased segregation of men and women. Men worked in teams clearing the land, while women worked together planting. In many horticultural societies that have been studied by ethnographers, men and women do not even live together but stay in separate houses. As people adopted horticulture in the Neolithic, there must have been a loss of prestige for the men, as they were forced to exchange the adventure of big-game hunting for the less skilled work of clearing land for women's planting. Finally, planting did not increase the amount of free time for the average person. People in simple horticultural societies worked at least twenty-five hours a week (Lenski, Lenski, and Nolan 1995), a significant increase from the fifteen to twenty hours estimated by Sahlins (1972) for hunter-gatherers.

Horticultural societies produced more food per capita than hunter-gatherer societies, but in important ways they were more vulnerable. Not only were horticulturalists more dependent on fellow social members, but they were more dependent on other groups for trade. Since they domesticated and planted only a narrow range of crops, and since they tended to stay in one place longer and thus could not access free-roaming game animals as well as nomadic hunter-gatherers could, horticulturalists did not enjoy as balanced a diet as their hunter-gatherer ancestors. The early gardeners were typically protein-deficient. The only way they could supplement their diets was through trade—producing more of what they could produce, and exchanging it for what they could not. Coordination of material production thus became a necessity. The society as a whole needed a subsystem to manage the economic exchange of goods that went beyond informal exchanges between families. The society required a public economy in addition to a domestic economy. A shift in economic exchange from generalized reciprocity to what Harris (1988) calls "egalitarian redistribution" coordinated by a "**big man**" was a solution to this problem.

"Big men" played the role of hardworking public-spirited individuals who exhorted their families and neighbors to work toward accumulating surplus food that could be given away at a big feast. During the feast, the big man ostentatiously redistributes the extra food, thus acquiring prestige and influence in the community. According to Harris (1977), regardless of how the big man rationalizes his own actions, or how members of the society make sense of what he is doing, he is in fact inadvertently training people to produce more than is needed for just the family and the kin group. By training himself and others to work this way, the big man is "teaching" all involved how to share in a more systematic and efficient way in a public economy. The big man is not an institutional office of all simple horticultural societies; where it occurs, it is voluntarily chosen by a few individuals who compete with each other as to who can throw the biggest party (i.e., accumulate the most food). One psychological interpretation of bigmanship and the male secret societies that first emerge in horticultural societies is that they offered some compensation to men for the deterioration of their occupational status from big-game hunters to forest clearers.

It is tempting to believe that the emergence of big men was the beginning of social stratification, because these individuals took on some leadership functions and were able to mobilize people to do what they wanted. While we are not suggesting that the big man's motives were selfless, his goals were influence and prestige, not an increase in material wealth at the expense of others. More importantly, as an unintended consequence, he encouraged the habit of producing a surplus, since not all of what was produced for the feast was consumed. The rest was stored, available either in case of a bad harvest, as wealth to trade for other products, or as "bait" in forming alliances.

If the big man had really been accumulating power, he would have needed some institutionalized coercive force to protect that power. Simple horticultural societies had no such institution—no police or military force to protect the big man from popular protests or to enforce his will. As Sahlins (1972) argues, the big men had to "make their own power" through acts of generosity, bravery, oratory skills, charisma, or managerial ability. The big man had to goad, bait, or persuade people to help him prepare for the feast. If the feast didn't go well and one of his competitors won the contest for generosity, his followers deserted him. His followers only helped him prepare for the party in the hope that he would outdo competing big men. His winning added to their own prestige.

How did those members of society not involved in the process of throwing these "parties" feel about them? They probably had mixed feelings. In times of bad harvest, people were likely glad for the leftovers collected and set aside for the feast. However, when the harvest was good, people might have thought the whole process of throwing feasts a little silly.

It is only in complex horticultural societies that the public economy becomes institutionalized, existing across generations. The "big man" was not an office that could be handed down. The death of a big man often meant the end of redistribution of goods within and between polities. In protein-deficient horticultural villages where moving was not an easy option, this was a dangerous situation.

Let us turn from the economies of simple horticulturalists to their marriage and child-rearing practices, as compared with those of hunting-and-gathering societies. According to O'Kelly and Carney (1986), in horticultural societies the spouse relationship is not as important as the relationship between brothers and sisters. In fact, kinship relations are generally built around brothers and sisters. This makes good sense in terms of promoting social stability. Planters rightly sensed that a brother or sister relationship was far less likely to "break up" than was a marriage relationship, with all its storm and stress. In addition, O'Kelly and Carney point out that the sexual attitude men have toward women changed in these societies. Women were seen by men as dangerous polluters (through menstruation), and men's attitude toward sex gained a strong element of fear that had never existed in foraging societies.

Polygamy (the practice of having more than one mate) typically exists in one of two forms: *polygyny*, in which a man has more than one wife, or *polyandry*, in which a woman has more than one husband. Anthropologists have found that in societies where polygamy exists, it is far more likely to take the form of polygyny than polyandry. Polygamy of either form is rare in hunter-gatherer societies. However, polygyny is common in simple horticultural societies, a fact that would seem to contradict the belief held by many that women in such societies enjoyed high status. Yet there are some circumstances in which polygyny can benefit women. In simple horticultural societies, where women are involved in communal work patterns and eat and sleep together, it can make life easier economically for a group of wives to live and work together in a domestic arrangement. In terms of labor load, a monogamous marriage may be far more demanding.

In all horticultural societies, people have more children than in foraging societies because planting lends itself to child labor more easily than hunting or gathering does. But as can be imagined, because people are living in proximity, children are raised to be obedient rather than independent, due to the added social pressure to get along.

Environmental Psychology of Hunter-Gatherers and Simple Horticulturalists

In our society we tend to take the separation of our psychological states from physical reality as given. We assume our psychological states are what is inside us: emotions, memories, and fantasies. Physical reality includes rivers, streams, rocks, and trees, and these are thought to have no psyche. But egalitarian foragers and planters experienced the physical world as having psychological characteristics. This is crucial for understanding their perception of their environment.

In hunting-and-gathering societies the psyche is diffused throughout the natural environment as well as the humanly built environment. Psychological experiences are not thought to originate inside people but to come from the outside. A typical individual in a core industrial society who is asked over the breakfast table about their dreams will probably begin with the statement, "I had a dream." This assumes that a person's psyche is completely under their control.

Before the Late Iron Age (500 BCE), people were far more likely to answer the same question with "A dream came to me." Furthermore, though the location of the origin of dreams might be some invisible dimension, it was mediated through the physical landscape. This means that people's psychological states were rooted in very specific places. Places in most of ancient history were far from neutral containers of events. Places *already had* psychological qualities that helped form events that occurred within them.

For example, before people in nonstate societies traveled to another village, they were expected to know which sacred presences ruled over the areas where they were traveling, and they were taught techniques to protect themselves from being attacked or displeasing these powers. There are no empty, secular geographies in tribal societies. All the land is filled with psyches that are inhabited by spiritual entities.

When foragers go on a hunt, according to Peter Wilson (1988), the land is thought to be teeming with spirits who are as mobile as the hunters are. Sacred spirits do not inhabit a bounded territory but reside in paths, tracks, haunts, waterholes, and landmarks. The landscape is understood as a mythical topographical map, a grid of ancestor tracks of sacred sites.

Places and Territories

Among nomadic foraging societies, areas in which people perform their most important daily activities both inside and outside the camp become places to them. Places are the psycho-physical arenas in which a sacred ecological feedback loop is enacted among the band-stones-animals-trees-rivers in which generalized reciprocity occurs. Places need to have norms in order to preserve their sacred feeling. One of the norms is to minimize commerce, gambling, and fighting, because these activities undermine group solidarity and contaminate the "psyche" of the place.

Foraging societies do not have clearly defined territories. The territory outside the immediate camp and the places where hunting and gathering occur becomes less clearly defined the further out they venture, tapering off in a mist until it overlaps with the places of other polities. These diffused territories are more likely to be zones in society in which secular activities take place, such as fighting, gambling, or bartering with members of other polities. These areas are usually less predictable and riskier to inhabit.

Lyn Lofland (1998) proposes that the social terrain can be divided into three areas—private, parochial, and public. The private realm is governed by ties of intimacy among primary groups who are located in households. The parochial realm includes areas where kin groups, friends, and enemies congregate and with whom one has a culture and history. This is typically called a "community." The public realm is the area of society where strangers meet. We will be applying these concepts to gardening societies shortly.

Peter Wilson (1988) argues that whether people live in built environments or whether they live in open environments affects their social relationships. In nomadic hunting-and-gathering societies the tenuousness of the architecture of the housing arrangements allows for more visual transparency. Being the subject of attention was relentless. Daily life goes on in full view of the camp, and whether people like it or not there is a sense of involuntary involvement. In these societies solitude is frowned on, and privacy within the camp can only be gotten with the collusion of others to be "civilly inattentive." The boundary between the parochial and the private was very weak.

In horticultural societies, places are more clearly defined and intensely bounded. Because horticultural societies are more sedentary, people become more attached to their places. In these societies, territorial boundaries that were diffused among nomadic foragers become hardened with definite cutoff points. They become territories. Furthermore, particular groups within the village "own" portions of this territory. When people settle down and plant, houses stand for at least a year and burial sites are given more attention. The distinction between the parochial and the private grows much stronger.

If the public realm consists of the areas that house the activities of strangers, the public realm did not exist within either foraging or horticultural societies. It existed only in the buffer zones between societies as either trading zones or war zones. According to Lofland (1973), the presence of strangers created an extreme reaction. In isolated egalitarian societies, strangers were not even seen as human. If they were different but powerful, they might be seen as gods or deceased ancestors. Egalitarian societies made strangers kin through a ritual, or they expelled or killed them.

As people become more settled, they build domestic environments that are opaque to others. With the adoption of closed-off domestic quarters, concentration is possible because it is easier to exclude and avoid others. However, this new arrangement heightens tension in egalitarian horticultural societies because it is easier to plot to get ahead of others. A closed environment increases the potential for exploiting possibilities behind closed doors as well as displaying things in the open. It can accentuate secrecy and paranoia among neighbors, leading to accusations of witchcraft. These problems also invite the emergence of social mechanisms for alleviating fears and building solidarity, such as the formation of kin groups to structure relationships and systematic hospitality to quell paranoia.

Impact of Enclosed Parochial Places: Witchcraft, Hospitality, and Kin Groups

For most of the history of sociology, sociologists, with rare exception, have treated the physical environment undialectically, that is, as a passive backdrop for socioeconomic and political activity. But Peter Wilson (1988) argues that the manner in which the physical environment is organized actually shapes some aspects of social organization, specifically the extent to which society has kin groups, institutionalizes hospitality, or possesses witchcraft. The invention of kin groups systematizes cooperation and normalizes exchanges among people living in close quarters where some social relationships occur behind closed doors and privacy and exclusiveness can be cultivated.

Hospitality in horticultural societies might be looked at as an attempt *to ward off the emergence of the public arena* within society by extending parochial places and their accompanying exchanges across the entire village. In some cases this involves thousands of people who will never get to know each other face-to-face.

Exchanges between large kin groups are permeated with a sense of tension between the muffled self-interest among competing groups who at the same time must act as if this tension did not exist. These kinship relations in some cases take on some elements of the civility of city life complete with formalized manners and good cheer while retaining tribal expectations of group solidarity. In order to show that public display of good cheer is not a complete sham, hospitality is expected.

In a simple horticultural society the relationship between host and guest was reciprocal. The need to keep reciprocity alive over time is justified by the nature of how the exchange is conceived:

> One gives away what is in reality a part of one's nature and substance, while to receive something is to receive a part of someone's spiritual essence. *To keep this thing is dangerous* . . . the thing given is not inert. It is alive and often personified . . . the benefits taken by man ought to be returned to their source, that it may be maintained as a source. (P. Wilson 1988, 113; italics added)

Perhaps the most important element of having people over to a kin group's private place is to show they have *nothing to hide*. Generosity is not only done out of respect but done out of transparency. In contrast, hospitality is not part of the lifestyle of nomadic hunter-gatherers:

> Whereas hospitality is invariably mentioned in the ethnography of domesticated societies, it is to my knowledge . . . never described among hunter/gatherer societies. Among the latter, people from one company certainly visit those of another, but when they do they are absorbed into the company rather than separately identified and treated as guests. . . . The sense of identity and proprietorship in regard to place implicit in the term "host" [is absent]. (P. Wilson 1988, 97)

In a foraging society it is more important to give, receive, and pay back gifts than to be known as a generous giver or gracious receiver. The latter are more elaborated and long term.

Despite the mechanisms of kin groups and hospitality, accusations of witchcraft are never far away. In order to understand the social function that witchcraft serves, it must be distinguished from shamanism on the one hand and ancestor worship on the other. Peter Wilson (1988) makes three very interesting distinctions between them.

Shamanism involves an individual possessing or being possessed by a spirit. Ancestor worship involves a relationship between the living and the dead. The ancestors may act of their own accord but usually for a reason. They are upset by some failure of the living to respect them, fulfill obligations, or observe the proper taboos. To address the problem, the living carry out propitiatory rites. Although other living members of society may have been responsible for displeasing the ancestors, the general misfortune of society is blamed on the ancestors. In both shamanism and ancestor worship, forces from the outside affect humanity.

Witchcraft is about using sacred forces to affect relationships *between people*. Witchcraft may enlist the aid of spirits through magical activities but only at the bidding of the practitioner whose desire is to affect others. In shamanism one is taken over by a spirit; when the ancestors are displeased, they impact the entire community. But when one is bewitched, one is taken over by a spirit in the *control of another person*. What does witchcraft have to do with kinship and hospitality?

The formation of kinship relationships and structured hospitality are attempts to forestall paranoia leading to accusations of witchcraft among people living in close quarters in egalitarian relationships. According to Peter Wilson (1988), it is an attempt to understand how some kin groups still do better than others in spite of political and economic egalitarianism. More specifically, witchcraft is especially likely to occur during the winter season, when people are working less and living in close quarters. They naturally get on each other's nerves and don't have an opportunity to let off steam or express their envies and suspicions to anyone.

> Witchcraft accusations came when people perceived their neighbors to be in some way remiss and delinquent toward their obligations to entertain, to loan, to respect; and accusations occurred when people seemed to be taking advantage: to be borrowing more than they loaned, to visit more than they were visited. Such importunity causes

> strain because it is hard to refuse a request for a loan. In a social community of equality . . . imbalance between people, exceptional talents and achievements appear contrary to the ideal. . . . The exceptional success of individuals even if based on natural endowment is likely to be seen as a result of that person's access to hidden powers. (P. Wilson 1988, 139)

In our terms, whenever people feel that a domestic household is putting the private realm before the parochial realm and is gaining from it, witchcraft accusations are likely. According to Peter Wilson (1988), witchcraft is noninstitutional justice.

At the beginning of this section we said that the parochial realm consists of friends, enemies, and neighbors. Peter Wilson (1988) points out that among the Azande all accusations of witchcraft take place between *neighbors*, not between kin, strangers, or people of different rank. Why is this? Between kin groups and members of different rank (if we are talking about complex horticultural societies) there are *clear boundaries*. Strangers are a very rare phenomenon in any tribal society. Neighbors, on the other hand, stand in the outer reaches between the parochial world and the protopublic world of peripheral markets. The relation between neighbors is the most vague. Relations between neighbors or distant kin are probably the weakest link in the parochial realm, and there is the least to lose from neighbors accusing each other of witchcraft. Peter Wilson (1988, 145–146) summarizes:

> Witchcraft addresses the problems and difficulties that arise from living in a state . . . called unsocial sociability. Settlement compresses people together more intensively and for longer periods than living in a temporary open camp. Friction between people that might otherwise be defused by a simple parting may smolder to ignition in the domestic situation . . . the presence of privacy barrier . . . leads directly to an increase in suspicion, uncertainty, improperly taken hints, half glimpsed shadows, distorted eccentricities, circumstantial evidence, furtive glances, impolitic stares, uninvited intrusions. . . . From these . . . accidents, good and bad luck, coincidences and discrepancies in talent . . . there arise frustrations, envy, jealousy, cunning deceit. Is failure to return something borrowed on time innocent negligence or calculated insult?

Time and Space

All these tensions within societies are overlain within a scaled macro-micro cyclical of magical cosmology. In hunting-and-gathering societies, *geographies move with time* (see Table 6.1). The

Table 6.1 Geography among hunter-gatherers and simple horticulturalists

Hunter-Gatherers	Horticulturalists
Private-parochial diffused	Private-parochial separated
Camps (nomadic)	Villages (sedentary)
Place/territory diffused	Place/territory separated and bounded
Graves not marked or visited	Burial sites more elaborate
Transparent housing	Opaque housing
Attention diffused across camp (attention achieved by leaving the camp)	Attention concentrated within houses
Involuntary transparency	Concealment/display
Nuclear families	Nuclear family and kin groups
Visitors incorporated into society	Visitors get hospitality
Gift giving	Generous receiving
Informal behavior	More formal behavior
Open landscape	Boundary: inclusion-exclusion
Ancestors reside in landmarks	Ancestors reside in territories
Places move with time	Time passes into one place structured by seasons
History swallowed up by dreamtime	History captured by architecture
Shamanism: possession by spirit	Ancestor reverence: dead and living
Witchcraft: magic between members of other societies, as noninstitutional justice	Witchcraft: magic between people, between members of same society (neighbors)

specific history of the group is swallowed up in sacred dreamtime. But in domesticated societies, as Peter Wilson (1988) says, time *passes through* place. Place receives time and structures it through the seasons. Time is captured and shaped into the cycle of the seasons. In addition, the presence of more permanent architecture captures time for the history of the group. In other words, the group experience of building closed structures houses the events that the group has experienced over time.

The house and the village are small and medium-sized replications of the structure of the macrocosm. According to Peter Wilson (1988), they fulfill at least three functions: (1) they link social life to the natural world, (2) they give structure to social life, and (3) they help elaborate the thinking about the structure of the world. In the center of the village is the sacred dancing grounds where all rituals are enacted. This is the middle realm between the house at the micro-level and the cosmos at the macro-level.

Who one is in egalitarian horticultural societies is so much a function of *where one stands* that a person's identity can be seriously distorted simply by moving the village around:

> Seen from the treetop or a roof, a Bororo village looks like a cartwheel. The . . . missionaries persuaded the Bororo to abandon their circular villages in favor of houses set out in parallel rows. This completely disoriented them and once they had been deprived of their bearings and were without the plan which acted as confirmation of their native lore, the Indians soon lost any feeling for tradition; it was as if their social and religions systems were too complex to exist without the pattern which was embodied in the plan of the village and of which their awareness was constantly being refreshed by their everyday activities. (P. Wilson 1988, 73)

The Self in Hunter-Gatherer and Horticultural Egalitarian Societies: Horizontal Collectivist Selves

Now we discuss the specific ways in which people in egalitarian societies differed in how they were socialized to use the building blocks and shape their collectivist selves. Horizontal collectivist children learned to distinguish themselves from their mother as they grew up, as all children do, but unlike the individualist self they never imagined themselves as separate and autonomous from their society or the natural world. Collectivists imagine their relationship with the social and natural world in an organic way, as if they were an organ in the body of society. The organ has a function to perform within the whole. If the organ gets separated from the body, it dies. However, while horizontal collectivists feel a kind of organic bond with other members of society, this does not extend outside their kin groups. Collectivists do not tolerate strangers. Strangers are either brought into the kin group through a ritual or ceremony or are expelled or killed.

As we will see shortly, in tribal societies there is no full-time division of labor where people occupy themselves with one job all day. Furthermore, there is no separation between people who do only mental work and people who do only physical work. As Ernest Gellner (1988) points out, there is a direct connection between the specialization of labor and the specialization of language.

Gellner contends that as people in tribal societies move from one work setting to another, the words they use to describe their work experiences are less specialized because they do not work long enough at any one activity to develop a specialized language that only people who do the same activity can understand. Secondly, people engage many of the same others in many different contexts. This means that when a female gatherer talks with another female gatherer they also have a relationship in many other contexts besides gathering. They may meet each other during childcare, in tanning leather, or in weaving or as participants in a ritual. In order to maintain group solidarity, the language must expand far enough to cover a variety of social contexts. This means that language must be intentionally ambiguous.

Collectivists (whether horizontal or vertical) are more likely to be better at role-taking than individualists. For one thing, collectivists accept their role in the way an organ "accepts" its role in the body. It is necessary to the functioning of the whole. In egalitarian societies, individuals play a number of roles, but they do not make a separation between their personality and the roles they play. Because the rate of change of their society is generally slow, collectivists are most at home in role-taking in routine situations rather than role-making. When a routine situation becomes problematic or becomes a crisis, there are a number of possible outcomes. One is that crisis situations can lead to degeneration, a return to a routine, or a transformation of the situation, which, in society as a whole, can lead to reform or revolution.

At the same time, this must not be carried too far. Nomadic egalitarian hunter-gatherers were probably better at role-making and dealing with crisis situations than egalitarian horticulturalists just because they were smaller in numbers, there was less material wealth, and a nomadic way of life made people more used to dealing with the role-making necessary in crisis situations. This is less the case in egalitarian horticultural societies because living in villages in a sedentary lifestyle tends to stabilize and deepen the habit of dealing with routine situations.

Earlier we said that cultivating a generalized other involved an expanding sense of time and space. This leads to the realization that the world is objective and independent of the individual's thoughts, emotions, or intentions. This includes comprehending that roles are multiple, detachable, global, and historical. How well do horizontal collectivists do in developing a generalized other?

Collectivist selves generally have a more difficult time being objective. However, horizontal collectivists will easily understand roles as multiple because of the lack of division of labor in these societies. Horizontal collectivists have a difficult time imagining roles as detachable, because their roles are an extension of their kin-group responsibilities that are linked to their ecological settings and their sacred worlds. Further, because collectivist societies are more provincial, they tend to absolutize the roles that are played and are less aware that the roles they play are similar to the roles played by other tribal societies in other areas. The collectivist self will have no trouble with the historicity of roles when it comes to understanding that they exist beyond the lifetime of their generation. In fact, they probably imagine these roles as eternal. What will be difficult is the notion that new roles emerge as part of the historical process, while other roles are marginalized or vanish. On the whole, collectivists are more intersubjective rather than objective.

Horizontal collectivists do not pay much attention to their biographical identity. Certainly the major landmarks such as initiation rites, marriages, and separations are remembered, but what matters for the collectivist is the *group* past and future. The individual's unique experiences are not reflected upon, taken apart, or imagined to be anything special.

Also related to the biographical self is the perceived locus of control. Cross-cultural psychologists make a distinction between "external" and "internal" loci of control. Collectivists have an external locus of control, meaning that what happens to the individual is generally believed to be caused by forces beyond his or her control. This can mean sorcery at the hands of other people, the unknown machinations of sacred presences, or just luck. For horizontal collectivists, their external locus of control only refers to the relationship between the individual and nature. Through communal magical rituals, horizontal collectivists believe they have a great deal of control over the natural world. This sacred belief is an expression of their political and economic relations. If these individuals as a collective actually have control over the basic resources of life and the political decision-making processes, this reality will tend to show itself in their sacred world.

In any individual identity, there are two major divisions: one's internal state and the outer world of actions. As it turns out, individualists and collectivists locate their biographical self on different sides of this identity. Luria (1976) compared the personalities of peasants still living in the rural areas of Russia approximately ten years after the revolution with the personalities of those who had moved to the cities and been subjected to industrialization. He found there was a difference in how they evaluated their personality.

He found that peasants inhabiting rural areas answered questions about their personality by referring to other people who they believed were a better judge of their personality than they were. They believed their actions in the world were the true test of who they were. They did not refer to their own assessment of their inner states to determine their identity. While the collectivist must self-reflect on the feedback received by others in order to become more sensitive to his social environment, the self-reflexive moment is in the service of others. The moment of self-reflection is not imagined as detachable from other actions. In other words, collectivists would find the invitation to self-reflect on one's identity that is encouraged in many forms of psychotherapy today to be very selfish and not likely to reveal the truth about a person.

In all societies, individuals have to face a potential conflict between their individual self-interest and the group self-interest. But for horizontal collectivists, the individual self-interest is almost always synonymous with the self-interest of society as a whole because the societies are egalitarian. So for horizontal collectivists, the "I-Me" dialogue was more or less fused. Though in most respects, women's and men's identities as horizontal selves were more or less the same, women's primary responsibility for child rearing would probably make her stress the "Me" part of the "I-Me" dialogue more than the men would.

From Simple to Complex Horticulture

The shift from foraging to horticulture provides more food per unit of land. In some areas this made possible the emergence of larger polities, a more complex division of labor, and greater hierarchy within societies. Some adults began to specialize in the production of tools, and so a division of labor emerged between tool producers and food producers. Some polities use resource endowment advantages they had to specialize in the production of goods for trade with other polities, and so an intervillage or interregional division of labor developed. And in some societies, certain families of kinship groups claimed superiority over other groups and began to build hierarchy into the way in which kinship was reckoned. These emerging elites tended to be more successful when they could justify their claims by providing coordination of collective accumulation or of exchange with other groups.

As villages eventually grew larger, trade networks did as well and craft specialists began producing for export and importing raw materials. Trade networks probably expanded and contracted along different spatial dimensions, as was the case in Northern California reported in Chapter 5. Some regions began displaying mortuary practices that indicated the emergence of social stratification. In Northern Mesopotamia this kind of society is evident in the Hassuna/Samarra archaeological tradition from 6000 BCE to 5500 BCE. Precious minerals were traded over larger and larger regions, and regionally defined pottery styles developed. The Halafian archaeological tradition in Northern Mesopotamia (5500 BCE–5000 BCE) had even larger villages, and some have argued that these were chiefdoms, yet they lacked clearly defined public buildings and definitive evidence of stratification.

Hunters Once Again: The Abandonment of Horticulture

Some students of social evolution assume that gardening is "better" than hunting and gathering, and so peoples will prefer to raise crops and domesticated animals whenever these options become available. But this conclusion is not warranted. There have been instances in which horticulturalists threw away their digging sticks and became hunter-gatherers once again. When the ancestral Maori arrived in New Zealand there were ten-foot-tall flightless birds—the Moa (Figure 6.1). These Polynesians gave up fishing and planting and became hunters of Moa until the

Figure 6.1 New Zealand Moa and ancestral Maori Moa hunters
Source: Wikipedia Commons.

Moa had been exterminated, and then the Maoris again adopted horticulture.

The first Polynesian settlers in the Hawaiian archipelago found a land full of food. For the first few hundred years, the Hawaiians derived a large portion of their protein from the meat of birds, including a species of flightless geese that had no natural predators until the arrival of humans. These early settlers spread out across the archipelago, occupying the prime sites for birding until the flightless geese had been exterminated. As population density increased and all the islands became populated, the Hawaiians returned to the horticulture and fishing that had been their mode of production in the locations from which they had traveled to Hawaii. Both the Maori and the Hawaiians demonstrate that people prefer hunting to horticulture when hunting can provide a great return.

Recall the question posed above as to why maize planting did not diffuse to California. It was not that native Californians were ignorant of the techniques of planting. Indeed, they did plant tobacco near their villages. And neither was it the "tyranny of distance" that prevented the carrying of corn seeds into California. A drive across the Mohave Desert suggests that this formidable land might have prevented indigenous peoples from bringing seeds from the Colorado River into the better-watered regions of the West Coast. But this is simply wrong. Indigenous peoples inhabited the Mohave for millennia, and trade goods did move across this desert as well as across the High Sierras to the north.

The reason why maize horticulture was not taken up by native West Coast societies is that hunting and gathering was still paying great returns despite high population densities. In California there were still some neutral territories that were uninhabited. Some of these may have been buffer zones in which conflicting groups avoided contact by not building villages near their adversaries. But others, such as the Marysville Buttes, an upwelling of high mountains in the midst of the Sacramento Valley inhabited by condors, were simply unclaimed land where different groups could occasionally visit to hunt or gather resources. California, despite rapid population growth since 1500 CE, had not yet reached **carrying capacity** for foraging because of the extreme productivity of its natural environment.

The peopling of the Americas and subsequent human sociocultural evolution produced a complicated geography of different kinds of societies with very different institutions despite that most of the original immigrants were culturally similar. We are still discovering new archaeological evidence about the nature of the peopling of the Americas and their subsequent development (C. Mann 2005). What is obvious is that Amerindian societies were far more diverse and developed than is commonly understood. The Web Chapter (http://www.paradigmpublishers.com/resrcs/other/1612053289_otherlink.pdf) describes what is known about the many regional world-systems that were emerging in that part of North America that eventually became the United States.

Suggested Readings

Diamond, Jared. 1997. *Guns, Germs and Steel: The Fates of Human Societies.* New York: Norton.

Kristiansen, Kristian. 1998. *Europe before History.* Cambridge: Cambridge University Press.

Mann, Charles C. 2005. *1491: New Revelations of the Americas before Columbus.* New York: Alfred A. Knopf.

7

The Sacred Chiefs

Chiefdoms have a form of leadership in which the chief has a more permanent claim to his or her position than do the headmen or big men of less stratified polities. Chiefs are held to be closer to the ancestors of the society in a way that legitimates their abilities to make decisions for the group. In chiefdoms, kinship has become hierarchically organized. Some lineages or clans (family groups) are defined as superior or more "senior" than others. Seniority here means a more direct descent from revered ancestors. In complex chiefdoms, lineages have often become divided into a class of chiefly families and a class of commoners, and this constitutes the beginning of true class societies. In such societies, commoners have lost legitimate rights over productive property (means of production), and so what was collective property of the whole society in less stratified polities has now become the property of the **chiefs**. Commoners are dependent on members of the chiefly class for access to necessary resources such as land or for access to social goods that are required in order to become an adult or to get married. Elites become enabled to exert influence over economic production and biological reproduction.[1]

Rise and Fall

What we have been calling "rise and fall" corresponds to changes in the centralization of political-military power in a set of polities. It is a question of the relative size of interacting polities and the distribution of power among these polities. The term "cycling" has been used to describe this phenomenon as it operates among chiefdoms (D. Anderson 1994). All world-systems in which there are hierarchical polities experience a cycle in which relatively larger polities grow in power and size and then decline. This applies to interchiefdom systems as well as interstate systems, to systems composed of empires, and to the modern rise and fall of hegemonic core powers (e.g., Britain and the United States). Very egalitarian and small-scale systems such as the sedentary foragers of Northern California do not display a cycle of rise and fall, though, as we have seen, they do exhibit the pulsation of trade network expansions and contractions.

The causal processes of rise and fall differ depending on the predominant mode of accumulation. Larger chiefly polities developed in some regions and then fell apart as the problems

[1] There is a large literature by archaeologists and anthropologists on chiefdoms (e.g., Earle 1991; Upham 1990).

that were caused by the emergence of hierarchy became too great for the larger polities to resolve. **Rise and fall** refers to the general tendency in interpolity systems for one society to emerge as most powerful and then to decline at a later point.

Figure 7.1 illustrates what is meant by the idea of rise and fall combined with a stairstep up to larger polity sizes. It is not meant to suggest that individual societies went through all these changes. Rather, the figure illustrates the variation in the size of the biggest polity within expanding political-military networks.

Rise and fall works somewhat differently in interchiefdom systems because the institutions that facilitate the extraction of resources from distant groups are less fully developed in these than those that eventually emerge in state-based systems. David G. Anderson's (1994) study of the rise and fall of Mississippian chiefdoms in the Savannah River valley provides an excellent and comprehensive review of the anthropological and sociological literature about what Anderson calls "cycling." Cycling is the processes by which a chiefly polity extended control over adjacent chiefdoms and erected a two-tiered hierarchy of administration over the tops of local communities (rise). At a later point these regionally centralized chiefly polities disintegrated back toward a system of smaller and less hierarchical polities (fall).

Chiefs relied more completely on hierarchical kinship relations, control of ritual hierarchies, and control of prestige goods imports than did the rulers of true states. These chiefly techniques of power are all highly dependent on normative integration and ideological consensus. States developed specialized organizations for extracting resources that chiefdoms lacked—standing armies and bureaucracies. And states and empires in the state-based world-systems were more dependent on the projection of armed force over great distances than modern hegemonic core states have been. The development of commodity production and mechanisms of financial control, as well as further development of bureaucratic techniques of power, has allowed modern hegemons to extract resources from faraway places with much less overhead cost. The development of techniques of power has made core/periphery relations ever more important for competition among core powers and has altered the way in which the rise-and-fall process works in other respects.

Chiefdom Formation

Chiefdom world-systems were those in which the largest and most complex polities were chiefdoms. These often also contained less complex societies that were in interaction with the chiefdoms. But

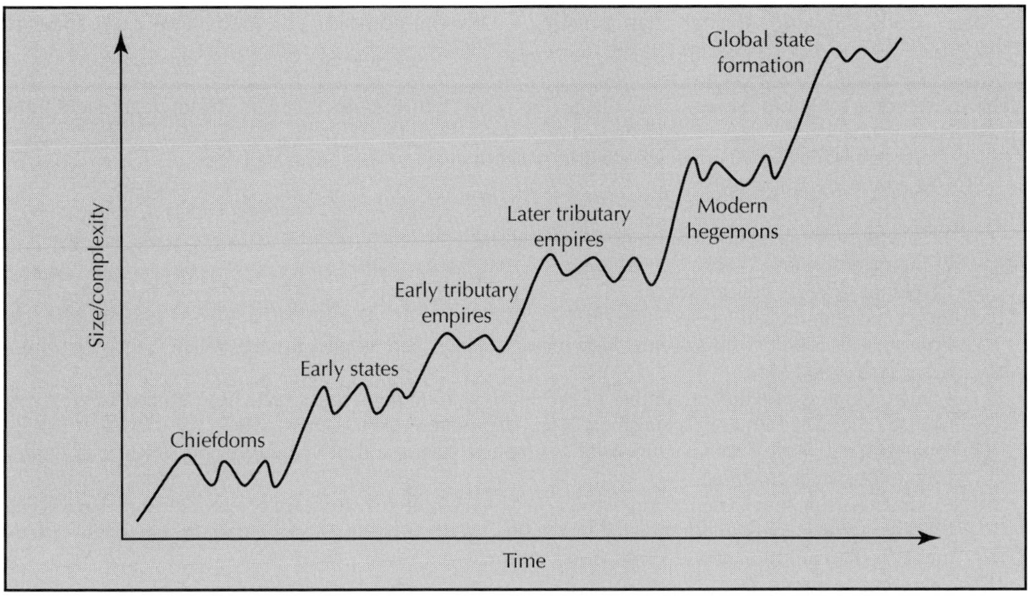

Figure 7.1 The rise-and-fall polities with occasional upward sweeps in size

once hierarchy exists within a system, there are often pressures for all the interacting societies to develop their own hierarchies in order to provide protection against hierarchical neighbors. Exceptions are people who live in mountainous terrain or other inaccessible and easily defended regions (e.g., the Swiss). It is costly to dominate and exploit such people, and so they may retain rather egalitarian forms of organization even in a context where they are surrounded by large and powerful neighbors.

Chiefdom formation undoubtedly occurred in several different ways. Jonathan Friedman's (1982) world-systems analysis of Pacific island societies distinguishes between chiefdoms based on **prestige goods systems**, in which the power of chiefs is based on their ability to monopolize imported status goods, and caste-like "feudal" systems like those found in Eastern Polynesia, including Hawaii.[2] Friedman stresses that chiefdom formation is reversible. He points out that, if chiefdoms automatically emerged with the passage of time, Melanesian societies should be the most hierarchical because Melanesia has been occupied for much longer than has Polynesia. But Eastern Polynesia, the most recently settled region, is also the region with the most stratified societies in the Pacific.

Jonathan Friedman (1982) contends that earlier Melanesian and Western Polynesian hierarchies that were based on the control of prestige goods declined in a context of increasing trade density (because chiefs lost their monopoly of prestige goods imports). Rather than prestige goods monopolies, the chiefdoms of Eastern Polynesia were based on staple finance (the appropriation of labor and products from dependent commoner populations by means of control over productive property). These sometimes collapsed because of overexploitation of the environment (e.g., Easter Island).

There were also cases in which chiefdom formation and political centralization became stalled. Kirch's (1991) analysis of the Marquesas Islands societies argues that relatively poor ecological conditions on the Marquesas prevented the emergence of island-wide polities and perpetuated a cycle of endemic warfare and cannibalism that performed the function of demographic regulator. This is the nasty bottom part of the iteration model discussed in Chapter 2.

The broad typology of world-systems proposed by Chase-Dunn and Hall (1997)[3] utilizes the structural distinctions proposed by Johnson and Earle (1987). They distinguish among big-man systems, simple chiefdoms, and complex chiefdoms. These types are mainly based on the degree of internal hierarchy, the nature of the institutionalized power of leaders, and the size of independent polities. Complex chiefdoms have rather large polities and class-stratified social structures based on a hierarchy that separates the class of chiefs from the commoners and strongly institutionalizes the control of the chiefs over resources that are necessary to the daily lives of commoners.

Johnson and Earle (1987) make the cut between complex chiefdoms and early states in

---

[2] This difference is similar to Earle's (1991) distinction between hierarchies based on wealth finance and those based on staple finance.

[3] Chase-Dunn and Hall's (1997) typology of world-systems:

- I. Kin-based mode dominant
  - A. Stateless, classless
    - 1. Sedentary foragers, horticulturalists, pastoralists
    - 2. Big-man systems
  - B. Chiefdoms (classes but not states)
- II. Tributary mode dominant (states, cities)
  - A. Primary state-based world-systems (Mesopotamia, Egypt, Indus valley, Ganges valley, China, Precolumbian Mexico, and Peru)
  - B. Primary empires in which a number of previously autonomous states have been unified by conquest (Akkad, Old Kingdom Egypt, Magahda, Zhou, Teotihuacan, Huari)
  - C. Multicentered world-systems composed of empires, states, and peripheral regions (Near East, India, China, Mesoamerica, Peru)
  - D. Commercializing state-based world-systems in which important aspects of commodification have developed but the system is still dominated by the logic of the tributary modes (Afroeurasian world-system, including Roman, Indian, and Chinese core regions)
- III. Capitalist mode dominant
  - A. The Europe-centered subsystem since the seventeenth century
  - B. The global modern world-system

terms of the emergence, in true states, of specialized institutions of regional control such as standing armies or permanent bureaucracies. Chiefdoms rely exclusively on kinship-based marriage alliances and a metaphor of lineage seniority for controlling distant regions, while states employ non-kin-based institutions of regional control. Johnson and Earle also utilize the polity size criterion in this distinction. States are usually larger than complex chiefdoms. Though these distinctions may be difficult to apply to particular cases, we agree with Johnson and Earle that the underlying dimensions of organizational differentiation that they specify are important for distinguishing between different types of systems.

All state-based systems exhibit certain analytically similar features. They went through a sequence of political centralization and decentralization in which a single state conquered a large chunk of the contiguous core region and then this conquest empire fell apart to once again take the form of a system of competing states (an interstate system). New core regions and dominant states emerged as these systems developed, with formerly semiperipheral regions attaining core status at later points in time.[4]

Chiefdom world-systems are much more similar to the modern system than indigenous California was. Chiefdom systems also experience a sequence of political centralization and decentralization in which larger conquest chiefdoms rise and then fall apart. Sahlins (1972, 141–148) described and analyzed this sequence of rise and fall for the Hawaiian case. And, like state-based systems, chiefdom systems occasionally go through radical expansions in which the whole scale of the system gets larger. And, in both state-based and complex chiefdom systems, conquest and the political-military cycles are connected to the dynamics of class exploitation within polities (Turchin and Nefadov 2009).

There are other important differences between chiefdom systems and state-based systems in addition to size and the degree of specialization of control institutions. The strategies of chiefdom formation and expansion differ in important ways from the strategies of state formation and expansion. And there are different strategies of chiefdom formation, as discussed by Jonathan Friedman (1982). The unspecialized nature of internal political hierarchies in chiefdom systems usually corresponds with an intermediate degree of core/periphery hierarchy because kin-based control institutions are relatively poor vehicles for exploiting and dominating distant regions.

Friedman and Rowlands (1977) were the first to formulate an evolutionary world-systems explanation of chiefdom formation that turns on the workings of regional relations among different polities. The following quotation makes this explicit:

> The model as presented thus far may appear to be localized to a particular concrete society where production and reproduction are determined by a local set of productive relations. This, however, is not the case, for we must take into account that reproduction is an areal phenomenon in which a number of separate social units are linked in a larger system. As production for exchange seems to be a constant factor in evolution we must deal with a system larger than the local political unit, whether it be a tribe or a state, if we are to understand its conditions of existence and transformation. (Friedman and Rowlands 1977, 204)

And further,

> The expansion of a tribe into a state occurs in the presence of other tribes connected by exchange and warfare to the evolving unit and which may be transformed into a politically acephalous[5] periphery of the emergent state which imports a large portion of their labor force and part of their product. Similarly, long-distance trade between emergent chiefdoms and states may help stimulate local intensification of production and the political development of local centers at

[4] The nature of the sequence of political centralization/decentralization altered with changes in the logic of accumulation. The predominance of capitalism in the modern world-system led to the replacement of the cycle of empire formation and decline by a cycle of the rise and fall of hegemonic core powers (e.g., the Dutch, the British, and the United States).

[5] "Acephalous" means headless or leaderless.

> the expense of their immediate peripheries. (Friedman and Rowlands 1977, 205)

They described the process of evolution from tribe to chiefdom in terms of three relations of production: the social appropriation of nature by local lineage production, relations among lineages (most importantly matrimonial exchange in which wife-givers have greater status than wife-takers), and relations between lineages and the community as a whole—the conversion of lineage surplus into distributive feasts. Friedman and Rowlands (1977) further note that prestige goods traded with other tribes may have more than a sumptuary (status-signifying) function. Among the Trobriand Islanders, for example, control over elite goods was a source of power over labor because these goods were necessary for marriage and other obligatory payments.

Friedman and Rowlands (1977) described the way kinship relations could operate in a tribal system to cumulate inequalities. They presumed the existence of strong lineages that are ranked by "social age," whereas in Northern California lineages were fluid and unranked. And they "assume for purposes of the model . . . that the local lineage is patrilineal and patrilocal so that it is groups of men who exchange women" (1977, 207).

They also stress the connection between lineage seniority and rank in the supernatural world. As they write,

> Economic activity in this system can only be understood as a relation between producers and the supernatural. . . . The entire universe is usually envisaged as a single segmentary structure in which the most powerful deities are no more than more distant ancestor-founders of larger groups. . . . The lineage that is able to produce a large enough surplus to feast the entire community can only do so because of its influence with the supernatural, and since influence is defined as genealogical proximity, the lineage in question must be nearer to such powers. This "genealogical" differential is expressed in terms of relative social age. Within the local community, such a lineage would be an older lineage, a direct descendent of the territorial founder ancestor spirit of that larger group. . . . Women are then given to other lower status groups in exchange for a bride price that measures the social value of the wife-giver. This relation is one where a given quantity of real wealth is exchanged for a kinship connection (matrilateral link) to the source of wealth. (Friedman and Rowlands 1977, 207)

This pattern of wife-giving in which a core lineage exchanges its daughters for wealth is the basis of chiefdom formation out of a tribal context as formulated by Friedman and Rowlands (1977). Peregrine (1991, 1992) has applied this prestige goods system model to explain the rise of complex Mississippian chiefdoms in precontact North America.

Friedman and Rowlands (1977) also consider the emergence of even more hierarchical systems containing social classes and early states. In these transformations, which typically involve the emergence of conical clans, there is a pattern in which the genealogically highest groups become wife-takers from lower-status groups. As Friedman and Rowlands say,

> In the previous system wife giving was a means of establishing relative rank, but now, as social position is determined from the start, hypogamy (wife giving) must lose its former function. On the contrary, wives will tend to move from lower to higher ranks as a form of tribute. This is merely a generalization of a form of exchange that already occurs in the chiefdom between the paramount and lineages of definitively lower status, especially in the case of secondary wives. (1977, 217)

Thus, the meaning of elite wife-giving or wife-taking varies depending on how kinship hierarchies and class relations are intertwined.

Earle (1977) disputes Service's (1975) contention that chiefdoms emerged to facilitate exchange among villages producing different types of goods. His analysis of Hawaiian chiefdoms shows that, even though the villages occupied very different ecological niches, they remained self-subsistent. The surplus appropriated by chiefs was used exclusively for the provisioning of the royals and for waging war, not for redistribution to commoners in different villages. Earle (1977, 215) distinguishes among several types of redistribution:

1. *Leveling mechanisms:* Any cultural institution in which the effect is to counteract the concentration of wealth by individuals or groups. Examples: ceremonial obligations, potlatching, progressive taxation.
2. *Share-out:* The allocation of goods produced by cooperative labor to participants and the owners of the factors of production. Example: distribution of meat resulting from cooperative hunts.
3. *Mobilization:* The appropriation of goods and services from a producing class for the benefit of an elite. Examples: tribute, taxation, and corvée labor.

It is this last type, attributed to Smelser (1959), that Earle claims is the major operant form in the Hawaiian chiefdoms. Note that "mobilization" is the institutional basis of what we call the tributary mode of accumulation. The identification of this type of accumulation in a complex chiefdom such as that which existed in Hawaii shows an important overlap with state-based world-systems.

Core/Periphery Relations in Interchiefdom Systems

The first sedentary foragers interacted with their still-nomadic neighbors. This constituted the first instance of core/periphery differentiation as we have defined it in Chapter 2. When horticulture emerged, farmers interacted with foragers in a somewhat different kind of core/periphery differentiation. But what about core/periphery hierarchies? This is the big question that was confronted in Chase-Dunn and Mann's (1998) study of indigenous California.

Among stateless systems, those containing complex chiefdoms had the most potential for arranging a core/periphery hierarchy. They had the rudiments of mobilizational resources and they engaged in conquest. The tribute demanded of conquered villages must be considered exploitative. Chiefly expansion was not very stable because the mobilizational institutions were weak, constrained as they were by the norms of reciprocity (see Sahlins's discussion of Hawaii below). The chief did not enjoy much relative autonomy.

Chiefdoms in Ancient Southwest Asia

In Chapters 5 and 6 we discussed the emergence of sedentary foragers and the first development of horticulture in the ancient Levant (what is now Lebanon, Palestine, and Israel). Near to this region was also the first to see the emergence of interchiefdom systems. Some areas began displaying mortuary practices that indicated the emergence of social stratification. In Northern Mesopotamia this kind of society is evident in the Hassuna/Samarra archaeological tradition from 6000 BCE to 5500 BCE. Precious minerals were traded over larger and larger regions, and regionally defined pottery styles developed. The Halafian archaeological tradition in Northern Mesopotamia (5500–5000 BCE) had even larger villages, and some have argued that these were chiefdoms, yet they lacked clearly defined public buildings and definitive evidence of stratification.

According to Nissen (1988, Chapter 3), the first three-tiered settlement system in Southwest Asia emerged on the Susiana Plain in the Ubaid period (5500–4000 BCE). This indicates the presence of complex chiefdoms, and Wright (1986) points to the importance of the existence of complex chiefdoms in a region as the necessary organizational prerequisite for the emergence (later) of pristine states. In other words, early states do not emerge directly from egalitarian societies.

Evidence from Uqair, Eridu, and Ouelli shows that there were also Ubaid towns on the Lower Mesopotamian floodplain, the drainages of the Tigris and Euphrates Rivers in what is now Iraq. These towns were as large as the sites on the Susiana Plain at this time. The Early Ubaid phase at Tell Ouelli on the floodplain shows remarkably complex architecture as early as anything in Susiana. Thus, there was an interregional interaction system of chiefdoms based on a mix of rain-watered and irrigated agriculture.

The Chesapeake System in the Time of Captain Smith

Captain John Smith's reconnaissance of the Chesapeake Bay in 1607 and 1608 and the detailed map that he prepared provides an illuminating window on the indigenous world-system of the

Chesapeake region before the coming of Europeans massively disrupted it. Smith learned to speak the Powhatan dialect of Algonquian well during his famous captivity among the Indians, and his geopolitical strategies made him pay close attention to the niceties of alliances and enmities among the native groups that he encountered (Potter 1993, 181).

The indigenous linguistic situation in the early sixteenth century CE had different dialects of the Eastern Algonquian language stock spoken on the entire Chesapeake. The Algonquian-speaking peoples may have migrated from the Great Lakes region in a number of waves over the past two millennia (Potter 1993, 3). To the west in the piedmont of the Blue Ridge Mountains were groups of Souixan speakers (the Monacans and the Mannahoacs), and on the Susquehanna River at the northern end of the Chesapeake Bay were the Iroquoian-speaking Susquehannocks. Another group of Iroquoian-speaking people, the Massawomecks, were raiding and trading into the Chesapeake from a homeland somewhere to the northwest (Pendergast 1991). To the south of the Chesapeake there were Algonquin speakers near the coast (Chawanoc, Weapemeoc, and Roanoke) and southern Iroquoian speakers near the fall line between the coastal plain and the piedmont terrain (Nottoway, Meherrin, and Tuscarora). Thus, there were three major language stocks, each with several dialects, and many of the dialects were mutually unintelligible.

Bounding the Chesapeake Interaction Networks

The place-centric approach to bounding of world-systems (see Chapter 2) requires that we begin at some point in space. The obvious choice, because of evidence and structure, is to put the Powhatan paramount chiefdom in the center and to survey the interaction networks and core/periphery relations from this vantage point. The Powhatan chiefdom is named after the individual (also called Wahunsenacawh) who held the position of paramount chief (mamanatowick) over about thirty smaller chiefdoms or districts, each with its own *werowance*, or chief. Powhatan's original home village was very near what is now Richmond, Virginia, on the James River. Chief Powhatan had inherited control of nine small districts on the upper portions of the James and York Rivers. In the last years of the sixteenth century, he initiated a series of campaigns of expansion by conquest that successfully extended his control over all the districts on the lower James and York Rivers as well as the south end of the Chesapeake Bay. The Powhatan paramountcy also induced tribute payments from districts on the Rappahannock and Potomac Rivers and from across the Chesapeake Bay (what is now Virginia's Eastern Shore).

Just north of the Powhatan paramountcy was another large polity on the north shore of the tidewater Potomac River just below what is now the District of Columbia, the so-called Conoy paramount chiefdom, whose paramount chief (*tayac*) was a Piscataway. The smaller chiefdoms of the Patuxent River were not part of the Conoy paramountcy, and neither were the groups along the southern shore of the tidewater Potomac. The Conoy paramountcy probably emerged by about 1500 as the first large chiefly polity of the protohistoric period. By the time Captain Smith arrived it had already begun to decline with the secession of the Patowomeke (Potter 1993, 150). Here is a Chesapeake instance of rise and fall, or at least rise and decline.

The Bulk Goods Network

The bulk goods network (BGN) was composed of a local subsistence system in which commoner families produced most of their own food by means of hunting, fishing, gathering, and horticulture, and a larger political economy of tribute in which local chiefs collected from their own commoners and passed food and other valuables on to regional paramount chiefs. Corn was transported across the Chesapeake from the Eastern Shore chiefdoms tributary to the Powhatan. Commoners stored food in concealed household storage pits while chiefs displayed their wealth in granaries and storehouses (Potter 1993, 172).

The subsistence of the Powhatan and surrounding groups was based on horticulture supplemented by hunting and gathering. It is estimated that over 50 percent of the food consumed was maize (Potter 1993, 40). Other crops were beans, squash, pumpkins, gourds, sunflowers, and tobacco. Deer hunting was done mainly in the winter in upland regions. Deer were scarce in the heavily populated riverine and estuarine regions. Shellfish and other marine resources were an important part of the diet. The political economy was primarily one in which matrilineal families supplied their own needs, but there was an important overarching structure of chiefly accumulation.

Class formation had emerged in these societies such that there was an important degree of inequality between chiefs and commoners. Chiefs were understood to be a special and powerful group with claims on the labor and produce of commoners. The holders of chiefly offices were served by priests and by war leaders chosen from among the commoners. Local chiefs collected food and other valuables and then paid tribute to paramount chiefs. The collected goods were stored in special mortuary temples that contained the remains of dead elites and that also served as storehouses containing maize, animal skins, copper, beads, pearls, and dyes (see Figure 7.2). Only priests and *werowances* were allowed to enter these mortuary temples. Chiefs and paramounts used the stored valuables to reward their followers and for trade.

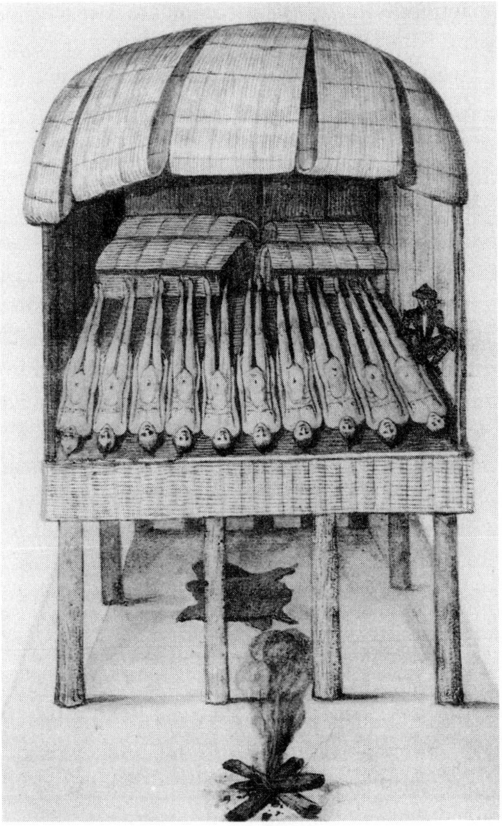

Figure 7.2 North Carolina mortuary temple/storehouse. Chesapeake Algonquin chiefdoms had similar structures. Watercolor by John White, circa 1585.
Source: D. C. Curry. 1999. *Feast of the Dead.* Crownsville, MD: Maryland Historical Trust Press. © The British Museum.

The Prestige Goods Network

Prestige goods moved locally and over great distances by means of both trade and direct procurement. The amount of long-distance trade was less than had been the case a few hundred years earlier, before the adoption of horticulture and the most recent rise of the chiefdoms (see the Web Chapter). Antimony, a silvery substance used for body paint, was mined near the head of Aquia Creek in the territory of the Patowomeke, an important chiefdom on the south shore of the tidewater Potomac. Antimony paint was observed in use on the south bank of the James River and was considered a luxury item by the Powhatans. Potter (1993, 161) contends that control of this valuable mineral enhanced the power of the Patowomeke *werowance*. Marine shells from the Atlantic, copper from the Blue Ridge and from the Great Lakes region, puccoon (a red pigment used to dye the skin) from the southern piedmont, and pearls (probably from the north) were all important prestige goods in the Powhatan and Conoy paramountcies (see Figure 7.3).

The scale of the prestige goods network (PGN) was not uniform regarding different luxury goods. Some of the copper came from the Great Lakes, while shells and shell beads came from the Eastern Shore. There are important questions regarding the form and institutional nature of exchange in this system. Obviously copper merchants were not traveling from Lake Superior to the Chesapeake to sell their wares. Copper must have been traded down the line, passing from group to group. And all the other goods could have also been traded in this manner in the absence of long-distance trading missions. But Rountree (1993b) contends that traders and travelers did make long journeys, and she cites accounts from the historical period about institutions of hospitality for travelers. Of course, the transportation situation changed greatly with the arrival of horses in the historic period, so these instances may not accurately reflect the prehistoric situation. The rather high level of warfare in this region (see below) would have made long-distance trade journeys quite risky.

Regarding the institutional nature of exchange, we know that paramount chiefs accumulated some

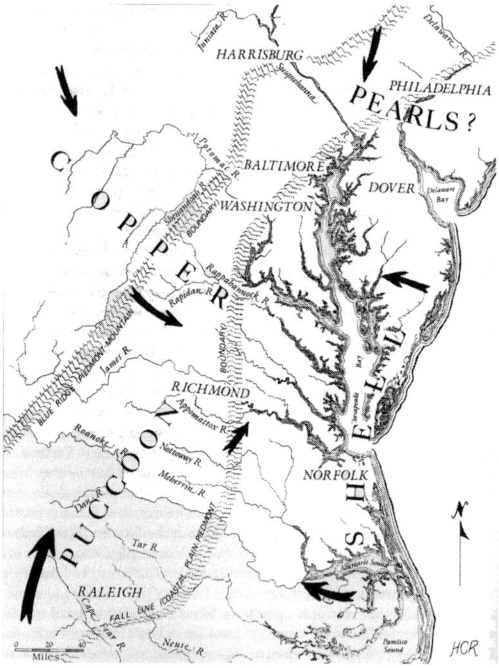

Figure 7.3 Luxury goods entering the Chesapeake in 1608
Source: Rountree 1993a, 221.
© University of Virginia Press.

luxury goods and maize as tribute and that gifts were given in order to secure military alliances among chiefdoms. There is little discussion of the existence of standardized media of exchange (money), and yet shell beads and copper were used to purchase goods. Apparently most of the disk-shaped shell bead strings used in trade, called "roanoke," were manufactured at Cuscarawaoke, a village on the Eastern Shore that was outside the Powhatan realm (E. R. Turner 1993, 83). The roanoke was taken on trade missions and used to purchase other goods. But was it a standardized medium such that rates of exchange (prices) were known and important features of trade? Davidson says, "Smith and other early English visitors to the Chesapeake region considered roanoke and peak to be types of Indian 'money,' and these beads were commonly used as currency by both the Indians and the English later in the seventeenth century" (1993, 145).

Another question is who the traders were. In many stateless world-systems only chiefs engaged in trade. But there seem to have been instances in the early historic Chesapeake in which commoners engaged in trade with the English, and so commoners may have engaged in certain kinds of trade in the prehistoric indigenous system.

The Political-Military Network

The political-military network (PMN) was an interchiefdom system in which each small chiefdom held a fixed territory with known boundaries. The best succinct description comes from Potter (1993, 179):

> In 1607, the year the English built James Fort in Virginia, relationships between Indian groups in the Chesapeake Bay region consisted of a complex web of trade and military alliances, raids and warfare. . . . To the north were the Susquehannocks who lived along the lower Susquehanna River in Lancaster County, Pennsylvania, but claimed as their territory the entire Susquehanna Valley and vast areas on either side of the Chesapeake Bay. . . . Susquehannock raiding parties were striking Algonquian villages along the Patuxent and Potomac Rivers. Somewhere northwest of the Susquehannocks were their "mortall enimies," the Massawomecks, who were busy trading with some Eastern Shore groups in the Tangier Sound region while attacking the Susquehannocks, the Tockwoghs and other Indian groups near the head of Chesapeake Bay, the Algonquians of the Patuxent and Potomac rivers, and the Mannahoacs of north-central piedmont Virginia. The Mannahoacs and their piedmont confederates, the Monacans, warred with and sometimes traded with the Algonquians living near the fall line from north of the Rappahanock River to the James River. . . . South of the tidal Rappahannock was the heartland of the Powhatan's paramount chiefdom, concentrated along the tidal York and James rivers. Most of the tidewater Algonquians living along the Rappahannock River and the south shore of the Potomac River were part of Powhatan's "ethnic fringe." . . . But two of the groups with territories on the Potomac's south shore, the Patawomekes and Tauxenents, probably were not within the Powhatan fold.

Figure 7.4 depicts the nature of political-military and trade relations in the Chesapeake region from the perspective of the Powhatan paramountcy.

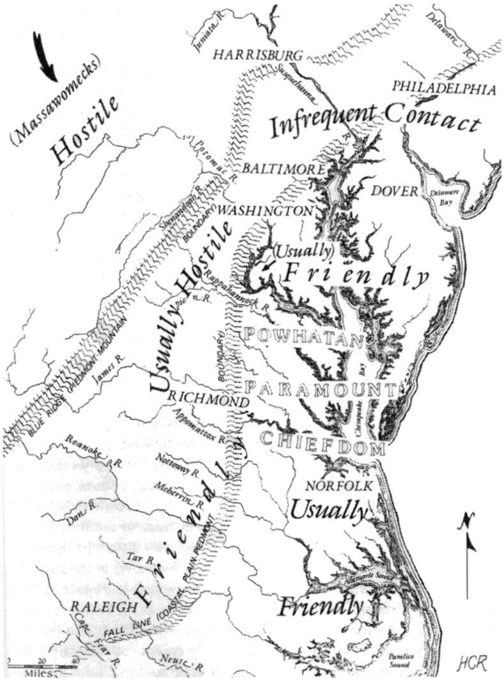

Figure 7.4 Political-military and trade relations of the Powhatans circa 1608

Source: Rountree 1993c, 214.

Figure 7.5 Theodor de Bry's 1585 engraving of Secoton, North Carolina. The Virginia Algonquian villages are thought to have been quite similar.

Source: Wikipedia Commons.

The settlement system was composed of small hamlets that surrounded larger villages. The largest villages were distinguished by the residence of a chief and usually had a nearby mortuary/storehouse temple. Villages varied in size from two to fifty houses, with from six to twenty residents in each house (Potter 1993, 23, 27). Most of the villages had houses and other features spread over a large area of the sort illustrated in Figure 7.5.

On the other hand, there were also palisaded villages in which the houses and other features were crowded close together and enclosed in a defensive wall of stakes set into the ground (see Figure 7.6). These palisaded villages were a recent development, and they tended to be either important political centers containing chiefs' houses and temple/mortuaries or else to be located along conflictive territorial boundaries.

Some of the polities had not yet adopted chiefdom-level organization. The Chickahominies, near the heartland of the Powhatan paramountcy, were governed by a council of elders and refused to accept a chief appointed by Powhatan (Potter 1993, 170).

Beyond the matrilineal inheritance of chiefships, not much is known about Chesapeake Algonquin kinship. This is unfortunate because chiefdom formation is a process of reorganizing kin relations to create social classes and to delineate claims to social authority based on hierarchized kinship. Kinship can facilitate or undercut the power of leaders depending on how it is structured, and it would be nice to know more about how the different Algonquian speakers reckoned blood relations.

Potter (1993, 211–213) contends that mortuary customs for deceased chiefs and priests were quite different from those for commoners. He also quotes John Smith about Algonquian beliefs regarding the afterlife. Chiefs and priests go beyond the mountains and the setting sun and dance and sing forever. And Smith says, "But the common people they suppose shall not live after death" (quoted in Potter 1993, 213). This implies a rather radical differentiation between the chiefly class and the commoners, though it is unknown whether the commoners also held these same beliefs. An additional element that indicates a

Figure 7.6 North Carolina Algonquian palisaded village similar to those known historically and archaeologically on the Chesapeake. Painting by John White, 1585.
Source: Wikipedia Commons.

substantial degree of inequality in Chesapeake societies is the institution of polygyny (a man has more than one wife). Many egalitarian societies have polygyny in which the headman has more than one wife, perhaps two or three or four. Chief Powhatan reportedly had over a hundred wives (Potter 1993, 17).

And yet Rountree (1993a, 7–13) argues strongly that the power of the paramount chief was greatly limited with regard to control over the actions and attitudes of commoners and district chiefs within the paramountcy. She gives many examples that illustrate a good degree of autonomy from the will of the paramount. It would also appear that authority was largely charismatic rather than bureaucratic.[6] Opechanecough, a younger brother of Powhatan, was the effective leader for many years after Powhatan died, despite that his older brother Opitchapam officially held the position of paramount (Potter 1993, 185).

A key question for class formation is the control of necessary resources such as land, water, mines, fishing places, hunting grounds, and so forth. In complex chiefdoms with severe class structures (e.g., Hawaii), the commoners have been separated from legitimate claims over necessaries and must rely on chiefs. In simple chiefdoms the chiefly class often tries to legitimate the accumulation of surplus product from commoners by monopolizing the importation of symbolic goods held necessary for social reproduction, marriage, and so forth, or by promoting an ideology in which the chiefs ritually intervene with powerful forces of the universe. It is most likely that the Algonquian chiefdoms were of the latter sort.

So two rather large paramountcies, the Powhatan and the Conoy, were surrounded mainly by rather more autonomous district chiefdoms and less hierarchical polities (see Figure 7.7). According to Hantman (1993), both the Monacans and the Mannahoacs had multidistrict polities in which several districts paid tribute to one. Clark and Rountree (1993) describe the organizational differences between the more centralized Conoy paramountcy and the confederation of district chiefdoms on the Patuxent River. According to Potter, "The people of the chiefdoms were more sedentary than their more egalitarian neighbors and the settlements were usually smaller, but there were more of them and they were closer together" (1993, 170).

The Souixan-speaking Monacans and Mannahoacs in the piedmont to the west of the Powhatan were traditional enemies, and a wide uninhabited buffer zone separated the Algonquians from the Souixans. Hantman (1993) has shown that the Monacans and Mannahoacs were maize agriculturalists who probably inhabited large villages and had multivillage polities. They were not nomadic hunter-gatherers as had been earlier surmised.

Thus, there was no radical core/periphery differentiation between the valley people and the

[6] Charismatic authority is generated by the inspiring personality of the leader, whereas bureaucratic authority is a feature of the leadership position rather than of the personality of the leader.

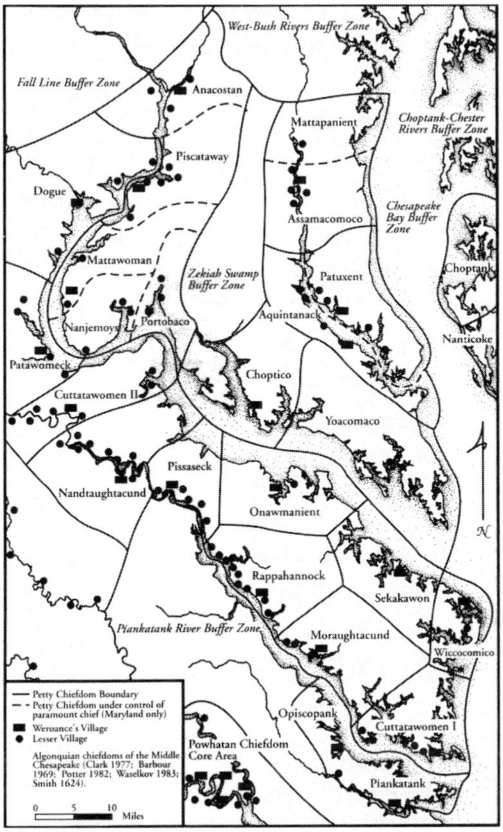

Figure 7.7 Map of Maryland and Northern Virginia Algonquians showing estimated chiefdom boundaries

Source: Rountree 1993a, 114.

hill people in the seventeenth century. There were also smaller uninhabited buffer zones between the districts of Algonquian speakers.

Anthropologists have disputed whether these uninhabited zones were neutral deer parks (E. R. Turner 1978) or were no-man's-lands (buffer zones) between conflicting groups (Mouer 1986). Based on the reports of Smith's reconnaissance, it is agreed that the entire northwestern portion of the Chesapeake Bay, including the Magothy, Patapsco, and Bush Rivers, was uninhabited in 1608. Smith's map indicates by the mark of a cross that he ascended the Patapsco River (which he named the "Bolus") past what is now Baltimore, and he reported seeing no indigenes or villages in this area. Both archaeologists and ethnohistorians contend that the northwest Chesapeake was a large buffer zone that was abandoned in about 1500, probably by Algonquian speakers who were escaping the predations of invading Iroquoians (Susquehannocks and Massawomecks) from the west and north.

All scholars agree that the Chesapeake system before the arrival of the Europeans was already experiencing a rather high level of warfare. Potter (1993, 147) contends that warfare had increased after 1400 and became endemic after 1500. Most observers also point out that the level of warfare among indigenous groups increased to an even higher level with the arrival of the Europeans as groups contended against one another to control the influx of trade goods and to make alliances with different European factions. But the indigenous system was already quite warlike. We have mentioned the existence of buffer zones, depopulated regions, and palisaded villages. Another indicator is the institution of the *huskenaw*, a warrior initiation rite for adolescent boys (except priests) who were trained to endure torture and to fight. The institutional channeling and intensification of aggressive male identity is a known aspect of societal adaptation to high levels of warfare.

Regarding the spatial scale of the Powhatan PMN, we generally surmise that important political-military interaction ranges include two or, at most, three indirect interactions. The direct interactions displayed in Figure 7.4 do not extend beyond the Blue Ridge Mountains to the west, or above the Susquehanna River to the north. But to the northwest, we have the mysterious Massawomeck. Much ink has been used on the question of the identity and homeland of these raiders and traders who came into the Chesapeake in birchbark canoes. In a most thorough review of the evidence, Pendergast (1991) concludes that the Massawomeck were a contingent of the Iroquois confederation who originally inhabited the Niagara River valley near Lake Erie and who moved south in protohistoric times driven by indigenous conflict and the desire to control European trade goods. Pendergast has the later Massawomeck homeland at the headwaters of the Potomac River or thereabouts.

It is not clear whether the long-distance movements of the Massawomecks should be considered a typical feature of the indigenous PMN, or to what extent these journeys were stimulated by the arrival of the French in the St. Lawrence Valley. The literature on incorporation into the modern world-system and incorporation processes in earlier systems shows that when a state-based system begins to engulf a stateless one, the amount of warfare in the "tribal zone" goes up (Ferguson and Whitehead 1992).

Potter (1993) casts doubt on Pendergast's claim that the Massawomeck were motivated to move into the Chesapeake because of a desire to control access to European goods. Potter does not find archaeological evidence of European goods in the protohistoric Chesapeake. But information does not show up in the archaeological record. The Chesapeake Bay appears on a Spanish map as early as 1527. It is not impossible that knowledge of European contact in the Chesapeake could have been a factor in the Massawomeck forays, but we agree with Potter that it is unlikely. If the Massawomeck were run out of Lake Erie by losing a struggle on Lake Erie and descended into the Chesapeake because of this, this would be an instance of one world-system impinging on another, but not an example of regularized interaction. We think the best guess about the Powhatan PMN's spatial extent is about a 300-mile (455-kilometer) radius from the Virginia tidewater.

Ethnogeography

Information networks (INs) and the cosmography[7] of peoples are important for understanding what is going on in any world-system. Information can flow across cultural and linguistic boundaries, and it may or may not accompany trade goods. Information falloff is usually rather rapid in a trade network organized as down-the-line trade. And in a situation of endemic warfare we can imagine not only barriers to information flows but also the probability of disinformation. In a geopolitically complex situation, actors may want to represent themselves as allies by telling lies about their relations with other players. John Smith did this when he traded with the Massawomeck and then displayed the received goods as prizes taken in battle to the Chesapeake Algonquians. This tactic may have also been employed in indigenous "diplomacy."

Regarding cosmography (ethnogeography), Helen Rountree (1993b) has argued that Chesapeake indigenes probably knew more about distant places than they were letting on to the Europeans. John Smith's map portrays a saltwater sea beyond the Blue Ridge Mountains on the shores of which are the four villages of the Massawomeck. Was this a misunderstanding spurred by English wishful thinking regarding the "northwest passage" to the Orient, or was Powhatan really quite ignorant about the territory beyond the mountains? Smith also reports that the Tockwoghs, Algonquian speakers at the north end of the Chesapeake, had little knowledge of the Powhatan at the south end of the bay. If this were so, the scale of the IN would be less than two hundred miles, at least in the north-south direction. Rountree (1993b, 22) reports that one Tockwogh spoke the Powhatan dialect, but her map (Rountree 1993c, 214) designates Powhatan relations with the north end of the bay in terms of "infrequent relations" (see Figure 7.4).

Chesapeake Core/ Periphery Relations

Were there core/periphery relations in the Chesapeake system? The comparative world-systems approach treats the issue of core/periphery structures as a question for research in each case. Earlier research has shown that state-based systems all have core/periphery structures, and very egalitarian systems of sedentary foragers have only mild ones (e.g., Chase-Dunn and Mann 1998). This makes world-systems composed of chiefdoms important, because it was in these that core/periphery relations first emerged and became important in processes of uneven development and institutional evolution.

Recall that there are two analytically separable aspects of core/periphery relations. The first, core/periphery differentiation, refers to a situation in which societies at different levels of complexity and internal hierarchy are interacting regularly and importantly with one another. The second, core/periphery hierarchy, refers to a situation in which one or more societies are exploiting and/or dominating other societies.

[7] Cosmography is geography in the heads of the actors—their consciousness about near and distant locations.

In practice, core/periphery differentiation usually involves not only differences in complexity and hierarchy but also differences in population density and modes of subsistence. In the Chesapeake in 1608, paramount chiefdoms were interacting with simple chiefdoms and with more egalitarian tribal societies. There were also important differences in the size and concentration of settlements that were probably related to important differences in social organization. Potter (1993) describes a somewhat unusual situation in which core areas with chiefdoms had slightly smaller villages that were closer together, while noncore neighbors had larger villages that were more spaced out.

The most relevant overview of the entire range of organizational diversity is Custer's (1994) survey of the Mid-Atlantic Region, which includes the Chesapeake as well as the Delaware and Susquehanna Rivers. Custer notes that the Lenape on the Delaware River never adopted maize planting and they remained at a band level of organization until European contact. These were the last foragers in the region. But other groups differed greatly in the extent to which they had become involved in maize planting. The Munsee were planting maize, but it was not a large component of their mode of subsistence. Custer makes several important distinctions regarding the continua of complexity and hierarchy. He distinguishes between bands and tribes. Tribes have pan-tribal sodalities, meaning kinship or other organizational categories that extend beyond the local group. Custer mentions age grades, clans, lineages, and secret societies. Bands do not have these features of intergroup social structure. Custer also distinguished two different kinds of tribes: cognatic and lineal.

Cognatic tribes have intergroup relations, but these are weak and do not promote intergroup economic cooperation. Segmental tribes have kinship structures that sustain obligations among kin groups when growing villages hive off—when a group leaves to found a new village. The lineage or clan then remains an important family tie in an intervillage cooperation network. Custer (1994) points out that this segmented tribal organization is most likely to develop in coarse-grained ecological situations that encourage exchange among different groups because of access to different kinds of natural resources. Custer contends that segmented lineage tribes are indicated in the archaeological record by longhouses in which extended families reside, whereas the people of cognatic tribes are more likely to live in smaller dwellings, each housing a nuclear family.

One key advantage in a system in which warfare is an important institutional form of competition is population density, because the ability to concentrate a greater number of warriors is crucial in a confrontation. Most of the groups living around the Chesapeake had adopted horticulture in the Late Woodland period, so there was not an important core/periphery differentiation based on interactions between farmers and foragers. But there were major differences among groups with regard to the degree of internal hierarchy and the nature of central authority. This was the important basis of core/periphery differentiation in the Chesapeake system.

Randolph Turner contends that the core area of the Powhatan paramountcy was the population-dense territory of the Pamunkey chiefdom (at the confluence of the Pamunkey and Mattoponi branches of the York River). The Pamunkey had a long-standing rivalry with the Chickahominies, also a powerful and population-dense core polity (see Figure 7.7). This rivalry and the strategic importance of the home district of Powhatan at the James River fall line, with regard to trade routes and protection from the piedmont Souixans, led to the formation of an alliance between Powhatan and Pamunkey that was the basis of the Powhatan expansion (E. R. Turner 1993, 86, 90–92).

If Turner is right, this sounds like an instance of semiperipheral development. Polities from semiperipheral regions are often able to take over older cores and to implement changes in the scale of polities and institutional structures, as we saw above. Semiperipheral marcher chiefdoms are known from Polynesia (Kirch 1984, 199–202), as we shall see below. The rise phase of the cycle is usually due to the action of semiperipheral chiefly polities, and the Powhatans were another example of this.

The most obvious instance of core/periphery hierarchy in the Chesapeake was the tribute extraction by paramount chiefs from local districts. This was core/periphery exploitation and unequal exchange. Most Powhatan scholars are quick to point out that it is a mistake to characterize the tribute system as "redistribution," because very little was redistributed to the original contributors. But as Davidson (1993) points out, it is often difficult to distinguish tribute-paying from exchange in interchiefdom systems. The contemporary accounts of corn and shell beads being brought in canoes from the Eastern Shore as tribute to Powhatan may not have represented exploitation if an equal value of goods was being returned. Davidson contends that this "tribute" was simply the continuation of a long tradition of east-west exchange across the bay. He supposes that the chiefdoms of the Eastern Shore would have been difficult for Powhatan to exploit because of the difficulties of projecting coercion so far.

There are a number of considerations here. Unequal exchange can take place in the absence of direct coercion if peripheral agents can be induced to exercise their own coercion over others in order to obtain core goods. An example is the slave trade in the Pacific Northwest discussed in the Web Chapter. It is possible that Eastern Shore chiefs were so desirous of copper or puccoon supplied by Powhatan that they were willing to extract beads and/or corn from their own people in order to obtain these valuables. It is also possible that Davidson is wrong about the spatial extent of the power capabilities of Powhatan. Canoes full of warriors may have been quite capable of threatening villages across the bay, as the example of the Susquehannocks in the northern bay demonstrates.

Davidson (1993) also points out that the Conoy paramountcy had similar relations with Eastern Shore groups north of those that were linked with Powhatan. This case is also problematic with regard to the question of core/periphery hierarchy. In 1660 the brother of the Piscataway *tayac* (paramount) testified that thirteen reigns earlier, a chief from the Eastern Shore whose name was Uttapoingassinem had led the Conoy (Potter 1993, 132). How could a peripheral chief become the paramount of a core group? The most likely scenario is that an important Conoy chiefess married an Eastern Shore chief and he moved to the Western Shore and rose to the top. If this is what happened, it would support the hypothesis of Davidson that the east-west interaction was between societies of approximately equal power.

It is likely that most core/periphery exploitation and domination was rather local in the Chesapeake system. The paramountcies did not sufficiently control trade valuables or produce great quantities of surplus food to make unequal exchange with distant regions possible. Nor were they able to project military power very far. Despite a rather high level of warfare among different groups, there were no conquest-based polities that were very large. The Powhatan expansion had probably gone about as far as it could go.

Mississippian Complex Chiefdoms

After 900 CE a new interaction sphere that archaeologists call Mississippian emerged along the central rivers of the North American mid-continent. This much more hierarchical cultural complex involved rituals that symbolized the sacredness of certain lineages and an important regional economy in which prestige goods were traded over long distances. Several large centers were established, usually at sites that were important for the regional and interregional trade networks.

Large urban centers at Cahokia (East St. Louis), Moundville in Alabama, and Spiro in Oklahoma were important controllers of long-distance trade and builders of large-scale monumental complexes. These were complex chiefdoms or early states. As with early states elsewhere, the death of a king was the occasion for the sacrifice of a large retinue to accompany him to the afterlife. The riverine locations of these centers were a function of the importance of large-scale maize agriculture and the control of long-distance trade (Peregrine 1995). Mississippian culture emerged about 900 CE. By 1200 Cahokia had collapsed, but other Mississippian centers, especially Moundville, continued to thrive until the fourteenth century. The Mississippian cultural complex spread to the Southeast. In the Savannah River valley, local chiefdoms emerged using the religious symbols of the Mississippian civilization (D. Anderson 1994).

By the twelfth century, a complex chiefdom (or early state) had emerged at Cahokia (Pauketat 2009). Cahokia was located on the Mississippi River near its confluence with the Missouri River near what is now East St. Louis. It was the preeminent center of what Peter Peregrine (1992) has called the Mississippian world-system. The population size of Cahokia proper was probably about 10,000, whereas the American Bottom—the region immediately surrounding Cahokia—probably held a population of about 40,000.

Whether the polity at Cahokia should be called a complex chiefdom or an early state is a matter that is in dispute. O'Brien (1992) characterizes the polity at Cahokia as the "Ramey state," and she reports that one of the excavated burial mounds contained the remains of seventy young women who were apparently sacrificed in a single ceremony in connection with the death of a sacred chief. This scale of ritual violence indicates a rather hierarchical system, but we have no way of knowing whether specialized non-kin-based institutions of regional control existed at Cahokia. Military specialists and a bureaucracy dedicated to regional control are the important organizational features that distinguish between a complex chiefdom and a state, according to the definition employed by Johnson and Earle (1987). But, whether or not these existed at Cahokia, it was a large, impressive, and quite hierarchical polity.

There were other large centers in the Mississippian system, especially Moundville (on the Black Warrior River in Alabama) and Spiro (Oklahoma). And there were hundreds of smaller chiefdoms that utilized the cultural equipment that is identified as Mississippian. Cahokia declined well before the arrival of the Europeans, but the remnants of its hierarchical kinship system were observed by European explorers in the institutions of the Natchez Indians, who continued to commemorate the death of a sacred chief by ritually sacrificing his family and friends. David Anderson's (1994) archaeological study of Mississippian chiefdoms in the Savannah River valley is a valuable contribution to our knowledge of how the system worked far from the large centers. His evidence shows that the cycle of the rise and fall of chiefdoms occurred in the periphery as well as in the core.

Many issues about the nature of the Mississippian system are unresolved. Peter Peregrine (1992, 1995) strongly contends that the prestige goods system model explains the rise and fall of the Mississippian system. Stephen Kowalewski (1996) argues that prestige goods are essentially symbols of power and that they do not work as mechanisms for controlling social labor in the absence of other, more compelling types of power. Kowalewski also contends that warfare was an important part of the dynamics of rise and fall in the Mississippian system. We will present insightful quotations from both of these authors. Peregrine (1995, 41) says:

> The lineage-focused social organization apparent in Late Woodland settlement patterns may have fostered competition between lineage heads and encouraged further social changes that increased their control over flows of prestige-goods. It is difficult, given the inadequacies of available data, to precisely describe the changes that took place, but I hypothesize that they may have included the development of sumptuary rules restricting consumption of higher-order goods to elders, new mechanisms of labor control for the manufacture and transportation of prestige-goods, and perhaps new forms of political structure or alliance for solidifying the control of trade routes (Peregrine 1991, 1992).
>
> These social transformations set the stage for a re-emergence of higher-level political leaders in the Early Mississippian period, and intensification of production necessary to sustain these emergent leaders followed. In prestige-good systems individuals find it necessary to support local (usually lineage) leaders, for they control the goods needed to fulfill social obligations and to maintain an adequate standard of living. The basic idea here is that individuals would have intensified production to support their local leaders in competitive exchanges of prestige-goods so that they would have had better access to these goods, and hence a better opportunity to socially reproduce themselves at acceptable levels. . . .
>
> As leaders competed for goods in the emergent Mississippian prestige-good system, those located at nodal points on trade routes, and who had a supportive population, may have been able to control those routes and the goods flowing through them (Peregrine 1991). Population would have been attracted to leaders who offered greater access to prestige-goods, and hence better opportunities to socially re-

produce (Friedman and Rowlands 1977). In this way social stratification, maize horticulture, and political centers with dense populations could have readily emerged in the central riverine valleys of the mid-continent, where riverine trade could be controlled, and where intensified production was possible.

Stephen Kowalewski's (1996, 30–31) critique of the idea of a prestige goods system goes as follows:

> Long-distance symbolic interaction can operate to transfer value from one point to another. In aboriginal North America, a returned pilgrim, a vision quester, one who acquires a new dance, or one who owns the rights to display a crest could acquire some prestige, power, or wealth useful in internal competition and perhaps useful for external recognition. Symbolic objects convey information about the social relations of givers and receivers. As symbols the stuff is completely arbitrary, except that items should be rare, light, exotic, or crafted. Here we can think of gold in the Old World, or copper bells, crests, or breastplates in North America; and as Mary Helms (1988) has shown, knowledge itself may be a prestige good.
>
> The informational value of a symbol, what specifically a symbol represents, or what other value it may be translated into, may not necessarily be mutually recognized by all parties in exchange. All that may be required is that the parties understand that the symbol is valuable in some way. It is not true that symbolic items will carry the same meanings within or between social groups across space. . . . The point is that biscuit, beads, copper, or other such preciosities in prestige goods exchange have values so arbitrary that they must be continually reaffirmed by something else, which in my opinion is power. In cross-cultural communication and generally in symbolic interaction, the parties to interchange have differing or contested values and interpretations, ultimately decided in the arena of power.

Both Kowalewski and Peregrine agree that power must necessarily stand behind prestige goods. Kowalewski's critique seems to assume that the prestige goods system theory requires that prestige goods operate in the absence of other sorts of power, either internally or across group boundaries. But what is claimed is that control over prestige imports can facilitate the rise to power of a local elite. Jonathan Friedman (1982) also argues that loss of control over prestige goods trade can cause stratified hierarchies based on this control to fall. The question of prestige goods being important in relations among different polities has not been addressed at a general level, but on this most scholars would probably agree that symbolic exchanges or ritual hierarchies are not likely to sustain domination or exploitation of one society by another in the absence of other forms of power such as military force or the monopoly of the supply of some more basic good such as food or raw materials needed for the everyday life of most members of the society. Ritual hierarchies are easily overturned if they are not backed up by something else.

What about core/periphery relations in the Mississippian system? It is unclear how far the powers of large centers like Cahokia and Moundville extended, and what means they used to draw resources from distant hinterlands. Kowalewski mentioned the importance of warfare in the Mississippian system, but this was thought to be primarily a matter of conflict among neighboring chiefdoms. No one has portrayed Cahokia or Moundville as the center of military empires of the sort that the Aztecs constructed. And, as discussed above, ritual superiority is not a sufficient basis for extracting surpluses from distant societies. It is possible that the Mississippian centers gained from their nodal locations on trade routes and that they exported some goods to distant societies in return for other goods, but most of the exchange in this system would have been reciprocal gift giving among elites of different polities. It is doubtful that true markets existed. And so it is unlikely that a hierarchical division of labor based on unequal exchange extended very far from the direct power of the core chiefdoms.

Dincauze and Hasenstab (1989) have argued that Iroquoian tribe formation—the establishment of matrilineal long houses—was caused by long-distance interaction with the Mississippian centers. This hypothesis was met with derision by the old guard of site-specific archaeologists. The controversy is reviewed by Peregrine and Feinman (1996, 41–43), who, despite his call for examining the patterns of large macroregions, finds that there are timing problems with the hypothesis that interaction with Mississippian centers caused Iroquoian development. It is likely that information flows and some trade goods did connect these distant regions. But were these connections strong enough to cause important social changes?

This case is different from the Delmarva Adena case (discussed in the Web Chapter) in that the Iroquois did not adopt rituals from the Mississippian core. Certainly, local conditions were important to the emergence of complexity, as they were elsewhere. And synchrony does not prove causality. In this case a somewhat synchronous rise in two distant areas could have occurred because local causes happened to co-occur in time, or as a response to something else entirely, such as climatic change.

The Hawaiian World-System

Precontact Hawaii had become a system of complex chiefdoms or archaic states with large polities and a radical separation between social classes (Kirch 2010). Archaeologists such as Peregrine (1992) and Kristiansen (1987) have studied world-systems containing complex chiefdoms, but it is difficult to determine the existence of core/periphery hierarchies based on archaeological evidence alone. It is better to combine archaeological evidence with ethnographic and documentary evidence. Elena Ermolaeva (1997) has done this for the case of precontact Hawaii. The Hawaiian Islands are easily understood as a whole system because they were relatively isolated from interactions with other areas in the Pacific before the arrival of Captain James Cook in 1778.[8]

The Hawaiian world-system was composed of a set of unevenly powerful chiefly polities that competed with one another for control of territory and labor. The kinship system was composed of conical clans in which each position was uniquely ranked in terms of its degree of seniority or theoretical closeness to the ancestors. Class formation had proceeded to the extent that there was a class of sacred chiefs and a class of commoners who had no kin-based claim to land.

The sacredness of high chiefs was symbolized in a set of ritual taboos. In some cases the shadow of a sacred chief was held to be deadly if it fell upon a commoner, and so these most sacred could not go forth except at night lest they kill their inferiors. Seniority was the product of the most direct link to the founding ancestors, and a sacred chief marrying a sibling could produce the highest possible rank. Thus, brother-sister marriage was legitimate among the senior sacred chiefs, further distinguishing them from their juniors and the commoners.

This system had evolved since ocean-voyaging Polynesians, probably from the Marquesas, first occupied the Hawaiian archipelago as early as the third century CE. The first settlers bore the cultural heritage of their Polynesian ancestors: knowledge of agriculture, sophisticated fishing techniques, boatbuilding, navigation, the principle of hierarchical kinship based on successive primogeniture, and the ideas of *mana* and *kapu* (taboo). Mana represents the powers of the universe as mediated by the sacred chiefs. In the succeeding centuries the Polynesians populated all the islands of the archipelago. We discussed in Chapter 6 how the first immigrants exploited the flocks of flightless geese found on the islands. As the populations grew and the land became inhabited, the Hawaiians developed irrigated and terraced agriculture and artificial coastal fishponds in which great quantities of fish were raised for food.

[8] The isolation of the Hawaiian archipelago before the arrival of the Europeans was an advantage because it reduced the frequency of exogenous impacts, though it did not eliminate them. The fact that the sweet potato somehow got from Peru to the Marquesas and thence to Hawaii made possible the development of dry field agriculture, which raised the human carrying capacity of the Hawaiian environment and provided an important alternative form of intensification of production. It is likely that institutional diffusions from Tahiti had some impact on Hawaiian religion and political organization in the twelfth or thirteenth century CE (but see Spriggs 1988, 68). These examples show that even such an isolated region as the Hawaiian archipelago, thousands of miles across the open ocean from other inhabited islands, was not completely free from exogenous impacts.

When Captain Cook first sighted Oahu and Kauai in 1778, the Hawaiian world-system was composed of four independent chiefdoms: Kauai and Niihau; Oahu and probably Molokai; most of Maui, Lanai, and Kahoolawe; and Hawai'i and part of East Maui (Spriggs 1988, 63–64). Each island was divided into major districts and these were further divided into *ahupua'a*, typically pie-shaped areas including seaside, flat land, and a section of mountainous area. In theory, each *ahupua'a* was self-sufficient because it contained all the necessary ecological zones from which food and raw materials were extracted. Each *ahupua'a* had a local chief, a *konohiki*, who was responsible for collecting and delivering food and other products of the commoners for the provisioning of the higher chiefs. The *konohiki* also acted to maintain the population of his *ahupua'a*. He encouraged marriage within the boundaries of his lands and sought to discourage emigration. The settlement system of the ancient Hawaiians was rather dispersed. Housing was located near fields or fishing places. People did not build houses close together in villages except under rare conditions in which a more dispersed pattern was made difficult by topography. There were big differences in the population densities of different areas, but these were due mainly to the uneven distribution across space of prime sites for agriculture and fishing (Weisler and Kirch 1985).

The interisland density of interaction must have been fairly high at the time of Captain Cook's arrival. Some authors have argued that the wide and dangerous channel between Kauai and Oahu limited interaction between Kauai and the other islands, and we know of historical incidents that support this contention. King Kamehameha was prevented from mounting an expedition of conquest against Kauai because a storm at sea disrupted his war-canoe navy. And yet we know that there were many intermarriages of chiefs from Kauai with chiefs of the other islands. Captain Cook discovered that it took venereal disease less than ten months to travel from Kauai to Maui, a distance of over two hundred nautical miles (Sahlins 1985, 1–3). There must have been fairly frequent interisland interactions for this to occur.

As we reported in Chapter 6, the first Polynesian settlers in the Hawaiian archipelago found a land full of food. For the first few hundred years they derived a large proportion of their protein from the meat of birds, including a species of flightless geese that had no natural predators until the arrival of humans. Hierarchy was probably minimal in these early settler societies as people spread out across the archipelago occupying the prime sites for agriculture, fishing, and birding. As population density increased and all the islands became populated, the ancestral Polynesian cultural script (contained in the principle of successive primogeniture and the ideas of *mana* and *kapu*) was used to fashion a more hierarchical society. Polity sizes grew and class stratification became more extreme.

Kirch (1984, 199–202) presents a simple model of this process of population growth and lineage stratification. The principle of successive primogeniture is organized in Hawaii and Polynesia on the basis of conical clans. Genealogical lines are ranked in terms of closeness to the original ancestor, and each person theoretically has a unique and intransitive position in this system of ranked seniority. In practice, this system operated as a theoretical ideal. Competing claims were settled by force, and genealogies were reconstructed according to the outcomes of struggles among contending chiefs. Nevertheless, the principle of genealogical seniority was an important one in legitimating rule, and this principle evolved, in Hawaii, to include a radical separation between chiefs and commoners, and the practice of brother-sister marriages among sacred chiefs and chiefesses to produce the highest possible seniority for offspring.

The case of Hawaiian chiefdoms illustrates important limitations on stateless efforts to expand redistribution. Hawaiian chiefdoms experienced a cycle of expansion, rebellion, and breaking up suggestive in some broad ways of the rise and fall of empires. Marshall Sahlins (1972, 144–145) describes:

> the tendency, on which traditions discourse at length, for chiefly domains to enlarge and contract, extended once by conquest only to be partitioned again by rebellion. And this cycle was geared to a second, such that the rotation of one would set off the other. Ruling chiefs showed a propensity to "eat the power of government too much"; that is, to oppress the people economically, which the chiefs found

forced to do when the political domain was enlarged, despite their obligations as kinsmen and chiefs to consider the people's welfare, which they nevertheless found it difficult to do even when the polity was reduced. . . . The chieftainship besides enjoyed no monopoly of force. It had to meet its diverse problems of rule organizationally then, by a certain administrative formation; a bloated political establishment that sought to cope with a proliferation of tasks by multiplication of personnel, at the same time as economizing its scarce real force by an awesome display of conspicuous consumption as intimidating to the people as it was glorifying to the chiefs. It fell especially on those nearest the paramount, within a range that made transport worthwhile and the threat of sanctions effective. Conscious, it seems, of the logistic burdens they were obliged to impose, the Hawaiian chiefs conceived several means to relieve the pressure, notably including a career of conquest with a view toward enlarging the tributary base. In the successful event, however, with the realm now stretched over distant and lately subdued hinterlands, the bureaucratic costs of rule apparently rose higher than the increases in revenue, so that the victorious chief merely succeeds in adding enemies abroad to a worse unrest at home.

Patrick Kirch (1984, 199–202) has proposed a model of colonization and development of Polynesian islands in which the original discoverers of an island settle in the most ecologically desirable location and form the most senior lineage (Figure 7.8). As the population grows, junior lineages move to the less desirable locations, and eventually the lineage hierarchy comes to map perfectly with the ecological structure of the island. The most senior lineages occupy the best locations, and the more junior lineages occupy less desirable locations. Polynesian islands are ecologically structured by the prevailing winds that carry moisture to the land. The windward side of the island received more rainfall and hence has more water, vegetation, and better soils than the leeward side. Thus, according to Kirch's model, the most senior lineage should occupy a deep valley with a good river and good agricultural land on the windward side. This model can also be applied to an archipelago such as the Hawaiian Islands, in which Kauai, the geologically oldest island with the best soil and rivers, was occupied earliest and held to most senior lineages.

Kirch (1984, 204) also suggests that the junior chiefs from the less desirable side of the island will have the strongest motive to try to conquer the older districts and to form an island-wide polity. This scenario has been termed one of "semiperipheral marcher chiefdoms" by Chase-Dunn and Hall (1997, Chapter 5). The Kirch model is suggestive of a widely known phenomenon that occurs in state systems in which semiperipheral states on the margins of an old core region are the powers that conquer the core states and form a larger core-wide empire.

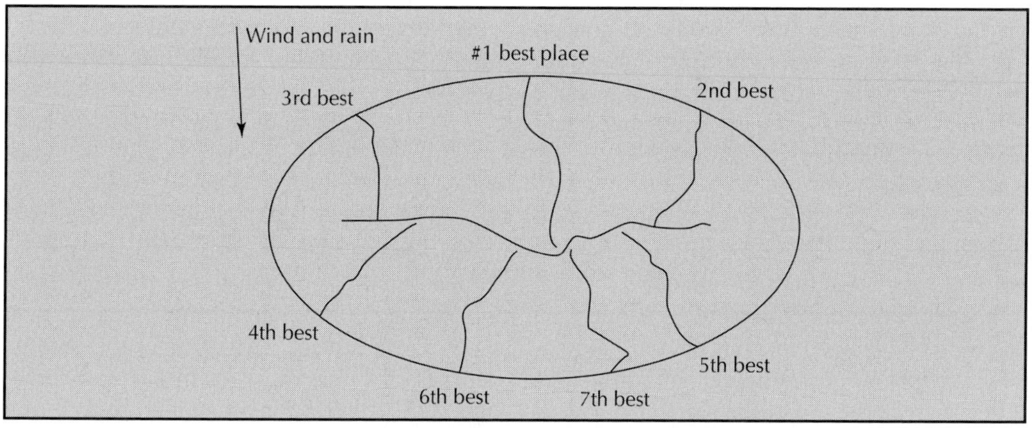

Figure 7.8 Kirch's (1984) model of island settlement

When Kirch's model is applied to the Hawaiian archipelago as a whole, the most desirable islands should have been settled first and should have been the first to experience population pressure. This eventually led to the populating of the less desirable islands. In Hawaii, the best soils, the flattest land, and the most navigable rivers are on the geologically older islands of the northwest—Kauai and Oahu. The Big Island of Hawaii, with still-active volcanoes and steep slopes, would be the last to develop population pressure and island-wide hierarchy formation. Hawaiian traditions assembled by Fornander (1880) support the idea that the island of Kauai was the home of the oldest and most senior chiefly lineages in the archipelago. The prohibition of chiefs marrying commoners was more strictly adhered to on Kauai than on the Big Island, indicating a stronger and older process of class formation. And Kamehameha, the sacred chief who unified the archipelago by conquest, came from the dry Kona district of the Big Island. First Kamehameha conquered the more senior districts on the windward side of the Big Island, and then he conquered all the islands of the archipelago. This fits the Kirch model nicely.

Gender Relations in Complex Chiefdoms

In her study on chiefdoms in the Tongan Islands, Christine Ward Gailey (1987) describes gender relations there as "ambiguous" rather than coerced. This means that the primary access to resources, power, prestige, influence, and privileges was never based solely on gender. Age, life experiences, rank, position within the descent group, skill in labor, and the value of products were also factored into who had power, privilege, prestige, and influence in any particular situation.

According to Gailey (1987), there was a multidimensional context for determining who was entitled to what they got and when they got it. Many of these dimensions of social life were controlled by females. Within the kin group as a whole, no one had unlimited authority, even if they were at the top of the hierarchy; and no one at the bottom was ever devoid of power and privilege in every situation. The variation in entitlements based on different contexts acted as a system of checks and balances. Kinship relations involved reciprocal support and obligations throughout the lifespan of all people related to each other through birth and marriage.

This did not mean that rights and privileges were equally shared. Rights and obligations were graded. Overall, chiefly groups had it best, followed by district managers and then commoners. Since chiefs and district managers were males, these men had more power and privilege than anyone else. Yet, chiefly power was limited. The chiefly group allocated land and resources to commoners, but the chiefs really could not refuse to do this. The process was a formality. The chief could not deny access to resources to commoners or confiscate their products with no promise of reciprocity. Chiefs had to produce something in return—prosperity, fertility, assurance, and protection.

All women, whether members of the chiefly kin group or not, were active in the public domain, and most work could be done by either sex. Commoners had hereditary use-rights to land. They did the bulk of the fishing, horticulture, and craft production. Male commoners worked on canoes and weapons, while women made carrying devices and storage containers, spun, wove, and made pottery.

Ultimate political and economic power originated from a structural role—the chief—which women never filled. And the male chief had differential access to the labor and products of all men and women. Despite the overall power of chiefs, in some local contexts women had more power than men. This made women's relationship to power and privilege ambiguous and diffused, rather than diminished equally in all dimensions of society.

What exactly do we mean by "social standing"? Within the village, there was still the problem of determining the value of the product in terms of reciprocal obligations. The value of a product produced by a woman was determined by the many dimensions of that woman's social standing, not just by the amount of labor necessary to produce the artifact. The status of the product depends on the occasion for which it is produced, how old the product is before it is received, and the rank of the person receiving it. Objectively speaking, the whole process of production and consumption under chiefdoms is inseparable from the sacred intention of building up group solidarity through developing the social personhood in each member. This means that at all stages of the laboring process, the participants know where the product is going and for whom it is destined. They also reexperience the fruits of their labor in the coming ceremony, whether what they produced was a craft or food for the ceremony.

Which products and processes of work were held in highest prestige? In an absolute sense, women's labor was more highly valued than men's labor because it was sacred. The men did the most demanding physical work and also the most menial tasks. What they produced were provisions for their society. For a man not to work was a sign of prestige because work was associated with the profane, mundane world. Work for men had little status. The products of all women, nonchiefly as well as chiefly, were considered special and used for sacred ceremonies—mats and sacred hangings for harvest festivals, rites of passage, and other special occasions. Chiefly women's products were the most sacred of all.

Women's labor was of the utmost value because it was a magical extension of her powers as a procreator. Women's production as workers was probably thought of as an extension of their production of babies. A woman must have been treated as if she were a goose that laid golden eggs. This was especially true of chiefly women, because without their production, the whole chiefly group would lose its legitimacy as a guarantor of fertility and the continuity of the whole society.

Let us examine how these "checks and balances" might work in favor of women. The male chief's power to demand more production was countered and tempered by the higher prestige of women's products. There were many other ambiguities in the status system. Which was more valuable, the product of a nonchiefly woman or that of a male member of the chiefly kin group? The answer is complex. The male member of the chiefly group had higher political status, but a woman's labor had higher status even if she were nonchiefly. This high status of women's labor would have kept male dominance in check. The relations of power between the sexes were no doubt tension filled and conflicted. There would, however, have been no tension between the product of a chiefly woman and that of a nonchiefly man; the woman's product would have been superior.

In Gailey's study, there was tension between a woman's role as a wife and her role as a sister. As a wife, she had to defer to her husband; as a sister, she had authority over her brother. So if a nonchiefly man married a chiefly woman, the woman's inferior status as a wife would have been countered by her superior position as a sister of a chiefly-class man. What she lost in one obligatory context she gained in another. Further, women were not economically dependent on men. The woman's status as a sister within her kin group guaranteed her subsistence rights.

Sometimes these crosscutting cleavages could work against women. We noted earlier that, in an absolute sense, the products of a chiefly woman were valued more highly than those of a nonchiefly man. But this could be an ambiguous power relation if the man was older, had more skill in what he made, or was producing for someone special and for an especially important occasion. So under extreme circumstances, a man's product could have more status than a woman's product.

How did these ambiguities play out in sexual expectations? In this domain, ambiguities existed not only between men and women but between women of different ranks. Prior to marriage, nonchiefly women could do as they pleased sexually, while chiefly women were closely watched. However, nonchiefly women were in danger of being raped, with no kin reprisal. The rape of a chiefly woman, on the other hand, would probably have meant death for the rapist. In fact, the kin group of a nonchiefly rapist might kill the man themselves to avoid the reprisals that would otherwise have been visited on them. Male chiefs had to attract women; they could not bully them into sexual engagements.

Among chiefly people there were other ambiguities. While male chiefs could have more than one spouse, chiefly women had to be formally monogamous. Once married, however, chiefly women often had affairs. Further, chiefly women also had control over secondary wives, and this could make the former's lives much easier.

On the whole, as long as population pressure and resource depletion were relatively stable in complex horticultural societies, institutionalized male dominance was tempered by crosscutting sets of rights and obligations.

The Self in Chiefdoms

Before the Late Iron Age all societies were overwhelmingly collectivist. Yet the leaders of these societies must have had elements of individualist selves growing, however weak. These would include headmen or shamans in foraging societies, and big men and chiefs in horticultural societies. We begin this discussion with chiefs as incipient individualist selves because these incipient individualist tendencies are great enough to merit commentary.

Broadly speaking, complex horticultural societies are a transition between horizontal and vertical collectivism. They are more vertically collectivist because there are definite rank or class differences and greater respect for the authority of the chief than egalitarian societies had for their leaders.

There is less social mobility, which means people are more likely to accept role-taking and routine situations as ways of life. There must have been the beginnings of a conflict of inner dialogue, not so much between an individual "I" and a "Me" (meaning what others expect) but between the interest of their group—commoners or administrators—and society as a whole.

What is more important is to locate the group that is most likely to develop an incipient individualism within these collectivist tendencies. That group would be the chiefly lineage and, more specifically, the chief. Chiefdoms are a somewhat specialized society but not to the degree that states are. Yet there is enough of a division of labor for the chief to work at activities that no other group engages in. At the same time, he must have been aware of his differences from the commoners and the district managers in terms of power and privileges. At the same time, the other factors that promote individualism that we identified in Table 4.3 in Chapter 4 are not operating.

Chiefdoms are usually land-based societies engaging in horticulture. There are no cities, and there is certainly a strong ideology of collectivism. Lastly, while the chief may see his role as different from other social groups, the chief does not imagine himself as standing against his lineage and against society as a whole the way, say, the Buddha or Confucius might in the Late Iron Age.

The Economic and Political Foundations of Sacred Traditions

How do the politics and economics of a society affect the sacred life of a people? As institutional materialists we see a very interesting relationship between the amount of inequality within a society and the degree of distance and amount of power a sacred power has over the human species (Lerro 2000). As Emile Durkheim (1915) contended, the characteristics of the sacred presences generally follow the form of social organization of a society.

For example, in egalitarian societies sacred spirits are mostly animalistic, earthly (as opposed to transcendental), and provincial (rather than cosmopolitan). Further, most sacred experience is unmediated by a specialist and is democratically accessible to everyone. We believe this is because of the material characteristics of hunting-and-gathering life—mobile, here-now, localistic, and relatively unspecialized.

As societies become more sedentary, occupy more or less permanent territories, the sacred powers of these societies are no longer mobile and diffuse but occupy provinces and have domains of power. Whereas in egalitarian societies the spirits of the earth are interdependent on humanity, as societies become more stratified the gods and goddesses become more independent of humanity.

In the case of chiefdoms, the ancestor spirits and totem animals and plants acquire more power than humanity. Whereas in egalitarian societies magical activities are understood to literally *recreate* the world, in chiefdoms human beings are more likely to be understood as helpers of more powerful beings. Whereas in nomadic foraging societies there are many spirits inhabiting small domains, in complex horticultural societies there are fewer spiritual presences presiding over larger domains.

Just as there is a relationship between politics and sacred worlds, there is a relationship between economics and sacred worlds. The movements from generalized reciprocity to egalitarian distribution by big men and partial redistribution by chiefs show the extent to which reciprocity between the sacred world and the material world became increasingly lopsided. At the beginning of his book *Primitive Religion* (1959), Paul Radin argued that religious beliefs evolve through four stages:

1. Object of sacred concern is under the power of spells
2. Object of sacred concern is more autonomous
3. Object of sacred concern is reciprocally engaged with humans
4. Object of sacred concern is fully independent of human influence

Each of these stages can be linked to egalitarian, rank, and stratified relationships. And they are related to generalized reciprocity, partial redistribution, and surplus expropriation in the economic world. We will come back to this issue as we explore agrarian civilizations and empires in Chapters 8 and 9.

Suggested Readings

Helms, Mary W. 1988. *Ulysses' Sail: An Ethnographic Odyssey of Power, Knowledge, and Geographical Distance.* Princeton, NJ: Princeton University Press.

Kirch, Patrick V. 1984. *The Evolution of Polynesian Chiefdoms.* Cambridge: Cambridge University Press.

Pauketat, Timothy R. 2009. *Cahokia.* New York: Viking.

PART

III

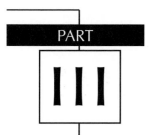

State-Based Systems

This section describes and explains the emergence of cities and states and tells the story of the first empires and the emergence of markets and money. We focus on the first time these features of society emerged in different regions, and so the telling is in chronological order by region. For example, cities and states emerged later in East Asia and the Americas than in West Asia, but we combine all these in the same chapter. The rise and fall of powerful states and empires is an important topic, as is the development of core/periphery relations. We consider the recurrent phenomenon in which semiperipheral and peripheral peoples conquer old core states and establish new empires. We explain the nature of political and economic institutions with a focus on the long rise of markets and money. Early on in the state-based world-systems, some autonomous groups in the spaces between the tributary states and empires specialized in long-distance trade. These semiperipheral capitalist city-states play an important role in expanding and deepening the trade networks of large regions. We trace the expansion of interaction networks that eventually makes continent-wide and intercontinental systems of linkages among very different kinds of societies in an emergent multicore Afroeurasian world-system.

8

The Temple and the Palace

Let us turn now to early state-based world-systems. Archaeologists refer to the formative and early florescent periods in which small states emerged and grew. **Pristine states**, or primary states, are those that emerge in a context in which there are no existing states in the region. Once states have emerged, the formation of additional states is termed **secondary state** formation. It is important to make the distinction between primary and secondary state formation because the processes involved are different. It is much more difficult for states to emerge in a situation in which there are no existing states, because new institutions need to be invented and implemented. Secondary state formation can be accomplished by borrowing organizational ideas from existing states and adapting them to local conditions.

Pristine State-Based World-Systems

The list of pristine early state emergences includes Uruk in Early Dynastic Mesopotamia, Peru long before the Incas, Egypt before the Old Empire, Shang China, and Mexico before the empire of Teotihuacan. There may have been similarly pristine state-based world-systems in other areas, such as Mayan Central America or Chibchan Northern Andes. And, as we have already discussed, some archaeologists argue that the Mississippian polity centered at Cahokia was an early state. Much of our focus here will be on the world-system that was centered on the Sumerian city-states of Southern Mesopotamia. This is because most experts agree that state formation occurred first in ancient Southwestern Asia.

The emergence of the primary states occurred at different times in Mesopotamia, Egypt, China, the Indus River valley, Mesoamerica, and Peru. Even though Southern Mesopotamia experienced this formative period earlier than other areas, diffusion has not been considered to have been very important in causing state formation in the other areas, especially the New World. Most scholars believe that largely parallel processes of evolution caused the emergence of states in these primary areas. Patrick Kirch (2010) contends that archaic states were emerging in the Hawaiian archipelago when Captain James Cook arrived in 1778.

A number of important changes were roughly contemporaneous during the formative period in all the areas where pristine states emerged. Population increased and so did the productivity of labor and land. In all areas, monumental religious centers emerged, and in most areas this was accompanied by the growth of urban populations. A more complex division of labor emerged with specialized forms of agriculture, production of manufactures by specialists, and a hierarchical administrative structure composed of religious and military leaders. A permanent class division between rulers and ruled emerged in which aristocratic lineages composed a nobility born to rule and institutionally entitled to support by laboring masses. Cultural elaboration of artistic production, the invention of writing, law, and other accoutrements of civilization eventually emerged in most of these regions. The formerly this-worldly religions of tribal societies in which gods, spirits, and ancestors were residents of the natural world where humans also lived became divided into the supernatural heavenly realm of the gods, accessible only to priests, and the profane world of everyday life below. The consensual normative regulations of community behavior became overlain by a structure of centrally codified laws.

Another regularity across these cases is that early states did not emerge one at a time, but rather they emerged together within the context of an existing interchiefdom system. Colin Renfrew (1975, 1986) has emphasized the importance of this "international" context with his notions of "early state modules" and "peer-polity interaction." Renfrew also argues that growing cultural integration and the formation of a regional civilizational culture is an important concomitant of the rise of early state systems.

Southwest Asia from Uruk to the Akkadian Empire

As we saw in earlier chapters, the region of Southwest Asia and the Levant was a fertile location for human social evolution. This region witnessed the emergence of sedentary foragers, Neolithic farmers, the first complex chiefdoms, and the first multitiered settlement systems. It also was the region that developed the first cities and states on Earth. And the Southwest Asian world-system developed the first relatively stable core/periphery hierarchies in which imperial core states exploited and dominated peripheral peoples. This region also witnessed the first instance on Earth of a core-wide empire resulting from the conquest of a set of older core states—the Akkadian Empire, a subject we shall consider in Chapter 10.

The rapid and dramatic emergence of states, cities, and writing in the Southwest Asian system in the fourth and third millennia was built on a set of prior developments that spread from the adjacent Levant over the previous 5,000 years. The metaphor of ecological succession is relevant for understanding the evolution of world-systems. Small plants breaking down rocks create soil. This produces what is necessary for larger plants and trees to grow. The analogue of soil is socially produced surplus product and the institutional structures that allow human societies to become larger and more hierarchical. But as with ecological succession, this is not a smooth upward accession from small to large. It is fraught with regressions and collapses and uneven development in space. The locations in which the first breakthroughs occurred are most often not the same locations in which later larger-scale developments emerged. It is a process of uneven development and the diffusion of innovations, as well as reactions to them, within a macroregion that establishes the economic, transportation, and communication bases for yet even larger, more complex, and more hierarchical human systems to emerge. The cultural and technological soil that made possible the growth of human social complexity and hierarchy first formed in the prehistoric Levant and ancient Southwestern Asia.

In the Uruk or Late Chalcolithic[1] period (from 4000 BCE to 3100 BCE), the first true city (Uruk, also called Warka or Erech) grew up on the floodplain of lower Mesopotamia, and other cities of similar large size soon emerged in this region. Surrounding these unprecedentedly large cities were smaller towns and villages that formed the first four-tiered settlement systems (Adams 1981). This was the original birth of "civilization," understood as the combination of irrigated agriculture, writing, cities, and states[2] (see Figure 8.1).States also emerged somewhat later during what is

[1] *Chalco* means "copper" in Greek, so this refers to the "copper age."

[2] A state is here understood as a specialized administrative apparatus of regional control that is at least partially independent of kinship organization.

Figure 8.1 Mesopotamian cuneiform writing

called the Uruk period on the adjacent Susiana Plain (Wright 1998), and these also developed four-tiered settlement systems (Flannery 1999b, 17). There was a transition from a regional inter-chiefdom system to an inter-city-state system that emerged first in Mesopotamia and then spread to the adjacent Susiana Plain.

The main architectural feature of these new cities was the temple. This monumental structure has long been considered to have been the primary institution of a theocratically (religiously based) organized political economy. A ziggurat, a multilevel mound with a shrine on top, was usually located adjacent to the main temple (see Figure 8.2). Later evidence about Sumerian civilization (based on documents written in the Sumerian language) shows that each city was represented by a god in the Sumerian pantheon (group of gods) and that the priests and populace were defined as the slaves of the city god—thus justifying the accumulation of surplus product (Postgate 1992). Flannery (1999b) claims that even the earliest archaic states often also had palaces—residential buildings for the war-leader king. But in Mesopotamia most scholars think that palaces were a later development that emerged with competitive warfare among the growing city-states (van de Mieroop 1999). Congruent with this is the evidence that shows an implosion of population from surrounding towns and villages to live within the protected confines of walled cities (Adams 1981). Thus was the early "peer polity" or "early state module" (Renfrew 1986) of coevolving archaic states transformed into an inter-city-state system of warring and allying states.

Flannery (1999b, 18) contends that Lagash, one of the Mesopotamian states, contained three cities as well as twenty towns and forty villages, and so he contests the characterization of Mesopotamian states as city-states. Experts on ancient Mesopotamia have long argued over the implications of certain texts regarding the territorial extent of the several states. Part of the problem is that the state territories expanded and contracted as states won or lost wars with one another or as their domination of peripheral regions expanded and contracted. We continue to use the term "city-state" because of the close identification of each state as an organization with its capital city. The Mesopotamian states were based on cults that focused on the god of the capital city as a main principal of organization and legitimation. As van de Mieroop (1999, 36) puts it, "The state was built around the city." It is in this sense that these were city-states even when they dominated other cities or regions.

Each city-state had its own god and cult, and each of these was recognized as an important

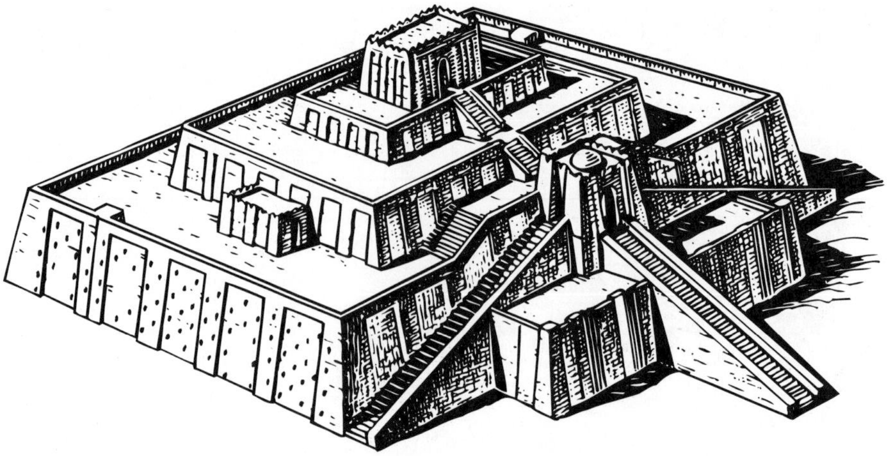

Figure 8.2 The ziggurat at Ur

member of the realm of gods in the regional pantheon. Though each city had its own main god, the emerging Sumerian civilization recognized all these gods as members of a single pantheon. The city of Nippur became recognized as a regional holy city of Sumeria because Nippur was where the gods were believed to gather. The priests of Nippur were asked to approve candidates for kingship of the city-states, and Nippur was recognized as a regional center of learning (van de Mieroop 1999).

The transition from theocracies to the primacy of warrior kings was an important development in the emergence of early states. The Sumerian cities erected their state institutions over the tops of kin-based normative institutions (Zagarell 1986). Assemblies of lineage elders long continued to play an important role in the politics of Mesopotamia. But the structures of institutional coercion—property and armies—became ever more important for maintaining power and accumulating wealth. One interesting apparent difference between the emergence of archaic states in Mesopotamia and instances of pristine state formation is the infrequent occurrence of ritual human sacrifice. A powerful way to dramatize the power of a king is to bury a lot of other people with him when he dies. Except for the royal cemetery during the Third Dynasty of Ur, there is little evidence of human sacrifice in Mesopotamia. The temple economy required contributions of goods and labor time, including animal sacrifices that were consumed in religious feasts. But the organized killing of humans in Mesopotamia was, as in modern civilization, mainly confined to warfare among states and capital punishment.

The story of the Uruk expansion in the fourth millennium is about the rise of the first state-based core/periphery hierarchy. The Uruk state extracted resources and founded colonies and colonial enclaves within existing towns across a vast region in order to gain access to desired goods and to control trade routes (Algaze 1993).

There is some disagreement as to the extent and degree of direct control that the Uruk state was able to exercise over distant peripheral regions. Gil Stein (1999) has formulated a "distance-parity" model of core/periphery relations that focuses on the spatial falloff of the ability of the core to project power. The effectiveness of military threats declines with distance from the center of political-military power, and so imperial core states must rely on equal exchange with peripheral peoples who are beyond the scope of intimidation. Stein's careful research at Hacinebe in Turkey has gone far to enlighten us about the nature of Uruk trading stations that were distant from the Mesopotamian heartland. Stein's research confirms the idea that core/periphery hierarchies in early state-based world-systems were limited in spatial scale and relatively unstable over time. Early states were not able to extract resources from distant peripheries, because they were unable to project military power very far and they did not have elaborate capitalistic mechanisms for facilitating unequal exchange. The "techniques of power" that eventually were invented to make long-distance imperialism possible (Mann 1986) were only beginning to be developed in the time of the Uruk expansion.[3] The Uruk expansion collapsed, though scholars do not agree as to the causes of the collapse. Both peripheral resistance and ecological degradation in the Sumerian heartland have been suggested.

Joyce Marcus (1998) points out that the interstate system of Mesopotamia exhibited a cycle of "rise and fall" in which the largest polities increase and then decrease in size, and that this phenomenon is also known in other cases of ancient state systems in the Andes and Mesoamerica. As we saw in earlier chapters, all hierarchical world-systems exhibit a structurally similar oscillation—from the "cycling" of chiefdoms (D. Anderson 1994) to the rise and fall of great empires, to the rise and fall of hegemonic core states in the modern world-system. The rise-and-fall phenomenon in Southwestern Asia is demonstrated with data on the territorial sizes of the largest states and empires from 2800 BCE to 1000 BCE in Figure 10.3 in Chapter 10. Following the Uruk expansion and collapse, the Jemdet Nasr and Early Dynastic periods saw the further growth of cities in Mesopotamia and seven centuries of an inter-city-state system with the rise and fall of hegemonic core states, but no successful formation of a core-wide empire.

This sequence is quite different from what happened in Egypt, where the emergence of cities and large-scale agriculture led to much larger territorial states and, very quickly, to a core-wide empire.[4] The explanations for these differences have long been alleged to be ecological, having to do with the differences in the communications and transportation possibilities in the two regions. Whereas the Nile is a single and quite navigable river, the Tigris and the Euphrates are much less navigable, and so communications and trade routes are more complex in Mesopotamia. In Egypt a state can easily get effective control of the entire agricultural heartland by controlling movement on the Nile, while in Mesopotamia central control of flows of information and goods is much more difficult to gain (Mann 1986). Thus the process of empire building took much longer in Southwest Asia than it did in Egypt. This ecological explanation is now often disparaged by those who compare Mesopotamia and Egypt in favor of cultural differences that may have led to the differences in political organization (e.g., Baines and Yoffee 1998). But it is equally plausible that the cultural differences themselves were largely consequences of different ecological and political structures.

The issue of how important interactions between Egypt and Mesopotamia may have been for the developments that occurred in each is still being contested, and new discoveries continue to be made that are relevant for this. It has been assumed that the somewhat earlier developments in Mesopotamia suggest that diffusion of ideas or inventions from there may have had some influence on the emergence of hierarchy and complexity in Egypt. But the rather different forms of writing and religious ideas that emerged in Egypt suggest a good degree of independent invention.

Another case where the issue of pristine versus secondary state formation is raised is the relationship between the states of central Mexico and the region in Guatemala where the highland Mayan states emerged. Teotihuacan was a huge empire centered in one colossal city in the Valley of Mexico in the fourth century CE. The huge pyramids of the monumental city may be seen today at an archaeological site that is thirty miles northeast of Mexico City. We will discuss Teotihuacan in Chapter 10 as the first core-wide empire to emerge in Mesoamerica. But of relevance here is the relationship between Teotihuacan and the emergence of states in distant Guatemala. Kaminaljuyu was a rather large city built in highland Guatemala (in what is now a suburb of Guatemala City) during the florescence of Mayan early states. But Kaminaljuyu built its pyramids in the architectural style of distant

[3] An evolutionary and comparative perspective on core/periphery hierarchies allows us to comprehend both the similarities and the differences between early regional world-systems and the global system of today. The institutional mechanisms of long-distance exploitation and domination evolved and became more effective, allowing for the expansion of larger and more complex world-systems.

[4] Though Egypt formed a core-wide empire early on, it continued to experience cycles of political centralization and decentralization, just as other state systems did.

Teotihuacan. Did the Teotihuacan Empire establish a colony in Guatemala in order to control trade routes?

Research carried out at Kaminaljuyu by Marion Popenoe de Hatch (1997) indicates that the builders of Kaminal were residents of the highlands who adopted the Teotihuacan religion and copied the architectural styles of highland Mexico to signify their adherence to the religion. Considerable continuity can be seen in the types of pots found at Kaminal, indicating an adaptation by local people rather than an incursion of immigrants. Hatch theorizes that forming an alliance with Teotihuacan and adopting the foreign religion gave the Kaminal state an important advantage over its Mayan neighbors in the control of the profitable prestige goods trade with the Mexican highlands. Mayans soon developed their own hierarchical religions and their own architectural and hieroglyphic styles that were quite different from those of highland Mexico, but the role of Kaminaljuyu makes this an interesting instance of secondary state formation.

State Building and Class Formation

Primary state formation was the emergence of the original organizations that had the capacity to monopolize legitimate violence and to effectively mobilize surplus product.[5] We will examine the nature of exchange relations (political and economic) within and between these first states and their hinterlands. Class formation is an important topic that must be considered in relation to state formation. The key organizational capability of a state is to have relatively autonomous access to resources produced by human labor (surplus product). These resources can come from a subordinated class within a society, from other societies, or from both. So pristine state formation involves the invention of institutions that allow the state to appropriate the labor services or the products of labor of a subordinated class. As we saw in Chapter 7, this process had already proceeded quite far in some of the complex chiefdoms, such as Hawaii. In early states, class formation often took the form of inventing legitimations for the appropriation of surplus product that were separate from the obligations of kinship. In Mesopotamia this legitimation was formulated as religious ideology in which all the members of society were held to be slaves of the god of the city, and so everyone had the obligation to provide labor or goods for the sustenance of the deity. The advantage of this principle is that it provided a source of labor and goods that was independent from and in addition to the obligations based on kinship. This allowed the state to undertake projects that were less constrained by the reciprocities of the kinship system and provided the priests and the emergent war leaders with an important degree of administrative autonomy from societal constraints.

Though most of the cultures in which primary states emerged eventually developed writing systems, the philological studies of their texts are often not well integrated with archaeological data (Adams 1984), and the great bulk of the surviving documents pertain to later periods in which empires had already arisen. It is risky to use insights based on documentary evidence from later periods to make inferences about the nature of processes of institutional change in earlier periods. In terms of our concern for regional and supra-regional economic patterns, the archaeological area surveys that reconstruct both urban and rural settlement patterns (Adams and Nissen 1972; Blanton et al. 1981) are a definite methodological advance over the previous tendency to focus mainly on the greatest monuments and cities.

Theories of Pristine State Formation

The general evolutionary iteration model for explaining hierarchy formation presented in Chapter 2 also applies to early state formation. A different perspective, but one that also uses world-systems as a framework for analysis, was presented by Jonathan Friedman and Michael Rowlands (1977). They were the first theorists to explain the process of early state formation using a world-systems approach that focuses on

[5] **Surplus product** is the labor time and products of direct producers that are appropriated by the ruling class in a class society.

the evolution of kinship, elite intermarriage, and class formation. Their perspective emphasizes the economic significance of kinship and religious institutions. State formation is understood here as a continuation of the conical clan formation that began within chiefdoms but that could only become fully elaborated in the context of an increasingly productive economic base. The monopolization of religion was the key to class formation, and wealth symbolized nearness to the deities. Surplus labor in the form of captive or purchased slaves was an important source of support for the emerging state. Relations with sublineages, formerly cemented by the chiefly lineage giving wives to lower-status lineages, became converted to wife-taking by the king. A prestige goods economy developed as a major form of exchange between the main center and regional centers, but this kind of economy was hard to regulate and encouraged regional centers to compete with, and sometimes overtake, former main centers. Thus a kind of uneven development based on competition resulted in the rise of competing centers. Long-distance trade relations for both scarce raw materials used for the production of prestige goods and more fundamental goods necessary for economic survival were carried out primarily on the basis of equal exchange in the Friedman-Rowlands model.

As trade networks increased in density, certain prestige goods became a more generalized medium of exchange and began to function as money. Local markets emerged around the ceremonial centers, and a monetary/property system emerged alongside the conical clan reciprocity and the prestige goods economy. Differentiation occurred within the governing class. Alongside the theocracy, a class of secular political leaders emerged and also a group of aristocrats who were private landholders. Eventually, empire formation led to the conversion of many long-distance trade relations to tribute gathering (unequal exchange) by the empire center.

Other theories of primary state and class formation have been proposed. Many social scientists have argued that it was population pressure on the land, due to either natural increase or immigration, that spurred the increase in agricultural productivity and eventually the emergence of states.[6]

Malcolm Webb (1975) and Charles Redman (1978) combined a version of the population pressure explanation with geographical circumscription and military competition. According to Webb, the early theocracies were more akin to chiefdoms than to real states. He attributed the early building of religious monuments to the problematic nature of authority in the incipient states. It was simpler to get agreement among lineage heads to allocate resources to temple building because this was easily legitimated as an activity devoted to the welfare of everyone. Webb disputed the theories that had contended that state formation resulted from the awe-inspiring psychological aspects of early hierarchical religions. He contended that a true state does not exist until there is an organization with a resource base large enough and independent enough to overcome the resistance of segmental kin structures within the society, and he pointed to the limitations on chiefs that we noted in Chapter 7. He contends these kinds of external resources could come from two sources:

- External trade
- The booty and tribute that result from conquest

Webb (1975) argued that external trade became important for secondary state formation (the creation of a state in a context in which there were already other existing states), when local leaders could use their control of imported goods to overcome the resistance of segmental lineage heads. But for primary state formation, it was not trade but conquest that provided the needed resources, according to Webb.

Conquest by itself does not explain why some chiefdoms were able to convert themselves into true states, however. Webb (1975) points out that warfare was endemic among chiefdoms in

[6] Blanton et al. (1981, 222–225) point out that population growth and population pressure are not necessarily the same thing. They report that although the population more than tripled in the valley of Oaxaca during the growth of Monte Alban (the capital city of the Zapotec Empire), it was still markedly below the level of population that could have been supported in the region.

many areas without producing states. It was the combination of the opportunity for conquest of relatively developed neighbors in a geographical context that limited population movement to new areas (circumscription) that, for Webb, was the set of conditions that allowed for pristine state formation. This is what accounts for the fact that the primary states all emerged in areas that were appropriate for productive agriculture but were surrounded by deserts and threatening nomads. This is the circumscription hypothesis originally proposed by Robert Carneiro (1970). Rising population pressure stimulates warfare among relatively developed chiefdoms in a situation where populations cannot escape to land that would allow them to continue a level of living similar to that which they have become accustomed.

The conquered areas continue to be populated by the original people, who now must pay tribute to the conquerors, and this tribute is great enough to permit true state formation within the conquering society. The iteration model of hierarchy formation described in Chapter 2 recapitulates this approach.

Karl Wittfogel's (1957) famous argument that the original states arose to administer large-scale irrigation projects has an element of truth, but there are problems with what is meant by large-scale. Some early states emerged where irrigation was possible on a decentralized basis, as with pot wells in the Valley of Oaxaca in Mexico. Investment in projects that increase the productivity of nature was undoubtedly important for enabling both complex chiefdoms and early states to succeed, but this was not always investment in irrigation. Hawaiian chiefdoms built huge enclosures along the coast for fish farming.

Elman Service (1975) proposed a functionalist theory of early state formation, arguing that states grew out of chiefdoms because the stabilization of order required a peaceful, institutionalized way for power to pass from one ruler to another. According to Service, primogeniture (inheritance of property and power by the first-born son) created an aristocracy and thus the emergence of a class structure. The state apparatus emerged because of the needs of society to preserve authority and order. The benefits to commoners included protection from outsiders, peaceful conflict resolution at home, the operation of a redistributive system that could overcome temporary and local shortages, and the mobilizing institutions needed for the development of more productive agriculture. In addition, the appropriation of surplus product allowed rulers to devote time and resources to the invention of the arts of civilization, according to Service.

Service (1975) critiques an argument he attributes to Friedrich Engels, that the first states were created to defend the privileges and profits of a merchant class. Service sees the state itself as the creator of class society and of large-scale and long-distance exchange, and he completely dismisses the notion that class struggle—struggle between rulers and ruled—was an important ingredient of state formation. In his interpretation the peasants of early states were silent, obedient, and pious believers in the hierarchical religions that legitimated the state. He claims that the political conflict and rebellion that did occur were primarily a matter of competition among aristocratic contenders.

Other eminent scholars such as Robert McCormick Adams (1966) and Morton Fried (1967) placed more emphasis on the contradictory interests of classes in the incipient chiefdoms and primary states. Fried (1967) contended that class society, or as he called it, "stratified society," emerged first and then brought forth the state. Stratified society is defined as "one in which members of the same sex and equivalent age status do not have equal access to the basic resources that sustain life" (Fried 1967, 186). This is what most scholars mean when they use the term "class society." Fried sees stratified societies as developing with institutions of private property and elite control over the means of production. Communal forms of property and unrestricted access to the means of production (land, water, and so on) characterized unstratified societies. Fried also included an intermediate form that he termed "rank society," in which kinship had become hierarchically organized, as we discussed in Chapter 7 on chiefdoms.

Unequal access to the means of basic production developed because of population pressures, shifts in customary postmarital residence patterns, contraction or sharp alteration of basic resources and shifts in subsistence patterns that arose from such factors as technological change or the impingement of a market system, and the development of managerial roles as an aspect of the maturation of a ceremonial system (Fried 1967, 196).

Once unequal access to the basic means of production exists, a state organization becomes necessary. The maintenance of class hierarchy demanded sanctions commanding power beyond the resources of a kinship system. By differentially distributing access to basic means of livelihood and by simultaneously making possible the exploitation of human labor, stratified societies created pressure unknown in egalitarian or rank societies, and these pressures could not be contained by internalized social controls or ideology alone (Fried 1967, 186). Thus, states had to develop institutionalized forms of coercion that protected property and the appropriation of surplus product from direct producers.

Thomas C. Patterson's (1990, 1997) explication of the emergence of states in the Andes employed an approach that was close to that of Fried. Class societies developed on the coast of Peru, where incredibly productive fishing grounds promoted a division of labor between fishing and farming villages. Cotton and maize horticulture soon produced class societies when irrigated agriculture used the snow melt streams running down from the Andes through dry, but irrigable, valleys near the coast to produce large agricultural surpluses. Patterson (1990) said that state formation occurred when temporarily appointed authorities did not want to give up power and were able to overcome resistance from kin-based community leaders.

Once they emerged on the coast, class societies and early states spread widely across the Andean region. Two empires emerged in the period between 500 CE and 900 CE. Huari (Wari) had a large capital city near modern-day Ayacucho in Peru.[7] The other empire (Tiwanaku) had a capital near Lake Titicaca in the highland basin of Bolivia. The Wari (Huari) and Tiwanaku empires had declined and the whole Andean region was in a decentralized situation of rather small polities and regional cults in the period before the rise of the Incan Empire (Stanish 2003). Cuzco, the homeland of the Incas, was located in between the old coastal and highland core regions.

Robert McCormick Adams (1966) placed less emphasis on private property and more on control over central institutions in his study of early class societies in Mesopotamia and Mesoamerica. But, citing the work of Igor Diakonoff (1974), Adams pointed to Mesopotamian land sale records from the Early Dynastic period. Though evidence is scarce, he suspected an early concentration of private landholdings by corporate kin groupings in addition to the lands held by the temple state. This may indicate the breakdown of communal, egalitarian control of landholdings and could constitute a case of Fried's unequal access to the basic means of production. Territorial residence seems to have increased as a basis for the control of land. Corporate landholding groups in both Mesopotamia and Mesoamerica were organized around lineages. In describing these units as combining features of both class and clan, Adams (1966, 88) quotes Eric Wolf (1959, 136), who describes **conical clans** as "kinship units which bind their members with common familial ties but which distribute wealth, social standing, and power most unequally among the members of the pseudo-family."

Adams's study focused on the growth of the state as an autonomous institution and its addition of functions. He argued that class contradictions were important causes of the differentiation of theocracies into states with temples and palaces, a sequence that can be seen in the development of both Mesopotamia and Mesoamerica. The earliest states were theocracies based on the donation of labor services to provision the gods. In Mesopotamia the main god or goddess of each city-state theoretically owned all the land within the jurisdiction of the city-state. Later separate military and administrative institutions emerged as signified by the erection of palaces apart from the temple.

The Institutional Nature of the Economy in Early States

There is great dispute about the relative importance of markets in the early state-based world-systems. There has been a resurgence of the use of market models to account for ancient

[7] Justin Jennings (2010) describes the rapid growth of the city of Huari and its influence on other regions as an early instance of globalization in which a large area becomes economically integrated and a global culture composed of both central and local features develops across a large region.

long-distance trade, and many have argued that growing market exchange figured in the emergence of the primary states. Karl Polanyi (1957a) claimed that the most important type of exchange was politically controlled redistribution organized by the state itself—**state-administered trade**. In Polanyi's interpretation, true price-setting markets had not yet emerged during the period of the early states. Exchange was structured and regulated by the political power of states. Trade between regions was understood by Polanyi as state-administered exchange in which agents of the king were authorized to carry out transactions in behalf of the state. The people who carried out this trade were seen as state agents rather than as merchants trading for their own profits.

Others have interpreted evidence as supporting the operation of markets within and among the early states. While the bulk of the available documents from Sumer describe the state-operated temple economy, there are occasional references to merchants who some claim were middlemen between states, sometimes trading on their own account and operating on a profit basis. Lamberg-Karlovsky (1975, 349) argues that:

> In Mesopotamia, in the late third millennium, there is ample evidence from textual sources that merchants specialized in the materials they traded. Thus, during Ur III times (2113–2006 B.C.), the merchant Ea-nasir, a member of the "group of seafaring merchants" (alik Telmun), received garments from Ur and took them to Dilmun (modern-day Bahrain), where he purchased large quantities of copper. . . . Ea-nasir obtained capital under contractual agreements, managing the money of others as a mutual fund, while also investing his own capital in copper-trading ventures. . . . It would appear that by the end of the third millennium there were specialized merchants dealing with large-scale exchange of goods in a wholesaling-retailing system.

Igor Diakonoff (1974) cites evidence about the size of the territory controlled by Lagash (one of the Sumerian states) that indicates that temple estates did not, as previously argued by others, occupy nearly the whole land area of the state. He also reports documents that refer to the sale of non-temple land that was in the hereditary possession of patriarchal families. Important administrators and kinsmen of the ruling princes purchased this land. These became the landholding nobility referred to by Ekholm and Friedman (1982) and also by Adams (1966). The existence of a market for alienable land, which composed a substantial portion of all land, is itself a grand challenge to Polanyi's position. In a note, Diakonoff (1974, 14) explains:

> The economy of Sumer being at this period still very primitive, cases of sale of land naturally happened but rarely. It should be noted that the prices of land are governed by the average ratio of profit that in the Ancient East can, for practical reasons, be conventionally equated to the average interest on loans. Thus, an average profit of 33% means that the average price of land will not exceed the price of three yearly crops. Therefore the price of land in Sumer was extremely low, not exceeding three or four yearly crops. . . . This was the reason why land was rarely sold unless the venders were in a critical economical or political situation.

This discussion of the average rate of profit on loans suggests that wealth, as well as land, was at least partially commodified in ancient Sumer. Struve's (1973) argument that Sumerian society was based on a slave mode of production documents the sale of slaves, after all a form of the commodification of labor, and Ekholm and Friedman (1982) even suggest the presence of some wage labor. But Diakonoff (1982), based on his analysis of documentary evidence, concludes that there was very little market exchange in ancient Sumer. The economy was mainly based on the coexistence of a temple-state sector with a private sector composed mainly of communal lineages. The ruling class was composed of temple and state aristocrats and heads of communal lineages.

The appropriation of surplus was accomplished by various kinds of labor dependency, of which slave labor (in the narrow sense of chattel slavery[8]) played a rather small part. In the communal sector, differentiation occurred such that lineage heads were able to benefit at the expense of their kinship brethren. Diakonoff (1982, 52) contends that communal groups carried on even "international" trade:

> This trade was maintained by "companies," essentially of a family-communal character, which tended to group together to form multi-branch associations having complex relations of mutual preferential crediting and clearing, this being due to insufficient money supply in general and to the overall essentially in-kind character of exchange even when it was carried out on an international scale.

In the temple-state sector of the economy, dependent workers did not pay taxes, but rather their whole product was taken by the state. They were either paid rations or given land to cultivate for their own use. At first, temple lands were, in principle, under the control of community assemblies, but later they became autonomous of these. Diakonoff (1982, 64) describes the original purpose of the temple economy to provide reserves, to ensure that certain necessities such as timber and metals were obtained from abroad, and to provide a reserve fund of working implements:

> The orientation of the temple economy towards the cult did by no means stand in the way of this above-mentioned main economic objective of the temple estate. On the contrary, it was, by the requirements of the times, in complete accord with that objective, since the sense of the cult, too, was to ensure the well-being of, and above all the fertility in, the community. The inadequacy of the religious-magical approach to this goal, as compared with the technical-economic one, could by no means be felt or recognized. The two aspects—the religious magical and the technical economic—were closely interconnected. E.g., the sacrifices may appear to us as an utter waste of products (since we know that the hopes for achieving affluence by virtue of magical sacrifices were indeed vain). But in effect they were not only of ideological but also of immediate and major economic significance. The participation in the sacrificial feasts opened the only opportunity for the people at large to get meat. Both the temple personnel and the entire community of believers who attended that particular temple were concerned.

Friedman and Rowlands (1977) analyze the political significance of feasting and of religious belief in the emergence of class society and the state. In their view, wealth was understood as an indication of nearness to the godly ancestors, and those who provided feasts were thereby closer to the deities. Sacrifice was not only an attempt to please the gods but a symbolic recognition of authority. Thus, burning of goods, sacrificing of children, and other completely "uneconomic" rites sustained the social order.

We mentioned above that ritual human sacrifice was often a characteristic of early states and that ancient Mesopotamia was unusual in having rather little of this. Recall from Chapter 7 that seventy decapitated young women were interred near a dead chief in Monk's Mound at Cahokia. Early states in China often buried whole detachments of soldiers and servants with a dead king. These ritual human sacrifices symbolized the importance of the hierarchy, especially when these hierarchies were not completely institutionalized and legitimated. Early states were erected over tops of, and still contend with, more egalitarian principles of organization. Modern states have laws, bureaucracies, courts, and police forces, as well as a moral order that supports states as dispensers of justice and public services. They are not usually competing with strong kin-based organizations for control of these functions. All this allows the Internal Revenue Service to collect taxes without having to dramatically symbolize its power by ritually sacrificing people.

Robert McCormick Adams (1984) has suggested that competition among the Sumerian cities for long-distance trade goods led to the operation of the principle of "protection rent."

[8] Chattel slavery means that slaves can be bought and sold as private property, as was the case in ancient Rome and the American South.

Frederic Lane (1979), on the basis of his studies of the Venetian city-state, proposed that protection costs for trade are an important determinant of profits and that an important function of states is their role as violence-producing organizations for the protection of trade. The state that could provide effective protection of economic activities at low cost would be favored by its own merchants and would be more successful in competing with other states. The returns due to lower protection costs are termed **protection rent**.

Adams (1984) claims that Sumerian city-states were under pressure to keep taxes on merchants low because, if they did not, alternative trade routes would be employed to sell goods to cities in which taxes were lower. Administered trade, in which exchange is determined by political agreements among state authorities, may respond to supply and demand. Political authorities must at least roughly take into account the availability of resources as well as labor and transport costs when they make agreements. And the agreed-upon rates of exchange must necessarily adjust to economic changes over long periods of time. A king cannot demand and receive tribute from a vassal that the vassal does not have or cannot possibly obtain. So, just as with reciprocal gift giving, administered exchange "prices" will approximately reflect real scarcities and costs even in the absence of a price-setting market, at least in the long run.

All scholars of the Bronze Age agree that sharing and reciprocity continued to be the most important forms of exchange within local lineages (e.g., Oppenheim 1974; Earle 2002), and that mobilization and redistribution by the temple state and, later, the militarized state were very important. The disagreement seems to be about the relative importance of markets for urban/rural trade, inter-city-state trade, and trade with distant locations. The contention that some markets existed does not prove that they operated in important ways to condition social development. It is agreed that the Sumerian city-states became enmeshed in a rather dense intraregional and interregional exchange network and that this had important consequences for their economic welfare and political stability. The institutional nature of these networks is in dispute. Booty, tribute, balanced reciprocity (gifts) among elites, and market exchanges were all mentioned, but which was most important is a matter of contention. Instances of a particular form do not tell us about the extent or importance of that form.

The Egyptian economy was certainly an example of a predominantly nonmarket politically structured system of exchange. McNeill (1963, 72) says, "Early Egypt was like a single temple community writ large." Because of the geography of the Nile valley, with the main transport being the Nile itself, control of exchange among regions became the key basis of support for the state. As McNeill (1963, 71, 74) writes:

> By controlling shipping, the king automatically and easily regulated all major movements of goods and people, and therewith possessed the means for effective rule over Egypt. . . . Trade and all large-scale economic enterprises were managed and controlled by officials of the divine household. At intervals the Pharoahs dispatched expeditions of a semimilitary character to Syria for timber, to Sinai for copper, to Nubia for gold, to Punt for myrrh; while within the country similar enterprises brought granite and other special stone from Upper Egypt and gathered taxes in kind into the royal treasuries. So far as the goods were not utilized directly by the god-king for the maintenance of his court or for the construction of his tomb and other buildings, they were distributed among the courtiers of the royal household.

Politics within the Early States

What was the political nature of these early states? We have already pointed to the importance of theocratic ideology. In the beginning, a city's pantheon was composed of the gods of those villages and lineages incorporated into the state, with the city's main deity as its parental head (Falkenstein 1974). Webb (1975) has attributed this to the weakness of the state, which could get agreement for centralized mobilization of resources only for religious purposes. In Sumer a circle of priests emerged to run the temple and to provide for the gods, as well as to guarantee the proper performance of ritual. At this stage there was also an assembly of lineage heads[9] that had important powers and elected a secular (nonreligious) leader to administrate those functions not carried out by the temple. Over time this secular leader took on more functions and became more autonomous, although for a long time military plans were supposed to be submitted to the assembly for approval. Some have described this system in its early phases as a democracy, although as with later ancient democracies, a large underclass of noncitizen slaves and temple servants had no say in the assembly. Diakonoff (1973) and many other scholars have argued that, as the leaders of the palace became hereditary, the polity became less democratic and more monarchical. But van de Mieroop (1999), contending against the notion of "oriental despotism" as applied to Mesopotamia, argues that the political powers of the citizenry increased over time rather than decreased. City subdivisions or quarters had their own courts and assemblies.

Early Interstate Systems

How were interstate relations in early state systems similar to or different from better-known interstate systems? During the late Uruk period in Southern Mesopotamia, there were at least 120 settlements in the Uruk region whose average size was one to two hectares. By the Early Dynastic period the number was reduced to less than fifty, with the average settlement occupying between six and ten hectares. During this period, cities became fortified and grew, indicating that population concentration resulted from rising military conflicts in the "heroic" age (Rhee 1981, 7). Interstate rivalry among Sumerian cities became rife, and warfare was frequent.

The Sumerian interstate system maintained a balance of power among eight or nine sovereign city-states during the early dynastic period from ca. 3000 BCE to ca. 2375 BCE. This is an instance of an early noncapitalist world economy and interstate system that refrained from turning into a core-wide empire for over six hundred years.[10] Descriptions of the interstate system of Sumer reveal that, though most of the time the separate cities were sovereign, occasionally one would conquer another, take booty, and extract tribute. Some of the more powerful states acted as mediators for other conflicting states, indicating the institution of diplomacy. McNeill (1963, 44) reports:

> Surviving records suggest that from about 2500 B.C., Lagash and Umma were the protagonists around which rival alliance systems formed. By degrees, the full autonomy of at least the weaker cities was reduced. Particularly strong rulers often created petty "empires" by uniting several communities under their rule; but such structures were highly unstable and broke apart whenever opportunity offered. Around 2375 B.C. the king Lugalzaggisi of Umma succeeded in temporarily uniting most of Sumer under his rule.

Several causes are asserted for the long period of city-state autonomy in Sumer and the long delay of a process of centralization by conquest. Rhee (1981) has pointed to the shared theocratic culture of Sumer, in which all the cities used the same language and recognized the same pantheon of gods, although each had its own most important god. This theological culture is alleged to have been the basis of a fierce independence that undermined attempts at unification. Ekholm and Friedman (1982) point instead to the geographical factors already mentioned above. Comparing Sumer with Egypt, where unification under a centralized theocracy came early, Ekholm and Friedman claim that in Egypt a central state was able to easily control long-distance trade because of the geographical

[9] Van de Mieroop (1999) argues that the assemblies were organizations of producer guilds and neighborhoods rather than kin groups.

[10] Immanuel Wallerstein's (1974b) formulation of the differences between the modern capitalist world economy and earlier state-based "world empires" emphasizes the importance of capitalism for preventing the European interstate system from being turned into an empire. Though the Mesopotamian system could not be construed as capitalist, it too was rather resistant to empire formation, whereas the Egyptian system rapidly became a single state (see above).

constraints that limited long-distance trade to the mouth of the Nile. In Southern Mesopotamia, the region of Sumer is open to long-distance trade by sea, but also overland in several directions. A central polity could not control the trade routes, and this delayed the unification of the region. Also, trade networks in Mesopotamia are thought to have been more dense and multicentric from the beginning, so alternative routes to the same destination could easily be found, making central control more difficult. The easily navigable Nile and the narrow agricultural region of the Nile floodplain created a linear system that was far easier to control than the much more complicated topography of Mesopotamia.

K. C. Chang (1980) has argued that the development of states and civilization occurs only in the context of interstate rivalry among a group of competing states. He concludes his study of the Chinese Shang dynasty with the contention that the "Three Dynasties" (Xia, Shang, and Zhou) were not sequential but rather composed an interactive interstate system (see also Liu and Chen 2003; Hui 2005). We know that states fought with one another over territory in the Yellow River valley that included a large number of sometimes sovereign, sometimes tributary states. According to Chang, the mythical Xia state in the center of this region was the first hegemonic state, and this was followed by a period of hegemony by the Shang in the East, and then a longer period of hegemony by the Western Zhou state in the West. Chang shows that most of the agricultural surplus was produced within each state, but that prestige goods were exchanged among the ruling classes of different states, and a long-distance trade with areas in Southern China already existed.

Core/Periphery Relations in Early State Systems

What can be said about core/periphery relationships in the early state-based world-systems? The idea of core/periphery hierarchy was originally developed to describe and account for the stratified relations of power and dependency among societies in the modern world-system. The comparative world-systems approach developed by Chase-Dunn and Hall (1997) and described in Chapter 2 distinguishes between core/periphery differentiation, in which there is important interaction among societies that have different degrees of population density, and core/periphery hierarchy, in which some societies are exercising domination or exploitation of other societies.

We discussed above the Mesopotamian Uruk expansion as characterized by Guillermo Algaze and critiqued by Gil Stein. Owen Lattimore (1940) described the emergence of a social frontier between agriculturalists and nomads along the ecological border between arable loess land and drier steppe, suited only for pasture, in North China. Originally horticulture was combined with hunting and gathering across the area. But specialization in agriculture drove the hunters out of the arable loess land. This produced the emergence of pastoral nomadism on the adjacent steppe lands. The Central Asian steppe nomads utilized horses to keep herds of domesticated pasture animals, mainly sheep. An exchange of meat and animal products for grains emerged across this frontier, and, along with military incursions by the nomads, this encouraged further intersocietal differentiation. The Chinese farmers, for their part, developed military-based states and walled cities. Chinese efforts to neutralize the nomads by engaging some of their leaders in tributary exchanges, and thereby to divide and conquer, were frustrated by an opposite process, the coming together of nomadic alliances under charismatic leaders who could occasionally form powerful steppe confederacies of tribes that could extract tribute from the Chinese core (see Barfield 1993). K. C. Chang (1980) contended that the military elite of the early Chinese states not only protected peasants from nomadic incursions but also utilized their coercive power against the peasants to suppress rebellions and to enforce taxation. So core/periphery relations had an important impact on early state formation in East Asia.

Elman Service (1975) suggested that the process of frontier formation that Lattimore described for China had also operated in Mesopotamia. Nomadic hill and desert tribes threatened the Sumerian cities, and the result was a militarily created depopulated no-man's-land (buffer zone) between the settled plains and the upland sanctuaries of the hill tribes and desert nomads. But eventually, peripheral areas became specialized in stockbreeding and nonirrigated agriculture (Diakonoff 1982, 22).

The cultural aspects of core/periphery relations can be seen in Sumerian literature. The famous epic of Gilgamesh describes the trials and triumphs of Gilgamesh, the king of Uruk (Silverberg 1985). This classic of Sumerian literature tells how Gilgamesh befriended a wild, uncivilized man by the name of Enkidu and of their adventures together. The distinction between the civilized lives of city dwellers and the uncivilized lives of barbarians and savages was an important feature of Sumerian consciousness (see also Chapter 10). Ekholm and Friedman (1982) and Algaze (1993) have characterized the Mesopotamian heartland as an imperialist center that exchanged manufactured goods (especially cloth) produced in the city-states for distant raw material imports. Ekholm and Friedman (1982, 97) noted that the expansion of the Mesopotamian trade system linked the entire region from the Indus to the Mediterranean during the Early Dynastic period. Timber, stone, copper, tin, rare minerals, and textiles are noted as imports (Marfoe 1987). During the third millennium BCE, both the temple and the palace were involved in long-distance trade using a group of merchants, the *dam-gar*. One of the important gods, Enlil, was known as "trader of the wide world." At Lagash the Baba Temple had 125 sailors and pilots to aid in water transportation and communications.

Diakonoff (1974) argued that the Mesopotamian political economy was not very dependent on core/periphery exploitation. Most economic exchanges with hinterlands, according to Diakonoff, were based on an equivalent exchange of goods. He contends that later warrior empires, such as the Assyrian Empire, were more reliant on the forcible exchange of goods with underdeveloped regions. Nevertheless, we can prove the existence of a hierarchical and somewhat stable core/periphery division of labor between Sumerian cities and peripheral hinterlands based on the historical documents of tributary relationships.

The greatest practical limit on long-distance overland exchange was the well-known exceedingly high cost of land transportation. This especially restricted the passage of bulk consumer goods. In Mesoamerica, without pack animals, a human long-distance carrier of maize would fairly quickly consume all the maize he could carry in order to have enough energy to make the trip (Drennan 1984). This did not preclude long-distance overland shipments of food, but it meant that such shipments required inputs beyond the value of the goods being moved. Even with the use of pack animals, transport costs were high. Lattimore (1940) reported that caravans traveling across the steppe, where open pasturage was available and free, could move goods economically across long distances, but as soon as they entered agricultural areas, where most of the land was planted and fodder had to be purchased, their economic range shortened greatly.

In ancient Southwest Asia and in Mesoamerica, all parties recognized certain neutral territories as international trade enclaves. These "ports of trade" (Revere 1957; Chapman 1957) allowed international exchange to go on even during periods of warfare between states. Some of these neutral territories were small cities near the boundaries of larger polities. But each Mesopotamian city also had a port district within it, and these city districts were often also treated as if they were neutral free-trade zones (van de Mieroop 1999). Scholars disagree about whether it was primarily administered trade or market trade that occurred in these enclaves. Ratnagar (1981, 226–227) contends that Dilmun (Bahrain) in the Persian Gulf performed this port-of-trade function in the exchanges between the Harappan civilization of the Indus River valley and Mesopotamia. He also cites evidence that indicates that the Dilmunites later took on the functions of middlemen/carriers operating between the great states, thus becoming early forebearers of the specialized trading city-states of the Phoenicians. This may have been the earliest example of the phenomenon that we have called the "semiperipheral capitalist city-state." If so, the merchants of Dilmun were not only trading on their own account but were actively promoting the production of surplus products for commodified exchange in the regions in which they traded. The question still remains as to how important commercialized exchange had become in the ancient Mesopotamian-centered system.

The Indus civilization produced two huge cities (Harappa and Mohenjo-daro) surrounded by a wide system of settlements in the drainage of the Indus River, which is now Pakistan. Jonathan Kenoyer (1998) has contended that these planned and well-designed cities do not suggest the presence of an elite (because no elite burials or residences have been found), and that there was little in the way of warfare. City walls have been interpreted as flood-control devices. While there is evidence of trade between the Indus cities and Mesopotamia, Kenoyer contends that the Indus florescence was substantially independent of Mesopotamian influence. We are still not able to decipher the writing system that developed on the Bronze Age Indus. Only a small corpus of texts has been found, and many now believe that the Harappan script was not a fully developed writing system but rather that it served only to mark certain kinds of tradeable goods. Thus, we do not yet have documentary evidence about the nature of this civilization. It is hard to imagine that such large cities could have been built in the absence of a ruling class, but this would seem to be the case. It is possible that in some cases class formation is a process that occurs only after an early state system has become militarized and competitive and that the Indus florescence did not survive long enough to reach this point. The Indus civilization declined and urban life disappeared from the region and did not reappear in South Asia until the emergence of states in the valley of the Ganges a millennium hence. The causes of the Indus decline may have been invasions or ecological degradation and flooding or some combination of these.

A process of state formation that appears very similar to that which we have described in Sumer began in the Ganges valley of the South Asian subcontinent during the first millennium. In the seventh century BCE, northern India was divided into sixteen *Majanapadas*, or "great states" (Chandra 1977, 50). Actually, some of these were probably still chiefdoms. In a slow process of alliance and conquest, the Mauryans of Magadha became dominant in this interstate system.

George Modelski's (1964) analysis of the third century BCE Indian interstate system is based primarily on the Arthasastra, allegedly written by the "Brahmin Machiavelli," Kautilya. Kautilya's prescriptions for the successful prince reveal some of the principles of the Hindu interstate system as it operated before the emergence of the Mauryan Empire. Implicitly comparing the Hindu system with the European interstate system of the modern era, Modelski notes the relative lack of development of an institutional apparatus for relations between equal states. The Indic geopolitical ideology assumed that relations are always hierarchical, and Kautilya prescribed the methods by which an aggressive prince can improve his power vis-à-vis other states.

The extent to which India was linked with the West Asian system in this period should not be overemphasized. The conquests of Alexander extended trade and cultural contact through to the Ganges valley, but in many respects the Hindu world remained an autonomous system. The Indian subcontinent remained a largely autonomous region within the multicentric Afroeurasian world-system with its own core/periphery hierarchy and interstate system. This is confirmed by Modelski's (1964, 555) description of the boundaries of the Hindu interstate system:

> That the international system within which Kautilya's princes exercised their status seeking existed in a "world" of its own is indicated in a number of passages. The Arthasastra refers several times to those who will conquer "the earth," or "the earth bounded by the four quarters." And in another place it indicates that this earth is to be understood roughly as the Indian sub-continent south of the Himalayas. This is the physical setting of Kautilya's international relations, and the arena in which the vijigishu (prince) could exercise his ambition.

Thapar (1980) makes a persuasive case against the use of the concept "Asiatic mode of production" to characterize the Indian civilization. The idea of an Asiatic mode of production refers to a state in which the king owns all the land. In addition to communally held village lands, there were privately owned lands, and both intraregional and long-distance trade were important. The regionally varying forms of caste institutions; the struggle between Brahminism, Buddhism, and Jainism; and the later expansion of economic and political influence over peripheral areas in Southern India, Sri Lanka, and Southeast Asia suggest a dynamic social system rather than a stagnant evolutionary cul de sac.

Trade and information exchange with West Asia and East Asia affected India to some extent. During the first millennium the states of the Ganges traded prestige goods including cotton and wool textiles, and elephants across the Great Road and by sea to the West and East, and this trade was in the nature of equal exchange.

The early state-based world-systems were fast becoming much like the world in which we now live. The basic institutional structures were in place, but the spatial range of these systems was still small. What came next was the invention of institutions that allowed for world-systems to become much larger and even more hierarchical. But what about the evolution of the personality during the rise of states and empires? That is the issue addressed in Chapter 9.

Suggested Readings

Adams, Robert McCormick. 1966. *The Evolution of Urban Society: Early Mesopotamia and Prehispanic Mexico.* Chicago: Aldine.

Algaze, Guillermo. 1993. *The Uruk World System: The Dynamics of Expansion of Early Mesopotamian Civilization.* Chicago: University of Chicago Press.

Anthony, David W. 2007. *The Horse, the Wheel, and Language*. Princeton, NJ: Princeton University Press.

Bibby, Geoffrey. 1969. *Looking for Dilmun*. New York: Knopf.

Chang, Kwang-chih. 1983. *Art, Myth and Ritual: The Path to Political Authority in Ancient China.* Cambridge, MA: Harvard University Press.

Jennings, Justin. 2010. *Globalizations and the Ancient World.* Cambridge: Cambridge University Press.

Lerro, Bruce. 2000. *From Earth Spirits to Sky Gods.* Lanham, MD: Lexington Press.

Silverberg, Robert. 1985. *Gilgamesh the King.* New York: Bantam.

Smith, Michael E. 2008. *Aztec City-State Capitals.* Gainesville: University Press of Florida.

9

Public Spaces, Self, and Cognitive Evolution in Early States

In this chapter we will expand our understanding of early agrarian states by first examining their class structure and their organization of the public realm, and then we will turn to the social psychology, spirituality, and psychology of their inhabitants by discussing the emergence of vertical collectivism, polytheism, and a new form of second order abstraction.

Social Classes in Agrarian States

Agrarian states were typically composed of eight or more stratified groups.[1] At the top were the king and queen and their family, followed by the priests and priestesses. Priests and priestesses were originally administrators who kept track of all transactions and interpreted the will of the goddesses and gods. They also reinterpreted and composed written sacred myths. The enhanced ability to store grain gave the king and the ecclesiastical hierarchy greater powers than the chiefs in complex horticultural societies had ever experienced. The job of the newly emergent military specialists was to protect the upper classes from the lower classes as well as to protect the state from other states.

Below the military were the merchants and artisans, who produced for an external market as well as for the royal household. Merchants traded the goods that the artisans produced. Merchants in agrarian states had much less autonomy than those in industrial capitalist states were to obtain.

In the city, the class below the artisans consisted of what Marx called the "lumpen proletariat." These were people living by their wits—beggars, thieves, and prostitutes. The urban population of large cities and towns was only about 10 percent of the total population of agrarian states. Most of the population of agrarian societies was composed of peasants who resided in rural villages (Lenski 1984).

The lowest class in the cities of agrarian states was composed of slaves, who were the property of the royal household or of the aristocratic class. Most of the slaves were women and

[1] The term "social class" can be understood generally to mean groups of families that have important institutionalized differences of power, prestige, and wealth. The term "caste" refers to class statuses that are inherited at birth rather than achieved. A society composed of castes has little upward or downward mobility, at least in the theory of inequality that it is institutionalized in that society. Sometimes the term "class" is used in contrast to "caste" and implies that mobility is possible.

children who worked in various jobs within the royal household. Women and children captured through conquest were valuable because the women could provide the king with children and perform menial tasks. Male slaves presented a problem because they were difficult to control.

The last class consisted of the peasantry living in the countryside—the main producers of food. The life of a peasant in an agrarian state was considerably worse than that of a commoner in a chiefdom. Peasants were heavily taxed, conscripted to fight in wars, and recruited to build public works such as irrigation systems and urban monuments. Why did peasants not run away? Emigration was usually discouraged because adjacent arable land was already occupied, and movement to nonarable lands would require a major change in subsistence strategy. This is the condition that we have called circumscription.

Life for about 90 percent of the population in agrarian states was less desirable than it had been for the inhabitants of pre-state societies. There was less warfare but more subjugation. In agrarian societies the ruling class controlled about 50 percent of the total wealth produced. Most of the rural and urban residents lived on a subsistence level—meaning they had just enough food to survive and to reproduce. The goods and services obtained through trading were mainly appropriated by the governing classes. The newly invented technologies such as wheeled vehicles were generally not used by the lower classes but reserved for the military purposes of the rulers or for public display. Long after writing had been invented, only the upper classes were literate. Citizenship was restricted to the elites. Power was hereditary, or conferred by appointment. Most people suffered from a lack of variety in their diet most of the time, which translated into vitamin, mineral, and protein deficiencies. In hunting-and-gathering societies, a more balanced diet had been achieved with far less labor.

The point here is that it is a mistake to think that the greater material wealth, better tools, and harnessing of greater amounts of nonhuman energy produced a better life for all. These things allowed for the emergence of larger settlements and for the expansion of a privileged elite.

Vertical Collectivism and Incipient Individualist Tendencies

The emergence of class stratification resulted in a conflict between the ideology of collectivism and the actual lived experience of class divisions among groups. The members of different classes have conflicting interests, and these conflicts of interest are much sharper than in chiefdoms. The conflicts act as a potential platform for the formation of an individualist self, which is what eventually emerged in the Late Iron Age. Vertical collectivist selves are more conflicted and less unified than the horizontal collectivist selves of pre-state societies.

In pre-state societies the boundaries between society, biophysical nature, and the individual were more porous. Both society and the individual were embedded in the temporal and spatial dynamics of the land and in the sky. In relatively larger-scale agrarian states, a stronger distinction emerges between culture (civilization) and nature. Civilization is tamed and nature is wild. While organic interdependence between humans and nature was intrinsic to the collectivist self, with vertical collectivism the organic whole becomes bounded to civilization and to those plants and animals that are domesticated.

Class distinctions make for different socialization processes within the various groups. Because there is little social mobility across class lines, these different socializing experiences create few internal conflicts within individuals. The socializing messages of religious, educational, and domestic settings more or less support each other. While there might be some loyalty conflicts between the peasant traditions in the villages and the expectations of the state, in most class societies peasants do not question their place in society most of the time. Peasants or artisans may complain about the abuses of a landlord or state official. Sometimes, as in early modern Europe, they created art forms imagining a reversal in class relations. But the idea of questioning the legitimacy of the entire system and presenting alternatives is something relatively rare and quite recent. Complaints are usually in the service of having things "get back to normal." Artisans and peasants lack the resources, free time, education, and ideological support to question the existing order. As James Scott (1990) has pointed out in *Domination and the Arts of Resistance*, peasants and artisans have their own material, status, and ideological disguised resistances.

The state did not have the infrastructural power to penetrate peasant traditions to control them in systematic ways. Tax collections were erratic, and spiritual and artistic traditions were not unified.

The emergence of a great division of labor between mental and manual work within these societies meant that these classes became more specialized in fewer work settings. According to Ernest Gellner (1988), this meant a more specialized language because people were becoming more skilled at what they did. In addition, as classes typically do not have frequent conversations with each other, except for perfunctory exchanges of deference to authority, the vocabulary of each class diverges from the whole.

In these societies, because there were fewer roles and the roles that were played were hierarchically organized, these roles tended to become routinized and rarely questioned. Because agricultural states are more sedentary than either hunting-and-gathering or horticultural societies, people were less at home with change. In symbolic interactionist terms, this meant they were much more at home with role-taking and routine situations than chiefly peoples. Having any experience in transforming situations would be more alien to them.

Vertical collectivists do not consider their personal past and future separate from their group past, and their locus of control was even more external than in complex horticultural societies. This is because both the biophysical environment and class relations were beyond their control. In Mead's "I-Me" dialogue, the "Me" side is far more developed since what is expected of others is far more important than what the "I" wants.

In earlier chapters we said that in complex horticultural societies the chief is the most likely candidate for developing an incipient individualist self. In agricultural states this tendency spreads to include the king, the priests and priestesses, and the merchants.

Reviewing our criteria for the conditions under which individualism might arise, we have already established that the increased specialization of labor, together with the increase in stratification, will support proto-individualist tendencies among all social groups. However, kings, priests, and priestesses are in a position to take this tendency further. First, agricultural states produce far greater absolute wealth than chiefdoms. This means all three classes have more leisure time, more accumulated wealth, and a greater opportunity for education than any chief has. Second, all three groups live in cities, which will further create a cosmopolitan attitude with fewer kinship responsibilities. While wealth in these societies was more land-based, parochial, and centralized (supporting collectivism), merchants regularly traded with other societies. This made them more relativistic in their loyalties than either kings or priests. At the same time, as priests began to master cuneiform script, their specialized knowledge increased and separated them from all other groups. As we will see, the emergence of numerical and literary tracking systems, along with the invention of monetary systems, also promotes the breakdown of kin groups and the emergence of a calculating, enclosed identity.

The status of women in agricultural states was worse than in any of the previous social formations. Women lost control of planting, as men worked plows harnessed to large animals. For the first time in history, most women did not work in public but rather in domestic households supporting the cottage industry of spinning, weaving, and canning. They became more economically dependent on their husbands and more isolated from other women.

Polygyny continued among the upper castes, as a means to either enhance status or seal political alliances. Birthrates were higher than in any previous type of society, as peasants reacted to their extreme poverty by producing as many sons as possible to labor in the fields. As might be expected, child-rearing practices emphasized discipline and obedience. This socialized children to reproduce the class system as adults.

Spiritual Culture in Mesopotamia

As it turns out, the rise of stratified societies and the increased control over the natural environment affect how religion is practiced. For one thing, the development of writing makes it possible to objectify sacred stories and create a high culture of gods and goddesses inhabiting cities.

Meanwhile, oral storytelling involving traditional spirits dominates among those living in rural areas. Secondly, the invention of bronze casting made it possible to fix the powers of gods and goddesses in monumental images, which must have added to an experience of awe, especially because the images in bronze are less subject to decay than those made from wood.

Thirdly, time is organized cyclically. Just as in agriculture there is a planting and a harvesting season, so, too, it is believed that the universe itself is eternally cycling through the seasons. This means that opposites are understood as polar and interdependent rather than dualistic and mutually exclusive. Just as spring could not exist without winter or winter without fall, the attributes of gods and goddesses complement each other within a closed harmonic cosmology. So, too, goddesses and gods have polarities built within them: strengths that can become weaknesses, and weaknesses that, in certain situations, can become strengths. Gods and goddesses are not understood as absolutely good or absolutely evil. This changed with the rise of universalistic religions between 1000 BCE and the sixth century CE.

The emergence of astrology in early state societies illustrates how both time and space are systematically organized according to cycles of the year. Every place in the heavens had a specific meaning because of its location. It was thought that events in the year could be predicted based on the time of the year and where the events occurred.

According to Tikva Frymer-Kensky (1992), the presence of goddesses in Mesopotamia expressed gender categories that people believed were immanent in the cosmos, culture, and society. The gods and goddesses engaged in the same activities writ large as men and women did. The natural elements controlled by goddesses were also *specific to their gender*. What were they expected to do? In weaving cloth, wool is represented by the goddess Ewe, while Uttu makes the wool into cloth. The growing of grain was done by the goddess Nisba. The goddess Ninkasi made beer, and the goddess Ninurra crafted pottery.

The wide range of roles goddesses performed was not limited to domestic activities. Other activities included dramatic performances such as singing at ceremonies for the dead, dream interpretation, medical healing, and wisdom writing and surveying.

From an institutional materialist perspective, there is a dialectical relationship between how the gods and goddesses interact and how actual men and women in society interact. In times of stable social relations there is a more general congruence between the two. When there is social instability and men's and women's roles are changing, the relationships between gods and goddesses generally run *behind* these changes. For the first few centuries, the Bronze Age Mesopotamia was socially stable, but the middle and late Bronze Age were characterized by many instabilities including wars and natural disasters and ecological degradation. These material changes are expressed in the changes in goddess-god responsibilities. Frymer-Kensky (1992) identifies three stages of the relationship between men's and women's roles, and the domains of gods and goddesses can be seen across the Bronze Age.

In the early Mesopotamian state, the roles of women and the domain of goddesses go together. But in the middle Bronze Age there is an interesting contradiction. Men take over many female roles, but *do it in the name of goddesses*. Finally, in the late Bronze Age, men perform these roles in the names of the gods. In the early Bronze Age, goddesses are subordinate to gods, but goddesses still have important roles to play. But between about 1900 BCE to the end of the Bronze Age in the twelfth century, the roles of goddesses go from subordinated to marginalized.

There is not always a direct correspondence between what the gods and men do or what the goddesses and women do:

> Although these cultural contributions of goddesses derive from the actions of women, the relationship between the activity of goddesses and that of women in cultural life is not a direct one-to-one match. At any given moment the portrayal of goddesses in culture reflect both the actual role of women at the time the literature was written and the cultural memory of the contribution of women to the development of civilization. (Frymer-Kensky 1992, 42)

As Frymer-Kensky (1992, 80) says: "The world by the end of the second millennium was a male's world, above and below."

Public, Parochial, and Private Spaces in Bronze Age Cities

What became of the private, parochial, and public realms with the rise of states and cities? Compared to villages, cities (whether agricultural or industrial):

- Are more *concentrated* (crowded)
- Are more *intense* in pace of movement (entering and leaving and exchange of information)
- Are more *diverse* in activities (cultural and recreational, food, education) and services
- Are more *exotic* in population (non-kin, less rooted)
- Have more variety of work opportunities and diversity of goods and services
- Are more *unpredictable* and *novel*
- Have less *interdependence* (more individualism)
- Have more *anonymity* (control over what people know about us)
- Have more *noise*
- Have more *danger*
- Have more homelessness

In short, urban existence is a profusion of audiovisual stimulation in a crowded, intense, exotic atmosphere where a greater number of rootless individuals seek to improve their situation.

Bronze Age cities are characterized by the rise of the public realm and the weakening of the parochial and private realms. According to Gideon Sjoberg (1960), there are many characteristics that distinguish preindustrial cities from industrial cities:

- In premodern cities, a larger proportion of space is spiritualized.
- Within premodern cities, a single space was used for many activities. In industrial cities there is a specialized use of spaces where one space is used for one activity.
- In ancient cities there *are unconcealed differences between classes in mannerisms, clothing, and dialect.* Lyn Lofland (1973) calls this "overt heterogeneity of the populace"; in industrial cities, differences within classes are hidden or understated. Lofland calls this a "masked heterogeneity" in public space.
- In premodern cities, space is less monopolized by commerce.

At the center of the Bronze Age city is a ceremonial center that acts as a little cosmos and that is usually set up, if possible, near a sacred plant or tree. From there the four directions radiate out through and beyond the city, which the gods and goddesses are thought to inhabit. Sack (1980) shows that there was no secular orientation to city planning. It is essentially psycho-spiritual arena:

> Often the most geographically permanent and regular features such as the sun, moon, stars, mountains, rivers and sea become the most . . . arresting. . . . Associations with the sun such as light, warmth, life and birth are placed in the sun's path, especially in the east and above. Their opposites such as darkness, cold and death belong to the west and below. In the mythical-magical mode, this means that directions actually are thought of as the places or "homes" of these feelings and functions. (Sack 1980, 152–153)

Sack gives examples from the Bronze Age city in China:

> Propitious sites for the location of settlements in China were determined by studying "earth currents." . . . The cosmic breath follows earthly channels in a way comparable to the flow of blood in the human body. Geomancy was used to locate Chinese cities and Chinese cities were conceived of as cosmological symbols. According to Chinese ritual books, cities were to be square in shape, orientation to the cardinal directions and enclosed by walls with twelve gates, one for each month. (Sack 1980, 157)

In agricultural states, at the beginning or end of the construction of any sacred or important building, there is a ceremony that integrates the new area or building into the sacred universe of the inhabitants.

The movement from village life to cities creates a special set of interpersonal problems for inhabitants of early cities. In the first place, in tribal societies face-to-face kin groups are the basic unit. Even in chiefdoms with thousands of people, the duties and obligations a person fulfilled were based, to some extent, on personal knowledge of specific kin members.

As we saw earlier, in nonstate societies the presence of strangers was not a taken-for-granted phenomenon. Tribal people either made strangers kin through a ritual or expelled or killed strangers. With the rise of cities, strangers had to be humanized in order for people to get along, especially in economic exchanges. This is because cities have far more strangers than kin members, and city people are far more mobile.

Early state cities are dominated by people in the streets. People with diseases or serious psychological problems wander the streets and are an integrated part of public life. There are no state agencies or hospitals to house the physically or mentally disabled. Punishment for crimes is publicly carried out, including beating, branding, scarlet letters, and having one's eyes plucked out or limbs cut off. There are no prisons. Sacred sacrifices were a normal part of street life.

Neither are there specialized places for children to play or to learn. Children play in the streets. When children were tutored they were taught wherever the tutor could find room outside the shops. There were no specialized places for public entertainment. Public squares and plazas could be used if room could be found.

The small amount of use of secular public spaces makes activities pile up on top of each other. Many activities go on in the same place at the same time. By contrast, in industrialized cities there are more single activities going on in different places at different times.

Compared to today, in ancient cities the rate of exchange of goods and information was far slower. This meant that the *experience* of the events was inseparable from *where* they were experienced. Distances were *experienced as sequences of encounters* with events as one moves from place to place. Much later on, in the modern West, as the rate of trade and information speeded up, the inseparability of time and the physical environment began to unravel in people's experience. *The experiential integration of space and time became separated from events.* The physical environment loses its psychological connection with events and becomes a mere neutral container for them.

In early state cities, the public realm emerges and the private realm declines, mostly because the lack of heat and light in houses drove people into the public. Unlike in modern cities, public space was not dominated by commerce. It was the domain for entertainment, festivals, games, and socializing.

Within public spaces in the ancient world there was little segregation of buildings. Warehouses and workshops were all mixed together. There was no spatial segregation of retail from wholesale items. Neither were animals completely separated from public life. Street life was filled with humans, horses, pigs, and barnyard animals. With the exception of Harappa-Mohenjo-Daro, in the first cities there were no sewers or indoor plumbing. Street life was an extreme mix of decay, feces, and urine mixed with the buying and selling at flea markets, storytelling, and parades. There were many more holidays celebrated in public than in modern cities.

There is an interesting problem between social stratification and spatial integration. Unlike industrialized societies, ancient cities were small by comparison and different social classes were crowded together in integrated neighborhoods. This creates a problem of social classes not being able to distinguish one class from another. The upper classes preserved differences by accentuating rigid codes of appearance and speech. Lower classes were legally bound not to wear clothes made of the same materials the upper classes wore. Peasants could be arrested for wearing the clothing material of the upper classes. There was no such thing as fashion in ancient cities. You wore the clothing appropriate to your social class. In this detribalized atmosphere of strangers, rigid codes of appearance and language were attempts at building a sense of predictability into social relationships.

In short, ancient cities must have been very intense, with the extremes of activities more or less randomly juxtaposed to each other: beggars walking near aristocrats; storytelling in the midst of public torture on one street, happening simultaneously with a parade on another; sacrifices occurring in one cluster while dancing and singing occur close by; children playing games of chance as prostitutes and the insane egg them on.

As Lyn Lofland (1973) argues, the city created a new kind of human being—the cosmopolitan who was able to relate to others in new ways that city living made not only possible but necessary. This individual gained the capacity for surface, fleeting, and restricted relationships that could be tolerated. The capacity to be "civil" means knowing how to behave in public in cities. Please see Table 9.1 for a summary of the characteristics of ancient cities.

Table 9.1 Characteristics of ancient cities

Characteristics of ancient cities	Description of ancient city life	Implied comparison with modern cities
1) Cities are primarily sacred	Cities are often built as a "little cosmos," that is, an expression of the organization of a larger spiritual cosmos in the stars	**Cities are primarily secular social organizations for capitalism**
2) Cities are smaller	**10,000–100,000 people**	**Cities are larger (millions of people)**
3) The commercial sector of public space is small	Commerce on the street (flea markets, haggling)	**Commercial sector of public space is large** Stores selling at fixed prices
4) Public realm is occupied more than private realm	Rich street life, robust public life: dancing, music, storytelling, parades; many holidays use public squares and plazas	**Public street life is marginalized** to make room for transportation and shopping
5a) Slow transportation	Walking for lower classes; litters, horses, or chariots for the upper classes	**Mass transportation**
5b) Slow communication	Town criers	**Mass communication—** newspapers, magazines, radio
6) Unitary experience of events with time and place	Events are experienced as inseparable from when and where they occur	The speeding up of transportation and communication separates experience of events from when and where they occur
7) Public activities are diffused across space and time	Many activities going on in the same place at the same time	**Public activities are focused and specialized** (single activities going on at different times and in different places)
8) Public institutions are less specialized	a) No hospitals (the maimed, diseased, and blind are untreated by institutions but part of public life)	**Public institutions are more specialized** **Hospitals**
	b) No places for public education (children are tutored in the streets)	**Public education**
	c) No sewers or indoor plumbing (body relief in public)	**Sewers and indoor plumbing**
	d) No prisons (public beatings, physical punishment: branding, loss of eye or limbs, and sacrifices)	**Prisons**
9) Public activities are integrated	Warehouses, workshops, houses all mixed together	Retail and wholesale zoning laws
	Farm animals—pigs and horses are part of city street life	Domesticated animals banished from city life except for pets
	Rich and poor are integrated within neighborhoods	Rich and poor are segregated in different neighborhoods
10) Class/caste differences are overt in language and appearance	a) People are what they wear; differentiation in design of dress, materials; costumes dictated by laws	a) People are where they stand; fashions
	b) Elite speech is blatantly different	b) Elite speech is more subtly different

The Emergence of Second Order Abstract Thinking

Usually we characterize abstraction as a private thinking process that goes on *in people's heads*, more or less separated from the point in history in which one is born. In other words, a headman in a hunter-gatherer society, a big man in a simple horticultural society, a chief in a complex horticultural society, and a priest in an agricultural state will all think at the same level of abstraction regardless of the type of society in which they live.

Following the sociohistorical school of Vygotsky and Luria, we challenge this assumption. We contend that abstract thinking:

- Is a social relationship between people both before and after it becomes internalized by an individual
- Is mediated and changed by inventions that occur over the course of history
- Is mediated by the social class one occupies within a given society

In Chapter 4 we argued briefly that the ability to think abstractly is rooted in a social institution—the development of verbal language. We said that the process of abstraction can be divided into three aspects—extraction, deliberation, and generalization. Further, we argued that the ability to learn to think abstractly is necessary for the development of the mature identity (the social self) of an individual. Abstraction is necessary for the development of the generalized other and the biographical self.

In Chapter 4 we also discussed several socializing forces, including religion, mass media, and education. But how do these socializing influences come to be imported inside the individual? In Chapter 1 we said that the process of cooperative learning can be understood as a mediator between the socializing influences of society and the psychology of individuals. These include (1) local, interpersonal, face-to-face interaction, (2) internalization, and (3) "global" interpersonal interactions where the individual applies what has been internalized to wider contexts than their local origins.

But what do Vygotsky's three stages of cooperative learning have to do with the three-stage process of abstraction? The basic movement of abstraction is social–psychological–social. The local interpersonal stage is social, the internalization phase is psychological, and the "global" interpersonal is social. *The moments of extraction, deliberation, and generalization are all part of the psychology of Vygotsky's internalization process.* What is interesting is that the need for abstraction starts with a reaction to a social situation—a problem that needs resolution—and it ends with a need to apply the results of abstraction to a new social situation. Thus, *the alpha and omega of abstraction is social, not psychological.*

A more visual description of what we've just said is as follows:

1. Socializing forces—religion, education, and mass media are focused and filtered by
2. Vygotsky's three stages of learning:
   a. Local interpersonal (social)
   b. Internalization (psychological): three phases of abstraction—extraction, deliberation, generalization
   c. Global interpersonal (social)
3. Building a social self that includes:
   a. Generalized other
   b. Biographical self

Vygotsky's work was concentrated in how children learn over a very short time in history. It tells us little about how *adults* learn over the course of generations. We are confident Vygotsky would say that adults *continue* to go through the same three phases of learning every time they learn to use a new tool or find a new occupation. But can Vygotsky's three stages of learning be applied to how a society learns over the course of history? In other words, what happens to adults and their children when a new tool emerges and new political and economic institutions get built over many generations?

In the specific time period we are studying, we want to address how counting tokens, the use of written symbols, and coined money forced priests, priestesses, and merchants to think in a new way in order to use these tools. In other words, new learning processes can be traced to whole classes as those classes learn to grapple with new symbols, currencies, and tools in the process of reorganizing their social institutions (see Table 9.2).[2]

The purpose of this section is to show how the invention of writing and money developed a new kind of mentality among elites in the early

---

[2] Vygotsky fully supported the work of his colleague Alexander Luria (1976) in researching the impact of the Russian Revolution and the transition from preindustrial to industrial society on the psychology of people. Though both Vygotsky and Luria certainly operated with the now-outdated theory of social evolution as progress, and although they failed to qualify the intelligence of peasants, we think the way they insist technological and economic revolutions revolutionize how people think is still useful and certainly consistent with Harris's (1979) cultural material theory of social evolution.

Table 9.2 Vygotsky's theory of learning: the micro-macro link

Micro-level of individual life cycle	Macro-level of history
Cause	
Socialization by parents for *child's individual* survival	Technological and economic innovation
Stage 1: Local interpersonal	
Engagement between parents and child in *playing and learning* new skills, roles in problem solving	Occupational *cooperation of adults of mental workers of the upper classes* as they *labor and learn* new technologies and economic and political systems
Stage 2: Internalization	
Private, independent problem solving of children	Private, independent problem solving of mental workers
Stage 3: Global interpersonal	
Application of new learning by the child to *nondomestic* contexts: school, play with peers or other adults	Application of new learning by the upper classes to *non-political-economic activities, sacred beliefs and practices, mathematics, art, child rearing, and recreation*
All higher psychological processes begin and end as social processes. They originate first in structured, meaningful, cooperative, and recursive local interpersonal relations between people. Only later do these skills become internalized, private, and independent skills that individuals can carry out alone. Finally, these skills are reapplied to the social world and to larger contexts.	

Source: Modified from Lerro 2000, 176.

Table 9.3 Social evolution from the Paleolithic to the Iron Age

Social evolution	Internal economic tracking	External economic exchange	Communication systems	Sacred systems	Form of abstraction
Paleolithic	Tallies	Barter	Oral (storytelling)	Animism	First order
Neolithic	Simple tokens				
Early Bronze Age	Complex tokens				
Middle Bronze Age	Tokens impressed on envelopes	Protomoney			
Late Bronze Age	Incised tablets, cuneiform		Writing, mathematics	Polytheism	Second order
Iron Age	Alphabet	Coined money	Writing	Monotheism	Second order

states of Mesopotamia, India, and Greece. This involved a move from a more concrete form of abstraction to what we call "second order" abstraction. We define second order abstraction as an *increase* in the ability to:

- Create *more distance* between oneself and a local place in the process of extracting the essential from the inessential
- *Project further back and forward in time* and in the process of deliberation
- Project further in space in the process of deliberation
- *Increase reflection on the thinking process itself*, independent of sensory experience in the process of deliberation
- Apply thinking to a *greater range of situations in the process of generalization*

Table 9.3 is an overview of where we are headed. There is a lot to think about here. We suggest you review this map to help you keep on track as we develop our discussion more deeply. Reading this table vertically you will see a kind of logic within a category. What we think is especially interesting is the relationship *across* categories. What is it, exactly, that unites incised cuneiform, protomoney, written communication, mathematics, and the rise of polytheism over animism in the middle Bronze Age? What do the alphabet, coined money, and monotheism have in common? One answer is the emergence of second order abstraction. The rest of this chapter is designed to tell how this story came about.

Economic Roots of Second Order Abstraction: Redistribution and Market Exchange

An increase in abstraction is driven by the economic and political reorganizations that accompany the emergence of social complexity and hierarchy. The upper classes in Bronze Age states had to learn to think more abstractly in order to manage the complex systems of production, accumulation, and redistribution that emerged. A proliferation of specialized agricultural and manufactured products constituted a complex temple economy that required commoners to contribute the products of their labor to the god of the city. The priests who managed this temple economy needed to keep track of who had contributed and how much. In smaller-scale redistribution systems such as the Hawaiian complex chiefdoms this was accomplished by local district chiefs who knew all the commoners in their district and were responsible for knowing who had contributed, when, and how much, as well as for passing on the contributed goods to the more senior interdistrict chiefs. But in the temple economies that emerged in the Sumerian city-states, populations were much larger and the whole centralized operation was more complex, so managing it required an increasingly formalized accounting system.

From Tallies to Complex Tokens in Mesopotamia

Denise Schmandt-Besserat (1992) shows that the antecedent of writing was not a simpler two-dimensional script, but rather three-dimensional counting devices that she calls simple and complex tokens. These tokens were used to keep track of transactions in the temple economy. We might think of this system as economic, but we need to recall that there was little distinction between the sacred and the economic in these early agricultural societies. All the commoners and the priests were held to be slaves of the god of the city who owed service. Religion was the economy, and the economy was religion. But it was the necessity of accounting in the complex redistributive economy that produced the standardized symbols that eventually evolved into writing, and only then was the new invention utilized to record written sacred traditions. It was only as a *by-product* of the writing on clay tablets for economic purposes that writing came to be used for sacred purposes.

Schmandt-Besserat (1992) distinguishes between two kinds of counting: reckoning and accounting. Reckoning is simply computing—making calculations of how many of an item there are. Accounting is a more complex process that reckons the movements of input and output within a complex network.

The history of human symbolic notations goes all the way back to the Upper Paleolithic when nomadic hunter-gatherers used notched sticks, etched bones, and antlers. According to Schmandt-Besserat (1992), these were simple tallies of many possible items—counting animal skins or the beginnings of a lunar calendar. Whatever the item being counted is, there is a matching of each unit of a group to be tallied with one notch.

> The tallies remained . . . a rudimentary device. First the notches were nonspecific since they could have an unlimited choice of interpretations. . . . The notched bones were limited to storing only quantitative information concerning things known by the tally-maker but remaining enigmatic to anyone else. The simple method of tallies could only be adequate in communities where only a few and obvious items were being recorded. (Schmandt-Besserat 1992, 160)

Yet even in this simple system there were elements of abstraction. As Robert Logan (1995) points out, the marks isolated the object from the context. Secondly, recording the item on the bone separates the information from a particular knower and makes the item recorded "public" knowledge. It displayed information that could be used by others, including those not immediately present.

In late Neolithic chiefdoms in Western Asia, notches and pebbles were at first supplemented and later replaced by clay. Clay was more adaptable to human notation than either bone, wood, or pebbles because of its plasticity, and yet it could be hardened by firing. Using clay allowed the tokens to be *designed* more freely for human purposes. More importantly, clay tokens easily lent themselves to being organized into a larger system of symbolic communication. Tokens were an interrelated system of symbols. For instance, a cone stood for a small measure of grain, a sphere stood for a large measure of grain, and an ovoid stood for a jar of oil. It becomes possible to measure with more precision a large quantity of information.

According to Logan (1986), these tokens could stand for the following commercial products:

- A ban (six liters) or bariga (thirty-six liters) of grain of which there were three varieties: barley, wheat, and emmet
- Jars of oil
- Containers of foodstuffs such as butter, berries, or dates
- Livestock, primarily sheep and goats—differentiated by age, sex, and breed in units of one, ten, and one hundred head
- Wool, cloth, and different types of garments
- Measures of land expressed in terms of the amount of seed required to sow it
- Service or labor expressed in the time units of days, weeks, and months

Clay was a wonderful medium because it was easy to find and easy to work with, and its flexibility made it possible to make tokens without the use of special tools or skills. For example, small tokens could be arranged and rearranged into groups of any composition and size, while notches engraved on bone, once marked, were not erasable. Tallying notations were *irreversible*. Once notches on a bone were made, the bone was "used up" as a means of tracking. On the other hand, plain tokens can be used and reused to track economic exchanges. Lastly, while tallies were limited to tracking only quantitative information, tokens convey qualitative information. The type of item counted was indicated by the token *shape*, while the number of units involved was shown by the corresponding number of tokens. This was certainly a great leap forward in the organization of social information. To summarize:

Tallies	Tokens
Probably counted time or objects	Counted economic items
Made of bone or pebble	Made of clay
Not systematically related	Systematically related
Fixed and irreversible	Can be reorganized and hence reversible
Quantitative only (nonspecific)	Quantitative and qualitative data
Independent of products	Tied to products

The tokens of ancient Western Asia were small three-dimensional geometrical shapes that stood for a certain type and quantity of goods. At the same time, tokens were less abstract than pictographic writing because the quantity recorded was never independent of the quality of a particular object. This meant that arithmetic, algebra, and geometry could not develop until it was possible for numbers to be abstracted from items and studied for their own sake. To study numbers independent of context is a good example of second order abstract reasoning, in which the inventions of the human mind (in this case, numbers) are reflected upon without the burden of a particular application.

Schmandt-Besserat (1992) has unearthed 8,000 specimens of tokens from 116 sites in Iran, Iraq, the Levant, and Turkey. The process of using representations began with twenty-four tokens sometime around 8000 BCE in simple horticultural societies and grew to more than two hundred tokens during the rise of states and cities in Mesopotamia around 3300 BCE. The shapes of tokens included spheres, discs, cylinders, cones, ovoids, triangles, and tetrahedrons. These were further differentiated with markings, incisions, and punched holes.

Tokens evolved following the movement from Neolithic villages to Bronze Age cities. At first, plain tokens were used for keeping track of the products of farming, such as animals or measures of cereals. These tokens were probably loose and exchanged hand to hand. As societies changed toward more complex chiefdoms, these plain tokens began to be enclosed in hollow clay envelopes.

It is presumed that the envelopes were used to consolidate all of the tokens employed in a single transaction. The surfaces of the envelopes were marked with the seals of the individuals involved in the transaction, and hence the clay envelopes may have served as a receipt or as an archival record of a tithe (Logan 1995, 89).

However, there was a problem with the new system in that the envelopes, when sealed, obscured the tokens inside. The contents could not be verified *without breaking the envelope open*. The solution to this problem was an inadvertent major advance in the evolution of writing:

> Accountants resolved the problem by imprinting the shapes of the tokens on the *surface* of the envelopes prior to enclosing them. The number of units of goods was still expressed by a corresponding number of markings. An envelope containing seven ovoids bore seven oval markings. . . . The seals signaled ownership, obligation or authority. (Schmandt-Besserat 1992, 7; italics added)

Corresponding to the increase in bureaucracy in Mesopotamia, *complex* tokens were developed to keep track of products manufactured in workshops, such as textiles, garments, luxury items, and other goods like bread and oil. Whereas plain tokens were simply smooth shapes, complex tokens had a greater variety of shapes and contained punctuated markings such as lines, dashes, and circles. These complex tokens were more refined and more uniform in character. In addition, for the most part, complex tokens were not stored in envelopes but rather were strung together by a solid bulla (leather thong), like the beads of a necklace. Furthermore, they were not passed on hand to hand but were kept in archives. The use of bullae solved the problem created by the envelopes (invisible content), but it did not lead to the next great leap.

We can see an abstract process at work in the movement from a three-dimensional handled symbol to a two-dimensional representation on the surface of a clay envelope. The drawing of signs of the object on the surface of the envelope combines the handling of the three-dimensional symbols and a two-dimensional writing system. *But the writing was not originally intended to be a substitute for the tokens.* According to Logan (1995), *it took at least fifty years for people to realize that the actual tokens in the envelope were redundant if the impressions were on the outside.* When this occurred, clay tablets with cuneiform symbols replaced hollow envelopes.

Cuneiform text was produced by using a wedge-shaped stylus (made from a reed) to make marks in soft clay, which was then hardened by firing. The envelopes became the small clay tablet troves that have been found in the archaeological sites of ancient Western Asia.

Schmandt-Besserat (1992, 7; italics added) continues:

> As a result, *tablets*, solid clay balls bearing markings replaced the hollow envelopes filled with tokens. . . . These markings became a system of their own that developed to include not only impressed markings but more legible signs traced with a pointed stylus. Both these types of symbols . . . derived from tokens were picture signs or pictographs. The signs were *not pictures of the items* they represented but *pictures of the tokens used as counters* in the previous accounting system.

We summarize here the differences between plain and complex tokens.

Plain tokens	**Complex tokens**
Smooth shapes	Perforated shapes with markings
Not stored (simple horticulture)	Stored in envelopes, on bullae (agricultural states)
Represented animals, cereals	Represented manufacturing products
Casually made (fired at low temperatures)	More standardized
Passed on hand to hand	Kept in archives

There were a number of complex forms of thinking at work as people learned to use these tokens. The general parts of the movement were as follows:

- From reckoning to accounting
- From irreversible markings on tallies to reversible use of tokens allowing repeated use
- From quantitative data to quantitative and qualitative data

- From tokens used at large to tokens contained in hollow envelopes or stringed bullae to clay tablets

The following is both a summary of what has been discussed and a preview of where we are headed. Up to now the movement from tokens to writing contained the following stages:

1. Types of tokens were at large and passed down hand to hand
2. The tokens were enclosed in an unmarked envelope
3. The tokens were enclosed in a marked envelope
4. Abandonment of envelopes for bullae or "stringed beads"

Where we are headed:

1. The abandonment of bullae for *tablets with impressed signs* that stand for abstract numbers
2. The abandonment of bullae for *tablets with incised signs* that stand for commodities made with a stylus
3. The development of *pictorial writing and the alphabet* from incised signs and used for purposes other than economics
4. The use of pictorial writing for self-reflection on numbers—mathematics
5. The use of the alphabet for self-reflection on words—sacred literature, myths

Table 9.4 contains a summary of this entire section that is helpful for keeping track of the big picture.

Table 9.4 From tallies to tokens to cuneiform

Time period	Type of counting	Material used	Containers	Contents counted	System application
Upper Paleolithic 29,000–15,000 BCE	Tallying One-to-one enumeration	Matched sticks, etched bones, antlers	At large	Time, animal skins Quantities, not qualities	Unsystematic reckoning
Mesolithic 15,000–8,000 BCE	Tallying	Pebbles, shells	At large	Time	Unsystematic reckoning
Neolithic 8,000–3,400 BCE	Plain tokens Concrete counting	Clay balls; tangible, tactile, three-dimensional	At large	Cereals, animals Quantity and quality are merged	Systematic accounting
Bronze Age cities 3,400–3,200 BCE	Complex tokens Concrete counting	Clay balls; incised, perforated, punctuated	Plain envelopes	Handicrafts, manufactured goods	Systematic accounting
3,250–3,150 BCE			Tokens impressed on envelopes, stored on stringed bullae		
3,150–3,100 BCE	No more tokens Writing Abstract counting	Clay	Impressed tablets; two-dimensional, visual		
3,100 BCE	Abstract counting	Clay	Incised tablets; two-dimensional, visual	Split between quantity and quality	Accounting, taxes, tribute, land surveying
			Concrete commodities; incised signs	Abstract numbers; impressed signs	Accounting
After 3,100 BCE	Second order Abstract counting	Clay	Numbers, words Picture writing/ ideograph Phonetic (alphabet)		Sacred texts, mathematics

Continuing with our story, tablets replaced both envelopes and bullae and with this came the development of what Logan (1995) calls the "logogram," which is a two-dimensional visual sign that abstractly represents the written form of a single word. Egyptian hieroglyphics and Chinese characters are examples.

Logan goes on to make a crucial distinction between the *impressed* tablet and the *incised* tablet. While the incised tablet led to the development of writing, the impressed tablet did not:

> It is important to note that the impressed logogram semantically was no different from a three-dimensional token. The logograms were two-dimensional negative imprints of the three-dimensional tokens. They were immediately recognizable to the users of the token system because they shared the same outline and bore the same markings as the actual tokens. In fact the first tablets are not true writing but merely the permanent records of an accounting system based on tokens in which the tokens themselves were actually discarded once their imprints had been made. (Logan 1995, 92)

However,

> The shift from three-dimensional artifacts to logograms in the form of negative images impressed on two-dimensional surfaces triggered a chain reaction that resulted in the invention of logographic writing, phonetic coding and abstract numerals. (Logan 1995, 93)

As Logan points out, the loss of volume, concreteness, and tactility in representations was the royal road to a higher form of abstraction:

> It removed the symbols one step further from the physical three-dimensional reality from which they stood. The display of information within a two-dimensional array, however permitted the user to see the information in a new light. By being able to observe more data at a single glance, the user of the tablet system began to think more "globally about the data. More abstract patterns of classifying and analyzing the data became possible." (Logan 1995, 94)

It was using a tablet with *incising marks* rather than impressing three-dimensional tokens that made possible these more abstract patterns of analysis and classification. According to Logan (1995), up to the invention of incisions on tablets, the movement from tokens to cuneiform went through five stages:

1. Plain tokens
2. Complex tokens
3. Tokens in clay envelopes (and strong bullae)
4. Impressed logographs on clay envelopes containing tokens
5. Impressed logographs on clay tablets

Up to this point, this movement is an evolution in the variety and number of tokens but not in their meaning or function. The limitations of tokens were also their strengths. While their three-dimensionality made them more flexible than notched tallies, their volume made them difficult to store. Small artifacts can be easily separated, and it is difficult to keep them in a particular order over long periods of time.

> The earliest tokens represented given quantities of given commodities. It required another quantum leap to conceptualize . . . the idea of *quantity apart* from any specific commodity. But once taken, this leap implied . . . the ability to represent any specific commodity apart from its dimensional representations of both numbers and commodities to the writing systems that emerged at the beginning of history. (Schmandt-Besserat 1992, xi)[3]

[3] Schmandt-Besserat (1992) here uses the word "commodities" in the conventional sense of any good produced for exchange. Recall that in Chapter 2 we used Marx's more restrictive definition of a commodity as a good that is produced for sale in a price-setting market in order to make a profit. We use the terms "goods" or "products" to designate items that have been produced for any kind of exchange outside the family, and reserve the term "commodity" for the above.

From Concrete Counting to Abstract Counting

Up until now we have discussed the movement from the concrete to the abstract in terms of objects used (tallies, tokens) and containers (envelopes or bullae). Now we will turn our attention to numbering systems. Each reckoning or accounting device was determined by a particular mode of counting. In simple hunting-and-gathering societies the repeated addition of one unit with no precise idea of total numbers is adequate to fulfill accounting in a society where goods are not usually stored.

Each mark tallied represented one unit of collection. Repeated addition of more tallies did not result in new numbers being attached to them. In other words, a set did not have a final number. A larger collection of coconuts would not be tallied as a precise number, such as forty-one, but rather "many." This way of tracking was adequate as long as the principal means of economic exchange was generalized reciprocity rather than a hierarchical redistribution center where precision mattered.

Concrete counting emerged in the token economies of the Neolithic and Bronze Age societies. In these redistributive systems, words for numbers were tied to the concrete objects that they stood for. The invention of tokens:

> provided new ways of handling data . . . cardinality and object specificity. Cardinality [is] the ability to assign arbitrary tags, such as number words, to each item of a collection, with the final number word of the series representing the number of the set. For example seven incised ovoids held in the Uruk envelope . . . stood [for] seven jars of oil. . . . Accounting with tokens implied grasping the notion of sets. . . . During the Neolithic, counting animals no longer consisted of adding "and one more" but one cylinder stood for 1 animal, two cylinders for 2 animals, three cylinders for 3 animals. (Schmandt-Besserat 1992, 189)

However, while adding qualifiers to quantifiers of tallying, plain and complex tokens *fused* quantity to quality. There were no abstract numbers such as one, two, and three. The second major change that tokens brought about was object specificity. The token system required particular counters to deal with each type of good:

> Ovoids were used to count jars of oil and spheres to count measures of grain; vice-versa jars of oil could only be counted with ovoids and measures of grain with spheres. . . . The fact that tokens varied with each good suggests that they reflected a conceptual level at which *only units of the same kind could be counted together*. In other words tokens seem to be conceived for manipulating data with a system of concrete counting. (Schmandt-Besserat 1992, 190; italics added)

To summarize thus far:

- Tallies—one-to-one correspondence—quantitative only
- Tokens—both simple and complex—concrete counting—quantitative and qualitative are fused

Abstract counting, on the other hand, involves the *separation* of numbers from the items:

> Our numbers 1, 2, 3 express the concepts of oneness, twoness, threeness as abstract entities divorced from any particular concrete entities. As a result, 1, 2, 3 are *universally* applicable. We can count men, canoes, and trees with the same numbers. . . . We can count for the sake of counting without any reference to any particular item. Whereas concrete counting probably did not allow counting beyond a score of objects, there is no limit to abstract counting. . . . Abstract counting thus marks the beginning of arithmetic. (Schmandt-Besserat 1992, 187)

The wedge, which originally meant a small quantity of grain, now stood for one; the circle, which represented a larger quantity of grain, was ten. The large wedge and punched wedge and the large circle were greater numbers (Schmandt-Besserat 1992, 193).

The Independence of Numerical and Writing Systems from Economic Redistribution

Once numbers become independent of economic transactions, words on paper soon after also become independent of economic accounting. However, the liberation of writing systems from economic redistribution did not occur until the late Bronze Age in Mesopotamia. On one hand, liberated numerical systems led to mathematics; on the other, liberated writing systems were used in the service of written myths.

At first, both numbers and words were embedded in economic institutions. But those classes working with these symbols (priests, priestesses, and merchants) begin to toy with and *deliberate* about the nature of these systems independently of their use in economic transactions. Lastly, years later they *generalize* into social use again. These inventions were applied to accounting in expanding storage systems in the case of mathematics and to the development of sacred myths in the case of the alphabet. Now abstract numbers and letters were both a product and a producer of second order abstraction.

Summarizing the above in terms of social evolution, we can say that:

> 8000–3500 BCE—concrete counting, fusion of quantity and quality
> 3500–3100 BCE—abstract counting applied to the number of commodities, separation of quantity and quality *in economics*
> After 3100 BCE—second order abstract counting, self-reflection on abstract counting applied to mathematics and sacred systems

Second Order Abstraction Applied to Evolution from Tokens to Cuneiform and from Concrete to Abstract Counting

All forms of notation, whether tallies, tokens, or writing, extract information from their context, separate knowledge from a specific knower, and become socially available. All notations express movements in collective abstraction. However, the later in history we go, the process of abstraction itself accelerates. At the beginning of this chapter we said there are three movements that can be traced in abstract thinking: extraction, deliberation, and generalization. What we will do now is apply this sequence to the evolution from tokens to writing and the evolution from concrete to abstract counting.

In the movement from concrete to abstract counting, the extraction moment is when quantities are extracted from qualities; the deliberation process includes self-reflection about the number independent of the specific items counted, which results in the extension of the number line and the beginnings of arithmetic. The generalization moment occurs when numbers are no longer tied to particular items, which results in:

- Expansion of storage possibilities because of the extension of the number line and the scope of the items that can be counted
- Expansion of the number of people who can use the codified information

We can also see the movement of second order abstraction in the movement from the use of tokens to the use of cuneiform script. Tokens were used at large and then they were collected in envelopes or strung on bullae. The movement of second order abstraction began when signs for the tokens and the numbers of the tokens were separated from the manipulation of the tokens. The deliberation process occurred when the accountants realized that holding the tokens in envelopes was no longer necessary if they were represented two-dimensionally on envelopes or tablets. The generalization occurred when the tablets were used to track goods by incised signs for the goods and for abstract numbers. A further generalization occurred when writing on tablets for accounting purposes opened up the possibility of writing about noneconomic aspects of human life (e.g., sacred traditions). Then letters became freed from their original context, just as numbers had been. Please see Table 9.5 for a summary.

A similar but different process of the invention of writing occurred in ancient China, where counting rods and inscriptions on oracle bones indicate the emergence of second order

Table 9.5 Comparison of first order and second order abstraction applied to internal economies

Devices used in tracking	Type of counting	Form of abstraction
Tokens in envelopes (3250 BCE)	Concrete counting (3250–3150 BCE)	First order
Tablets	3150–3100 BCE	Second order

Steps in the process of building second order abstractions applied to internal economies

Devices used in tracking	Stage 1: Extraction	Stage 2: Deliberation	Stage 3: Generalization
Tablets	Separation/elimination of three-dimensional containers	Reflection on container	Tablets with incised signs or impressed signs
Abstract counting	Numbers are extracted from items	Deliberation about numbers	Extension of the number line and the beginning of mathematics; expansion of storage; food more systematically distributed

abstraction (Needham 1959). Knotted strings (*quipu*) were used to record contributions of goods in the Andes, and hieroglyphics were well developed in Mayan and Mesoamerican civilizations.

The Invention of Money

The history of the invention of money did not begin with the early emergence of market exchange; rather, it began much earlier in societies of sedentary foragers and horticulturalists. Symbols of value began as prestige goods—precious and rare items that were used as status ornaments. These were often exchanged as gifts among elites to symbolize alliances. The Kula Ring of the Trobriand Islands in the South Pacific (studied by Bronislaw Malinowski) is the most famous example.

But standardized symbols of value were also used to facilitate the exchange of food among interdependent groups. We saw in prehistoric California (Web Chapter) the use of what we call "protomoney"—clamshell disk beads. These beads were produced by grinding clamshells into round and equivalently sized disks, drilling a hole in them, and stringing them onto a leather thong. Village headmen often had tattoos on their arms for measuring equivalent lengths of these strings of beads, and the beads were used in intergroup trading for both local and long-distance goods. This was not market exchange, because the rates of exchange (prices) were not set by competitive buying and selling among a large number of independent sellers and buyers trying to get the best returns. That is the definition of a price-setting market. In California the exchange of clamshell disk beads for food, obsidian, woodpecker scalps, bow-staves, and so on, was carried out in the context of trade feasts in which one village would invite neighboring villages to a multiday celebration. The trade was carried out by the headmen of the villages, and rather than trying to get the best deal, they were symbolizing their generosity and trust of one another in order to cement intervillage alliances. This was not market trade. It was generalized reciprocity using protomoney. But the existence of protomoney facilitated the emergence of true money once real markets and commodity production began to emerge. This began to happen within the complex agrarian states of Mesopotamia, China, and Mesoamerica.

A different kind of economic relationship began to emerge in the Bronze Age—commodity production for market exchange. The evolution of money from prestige goods involved the spread of its use from intersocietal relations among elites toward more general usage by commoners in smaller denominations. At first this was only an occasional and insignificant adjunct to the redistributive temple economy. Exchanges between societies mainly took the form of gift giving among elites or the payment of tribute from conquered provinces to the conquering king.

The invention of coined money in India and Greece between the tenth and seventh centuries BCE allowed people to organize all products in terms of a single price. Now a purchaser could bring money to a market without bringing any products. Karl Polanyi's famous essay, "Aristotle discovers the economy," describes how it had become possible in classical Greece to buy ready-to-eat food in the marketplace. Greek society had become relatively commodified with a large part of the overall economy carried out by means of production and exchange in price-setting markets.

The widening and deepening use of money involved people in market transactions and developed the use of quantitative calculations in the service of efficiency and in making decisions about alternative uses of scarce resources. The increasing use of money develops second order abstractions from another angle. Thanks to the work of Alfred Sohn-Rethel (1978) we can see that coined money is a *social* abstraction that teaches people to think beyond local space and present time. How is this so?

Trade was originally carried out by means of barter, in which the actual goods produced were exchanged for other goods needed by the producer. But barter is a rather cumbersome mechanism because it is often difficult for a seller to find a buyer who has exactly what she or he needs and wants what she or he has. What this does is to force people in their exchanges to focus on local space and present time. One does not want to go away empty-handed, but to bring back the goods to one's home base. The invention of money allows people to go to the market with nothing and browse without feeling pressured to exchange something. Money, a universal equivalent medium of exchange that symbolizes abstract value, is the solution to this problem. Using money not only buys time but also buys space. With money as a universal equivalent, trade relations across longer distances are easier. One of the essential parts of all abstract thinking is time-place displacement. The use of coined money covers three of the characteristics of second order abstract reasoning.

How do the three stages of abstraction apply to the use of coined money? The moment of extraction includes separating the quantity or standard (the essential) from the many accidental and particularistic characteristics that were part of pre-money economies. This facilitated ignoring all those qualitative properties of commodities that are irrelevant to their money value. Market interaction encouraged the ignoring of social status and other attributes of the person buying, other than ability to pay. The reduction of these qualitative differences to a price is roughly equivalent to the first moment of abstraction—extracting the essential from the inessential.

The moment of deliberation occurs in using money because it allows deliberation between the time of purchase and the time of sale. Money buys time. It allows people time to think about whether they want to buy something, because the physical burden of bringing objects to and from the market is eliminated. To trust in a coin that has no immediate use value (it cannot itself be eaten or used) requires an acceptance of the reliability of the value of money and the market economy to which it allows access.

The third moment of abstraction is generalization. Coined money makes for an expansion of trade within and between societies because it serves as a general system of value equivalence. Market economy provided an alternative to participation in kin-based and state-based sectors of the economy. This was useful to some of the elites, and it stimulated greater competition among them. It was also useful to commoners, who now had more options for obtaining needed resources.

But there was also a downside to the emergence of market rationality. The use of money concentrated people's attention on cost and alternative uses of commodities, and tended to obscure the relationships among people's labor that is actually the basis of a complex market society. The focus on one's own efforts to obtain money and to use it to buy commodities tends to take the foreground, while knowledge of the sources of the commodities bought, or the final destinations of commodities produced, recedes, at least compared to simpler, more local, and more normatively regulated economic systems. Marx referred to this phenomenon as the "fetishism of commodities." It produces a type of rationality that is focused on the question of how an individual can maximize his or her returns and tends to undercut those institutions that try to calculate in terms of collective rationality.

The Emergence of Mental Work Is the Foundation for Second Order Abstraction

The evolution of counting and accounting systems, together with the impact of writing systems, is inseparable from the class issue of who gets to count and who gets to write. As a result of the wealth in crop production created by use of the plow and large-scale irrigation, it became possible for the first time in history to divide the labor force into full-time mental workers and full-time physical workers. This centralized political process means that mental workers "think" much more than they "do," while physical workers of the lower classes "do" more than they are publicly supposed to "think." The priests and advisors to the kings were the full-time mental workers who made their living working with symbols.

In order to do the job of politically centralizing a society, a mental worker must cultivate the abstract thinking skills of coordination of the input and output of the redistribution center, the systematic supervision of others, and the ability to project plans for the society in the future. Coordinating, supervising, and planning require that administrators not allow themselves to be buried in inessential details. They must *extract* the essential from the inessential of the goods they are handling. They must stay focused on coordinating the details in one area with details from other parts of the system. The priest or priestess must also *deliberate* and think about how to coordinate the actions of others before ordering these actions. Lastly, in order to plan for society, the administrator has to *generalize* by imagining future contexts that anticipate what will probably happen before it actually happens.

One of the fruits of a class-based mental-physical division of labor in the Bronze Age is that upper-class mental workers had both the time and the occupational responsibility to *think about thinking*. This reflective process probably would not get very far without writing, because writing captures thoughts and allows them to be reorganized, improved, and self-consciously manipulated. The ability of the priests and priestesses in the upper classes of Bronze Age states to mobilize the labor of commoners allowed them to cultivate a private relationship where reading–thinking–writing–more thinking could develop and take on a life of its own. This led to *thinking about the thinking process itself and how knowledge is acquired* (epistemology). This meant that it became easier to organize thinking processes into categories, to compare them with other categories, to prioritize the categories, and to work out the logical inconsistencies between thoughts. Among the Greeks of the Iron Age, this became the basis of deductive reasoning and formal logic.

In everyday life, we are presented with problems. We use our minds to solve them and then new problems arise. Thinking is generally rooted in the need to take action to solve problems. In tribal societies, thinking and doing go together across a wide variety of semi-specialized activities. This we call "first order abstraction." But when people cannot "see" their cognitive processes through some kind of external storage system, the thought processes fade when conversations with others end or when projects get resolved either in successes or in failures. The idea of extracting thinking from this process of problem solving and *scrutinizing it for separate examination* can only come about through some kind of external storage system. It can also only come about once people are paid to think and become full-time mental workers.

Hieroglyphics, the Alphabet, and Second Order Abstraction

All societies have to determine how to transmit their most important social knowledge across generations. One of the by-products of the evolution of writing is that it serves as an external storage system for social knowledge. But how does a society transmit cultural knowledge when there are no writing systems?

As Eric Havelock (1963, 1971) has pointed out, people in oral cultures have developed very sophisticated memory devices using story, drama, poetry, music, and dance that provided a unified experience and allowed people to remember what was important in their society by saturating the senses and creating an altered state of consciousness. Therefore, religious practices not only served sacred purposes by emotionally involving people but fulfilled the pragmatic function of a memory theater.

The stories told are dynamic and easy to understand because they appear to be based on the common experiences of all members of the society. Conflicts around polarities such as danger and security, love and betrayal, leaving and joining others, and aggression and justice are just some of these tensions. The sacred beings that undergo these struggles have their unique strengths and weaknesses that allow people to identify with them. The stories have rhythm because they are connected to very particular times of the year and particular places. The stories are grounded in time and space. When combined with song and dance, the memories are located in the body and these memories return as soon as the music and movement opportunities present themselves. The rituals resemble a kind of public phenomenon in which each participant dramatizes the cultural legacy.

The emergence of hieroglyphics in the Bronze Age and the alphabet during the Iron Age loosened the necessity of using myths, dramatization, dance, and the arts to support collective memory and cultural legacy. With writing, these traditions became detached from the people enacting the story, the storyteller, the time and place of the ritual, and the sense data and emotions that go with it. The stories become isolated, enshrined, privatized, and deliberated about. This partly explains the differences between monotheism on the one hand and animism on the other. (For a detailed account of this see Lerro 2000, 2005.)

Especially in the case of the alphabet, those who can read and write can communicate with strangers, and this undermines loyalty to one's own kin group and community. A reader can see their culture more objectively and more independently of the need for storing memories. With the emergence of a secular science in the Late Iron Age, the sensuous present of storytelling was joined by a logical literary presentation of cause and effect, or a linear sequence from beginning to middle to end.

David Abram (1996) makes an excellent point in that human language did not always separate us so dramatically from biophysical nature. The language of hunter-gatherers includes making and listening to the sounds of other animals as part of their language. In order to survive in the jungles, foragers must become sensitive to the sounds and cries of other animals in order to catch them. Further, they must be able to imitate these sounds in order to lure these animals out of hiding. It takes years of practice to refine these techniques. To make exclusively *human* sounds when living in the jungle would keep potential prey away. On the other hand, to be incapable of listening to the sounds of dangerous animals would be life-threatening. It was *written language* that modified this. It was written language that expanded human-to-human communication across local boundaries, while using language to mimic the sounds of other animals declined.

The rise of picture writing (hieroglyphics) involved the transfer of attention from biophysical nature to the two-dimensional surface of parchment or tablets. Symbols of objects and animals rather than call-and-response relationships became the focus of attention. Even so, with picture writing, animals are visually depicted even though it is in static images. With the use of the alphabet, all visual images are left behind, as all sounds and letters refer to the human world of speech. As Marshall McLuhan (1969) has pointed out, learning to write and read transforms biophysical relationships based on *hearing* into social relationships based on *seeing*.

Hieroglyphics use pictures to represent words or ideas, while a phonetic alphabet represents the sounds of spoken words. One big advantage of an alphabet is that it takes only thirty or forty symbols to represent all the sounds you need to reproduce spoken language, whereas a system of hieroglyphs employs thousands of symbols that take a long time to learn. Hieroglyphic systems worked in societies that had a small full-time class of literacy specialists who could spend years mastering the great texts, but the trickling-down of writing to the practical world of commerce was greatly facilitated by the invention of alphabets.

It is no accident that Sumerian, Egyptian, Chinese, and Harappan civilizations are land-based river-valley agrarian states that contributed to the development of pictographs but not the alphabet. The movement to develop the alphabet was the work of more mobile herding, trading, and maritime societies—the Hebrews, the Arabs, the Phoenicians, and the Greeks. This is probably because these peripheral and semi-peripheral societies needed more portable and efficient writing systems for conducting business.[4]

The movement of writing from hieroglyphics in the Bronze Age to the alphabet in the Late Iron Age also occurred during the transition from polytheism to "universalistic" world religions based on monotheism. This movement went with changes in the law. For example, in the case of the Babylonians, the code of Hammurabi (1900 BCE) advanced the theory of jurisprudence because, in reaction to the task of organizing and centralizing local groups separated by language, race, and subculture:

> Hammurabi . . . had to appease each element of the society and satisfy them that they were being treated fairly and equally with all the rest . . . ensuring uniformity of measures, good prices, professional fees and transport tariffs throughout the empire. (Logan 1986, 76–77)

Before the Hebrews developed a writing system, their gods were sensuous and pluralistic. Yahweh at the time of Abraham, Isaac, and Jacob was just another tribal god of this herding society. But this soon changed:

> The God of Moses takes on an even more abstract formulation reflecting the abstraction of alphabetic writing. . . . YHWH is invisible to his people. He cannot be looked upon or the people will perish. The people are forbidden to make any visible image of their god. (Logan 1986, 91)

Table 9.6 summarizes the commonalities in building second order abstraction thinking in internal and external economic exchanges, in communication systems, and in sacred beliefs. Pay special attention to the commonalities in the stages of abstraction as they apply across the three stages (the parts of the table that are in italics).

Theoretical Implications: The Sociohistorical Nature of Abstraction

At the beginning of this chapter we showed the parallels between Vygotsky's stages of cooperative learning in children and how they could be applied to world history across generations. We will close this chapter by showing how these three stages could be applied intergenerationally in the use of tokens, writing systems, number systems, and sacred beliefs. To begin with, all new psychological skills are driven by necessity. In the case of individual development, the child must be socialized by parents in order to survive in society. In the case of world history, necessity comes calling in the form of technological innovation and economic reorganization. The invention of new technologies and the reorganization of political economies temporarily resolve a social crisis, and in the process of resolving the crisis, adults learn new psychological skills, specifically second order abstraction.

The three-stage process of learning occurs in individual development and in world history. In individual development the local interpersonal stage is the domestic household, usually between caretakers and children. In the realm of world history the local interpersonal stage occurs in the economic and political work settings of priests and royal political advisors. In the internalization stage of individual development, children internalize what they have learned from their caretakers; in the internalization stage of world history, adults internalize what they have learned from technological, economic, and political realms as their own. In the "global" interpersonal stage of individual development, children or teenagers take these internalized

[4] The late arrival of phonetic alphabets in East Asia may have been a consequence of the relatively more centralized Chinese dynasties compared to the multicentric and very competitive Central political-military network (PMN) at the western end of Eurasia. The more rapid turnover of political power and the frequent rise of semiperipheral marcher states allowed new communications technologies to become institutionalized more rapidly in the Central PMN.

Table 9.6 Commonalities in building second order abstraction across economic, communication, and sacred systems

	Type of abstraction used	Stage of abstraction	Stage of abstraction	Stage of abstraction
Internal economic exchanges				
Tokens in envelopes	First order	Extraction	Deliberation	Generalization
Tablets replace envelopes	*Second order*		*Reflection on container*	*Tablets with incised signs or impressed signs*
Concrete counting	First order	Extraction	Deliberation	Generalization
Abstract counting	*Second order*	*Numbers extracted from items*	*Deliberation about numbers; extension of the number line and beginning of mathematics*	*Generalization of numbers across categories of items; expansion and precision of storage; food more systematically distributed*
External economic exchanges				
Bartering	First order	Extraction	Deliberation	Generalization
Coined money	*Second order*	*Essential qualities of objects are reduced to a price*	*Deliberation; reflection between the time of purchase and the time of sale*	*Generalization; universal currency within society; buying and selling replace kinship rights and obligations*
Communication systems				
Oral (storytelling)	First order	Extraction	Deliberation	Generalization
Written (hieroglyphics 3000–1000 BCE, alphabet 1000–800 BCE)	*Second order*	*Thinking abstracted from conversation and action*	*Mental laborers plan, supervise, and coordinate work processes*	*Political centralization, empire building*
Sacred beliefs				
Animism	First order	Extraction	Deliberation	Generalization
Monotheism (1000 BCE)	*Second order*	*Essential (god) extracted from accidental properties of Nature*	*God has a plan for the universe*	*God is everywhere, God is transcendental*

skills outside the domestic household to the larger world, engaging teachers, friends, neighbors, and the media. In the "global" interpersonal stage of world history, the adult applies the skills learned at work to nonlaboring contexts.

Table 9.7 shows how these stages might be applied to the invention of new tools in the movement from the Neolithic to the Bronze Age.

Let us walk through this together. Begin by reading across and scanning the first three columns and the first four cells for orientation. Notice that the time frame is from the late Neolithic to the late Bronze Age. In the second three cells we are trying to show how skills are passed down from parents to children—the children internalize the skills and then as they grow up they must use the skills they learn in new work settings at a later point in history. The third grouping of cells is showing scale—from the macro-world of history to the micro-world of the individual, back to the macro-world of society. The last of the four cells simply shows what drives change. In the case of macro-history one, it is technology and the economy, and in the micro-world it is the need of the child to be socialized. In the third column, at a later point in history there is another wave of technological and economic reorganization.

Table 9.7 Intergenerational emergence of second order abstract thinking from the Neolithic to the Bronze Age among priests, priestesses, and merchants

Late Neolithic Age	Early Bronze Age	Late Bronze Age
Social-historical change in parents	**Ontogenetic change in teenagers of parents**	**Sociohistorical change as teenagers become new adults**
Macro-level 1	**Micro-level 1**	**Macro-level 2**
Cause: technological and economic innovation	**Cause: individual adaptation by being taught socialization skills by parents**	**Cause: a new technological and economic innovation**
VYGOTSKY'S THREE STAGES OF LEARNING THROUGH THE NEOLITHIC	**VYGOTSKY'S THREE STAGES OF LEARNING THROUGH THE EARLY BRONZE AGE**	**VYGOTSKY'S THREE STAGES OF LEARNING THROUGH THE LATE BRONZE AGE**
1) Local interpersonal change in laboring Practices: Cooperative learning and problem solving in new laboring practices in technology and economics; *use of plain tokens and complex tokens; commodity production*	**4) Local interpersonal: parenting** Priests, priestesses, and merchants teach second order abstraction skills to their teenagers in problem solving; role-playing in handling tools, artifacts; and game playing	**7) Local interpersonal** As adults, these priests, priestesses, and merchants must use second order abstract thinking to resolve new ecological-demographic crises (picture writing, use of gold and silver bars)
2) Internalization Priests, priestesses, and merchants learn to extract, deliberate, and generalize *Economic redistribution learned to extract images from tokens and apply to tablets with impressed or incised signs*	**5) Internalization** Teenagers extract, deliberate, and generalize *privately in the absence of adult supervision*	**8) Internalization** Priests, priestesses, and merchants learn to extract, deliberate, and generalize abstract counting
3) Global interpersonal Application of new skills to noneconomic contexts: *sacred beliefs, rituals, child rearing, and games*	**6) Global interpersonal** *Teenagers practice second order abstraction thinking when playing with peers and working; occupation of a priest, priestess, or merchant prior to a crisis*	**9) Global interpersonal** Application of second order abstraction to a more abstract polytheism and to the development of mathematics independent of surveying and weights and measures

In the second half of the table we show how Vygotsky's three stages of learning would play out over the course of history by recurring in three nonrepeating cycles between the late Neolithic Age and the late Bronze Age. The figure is best read top to bottom, following the numbers. Numbers one to three are cycle one, numbers four to six are cycle two, and numbers seven through nine are cycle three.

Women and Second Order Abstraction

According to Vygotsky's theory, the extent to which women used second order abstract reasoning is related to how often they got a chance to use complex tokens and hieroglyphics in the redistribution systems of the Bronze Age. During the Late Iron Age, how often were they able to use money and the alphabet when these emerged?

In terms of the development of plain and complex tokens, given that women more often than men made clay pots, it is likely that women were actively responsible for making these tokens. The handicraft production of these tokens, however, is not the same as *using* them. It was the priests in agricultural states who were responsible for using these tokens for redistribution/accounting purposes. This class was a small fraction of the entire agricultural state population—about 1 percent, according to Lenski and Lenski (1987).

It is important to remember that 99 percent of the men did not have access to this technology, so the lack of this tool affected lower castes of men as well as women.

As pointed out by Schmandt-Besserat (1992), when hieroglyphics emerged on two-dimensional tablets, those who first worked with them (whether for economic purposes or for sacred purposes) were men. Further, the invention of writing was important in justifying both gender and class stratification. The new mythology was powerful not only because it became male dominated but because it was *written down*. But why would writing the myths down have provided political clout for the elite? How would this differ from *orally* passing myths on?

Oral myths are more easily changed, if for no other reason than there are more limits to the human memory than there are to a written scroll. In oral myths, each generation must have left out certain elements of the myth and added new parts. In contrast to this, once the stories were written down, they were less subject to change unless deliberately intended. Written myths must have acquired an awesome quality and a formality that the oral myths lacked. Since *elite men* were in control by the time writing was invented, it was *their* myths that became awe-inspiring.

Writing must have increased gender inequality in another way. The gender-stratified moral order became *codified in laws*. Activities that deviate from codes that are written on tablets and scrolls must have been far more illegitimate and forbidding. This would have made it more difficult to protest.

As we said earlier, the emergence of the alphabet was a more democratic tool, because it was easier to learn and to use than earlier hieroglyphic scripts. The alphabet, not only in Greece but in China and Japan as well, spread to the middle classes and perhaps to some lower-class farmers, but the vast majority of people who learned to use it were men. If formal political participation in the polis was open to only about 20 percent of the male population, it is doubtful that women, who were excluded from direct political participation, would have learned to use the alphabet.

The emergence of coined money was different. As goods production and markets expanded in the Late Iron Age, those merchants involved in external trade involving ships were generally men. However, women were involved in both internal and external local trade in Greece and must have developed second order abstraction.

In short, hieroglyphics, the alphabet, and coined money increased the distance between some men and most other men and women and codified existing and expanding forms of patriarchy into institutionalized laws and daily practices. Emerging class and gender differentiation in social structures of the family, religion, and the state also became embedded in the differentiated selves within society. But class and gender struggles contested these developments, and the rationality developed by the rulers to protect their own interests was contested by a different rationality from below as the tools of symbolization filtered down.

Suggested Readings

Gellner, Ernest. 1988. *Plough, Sword and Book*. 5th ed. Chicago: University of Chicago Press.

Goody, Jack. 1977. *The Domestication of the Savage Mind*. London: Cambridge University Press.

Lerro, Bruce. 2000. *From Earth Spirits to Sky Gods*. Lanham, MD: Lexington Press.

———. 2005. *Power in Eden*. Victoria, BC: Trafford Press.

Logan, Robert. 1995. *The Fifth Language*. Toronto, Ontario: Stoddart.

Mumford, Lewis. 1956. *The Transformations of Man*. New York: Harper.

10

The Early Empires: Semiperipheral Conquerors and Capitalist City-States

This chapter is about the rise of the early empires in those regions of Afroeurasia and the Americas where early states had already arisen. It focuses on "pristine" or "primary" empire formation, in which large polities emerge in regions where they had never existed before and in the absence of contact with other very large polities. It is also about two kinds of semiperipheral development:

- The emergence of semiperipheral marcher states that create new large empires by means of conquest
- The emergence of semiperipheral capitalist city-states, autonomous states pursuing strategies of merchant capitalist trade, and the production of commodities in the context of world-systems in which the predominant mode of accumulation is based on the extraction of tribute and taxes by means of state-organized institutionalized coercion

An empire is a state that has conquered other polities and peoples. **Imperialism**, understood generally, is the exercise of intersocietal power—the domination and exploitation of a group of people by people from a different polity. In this general sense, core/periphery hierarchies in interchiefdom systems could be termed imperialism, but this term is more commonly used when the polity that is doing the exploiting and dominating is a state or an empire. A **core-wide empire** comes into existence when a single state unifies a whole core region of states by means of conquest.

Figure 10.1 plots Rein Taagepera's estimates of the territorial sizes of the largest and second-largest empires in the Central System for the purpose of identifying empire upsweeps. We know that the first upsweep was that of Uruk and the Uruk expansion that began on the floodplain of Southern Mesopotamia (Algaze 1993), but we do not have quantitative estimates of the territorial size of the Uruk polity. After a long period of competing city-states in Mesopotamia, the Akkadian Empire emerged as the first core-wide empire. Its territorial size is estimated by Taagepera, and so it appears in Figure 10.1.

The hegemonic sequence (the rise and fall of hegemonic core states) is the modern version of an ancient oscillation between more and less centralized interstate systems. All hierarchical systems experience a cycle of rise and fall, from "cycling" in interchiefdom systems to the rise and fall of empires to the modern sequence of hegemonic rise and fall. In state-based (tributary) world-systems, this oscillation typically takes the form of semiperipheral marcher states conquering older core states to form a core-wide "universal" empire (see Figure 10.2).

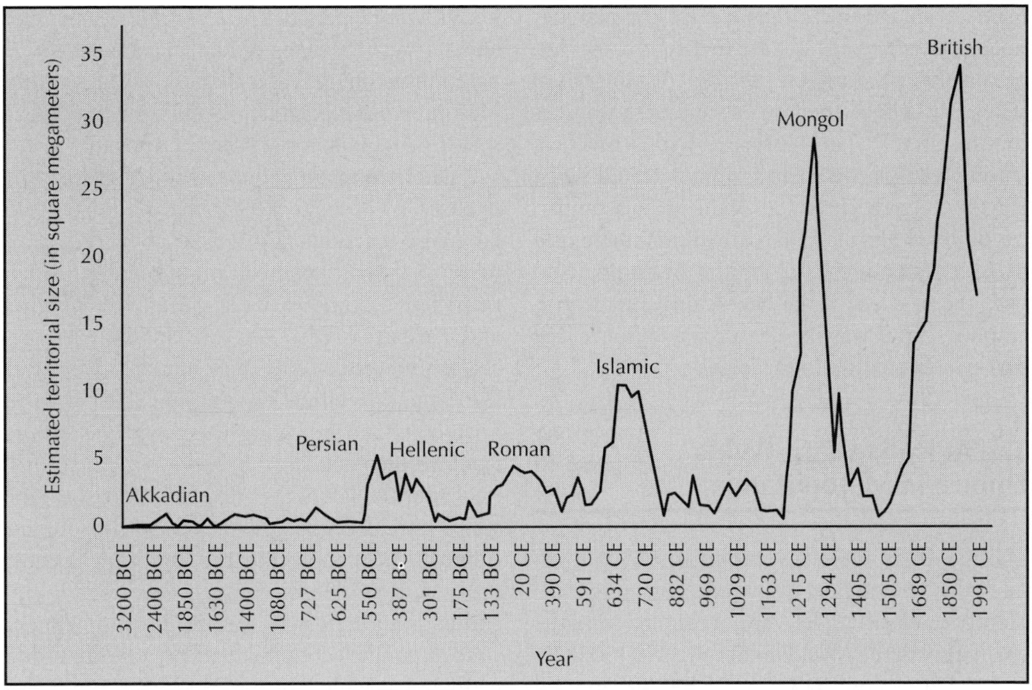

Figure 10.1 Territorial sizes of the largest states and empires, 3200 BCE to 1991 CE

Sources: Taagepera 1978a, 1978b, 1979.

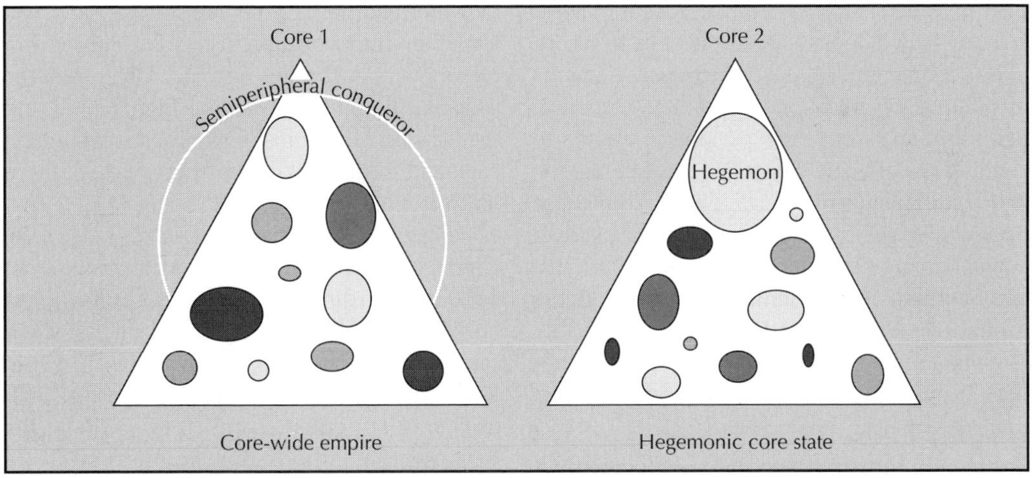

Figure 10.2 Core-wide empire versus hegemonic core state

Peripheral peoples sometimes overran civilizations that were in decline, despoiled them, and left only a scattered remnant of the former complex and hierarchical society. This is probably what happened to the Harappan civilization of the Indus River valley. In Mesoamerica, the empires of Teotihuacan, Tula, and Monte Alban may have suffered a similar fate. But a more common pattern was that of the **semiperipheral marcher state** recently founded on the edge of an old core region conquering the core states to form a new larger empire. William H. McNeill (1963) referred to semiperipheral states as "high barbarians." Randall Collins (1978, 1999) contends that the main advantage held by semiperipheral marcher states is that they do not have to defend their rear, because they are out on the edge of a region of states. This allows them to concentrate resources for the attack. The first core-wide conquest empire was the Akkadian Empire, created when Sargon of Agade subjected all the Mesopotamian city-states to his rule in the early third millennium BCE. It was not a large empire in comparison with the vastness of the later Mongol or British empires, but it was the largest single polity that had ever existed up to that time.

The Akkadian Core-Wide Empire in Mesopotamia

Though there were several efforts by powerful states to conquer the whole core region of Mesopotamia, this goal was not reached until the emergence of the Akkadian Empire in 2350 BCE. Chase-Dunn and Hall (1997, 84–89) argued that this first core-wide empire was a semiperipheral marcher state conquest. This was based on the notion that the Akkadian-speaking conquerors were semiperipheral because they were recently settled nomadic pastoralists in Northern Mesopotamia and because they used elements of political organization and military technology stemming from their peripheral origins to conquer the old core city-states and to erect the core-wide Akkadian Empire. This portrayal has been challenged by evidence that the Akkadian language had long been present in both Northern and Southern Mesopotamia and that Agade, the capital of the Akkadian Empire, was probably established after the Sargonic conquest rather than being a city populated by recently settled nomads (Postgate 1992, 36).

By the time of the Sargonic conquest, the characterization of Northern Mesopotamia as semiperipheral is problematic. The northern part of the alluvium was more heavily urbanized than the south in the Early Uruk period (Adams 1981), but the situation reversed toward the end of the Uruk period with the exponential growth of the city of Uruk. The north may have had a greater concentration of Akkadian speakers (Postgate 1992, 38), but some of the northern cities (e.g., Kish) had long been among the contenders for hegemony in the inter-city-state system of the Early Dynastic period. These considerations favor an interpretation of the Akkadian conquest that is based more on class and ethnic cleavages within Mesopotamia (e.g., Yoffee 1991) than on the idea that the Akkadians were semiperipheral.

The Akkadian regime, called an "upstart dynasty" by Postgate (1992), made the Akkadian language the official language of record, and, under Sargon's son, Naram-sin (2291 BCE), imposed a standardized system of weights and measures across the Mesopotamian core. Naram-sin extended direct imperial rule over the Sumerian cities, eliminating the old local aristocrats and replacing them with governors from his own family.

After the fall of the Akkadian dynasty, there was a period of disorder in which the Gutians (nomadic hill people from the Zagros Mountains) infiltrated the Mesopotamian core region and contended for power. The north-south dimension of conflict continued to be a cultural and geopolitical fault line. In 2113 BCE the Third Dynasty of Ur (Ur III) reasserted southern dominance and Sumerian culture. David Wilkinson (1991) notes a pattern that he calls "shuttling," in which centralized power shifted back and forth between two adjacent regions. Subsequent Mesopotamian empires were not larger than the Akkadian Empire had been (see Figure 10.3), and the location of the most powerful states shuttled back and forth between Northern and Southern Mesopotamia.

Figure 10.3 graphs the territorial sizes of the largest states and empires in Mesopotamia from 2600 BCE to 1000 BCE as estimated by Taagepera (1978a, 1978b). The rise-and-fall phenomenon can clearly be seen. Also, the great upward sweep of the Akkadian Empire (6.5 square megameters) was not equaled until 800 BCE by the Neo-Assyrians, who then went on to create an empire that ruled fourteen square megameters in 650 BCE. This was a new upward sweep of political integration of territory more than twice the size of the Akkadian Empire. We also have data on the sizes of many of the largest cities in Mesopotamia. This indicates that, as would be expected, large empires build large cities, and the processes that cause growth and decline phases affect both urbanization and empire formation.

As Elman Service (1975) and William H. McNeill (1963) have pointed out, the main problem

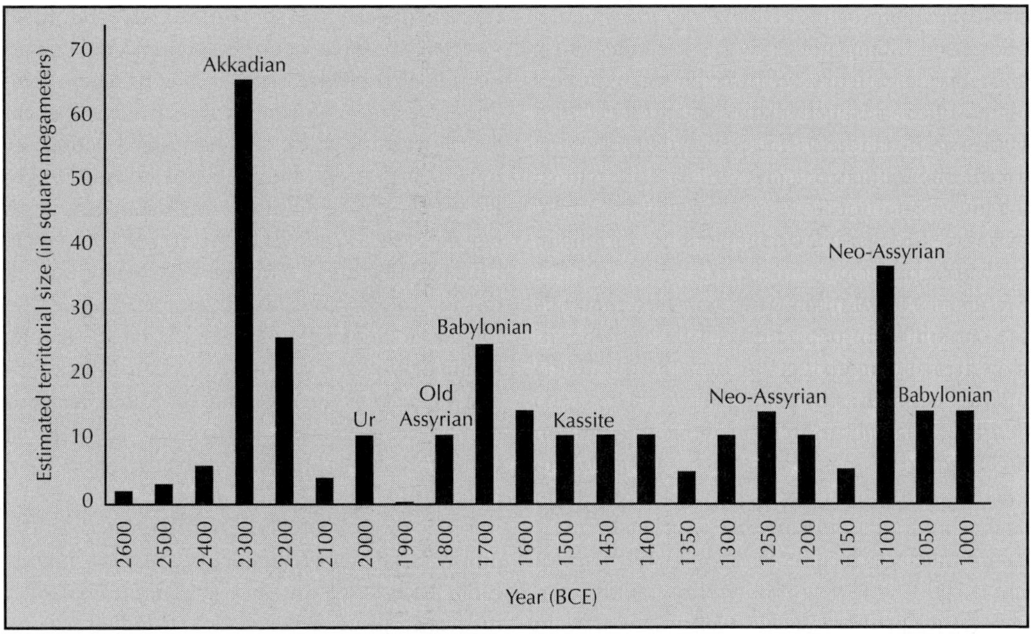

Figure 10.3 Territorial sizes of Mesopotamian states and empires, 2600 BCE to 1000 BCE
Sources: Taagepera 1978a, 1978b.

for the civilizations of the river valleys was not how to exploit peripheral peoples but how to fend them off. The accumulation of stored wealth was greater than ever before, and this constituted a license to steal for peripheral nomads. This led to a racist ideology of "subhuman barbarism." Jerrold Cooper (1983) contends that the Mesopotamians did not generally vilify different ethnic groups, but:

> There are two important exceptions to this absence of ethnic stereotypes: the Gutians and the Amorites, who represent the nomadic and seminomadic hordes of the mountains to the north and east and the desert to the north and west, respectively. Both are described as subhuman, but in somewhat different terms. The Gutians are characterized as savage, beastlike imbeciles, whereas the Amorites are usually curious primitives, less horrible, if every bit as threatening militarily, than the Guti.
>
> Even though the Gutians and Amorites did conquer, temporarily, in the lowlands their lack of familiarity with civilized culture made their rule short. Of course the (Sumerian) priests interpreted this in terms of their failure to understand how to worship the gods, much as the failures of more civilized dynasts were attributed to impiety. The maintenance of power required political savvy as well as military prowess, and in this the nomads were lacking.

Cooper's characterization of the Sumerian beliefs about the Gutians and the Amorites reminds us that something like racism is not a uniquely modern phenomenon.

Semiperipheral Conquerors: "Barbarians" on the Edge

The most serious incursions of peripheral tribes occurred during periods of political disorder in the core regions. There were probably both "push" and "pull" factors involved in this pattern of recurrent incursions. Disorder among the "civilized" states made them vulnerable and encouraged interlopers. And nomadic pastoralists and hill tribes had their own organizational dynamics (Hall 1991). We know from other areas that nomadic pastoralists have their own cycles of centralization and decentralization (Barfield 1989). And climate changes affected both the abilities of the agrarian states to produce food and the abilities of the nomads to raise herds. Thompson (2006) indicates that there is a fairly good correspondence over time between the size of the largest Mesopotamian state and the Tigris/Euphrates River levels. This is encouraging for the hypothesis that climate change played a part in the causation of the rise and fall of empires, and it may have been an important factor in peripheral incursions as well.

The Amorite tribes were nomadic pastoralists coming from the deserts of the northwest. In order to prevent their incursions, the Ur III dynasty constructed a defensive wall across the northern edge of the Mesopotamian core region (Postgate 1992, 43). Thus did the core/periphery interaction in Southwest Asia produce a feature of the built environment that is a smaller version of the much more famous Great Wall of China. But there were also new invasions from the east by Elamites, and it was a combination of Amorite and Elamite incursions that led to the fall of the Third Dynasty of Ur. There followed the Isin-Larsa period, in which small independent states each had an Amorite ruling house. The Old Babylonian period that followed was a system of rather large multicity states. The Amorite kings of Babylon, including the famous Hammurabi, expanded their empire to create the Babylonian Empire depicted in Figure 10.3. This is an example of semiperipheral marcher state conquest that we shall see repeated in the sequence of the rise of larger and larger core-wide empires. The Babylonian Amorites can be considered to be semiperipheral rather than peripheral people because they had lived in cities and states within the Mesopotamian interstate system for at least a century. Babylon itself was conquered in 1595 BCE by a new group of nomadic invaders, the Hittites, led by Murcilis. The conquest empire of the Hittites was a case of a marcher state strategy in which peripheral nomads overwhelmed an interstate system and created a new core-wide empire. Thus in the Bronze Age Mesopotamian world-system, we find both semiperipheral and **peripheral marcher states** creating new core-wide empires.

The distinction between peripheral and semiperipheral peoples is important for understanding the processes of social change in the ancient world. Peripheral nomads sometimes were successful in conquering sedentary core regions, but when they did the core region usually collapsed or the new dynasty was short-lived. Semiperipheral people were former peripheral nomads who had been settled on the edges of a core region long enough to make some changes in their internal social organization. If semiperipheral people set out on the path of conquest, they were much more likely to be able to build a longer-lasting core-wide empire. The Akkadians of the Sargonic conquest (discussed above) had been in Mesopotamia too long to be considered semiperipheral. The Akkadian language is part of the larger Semitic language family, and so the Akkadians were probably more recent arrivals than the Sumerians. But immigrants who have been around longer than a century become domestic ethnicities rather than semiperipheral outsiders.

The old Babylonian Empire created by the Amorites saw the emergence of the most famous early instance of the law—Hammurabi's Code. Institutionalized written law and judicial courts already existed in the early Sumerian states of Mesopotamia. But with the rise of the empires, the law took on a new importance by facilitating the ability of a conquering state to rule peoples with different cultures. The law is important as a means of governance in societies in which the moral order based on consensus about the norms of behavior is no longer able to serve as an effective glue for holding the social order together. Hammurabi's Code allowed the Babylonian Empire to impose its own rules over the ethnically different communities it had conquered.

The institution of the **law** can be defined as written rules that are legitimized by a state and backed up by state-organized rewards and punishments. All societies have rules, but not all have the law. The moral order is originally constituted linguistically as people's agreements about definitions of right and wrong, obligations, and legitimate conflicts. Kinship is the original basis of the moral order. This kind of orally constituted moral order works best in small egalitarian societies or within small subgroups of larger societies where people share consensual ideas about ethics and morality. In order to have law, a society must have a written language. The law is one of the institutions of regional regulations that are the defining characteristics that distinguish a chiefdom from a state. Other such institutions are bureaucracies and armies, and these are usually the mechanisms by which the law is enforced. The law requires institutionalized coercion to back it up. The law is not just the rules as they exist in peoples' consciousness. It is the rules as officially designated and enforced by the state. This is why state-based modes of accumulation are often described as being based on institutionalized coercion.

East Asian Marcher States

Owen Lattimore (1940, 305–306), in his famous book *Inner Asian Frontiers of China*, describes similar processes of semiperipheral marcher conquest operating in the interstate system of ancient China:

> Other groups began to follow, though more slowly, the same line of evolution as the Shang, some of them becoming tributaries while others remained independent and hostile though imitating as far as they could the characteristics that had given strength to the Shang. Some of these groups, which had not been sufficiently advanced in general culture to develop for themselves the technique of working in bronze as the Shang had developed it, were able to take over this technique once it had been developed. This narrowed the gap in military efficiency between what had now become backward or "less-Chinese" groups and the progressive Shang or "more Chinese" group. . . . As the backward groups became more formidable in war the most advanced and cultured group became more vulnerable. War, for the Shang people, came to mean not only the raiding of others but the protection of their own slaves, granaries, wealth, and lands. The difference between slave cultivators and ruling warriors meant that interest in war was not equal throughout the society. More backward groups with fewer slaves and more free warriors, even though they were less "noble" than the Shang aristocracy, became able to hold their own in war against the Shang. . . . When this equalizing process had gone far enough it was only a matter of time until the Shang would be overthrown by a cruder people who were not necessarily invaders from beyond the horizon of what was now definitely the early Chinese culture, but a people already belonging to the Chinese culture, although not to its most refined and advanced form.

The Chinese system shifted back and forth between "marcher states" nearer the frontier and lowland centers that led "nativist" reactions to the upland conquerors. The Zhou dynasty, attacked by new barbarians in the West, moved its capital further east toward the Great Plain and then declined. It was followed by the Qin, another semiperipheral marcher state from the West that succeeded in founding the first unified Chinese empire. The Qin conquered the Great Plains but never completely subdued the Yangtze valley state of Ch'u. Drawing on resistance from the Huai and Yangtze peoples, the Han dynasty (firmly based on the Great Plains) was founded in 206 BCE (Lattimore 1940, 311).

Lattimore (1940, 531) also graphically describes the cycle of Chinese dynasties that corresponds with our notion of the rise and fall of powerful states:

> Although the social outlook of the Chinese is notable for the small honor it pays to war, and although their social system does not give the soldier a high position, every Chinese dynasty has risen out of a period of war, and usually a long period. Peasant rebellions have been as recurrent as barbarian invasions. Frequently the two kinds of war have been simultaneous; both have usually been accompanied by famine and devastation, and peace has never been restored without savage repression. The brief chronicle of a Chinese dynasty is very simple: a Chinese general or a barbarian conqueror establishes a peace which is usually a peace of exhaustion. There follows a period of gradually increasing prosperity as land is brought back under cultivation, and this passes into a period of apparently unchanging stability.
>
> Gradually, however, weak administration and corrupt government choke the flow of trade and taxes. Discontent and poverty spread. The last emperor of the dynasty is often vicious and always weak—as weak as the founder of the dynasty was ruthless. The great fight each other for power, and the poor turn against all government. The dynasty ends, and after an

interval another begins, exactly as the last began, and runs the same course.

Lattimore goes on to qualify this characterization for different periods. Here we are concerned with the Qin and Han empires and their relationship with peripheral regions. It was not until the first century BCE that the Silk Road became a safe route for caravans with the establishment of a chain of empires linking the Han China, Kushan, Parthian, and Roman empires. Before that, diffusion was limited to down-the-line trade among oasis settlements and/or the carrying of cultural elements by migrating steppe nomads. Some have argued that original Chinese state formation by the Shang may have been spurred by an invasion of chariot-making barbarians from the West (e.g., McNeill 1963). It is true that bronze making probably diffused from its point of invention in Asia Minor across Central Asia to East Asia. But little evidence supports the conquest theory, and most scholars believe that state formation in China was mainly an autochthonous regional process that was not much affected by interaction with the older core states and cities of the Central System in the West Asian–Mediterranean region.

The relative isolation of Chinese civilization also prevented the diffusion of alphabetic writing. By the time contact with the West became more common, the Chinese already had a substantial investment in a great literature written in their complicated ideographic script.

Mesoamerican Marcher States

The Mesoamerican world-system also experienced the rise and fall of empires with semiperipheral marcher states as the conquerors that created large empires. The early states of Teotihuacan and Tula in the Valley of Mexico (central highland Mexico where Mexico City is now) fell in part because of invasions of peripheral nomadic peoples (generically called *Chichimecs*, or "dog-eaters") from the northern deserts. Recall from Chapter 8 that Teotihuacan was the large city that produced the monumental pyramids and temples that may be seen today about fifty kilometers northeast of Mexico City. The empire of Teotihuacan was very large, and the religion and architectural styles developed by this highland culture spread as far as the Mayan highland region to Kaminaljuyo, a large city that was in what is now a suburb of Guatemala City.

At Teotihuacan, the first urbanized empire in the Valley of Mexico, a community of artisans produced obsidian tools for mass consumption using chunks of raw material imported from distant mining sites (Spence 1982). These artisans lived and worked in their own district of the city, and archaeological evidence indicates an important transition in the organization of their supplies. At first, each workshop obtained its own supplies of obsidian, but later supplies were centralized, presumably by the state, and divided equally among workshops. Artisans supplied specialized high-quality products to the state by working part-time in state workshops located near the temple complex. These better-worked prestige goods were used in state-administered exchanges with other states in Mesoamerica. Recall from the Web Chapter that turquoise mined in what became the southwestern region of the United States (Arizona and New Mexico) found its way to the workshops of Teotihuacan and the homes of the core elites. The fall of Teotihuacan appears to have been a rather violent set of events in which the monumental parts of the city were intentionally destroyed. We do not know whether this collapse was due to an incursion of invaders or a conflict that emerged within the society of the core empire.

After the fall of Teotihuacan there was a period of small contending states in the Valley of Mexico before a new core state emerged with its capital at the city of Tula—the empire of the Toltecs. The Toltecs had a similarly far-flung empire. Charles Di Peso (1974) argued that "pochtecha" traders representing the Toltec kings were an important force behind the building of the great houses at Chaco Canyon in what is now northwestern New Mexico.

After the fall of Tula, the Valley of Mexico lost population, and no central state emerged to integrate the advanced horticultural economy for around 250 years. One of the Chichimec groups that moved into the valley was the Mexica-Culhua, a band of nomadic hunter-gatherers from the north. These are the people who became known to history as the Aztecs. As Richard Blanton et al. (1981, 152–153) put it:

> They rapidly adopted the behavior and technology of the Valley's more urbanized dwellers, however, and soon rose to political prominence. The story of one of these immigrant groups—the Mexica—is one of the greatest tales of epic progress from rags to riches ever recorded. The Mexica were originally considered to be so undesirable that they were forced to live on a series of low, swampy, bug-ridden islands in the middle of brackish Lake Texcoco. They survived by exploiting the meagre lacustrine resources, and by selling themselves as mercenary soldiers. Through cunning and generally shabby behavior they eventually established themselves and their island city of Tenochtitlan as a force to be reckoned with.

Within a century after its founding, Tenochtitlan had become an independent city, and from then until the Spanish conquest it carried on an aggressive policy of military expansion and alliance that created a large empire extending far beyond the boundaries of the Valley of Mexico. Although the Mexica could not be described as semiperipheral at the time of their arrival in the valley, after a hundred years of adopting "the behavior and technology of the Valley's more urbanized dwellers" they might easily be so considered. And though they were not pastoralists, their egalitarian kin-based mode of integration may have given them greater solidarity (**asabiyah**)[1] and a military advantage over their more stratified neighbors that Lattimore (1940) attributed to the Zhou marcher state in China (above).

The Mexica reorganized their own society during their adaptation to sedentary life in the Valley of Mexico. Their kin-based social structure had been constituted as a collection of equal lineages, but as they took up the role of military mercenaries contending with the older core states they underwent a process of class formation. An elite emerged (the *pipiltin*) that claimed descent from the Toltecs of Tula, the now-legendary former empire state in Central Mexico. The new hereditary elite was distinguished from the class of commoners, and this transformation to a class society expanded as success in war led to a new conquest empire.

Although historians refer to the Aztec Empire as if it were strong and centralized, the Aztecs always ruled in alliance with other city-states in the Valley of Mexico. And, while Tenochtitlan was the political-military center, Tlateloco, a neighboring city, was the main market center of the regional economy. The relatively weak and somewhat illegitimate character of Aztec rule may partly account for the politics of terror by which the Aztecs attempted to maintain the subservience of their own commoners and tributary states.

The large rituals of human sacrifice carried out by the Aztec priest-kings are hard to comprehend. The Aztec elites were fond of human flesh, and the bodies of the sacrificial victims were not wasted. The increasing scale of the rituals suggests that the priest-kings were trying to outdo one another in a competitive game of vaster and bloodier proportions.

R. C. Padden (1967) contends that the relative ease with which Hernan Cortez was able to conquer the Aztecs with a small force of Spanish soldiers was importantly due to the moral superiority that Cortez felt over the Aztecs. Cortez saw himself as the bearer of Christian civilization. When Montezuma, the Aztec emperor, showed Cortez the statue of Huitzilopochli (the Aztec God of War) in the temple on top of the main pyramid in Tenochtitlan, Cortez leaped up the stairs to the statue and pushed it down, smashing the idol. The Virgin Mary, symbol of the Christian god of grace and mercy, was strong medicine in the mind of the conqueror. Jared Diamond (1997) stresses another advantage that the Spaniards had. They carried with them pathogenic diseases that had been developed in the urbanized regions of the Old World and to which the New Worlders had no immunity (see also C. Mann 2005). Cortez was also able to easily mobilize indigenous allies against the Aztecs.

---

[1] "Asabiyah" means social solidarity—the "we-feeling" and trust among a group of people that facilitates collective action. This term was used by Ibn Khaldun (1958) to explain the military advantage that nomadic desert tribes had over urbanized societies.

Marvin Harris's (1977) explanation of the rise of world religions focuses on their advantages for the process of empire formation. If the conquering emperor's god is a tribal or city god, the conquered may end up as a ritual sacrifice for dinner. But if the conqueror's god is a "universal" god of mercy, the conquered can, in principle, become part of the moral community of the empire. The world religions also separate the moral community from kinship by locating the responsibility for commitment to authority within the individual, who must confess belief or undergo baptism. This allows religiously based morality to incorporate individuals from different families and ethnic groups into the same moral community.

Karl Polanyi's colleague Anne C. Chapman (1957) studied a coastal "port of trade" in a region that was intermediate between the Mexican and Mayan regions of Mesoamerica. According to Chapman, this was a neutral zone in which "state-administered trade" between different states was carried out (but see below). Recall that state-administered trade is based on political deals among states. The state traders in Mesoamerica were called *pochteca* by the Aztecs. The **pochteca** were agents of kings who combined religious, trade, and spying functions on their missions to distant lands. The Polanyian approach claimed that Mesoamerican trade was marketless.

More recently, scholars of Mesoamerican trade have found ample evidence of market exchange (e.g., Blanton et al. 1981). Blanton et al. contend that archaeological and documentary evidence from the valleys of Oaxaca and Mexico and the lowland Mayan area shows that market interactions existed and that the importance of markets ebbed and flowed countercyclically with the efforts of states to exercise political control over exchange (see also Hassig 1985, 67–84). As evidence of the existence of a profit motive in ancient Mesoamerica, Blanton et al. (1981, 38–39) write:

> Why for instance, would cacao-bean money have been counterfeited? Judges in the markets punished those who committed fraud in transactions. "Good" merchants were distinguished from "bad" ones. The latter profited excessively by selling fake stones as precious stones, or bad-tasting, old tamales as fresh ones, and so on. This sort of thing sounds very much like "business as usual," and certainly provides overwhelming evidence for a profit motive.

Ross Hassig's (1985, chapter 6) description of the economy of the Valley of Mexico under the Aztec Empire also sees an interaction between market processes and state regulation. Hassig describes how the Aztecs used political coercion to extract tribute and to promote a structure of market exchange that concentrated manufacturing in Tenochtitlan and production of less processed goods in other cities. Hassig implies that the Aztec policy deindustrialized the other cities. As Hassig (1985, 130) puts it:

> Tenochtitlan altered this pattern by encouraging primary production throughout the Valley of Mexico while simultaneously discouraging secondary production. It did so by controlling the flow of tribute and by exercising monopolistic control over much pochteca trade, rendering the valley cities incapable of effectively competing with the secondary production of Tenochtitlan for several reasons. First, overall craft specialization in these cities was weakened by the influx of competing tribute goods from the outside. . . . These goods consisted primarily of finished goods that could be rechanneled into the valley economy through the markets. The cost of tribute goods to the recipients was nil. There were, of course, both military and administrative costs involved in tribute, but the costs weighed more heavily on the commoners than on the nobility while benefiting the latter disproportionately. These tribute goods could be sold at or below the cost of production of similar wares produced in the Valley of Mexico.

It is impossible to say how important these forms of core/periphery exploitation were for the Aztec political economy, but the interaction between tribute from conquered hinterlands and the creation of a more hierarchical division of labor in the Valley of Mexico is a fascinating instance of the use of both imperial and market mechanisms to restructure a core/periphery division of labor in favor of the imperial center.

Empires in the Andes

The northwestern region of South America where early chiefdoms and states emerged is an ecologically dramatic region in which the biosphere and the geosphere generate radically different climates, topographies, and natural resources that are close to one another. This is what ecologists call a coarse-grained ecology. The deepness of the ocean and the prevailing currents produce an amazingly productive marine environment that has been exploited by humans since their arrival in the region. Radical shifts in the productivity of the ocean are caused by the powerful El Niño–Southern Ocean oscillation, and this also changes the climate of the land. The normally dry coastal region is watered by snow-fed streams coming down from the Andes, but an El Niño brings torrential rains to the coastal desert that tend to destroy the irrigation systems built to bring the river waters to agricultural fields. The productive but unstable environment of the coast produced complex chiefdoms that sought the mineral and agricultural resources of the highlands, and so the Andean world-system formed around the exchange of goods flowing up and down what John Murra (1980) called the "vertical archipelago."

Irrigated horticulture, a highly productive fishing economy, and state formation first occurred in the coastal river valleys, but the states that created the early Andean empires were the highland Wari and Tiwanaku. Elman Service (1975, 197) describes these as "cultural outposts" of the developed coastal region and ascribes their motivation for conquest as based on the need to control trade in the context of a coarse-grained ecology that linked the highlands with the coast.[2] As they became more specialized as pastoral and agricultural producers for exchange with the valley agriculturalists, they came to depend on imports for their livelihood. When political disorder disrupted the exchange networks, these peripheral peoples were motivated to conquer the lowlands in order to control the exchange network of which they had become a part.

As mentioned in Chapter 8, the Wari and Tiwanaku highland states had declined and the whole region was in a situation of rather small polities and regional cults in the period before the rise of the Incan Empire. Cuzco, the homeland of the Incas, was located in between the old coastal and highland core regions. This was a case in which the peoples of a region that was intermediate between two older core regions arose to create a much larger empire that incorporated both of the old core regions.

Murra's (1980) study of the Incan economy supposes that the state-organized system of marketless exchange had been imposed to regulate what had been a rather unstable system of trade among the ecologically differentiated areas of the Andean region. The trade in the vertical archipelago had been based on reciprocity within lineages rather than market exchange. Murra contends that each lineage established families in each of the ecologically different niches of the vertical archipelago so that reciprocity within the lineage would bring the resources of each region to the relatives located in the other regions. In principle, such a system could operate in the absence of a centralized state, but strong competition for control of resources and trade apparently created a chaotic situation that was ripe for the emergence of a centralized political structure.

Strong support for the existence of a nonmarket politically centralized economy is found in studies of the Andean system under the Incas (La Lone 1982, 1993; Patterson 1997). The Incan state erected large storehouses for the accumulation of food and cloth produced by the labor services of community members on state and church lands, as well as by a staff of state workers. A specialized group of "chosen" women weavers (*accla*) directly employed by the state cult produced fine types of cloth used in ritual ceremonies. All those donating labor services to the state or church were fed and clothed during the period of their labor out of rations from the state stores. Immense magazines overflowing with stored goods were found by the Spanish conquerors throughout the Incan Empire. These were utilized as a method of state finance for public works and military efforts. They did not play a role in the provisioning of interregional trade for the consumption of commoners. The subsistence of commoners

[2] William H. McNeill (1963) described a similar force driving hill peoples near the Mesopotamian heartland.

was provided by community redistributional mechanisms that had predated the Incan state. As mentioned above, lineages in one ecological zone had earlier colonized other zones where lineage members produced the products that could only be obtained within each of the several ecological zones of the "vertical archipelago." These goods were then reciprocally exchanged within each lineage. The Incan state adapted a version of this form of production and exchange to its own uses, sending colonists to intensify production in newly conquered territories. Murra (1980) contends that those who have understood the Incan political economy as a socialist welfare state have mistakenly attributed the redistributional communities that continued to function within the empire to Incan invention.

Only members of the royal family inhabited the capital city of Cuzco, and weekly distributions of tributary goods to the royal lineages in the main square were mistakenly identified as markets by the Spanish conquerors. La Lone (1982) points to the importance of reciprocity as an ideology at the highest level of the Incan state. The Inca himself, a priest-king, son of the Sun, participated in ritual labor with the planting of the first maize. Godelier (1977) contends that religious ideology was an "internal element in the relations of production" in the Incan political economy.

The Incan political system was a form of indirect rule in which the kings and chiefs of local states were given official titles and were "given" land that had formerly been theirs but, under the Incas, was defined as belonging to the state. These local kings and leaders brought tribute to Cuzco and in return were given prestige goods such as the clothes of the Inca and other items of high status. Murra (1980) contends that the Incas required primarily labor services rather than tribute in kind. This principle is reflected in the way in which state farms were worked. A broad field in one of the mountain valleys was divided into strips, and each strip was, in theory, the responsibility of a different lineage. Lineage heads and village leaders were responsible for sending a crew of laborers to meet their corvée obligations. This system, called the "mita," was utilized in modified form by the Spaniards to provide labor for the mines at Potosí, where over 8 million indigenous workers met their deaths digging and transporting silver for the European conquerors (Frank 1978). But this runs ahead of our story.

Early Semiperipheral Capitalist City-States

The rise of the early empires was accompanied by the continued expansion and deepening of trade networks (Jennings 2010). Periods of peace and the extension of imperial governance allowed trade to become more intense and goods to travel farther. As mentioned in Chapter 8, the kingdom of Dilmun, probably located on what is now Bahrain (an island in the Persian Gulf), carried on a brisk carrying trade that linked Mesopotamia with the civilization of the Indus River valley (Bibby 1969). This may have been the first **semiperipheral capitalist city-state**. The commodification of goods and wealth had long been emerging within and between the states of Mesopotamia. Contracts of sale of lands and interest-bearing loans were known from the Early Dynastic period, and prices were clearly reflecting shortages in the Ur III period. In the Old Babylonian period we find a clear instance of a semiperipheral capitalist city-state. This was the Old Assyrian merchant dynasty centered in the city of Assur on the upper Tigris (in what is now Syria), with its colonial enclaves of Assyrian merchants located in distant cities far up into Anatolia (what is now Turkey) (Larsen 1976, 1987). Assur was a land-based merchant capitalist city-state with a far-flung set of colonies in the midst of an interstate system in which most states were still extracting surplus from their own peasants and pursuing a strategy of territorial expansion by means of conquest.

The capitalist city-state phenomenon is clearly a different kind of semiperipheral development from that of the semiperipheral marcher state. These states pursued a policy of profit making rather than the acquisition of territory and the use of state power to tax and extract tribute. They emerged in the "interstices," the spaces between the territorial states in world-economies in which wealth could be had by "buying cheap and selling dear" (merchant capitalism). One of their consequences was the expansion of trade networks because their commercial activities provided incentives for farmers and craftsmen to produce a surplus for trade with distant areas. Thus the capitalist city-states were promoters of commodification and interregional economic integration.

The merchant capitalism of Assur, unlike that of most capitalist city-states, was not based on sea trade (as were, for example, the Phoenician, Italian, and German city-states). But the Old Assyrians did occupy a key transportation site on the Tigris that enabled them to tap into profit streams generated by the exchange of eastern tin and Mesopotamian textiles for silver. Bronze was being produced in Anatolia using copper from the north and tin imported from the east, probably from regions that are now part of Afghanistan. The demand for tin was great, and the merchants of Assur were able to make large profits by negotiating trade treaties with the many states along the trade routes that allowed them access to markets at agreed-upon taxation rates. They also organized the transportation of goods over long distances by means of donkey caravans, and they maintained an effective structure of self-governance and religious devotion to the god of Assur that allowed them to coordinate the activities of their central city and its distant colonies. This is an early instance of what Philip Curtin (1984) calls a "trade diaspora," in which an ethnic or religious group specializes in cross-cultural trade in a region of great cultural diversity.[3]

Much of the evidence that we have about the Old Assyrian city-state and its colonies comes from the Kultepe tablets at Kanesh, an archive of business records and letters that show how the merchants organized and governed their business activities (Veenhof 1995). The records show that the merchants were trading on their own accounts for profit. They were not agents of the Assyrian state carrying out **administered trade** akin to tribute exchanges among states. Karl Polanyi (1957a) had used an early and inaccurate examination of the Kultepe tablets as evidence that the Assyrian trade was state-organized exchange rather than market exchange. Though Polanyi was wrong in his designation of the Old Assyrian economy as "marketless trade," his theoretical perspective on the evolution of institutional modes of exchange remains an important contribution to our understanding of the qualitative differences among kin-based, state-based, and market forms of integration. Polanyi simply underestimated the age of market-based exchange. But he was right to claim that market exchange was an invention that emerged slowly in the context of kin-based reciprocity and state-based administered trade.

The later history of Assur is also an interesting case that is relevant for our understanding of semiperipheral development. The Old Assyrians and the city of Assur were conquered by Hammurabi, the Amorite king of Babylon, in 1756 BCE. The Amorites were originally Semitic-speaking nomadic people from the mountains of Syria, but they conquered states in Mesopotamia and established kingdoms in the late Bronze Age. Thus the status of the claim that the Neo-Assyrians were a semiperipheral marcher state is based on the originally semiperipheral location of the capital far up the Tigris and on the conquest of the capital by formerly peripheral Amorites.

The Amorites became the ruling class, though they adopted the language and some of the religion of the Assyrians. Their much later reemergence as the Neo-Assyrian Empire is a fascinating instance in which what had earlier been a semiperipheral capitalist city-state eventually adopted the marcher-state strategy of conquest,[4] and their success in this latter venture created an upward sweep of empire that was larger than any other before it in Southwestern Asia.

---

[3] Gil Stein (1999) uses the concept of "trade diaspora" in a somewhat different way to apply to trading enclaves set up by the Uruk core state to supply itself with certain goods from a distant region. Curtin's (1984) original idea applies to culturally specialized trading ethnicities rather than to trade outposts of urbanized core societies.

[4] Another instance of this kind of "niche switching" is the case of Hannibal. The Carthaginians had for centuries pursued the maritime capitalist city-state strategy in which they combined merchant capitalism with production capitalism by manufacturing profitable products for the carrying trade. Hannibal abandoned this profit strategy for the marcher-state approach, and he nearly succeeded in conquering Rome. His failure was partly due to the reticence of the Carthaginians, who were not fully convinced of the wisdom of territorial conquest. They failed to support his venture at a critical juncture.

Capitalist City-States and Ports of Trade

Sabloff and Rathje (1975) contend that the same settlement can oscillate between being a "port of trade" (neutral territory that is used for administered trade between different competing states and empires—see Polanyi, Arensberg, and Pearson 1957) and being a "trading port" (an autonomous and sovereign polity that actively pursues policies that facilitate profitable trade). The latter corresponds to what we mean by a semiperipheral capitalist city-state. Sabloff and Rathje also contend that a trading port is more likely to emerge during a period in which other states within the same region are weak, whereas a port of trade is more likely during a period in which there are large, strong states. Sabloff and Rathje carried out an archaeological investigation of Cozumel, an island off the coast of the Yucatan Peninsula in Mexico. Their project on Cozumel was designed to test the hypothesis that it had been a trading state with a cosmopolitan and tolerant elite during the so-called Late Post-classic period of the Mayan state system just before the arrival of the Spanish in the sixteenth century (see also Kepecs, Feinman, and Boucher 1994). There had long been a busy coastal trade network based on transportation in large dugout canoes among Mayan and Mexican polities along the Caribbean coast of Mesoamerica (McKillop 2005 and see Figure 10.4). If Sabloff and Rathje are right, trading ports (semiperipheral capitalist city-states) are more likely to emerge during the "fall" part of the cycle of rise and fall of empires that all state systems seem to exhibit.

This general idea also corresponds with the notion that world-systems have oscillated between periods in which they are more integrated by horizontal networks of exchange and periods in which corporate and hierarchical organization is more predominant (Ekholm and Friedman 1982). Such oscillations may have been based on the alternative successes and failures of tributary marcher states and capitalist city-states, but in the long run it was the capitalist city-states that transformed the state-based systems into the global capitalist system of today.

The upward sweeps of empires in which very large empires emerged in regional world-systems for the first time may have been facilitated by the actions of specialized trading states. If semiperipheral capitalist city-states were major agents of the spread of commodified exchange and the

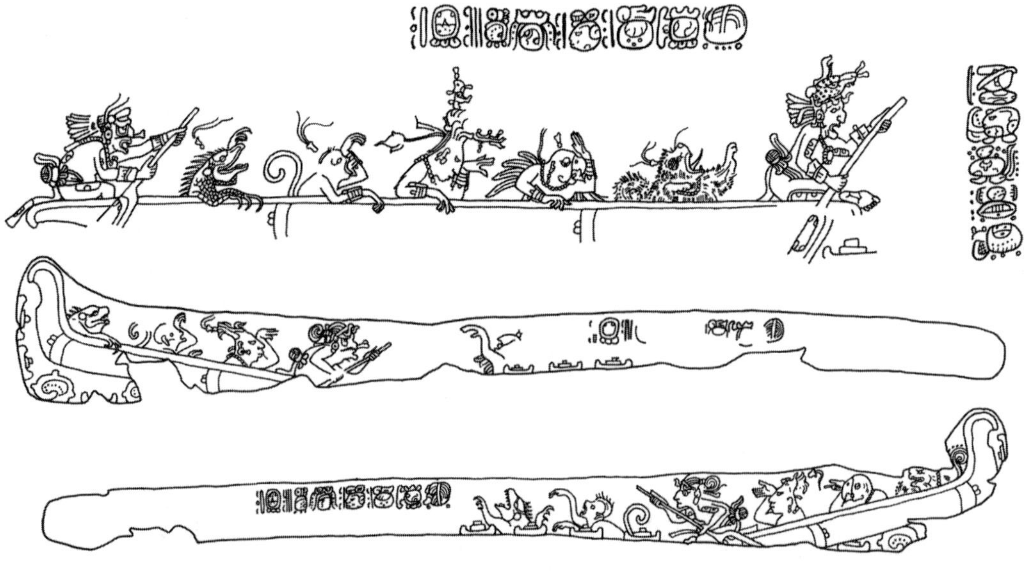

Figure 10.4 Drawing from an incised bone found at Tikal, showing a number of Mayan paddler gods carrying a maize god in a dugout canoe

Source: © David Schele, Foundation for the Advancement of Mesoamerican Studies, Inc. http://www.famsi.org.

expansion and intensification of trade networks, then upward sweeps in which larger states emerged to encompass regions that had already been unified by trade should have occurred after a period in which semiperipheral capitalist city-states had been flourishing. Regarding upward sweeps of the population sizes of cities, these generally followed upward sweeps of empires because it was empires that built the largest cities as their capitals. The settlements of semiperipheral capitalist city-states were usually much smaller than the capital cities of empires.[5] It was not until the rise of London that a capitalist city became the largest city in a world-system. We now turn to an examination of the larger states, empires, and cities that emerged in Afroeurasia and their relations with nomadic pastoralists.

Suggested Readings

Berdan, Frances F. 2005. *The Aztecs of Central Mexico: An Imperial Society*. Belmont, CA: Thomson Wadsworth.

Diamond, Jared. 2005. *Collapse*. New York: Viking.

Forte, Angelo, Richard Oram, and Frederik Pedersen. 2005. *Viking Empires*. Cambridge: Cambridge University Press.

Hui, Victoria Tin-bor. 2005. *War and State Formation in Ancient China and Early Modern Europe*. Cambridge: Cambridge University Press.

Jennings, Justin. 2010. *Globalizations and the Ancient World*. Cambridge: Cambridge University Press.

McKillop, Heather I. 2005. *In Search of Maya Sea Traders*. College Station: Texas A&M University Press.

[5] Carthage was an exception to this. It was the largest city in the Central PMN before the rise of Alexandria and Rome.

11

The Central System

This chapter presents an overview of the expansion of the state-based and citified Mesopotamian and Egyptian systems, their merger into what we will call the Central world-system, and its expansion and incorporation of other systems over the past 3,500 years. We will also tell the story of the rise and fall of empires in West Asia, South Asia, and East Asia and the increasing links among them in the emergence of a multi-core Afroeurasian supersystem (Figure 11.1). Also

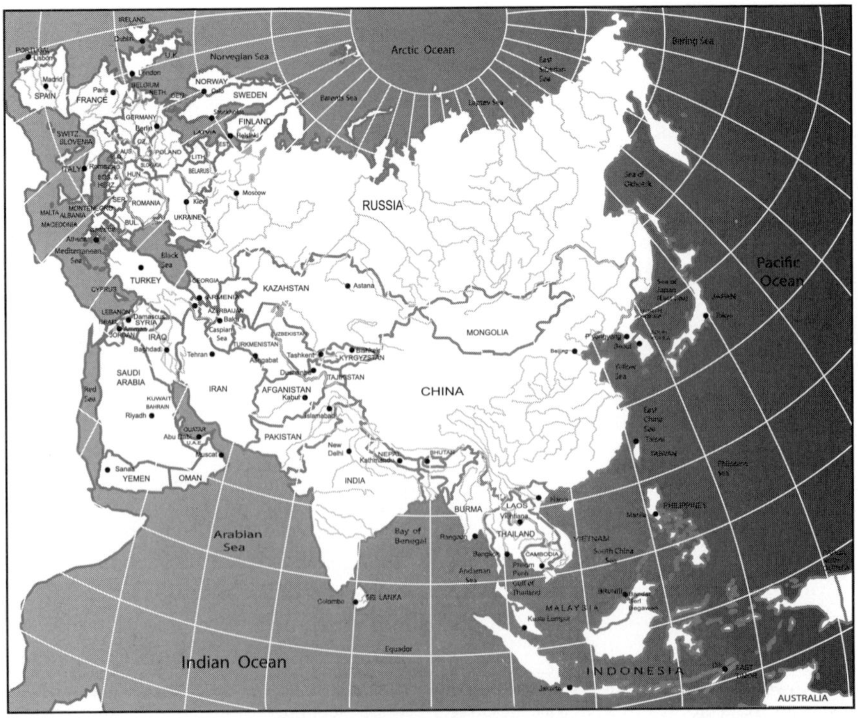

Figure 11.1 Map of Eurasia

told are more stories of semiperipheral marcher states and increasing numbers of semiperipheral capitalist city-states. Strong challenges to the great agrarian empires emanated from peripheral nomads from the time of the emergence of states and cities, but the core states eventually developed techniques of power that eliminated direct challenges from the periphery.

The Big Picture

If we focus only on world-systems that contain cities and states (ignoring the kinds of systems that were the focus of Part II of this book), we can produce a spatiotemporal map that shows the expansion of the interaction networks of these state-based systems over the millennia. As we have seen, about 5,000 years ago in ancient Southwestern Asia (Mesopotamia) the first cities emerged in the sense of settlements with over 10,000 people living closely together. In Chapters 7, 8, and 9 we examined the developmental history of the Mesopotamian world-system, but in this chapter we will use what we found as a starting point for examining the emergence of what we call the Central world-system. The Central System is called "central" because it developed cities and states first and because it eventually incorporated the rest of the regional world-systems into itself to form the global system of today.[1] It is not the *whole* story of social evolution but rather a slice of what happened in human history starting from the cutting edge of expansion of the oldest state-based political-military network (PMN).

Figure 11.2 shows how the Mesopotamian PMN merged with the Egyptian PMN around

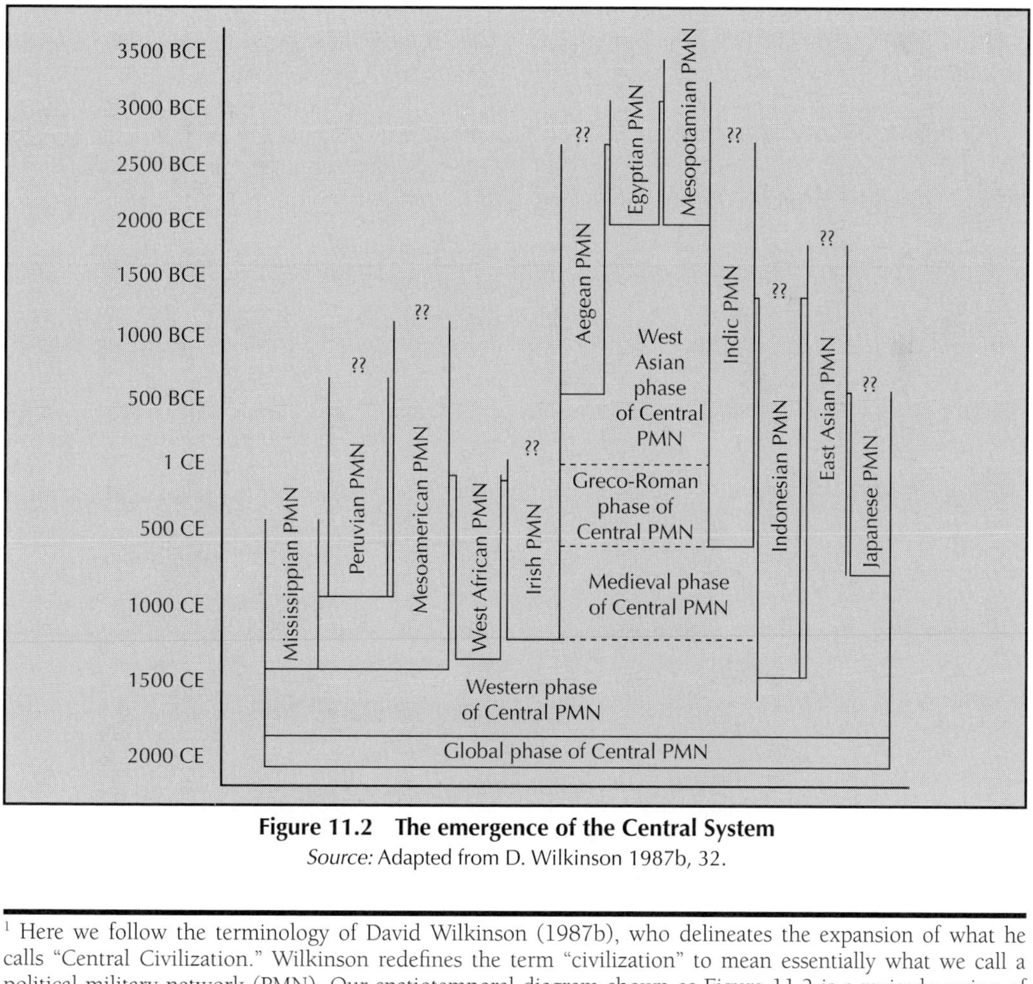

Figure 11.2 The emergence of the Central System
Source: Adapted from D. Wilkinson 1987b, 32.

[1] Here we follow the terminology of David Wilkinson (1987b), who delineates the expansion of what he calls "Central Civilization." Wilkinson redefines the term "civilization" to mean essentially what we call a political-military network (PMN). Our spatiotemporal diagram shown as Figure 11.2 is a revised version of Wilkinson's chronograph of the expansion of Central Civilization.

1500 BCE, and then this West Asian PMN incorporated the Aegean, the Indic, the Irish, and all the other state-based PMNs. It also incorporated all the regions in which there were no states. Eventually it became the modern world-system. Like a river system, the streams come together, merging as the larger and more powerful ones engulf the smaller and less powerful ones.

Recall Figure 2.2 in Chapter 2, which shows that PMNs are middle-sized interaction networks that typically contain smaller bulk goods networks (BGNs) and are parts of larger prestige goods networks (PGNs) and information networks (INs). The larger INs and PGNs became linked before the PMNs did. And the smaller BGNs got linked after the PMNs did. The rest of this book is about the waves of expansion and incorporation depicted in Figure 11.2. The most recent wave of expansion and incorporation (now called globalization) that has occurred since World War II is just the most recent of these oscillations that have brought all the humans of the earth more and more tightly together in a single global system.

Within the process of world-system expansion and incorporation there were rivers within rivers. Figure 11.3 depicts both the PMNs and the PGNs of the Central and East Asian systems. It shows the temporal pulsations and the phenomenon in which systems came together and then separated, before they eventually became strongly linked. Similar oscillations of expansion and contraction occurred on different scales in many regions of the earth.

By the second century BCE, China became linked to the Indic, Southwest Asian, and Mediterranean PGNs in a vast trading system in which land and sea routes connected the three regions. Once linked, the Central PGN cohered across three windows of time: 200 BCE–200 CE, 500–900 CE, and 1200–1400 CE.

Before the opening of the Silk Roads[2] across Central Asia, there were three large-scale PGNs in Afroeurasia: the West Asian-Mediterranean, the South Asian, and the East Asian. These core regions expanded and incorporated smaller world-systems in West Africa and Southeast Asia. The nomadic horse pastoralists of Central Asia played a key role during recurring periods in which they formed large tribal confederations. The most famous of these was the Mongol Empire, which conquered most of Eurasia in the thirteenth century CE.

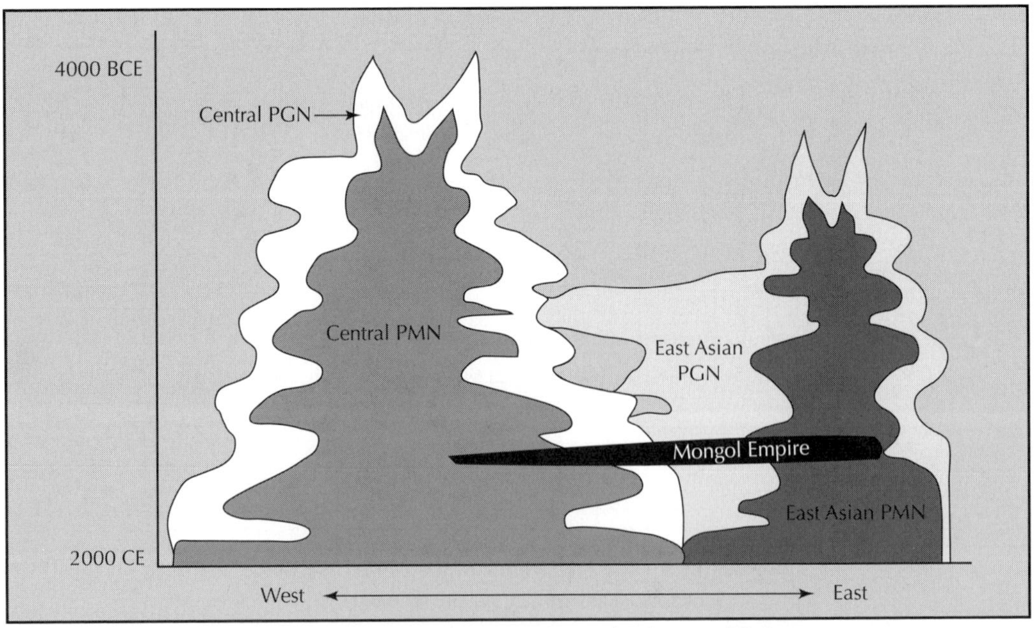

Figure 11.3 Central and East Asian pulsations and linkages
Source: Adapted from Chase-Dunn and Babones 2006, with permission from Johns Hopkins University Press.

[2] There were alternate routes, and the caravans could shift off each and any of those routes as conditions warranted.

The Mesopotamian and Egyptian core regions became firmly linked by trade no later than around 3000 BCE. This was when their PGNs joined. The West Asian PGN also came to include the Indus River valley civilization. But the three core regions did not yet form a single PMN. The merger of the Mesopotamian and Egyptian interpolity systems began as a result of Eighteenth Dynasty Egypt's invasions, conquests, and diplomatic relations with states of the Southwest Asian (Mesopotamian) system—first of all Mitanni, then the Hittites, Babylon, and Assyria. The signal event was Thutmosis I's invasion of Syria around 1505 BCE. The fusion of the systems began and then enlarged and intensified until 1350 BCE. Thutmosis III's many campaigns in Syria and the establishment of tributary relations, wars, and peacemaking under Amenhotep II, as well as the peaceful relations and alliance with Mitanni by Thutmosis IV, eventually led to Egyptian hegemony under Amenhotep III (Inoue et al. 2012).

Economics and Politics in the Tributary Empires

The rise of large empires, especially the Assyrian and Persian empires, brought most of the core region into a single core-wide state. In India, despite local state development in the northwest region, it was not until 321 CE under Mauryan rule that anything approximating a core-wide empire developed. The conquest of India by Alexander in the fourth century BCE Hellenized the West Asian/Mediterranean core, but it was only a temporary linking of the Central and Indic PMNs that dissolved when the Greek states were pushed out of South Asia.

The foremost characteristic of the large empires that emerged in the early Central System is their completely military nature. They are termed "warrior empires" by Diakonoff (1969). Utilizing the horse-drawn chariot as a tool of war, the Assyrians, based in Assur, were able to conquer a very large portion of the existing economic network of the West Asian world-system. According to Schumpeter (1951), this war-machine state expanded according to an internal logic that drove it to conquer areas for which there was no economic motive at all. Schumpeter maintained that a psychology of conquest drove the Assyrians and that they required warfare in order to sustain their self-conception as a conquering people. Diakonoff (1969), on the other hand, maintained that the Assyrians were able to consolidate their empire because of the central location of Assur near the main trade route between the Tigris-Euphrates and the Mediterranean.

The Assyrians politically united the Nile and the Tigris-Euphrates, temporarily consolidating the two older core areas into a single core-wide empire. Diakonoff (1969) described the motive of the Assyrian conquests as "forcible exchange," at first simply the accumulation of booty but later evolving into more regularized tribute taking. For the first time, a world-system had become primarily organized around a coercive core/periphery relationship.

The organizational problem for the conquerors, once they had extracted all the booty they could within their range of conquest, was to convert pillage into tribute taking (Allen 2005). And if they succeeded at this, they became "civilized" men trying to keep together a large political entity through a combination of force and co-optation. Military cadre settled down on the lands they acquired, had children, learned the pleasures of a peacetime life, and became reticent to personally heed the call to arms. Mercenary soldiers from outlying provinces were hired to fight, and they soon learned that the old rulers had become weak. This set the stage for conquest by new semiperipheral marcher states—the Hittites, Medes, or Persians.

Other factors, of course, entered in. At first, a warrior-state tried to convert all trade to state-administered exchange. But eventually, in part because of the enforced peace and the differentiation of power that allowed private accumulation, a long-distance market reasserted itself. This created sources of wealth outside the state apparatus, and these are likely to have been the basis of political strife over succession to the monarchy as well as challenges from regional centers of power. Within the warrior states, many areas such as Babylon maintained a certain autonomy that became the basis of challenges to the empire.

Another factor that played a role in the success of marcher states was changes in military technology. The development of cheaper and stronger iron weapons, first perfected in Anatolia, undercut the Bronze Age reliance on noble charioteers. The chariots could not match the new heavily armed infantry, and thus warfare became less an honorable profession of Bronze

Age aristocrats and more a mass-based confrontation between hordes of infantrymen with iron weapons.

The consequences of the policy of looting were not easy to mend. Vast areas were ruined and depopulated. In order to convert to a tribute-taking basis, these areas had to be reconstructed as productive. The Assyrians accomplished this by the mass deportation of peoples from peripheral areas to the old centers of high production (Oded 1979).

Diakonoff (1969, 31) develops his argument about the economic basis of the warrior empires as follows:

> The main economic role of the warrior empires was . . . the establishment of "forcible exchange" in the interests of agricultural and handicrafts in the more developed countries, such as Babylonia, partly Assyria, and later on probably also Phoenicia. This means that behind the activities of the warriors we must seek for a social stratum which profited by these activities. It was not merely the top military bureaucracy, hoarding wealth from their part in the loot and receiving from the king estates immune from taxation and corvée, and peopled with deportees. It was also such privileged cities, centres of handicrafts and agriculture, as Harran, Assur, Babylon, Sippar, Nippur, Uruk and later also the Phoenician autonomous cities. These cities continued to be governed by a Council of Elders and an Assembly; their citizens thus enjoyed full political rights and, moreover, were exempt from empire taxes and levies. These citizens were priests, merchants, owners of handicraft shops with slave labor, or of land, being in all cases either free land-holding producers or slave-owners depending on slavery economy.

Diakonoff contends that the problem of the relationship between the autonomous cities and the royal power was one of the main political problems of the warrior empires. In a footnote he clarifies the interaction and shows that Schumpeter's characterization (above) is not totally without foundation.

> The political relations between such cities and the royal power were subject to change. There seems to have existed a party (represented e.g. by Sennacherib) which did not favor city and temple privileges and preferred uninterrupted looting of the peripheral regions (as a means of keeping the warriors content) to the relative stability of the political situation needed by such trading centers as Babylon, Harran, etc. For this party the wars of the empire were an economic goal in itself, irrespective of the causes which had started them. (Diakonoff 1969, 31, n. 3)

From where did the conquering peoples who created the warrior empires come? The domestication of horses, the invention in Mesopotamia of the chariot, and the spread of bronze technology to the peoples of the desert, steppe, and mountains surrounding the valley civilizations created a grave threat to the cities. At the same time, the increased density of interregional trade and the spread of a more productive agriculture to the upland, rain-watered areas, as well as the previous political integration carried out by the primary empires within regions, created the organizational possibility for larger empires. The conquerors that created these empires were of different backgrounds. Assur, the city from whence the old Assyrians came, was on the main trade route between Mesopotamia and the Mediterranean. As we saw in Chapter 10, this was the home city of a large trade diaspora of merchants in the Bronze Age. The Medes and the Persians were upland people, nomadic pastoralists, who had only recently adopted agriculture when they began their campaigns of conquest.

The Persian king Darius "transformed an Aryan feudal kingship into an oriental despotism," according to John Cook (1983, 76). The later nomadic Scythian and Mongol horsemen who showered the infantries of civilizations with arrows were less involved in the exchange networks of civilization before the time of their conquests and thus may be best categorized as peripheral rather than semiperipheral marchers. Of course, they rapidly adopted many of the ways of the people they conquered after establishing their power over old core areas.

Egypt maintained a studied isolationism from the other centers of the Near East before the invasion of the charioteering Hyksos. There was tribute taking from Nubia, cedars were received from Byblos, and there was some trade with the Minoans and, through Syria, with Mesopotamia. But the inward-looking culture of the Egyptian system considered the outside world to be inferior and not worthy of much consideration. This attitude was rudely challenged by the nomadic Hyksos, and after a long struggle to expel the aliens, the Egyptians developed a more outward-looking policy. They engaged in an imperial expansion that subjected part of the Asian continent to their rule, and the pharaoh Ikhnaton tried to suppress the older Egyptian gods in favor of the single great god of the Sun, which shined on all lands, not just Egypt. The expansionary phase established more formal domination over Nubia, as described by William Adams (1977).

But Egypt's experiment with imperial expansion and cosmopolitan culture was partial and temporary. A more efficient alphabetic form of writing was successfully introduced, but the party of monotheism was overthrown by a resurgence of the local priests. Ikhnaton's policy of military expansion was stemmed, and a traditionalist revival of the old ways triumphed. Even the king of tiny Byblos refused to supply cedar logs on demand (Herm 1975). Egypt's move to become a significant player in the arena of the warrior empires failed, and it became only a regional center, sometimes independent, often tributary to the larger empires of the East. Not until it was Hellenized was Egypt to again play the role of great power in the Central System.

Taagepera (1978a) and Michael Mann (1986) have argued that the great upward sweeps of the empires were made possible by innovations in the delegation of authority, or what Mann calls "techniques of power" (see also Allen 2005). But when we look at the political forms used by the Persians in their rule over various satrapies and relatively autonomous cities (J. Cook 1983, Chapter 8), we do not find anything radically different from the smaller Assyrian warrior empire or even the primary empires studied in Chapter 7. A broad range of organizational forms, from feudal fiefs to multitiered bureaucracies, was used in various parts of the Persian Empire, depending on local circumstances.

The one policy that seems to stand out as different from earlier unifying empires was the Persian support of local religious leaders who were unhappy with their own military leaders—supporting the temple against the palace. Great King Darius of Persia funded the reconstruction of the temple at Jerusalem and restructured the state of Israel along more hierarchical lines with the support of the rabbis. This type of policy gained the Persians valuable allies in many regions and undermined local military leaders, but such divide-and-conquer tactics had been used before. It was probably both innovations in organizational techniques and greater economic and cultural integration (trade networks and methods of communication) that had been attained over a wider area that made it possible for the empires to expand.

The tension between independent cities and the royal institutions of the empire was a central one in the late Bronze Age world-systems. Diakonoff (1969, 31–32) writes:

> The Achaemenian (Persian) kings vacillated between regarding an autonomous city as a menace to the stability of the empire, and regarding the former as one of the chief economic and political mainstays of the latter. . . . The Hellenistic monarchs were staunch adherents of the second point of view, which resulted in the foundation of hundreds of new privileged cities after the pattern of the Greek poleis. . . . Moreover, alongside the Hellenistic poleis with a Greek constitution there existed—and were being founded—a number of cities with a local constitution but enjoying the same rights and privilege as a polis (the constitution being usually that of temple-city). The existence of a polis or a temple-city safeguarded the households and the political rights of the slave-owners and the free citizens in general from arbitrary actions of the royal power; their constitution guaranteed free development of handicrafts and commerce, of private agricultural estates, and of the new money economy.

More Capitalist City-States: The Phoenicians

In the Eastern Mediterranean, the Minoans on Crete, and perhaps also the Mycenaeans in the Aegean, had carried on the early seagoing trade. During the second millennium BCE, the

Mediterranean was upset by migrations from the north, peripheral peoples whom the Egyptians called the "Sea Peoples." These seagoing raiders disrupted the seaborne trade relations between Egypt and the Levant. The early Lebanese town of Byblos had long been a tributary supplier of cedar to Egypt, but the arrival of the Sea Peoples interfered with this trade.

Eventually the new peoples settled on the Lebanese and Palestinian coast and mixed with the older Semitic tribes there. Out of this admixture the Phoenician cities of Tyre and Sidon emerged, transforming piracy into merchant capitalism. The Phoenicians specialized in trading across the whole Mediterranean, especially in exchanging with primitive peoples to whom the products of the old East were, at first, prestige goods. They also maintained a degree of autonomy as carriers of goods between empires, especially the Egyptian and Assyrian empires. The Phoenicians established a colony for the production of copper on Cyprus and began a manufacturing industry that provided inexpensive glass vases to mass markets throughout the Mediterranean. They had stolen the Egyptian secret of glass production and improved upon it for use in the carrying trade (Herm 1975; Markoe 2000).

Thus the Phoenicians began a process of exchanging unequals, which is trading between systems not previously integrated by exchange. Buying (or producing) cheap and selling dear was their specialized purpose, and these independent temple-cities of Lebanon were early examples of autonomous capitalist states in which profit taking through commerce was the dominant raison d'état (purpose of the state). Their domain eventually spread as far as present-day Cadiz (Gades) on the Atlantic coast of Spain, and they traded down the Red Sea to East Africa and India and down the west coast of Africa, where they had a port at Moghador. They had alliances with the land-based Hebrew states of Judah and Israel, building the temple at Jerusalem under contract.

There are intermediate forms between a completely uncommodified exchange network and one in which commodification is the predominant form. Land, wealth, and labor are never perfect commodities in any historical system, even in the present. Rather, commodification is a matter of degree. The Phoenicians engaged in **merchant capitalism** by buying and selling the products of different, relatively isolated areas around the shores of the Mediterranean Sea. In doing this they brought the separate economies of these areas into interaction, subjecting the division of labor within each to the market forces generated in the network as a whole. The Phoenicians also produced manufactured goods for export, and these were not only prestige goods. They specialized in producing cheap copies that could expand market demand by lowering prices. The Phoenician glass implements industry and the textile industry were not merchant capitalism but rather production capitalism that imported technical knowledge and applied it to the mass production of commodities (Herm 1975, 80). We do not know how the logic of costs was applied to raw materials, built environment, and labor in the cities of Tyre and Sidon where these industries were located. The commodification of labor power may have been constrained in many ways, by kin networks or state regulation. But it seems reasonable to assume that these forms of labor control, however they were organized, were subjected to the competitive logic of the larger Mediterranean political economy.

Dominant powers at sea, the Phoenicians built their cities on promontories or islands where they could be protected from land attack. Tyre was built on a rocky reef separated from the shore by open water. It was only conquered after Alexander's army built a causeway to it (Markoe 2000). Although fairly autonomous, as mentioned by Diakonoff (1969) above, the Phoenicians were not averse to paying tribute to whichever land-based empire was currently responsible for the peace. They allied with the Persians in their war against Greece, thereby gaining the permanent enmity of the Greeks, who characterized them as "pirates." The Phoenicians never achieved political unity among their far-flung cities, and one of their split-off groups founded Carthage, to become the center of a largely independent trade network in the Western Mediterranean. The Carthaginians battled with the Greeks over Sardinia, and in one of their temporary conquests of a Greek colony they discovered the superior art and craft products of Greek culture. After this, statues of Greek gods appeared in the gardens of Carthaginian aristocrats, although when they were direly pressed by a Greek conqueror from Sardinia, they flooded back to their old religion, carrying out a massive human sacrifice to try to appease their old gods.

The Greek city-states invented a new type of polity and combined seaborne trade with advanced commodity production in agriculture. The Phoenician temple-cities were so specialized in trade that they did not concern themselves with revenues or profits from agricultural land, preferring to import most of their food. Their colonies in the Western Mediterranean, like the original cities on the Lebanese coast, were set up on promontories and oriented toward the sea.

The Greek polis, on the other hand, was an association of landholders. Its uniqueness was not in its autonomy from imperial rule. This was shared by other autonomous cities of West Asia and the Mediterranean. What made the Greek cities different was the small and inconsequential nature of the state sector compared with the private sector (Diakonoff 1982). Sparta, of course, was a notable exception.

The polity of most Greek city-states was primarily an association of private landowners rather than itself a major landowner and economic sector. This, and the high level of commodity production, was the main feature that made Greek society different. Unlike the Phoenicians, who only set up trading cities, the Greeks had more traditional attitudes toward expansion and conquest. The purpose of conquest was booty, and the purpose of colonies was to settle citizens who could farm and provide food for the mother city. The cultural disapproval of merchants did not prevent Greeks from engaging in trade, but it may have partly accounted for the large number of foreigners (metics) who lived in Athens. While most Greek colonies were established for the purposes designated above, there were a few that specialized in trade (Curtin 1984). And as the cultural Hellenization of the Central System proceeded, the Greeks, or at least many of them, became long-distance traders.

Karl Polanyi (1957b, 87) argued in favor of the existence of price-setting markets at Athens in his essay "Aristotle Discovers the Economy." He contended that coinage in small denominations indicates a real peoples' market in which it was possible to buy a prepared meal on the street. Greek generals undertook to provide meals for their troops on the road by encouraging local provisioners to set up markets ahead of the army's arrival. Polanyi saw these as indicators that a generalized commodity economy had emerged within the Greek sphere of influence.

How can we describe the political economy of the early Central System? Within the great empires, trade and production for exchange grew, but two tendencies limited it. As of old, the empire, and most of the competing polities within empires, tried to monopolize exchange. This was accomplished by converting long-distance trade into tribute taking and local trade into royal monopolies producing revenues utilizing a dependent population receiving rations or subsistence plots. Nevertheless, private trade and markets tended to grow, but they were stifled by the lack of a generalized monetary system and the scarcity of money.

In the spaces (interstices) between the empires, as along the Lebanese coast, and in other peripheral and semiperipheral areas, market forces were less constrained. This is where the early capitalist city-states emerged, the purest cases being the autonomous Phoenician cities. The Greeks, especially at Athens, demonstrated that even an agricultural state can adapt to market forces and benefit from them (rather than trying to consume them) while still remaining a predominantly land-based agricultural society. This trick, the coexistence of a tributary mode of accumulation with a large measure of commercialization, was invented in semiperipheral Athens but was later learned by large commercialized empires (Sanderson 1995a).

Greeks and Hellenization

Along the steppe frontier from Europe to China, the migrations of peripheral nomadic pastoralists and invasions by war alliances among these tribal horsemen exercised an oscillating pressure against the great agrarian empires on both the east and west ends of the "world island" (Eurasia). The Central System underwent a shifting cultural and economic florescence. First, the dynamic semiperipheral Greek interstate system exhibited rapid development and was the basis of cultural Hellenization in the West, as well as a new wave of empire formation that affected the Mediterranean littoral (shore), the old West Asian core region, and the northwestern corner of the South Asian subcontinent. The expansion of Hellenization was followed by a powerful irruption from the West, the Roman Empire.

The Greek polis was mentioned above as an important social structural development.

The relative weakness of monarchical power in most of the Greek city-states, and the long gestation period before the Greek interstate system was converted into an empire, along with the existence of a cross-cultural trading network throughout the Mediterranean littoral, were the conditions for an expanding commercialization that involved both the urban manufacturing industry and a commercialized agriculture producing olive oil and wine.

Within the Mediterranean region the Greeks enjoyed the profits of a hierarchical division of labor. The terms of trade at which they exchanged their manufactures, oil and wine, for the timber, metals, and grain of less developed areas were quite favorable (Hopper 1979). Their success in staving off the Persian invasion of Attica provided the impetus for the Athenians and the Spartans to liberate the Greek Ionian cities of Asia Minor that had been under Persian rule (Pagden 2008).

The long struggle between Sparta, a predominantly land-based power, and Athens, the inheritor from the Eastern Phoenicians of predominance at sea, led eventually to a partial Spartan victory in the Peloponnesian wars. Greek culture, like most classical cultures, gives merchants a low place in the social order. Hermes, the thief, was the patron god of Greek merchants. Nevertheless, Greek society increasingly made room for commercial exchange and profit making. Foreign merchants were protected under Greek law, and commodity production became an important source of wealth for the Greek city-states.

The victory of the Spartans and Athenians over the Persians was understood by Herodotus, and by most modern historians, to be the result of political differences between East and West. In this version it was Western democracy that created a motivated citizen army defending its own livelihood and its own state, while the mercenary and enslaved soldiers of the Persians demonstrated the political weakness of "oriental despotism." But if we place this victory of a relatively less-stratified semiperipheral army over a relatively more hierarchical and encrusted older empire into a long-run comparative perspective, we will see that this is another instance in which a semiperipheral society had advantages over a core state. A less stratified polity was not a monopoly of the West. The Persians themselves had been such a polity when, as a young marcher state, they conquered earlier empires. Indeed, Athens and Sparta were to meet their own semiperipheral conquerors, the Macedonians led by Alexander (Thompson 1995).

The very success of Greek culture and economy created problems for the Attican core states of the Greek regional subsystem. Both manufacturing and commercial production of olive oil and wine were spread by Greek colonists to areas all around the fringes and islands of the Mediterranean Sea. According to Rostovzeff (1941) this created an economic slump in Attica as competition increased. This phenomenon of the diffusion of comparative advantage and decline of the original region of innovation is well known in the modern world-system. An important similarity should be noted, however. Athens, the economic hegemon within the Hellenic region, reacted to this crisis by pursuing a policy of empire formation. This policy was opposed by another core power within the Attican subsystem, Sparta, and the attempt by Athens to convert the Aegean into an empire was unsuccessful. The unsuccessful effort of Athens to create an empire in order to make up for the decline of its economic hegemony suggests the pattern of overextension that may be common to both classical and modern hegemons, including the contemporary United States.

The Hellenization of Western Asia was also, of course, the Asianization of the Greeks. Alexander married a Persian noblewoman and arranged for 10,000 of his soldiers to marry Persian women. Macedonian soldiers never liked urban Greeks in the Aegean, but running the three empires that fell out of Alexander's conquests required skilled personnel and Greek immigrants were used everywhere. Ptolemaic Egypt became an important repository of Greek art and literature as well as a manufacturer of copies of Attican statuary for export. The Central System became increasingly integrated by both tributary accumulation and commercial trade links, as well as shared culture as a result of the Hellenization process. Rostovzeff's (1941, 2:1248–1271) discussion of the trends among the Hellenized empires demonstrates the extent to which these were part of a single economic network circulating grain, wine, olive oil, fish, timber, metals, manufactured articles, and slaves.

When we speak of the Mediterranean shores as the economic center of the Central System, we should not ignore the extent to which overland trade had very early on begun to penetrate the inland areas of Europe. As early as 500 BCE Etruscan and Greek products such as bronze bowls were carried over the Alps to the valleys of the Danube and Rhine Rivers. Wells (1980) and Sherratt (1993a, 1993b) used archaeological evidence to reconstruct the consequences that the trade in prestige goods had for the tribal cultures of Europe. Some of these seem to have been stimulated toward chiefdom formation by the trading relationship with Western Asia and the Mediterranean. The Etruscans of the Italian Peninsula were probably migrants from the older core regions of the Eastern Mediterranean. They lived in hilltop cities, were literate and artistic, and practiced sophisticated agriculture and industry.

The Roman Rise

In the central Mediterranean, three powers were in competition for dominance: the Greeks, the Etruscans, and the Carthaginians. As mentioned above, Carthage was a Phoenician city-state in what is now Tunisia on the southern shore of the Western Mediterranean. Carthaginians and Greeks had been fighting over Sicily for two centuries when a rising power, Rome, conquered Sicily, its first province beyond the Italian Peninsula. The Romans were Latin-speaking farmers and neighbors to the city-living Etruscans. The Romans, as did earlier semiperipheral peoples, underwent secondary state and class formation while they were interacting with their citified Etruscan neighbors. And then they began a policy of expansion in which they subdued the Latin and Etruscan cities of the Italian Peninsula. The semiperipheral marcher Roman polity was a land power, based on a peasant army that was committed, at first, to a relatively egalitarian polity. Once they had become engaged with the Carthaginians over Sicily, the Romans hastily constructed a fleet of warships, incorporating a new feature—boarding planks—that would allow their soldiers (marines) to rapidly invade an enemy ship. Without skilled pilots, but with their soldiers and boarding planks, they defeated the Carthaginian lords of the sea in the first Punic war.

After this defeat the Carthaginians began to question the sustainability of their supremacy on the seas. After long specializing in the seaborne trade, they were willing to consider a switch in strategy toward the establishment of a land-based empire. Hamilcar Barca, Hannibal's father, hated the Romans because he had been defeated by them on Sicily. Hamilcar began the expansion of Carthaginian power in Spain with the founding of Gades (Cadiz). This expansion eventually led to another war with Rome (second Punic war), in which Hannibal crossed the Alps from Spain with his army and elephants and won four major battles against the Romans in Italy. Hannibal rested his troops in a city very near to Rome while waiting for reinforcements from Carthage that never came, and so he lost his momentum. The Romans recovered, and their obliteration of Carthage greatly diminished the importance of Phoenician merchant capitalism in the Mediterranean (Livy 2006; Hoyos 2003).

The Roman Republic, like earlier semiperipheral marcher states, became the Roman Empire. The citizen army became an army of professionals, and eventually an army of mercenaries. The peasant smallholders of the Italian countryside were replaced by commercial slave-worked *latifundia* (large farms) owned by the Roman patricians. The empire remained strong as long as it expanded, and it expanded a long way. It extended the boundaries of the Central System deep into Europe and conquered most of the Mediterranean littoral, including Egypt and Palestine. Keith Hopkins (1978) proposed a model that captures the logic of the Roman system, a logic based on conquest, booty, slave-gathering, and tribute extraction. Moses Finley (1973) presents convincing evidence that the Roman elite, despite that much of its wealth was based on agricultural commodity production, did not view life as a search for commercial profits. They saw politics and status within the Roman community as the arena of meaningful action.

Although we agree that Rome was not a social system in which capitalism was the dominant mode of accumulation, there was a lot of commodity production and market exchange in Rome. The use of money and the commercialization of the economy were greater than in any preceding empire. Wage labor and various types of slavery, tenancy, and clientalism as well as kin-based obligations constituted a complex constellation of institutions for the mobilization of labor in Rome (Finley 1973; De Ste. Croix 1981). Efforts to demonstrate the effects of a nascent capitalism on Roman politics have been the subject of much controversy, but all agree that Roman law, especially the law of contract, reflected and served the needs of a strong market economy.

The Roman Empire was never in itself a whole world-system. Rather, it became the Western part of the Central System and it extended the Central System more deeply into Europe and North Africa. Perry Anderson (1974a) discussed the role of Roman slave-gathering and trade in promoting state formation among peripheral German tribes (see also Luttwak 1976). Roman trade with India also strengthened the ties with the South Asian part of the Afroeurasian PGN, and trade with China across the Silk Roads also developed an important link that decreased the extent to which the East Asian system was isolated from the Central System.

Commercialization of the Post-Roman Central Empires

When the Western Roman Empire fell apart and the center of power moved back toward the old West Asian/Eastern Mediterranean core region, the market economy created and extended by the Romans continued to function. Not until the Islamic empires blocked European access to the Levant did extreme economic devolution visit Europe (Pirenne 1980). The Hellenic and philhellenic empires of the Central System also experienced increasing commercialization, with the autonomous cities of the old core continuing to prosper on the basis of long-distance trade in spite of periods of political instability. The Parthian Empire exhibited a strong tendency to support commerce in the Mesopotamian cities, preferring taxation of the caravan trade to direct state monopolization of enterprises (McNeill 1963, 285).

The emergence of Islam in Mecca and Medina, semiperipheral city-states on the Arabian Peninsula in a space of stateless societies between the Sassanian and Byzantine empires, is another instance of semiperipheral state formation that led to a marcher conquest empire. All the world religions that spread widely emerged from semiperipheral regions in which moral entrepreneurs were aware of the competing theologies and yet were free to synthesize new versions of divine authority. The Bedouin tribes of the Arabian Peninsula had become deeply involved in both the trade routes of the larger world economy and the geopolitics of competition among the adjacent empires. Bedouins were often employed as mercenaries by contending states in the region (Hodgson 1974).

The rise of Islam as a world religion, while it is similar to the earlier emergence of world religions in semiperipheral regions in some respects, is somewhat different with regard to the connection between religion and state formation. The earlier world religions emerged in a context in which there were already powerful states. Islam emerged in a context of a tribal society that was undergoing nascent state formation, and *the two processes became linked*. The status of the Islamic religious leader as simultaneously the head of the military organization was a structural detail that reunited the palace and the temple and gave empire formation by conquest a strong dose of ideological zeal (asabiyah on steroids).

This said, the trajectory of the rapidly expansionist Islamic empires is quite similar in its broad aspects with earlier and later rapidly expanding empires, especially the Alexandrian and the Mongol. A process of rapid expansion and overshoot was followed by a breaking up of the gigantic conquest empire into governable subsections.

The great commercialization of many areas that were incorporated into the Islamic empires raises the question of the extent to which they were capitalist (Rodinson 1981). Weber's (1978, 1981) rather restrictive definition of rational capitalism excludes the Phoenicians, who adapted magic-based religion to their commercial needs. But if we have profit-oriented trade in a price-setting market, what difference does it make about the content of the religious beliefs of the merchants? The important thing about religion is the same thing that is important about ethnicity and kinship. It is an ideology that allows people to trust one another, and so it reduces the risk of transactions.

Samir Amin (1978), inspired by Ibn Khaldun (1958), described the mode of accumulation of the Arab societies of the Mahgreb and the Arabian Peninsula (but not Egypt) as based on the profits derived from the long-distance trade between different zones. He pointed out that merchant capitalist ideology is evident in Islamic theology, and he describes the Arab Islamic conquerors as "warrior-merchants" who expanded out of the Arabian Peninsula when their livelihood, based on the long-distance trade, was threatened by disruption of their trade monopoly. Although

Amin described the above as a tributary mode of production, the high level of commercialization and the devotion of states to the end of profitable merchant capitalism are evident from his analysis.

The penetration of Islam into Africa created trading cities in which merchants were the ruling class (Willard 1993). Like the Phoenician city-states, these cities were not only heavily involved in commercial relations but politically dominated by merchant interests (Curtin 1984). Contrary to Max Weber's (1958b) distinction between Occidental and Oriental medieval cities, which argues that capitalist rationality became predominant only in the West, these cities developed legal systems that were conducive to commerce, and commerce itself was the main goal of policy. Amin (1980, 69) contended that the Islamic-Arabic cities were indeed moving toward the consolidation of a regional capitalist mode of production when they were peripheralized by the newly emerging European core capitalism. And Ekholm and Friedman (1980, 71) observe, "Just as the capitalistic world contained different forms of exploitation such as slavery, serfdom, metayage[3] as well as wage labor in the center, so the Medieval Arab system had mostly wage labor in centers such as Baghdad, but feudal exploitation, slave plantations and free peasantry elsewhere."

The Development of Capitalism in China

In East Asia the still substantially separate Chinese core-wide empire expanded its political jurisdiction to marginal areas. The East Asian system was centered on China. The economies of Korea, Japan, and the South China Sea were integrated into the Sino-centric trade-tribute system. Malacca, a theoretical protectorate of the Chinese Empire, played the role of semiperipheral capitalist city-state in the Malaysian and Indonesian archipelagos. The commercialization of the Chinese economy was already well developed by the eighth century CE. Monetization and credit mechanisms such as "flying money" emerged and were periodically subjected to state control (Elvin 1973). Capitalism nearly became predominant in China during the Sung dynasty (Balazs 1968, 34–54; Shiba 1970). The development of an excellent system of waterways allowed for the commercially profitable transportation of bulk goods across a large area. Industrial production of iron and steel in eleventh-century China had a greater output than the British iron industry of the eighteenth century (Hartwell 1966). Conversion to money rents was widespread, and an extensive foreign trade with the South Seas and across the Silk Roads to the West further stimulated commercialization within China. The Chinese city-system also filled out because of the growth of medium-sized cities based on serving local and regional markets (Rozman 1973).

Monopolization of profitable commerce by the Chinese state faced challenges from market forces (Worthy 1975), and eventually the state, rather than trying to control and restrict this development, learned to gain greater revenues by encouraging private enterprise and then taxing it (Hartwell 1971). This and the Islamic states are the most important instances—prior to the emergence of capitalism in Europe—in which a core state adapted its accumulation logic to the capitalist economy in order to benefit from it, rather than simply monopolizing profitable enterprises.

This period of capitalist growth in China led, in the Ming dynasty, to overseas explorations in which a Chinese fleet of ocean-crossing junks sailed down the East Coast of Africa led by the Imperial eunuch Admiral Zheng He. A main part of the motivation for these explorations was commercial trade.

But a reaction against the power of private wealth and the forces it created resulted in a series of dramatic reversals (McNeill 1982; Wallerstein 1974b). The Chinese imperial state clamped down on private enterprises and repealed the policies that had promoted capitalist development. State control of the economy was reasserted and the overseas explorations were ended. The logic of an imperial tributary mode of production was reasserted, and it prevented the emergence to predominance of the logic of capitalism (see Chapter 14). A transformation of world-historical significance was thus left for others, inhabitants of that Western land (Europe) that French essayist Paul Valéry called "the tiny promontory of Asia."

---

[3] Metayage is the cultivation of land for a proprietor by one who receives a proportion of the produce—a kind of sharecropping.

Commercialization in India and the Indian Ocean

The Indian subcontinent also expanded its cultural, political, and economic reach. Southern India became incorporated into the civilization that had emerged in the Ganges River valley in the north, and Indian traders ranged far to the East toward the Malay peninsula, Indochina, and beyond. Even though priestly Brahmins were theoretically forbidden to travel overseas (to avoid pollution by contact with foreigners), many did. Wheatley (1975) discusses the Hinduization of Southeast Asia by traders and priests, the latter imported by local rulers to sanctify the creation of divine kingships. The main stimulus and source of outside resources that spurred state formation in Southeast Asia was the trade with Indian merchants. This was not tributary exchange or reciprocal gift giving. Indian merchant entrepreneurs brought highly valued goods across the sea to trade for scarce metals and other goods that the local economies could produce. Control over access to the Indian goods enabled local leaders to create redistributive states and provided the motivation for increased production for exchange in the overseas trade.

The multicentric nature of the Indian Ocean trade network made commerce competitive. Both Indian and Chinese core areas traded with the Southeast Asia periphery, and important groups of trading middlemen emerged. Specialized trade diasporas developed to service the local bulk sea trade (Curtin 1984), while Chinese and Indian merchants kept the importation of core commodities in their own hands (Meilink-Roelofsz 1962).

In his fascinating study of merchant capitalism on the Indian Ocean, K. N. Chaudhuri (1985) examined the same kinds of details of material life and exchange that Fernand Braudel (1972) provided for the Mediterranean (see also Beaujard 2005). Chaudhuri's study strongly supports the notion of a commercializing South Asian regional system within a larger multicore Afroeurasian macrosystem. On prestige goods and fundamental commodities, he says:

> It has been pointed out how certain items of trade—gold and silver, silk, fine muslins, spices, incense, and horses—were looked upon as great products of civilization, indispensable accompaniments to a refined and luxurious way of life. But we also know that the trans-oceanic trade of Eurasia was not supported by high-value precious goods alone. The technology of sailing-ships demanded the transport of bulk goods in combination with precious articles. Moreover, many regions around the Indian Ocean supplemented their food production with imports from areas of high agricultural surplus. An active trade in food grains and many different kinds of foodstuffs enabled the chronically deficient regions to specialize in the production of commodities for which there was a steady demand. The level of production in these areas was conditioned not only by the local geography and economy but also by the volume of long-distance trade. The strength of urban centers in different parts of Asia—the Middle East, Central Asia, and China—was derived precisely from the strong flow of maritime and caravan trade. In the Red Sea and the Persian Gulf, entire communities depended on food imports from Egypt and India for their daily survival. (Chaudhuri 1985, 203–204)

Even though the Chinese Empire tried to constrain and control foreign trade, it burgeoned. Many subterfuges and legal loopholes were employed by private entrepreneurs in the trade between China and Southeast Asia (Viraphol 1977). By the time the Europeans entered the Indian Ocean trade, the direct and indirect links between China and India had strengthened to the point that we can no longer speak of an entirely separate East Asian world-system. Instead, European, Indian, and Chinese subsystems were linked directly by substantial long-distance trade, and the Indian and Chinese subsystems were linked indirectly by their competition for profits in the South Seas.

A single state-based world-system that stretched from Europe through Southwestern Asia to India and China had emerged, but direct political-military interaction between East Asian and European states did not occur until the nineteenth century. As Jane Schneider (1977) and Janet Abu-Lughod (1989) contended, there was a precapitalist Afroeurasian-wide world-system. And there was a lot of capitalism in it, although this mode of accumulation was strongest in semiperipheral areas. In core areas the states and empires continued to be dominated by noncapitalist classes, and the predominant logic of expansion and contraction continued to be based on political-military power, tribute gathering, and taxation. But even within these tributary empires the states had begun to accommodate rather than suppress markets and profit making, and in the spaces between the empires and in some semiperipheral areas, capitalism had achieved political power in what we have called semiperipheral capitalist city-states.

Philip Curtin's (1984) discussion of **trade diasporas** sheds light on the processes by which a more integrated market economy emerged that linked the different cultural areas that composed the Afroeurasian macrosystem. The purveyors of cross-cultural trade that Curtin studied are those specialized ethnic groups (trade diasporas) that use kin-based ethnic and religious solidarities as institutional support for long-distance trust that facilitates trade between culturally different regions. Curtin points out that trade diasporas lose their reason for existence when a "**trade ecumene**"—a set of institutions and agreements that is transcultural—emerges and states set up mechanisms to protect foreign merchants and to enforce intercultural contracts. The trade ecumene is the beginning of a system-wide set of normative agreements and institutional structures that provides the basis for global culture.

Core/Periphery Relations in the Central System

Invasions by peripheral peoples and conquests by semiperipheral marcher states continued to be important aspects of core/periphery relations. Increased population density on the Central Asian steppes and confrontations with the civilized empires stimulated the formation of vast nomadic confederations around warrior kings. These peripheral warrior confederations threatened the borders of the civilized empires all along the steppe frontiers from Europe to East Asia. Often their incursions were merely temporary desolations or conquests of border areas, but sometimes they succeeded in setting up a new dynasty to rule over the old core areas.

When nomads or other peripheral peoples did occasionally conquer an agrarian empire in the East, the striking thing is how little difference there was between the old Chinese dynasties and the new conquest states. The Mongols and Manchus were rather quickly assimilated to Chinese ways, and their dynasties soon faced the same problems that the older indigenous ones had. When agrarian China paid tribute to peripheral nomads, this constituted a situation in which the periphery was exploiting the core. Conflict on the border was usually eventually converted into a peaceful arrangement: the employment of nomadic mercenaries by the Chinese and the shipping of prestige goods to the nomads, as well as a continuing division of labor and trade between steppe husbandry and Chinese agriculture.

The steppe confederations used what Thomas Barfield (1989) has called the inner- and outer-frontier strategies. The outer-frontier strategy involves a dominant nomad leader using violent attacks to terrify agrarian state officials for the purpose of extracting tribute payments and improving the terms of trade, while also *avoiding* the takeover of agrarian territory. The inner-frontier strategy occurred when a nomadic confederation began to disintegrate. One of the weaker factions would seek alliance with agrarian allies, the factions hoping to obtain the tribute goods that the agrarian state would send their rivals. The agrarian state officials would often go along with this as a "divide and conquer" tactic. The inner-frontier strategy gave the nomad leaders two choices—use their power to unify nomadic groups and return to an outer-frontier strategy, or leave them politically fragmented and strengthen their power over a limited region. There was a positive feedback loop between the strength of the agrarian state and the strategy of the nomadic confederation. When the empire was stronger, the nomads adopted an outer-frontier strategy; when it was weak, they used an inner-frontier strategy.

The development of larger horses capable of carrying heavy metal armor, along with the diffusion of the stirrup, eventually provided a response to the arrow showers of the nomadic light cavalry. Nomads could not afford knightly armor, and the larger horses could not be sustained on the sparse pasturage of the steppe (McNeill 1963). Thus did the weight of peripheral incursions from the steppes decrease as a factor in the processes of social evolution in the Afroeurasian macrosystem. Other peripheral peoples, such as the Scandinavians and the Manchurians, were to sweep down upon and conquer areas of the old core, but the long history of strong interaction between peripheral raiders and the agrarian empires was winding down.

This form of interaction had affected the development of military technology in the centers of civilization since the first emergence of cities in Mesopotamia, but this pressure tapered off after the Middle Ages. The Manchu (Qing) dynasty was the last successful conquest of an old core area by a semiperipheral marcher state. Peripheral nomads remained on the steppes, but they no longer presented strong challenges. Their importance was reduced to that of mercenaries in border areas between empires—for example, Tartars and Cossacks in the buffer zone between the Russian, Ottoman, and Hapsburg empires (McNeill 1964). Of course, peripheral state formation and other forms of resistance continued to influence the development of core regions because effective exploitation of peripheries was an important factor affecting the competition among core states. But these no longer directly threatened the core areas. Thus, the old pattern, in which both semiperipheral and peripheral areas sometimes gave birth to new core states, was replaced by a new one in which peripheral areas were permanently exposed to the **development of underdevelopment**, while new challenges to core states came primarily from the semiperiphery.

Patterns of Change in Afroeurasia

There were similar patterns of change at the western and eastern ends of Afroeurasia and evidence that they were connected into a single system much earlier than many historians have thought. The Central Asian steppe confederations and the South Asian states followed a somewhat different pattern, playing a middleman role in exchange between the East and West core regions. The steppe confederations were large but short-lived. The states and cities of India remained relatively small after the fall of the Mauryan Empire.

The history of the Afroeurasian world-system shows that incorporation need not automatically imply peripheralization. Incorporation was involved in the transformation of three formerly autonomous core regions into one larger, multicentric world-system. Religions such as Buddhism, Christianity, and Islam were important innovations in the information net and represented new techniques of ideological power that had big effects on the processes of state formation and interregional trade. Stirrups, gunpowder, and shock combat were important innovations in the political-military net. The compass was important for both the PGNs and BGNs.

The Afroeurasian system set the stage for the emergence of a global world-system by further developing the institutions of large-scale political control and long-range trade. The development of large states and empires occurred in the context of a trade network that was larger than any state. Thus, the political structure was most often multicentric, and this encouraged rulers to allow more autonomy to merchants. The growing commercialization of the tributary empires was reflected in the increasing commodification of land, labor, and wealth. The pulsation of the scope and strength of large-scale PGNs created local demand for food and basic goods and stimulated the expansion of BGNs. The growth of cities created a demand for the production of food for exchange. In the tributary empires, the main mechanism for ensuring the availability of supplies for the cities was the coercive institutions of the state, especially armies and navies. But markets played a larger and larger role in the later commercialized empires. As a result, the institutions that eventually allowed capitalism to become the predominant form of accumulation in Europe were developed in the commercialized agrarian empires, especially the semiperipheral capitalist city-states of Afroeurasia.

Suggested Readings

Barfield, Thomas J. 1989. *The Perilous Frontier: Nomadic Empires and China*. Cambridge, MA: Basil Blackwell.

Beckwith, I. Christopher. 2009. *Empires of the Silk Road*. Princeton, NJ: Princeton University Press.

Bentley, Jerry H. 1993. *Old World Encounters: Cross-Cultural Contacts and Exchanges in Pre-Modern Times*. Oxford: Oxford University Press.

Hopkins, Keith. 1978. *Conquerors and Slaves*. Cambridge: Cambridge University Press.

Scheidel, Walter, and Ian Morris. 2009. *The Dynamics of Ancient Empires*. New York: Oxford University Press.

Turchin, Peter. 2005. *War and Peace and War: The Life Cycles of Imperial Nations*. New York: Pi Press.

Wilkinson, David O. 1987. "Central Civilization." *Comparative Civilizations Review* 17 (Fall): 31–59.

PART

IV

The Long Rise of Capitalism

The development of capitalism in world history needs to be understood as the slow and uneven emergence of institutions that made commodified social relations possible. These include the development of money as commodified wealth, the development of commodified property, commodified labor, and legal institutions such as contract law that facilitate capitalist economic relations. We examine the emergence of social conceptions of the self that facilitated marketized relations. The production of commodities was stimulated within the tributary empires and surrounding kin-based societies by capitalist city-states that carried on long-distance trade, manufactured products for the carrying trade, and encouraged commodity production wherever they traded.

Rome in ruins

The increasing density of capitalist city-states and the slow and uneven commercialization that occurred within the tributary empires over millennia eventually produced the possibility that capitalism—a system based mainly on the production of commodities and the accumulation of profits—could emerge as a predominant mode of accumulation. It was in semiperipheral Europe, long a distant periphery of the old West Asian/Eastern Mediterranean core region, that capitalism first became predominant over the tributary modes of accumulation. This occurred after Europe had been cut off from the long-distance trade with Eurasia. When the long-distance trade was reestablished, the emergence of strong groups of European merchants in cities occurred in a context in which tributary states were small and relatively weak.

The relative density of capitalist city-states on the Italian Peninsula and the German Hanse cities of the Baltic was linked with commercial interests elsewhere in Europe. When larger states emerged in a competitive context of frequent interstate warfare, they were dependent on the capitalists within for financial resources as well as those in the still-independent city-states (Tilly 1990). Thus the European interstate system combined the commercialized institutions of the classical world and the contemporary adjacent commercialized Islamic empires to develop new institutions that were friendly toward marketized social relations.

Chapter 12 casts the rise of European hegemony in the context of the larger Afroeurasian system. Europe had long been a peripheral area to the more developed civilizations of the Near East (Western Asia) and the Eastern Mediterranean. European hegemony and the transformation to a fully capitalist system could not have occurred without the prior development of the institutions of capitalism and the networks of commodified trade in the larger system. Indeed, Europe was another instance of semiperipheral upward mobility, but this time of a whole world region. We will consider the question of European uniqueness and the "rise of the West" from a humanocentric perspective and as an instance of continuing sociocultural evolution. The emergence of the hegemony of the Dutch Republic in the seventeenth century is considered in some detail as the key development that led to the coming of a fully developed capitalism in Europe. The Dutch Republic was not the first capitalist state, but it was the first capitalist state that was not a city-state. It was the emergence of a strongly capitalist political economy that allowed Europe to become hegemonic over the other core and peripheral areas of the world-system, though Europe did not outperform China until the late eighteenth century.

How did the rise of capitalism affect people's psychology? While the **vertical individualist self** had its roots in the Late Iron Age, this form of identity really came into its own with the development of capitalism in Europe. The emergence of a completely secular science and the invention of the printing press paved the way for more abstract thinking for those literate classes who worked in the sciences and were able to buy books.

Chapter 12 tells the story of Europe's peripheral position in the West Asian/Mediterranean world-system of the Bronze Age and the long and temporally uneven rise of the West. The Roman semiperipheral marcher state created a Western core region, but the demise of Rome and moving of the Roman (Byzantine) capital back to the old Eastern core region (Constantinople) led to a reperipheralization of Western Europe that was the heyday of European feudalism. European feudalism was a peripheral and decentralized version of the tributary mode of accumulation. The subsequent renewed rise of Europe began with the Crusades. Under the banner of rescuing the Holy Land from the Moslem infidels, European armies invaded the old Near Eastern core region. But in addition to religious zeal, this effort was spurred on by Venice, a prototypical capitalist city-state that wanted to break the Islamic blockade of trade from Asia. Another significant element in the Crusades was the role played by the Norman semiperipheral marcher states recently established in Sicily and the kingdom of Naples. The expansionary Norman conquerors and the entrepreneurial and manipulative Venetians mobilized the European Christians to attack and sack not only the Holy Land but also the Byzantine (Christian) capital of Constantinople. This preemptive war succeeded in opening up the trade connections between Europe and the distant South and East Asian core regions that had been largely cut off by the emergence of the Islamic empires.

Chapter 13 is about the modern Europe-centered world-system since the long sixteenth century. It is the story of the rise to global hegemony of the European core states; the emergent predominance of capitalism; the construction of colonial empires in Africa, Asia, and the Americas; and the hegemonic rivalry among European core states. We shall tell the story of the rise to economic hegemony of the Dutch Republic in the seventeenth century, the struggle between Britain and France in the eighteenth century, the British hegemony of the nineteenth century, and the hegemony of the United States in the twentieth century in subsequent chapters.

Chapter 13 focuses on the modern world-system in which we now live. Its basic structures and processes are described, and an overview of its structural history is provided. The developmental trends and cyclical processes of the modern system are explained. The hegemonies of the Dutch, the British, and the United States are compared. The incorporation of the remaining regions of the earth by European expansion is described, as is the changing nature of core/periphery relations in the modern world-system.

Chapter 14 compares the early modern regional systems in the fifteenth through eighteenth centuries with each other to illuminate both similarities and differences. Chapter 15 analyzes the great wave of capitalist globalization that occurred under British hegemony in the nineteenth century. The rapid acceleration of communications and transportation technology, the growth of international trade and investment, the further marketization of agriculture and mining in the less developed countries, the last wave of European colonialism, and the growing integration of a global capitalist class were all important features of the nineteenth-century wave of globalization. Chapter 16 further considers the development of the modern individual in the context of complex capitalist societies. Chapter 17 discusses the first half of the twentieth century in world-historical perspective, and Chapter 18 examines the second half of the twentieth century.

12

The Long Rise of the West

This chapter further examines the similarities and differences between Europe and the other core regions of Afroeurasia, as well as the emergence of links among these regions. We begin with a short discussion of Eurocentrism and the difficulties of attempting to be truly objective about the human past. Then we discuss four regions in Afroeurasia in terms of which had the largest cities over the past 4,000 years. This shows the trajectory of the European rise. Then we characterize the integration of Europe into the old Central System. Europe was the locus of small-scale egalitarian world-systems until it became a distant periphery of the old West Asian Central System. The emergence of European chiefdoms and early states occurred in distant indirect interaction with the

Dutch capital-intensive agriculture

core of the old Central System. The rise of the Roman semiperipheral marcher state expanded the core region of the Central System toward the west, but the demise of the Roman Empire and the rise of the Islamic empires returned most of Europe to peripheral status.

The Moslem blockade of European trade with Asia deepened the devolution of the European regional economy and produced a very decentralized version of the tributary mode of accumulation—European feudalism. But then the ability of the Islamic empires to monopolize trade with the East declined as they broke up into competing states and as the Europeans launched their first wave of expansion under the banner of restoring Christian rule to the Holy Land. The Crusades were based on a combination of religious fervor that was spurred on by Norman marchers looking for new conquests and the savvy Venetian **doges** (merchant princes who governed Venice) who sought freer access to prestige goods from Asia. European cities began to grow again, and Europe formed its own regional core composed of capitalist city-states on the Italian Peninsula and north of the Alps.

The emergence of predominant capitalism in semiperipheral Europe was made possible because the institutional and cultural elements of commodified society were already present in the classical heritage from Rome and in the contemporary adjacent and quite commercialized, but still predominantly tributary, Islamic states and Byzantium. These institutions, and the new capitalist class that benefited from them, were able to become powerful in Europe because of the weakness of European tributary states. This made it possible for merchants, producers of commodities, and finance capitalists to gain institutionalized power in the emerging city-states and nation-states of Europe.

Europe enjoyed a semiperipheral advantage in the Central System and was in the right place at the right time to make the transition to capitalism before the other commercialized regions of Afroeurasia could. Thus the rise of Europe was due to a combination of characteristics within Europe and its relationships with the larger Afroeurasian world.[1]

After a fuller discussion of the above, this chapter examines what happened in Europe after the fall of Rome—the involution of the economy and the decentralization of the polity that eventuated in classical European feudalism. Then we consider the crisis of feudalism and the emergence of capitalism in Europe. And then we will turn to an examination of the development of individualism in medieval Europe. The rest of the chapter focuses on developments during the first half of the second millennium CE in other regions of Afroeurasia and their connections with Europe.

Eurocentrism versus Humanocentric and Cosmocentric Objectivity

Much of our knowledge about human social change has been influenced by the fact of the rise of European societies to world power over the last few centuries. Modern ethnography and archaeology, as well as much of what has been written by historians, have largely been produced by Europeans or peoples of European descent, and much of what has been produced as scientific knowledge of human social change has been influenced by assumptions about the superiority of European peoples and their social institutions. Nineteenth-century social Darwinists used a Eurocentric version of social science to legitimate class, race, gender, and core/periphery exploitation and domination.

"Europe" is a socially constructed category that some people have used to differentiate themselves from others. All peoples who share a common culture define that culture in part by comparing it with others. There is no European continent in strictly geographical terms. The Eurasian "World Island" is a continuous landmass from the Atlantic to the Pacific Oceans. Drawing a line along inland bodies of water or mountain ranges does not produce a continent in geographical terms. The motivation for creating the entity "Europe" and calling it a continent has been what many social theorists have called "orientalism." **Orientalism** involves making East/West social distinctions that are understood in evaluative terms, although these evaluations are often

[1] Thus the rise of the West was not entirely occidental ☺.

buried under claims about objectivity. The Greek historian Herodotus portrayed (Persian) Asia as the land of despotism and Greek Europe as the land of freedom. Modern political theorists have elaborated this distinction and sought the roots of later European democracy in classical Greece, a discussion that we engaged in Chapters 9 and 10.

Andre Gunder Frank's (1998) provocative study of the global economy from 1400 CE to 1800 CE contended that China had long been the center of the global system. Frank also argued that the rise of European hegemony was a *sudden and conjunctural* development caused by the late emergence in China of a "high level equilibrium trap"[2] and the success of Europeans in using silver extracted from the Americas to buy their way into Chinese technological, financial, and productive success. Frank also contended that Eurocentric ignorance of the importance of China invalidates all the social science theories that have tried to explain the rise of the West based on the differences between the East and the West. In Frank's view there never was a transition from feudalism to capitalism that distinguished Europe from other regions of the world. He argued that the basic dynamics of development have been similar in the global system for 5,000 years (Frank and Gills 1993).

In recent decades there have been serious efforts to overcome Eurocentric biases by world historians and anthropologists. Theories of social evolution have been purged of their nonscientific assumptions (e.g., Sanderson 1990, and Chapter 1 of this book). World historians have paid more attention to the histories of non-Europeans, and anthropologists have tried to look at the world from the perspective of the "people without history" (Wolf 1982).

These efforts may not have been completely successful, and so it is a good idea to be critically aware of how institutionalized power can affect social science. We have endeavored to be objective from a humanocentric and a cosmocentric perspective on human social change—one that looks from the point of view of the whole human species and also from the point of view of the physical and biological universe. But objectivity is a very daunting goal, and we do not presume to claim that we have attained it. After all, we are thinking and writing in a particular language (English). We are citizens of the most powerful state on Earth (the United States). We are academic professionals from particular disciplines, members of families, and inheritors of a body of social science and general culture that has been produced by a particular period of human history. So we encourage our readers to ask to what extent we have been able to live up to our intention of objectivity. These issues become more pressing as we move closer to our own time, especially when we try to peer into the future.

City Growth in the Core Regions of Afroeurasia

One way to compare the relative development of different regions is to examine the sizes of their cities. Figure 12.1 shows the population-weighted percentages that four regions held of the twenty largest cities on Earth from 2000 BCE to 1988 CE.

In Figure 12.1 we see the emergence of the world's first cities in Mesopotamia and Egypt, represented here by the designation West Asia/North Africa. In the upper-left-hand corner of the graph, the dashed line shows that this region had 100 percent of the largest cities on Earth in 2000 BCE. As other regions developed large cities, this monopoly necessarily diminished, and 4,000 years later only a very small percentage of the world's largest cities were in this region. This is strong evidence of the notion of uneven development and the geographical movement of the cutting edge of sociocultural complexity.

The relative sizes of the largest European cities (indicated by the solid black line) show a long oscillation around a low level, indicating Europe's peripheral and semiperipheral location in the old Central System. Europe had been firmly incorporated into the trade networks of the Central System during the Bronze and Iron Ages. Figure 12.1 indicates that around 1450 CE, Europe's cities began a long rise in terms of their sizes relative to the other largest cities on Earth.

[2] A **high level equilibrium trap** is a situation in which labor is so cheap that producers have no incentive to invest in labor-saving technological change.

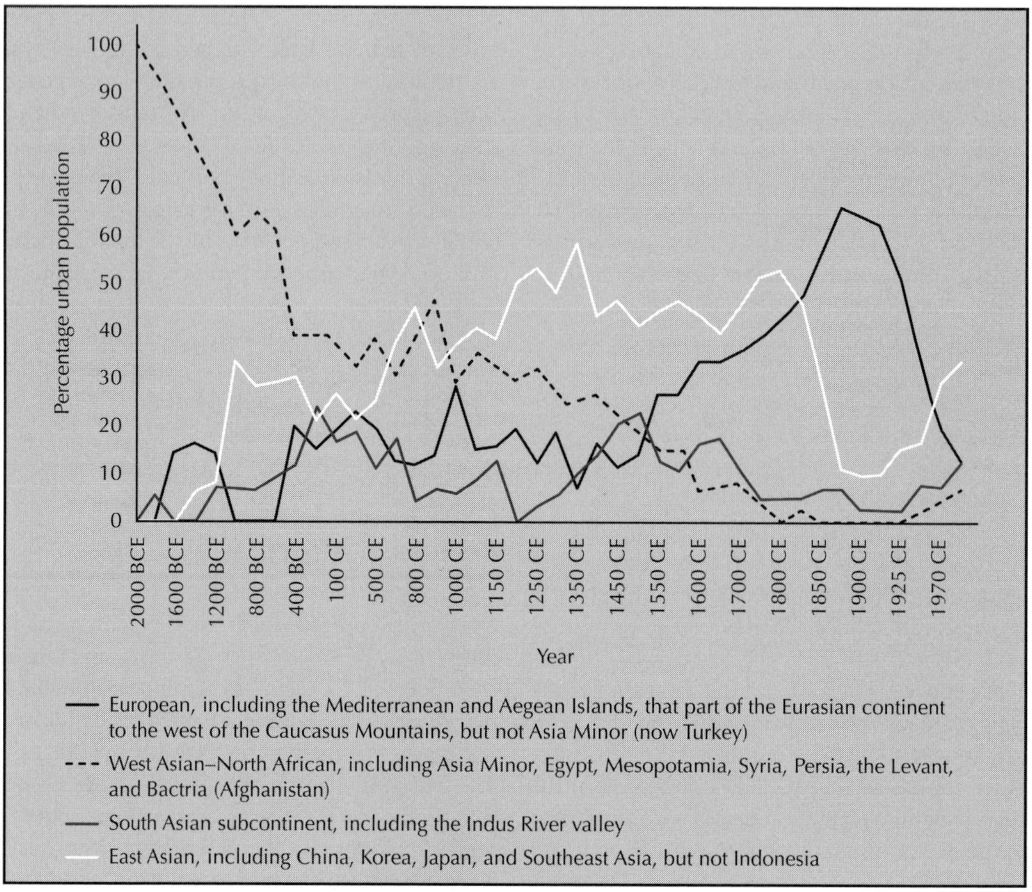

Figure 12.1 Regional urban population as a percentage of the world's twenty largest cities, 2000 BCE to 1988 CE[3]

Sources: Estimates of the sizes of the largest cities are from Modelski (2003), Ian Morris (2010, 2013), and Chandler (1987).

Europe's cities passed those of East Asia in 1825 CE and peaked in 1875, and then underwent a rapid decline in importance because of the rise of large cities in North America and the continued growth of cities in Asia (see also I. Morris 2013).

All twenty cities, including those in the Americas, are in the denominator of the indicator of relative urban size in Figure 12.1. So in the decades of the twentieth century, the percentages shown in Figure 12.1 do not add up to 100 percent, because some of the largest cities are not in any of the regions tracked (e.g., New York City, Mexico City). Thus Figure 12.1 indicates that the relatively smaller and older European cities (e.g., London and Paris) were surpassed by the much larger American and Japanese cities in the twentieth century.

The trajectory of Europe displayed in Figure 12.1 supports part of Andre Gunder Frank's (1998) contention that China was long the center of the world-system, but contradicts another part. The small cities of Europe in the early period indicate its peripheral status vis-à-vis the core regions of West Asia/North Africa, South Asia, and East Asia. As Frank argues, Europe did not best East Asia (as indicated by city sizes) until the

[3] A different approach would be to use PMNs as the units of comparison even though the spatial boundaries of these change over time. More details about this analysis of relative city sizes can be found in Chase-Dunn and Manning (2002).

eighteenth century. But the long European rise, beginning in the fifteenth century, contradicts Frank's depiction of a sudden and conjunctural emergence of European hegemony in the eighteenth century. Based on relative city sizes it appears that the rise of Europe occurred over a period of five hundred years. This upward trajectory began during Europe's second wave of expansion (see below) in the fifteenth century.

For East Asia, we see in Figure 12.1 a rapid rise that began in 1200 BCE with the emergence of the first states and cities in the Yellow River Valley. This was followed by a small decline, then another burst of relative urban growth that began in 361 CE and rose to a peak in 800 CE, then another decline, and then a further rise to the highest peak of all in 1350 CE. Then there was a small decline and another peak in 1800. Not until 1825 was East Asia bested by the European cities after a decline that started in 1800 and continued until 1914, when a recovery began. The European cities were bested again by the East Asian cities between 1950 and 1970 during the rapid decline of the European cities in terms of their size and importance among the world's twenty largest cities. This most recent rise of the East Asian cities is a consequence of the upward mobility of Japan and China in the global political economy of the twentieth century.

The South Asian cities indicate how this region has fared during the long integration of Afroeurasia. In Figure 12.1, South Asia is shown by the solid gray line. The early emergence of cities in the Indus River valley can be seen, as well as their demise, and then the rise of the Gangetic states that peaked, in terms of city-size importance, in 200 BCE. The Indic cities disappeared completely from the world's twenty largest cities in 1200 CE but then rose to another peak in 1500 CE corresponding with the Mughal Empire. In 1988 the South Asian cities had risen once again to a level as high as they had between 1650 CE and 1700 CE.

While the "European" rise began much earlier than Frank contends (as indicated by Figure 12.1), this early rise was mainly due to the growth of Ottoman Constantinople (Istanbul). Constantinople was within the continent of Europe as we have defined it. The second- and third-largest cities in Europe in 1500 were Paris and Venice, followed by Naples and Milan. From 1500 to 1600 the Parisian population grew from 185,000 to 245,000, and the other large cities of Europe grew at a similar pace. So the early European upsurge seen in Figure 12.1 was not due only to the growth of Constantinople. Christian Europe was also experiencing a sixteenth-century boom period. This does not dispute the relatively greater centrality of China in this period, but it does show that Europe did not remain a peripheral backwater until it finally sprang to hegemony in the late eighteenth century.

Constantinople's population leveled off at 700,000 in 1600 and stayed at that size until 1700, after which it began to decline. In this same period the largest cities of Western Europe were growing rapidly. London had grown larger than Constantinople by 1750. Now that we have scanned the horizon of the development of Afroeurasian regions using the telescope of comparative city sizes, let us look more closely at Europe and its relationship with the other regions to see what was going on closer to the ground.

Europe's Place in the Old Central System

Europe's human inhabitants had long been hunter-gatherers living in largely independent and small-scale egalitarian world-systems. The diffusion of Neolithic farming practices and the arrival of immigrant gardeners from the East produced a local core/periphery differentiation in which sedentary horticulturalists traded and sometimes fought with more nomadic hunter-gatherers (Renfrew 1987; Gregg 1988). Pastoralism based on the raising of domesticated animals, especially cattle, was adopted, and Europeans developed the biological ability to digest cow and goat milk as adults that still distinguishes them from many other human populations. Difficult communications and transportation conditions limited the spatial size of both BGNs and PMNs in Neolithic and Bronze Age Europe. Nevertheless, Europe became slowly linked with the INs and PGNs of the expanding state-based West Asian/East Mediterranean world-system.

An indicator that something was going on in Europe was the building of large stone megaliths (such as the famous one at Stonehenge in England) in the late third millennium BCE.

The construction of these monuments seems to have begun in southwestern Europe and then spread to northwestern Europe. This was probably indicative of the emergence of chiefdoms in these regions, and it has been supposed that these changes were stimulated in part by trade connections and information flows from the old Central System. Yet the links were not very strong until Europe became more heavily involved in the Central PGN during the late Bronze Age. Prestige goods such as copper, bronze, and amber linked the Mediterranean, temperate Europe, and Scandinavia to the West Asian states. This, and increasing population densities, led to the development and spread of new religions and the formation of local chiefdoms as indicated by elite burials that contained bronze axes (Kristiansen 1998).

Population densities continued to rise with the diffusion of iron tools and weapons from the Central System. Iron hoes allowed farmers to dig deeper into the ground, producing larger crops. Sherratt (1993a, 1993b) contends that it was during the Iron Age that Europeans became seriously integrated into the West Asian BGN as producers of raw materials in exchange for the manufactured goods of the eastern Mediterranean core. The Phoenician city-states played an important role by linking the trade of the Mediterranean and the Iberian Peninsula with West Asia and beyond. The Etruscans, who built the first cities on the Italian Peninsula, probably migrated to Italy from the old Near Eastern core region of the Central System. This, and the establishment of Greek colonies on Sicily, pulled Europe into the Central PMN.

The rise of the Roman semiperipheral marcher state integrated the rest of Europe into the Mediterranean system of food production. This made Europe a solid part of the Central System, from which it was never separated from this time forward. The establishment of a strong empire centered on the Italian Peninsula expanded the core region of the old Central System toward the west. So after the Bronze Age, Europe was always part of the Central System. The rise of Islam temporarily interfered with Europe's connection to Asian trade networks, but this was possible only because Europe and the Islamic states were engaged in intense political/military conflict, an important type of interaction in all world-systems.

European feudalism has been thought of as a "stage" of social evolution and as a distinct mode of production in many theories of social change. But many contend that it was a decentralized version of the tributary mode of accumulation. The processes of economic and political involution that produced European feudalism occurred in waves after the demise of the Western Roman Empire. The abandonment of Rome caused the city to rapidly shrink in size as the tentacles of the empire were no longer operating to supply it. Steppe nomads and semiperipheral marchers moved into the former territories of the Roman Empire in Europe and this disrupted the local economy and long-distance trade to some extent. But towns continued to produce goods and to exchange them for the produce of the countryside. The biggest wave of involution, the greatest shrinkage of the European towns, and the peak of feudalism based on the self-subsistent manor (see below) did not occur until the newly emergent Islamic states were able to greatly constrain Europe's trade with Asia.

The weakness of territorial states in Europe was ultimately a function of the demise of the (Western) Roman Empire and the rise of the Islamic blockade. This weakness of centralized states made it possible for capitalist city-states to bunch closely to one another and to develop a strong regional system of commodity production and commercial finance once the regional economy began to rebound. Though capitalist city-states had existed for millennia in the old Central System, the concentration of a number of them on the Italian Peninsula and north of the Alps was unique. The weak and decentralized tributary system (feudalism) was a major structural condition that allowed the European merchants to accumulate capital without significant intervention from the tribute-gathering classes and to eventually attain state power itself. It was the continued strength of the tributary states in West, South, and East Asia that prevented capitalism from becoming predominant in those regions.

European Feudalism

Classical European feudalism reached its zenith in the ninth century CE. The regional states were extremely weak alliances in which the "king" was simply the landlord who could mobilize a sizeable contingent of local knights to support him. This characterization applies even to those kings who made the greatest efforts to construct a centralized regional state—the Carolingian "Empire" of Charlemagne. Edward Fox (1971, 1991) contends that this political devolution was the result of the emergence of heavy cavalry made possible by the diffusion of the stirrup. Heavily armored knights riding huge warhorses emerged during the Carolingian period as the predominant military formation of the day. Fox argues that the massive consumption of hay and grain by these horses made a centralized and concentrated army logistically impossible under the conditions of difficult land transportation that existed in medieval Europe. Only a decentralized system of agricultural manors could supply the warhorses, and so the polity and the economy became decentralized.

The **manorial economy** was very decentralized. In principle, each manor was under the legal jurisdiction of its lord, a warrior-knight. And in principle, the manor was intended to be economically, politically, and religiously self-sufficient. Serfs contributed the labor power of the manor. The serfs were part of the property held by the landlord and contributed their labor in exchange for protection and access to a small parcel of land. In fact, serfdom and enserfment were institutions that varied over time and space depending on local conditions of security and other factors. For peasants, the question was one of survival, and it was sometimes better to become enserfed than to starve or to be killed in violent conflict over access to land.

The manor was the real unit of political and military sovereignty. The lord controlled the rule of law, and it was he who retained the priest who served the manor. The serfs were part of his property. They were theoretically not free to leave. They provided labor services to the lord by working on the **desmesne** (pronounced "demain"), that part of the tilled land of the manor from which all produce went to the castle (see Figure 12.2). In exchange for this and other services, the serfs were given access to tenant plots to raise their own food, and the landlord, a knight in shining armor, provided the serfs protection from others who might try to pillage the manor. In principle, the manor also had skilled craftsmen who produced the tools and other manufactures needed for agriculture and the household.

It has been suggested by anthropologists (e.g., Johnson and Earle 1987) that European feudalism was reminiscent of complex chiefdoms in that these were small polities, there was a radical

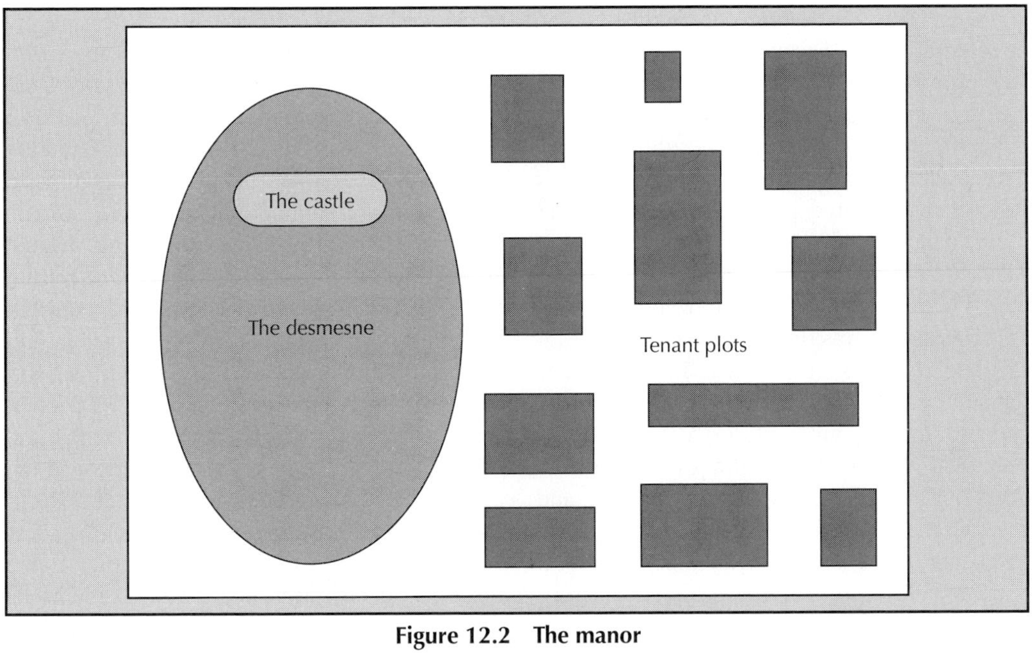

Figure 12.2 The manor

distinction between the rulers and the ruled, and generalized authority was concentrated in the person of the lord of the manor. The radical distinction in feudalism between nobles and peasants—with the nobles conceived as people who were born to rule, and the peasants understood as "drawers of water and hewers of wood"—is similar to the radical distinction in some complex chiefdoms or archaic states between sacred chiefs and commoners (e.g., precontact Hawaii). The chiefdom analogy is somewhat apt, but the European lords lived in a culture that contained the institutional remnants of true states—laws, writing, world religions, the memory of bureaucratic administration, money, and markets. Knowledge of these institutions, even when they were not actually present in feudal society, altered the flavor of feudalism, and when new conditions arrived, these things did not need to be invented.

The manorial property itself was not commodified property. It was not a "freehold" that could be sold. Rather, the manor was held at the behest of the king, and its inheritance was subject to the institution of fealty. **Fealty** is a ritual swearing of loyalty by tenants and vassals to their lord. It is a voluntary bond among individuals who are not necessarily related by kinship, and this institution is another way in which feudalism was different from most pre-state chiefdoms, where alliances were socially constructed as kin relations (conical clans and ranked lineages).

Once land has become commodified it can be sold for money. The existence of a market for "real property" allows people with money to have a lot of power. The situation of feudalism was very different. Manorial property was controlled by a decentralized and competitive political/military logic of security and protection. Property was not an adjunct to commodity production, but was instead a direct mobilizer of production by means of institutionalized coercive power.

The manor was the basic economic, political, and religious unit of feudal society. The self-sufficiency of the manor was never complete, and even in those times and places where it was very great, the feudal economy still contained a degree of market exchange among manors and between manors and towns. But the theoretical sovereignty of the manor was an important aspect of the social structure of European feudalism.

When the shrunken European cities began to grow again, they were able to obtain the same relatively high level of autonomous sovereignty held by the manors. Thus serfs who managed to escape from the manors were often able to find respite and protection in the relatively sovereign cities. The notion of *stadtluft macht frei* (city air makes you free) became part of the culture of European feudalism. And when urban revolutions brought merchants or entrepreneurial aristocrats to power within cities, they could use the autonomous power of the urban polity to pursue policies that were friendly to their own businesses.

Something like feudalism existed in many other places besides Europe whenever an empire broke down into "warlordism." In most places this kind of tributary decentralization was followed fairly quickly by the emergence of a new empire, usually at the hands of a semiperipheral marcher state. But the European warlordism lasted for a thousand years after the demise of Rome.

The peak of European feudalism occurred in the centuries just after the peak of the Islamic caliphates in the old Central System. As discussed in Chapter 11, the rise of Islam was a classical case of semiperipheral marcher conquest but with a particularly fervent religious aspect. The nomadic Bedouins of the Arabian Peninsula had long served as mercenary soldiers for the agrarian empires of the old Mesopotamian heartland. Camel caravans made transportation of prestige goods across the deserts of the Arabian Peninsula possible, and trade-based cities populated by urbanized Arabs and other trading peoples emerged on the Arabian Peninsula. The emergence of Islam was part of a process of state formation that occurred in a region that had been peripheral, but in the midst of earlier tributary empires—the Arabian Peninsula. The Abbasid caliphate was a semiperipheral marcher empire that emerged from the new Arabian world religion (Islam) and the process of Arabian state formation. It was a large and strong empire that built the huge city of Baghdad in Mesopotamia and tried to monopolize the trade between Asia and the West. The Islamic conquest of both Byzantine Egypt and the Sassanian (Persian) Empire that had controlled Mesopotamia put a huge dent in the Asian goods that passed through Western Asia to Europe, despite that the Arabian Moslems never conquered Byzantine Constantinople. Henri Pirenne's (1980) *Mohammed and Charlemagne* describes the Mediterranean Sea in the period of the Abbasid caliphate as a "Moslem Lake."

At the very same time that Europe was being cut off from the Eastern trade by the Islamic marcher states, another power was emerging from the far north. The Vikings lived in seagoing chiefdoms with strong military traditions. As population pressure visited the Scandinavian homelands, the losers of local conflicts were expelled and set off on voyages of conquest. Some made it to Iceland, Greenland, and North America (Diamond 2005). Many marauded England, Scotland, and Ireland. And an important contingent established a new kingdom in Normandy on the coast of France, where they adopted Christianity and a more semiperipheral political structure. From Normandy they launched a successful conquest of England. But the Normans continued to fight among themselves, and parties set off to conquer new lands as far away as the Mediterranean. Sicily and the kingdom of Naples were conquered by Normans, and these semiperipheral marchers were an important component of the European Christian Crusades against Moslem control of the Old West Asian core region.

In the late tenth and early eleventh centuries, Christendom spread to Scandinavia, Poland, and Hungary, further culturally integrating Europe and facilitating trade. As trade increased, the towns began to grow. By playing one lord against another, and by using wealth to purchase independence, a rare capitalist type of town began to spread throughout northwest Europe. These towns were rather more independent of any noble ruler and accustomed to self-governance.

European towns became attractive to peasants who often left harsh conditions on manors to take up urban residence and employment. While European towns offered opportunities for advancement that were not possible on the manor, they also were frequently lethal to newcomers not adjusted to diseases borne of high-density living. The availability of towns as an alternative to the manor gave European peasants an improved bargaining position vis-à-vis nobles (Bartlett 1993).

The commercial success of the Venetian capitalist city-state was enhanced by the breakup of the Abbasid caliphate into competing Islamic states and the Mongol conquest of Baghdad, which loosened up Islamic control of the Eastern trade. The Venetian doges supported their trading ventures with a strong navy that supplied protection and expanded the profitability of merchant capitalism by strategic interventions in the power politics of the Central System (Lane 1973). In 1204 the Venetians managed to convince the Christian crusaders to sack Christian Constantinople, a major competitor of the Venetians in the Eastern trade (Lane 1979, 28). Thus, the combination of the Norman marcher states, an entrepreneurial Venetian capitalist city-state, and the religious fervor provided by Christian concerns about control of the Holy Land by Moslem "infidels" enabled semiperipheral Europe to reestablish its connections with the Asian trade networks. This provided the economic stimulus for further intensification of commodity production and market relations within Europe. The cities grew again, and the balance of power within states shifted in favor of those who employed their capital in commodity production and trade. Despite the ascendancy of the Venetian semiperipheral capitalist city-state, the new prosperity in northern Europe brought population growth and moved the "center of gravity" of Europe north of the Alps for the first time. A new core region emerged, what Peter Spufford (2003) has called the "blue banana," a region of strong capitalist city-states from the Italian Peninsula across the Alps and into the valley of the Rhine. This region sat betwixt larger tributary states of the old kind, but they were too slow and weak to grab the banana.

The Long Rise of European Global Power

The modern world-system is arguably different from any earlier system in that there was a qualitative change in the mode of accumulation with the rise of Europe.[4] Within Europe the feudal

[4] We mentioned earlier that Andre Gunder Frank (1998) contended that there was no transition to capitalism in Europe. Even among the many scholars who do see a qualitative transformation, there are great differences regarding the nature, causes, timing, and locations of the transition. Our portrayal is consistent with the theoretical perspective we have employed to study social change, but we do not claim that this is the last word on these controversial topics.

mode of production was challenged and then superseded by the emergence of a strong urban and agricultural capitalism in the sixteenth and seventeenth centuries.

The emergence of predominant capitalism in Europe occurred in a series of waves, which explains why so many scholars disagree about the timing of the transition. The transition did not occur all at once, but in a series of what Giovanni Arrighi (1994) has called "systemic cycles of accumulation," in which the power of money penetrated deeper and deeper into the societies of the modern system. We have already outlined the basic structural features that made the transition possible: the existence of appropriately commodified institutions—money, markets, contract law—and the weak and decentralized nature of European tributary structures. But these structural features combined with a number of conjunctural elements to allow capitalists to become more and more predominant in Europe.

The nature of Europe's connection with the Central System had changed radically over time. With regard to bulk goods and prestige goods, Europe was temporarily disconnected from Asia during the Islamic blockade. Within Europe the feudal manorial economy was based mainly on local self-subsistence. But Europe continued to be strongly linked with the Central PMN despite the temporary bulk and prestige goods disconnect. When trade connections with Asia were reestablished, Europe's cities began to grow again in the context of a rather decentralized version of the tributary mode of accumulation. The formation of a new core region within Europe allowed improved terms of trade with Asia. Janet Abu-Lughod (1987, 1989) depicts the Afroeurasian world-system of the thirteenth century as a multicore system in which trade relations were mainly based on equal exchange among the urbanized core regions of East Asia, South Asia, West Asia, North Africa, and Europe.

The Mongol conquests did not have the same repercussions in Europe that they did throughout West Asia in terms of political alignments. Northwest Europe was the only part of Eurasia that was not significantly disrupted directly by the Mongol conquests. In 1348 the bubonic plague, spread by traders traveling across the steppe, swept into Europe, killing between one-third and one-half of the population. Like earlier epidemics, this one returned periodically for several decades. These massive die-offs disrupted European development. The European population did not fully recover until sometime in the sixteenth century. European prosperity was undermined and conditions remained uncertain. The shortage of labor favored the bargaining power of peasants vis-à-vis landlords and encouraged the transition to capitalist agriculture in the countryside and the emergence of capitalism in the cities.

An important cause of the transition was what has been called the "crisis of feudalism." The twelfth and thirteenth centuries in Europe saw the growth of cities and long-distance trade (described above), and also the growth of the rural population and the bringing of additional lands into agricultural production. But in the fourteenth century, these growth trends were reversed. Part of the reversal was due to a worsening of the climate and the arrival of the Black Death (bubonic plague). Colder climates and heavier storms reduced agricultural productivity, and the Black Death killed off a large number of people. Some lands that had been brought under cultivation during the upswing were again abandoned.

These declines combined with the long-run consequences of the growth of the urban economy to produce a reduction in the incomes of the landlords, the so-called crisis of seigniorial revenues. The landed aristocracy had grown larger during the growth period. Peasants found it possible to make a living in the towns, and so the power of the lords over their workforce declined. When the landlords tried to extract more labor from their serfs based on feudal dues, the peasants either ran away or revolted. Peasant revolts were widespread across Europe after the fourteenth century.

Thus, contraction during the fourteenth and fifteenth centuries induced large numbers of feudal lords to supplement their feudal incomes by means of converting their lands to commodity production, and this trend increased when the economy began to grow again in the fifteenth century. So agriculture, as well as the urban economy, moved toward capitalist commodity production. And the search for new sources of elite income also stimulated another wave of European external conquest and the peripheralization of distant lands. Thus did the crisis of feudalism usher in an important wave of commodification that

Immanuel Wallerstein (1974b) has called the "long sixteenth century" (1450–1640).

The Crusades were followed by the expulsion of the Islamic moors from the Iberian Peninsula and then by the Portuguese establishment of colonial ports down the west coast of Africa. The first Portuguese colony in Africa was Ceuta, just across the Strait of Gibraltar, taken in 1415. Then the Portuguese, with financial help from Genoa, attempted to monopolize the spice trade with the East Indies (Lane 1979, 31–34).

Europeans began growing sugar cane on the islands of the Mediterranean and in the Canary Islands in the Atlantic. This was the birth of what Philip Curtin (1990) has called the "plantation complex," a system of peripheral capitalism that produced tropical agricultural raw materials for the European core. Its institutional roots were in the Roman *latifundia* and the great Arab estates. The plantation complex was later expanded into the Western Hemisphere, where it enjoyed a long history in which chattel slavery was used for the production of agricultural commodities—an ironic combination of capitalism and coercion that we call **peripheral capitalism**. The expansion of European power into Africa and the Americas further stimulated the development of capitalism in Europe, though the effects in Europe of the wealth extracted from the new peripheries were complicated and uneven.

Europe's continued struggle with states in West Asia and its technological backwardness relative to industries in China and India encouraged European expansion into regions where the Europeans had a technological and political/military upper hand—Africa and the Americas. European naval power and sailing capability developed quickly because of intense competition among the European states. It was Ferdinand Magellan, a Portuguese navigator, who first circumnavigated the earth,[5] and Europeans were the main developers of the techniques of ocean-crossing shipping that eventually made a global world-system possible.

The rise of European hegemony was one more example of semiperipheral upward mobility. But it was also a new departure for two reasons:

1. Because of the spatial scale involved—a whole region eventually became dominant and created a single global world-system with a single integrated and directly interconnected interstate system of core states
2. The region that became dominant underwent a transformation of the mode of accumulation—capitalist commodity production superseded state taxation and tribute gathering as the main form of accumulating wealth and power

What occurred in Europe after feudalism waned was the emergence of a regional core within which capitalism became the predominant mode of accumulation. Capitalism had had a long gestation period in Afroeurasia as the tributary empires had become more commercialized and semiperipheral capitalist city-states had become more important. The Roman Empire, China, and the Islamic states all had elaborately commodified trade, wealth, and property relations, but in each of these the logic of state expansion remained the main game. And the process by which semiperipheral marcher states created core-wide empires by means of conquest remained the predominant mechanism of social change within the tributary state-based world-systems. But in Europe, the old rise and fall of empires was transformed into a new kind of rise and fall—that of hegemonic capitalist core states (see Chapter 14).

The Development of Individualism in Medieval Europe

The roots of individualism go all the way back to the Indo-Europeans. Hallpike (1988, 2008) points out that kinship relations among the Germans and Celts did not exist much beyond the level of the family and were governed by a contract of loyalty. There was private property

[5] Actually, Magellan himself never made it all the way around. He was killed in the Philippines in 1526, but one of the ships of his expedition, the Victoria (under the command of Juan Sebastian del Cano), completed the circumnavigation.

of cattle and voluntary organization into guilds. Politically there were assemblies of freedmen, and kings were elected. Truth was tested through competition and debate. All these characteristics are typical of individualism.

Many scholars have argued that ecological and geographical conditions in Europe acted to inhibit the formation of a single centralized European state. The mountainous terrain of Europe made communication and transportation difficult. Centralized states emerged in many other regions in order to build and manage large-scale irrigation systems. Europe's adequately rain-watered agriculture did not require the development of large-scale irrigation systems, and so this functional legitimation for large and centralized states was missing. And yet the Roman Empire had succeeded in bringing most of Europe under the jurisdiction of a single state apparatus. Nevertheless, the absence of a centralized state after the fall of Rome has implications for the study of personality, because state centralization is most often accompanied by vertical collectivism, while a system composed of smaller and more competitive states may facilitate individualism. We have also argued that capitalism and market relations became unusually strong in Europe, and these elements of social structure are also usually associated with greater individualism.

According to Colin Morris (2000), social conditions in Europe between 1050 CE and 1200 CE made individualism more likely to spread beyond the aristocracy. Improved agricultural techniques allowed the cultivation of wastelands and the clearance of forests, making it possible to grow more crops and to feed more people. A larger population allowed for more specialization and new types of occupations. While there was an incipient individualism among the aristocrats of ancient civilizations, what was new was the spread of individualistic personalities to other social classes. This tendency increased in the fourteenth century as a shortage of agricultural labor emerged. Peasants ran away to the towns to try their hand at a new life. Both craft production and trade demanded more initiative and rational activity than agriculture, and more individualism.

Demographic and economic growth coincided with a managerial revolution in both the state and the church. Both needed skilled lawyers and literate clerks. As cathedral schools and universities emerged to meet these needs, the middle classes had a wider range of choices of vocations—teacher, monk, administrator, scholar-lawyer. The new choices both promoted individualism and raised anxiety. This situation made people uncertain about the roles and rules of their new professions. Consensus about morality and ethics decreased. The resulting anxiety often stimulated either otherworldly renunciation (monasticism) or a newfound optimism about the future (Morris 2000).

Between 1050 CE and 1200 CE, the church underwent a number of reforms that Europeans could not help but find unsettling. The organization and texts of the church became increasingly anachronistic. Morris (2000, 24) argues:

> For the early Church to become a Christian was a deliberate personal choice, involving both an interior change (repentance) and an exterior one (baptism). . . . Service of Christ thus consisted of both an individual decision and membership in a close community. . . . Neither of these experiences could be meaningful to the men of the tenth century. It required no personal choice to become a Christian nor did the believer find himself to be part of a community distinct from society as a whole.

This resulted in a shift from the New Testament teachings of St. Paul to the Old Testament doctrines of King David. More disturbing for the individual was the fact that authorities did not always agree on the interpretations of biblical texts. The veracity and reliability of the scriptures were called into question with the rise of a new class of educated church bureaucrats.

Another development was an interesting shift in the church's attitude toward salvation. According to Morris, until the eleventh and twelfth centuries, salvation had been understood as the salvation of *mankind*. After this time there was more concern with the salvation of the individual through acts of personal piety:

> Earlier eschatology had kept a balance . . . between an individual and a corporate ex-

> pectation. The particular person might look forward to his own release, but he did not normally count upon the perfection of his happiness until the renewal of the creation at its final perfection in the general resurrection. . . . [But later] the whole strength of eschatology now became attached to the individual. . . . Attention was concentrated upon one's personal answer and personal hope of heaven, if necessary, after a stay in purgatory. . . . The destiny of the individual was becoming the center of attention, and the theme of the renewal of all things was slipping into a secondary place. (Morris 2000, 147–148)

Because the psychology of people who lived hundreds of years ago is difficult to study empirically, we must rely on documentary evidence for clues as to changes in the social self. Most of us find it hard to believe that uniqueness, that is, what makes one individual different from another, was not a preoccupation. But according to Morris (2000), the notion of individual uniqueness was quite rare in the ancient world, and it only became more frequent in Europe in the late eleventh century. According to Aaron Gurevich (1995), words with the prefix "self" (e.g., self-aware, self-support) that indicate an awareness of self have expanded widely only since the Protestant Reformation. Early instances of individualism were not usually associated with the notion of uniqueness. For example, though some of the people in classical Greece were certainly individualists (e.g., the nature philosophers Plato, Socrates, and Aristotle), individuality was not usually conceived of as uniqueness.

Gurevich (1995, 91) says that self-reflection and individual uniqueness were rarely found in premodern societies:

> The inner psychological essence of the human being in the Greek World was not the object of tenacious quests and investigations. In Ancient Rome the position was slightly different. Certain writers manifested a tendency to engage in self-examination (Seneca, Marcus Aurelius), but the genuine breakthrough to psychological introspection . . . was that undertaken by St. Augustine.

Most of these early thinkers were not interested in the qualities that made individuals different from one another. Even in Medieval Europe originality or idiosyncrasy were often interpreted as grounds for charges of religious heresy.

Art is another arena in which individuality was not understood as uniqueness. The overwhelming majority of Greek sculptures, like those of other ancient civilizations, were not portraits of particular individuals but were embodiments of universal principles and expressions of the social status of individuals.

Throughout the ancient world, even those we would consider individualists still appeared to feel that ultimately it was Fate or the gods that determined what became of them. When Augustine declared that it was the individual, not Fate, Destiny, or the devil, that determined what became of them, he said something very unusual for those times.

In the Middle Ages we can see a number of individualistic tendencies that are nested in the bosom of the Catholic Church. These include personal confessions, mystical visions, autobiography, individual meditation, personal atonement, and the importance of intention. All these had proto-individualistic elements, but those tendencies were countered by subordination to God, to one's extended family or clan, or to one's vocation. People were also supposed to emulate archetypes such as heroes of the pagan past or figures from the Gospels.

Though biography is known in the classical world (e.g., Plutarch's *Lives*), the first experiments in *auto*biography (after St. Augustine) appeared in the tenth and eleventh centuries, and these occurred more frequently in the literature of the twelfth and thirteenth centuries. Yet these autobiographies do not go into old age, but only up to the point where they reach their spiritual goal. Medieval autobiography was not a self-generating activity for its own sake, but a means for attaining spiritual enlightenment.

While few people wrote their autobiographies, it was a practical requirement of every Christian to make a confession to a priest once a year. Confession required self-analysis over a relatively long stretch of time. Visions were another vehicle through which individuals were allowed to tell their story, not for its own sake but for depicting the visions as stages of conversion.

Through these forms of expression, feelings of fear, depression, suppressed desires, and so forth, could be expressed, but in the service of some "higher purpose."

Another sign of individualism was the growth of the spiritual practice of meditation and the ritual receiving of sacraments by individuals. Colin Morris (2000) notes that interest in atonement and repentance (involving introspection) challenged the need for external punishment such as public penance. In monasteries monks strove to see others objectively, independent of their needs, and they understood being open to the feelings and views of others as a virtue.

In marriages, as individuals began to free themselves from loyalties to institutions, they formed relations with others based on personal choice rather than just on economic considerations. The troubadours introduced romantic love outside of marriage, but this was limited to the aristocracy.

Landed aristocrats, knights, merchants, and artisans were most likely to express individualistic tendencies. The life of a knight sometimes took him far from home and weakened his loyalty to clan and family.

> In battle a knight had to rely primarily on his own strength and valor, for he was usually fighting on his own rather than among other fighting men. He was protected not by a compact battle formation, but by chain mail or armor, the speed of his own reactions and his mount's training. On horseback, a knight resembled a self-contained mobile fortress. (Gurevich 1995, 178–179)

The troubadours were champions of romantic love who wrote lyric poetry (based on revelations of personal experiences) as opposed to epic poetry (which is about the trials, tribulations, and victories of charismatic heroes). The medieval troubadours advocated the virtues of fidelity, prowess, joy, and courtesy. They developed an ideology of romantic love that challenged the institution of religiously sanctified marriage based on considerations of politics and property. But while the monks tried to develop an appreciation of the unique qualities of others, the troubadours paid little attention to the personally unique qualities of their mistresses. According to Morris, the point of courtly love and romance was to develop an understanding of one's own emotional life:

> The poets showed little interest in their ladies' character. The twelfth century felt a persistent attraction for the legend of Narcissus and the symbol of the mirror, which were used to describe "the birth of self-consciousness through love." . . . The center of interest was not the friend or the mistress, but one's own self, the thoughts inspired, the passions aroused, by the distant beloved. (Morris 2000, 118–119)

If the tools of knightly individualism were military, the tools of the merchant were commercial—the abacus and the ledger for accounting. Engaging in commercial operations demanded not only attention to detail but an ability to take entrepreneurial risks, an ability to anticipate future needs, and a capacity for reasoned calculation of costs and benefits that were somewhat independent of loyalty to specific groups. The merchant had to master calculation, and the easiest calculable rationality is individualistic. The nature of risk taking created in the merchant a unique combination of rationality regarding the processes he could control and an acceptance of the power of chance.

> Confidence in themselves and in their abilities was to be found side by side with "melancholy" in the minds of merchants and financiers, side by side with visions of destiny as an all-powerful and capricious force that would bring either sudden success or just as easily, unexpected disaster. . . . The image of Fortuna, tirelessly turning her wheel, on which people of various social estates first climb aloft and then inevitably fall, became very popular in the twelfth and thirteenth centuries. (Gurevich 1995, 94)

According to Richard Sennett (1990), in the ancient world, Fortune was impartial and made by the gods. But in the Renaissance, Fortune was wedded to chance that was made by humanity. This is one of the first signs that while individual lives may remain uncontrollable, the external forces responsible were no longer understood as cosmic or natural but rather as social and historical.

The emergence of humanism in the European Renaissance and later in the Enlightenment was linked to the development of individualism. Humanism put the human species at the center of morality and ethics. Some medieval humanists dealt with the anxiety of living in a rapidly changing society optimistically, and others pessimistically. Some humanists became satirists, attacking the church for its corruption or for the exclusion of critics. Others such as Petrarch saw in humanism the birth of a new world.

Petrarch was an early proponent of a humanist tradition that did not unhinge individual consciousness from its immediate social connections but expanded intersubjectivity beyond everyday life, the recent past, and the immediate future into the deep past and the distant future. For example, Petrarch did not rely on a mentor from his own time. He chose St. Augustine, who lived a thousand years earlier, to be his intimate teacher. Gurevich says of Petrarch:

> He used to rise while it was still dark and leave the house as the first rays of sunlight appeared: he would contemplate, read, write and consort with his friends. Yet, who were his friends? They were not only the individuals with whom he came into contact in his day-to-day life but also those who had died centuries before and who were known to him only through their works. "I assemble them from any place and any age. . . . I am happier to converse with them than with those who imagine themselves to be alive, . . . Petrarch sees himself as belonging to 'extended time': he is able with infinite ease to move from era to era feeling at home wherever he goes." (Gurevich 1995, 233)
>
> Petrarch is clearly anxious not just to be a man of his times but . . . to be a man of the classical past, which he is bringing back to life . . . and at the same time to be able to link himself with the future. (Gurevich 1995, 236)

According to Gurevich, Scandinavians had a more advanced form of individualism than did Western Europe because the Catholic Church had not affected them with accusations of sin or pride or the need for humility. For example, the hero in Scandinavian mythology identified more with great deeds than blind loyalty to family. His extraordinary feats lived on in the minds of individuals through his reputation.

But here also there were limits to individualism. For example, the hero's source of identity was not a mental attunement with a spiritual world the way it would have been for St. Augustine or Plato, but rather physical deeds. Intentions and moods were not introspected but were revealed through actions. The conflicts that might have existed within the personalities of the epic heroes were projected as being between individuals. This does not mean that the hero had no loyalty to his clan. It just means that, since his actions were determined by Fate, his clan would forgive him no matter what he did. And because the hero's actions were determined by Fate, there was no conscience. There was no weighing the pros and cons or consideration of different viewpoints before deciding:

> The concept of conscience is hardly appropriate here, demanding as it does moral self-control on the part of the individual who independently formulates moral precepts and evaluates these. In a society where clan traditions hold sway and where personality emerges as clan personality, moral issues regarding the individual could not yet have acquired any substantial importance. (Gurevich 1995, 38)

It is important to realize that just as human societies do not evolve in a unilinear way, neither does the self. By most standards, the Greek philosophers and St. Augustine are much closer to modern individualism than any individual in the Middle Ages. Yet within the Middle Ages it was becoming easier for more than exceptional persons to develop an individual identity.

Below is a summary list of the influences on medieval individualism:

- Writing autobiographies
  - Confession
  - New occupations
  - Mystical visions

Meditation/introspection (vs. public penance)
Importance of intentions (vs. actions)
Humanism
Troubadours and romantic love
Lyric poetry (as opposed to epic poetry)

Justice from Drama to Documentation

M. T. Clanchy (1979) described in wonderful detail how the increasing use of documentation changed the justice system in England from the Norman Conquest to the death of Edward the First in 1307 CE (see Table 12.1).

In an oral society, a man has to stand by his word by taking an oath. An oath is a conditional curse called upon oneself in the event he should become unfaithful while swearing. Prior to the reliance on documents, ownership of a piece of property would be transferred by a witnessed ceremony, and then the transfer of a symbolic object would follow. Even when written deeds came to be used, they were accompanied by something physical, like a clod of earth.

Beginning in the thirteenth century, texts began their transformation from these dramas into documents. Under the literate regime, the oath must compete with the manuscript. By the end of the thirteenth century, a legal charter or deed was no longer an oral ceremony. The notion of a jury also changed from sworn testimony, when jurors were witnesses, to the jury becoming an unbiased body who no longer witnessed what happened but were capable of a *critical assessment* of testimony. Proof also changed from being an act carried out by the accused, whether by battle, ordeal, or oath, to a way of proof by trial by jury. What is the pattern here? Written records create distance, distance from face-to-face engagements to a cooler, more objective distance.

The Reign of Quantity and Measurement and the Rise of Sight

In his book *The Measure of Reality*, Alfred Crosby (1997) compares the worldview of the early Middle Ages with that of the High Middle Ages, the Renaissance, and the Reformation prior to the scientific revolution. Since the changes in historical institutions have been told many times, we will not go into detail. However, there are at least two points we wish to make.

Crosby argues that between 1250 and 1600 there was a growing desire for measurement. Spatially, things are broken into leagues, miles, and degrees of angles. Astronomically, planets are broken down into orbits; paintings into geometrical lines, squares, and circles; music is quantified by staff notations; commercial transactions are organized into ledgers and columns with accounts received and payable. Clocks break time into hours and minutes.

Crosby identifies four steps necessary in order to quantify:

1. Reduce what we are studying into a minimum amount required by its definition
2. Visualize it on paper
3. Divide the amount into equal quanta
4. Measure it by counting the quanta

Crosby says that by the fifteenth century, modern Europeans knew more about wheels, levers, and gears than anyone in the Middle Ages, and more than any other culture as well. See Table 12.2 for a summary of the changes in mathematics, painting, and music.

Table 12.1 Impact of documentation on medieval legal standards

Category of comparison	Norman Conquest (1066)	Death of King Edward (1307)
Transfer of property	Legal charter an oral ceremony	Legal charter is a sealed document
Kind of jury	Juries were witnesses who could swear the truth of a claim	Unbiased persons who could carry out a critical assessment of testimony of others
Proof	Carried by accused by battle, ordeal, or oath	Trial by jury
How can legality be characterized?	Drama	Documentation

Table 12.2 The power of measurement

Category of comparison	Middle Ages	Early modern period
Space	Relative—finite, spherical, and qualitative Cardinal directions had qualities Plenum with no void	Absolute, infinite, quantitative Cardinal directions are neutral Void
Astronomy	Earth-centered cosmos Fixed stars, planets in circular rotations	Copernicus: Earth revolves around the sun Stars have a birth and death Kepler: planets rotate elliptically
Cartography	Maps inseparable from deities and sacred places	Maritime chart "Portolano"—utilitarian drawing for enclosed waters like the Mediterranean and the North and Baltic Seas
Time and timing	Contextual time—inseparable from the seasons, human events (church bells)	Absolute time—independent of seasons, human events (clocks)
Commerce	Little loaning of currency Little debts or loans Peddlers	More loaning of currency Calculation of interest Merchants
Accounting	No accounts receivable or payable (difficulty tracking bills of exchange, promissory notes, inventory, loans, debts or economic trends; no annuities)	Double-entry bookkeeping allowed for tracking bills of exchange, promissory notes, inventory, loans, and debts; balancing accounts; projecting trends; and taking out annuities
Mathematics	Lack of precision—general and impressionistic or exaggeration	Precise, specific, and concrete (balance scale, yardstick)
Number systems	Roman numerals	Use of Hindu-Arabic numbers
Operations	Counting and simple arithmetic, with the rest expressed verbally No operations of addition, subtraction	Algebra Operations signs of addition, subtraction, and equals
Devices	Use of abacus—could not handle very large or very small numbers Computing, not recording	Computing and recording
Secularization or spiritualization of numbers	Numbers mixed with spiritual meaning	Numbers separated from spiritual meaning Specific quantities Specific qualities: Fibonacci
Painting	Flat picture plane No use of Euclidean geometry	Three-dimensional picture plane Creating illusion of third dimension by use of Euclidean geometry to show parallel lines receding
Music	No written musical texts Gregorian chants	Written musical scores Polyphonic singing
Military operations	"Close-in" fighting	Distant weaponry (pikes, crossbows, muskets)
Sense ratios	Proximate senses—touch, smell, taste	Predominance of sight
Forms of abstraction	First or second order	Beginnings of third order

To detail just one of the comparisons in Crosby's work, the invention of double-entry bookkeeping allowed merchants to sort out and track bills of exchange and promissory notes from barge ships and mule trains, balance their accounts, take an inventory of their stock, track the currency used to make each transaction, make loans with payable time schedules, and have some measure of prediction of short- and long-term trends. Double-entry bookkeeping made it possible to freeze, hold in suspension, and then arrange and make sense of the masses of data that previously had been overflowing and lost. It allowed merchants to go into debt consciously understanding what they were getting into. Double-entry bookkeeping made it easier to calculate interest, expand the quantity and variety of products, form partnerships, pool their money, and take out insurance policies to hedge against failure.

But what is the relationship between measuring the world and the five senses? Are touch, taste, sight, smell, and hearing all equal candidates for measuring the world? If measurement is quantification, and if quantification involves breaking things down into parts that are uniform and then counting them, can this process be done with all five senses, or are some senses better at this than others?

Crosby argues that there is a direct line between *sight*, measurement, mathematical symbols, logical symbols, rational analysis, and universal scientific judgments. Therefore, a revolution in the organization of sense ratios must accompany the revolution in painting, music, commerce, and mathematics.

According to geographer Yi-Fu Tuan (1982), what is common to the proximate senses of smell, touch, taste, and hearing is that they are wrap-around, pervasive senses that are hard to measure because the boundaries between these senses and the world are permeable. Unlike the ear and the nose, which are open to the world without humans deciding to open or close them, *the eyes can be closed* to the world or focused in a particular direction. Of the five senses, sight is the most distancing and has the most potential for objectivity. However, as long as sight was just one sense among the others, the precision required of measurement would not be able to develop. There was a revolution in human perception in which sight took over and subordinated the proximate senses.

If we examine all the activities in Table 12.2, most, if not all, are dominated by visualization. Visualization underlines reading, commercial calculation, painting, and singing to musical scores. The activities in our table are about a certain kind of measurement, *visual* measurement. Composers, painters, and bookkeepers were committed to quantitative visual perception in the material of their craft. Counting was involved in singing, making pictures, and balancing their accounts. And the foundation of counting is predominantly seeing.

To give but two examples of how this reorganization of sense ratios evolved, Crosby tells us that the word "audit" came from the same root as "audible," which has to do with *hearing*. In law it meant deciding about the quality of evidence by *listening* to testimony. After the visualization revolution, auditing became unhinged from its hearing roots and became a word used in law courts to *visually* examine archival documents in silence. In accounting, auditing came to mean examining one's commercial books by the same visual process, by auditing them. Before the thirteenth century, sacred pictures showed God and his angels and saints always communicating with humans *by speech*. Shortly after 1300 an Anglo-French prayer book showed the Virgin Mary pointing to *words in a book* in order to communicate.

Consider the changes in cartography, mathematics, painting, music, accounting, and time and space categorizing that occurred in early modern Europe. The use of Hindu-Arabic mathematics, musical notions, linear perspective, and double-entry bookkeeping might have required a new order of abstraction. All of them seem to require that the world of reality and the world of the mind need to become separated before each can be reflected upon.

Cognitive Revolution in Theater and Literature

In his book *The Cognitive Revolution in Western Culture*, Don LePan (1989) argues that between the twelfth century and the middle of the sixteenth century in England, there were major historical changes in theater, including plot construction, character development, audience expectations, the relationship between the stage and audience, the necessity of creating illusions, and techniques for creating altered states of consciousness in the audience. LePan's point is that playwrights and audiences had to begin to use newer forms of abstraction to engage these forms of entertainment. A summary of LePan's understanding of the changes in theater and literature from the Middle Ages to the sixteenth century is in Table 12.3.

Table 12.3 Theatrical differences as a function of cognitive evolution

Category of comparison	Medieval literature	Modern literature
Examples	Beowulf, Noah's Flood, King Herod	Shakespeare, Gawain, and Chaucer
Relationship between actions and intentions of characters	Actions only; intentions unknown or unimportant	Intentions, human actions, and external events are distinguished and used to build suspense
What is the relationship among expectations, hopes, wishes?	Expectations are mixed up with hopes and wishes	Expectations are distinguished from the objective odds in the real world
Where is meaning?	Meaning lies within each event taken separately (hypostatization)	Meaning lies within the relationship between events
Type of plot (time/space parameters)	Simple plot—set in a temporal and spatial vacuum Infinite number of characters; introduction of new characters in the middle or end of the play	Complex plot—temporal time and place established (often one day, specific place) Finite number of characters; no new characters once play is under way
How are the parts of a play put together?	Episodes—parts of play are juxtaposed to each other without an explicit relationship ("and then," "meanwhile")	Organic interdependent parts—parts of play are integrated into a specific relationship, linear and progressive ("because")
Relationship between direct presentation and exposition by characters	The story remains virtually inseparable from the direct presentation of the action throughout	More blending of direct presentation and exposition
Relationship between offstage and onstage	Nothing is done offstage and reported	Things happen offstage that characters report
Perspective and foreshortening	Field of vision provides little perspective or foreshortening	Provides perspective and foreshortening
Anticipated audience reaction	Shell-shocked, incredulous; anything is possible	Suspense; degree of likelihood, but anything is not possible; tragic expectation
Interpretational style	Literal	Metaphorical
Is the ending foretold?	Foretold but does not allow continual formation of expectations	Not foretold, audience asks
Does drama have illusion?	"What are the odds?"	Drama with illusion—creation of an imaginary world audience can believe in, suspend real life, and make believe that the stage, actors/actresses, and objects are real life
How to create altered state in the audience	Magical appearances and disappearances Changes of perception in space	Use of imagination in the mind's eye Changes in anticipated future through expectation
Relationship between stage and auditorium	Porous boundaries	Hard boundaries
Characters' relationship with audience	Characters mix with audience; with comic appeal or allegories	Audience separated from characters; the play may be preceded and followed by introductions and epilogues in which the actors appear as actors, but during the play characters do not talk to audience
Audience relationship with characters	Audience sometimes enters the stage and acts themselves	Audience remains passive and watches the play
Intensity of interaction between characters	Weak—characters isolated from each other	Strong—characters mix more
Relationship between characters mixing and scenic breaks	Scenes involving the same characters entering again directly after they have made their exits	Introduction of new characters at scenic breaks to give a feeling that things are going on at the same time in other places
Form of cognition	First or second order abstraction	Beginning of third order abstraction

Source: LePan 1989.

The Central System and East Asia in the Twelfth to the Sixteenth Centuries

The most famous of the Central Asian steppe nomad conquests is the Mongol Empire. The steppe confederacy of tribes organized and led by Chinggis Khan got its act together at a somewhat unfortunate time, at least for the successful pursuit of the outer-frontier strategy of extracting tribute from the East Asian agrarian states. China had fallen under the power of a different semiperipheral marcher, the Jurchen of the Manchurian forests, and the Jurchen refused to meet the Mongol demands for tribute despite increasingly destructive marauding. In a fit of frustration, Chinggis Khan conquered the Chinese cities and continued expanding the Mongol state toward the West. Chinggis's grandson Hülegü Khan conquered Baghdad on the Tigris in 1248. This unification of West and East Asia under a single polity was the first time that the two distant PMNs had been directly linked together, but it was not to last. The Mongol Empire quickly broke up into smaller dynasties, and the Central PMN did not directly incorporate East Asia again until the European powers penetrated nineteenth-century Qing China with "treaty ports." The Mongol Empire was the largest single polity on Earth in terms of territorial size, until the British Empire reached its zenith in the nineteenth century (see Figure 10.1 in Chapter 10).

The Mongols were horse pastoralists who disdained sedentism and agriculture. Their military superiority was based on huge groups of skilled horsemen who could accurately shoot arrows from extremely powerful bows while riding very fast. Korakoram, a large encampment on the Central Asian steppe, was their capital. The conquest of China was not what the Mongols intended, because they did not want to administer an agrarian empire. Nevertheless, their conquest left no Chinese state capable of extracting food and taxes from the Chinese peasants, and so the Mongols reluctantly inserted themselves into the vacuum to create the Yuan dynasty in China.

Mongol unity lasted little more than a century, but it brought major changes to Eurasia. It opened a third, northern trade route between China and Europe, directly over the steppes, bypassing the routes through southern Iran and Iraq or the maritime Indian Ocean route. The increased traffic across the steppes opened other circuits of trade: "Gradually a north–south exchange of slaves and furs for the goods of civilization supplemented the east–west flow of goods that initially sustained the caravans" (Bentley 1993, 56).

The existence of a new, third route between East and West was very important. It meant that trade could not be monopolized entirely at any one choke point. This, and the Mongols' pragmatic attitudes toward religion, cuisine, and culture, radically increased the rate of diffusion of cultural artifacts across the Eurasian **ecumene** (E. Anderson 2004).

One of the most important consequences of Mongol unification of Eurasia was the transmission of a hitherto isolated strain of the rat-and-flea-borne Black Death (bubonic plague) to Europe and China (McNeill 1976; Abu-Lughod 1989). The Black Death first swept through China in 1331 and through Europe in 1348, ultimately killing one-third to one-half of the population, which fundamentally altered the relations between lord and peasant. It took Europe over a century to recover.

The bubonic plague was not new to Europe. An earlier strain had ravaged the Byzantine Empire in the 500s. China had an endemic version of the plague in the countryside, so there was not much transmission to the city and there was some immunity, which is why the death rate was lower in China than in Europe.

In addition to being an exception to the steppe nomad pattern, the Mongol Empire was an anomaly in world-system terms: It was a peripheral marcher state that became a core power by virtue of its middleman and military roles. It was not a typical semiperipheral state (in which nomads had recently become sedentary and undergone class and state formation). Rather, the Mongols were a peripheral power that overplayed the outer-frontier strategy. Instead of using violence to extort resources from surrounding states or to exact better terms of trade, the Mongols attacked too vigorously and actually conquered the agrarian states, including China.

It has long been observed that an empire can be conquered from horseback, but it cannot be ruled from the back of a horse.[6] The power of the Mongols derived from a novel use of a nomadic **segmentary lineage** kinship system that allowed convenient inclusion of new members based on political trust. But this same system generated disputes over leadership upon the death of a reigning khan. To institutionalize a rule of succession would have undermined the very social features that allowed the amassing of large conquest armies. In short, Mongols could not institutionalize kingship and remain Mongols (Barfield 1989; Hall 1991). This is why Mongols, and steppe nomads in general, so often melded into the societies they conquered: They had to adopt the culture of the sedentary societies they conquered in order to rule.

The Mongol conquest, in world-system terms, transformed Afroeurasia into a single PMN. However, this new, vast PMN was unstable. The empire was simply too large to be maintained logistically. None of the potential hegemonic core powers—the Yuan or Ming China, the Ottoman Empire, or any of the states of South Asia—could mount an expedition to conquer any of the others. Tamerlane's effort to rebuild the Pan-Asian Empire (1360–1405) disintegrated upon his death. Furthermore, the Mongols did not produce anything of great economic value to the world market (except sheep and horses). They were an interesting variant of what William McNeill (1982) has called "macroparasites." Their wealth came from extorting tribute from adjacent agrarian states and taxing the trade that traversed their territory.

The Mongol conquest did, however, bring massive changes in the relative balances among the three old core regions of Afroeurasia. In the early Ming dynasty, an expansionist foreign policy financed voyages of discovery. As mentioned in Chapter 11, the famous eunuch Admiral Zheng He sailed a fleet of huge Chinese junks to Africa and back. But China's growing lead in technology and productivity was set back to some extent when the Ming dynasty turned its main efforts toward protecting the northern border from further nomadic incursions by extending and strengthening the Great Wall. The new overland trade across the steppes largely bypassed India. West Asia was shattered by a series of nomad incursions that reshaped the states and undermined any semblance of Islamic unity.

Meanwhile in Europe, growing trade began the long process of increasing the strength of merchants compared to the kings, the nobility, and the church. The opening of new trade routes and increased favor toward merchants had opened China, and East Asia generally, to European explorers. These actions whetted European appetites for further trade, and ultimately for more direct routes to the East. This was the major spur to European exploration of the globe in the following centuries.

West Asia

Around 1000 CE, Turkish tribes began moving from Central Asia into Western Asia. The movement seems to have been motivated by the usual Central Asian factors: fierce competition from other Central Asian peoples and more attractive lands in the West. Most of the Turks accepted Islam, albeit lightly. Many Turks became effective, if troublesome, troops for the Abbasid rulers in Baghdad. Their acceptance into the Islamic world generated a great deal of political unrest and disorganization. Still, they were a major asset in subsequent Moslem expansion.

In 1071 the Seljuk Turks conquered Byzantium and invaded most of Asia Minor. This provided an important justification for the first European Crusade of 1096. By 1099 the crusaders had captured Jerusalem and created a series of small Christian states along the eastern shore of the Mediterranean. Their success was as much due to political disarray in the Islamic states as it was to their own efforts. This was the only crusade to actually reach Jerusalem. Jerusalem was recaptured by Saladin in 1187 and nearly all of the Christian Frankish states were destroyed.

Moslem traders spread down the coast of East Africa, and caravan traders crossed the Sahara connecting West Africa with Northern Africa. These connections and the conversions of

[6] This was originally observed by the top aide to Liu Bang when Liu (one of the two commoners to found a dynasty in China) overthrew Qin and founded the Han dynasty.

some African ruling dynasties to Islam are often portrayed as having been the major factors causing the emergence of states in West Africa. But recently published archaeological studies indicate that there had long been complex polities on the great bend of the Niger River in West Africa. Ray Kea (2004) convincingly argues that these polities contributed major logistical support to the Mauritanian Almoravid dynasties' conquest of Morocco and a large part of the Iberian Peninsula in the early twelfth century.

Many Central Asian groups were converted to Islam, and a few Moslem communities developed in Western China. Between 1000 and 1200, Moslems nearly doubled the territory they held. In the thirteenth century, the Mongols overran much of Moslem territory, sacking Baghdad in 1258. Turkish warriors built the Ottoman Empire, and in 1389 they crossed into Europe and defeated the Serbs at Kosovo. While the territory influenced by the Islamic religion continued to expand, the Mongol conquests shattered Islamic unity and the West Asian region never regained its world-historical prominence.

South Asia

Shortly after 1000, certain Turkish groups that had been resident in West Asia invaded northern India. The final linking of the South Asian PMN with the Central PMN was begun by the incursion of Mahmud of Ghazni in 1008 CE. Alexander of Macedon's earlier incursion in the fourth century BCE had been a temporary connection between the Central and the South Asian PMNs that ceased after the Greek conquest states in South Asia had been expelled. The connection was made permanent by Mahmud of Ghazni. Because these Turks wore their Islam lightly, they were able to compromise with their Hindu subjects, though Hindu dynasties in the valley of the Ganges continued to strongly contest the rule of Moslems until the rise of the Mughal dynasty in the sixteenth century. This accommodation, and the absence of any Mongol invasions, contributed to the stability of the Mughal Empire in India. But the Mughals' main focus was on internal extraction of wealth from the peasants of India. They largely ignored the larger world market, leaving the way open for the Portuguese.

Suggested Readings

Abu-Lughod, Janet L. 1989. *Before European Hegemony: The World System A.D. 1250–1350*. Oxford: Oxford University Press.

Braudel, Fernand. 1972. *The Mediterranean and the Mediterranean World in the Age of Philip II*. 2 vols. New York: Harper and Row.

Hodgson, Marshall G. S. 1974. *The Classical Age of Islam*. Vol. 1 of *The Venture of Islam: Conscience and History in a World Civilization*. Chicago: University of Chicago Press.

Mann, Charles C. 2011. *1493: Discovering the New World Columbus Created*. New York: Alfred A. Knopf.

Morris, Ian. 2010. *Why the West Rules—For Now*. New York: Farrar, Straus and Giroux.

Spufford, Peter. 2003. *Power and Profit: The Merchant in Medieval Europe*. London: Thames and Hudson.

13

The Modern World-System

Five chapters that tell the story of the modern system chronologically since the fifteenth century follow. But the unfolding story obscures certain general patterns that can only be seen by looking at the whole system over the entire period of time since the fifteenth century. These patterns are the subject of this chapter. The modern system shares many similarities with earlier regional world-systems, but it is also qualitatively different from them in some important ways. Obviously it is larger, becoming global (earth-wide) with the incorporation of all the remaining separate regions during the nineteenth century. The key defining feature of the modern world-system is capitalism. We have already seen the long emergence of those institutions that are crucial for

Mill at Bruges by W. O. J. Nieuwenkamp

capitalism (private property, commodity production, money, contract law, price-setting markets, commodified labor) over the previous millennia in Afroeurasia. But it was in Europe and its colonial empires that these institutions were able to take most strongly and to direct the fundamental dynamics of social change to so great an extent that we can speak of the first world-system in which capitalism became the predominant logic of development.

Capitalism has many definitions, and its fundamental nature is still a matter of lively debate.[1] We agree with those who define capitalism as a set of economic and political processes that are based on the accumulation of profits. This involves the production of commodities by large private owners of the means of production and also a geopolitical process of state building, competition among states, and increasingly large-scale political regulation involving institutions of coercion and governance. Capitalism is not solely an economic logic. It is also a type of political logic.

Some theorists have contended that state power and "violence-producing enterprises" were only involved in setting up the basic underlying institutional conditions for capitalism during an early age of "primitive accumulation" and that once these institutions were in place, capitalism began to operate as a purely economic logic of production, distribution, and profit making—so-called expanded reproduction.[2] The comparative world-systems perspective allows us to see that both economic and political institutions have continued to evolve, and the central logic of capitalism is embedded in the dialectical dance of their coevolution and expansion.

From a world-systems perspective, the political body of capitalism is the interstate system rather than the single state. Single states and national societies exist within a larger structure and set of processes that heavily influence the possibilities for social change. And the interstate system interacts with a core/periphery hierarchy in which wealthy and powerful national states in the core exploit and dominate less powerful and poorer regions in the noncore.

States are organizations that claim to exercise a monopoly of legitimate violence within a particular territory. They are not whole autonomous systems, and they never have been. Much of contemporary social science continues to treat national societies as if they were on the moon, with completely self-contained (endogenous) patterns of social change. The growing awareness of globalization has challenged the notion that national societies are separate and unconnected entities. The world-systems perspective extends this notion of interconnectedness of national societies back to the fifteenth century, and the comparative world-systems perspective that we have employed in this book notes that human societies have importantly and systemically interacted with neighboring societies throughout the period of sociocultural evolution.

---

[1] The definition we employ is explained and discussed in Chapter 2: "Capitalism is based on the accumulation of profits by the owners of major means of the production of commodities in a context in which labor and the other main elements of production are commodified."

[2] Karl Marx's theory of expanded reproduction presented in Volume 1 of *Capital* proposes such an understanding. Marx defined capitalism as commodity production using wage labor, and so fully developed capitalism only emerged with the English Industrial Revolution. He saw modern colonialism as precapitalist because coercion was often directly used in the mobilization of labor power (e.g., slavery). World-systems theorists contend that what happens in the periphery and the semiperiphery was, and continues to be, essential for what occurs in the core, and peripheral capitalism must be understood as a constitutive and necessary element that is part and parcel of the structural logic of capitalism. This said, Marx's pithy portrayal (as translated from German by Moore and Aveling) of the run-up to industrial capitalism remains one of the most powerful brief renditions of the roots of modernity:

> The discovery of gold and silver in America, the extirpation, enslavement and entombment in mines of the aboriginal population, the beginning of the conquest and looting of the East Indies, the turning of Africa into a warren for the commercial hunting of black skins, signalized the rosy dawn of the era of capitalist production. These idyllic proceedings are the chief momenta of primitive accumulation. On their heels treads the commercial war of the European nations, with the globe for a theatre. It begins with the revolt of the Netherlands from Spain, assumes giant dimensions in England's Anti-Jacobin War, and is still going on in the opium wars against China, &c. (Marx 1967, 751)

Capitalism and capitalist states existed in earlier regional world-systems, but capitalism was only a sideshow within the commercializing tributary empires, while real capitalist states were confined to the semiperiphery. Capitalism became predominant in the modern system by becoming potent in the core. This happened for the first time in world history with the emergence of the Dutch hegemony in the seventeenth century. In the modern system the most successful states became those in which state power was used at the behest of groups that were engaged in commodity production, trade, and financial services. State powers to tax and collect tributes did not disappear, but these sources of accumulation became less important than, and largely subordinate to, the logic of profit making.

The very logic of capitalism produces economic, social, and political crises in which elites jockey for position and less favored groups try to protect themselves and/or fundamentally change the system. Capitalism does not abolish imperialism; rather, it produces new kinds of imperialism. Neither does it abolish warfare. It is not a pacific (warless) mode of accumulation as some have claimed (e.g., Schumpeter 1951). Rather, the instruments of violence and the dynamics of interstate competition by means of warfare have been increasingly turned to serve the purposes of profitable commodity production and financial manipulations rather than the extraction of tribute. And the increasing "efficiency" of military technology in the capitalist world-system has made warfare much more destructive.

Core/periphery hierarchy is not abolished by the development of capitalism. On the contrary, the institutional mechanisms by which some societies can exploit and dominate others have become more powerful and efficient and are increasingly justified by ideologies of civilization, development, and foreign investment. "Backwardness" is reproduced and the world-system becomes ever more polarized between the core and the noncore than were earlier systems. The growing inequalities within and between national societies are justified by ideologies of productivity and efficiency, with underlying implications that some people are simply more fit for modernity than others. Nationalism, racism, and gender hierarchies are both challenged and reproduced in a context in which the real material inequalities among the peoples of the world are huge. This occurs within a context in which the values of human rights and equality have become more and more institutionalized, and so important movements of protest occur. All this is characteristic not only of the most recent period of globalization and globalization backlash, but of the whole history of the expansion of modern capitalism. The modern world-system experiences recurrent waves of **world revolution** in which local protests and rebellions cluster together in time and challenge the structures of domination and exploitation.

The similarities with earlier world-systems are important. There is a political-military system of allying and competing polities, now taking the form of the modern international system (studied mainly by political scientists who focus on international relations). There are still different kinds of interaction networks with different spatial scales, though in the modern system many of the formerly smaller networks have caught up with the spatial size of the largest networks. Much of the BGN is now global. One of the unusual features of the modern system in comparative perspective is that the differences in spatial scales among different kinds of networks have been greatly reduced, which makes it far easier for people to perceive the large-scale international and transnational interaction networks in which they are involved.

The phenomenon of rise and fall remains an important pattern, albeit with some significant differences. As with earlier state-based systems, there is a structurally important interaction between core regions and less powerful peripheral regions. There remains an important component of multiculturalism in the system as a whole, a feature that is typical of most world-systems. Semiperipheral development continues. As discussed in Chapter 12, the rise of Europe was itself an instance of the emergence to global power of a region that was previously semiperipheral. And semiperipheral societies within the modern system have been and continue to be upwardly mobile and to restructure the institutions of the system. In these respects the modern system is quite similar to most of the earlier regional world-systems that contained states and hierarchies.

But the nature of the mode of accumulation is quite different, and there are other related differences that are connected with the emergent predominance of capitalism. Both the pattern of rise and fall and the nature of core/periphery relations have changed. Since accumulation is predominantly capitalist and the most powerful core states are also the most important centers of capitalist accumulation, they do not use their military power to conquer other core states in order to extract revenues from them. In world-systems in which the tributary mode of accumulation is predominant, semiperipheral marcher states conquer adjacent core states in order to extract resources and erect "universal" empires. Similar versions of this strategy have been attempted in the modern system (e.g., the Hapsburgs in the sixteenth century, Napoleon at the end of the eighteenth century, and Germany in the twentieth century), but they have failed. The tributary mode of production is not gone, and indeed even modern capitalist hegemons employ "accumulation by dispossession" (Harvey 2003), especially when they are in decline. But a major difference between the modern capitalist world-system and earlier tributary systems is that the balance between coercion and consensus has shifted in favor of consensus. This is an important part of what Karl Marx meant when he claimed that capitalism, though not the best of all possible worlds, is indeed progressive relative to systems in which the tributary modes of accumulation were predominant.

Another sense in which capitalism may be thought of as progressive is its effects on technological change. Technological change has been a crucial aspect of human social evolution since the emergence of speech. The rate of innovation and implementation increased slowly as societies became more complex, but capitalism shoves the rate of technological change toward the sky. This is because economic rewards are more directly linked to technological innovation and improvements in production processes. There are, to be sure, countervailing forces within real capitalism, as when large companies sit on new technologies that would threaten their existing profitable operations. But because permanent worldwide monopolies do not exist (in the absence of a world state), the efforts of the powerful to protect their profits have repeatedly come under attack by a dynamic market system and competition among states. The institutionalization of scientific research and development has also boosted the development and implementation of new technologies; thus, in the most developed countries, rapid technological change and accompanying social changes have become acceptable to people despite their disruptive aspects. This is a major way in which the modern world-system differs from earlier systems. Social change of all kinds has speeded up.

Another major difference between the modern system and earlier state-based systems is the way in which the cycle of rise and fall occurs. The hegemonic sequence (the rise and fall of hegemonic core states) is the modern version of the ancient oscillation between more and less centralized interpolity systems. As we have seen, all hierarchical systems experience a cycle of rise and fall, from "cycling" in interchiefdom systems, to the rise and fall of empires, to the modern sequence of hegemonic rise and fall.[3] In tributary world-systems, this oscillation typically takes the form of semiperipheral marcher states conquering older core states to form core-wide empires.[4] (See Figure 10.2 in Chapter 10, which contrasts the structure of a core-wide empire with that of a more multicentric system in which one state is the hegemon.)

One important consequence of the coming to predominance of capitalist accumulation has been the conversion of the rise-and-fall process from semiperipheral marcher conquest to the rise and fall of capitalist hegemons that do not take over other core states. The hegemons rise to economic and political/military preeminence from the semiperiphery, but they do not construct a core-wide world state by means of conquest. Rather, the core of the modern system oscillates between a condition in which there is a powerful hegemon

[3] This is likely to be true of future world-systems as well, though the form taken by the power cycle may change yet again.

[4] A core-wide empire has sometimes been called a "universal empire" by world historians such as Arnold Toynbee (1947). Immanuel Wallerstein's (1974b) distinction between a world-empire and a world economy points to this same difference in the degree of centralization of a state system. The term "world-empire" has sometimes been used to refer to single tributary states such as Sassanid Iran (e.g., Foran 1993), but this is a mistaken usage because all tributary states are involved in trade of basic goods with other regions. Thus they are not whole world-systems but rather parts of systems.

interacting with other core states and a situation of hegemonic rivalry in which a number of core states and semiperipheral challengers contend for predominance.

Capitalist accumulation usually favors a multicentric interstate system because this provides greater opportunities for the maneuverability of capital than would exist in a world state. Big capitals can play states against one another and can escape movements that try to regulate investment or redistribute profits by abandoning the states in which such movements attain political power.

Another difference produced by the rise of capitalism is the way in which imperialism is organized. The predominant form of modern imperialism has been what are called **colonial empires**. Rather than conquering one's immediate neighbors to make a contiguous empire, the most successful form of core/periphery exploitation in the modern system has involved European core states establishing political and economic controls over distant colonies in the Americas, Asia, and Africa. To be sure, the old kind of imperialism continued to exist during recent centuries as the Ottoman and Russian empires expanded, and the Manchus from semiperipheral northern Asia managed to conquer China in a classic example of a semiperipheral marcher state. Even in Europe the old strategy did not disappear. We have already mentioned the Hapsburg attempt to convert the nascent capitalist world economy into a tributary empire, and the French and German efforts of much more recent centuries also bear some of the marks of the older form of empire. But the most successful form was the colonial empire, and it evolved from the early efforts by Portugal and Spain into the later Dutch, French, and British empires and then morphed into a less obvious kind of neocolonialism in the relationship between the United States and Latin America after the 1880s.[5]

There is another important difference between the modern Europe-centered core/periphery hierarchy and the earlier tributary world-systems in the nature of core/periphery relations. The ability to extract resources from peripheral areas has long been an important component of successful accumulation in state-based world-systems, and this is also true for the modern world-system. But there is an interesting and important difference—the reversal of the location of relative intrasocietal inequalities. In state-based world-systems, core societies had relatively greater internal inequalities than did peripheral societies. Typical core states were urbanized and class-stratified, while peripheral societies were nomadic pastoralists or horticulturalists or less densely concentrated peoples living in smaller towns or villages. These kinds of peripheral groups usually had less internal inequality than did the core states with which they were interacting.

In the modern world-system this situation has reversed. Core societies typically have less (relative) internal inequality than do peripheral societies. The kinds of jobs that are concentrated in the core, and the eventual development of welfare states in the core, have expanded the size of the middle classes within core societies to produce a more-or-less diamond-shaped distribution of income that bulges in the middle. Typical peripheral societies, on the other hand, have a more pyramid-shaped income distribution in which there is a small rich elite, a rather small middle class, and a very large mass of very poor people.[6]

This reversal in the location of relative internal inequality between cores and peripheries was mainly a consequence of the development and concentration of complex economies needing skilled labor in the core and the politics of democracy and the welfare state that have accompanied capitalist industrialization.

These processes have occurred in tandem with, and are dependent on, the development of peripheral capitalism, colonialism, and neocolonialism in the periphery, which have produced the greater relative inequalities within peripheral societies. Core capitalism is dependent on peripheral capitalism in part because exploitation of the periphery provides some of the resources that core

[5] Earlier examples of colonial empires were the seaborne imperial enterprises of those maritime semiperipheral capitalist city-states that captured distant political and economic vantage points in order to carry out long-distance trade.

[6] The increased inequality of wealth and income in the United States since the 1980s has been going in the direction of a Third World–like stratification system, but the remaining differences are still very large (see Chapter 18).

capital sometimes uses to pay higher incomes to core workers. Furthermore, the reproduction of an underdeveloped periphery legitimates the national capital/labor alliances that have provided a relative harmony of class relations in the core and undercut radical challenges to capitalist power (Chase-Dunn 1998, Chapter 11). It is not the case that all core workers compose a "labor aristocracy" in the modern world-system. Obviously groups within the core working class compete against one another, and some are downsized, streamlined, and so forth, in the competition of core capitalists with one another. But the overall effect of core/periphery relations has been to undercut challenges to capitalism within core states by paying off some core workers and groups and convincing others that they should support and identify with the "winners."

In premodern systems, core/periphery relations were also important for sustaining the social order of the core (e.g., the bread and circuses of Rome), but not to the same extent, because the system did not produce relatively more equal distributions of income and political power in the core than in the periphery. Thus the core/periphery hierarchy has become an even more important structural feature of the modern world-system than it was in earlier tributary systems. This change in structure corresponds to the relatively greater stability of power structures in the modern world-system because of the relatively greater harmony of class interests within the core. While bread-and-circus dynamics operated in Rome, they were far less developed than the welfare state apparatus and entertainment industries of the late modern system.

Another important difference is that the Central System before 1800 contained three nonadjacent core regions (Europe/West Asia, South Asia, and East Asia), each with its "own" core/periphery hierarchy, whereas the rise of the European core produced a global system with a single integrated set of core states and a global core/periphery hierarchy. This brought about the complete unification of the formerly somewhat separate regional world histories into a single global history.

Political ecologists have argued that capitalism is fundamentally different from earlier modes of accumulation with respect to its relationship to the natural environment (O'Conner 1989; Foster 2000). There is little doubt that the expansion and deepening of the modern system of global capitalism has had much larger effects on the biogeosphere than any earlier system. There are many more people using hugely increased amounts of energy and raw materials, and the global nature of the human system has global impacts on the environment. Smaller systems were able to migrate when they depleted local supplies or polluted local natural resources, and this relationship with the environment has been a driving force of human social change since the Paleolithic. But is all this due only to capitalism's greater size and intensity, or is there something else that encourages capitalists to "externalize" the natural costs of production and distribution and produces a destructive "metabolic rift" between capitalism and nature (Foster 2000)?

Capitalism, in addition to being about market exchange and commodification, is also fundamentally about a certain kind of property—private property in the major means of production. Within modern capitalism there has been an oscillating debate about the virtues of public and private property, with the shift since the 1980s toward the desirability of "privatization" being only the most recent round of a struggle that has gone on since the enclosures of the commons in Europe.

The ongoing debate about the idea of the "commons"—collective property—is germane to understanding the relationship between capitalism and nature. The powerful claims about the commons being a "tragedy" because no one cares enough to take care of and invest in public property carries a powerful baggage that supports the notion that private ownership is superior. Private owners are supposed to have an interest in the future value of the property, and so they will keep it up and possibly invest in it. But whether this is better than a more public or communal form of ownership depends entirely on how these more collective forms of property are themselves organized.

Capitalism seems to contain a powerful incentive to externalize the natural costs of production and other economic activities, and individual capitalists are loathe to pay for the actual environmental costs of their activities as long as their competitors are getting a free ride. This is a political issue in which core countries in the modern capitalist system have been far more successful at building institutions for protecting the national environment than noncore countries. And, indeed, there is convincing evidence that core countries export pollution and environmental degradation to the noncore countries (Jorgenson 2004).

Certainly, modern capitalism has been more destructive of the natural environment than any earlier system. But it is important to know whether this is completely due to its effects on technology and the rapidity of economic growth or whether there is an additional element that is connected to the specific institutions and contradictions of capitalism. Technological development, demographic expansion, and economic growth cause problems for the environment. But are there better alternatives? And is capitalism more destructive of the environment than earlier modes of accumulation net of its demographic and technological effects?

The human species can and must do better at inventing institutions that protect the biogeosphere. Regarding earlier modes of accumulation, certainly some cultures did better than others at protecting the environment. The institutions of law, the state, and property evolved, in part, as a response to environmental degradation (recall our iteration model in Chapter 2). It is not obvious that contemporary capitalist institutions are worse than earlier ones in this regard. The main problem is that the scale and scope of environmental degradation has increased so greatly that very powerful institutions and social movements will be required to bring about a sustainable human civilization. Capitalism may not be capable of doing this, and so those theoretical perspectives that point to the need for a major overhaul may be closer to the point than those that contend that capitalism itself can be reformed to become sustainable.

The Schema of Constants, Cycles, Trends, and Cyclical Trends

Most histories of the modern world tell a story, and we shall do the same in the following chapters. But here we will begin with a model, as if the modern world-system were a great machine or a superorganism. The systemic analogy will be stressed at this point so that we can see whether, and in what ways, the basic system has changed in the chapters that follow. One way to help us think about the modern world-system as a whole is to describe its structures and processes in terms of patterns that are more or less constant, that are cyclical, and that are upward (or downward) trends. Some important characteristics of the whole system, like globalization, are both cycles and trends. This means that there are waves of globalization in the sense of larger and more intense interactions, and that these waves also go up over time—an upward trend. Patterns of this kind are called "trending cycles." Figure 13.1 illustrates what we mean by constants, cycles, trends, and trending cycles of the Europe-centered modern world-system since the fifteenth century.

The systemic constants are:

1. Capitalism—the accumulation of resources by means of the production and sale of commodities for profit under conditions in which most of the major means of production are privately held by an elite class of capitalists
2. An interstate system—a system of unequally powerful sovereign states that compete for resources by supporting profitable commodity production and by engaging in geopolitical and military competition
3. A core/periphery hierarchy—in which core regions have strong states and specialize in high-technology, high-wage production while peripheral regions have weak states and specialize in labor-intensive and low-wage production

These general systemic features of the modern system are continuous and reproduced, but they also have evolved.[7] They are interlinked and interdependent with one another such that any

[7] All three of the systemic constants have evolved and expanded over the past centuries. Capitalism has expanded and deepened, which is part of the reason why scholars disagree about when it became the predominant mode of accumulation. The interstate system has expanded to the periphery and has become evermore institutionalized; even political globalization has established a number of important international organizations that constitute a world protostate. The core/periphery hierarchy has been reorganized with decolonization and neocolonial institutions such as the IMF and the global regime of foreign investments. Nevertheless, it is useful to characterize capitalism, the interstate system, and the core/periphery hierarchy as constitutive structures of the modern world-system.

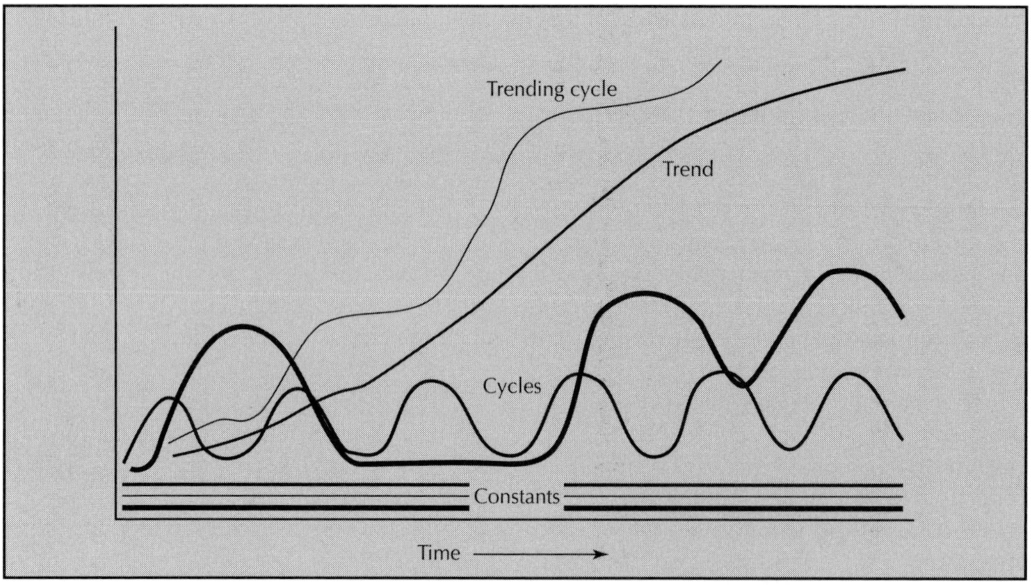

Figure 13.1 Constants, cycles, trends, and trending cycles

major change in one would necessarily alter the others in fundamental ways (Chase-Dunn 1998).

In addition to these systemic constants, there are several other systemic continuities that have displayed patterned change. These are the systemic cycles, the systemic trends, and the trending cycles.

The basic systemic cycles are:

1. The **Kondratieff wave** (K-wave)—a worldwide economic cycle with a period of forty to sixty years in which the relative rate of economic activity increases (during "A-phase" upswings) and then decreases (during "B-phase" periods of slower growth or stagnation).
2. The hegemonic sequence—the rise and fall of hegemonic core powers in which military power and economic comparative advantage are concentrated into a single hegemonic core state during some periods, and these are followed by periods in which wealth and power are more evenly distributed among core states. Examples of hegemons are the United Provinces of the Netherlands in the seventeenth century, the United Kingdom of Great Britain in the nineteenth century, and the United States in the twentieth century.
3. The cycle of core war severity—the severity (battle deaths per year) of wars among core states (world wars) displays a cyclical pattern that has closely tracked the K-wave since the sixteenth century (Goldstein 1988).

The systemic trends that are normal operating procedure in the modern system are:

1. Expansion and deepening of commodity relations—land, labor, and wealth have been increasingly mediated by market-like institutions in both the core and the periphery.
2. State formation—the power of states over their populations has increased everywhere, though this trend is sometimes slowed down by efforts to deregulate. State regulation has grown secularly while political battles rage over the nature and objects of regulation.
3. Increased size of economic enterprises—while a large competitive sector of small firms is reproduced, the largest firms (those occupying what is called the monopoly sector) have continually grown in size. This remains true even in the most recent period despite its characterization by some analysts as a new "accumulation regime" of **flexible specialization**, in which small firms compete for shares of the global market.
4. Increasing capital-intensity of production and mechanization—several industrial revolutions since the sixteenth century have

increased the productivity of labor in agriculture, industry, and services.

5. Proletarianization—the world workforce has increasingly depended on labor markets for meeting its basic needs. This long-term trend may be temporarily slowed or even reversed in some areas during periods of economic stagnation, but the secular shift away from subsistence production has a long history that continues in the most recent period. The expansion of the informal sector is part of this trend despite its functional similarities with earlier rural subsistence redoubts.

And there have been two trending cycles that oscillate up and down with intermittent peaks that are higher than all those before:

1. International economic integration (**economic globalization**)—the periodic and long-term growth of trade interconnectedness and the transnationalization of capital. Capital has crossed state boundaries since the sixteenth century, but the proportion of all production that is due to the operation of transnational firms has increased in every epoch.[8] Trending waves of trade and investment globalization have been quantitatively measured since the early nineteenth century (Chase-Dunn, Kawano, and Brewer 2000).
2. International political integration (**political globalization**)—the emergence of stronger international institutions for regulating economic and political interactions. This is a trend since the rise of the Concert of Europe after the defeat of Napoleon. The League of Nations, the United Nations (UN), and such international financial institutions as the World Bank and the International Monetary Fund (IMF) show an upward trend toward increasing **global governance**.
3. Global culture formation (**cultural globalization** or **geoculture**)—the emergence over the tops of the civilizational and national cultures of a global culture in which assumptions about what exists (ontology) and what is good (ethics, morality, values) are coming to be shared across the whole Earth. This process proceeds as the constitution of a series of world orders and their contestation in a series of world revolutions that challenge the old hegemonic assumptions and produce newly evolved versions of the global culture (Wallerstein 1991). The Protestant Reformation was the first of these world revolutions, and the waves of decolonization discussed below were parts of later world revolutions.

The above conceptual model of the modern system is not posited to deny that the system has evolved, but rather to make it possible to see clearly the new organizational features that have emerged over the past six hundred years and to enable us to accurately compare new developments with the relevant features of the past. The schema above suggests a system that is experiencing expanding cycles of growth and confronting contradictions that require new organizational solutions, but this is not to suggest a purely functionalist process of adaptation and learning. Struggle over the very nature of social change has been present all along and remains entirely relevant for comprehending the emerging situation of the twenty-first century.

The trends in the shares of world population shown in Figure 13.2 confirm observations that were discussed in Chapter 12. Figure 13.2 shows shares of the total global population since the beginning of the Common Era 2,000 years ago according to Maddison's (2001) estimates. The time scale on the horizontal axis of Figure 13.2 is misleading because the intervals are not equal. Keeping this in mind, we can see that the countries that became hegemonic in recent centuries did not change much in terms of their shares of world population. The countries with the big shares, India and China, still have huge shares, though India declined quite a lot until 1950 and then began to rise again. China peaked in 1820 and has mainly been declining since then. The United States rose above 5 percent of world

[8] The contemporary focus on transnational corporate sourcing and the single interdependent global economy is the heightened awareness produced by a trending cycle long in operation.

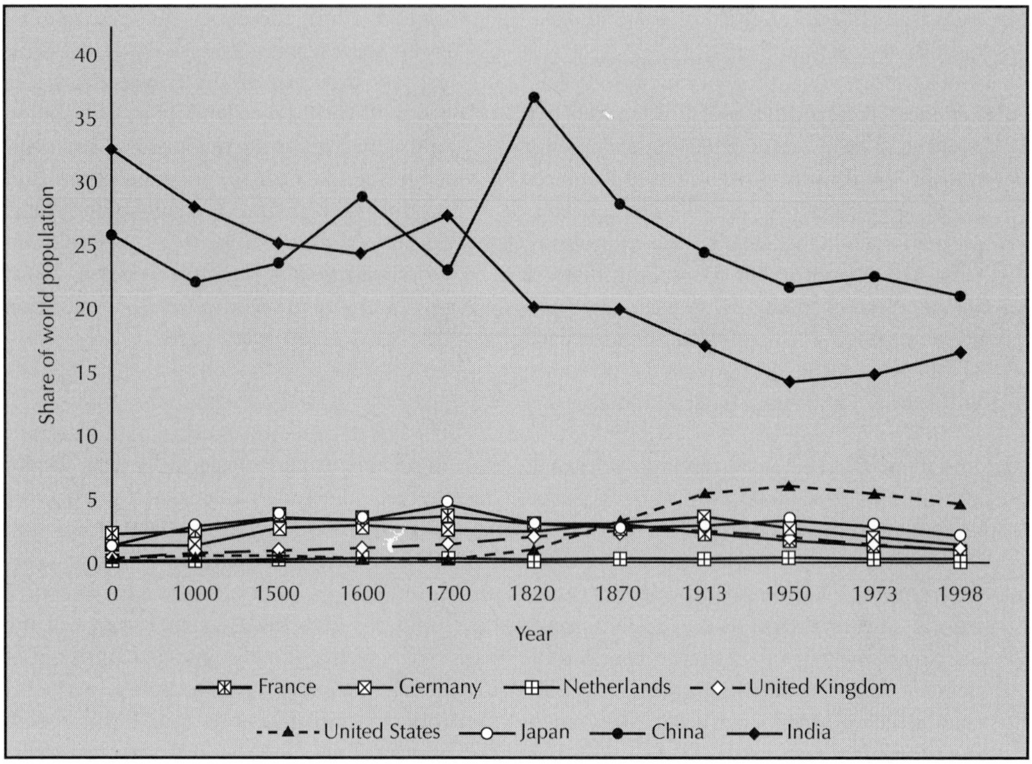

Figure 13.2 Shares of world population
Source: Data from Maddison 2001.

population in 1913 and dropped below that level in about 1985. East Asia and South Asia have long been the demographic centers of the earth but have become somewhat less so over the past two millennia.

Maddison's (2001) estimates of gross domestic product (GDP) allow us to examine the ratio between GDP per capita in regions and countries to the world average GDP per capita. This is a useful indicator of economic hegemony, though it does not capture military, cultural, or the finer points of economic power. Figure 13.3 traces this ratio for some of the European "great powers," the United States, and Japan since 1500. Again, the time dimension is distorted, with earlier years contracted on the horizontal axis and later years expanded.

Figure 13.3 shows the three hegemonies of the modern world-system (the Dutch in the seventeenth century, the British in the nineteenth century, and the United States in the twentieth century). It also shows that each of these successive hegemonies achieved a higher level of economic development relative to the general world level than its predecessor.

Waves of Colonial Expansion and Decolonization

The crusades against Moslem control of the old West Asian core and the reconquest of the Iberian Peninsula constitute the first wave of European expansion, as discussed in Chapter 12. This was the effort of a reviving Europe to strike back against the expansion of the Islamic empire-states and to reopen trade with Asia. It was followed by another wave of expansion that began slowly in the fifteenth century with Portugal's establishment of colonial control of Ceuta (in Africa just across the Strait of Gibraltar) in 1415 and of Madeira, an island in the Atlantic that was important for sailing down the coast of Africa.

Under Prince Henry the Navigator, the Portuguese were set on a course of rounding the

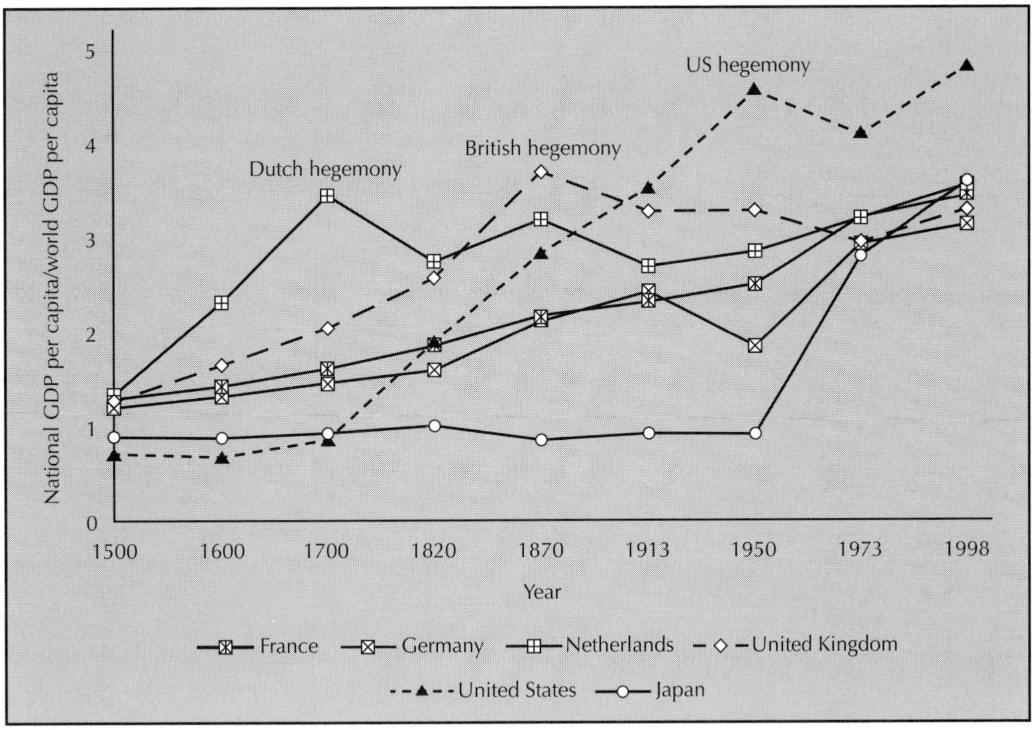

Figure 13.3 Country GDP per capita as a ratio to average world GDP per capita, 1500–1998
Source: Data from Maddison 2001.

African continent as a route to the East in order to break the Venetian monopoly on the spice trade (Lane 1979, 31–34). On the way they were able to gain access to important sources of West African gold and to develop an interest in the slave trade. This was the first burst of modern European colonial empire of the type described above. The Portuguese were encouraged and financed by the bankers of Genoa, who were competing with Venice for a better position in the Eastern trade. Thus did a semiperipheral capitalist city-state (Genoa) throw in with an ambitious nation-state (Portugal) on a global gamble that would have vast implications for the rise of the West. As Immanuel Wallerstein (1974b) has pointed out, there was no emperor of Europe to tell Prince Henry and the Genovese that they could not do this. At about the same time, the Ming dynasty in China was recalling its fleets and battening down to concentrate its resources on expanding the Great Wall against Central Asian steppe nomads. The European interstate system was becoming institutionalized around the diplomatic protocols developed on the Italian Peninsula among capitalist city-states in the southern sector of the "blue banana."

The years between 1415 and 1420 saw the beginning of Portugal's long circumcolonization of Africa. This is the first bump that one can see on the left side of Figure 13.4—the settlement and establishment of sovereignty over Ceuta and Madeira. The Spanish grabbed the Canary Islands off the coast of Africa beginning in 1479 and then went for the New World.

Portugal and Spain were the major players in the sixteenth-century wave of European colonial expansion. In the seventeenth century, the Dutch, English, and French moved out to produce another wave of expansion, in which the Spanish and the Portuguese also continued to expand their control of overseas territories. Figure 13.4 combines the colonies established by all the European "mother" countries to show the waves of modern colonial expansion.

The waves of European colonial expansion were carried out by different countries in different time periods. The colonial empires had important cultural and structural differences as well, and

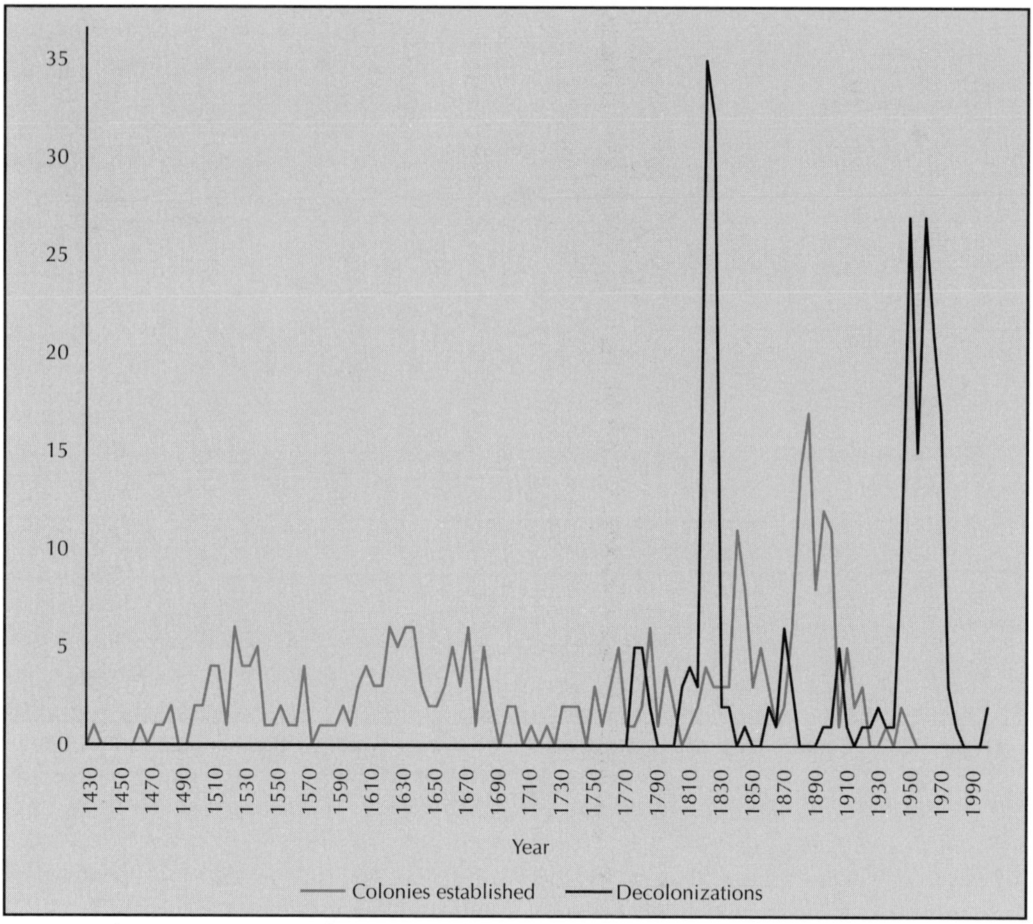

Figure 13.4 Waves of European colonial expansion and waves of decolonization
Source: Data from Henige 1970.[9]

the eras of colonialism were different because the needs and natures of both the colonizers and the colonized varied (Abernethy 2000). Nevertheless, there is an important overarching reality to the whole process of European expansion that is shown by the gray line in Figure 13.4.

The black line in Figure 13.4 depicts the waves of decolonization. The victims of colonialism were not inert or faceless peoples who simply were overwhelmed by the Europeans. They fought back, and eventually they succeeded at establishing, or reestablishing, at least formal sovereignty and political self-governance. The waves of decolonization started only in the late eighteenth century, the most famous example of which is the American Revolution. Sometimes called "the first new nation," the English colonies that became the United States were harbingers of

[9] The Ottoman and Manchu conquests were not included, because they were not included in Henige (1970) and are not understood to have been products of modern colonialism. Also not included are new colonies created from old colonies, redivisions of existing colonies, and colonial transfers (colonies taken from other powers). Two criteria were used to determine when a colony should be included: it had to be both claimed and settled, and it could not previously have been settled and claimed by another European power. Territorial expansions were also documented in the data sets. Double counting was avoided. So territories taken from other modern colonial powers were not counted. Temporary settlements of short duration (e.g., Roanoke) were not counted. The idea was to capture the territorial expansion of European colonial sovereignty.

rebellion against the colonial empires and modern imperialism, a story we shall retell from the perspective of the world in Chapter 16. While the British burned the capitol building in Washington to the ground in 1812 trying to recoup their losses, British covert policy, agents, money, and "privateers" supported rebellions in Latin America against the Spanish, the Portuguese, and the French. The early nineteenth-century liberation of Spanish America was also supported by the fledgling United States, then still a semiperipheral state in the larger system.

The next big wave of decolonization began mainly after World War II and lasted well into the 1960s. This was the final establishment of formal sovereignty and the extension of membership in the interstate system to Asia, Africa, and the Pacific. Like the waves of colonial expansion, the waves of decolonization were somewhat different from one another. But as a singular phenomenon of the world-system as a whole, these constituted a major restructuring of the system from one of colonial empires to a globe-wide interstate system based on formalities of national sovereignty and the equality of nations.

The other side of this story is about neocolonialism. In part because of its own history as former colonies, the United States spurned formal colonialism, but its rise to core status and eventual hegemony required the development of techniques for controlling and exploiting peripheral regions in the absence of the trappings of a formal empire. The United States began practicing "gun boat diplomacy" in Latin America in order to get its way in local politics, and the institutional capabilities of informal control made possible what has been termed "neocolonialism." The power disparities between the core and the periphery continued to expand despite the abolition of the colonial empires, though the achievement of formal sovereignty has led to an increased level of autonomy in the noncore. Like the British in the early nineteenth century, the United States in the twentieth century generally supported the decolonization of the empires of competing core powers, while at the same time it fought wars to prevent the emergence of regimes that were deemed to threaten its interests. So Cuba, the Philippines, Puerto Rico, Guatemala, the Dominican Republic, and Vietnam saw US military intervention as the raw face of neocolonialism. The colonial empires are gone, but not imperialism.

Suggested Readings

Abernethy, David B. 2000. *The Dynamics of Global Dominance: European Overseas Empires, 1415–1980.* New Haven, CT: Yale University Press.

Chase-Dunn, Christopher. 1998. *Global Formation: Structures of the World-Economy*. 2nd ed. Lanham, MD: Rowman and Littlefield.

Frank, Andre Gunder. 1978. *World Accumulation, 1492–1789.* New York: Monthly Review Press.

Lane, Frederic C. 1979. *Profits from Power: Readings in Protection Rent and Violence-Controlling Enterprises.* Albany, NY: SUNY Press.

Martin, William G., Tuba Agartan, Caleb M. Bush, Woo-Young Choi, Tu Huynh, Foad Kalouche, Eric Mielants, and Rochelle Morris. 2008. *Making Waves: Worldwide Social Movements, 1750–2005*. Boulder, CO: Paradigm Publishers.

Shannon, Thomas R. 1996. *An Introduction to the World-System Perspective.* 2nd ed. Boulder, CO: Westview Press.

Wallerstein, Immanuel. 2004. *World-Systems Analysis.* Durham, NC: Duke University Press.

14

The Early Modern Systems in the Fifteenth to the Eighteenth Centuries

This chapter tells the story of the continuing rise of European global predominance based on the emerging strength of capitalism in Europe and its colonies. It also tells of the expansion of production, urbanization, and population growth, especially in East Asia and South Asia. In Europe there were important alliances among bankers from Genoa with the expanding Portuguese and Spanish monarchies. The effort by the Hapsburg dynasty to erect a tributary empire over the core

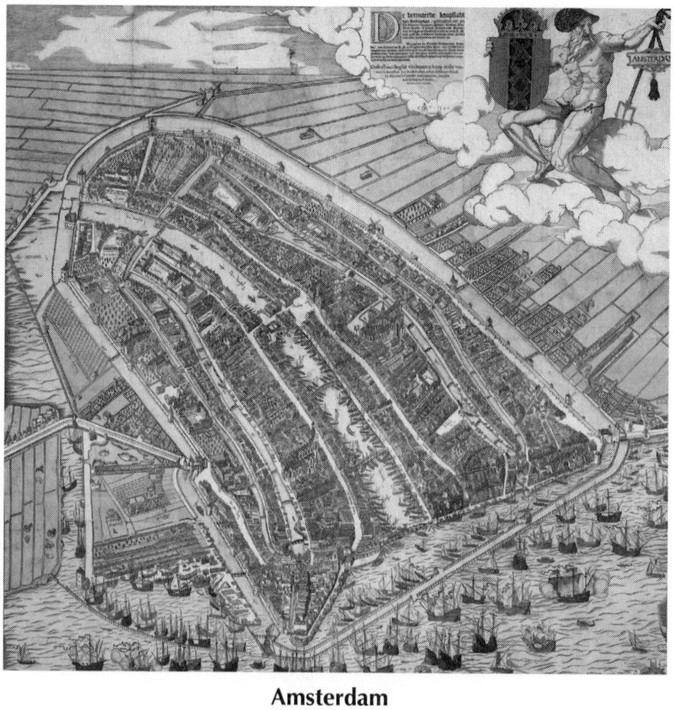

Amsterdam
Source: Wikipedia Commons.

states of Europe in the sixteenth century nearly squelched the emerging predominance of capitalist accumulation, but the rise of Dutch hegemony in the seventeenth century produced the world's first capitalist core state. We also will examine the further institutionalization of the interstate system in the treaty of Westphalia, and the contention between Britain and France for global dominance in the eighteenth century. The new social institutions and technologies that emerged in this period changed human societies all over the earth.

Institutional Developments in the Early Modern World Regions

The early modern world regions of East and West saw huge changes in production, transportation, and communications technologies as well as important new departures in religion, philosophy, science, commerce, and mathematics. These developments occurred both in Europe and in the older core regions of the Near East, South Asia, and East Asia. Because of new forms of transportation and communications, inventions, products, new crops, and diseases spread rapidly back and forth across Eurasia and between the Old World and the New World. The emergence of capitalist accumulation in Europe radically increased the economic incentives to develop and implement profitable new techniques. The competitiveness of the European interstate system used a lot of the wealth generated by economic growth to rapidly develop new military technologies, and the diffusion of the knowledge of how to make gunpowder from China fueled a new wave of expansions of tributary states, the so-called gunpowder empires (e.g., the Ottoman Empire, the Mughal Empire in India, and the Manchu conquest of China). The Chinese also developed a compass based on floating a magnetized needle in a bowl of water, and Islamic monsoon sailors began to understand that the angle between the horizon and celestial objects could be used to estimate one's latitude—distance from the equator. The lateen sail used on Arab dhows allowed for sailing across, and sometimes even into, the wind, and knowledge of the seasonal monsoon reversal of the winds allowed for long-distance return trips from the East Coast of Africa to the South Asian subcontinent and beyond. These technologies were further developed by the Portuguese and other European explorers and traders during the early modern period (see below).

The building of roads and the development of lighter and faster horse-drawn vehicles allowed for faster and cheaper land transportation, more strongly linking rural hinterlands with towns and linking towns with one another. Canal building also facilitated bulk goods transportation. The narrow small-boat canals of Venice were expanded in Amsterdam to accommodate larger vessels that could more easily bring large loads into the city. The invention of moveable type and the printing press lowered the cost of text production and made the expansion of literacy feasible. The transfer of crops between the Americas and the Old World—the so-called Columbian exchange (Crosby 1972)—raised the productivity of agriculture in some regions, while it helped to destroy the livelihoods of hunter-gatherers and horticulturalists in others.

Human population growth, the growing sizes of towns and cities, the expansion of larger-scale agriculture, and the advance of manufacturing placed new demands on local resources that led to depletion and pollution, but the cheapening of long-distance transportation allowed imported resources to be substituted for locally depleted ones. The more rapid revolutionizing of production technologies allowed old resources to be exploited more thoroughly and new local resources to be used. Thus the processes of population pressures and environmental degradation that are central to the iteration model became increasingly mediated by markets and price changes, and by states that sought to protect their own natural capital and to exploit the natural capital of others. Expansion into the New World and the tapping of Africa as a reserve army of labor added greatly to the stock of natural and human capital available for exploitation by the expanding European core and greatly facilitated Europe's rise to global hegemony over the older core regions of Eurasia.

The emergence of the Dutch hegemony in the late sixteenth and early seventeenth centuries was a key development that led to the further deepening and widening of capitalism in Europe and in those parts of the world that were coming under the sway of the European powers. The Dutch Republic was not the first capitalist state, but it was the first capitalist state that was more than a city-state. It was the emergence of a strongly capitalist political economy that eventually allowed Europe to become hegemonic over the other core and peripheral areas of the world-system, though Europe did not outperform China economically until the late eighteenth century and did not dominate China until the nineteenth century.

The Second Expansion of Europe

As we saw in Chapter 12, the fifteenth century saw the rise of a second wave of European expansion.[1] The main engines of European global expansion in this second wave were Portugal and Spain, fueled by Genoese financial support. The Portuguese were encouraged and supported by Genoese merchants and bankers who were competing with Venice for the Eastern spice trade. They began the circumnavigation of Africa and the establishment of trade enclaves in India, the East Indies, and Southern China (Macao). The Portuguese king Henry the Navigator established a school for the study of oceanic navigation on a cape overlooking the Atlantic (Boxer 1969). King Henry brought scholars and navigators from all over the Mediterranean, including the Islamic states, to his school. There they perfected the quadrant—an instrument used to measure the angle between a celestial object (e.g., sun, moon, stars) and the horizon for estimating latitude (distance from the equator). This investment in blue-water navigation technology emboldened the Portuguese to sail far away from the coast in order to use prevailing winds to round Africa by sea.

The Venetians had a lock on the importation of spices from the East Indies into Europe because of their domination of the overland, Persian Gulf, and Red Sea trade routes. Genoa, a competing capitalist city-state on the Italian Peninsula, wanted to break the Venetian monopoly, and so Genoese bankers financed King Henry's navigation research and the naval effort to develop a string of trading ports around Africa that would enable an alternative route for the spice trade. The Portuguese navy not only rounded the African Cape of Good Hope and built colonial enclaves in Mozambique and Angola that would remain Portuguese colonies until the final wave of decolonization in the twentieth century, but they conquered colonial outposts in India (Goa) and in the spice islands of the East Indies that allowed them to successfully foil the Venetian spice monopoly. They rewired the global trade network.

The first Portuguese colony, conquered in 1415, was Ceuta on the African side of the Strait of Gibraltar just opposite the great rock. This was a strategic point for observing and potentially controlling access to the Mediterranean from the Atlantic Ocean. The Portuguese followed the Venetian strategy of "armed trade," a profit-oriented policy that relied greatly on the deft application of organized violence (especially naval power). The Portuguese were also conscious bearers of the Christian god, especially in the guise of the Virgin Mary. Like the Spanish conquistadors, the Portuguese saw their adventures as a continuation of the battle against religious infidels that had begun with the expulsion of the Islamic Moors from the Iberian Peninsula.

In this respect, the second wave of European expansion was similar to the first wave. It was carried out by an alliance of merchants, bankers, and religious military adventurers, but the states that supplied the main muscle of conquest were larger and more organized in the second wave—the Portuguese and Spanish monarchies. Genoese financial capital partnered with Spanish and Portuguese colonial empires to further expand European hegemony. Thus it was transnational alliances among monarchs and bankers that played the hegemonic role in the fifteenth-century Central political-military network (PMN).[2]

[1] The first wave of European expansion, if we do not count the Roman Empire, was the crusaders' attack on the Holy Lands.

[2] Giovanni Arrighi (1994) presents this as the first of a series of four "systemic cycles of accumulation." This is his term for what is called the "hegemonic sequence" in Chapter 13. The later systemic cycles analyzed by Arrighi are focused on the Dutch in the seventeenth century, the British in the nineteenth century, and the United States in the twentieth century.

Ming Expansion and Withdrawal

The second wave of European expansion occurred during an age of intercontinental exploration that began when Moslem fleets sailed from Africa to Southeast Asia and Chinese fleets sailed to the Persian Gulf. Andre Gunder Frank (1997) has shown that China remained the predominant center of the Eurasian multicore world-system until the eighteenth century. The Mongol-founded Yuan dynasty in China was overthrown and the ethnically Chinese (Han) Ming dynasty was reestablished in the late thirteenth century. The Ming emperor Zhi Di funded huge intercontinental seagoing explorations and trading ventures. The famous eunuch Admiral Zheng He three times sailed huge fleets of four-hundred-foot treasure ships from Nanjing to Africa and back to Nanjing in the early fifteenth century (Viviano 2005; see Figure 14.1).

Indeed, the very same year that the Portuguese took their first African colony at Ceuta (1415), Zheng He's fleet was at the Strait of Hormuz, the entrance to the Persian Gulf. But these Chinese seagoing explorations were curtailed when the Ming dynasty experienced internal troubles, new attacks from Central Asian steppe pastoralists, and troubles with Japanese pirates. Chinese state expenditures were concentrated on rebuilding the Great Wall. The Ming dynasty turned inward and the great overseas voyages were discontinued, leaving the rest of the age of exploration to the Europeans. In 1522 Ferdinand Magellan's personal slave and seventeen members of his crew became the first men to travel all the way around the earth. Magellan himself died in the Philippines in 1521.

Europeans incorporated much of Africa, the Americas, and some of Asia into the expanding Central PMN in the sixteenth and seventeenth centuries. The Afroeurasian prestige goods network (PGN) and the Central PMN expanded to include parts of the Americas. But the East Asian PMN remained substantially separate from the Europe-centered PMN until the nineteenth century, while the long-standing PGNs linking East Asia with the West continued to intensify. There was very little direct military interaction between the East Asian PMN (China, Korea, Japan, and so forth) and the European states in these centuries. Portuguese Jesuits and merchants were thrown out of Japan by the Tokogawa shogunate (Batten 2003).

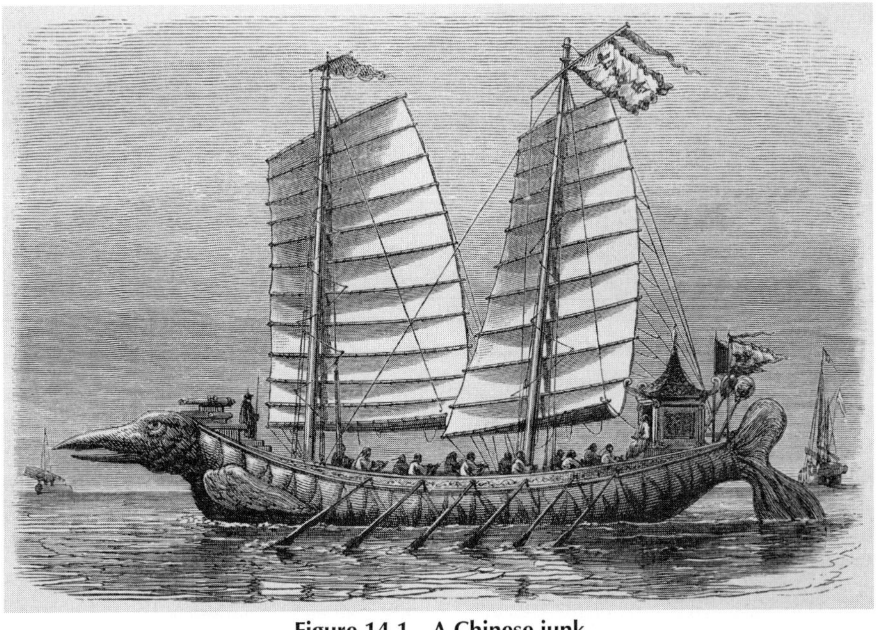

Figure 14.1 A Chinese junk

Expansion and Peripheralization

As Europe continued the formation of its own regional core, it also forged new global networks, mainly motivated by the desire for East Asian–manufactured prestige goods and valuable metals (silver, gold) with which to pay for them. The conquests of Mexico and Peru by the Spanish conquistadors brought vast new quantities of gold and silver into the system, while they devastated the Native American populations with Eurasian epidemic diseases for which they had no immunity (Crosby 1972; Diamond 1997). Starting in 1565 the Spanish sailed the Manila Galleon every year from Acapulco on the Pacific coast of Mexico across the Pacific to the Philippines to buy Chinese silks and porcelain ("china") with American silver (Schurz 1959). The Manila Galleon was the first regularly scheduled trade link connecting the Americas with East Asia.

The mercantile aggressiveness of the Portuguese served as the vanguard of the second wave of European expansion, but like the later centrality of Spanish Seville, Portuguese Lisbon did not develop an important economic center based on production of high-technology commodities. The "primitive accumulation" of American gold and silver by the Spanish had positive effects on the development of business enterprise across Europe (Wallerstein 1974b, 67–84), but it did not lead to the development of capitalist core production in Spain. Somewhat like the case of France, Spain included regions that had contradictory economic interests. The Spanish monarchy was weighed down and made indecisive and inflexible by the necessity of holding together these centrifugal regions. Spain and Portugal, while very important to the formation of the newly emerging capitalist world region, were not themselves fully formed hegemonic core states of that system. Capitalists had state power in smaller city-states in this period (Venice, Antwerp, Genoa, Florence), but the larger states were still dominated by tribute-oriented classes, though they were pursuing increasingly mercantilist policies under the influence of the capitalist city-states.[3]

The first period of Spanish peripheralization of the New World focused on the extraction of raw materials that were valuable prestige goods in the Afroeurasian PGN—gold, silver, and pearls. Hernan Cortez substituted himself and his soldiers for the Aztec ruling class, appropriated the gold and silver that the Aztecs had accumulated, and began the search for mines and pearling sites. Francisco Pizarro did the same thing in the Andes. When a mountain of silver was discovered high in what is now Bolivia, the Spaniards mobilized indigenous peoples to work in the mines at Potosi using a system of corvée labor mobilization (the *mita*) developed by the Inca in which each village was obliged to supply workers. In both Mexico and the Andes, the heavy exploitation of indigenous workers in the mines combined with epidemic diseases to produce a demographic holocaust from which it took centuries for these populations to recover.

In his influential article entitled "Three Paths of National Development in 16th Century Europe," Immanuel Wallerstein (1972) presented the structural history of the modern world-system as the interlinked development of a Northwestern European core region, peripheralized regions in Latin America and Eastern Europe, and an increasingly semiperipheral region in the Christian Mediterranean. Dependency theorists had been critiquing modernization theorists' interpretations of Latin America as an undeveloped backwater of traditional societies by

[3] Many stage theories of capitalism posit a mercantilist stage in which states actively intervened in the economy. This was allegedly followed by a free market stage in which states followed the policy of laissez-faire (let the people do as they will). In the world-historical framework, which includes both core and noncore regions, we can see that state intervention does vary over time in degree and content, but it is always important. Free trade and free market ideologies and policies are characteristically found in states that either have a comparative advantage in some key economic activity or have very little leverage over the world economy because they are dependent on economically dominant states. Protectionist and interventionist policies are likely to be adopted when a state with potential and aspirations is trying to move up in the global food chain. The content of state regulation and intervention is also important. Some states, mainly in the periphery, are merely tools for the extraction of rents by a state elite. Others intervene to promote economic development, and use political leverage to open new markets and investment opportunities abroad. Stages of world capitalism are not easily demarcated as mercantilist or free trade, because these policies vary across countries as well as across periods.

pointing to the hundreds of years in which Latin America was subjected to imperial controls by Spain and Portugal and the more recent exercise of neocolonial power by the United States. Wallerstein read Marian Malowist's (1966) analysis of uneven development in Eastern and Western Europe and realized that core/periphery relations—institutionalized power-dependence relations among national societies—were important in the emergence of capitalism within Europe as well as between Europe and the Americas.

Poland in the sixteenth century was becoming a dependent producer of serf-produced grain that was exported to Northwestern Europe in exchange for imported manufactured goods. Historians called the expansion of large export-producing farms owned by Polish aristocrats the "second serfdom" because it followed the period of enserfment that occurred during the earlier period of feudalism in Western Europe. But for Poland and the other countries of Eastern Europe, and for Russia, it was the first time that rural producers had become legally tied to the land (enserfed). Wallerstein recognized the similarity of this process of enserfment with the expansion of slavery in the New World, and he came to see these as two types of "coerced cash crop labor mobilization" that were important defining characteristics of peripheral capitalism. The contrast between "free labor" (i.e., wage labor) in the core and coerced labor (e.g., slavery, serfdom, indentured servitude) in the periphery became a defining feature of Wallerstein's modern world-system, and one that survived the abolition of slavery and serfdom because labor remains less protected from exploitation and state coercion in the periphery than it is in the core.

Core-Wide Empire or Capitalist World Economy? The Hapsburg Empire

France, England, Spain, and Portugal had all formed more centralized state structures (relative to decentralized feudalism) based on the political theory of absolute monarchy and the divine right of kings. The process of state formation proceeded by expanding the feudatory privileges of the king's household into an institutionalized fiscal structure that would support state bureaucracies and a centrally controlled military apparatus. This occurred differently in the several European states, and very differently in Eastern Europe, depending on the relative power of several kinds of elite groups (the landed aristocracy, the church, the military, merchants, and bankers) (P. Anderson 1974b; Tilly 1990). But the outcome was most often a centralized state apparatus and the beginnings of a process of nation building in which elites and commoners shared a single national language and culture. While these were still primarily tributary (not capitalist) states oriented toward the control of land and the extraction of taxes and expansion into adjacent territories, this formation of larger states in Europe occurred in a context in which both urban and agrarian capitalism were becoming stronger. The clustered capitalist city-states of Italy provided the legal, diplomatic, and cultural institutions of the Renaissance as well as substantial financial support to the emerging monarchs of Europe.

The effort by the Hapsburg dynasty to impose an empire on the not yet fully developed capitalist system in Europe represented the attempted reassertion of the logic of tributary domination. The Hapsburg dynasty, based in German-speaking Austria, was semiperipheral to the larger and more dynamic states of Portugal, Spain, and France in the sixteenth century. The Hapsburg emperor Charles V created a strong alliance with Spain by marriage and proceeded to build a large state in Western and Eastern Europe. The Hapsburg Empire included most of those regions in Italy and Northern Europe that had contained the capitalist city-states that had emerged during the first wave of European expansion—the so-called blue banana described in Chapter 12. The Hapsburg dynasty fought a war with France, and if it had won, the whole of continental Europe would have been united under a single imperial state.

The Hapsburg effort to transform nascently capitalist Europe into a tributary empire fell victim to three circumstances:

1. Its own inadequate fiscal resources
2. Only weak support from the capitalist city-states
3. Strong resistance from France and the Ottoman Empire

The defeat of the Hapsburgs was an important event in the development of Europe because the Hapsburg effort represented the reassertion of the old logic of tribute trying to impose a single tributary world state in place of the emerging capitalistic European interstate system. Challenges of this kind were repeated in later centuries by Napoleonic France and by Germany in the twentieth century, so it is important to understand how the Hapsburg effort was similar to or different from these later efforts.

The Ottoman Turks were migrants from Central Asia who had served as soldiers in the Byzantine Empire and then, in the fifteenth century, conquered a large swath of the old Central System in Western Asia and the Eastern Mediterranean. It was another case of a semiperipheral marcher state creating a large empire by conquest. The Ottomans adopted Islam and took Constantinople as their capital.

Interaction Networks and Capitalism in the Rise of Europe

Immanuel Wallerstein's (1974b) study of the emerging predominance of agrarian and urban capitalism in Europe and the European colonies in the "long sixteenth century"[4] defined the European capitalist world-system as spatially bounded by the capitalist mode of production,[5] which was alleged to be coterminous with European Christendom. Wallerstein argued that the Ottoman Empire was a separate noncapitalist "world-empire" and that it was located in an "**external arena**" outside the capitalist European world economy. Aristide Zolberg (1981) criticized Wallerstein's alleged overemphasis on the importance of capitalism in the sixteenth century. Zolberg claimed that Wallerstein ignored the autonomous importance of politics and statecraft. In support of his contention, Zolberg pointed to the fact that the European interstate system was importantly influenced by powers that were outside Wallerstein's bounding of the capitalist world economy during the sixteenth century—the important alliance between France and the Ottoman Empire against the house of Hapsburg. Zolberg contended that the French-Ottoman alliance, which was vital for France's ability to resist the Hapsburgs, proves the autonomy of the interstate system and geopolitics from the logic of capitalism. It is true that this alliance greatly affected the course of European development. Without this crucial alliance, the emergence of capitalism in Europe might have been long postponed. The conversion of the European interstate system into a single empire would have constrained the development of capitalism. Max Weber (1981) and most other analysts of the development of capitalism in Europe contended that the existence of a competitive interstate system among the European core states was an important element in the strong development of capitalism. The existence of large tributary empires such as the Ottoman Empire in the Near East, the Mughal Empire in India, and the Ming dynasty in China placed substantial limits on the development of capitalism in these regions because state power in the hands of tribute-taking accumulators was often used to extract wealth from businessmen, and the state policies pursued by these tributary empires were often inconsistent with the business interests of capitalists. A competitive interstate system of small and medium-sized states allows capital great maneuverability, and so capitalists tend to oppose the emergence of a world state under most conditions.

The Hapsburg effort to convert the nascent capitalist region in Europe into a tributary world-empire was stemmed by both the opposition of capitalists and the alliance between the French monarchy and the Ottoman Turks. Later efforts by semiperipheral marcher states to create core-wide empires were put down by alliances between declining capitalist hegemons and newly arising semiperipheral capitalist nation-states. Zolberg was right in pointing to the French-Ottoman alliance as evidence of the

[4] Wallerstein (1974b) calls the period between 1450 and 1640 the "long sixteenth century." It is in this period, he contends, that capitalism first emerged to predominance out of European feudalism.

[5] According to Wallerstein (1974b), the capitalist mode of production is a feature of the whole world-system, not its parts, and it includes both core and peripheral forms of capitalism. Peripheral capitalism uses coerced labor (slaves, serfs, and so on) to produce commodities for export.

continuing importance of the interstate system and geopolitics, especially in the sixteenth century, but he fails to see how the unusually concentrated development of capitalism in Europe also played an important role in the defeat of the Hapsburgs.

The Wallerstein-Zolberg debate served to clarify two important conceptual issues in the comparative study of world-systems. The first is that intersocietal interaction networks should be defined empirically as all the important interactions irrespective of the social characteristics of the entities that are interacting. Wallerstein's idea that Europe was a separate system because it was capitalistic was a mistake. Europe was developing strong capitalism, but it had not been a separate system in terms of prestige goods trade and political-military interaction since the Bronze Age. The development of capitalism in Europe did not separate it from the larger system from which it had long been a part. Indeed, its semiperipheral status in that larger system and the heritage of institutions developed in the larger system were what made the emergence of capitalism in Europe possible. The Ottoman Empire and the European states were linked into a single PMN despite that capitalism was developing rapidly in Europe but not in the Ottoman Empire.

And the continuing importance of geopolitics as part of the logic of capitalism is the other important conceptual point that comes out of the Wallerstein-Zolberg debate. Capitalism cannot be understood as solely an economic process. States, the law, property, and the provision of security are part of capitalism as a social process. What happened in the transition from the precapitalist tributary mode of accumulation is that the accumulation of profits based on commodity production, trade, and financial services became relatively more important. This altered the purposes for which state power was deployed and changed the nature of geopolitical competition within the core from that of semiperipheral marcher conquest to that of the rise and fall of capitalist hegemons that also emerged from the semiperiphery.

The Protestant Reformation as the First World Revolution

The influx of silver and gold brought by the Spanish conquerors of the Americas into the European economy caused a long-term rise in prices and the expansion of production and trade, which created opportunities for business enterprise across Europe. The growing power of Catholic Spain and the attempt by the Hapsburg dynasty to conquer Europe provoked a religious and political reaction among those Christians who resisted the centralized hierarchy of the Roman Catholic Church and the power of the Catholic states. The Protestant Reformation took somewhat different forms in different regions, but it reemphasized the confessional, individualistic, and locally controlled aspects of the relationship with the deity against the priest-mediated and centrally controlled hierarchy of the Catholics. This was the first of a series of world revolutions in which the hegemonic institutional structures of the modern system have been challenged and restructured by transnational social movements of resistance (Boswell and Chase-Dunn 2000). Of course, the Protestant Reformation was not a global development, but its effects on the emerging European world order were eventually to have global consequences.

Max Weber (1958a) also famously argued that the doctrinal content of Calvinist Protestantism facilitated the "spirit of capitalism" by providing religious legitimation for saving, investing, and deferring gratification. We contend that the Protestant Reformation did play an important role in the development of European capitalism, but not the role described by Weber. Catholic religious ideology cannot be greatly deficient with regard to the spirit of capitalism even though the medieval Christian church disapproved of usury (high interest on loans), because the Italian city-states were full of prodigious capitalists who were also Catholics. The main way in which the Protestant Reformation influenced the emergence of capitalism in Europe is described below, by enabling the Dutch Revolution.

World Party Formation

The Catholic reaction to the Protestant Reformation produced new institutions as well. The Society of Jesus (Jesuits) was a monastic order organized to save souls, but also to play a covert role in European politics. The Jesuits were explicitly internationalist in outlook and intent. Their policy was to organize groups of missionary priests from different European national cultures (e.g., Germany, Italy, Spain) in order to produce a Pan-European consciousness. Whenever the Jesuits sent a team of priests to establish a new mission to convert the heathens, they tried to include men from different European countries. Their machinations in the politics of European states produced a backlash in the seventeenth and eighteenth centuries in which the Jesuit order was banned from many activities and was replaced by other orders, especially the Franciscans. The Jesuits represent an early "world party" organized explicitly to influence and transform the emerging global system.

International and transnational organizations[6] with world-level political intentions have included churches, secret societies, professional associations, and religious sects as well as international political parties. Such organizations have existed for centuries and have played an important role, along with states, in the evolution of a succession of world orders and emergent forms of international and global governance. The discussion of political parties in world-historical perspective requires us to use a rather broad and flexible definition of parties that includes both religious and secular organizations[7] as well as organizations that do not claim a broad or formal representative structure regarding members or constituents.[8] We combine the current notion of nongovernment organizations (NGOs) and the idea of "transnational advocacy networks" (Keck and Sikkink 1998) into our broad conception of political parties for the purposes of studying world history over long periods of time. The literature on "epistemic communities" in international relations is also germane to studying contestation within the world polity (Haas 1992; Whiteneck 1996). We also contest the idea that a political party must necessarily struggle for power within a single state, and so there can be no global political parties because there is no global state. Political parties can contest for power and influence within a multistate system, just as they do in a federal system.

It is often supposed that in past centuries, world politics was mainly the province of economic, political, and religious elites, and that nonelites only rarely engaged in actions that were intended to have transnational consequences. If we consider both secular and religious movements, even this way of segregating the present from the past does not work. Certainly the diplomacy and war making of statesmen, the profit making of businessmen, and the preachings of churchmen have always operated in a transnational and international arena. And there have been transnational secret societies with counter-hegemonic intentions all along. We can mention the Knights Templar, the Jesuits, the Masons, and the many mystical and millenarian sects and cults that have intended to alter the world orders of the past. The Protestant Reformation was a political movement with a religious ideology that had large consequences for the European world order of the sixteenth and seventeenth centuries, including playing a crucial role in the rise of the Dutch hegemony.

The Dutch Hegemony: The First Capitalist Core State

The main difference between the modern world-system and earlier world-systems is that commodity production and profit making have become the predominant modes of accumulation at the center of the system. In the Roman Empire and many other precapitalist world-systems, there was much commodity production and market exchange, but it flourished mainly on the

[6] International organizations have explicitly national subunits, while transnational organizations do not, but the memberships cross international boundaries.

[7] The notion that non-secular political organizations were "traditional" and that functional groups would be mainly represented by secular organizations has allowed social movement theory to largely ignore religious movements and organizations. This is a huge problem for understanding both the early modern world-systems and the contemporary scene.

[8] Stephen Gill (2000, 2003) adopts a similarly broad and flexible definition of "political party" in order to discuss contemporary developments. Gill also makes the important point that all global political parties are not progressive. A more complete survey would include these.

edges or in the spaces between the institutions of state-based accumulation. In Rome (a relatively commercialized but still predominantly tributary system), production for the market and retail commerce was mainly the business of dependents of the ruling-class families and freed slaves, or the specialty of semiperipheral trading states such as the Phoenicians. The "perspective of the world" was a game played mainly by men who used state power as the primary instrument for obtaining wealth and prestige. It was the emergence of a different kind of state in the core region of the European world economy, the hegemonic Dutch state employing its military capabilities primarily to provide protection rent[9] to its capitalists, that signaled the consolidation of a world region in which capitalism had become the predominant mode of production.

The Dutch revolution was perhaps the most significant development in which the Protestant Reformation played an important role in the development of capitalism. The growing trade connections between the Baltic Sea and the North Sea (forged by the Hanseatic League of German city-states) with the Eastern Atlantic and the Mediterranean Sea provided a central network niche for the merchants of Antwerp in Burgundy (now Belgium). Antwerp was the key world city linking all these regions in the sixteenth century (Braudel 1984). The Protestants were strong in Burgundy, a state that was tributary to Philip II, the "most Catholic king" of Spain. Philip organized the Spanish Inquisition to expose the heretics, especially Moors and Jews who had converted to Catholicism after the Christians had reconquered Southern Spain. When Protestant extremists burned down the cathedral in Antwerp, Philip sent a large army under the Duke of Alva, and also the huge Spanish Armada of warships by sea, to bring the rebellion to heel. The Protestant forces had to retreat into a nearly impenetrable wetland region, later to be known as the Netherlands. With the help of the English navy and a violent storm in the English Channel, the newly formed Dutch navy defeated the Spanish Armada in 1588, and the Duke of Alva's soldiers bogged down in the swamps. The rebels founded a new city, Amsterdam, and invited immigrants from all over Europe, and especially victims of the Inquisition, to become citizens of this unusually cosmopolitan city.

The newly formed Dutch Republic was a constitutional federation of provinces in which the central government had formally limited powers. Within this confederation of provinces, Holland (the province of Amsterdam) played a leading role. The House of Orange, a landowning aristocratic lineage, served as hereditary nobility, a political necessity for becoming a player in the still-monarchical state system of Europe. Amsterdam struggled with the land-based House of Orange, but this did not much interfere with the profit-oriented policies of the Dutch state. The Dutch nobles were greatly dependent on the wealth and international connections of the merchants and bankers of Amsterdam, who used Dutch naval power to insert themselves into the commercial niche formerly held by Antwerp.

The Dutch revolution produced a rather democratic and federally structured state that was mainly under the control of capitalist merchants, capital-intensive farmers, and finance capitalists. This was the most significant outcome of the first world revolution. A semiperipheral region had risen to core status and formed a core nation-state under the control of capitalists. This was very significant for the process of core formation in Europe and the emergence of a capitalist world region.

Amsterdam replaced Antwerp as the predominant world city of the era because the Dutch navy was able to blockade Antwerp's access to the sea. Dutch merchant capitalism brought the products of the European continent, the Baltic,

[9] As explained in Chapter 8, the concept of "protection rent" was developed by Frederic Lane (1979), the historian of Venice (1973), to explain the relationship between profit making and the provision of security by "violence-controlling enterprises" such as the Venetian state. Protection rent is not the returns to the state for providing protection; rather, it is the additional returns obtained by a businessman who receives protection at (or below) cost compared with competing businessmen in other states who are charged more for their protection than it costs. Lane understood that Venetian capitalists were making greater returns than were the businessmen of other states with whom they were competing because the government of Venice was providing naval protection for overseas trade enterprises at cost.

the Mediterranean, and the East and West Indies to the warehouses of Amsterdam (Misra and Boswell 1997). It was purportedly cheaper to buy French wine in Amsterdam than to buy it in France because the huge volume of trade allowed the Dutch merchants great leverage with producers. These were the "buyer-driven **commodity chains**" of the seventeenth century. Students of contemporary globalization describe this very kind of business organization, in which large retailers such as Walmart dominate small producers. Buyer-driven commodity chains and supply chain capitalism are not forms of business organization that are unique to the last few decades.

But Dutch capitalism was not only merchant capitalism (buying cheap and selling dear). It was also financial capital, production capital, and agricultural capital. Indeed, the Dutch economy underwent an industrial revolution in the late sixteenth and early seventeenth centuries that was comparable in scope to the more famous Industrial Revolution in England in the eighteenth and nineteenth centuries. The Amsterdam Bourse was a modern stock and commodity exchange that traded the shares of great chartered companies—the precursors of the modern multinational corporations. The VOC (the Dutch East India Company) organized trade and production on a global scale in the early seventeenth century.

The Dutch Revolution created a republican federation in which the seafaring capitalists of Amsterdam held considerable power. The religious wars of the Protestant Reformation and the Catholic Restoration brought refugees to tolerant Amsterdam with their skills and whatever capital they could manage to bring with them. Citizenship in Amsterdam could be purchased for a nominal sum of money (Barbour 1963). Competitive advantage in production was first developed in the herring fisheries, which captured a large share of this staple food market in the expanding Atlantic economy. Salted herring is a source of protein that can be stored for long periods, making it a valuable commodity for long-distance trade.

Shipbuilding was another leg of Dutch core production that enabled merchants to outcompete Hanse and English competitors in the carrying trade. The cost-efficient fluyt was easily adapted to many specialized uses and effectively manned by small crews. Angus Maddison (1982, 35, table 2.2) shows that the Dutch economy was much more industrialized in 1700 than was the British economy. Both Maddison and Wallerstein (1974b) contend that the Dutch hegemony was based on production capital in lead industries, contrary to those who have seen the Dutch primarily as merchant capitalists.

The Dutch shipbuilding industry not only supplied the navy with ships and bronze canons (manufactured by Dutch-owned canon foundries in Sweden), but also produced customized and efficient ships for the slave trade and the herring fishery. Using timber imported from the Baltic, a standardized capacious hull design was fitted out for specialized purposes. Dutch herring ships have been described as factories on the sea, catching and salting herring to produce this valuable food export. The slave ships were designed to securely transport as many as three hundred slaves with a small crew of seven sailors (see Figure 14.2). Dutch slavers used these ships to carry Africans to the Americas, and the customized ships were also profitably sold as capital goods to the slavers of other European powers.

The Dutch hegemony was made possible by state support for private profit making in the world economy and a comparative advantage in emerging very profitable key industries and trades. In more recent parlance this is called the "developmental state." The Dutch economic and political hegemony peaked in the middle decades of the seventeenth century. The Dutch Golden Age was contemporaneous with the economic and demographic contraction that occurred in most of the rest of Europe and much of Asia during the seventeenth century. Dutch art, science, philosophy, and political-economic theory were at the cutting edge of the European Enlightenment. The Stadtholder (mayor) of Amsterdam, Johan DeWitt, wrote a defense of the universal superiority of free trade that was an important precursor of the economic theory of Scottish moral philosopher Adam Smith. Smith's *Wealth of Nations* was not published until 1776. Hugo Grotius, a Dutch legal philosopher and founder of international law, propounded the idea that the oceans should be a global commons with free access unobstructed by any state. The alliance with the English against Spain eventually foundered and devolved into the Anglo-Dutch wars over competing business and colonial interests.

Figure 14.2 The Dutch fluyt (replica)

The Dutch colonial empire followed the Portuguese into the East Indies and established outposts in the Americas, including New Amsterdam, later to become New York under the English. The Dutch East India Company and the Amsterdam Bourse thrived even while the boom of the long sixteenth century slowed down to become the crisis of the seventeenth century.

The Dutch state is often seen as small relative to the other European states of the time. It was not large, but it was unusually strong because it received great support from a wealthy business class (Braudel 1984, 193–195). DeWitt could sell enough bonds in a day on the Amsterdam Bourse to defeat any sea power in the world. It has been said that the Dutch state was often in turmoil because of differences between the business interests of Amsterdam and those of the land-oriented House of Orange, but in comparison to the other contemporary core states, the capitalists had great sway indeed. During national calamities, the princes of Orange rallied the populace to defend the nation, while during peacetime the less patriotic urban capitalists had their way.[10] The federation and the republican form of government enabled the state to adapt easily to changing economic and military contingencies and the shifting interests of the political coalition of businessmen that was its main constituency.

The Dutch intelligentsia propagated the ideology of free trade and the rights of all nations to use of the seas during the period in which economic competitive advantage enabled the Amsterdam capitalists to undersell all competitors (C. H. Wilson 1957). This was quite compatible with the policy of "armed trade" employed in the periphery to deprive the Portuguese of their monopoly of spices from the East Indies (Parry 1966). Violet Barbour (1963) has contended that in many respects Amsterdam was a city-state, more similar to Venice and Genoa than to England or the United States, and Fernand Braudel (1984) concurs. The Dutch orientation toward the seafaring international market was undiluted by commitments to continental territorial

[10] The transnational links and activities of the Dutch capitalists were strong enough to overcome whatever patriotic qualms they may have had. Dutch-owned canon-making firms in Sweden were suspected of selling weapons to states that were actively engaged in wars with the United Provinces of the Netherlands.

aggrandizement. In this respect it was much like Venice. Recall that the Venetian city-state was the leading semiperipheral capitalist city-state during the first wave of European expansion. Peter Burke's (1974) fascinating comparison of Dutch and Venetian entrepreneurs (venture capitalists) and rentiers (coupon-clipping finance capitalists who collect rents and loan money at interest) shows the growth of rentier activity as comparative advantages in production declined in both Venice and the Dutch Republic. Barbour's contention that Amsterdam was a city-state suggests a succession from true city-state (Venice, Genoa), to half-nation state (the Dutch Republic), to full nation-state (the United Kingdom), to continental-sized federal nation-state (the United States). Capitalist hegemons have become larger and larger as capitalism has become more predominant and as the Central PMN has become global.

Frederic Lane, the great historian of Venice (1973), observed that the Venetian ruling classes became land oriented during the period of their decline, and he interprets this as an attempt to form a larger nation-state that could compete with the other emerging national states of Europe. The United Provinces of the Netherlands may seem to have been rather small in terms of land area and population size compared to the other states of Europe, but it nevertheless played the role of hegemonic core state rather effectively during the seventeenth century. It was an economic fore-reacher, and it also played an important geopolitical role in the further institutionalization of state sovereignty and international law in the European interstate system. As mentioned above, the Dutch Republic may be seen as a kind of midpoint between Venice and England in the sequence of the development of capitalist states and modern hegemons. The hegemonic state became increasingly a nation-state, and the size of the national market became larger and larger, with the US national market being an immense share of the world economy in which it has been hegemonic.

The War of Spanish Succession (1701–1748) resulted in the exhaustion of Dutch resources and the fall of the Netherlands from leading status, but it did not result in the immediate emergence of a successor hegemonic state. France was weakened but still strong, maintaining possession of some of its European conquests, including the rich province of Alsace and the city of Strasbourg. Its colonial empire was still extensive and Louis XIV's grandson retained the throne of Spain. England was strengthened but not yet preponderant. Spain held on to its American empire, and Austria gained extensive territories on the European continent. Louis XIV (the French Sun King who built Versailles) tried unsuccessfully to expand his monarchy over other lands during the decline of Dutch hegemony, but this effort was quelled by a coalition led by the still-influential Dutch Republic.

The Dutch case fits Immanuel Wallerstein's three stages of hegemony rather well. Wallerstein (1984) contended that hegemonic economic comparative advantage first emerges in the production of new consumption goods. This advantage is lost as foreign competitors adopt and improve upon the production of these goods. In the case of the Dutch, this was the herring fishery, the Baltic trades, and the production of dairy-based food products. Wallerstein's second stage of economic hegemony is based on capital goods. Here the Dutch sold ships and canons, and invested in further land reclamation projects based on the building of dikes and the draining of wetlands. When the comparative advantage in capital goods passes, as foreign competition emerges, the capitalists of the hegemonic state increasingly shift over to financial services: international banking, investments abroad, insurance, the selling of securities, and making money by buying and selling money. The hegemon exploits the centrality of the position it has developed in the world economy based on its earlier comparative advantages in consumer and capital goods. In the case of the Dutch, this financialization stage was seen in the shift toward financial services, the export of capital, and the transformation of the Dutch capitalists from entrepreneurs to rentiers (Burke 1974).[11] Amsterdam remains an important center of international commerce and financial services three hundred years after it lost first position.

[11] The queen of the Netherlands owns buildings on Washington, DC's Massachusetts Avenue that are rented as the embassies of many nations.

National Sovereignty and the Peace of Westphalia

In 1648 the Peace of Westphalia officially ended the Thirty Years' War and firmly established the principle of national sovereignty in the European state system. Many earlier interpolity systems had evolved formal institutions for regulating conflict, protecting the sovereignty of polities, guaranteeing safe passage and trade, and so on. Ethnographic evidence tells of some of these institutions in interchiefdom systems, and archaeological evidence indicates the existence of buffer zones between warring chiefdoms. The Sumerian interstate system maintained a balance of power among eight or nine sovereign city-states during the early dynastic period from ca. 3000 BCE to ca. 2375 BCE. This was an instance of an early noncapitalist world economy and interstate system that refrained from turning into a core-wide empire for over six hundred years.

The Peace of Westphalia further institutionalized and codified the interstate system of competing and sovereign states in the European core and set up institutions to protect national self-determination. Some call this a world revolution in which the old imperial world order was restructured into a new world order based on national sovereignty. But the rules did not apply to the regions of the rest of the world that were becoming increasingly peripheralized as the colonial empires of European core states. It was only after the most recent wave of decolonization in the 1960s that the rest of the world was incorporated into the system of sovereign states that was encoded at Westphalia.

The Westphalian treaty can be understood as extending and expanding the international laws and practices that had been developed on the Italian Peninsula among the city-states of the first wave of European expansion. The Italian system of competing and allying city-states that was presumed in Machiavelli's *The Prince* was expanded into a Europe-wide system of increasingly national states. The institutions of diplomacy (e.g., diplomatic immunity) were well developed by the Italians. Westphalia further elaborated international law[12] and formalized the sovereign right of states to defend themselves against aggression. The balance of power mechanism that was codified was the notion of general war, in which any "rogue state" that attacks another state is vulnerable to legitimate retaliation by all the other states in the system. This commits all the signatories to the protection of the sovereignty of each. It is a rule that defends the individual players against the "duck shoot strategy," in which one aggressor state picks on the weakest of a set of states, builds up its power in a series of conquests, and then "rolls up the system."

The general game logic of the balance of power, in which smaller polities ally against larger ones, undoubtedly operated in interchiefdom systems and early interstate systems. But codifying the responsibilities of member states to defend one another's sovereignty has been an important factor, along with the emergence of capitalism, protecting the modern interstate system against the formation of a world state by conquest.

Semiperipheral England in the seventeenth century experienced a complex revolution in which Protestants cut off the king's head and Parliament exercised the power of a new class of business elites against the traditional privileges of the landed aristocracy. The waves of privatization that were the enclosures of the commons engendered resistance from those who lost their rights to use the formerly public lands. These "commonists" found support in the Bible (e.g., Jubilee, Book of James) for their claims to popular access to land. The most radical of these were the True Levelers, or Diggers, who organized collective rural communes and protested exclusion from formerly public lands by planting turnips on the king's land. The Diggers renounced violence and embraced civil disobedience. Gerrard Winstanley (1609–1676), one of the founders of the True Levelers, coauthored a famous pamphlet called the "True Levelers Standard Advanced," which proclaimed:

> And we shall not do this through force of Arms, we abhorre it, For that is the work

[12] International law is a set of codified rules that are agreed upon in treaties among sovereign states. International law is not true law in the sense meant by Max Weber (1978, 33–36), because no state exercises legitimate coercion to enforce international law. To have true world law in the Weberian sense would require a world state.

> of the *Midianites* to kill one another; But by obeying the Lord of Hosts, who hath Revealed himself in us, and to us, by labouring the Earth in righteousness together, to eate our bread with the sweat of our brows, neither giving hire, nor taking hire, but working together, and eating together, as one man, or as one house of Israel restored from Bondage; and so by the power of Reason, the Law of righteousness in us, we endeavour to lift up the Creation from that bondage of Civil Propriety, which it groans under.

At the same time, multicultural and interracial challenges by slaves, impressed sailors, indentured servants, landless farmers, and disgruntled tradesmen to hierarchical power in England and the Atlantic world were given additional impetus by the reports of relatively egalitarian and communal societies discovered by the colonists of the New World. John Smith's published observations of his life with the indigenous Powhatans on the James River in Virginia painted a picture of natural freedom that would have a powerful effect on the imaginations of the egalitarian rebels in England (Linebaugh and Rediker 2000; see Figure 14.3).

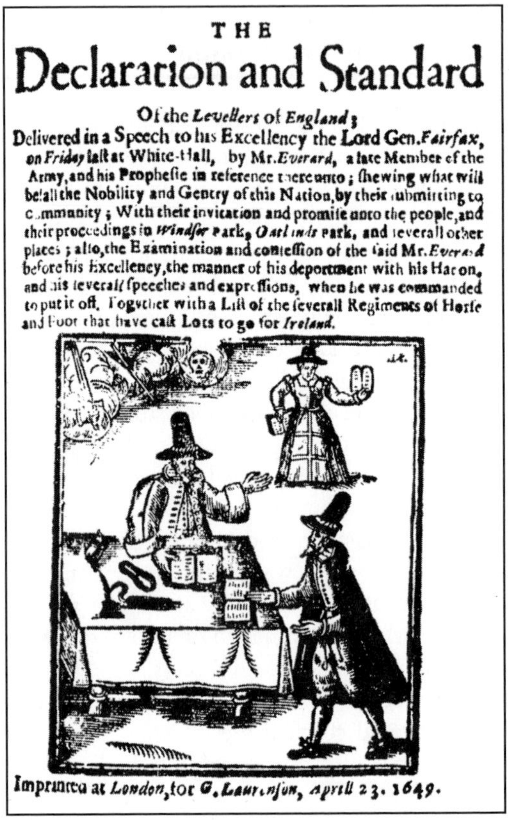
THE

Declaration and Standard

Of the *Levellers* of *England*;

Delivered in a Speech to his Excellency the Lord Gen. *Fairfax*, on *Friday* last at White-Hall, by Mr. *Everard*, a late Member of the Army, and his Prophesie in reference thereunto; shewing what will befall the Nobility and Gentry of this Nation, by their submitting to community; With their invitation and promise unto the people, and their proceedings in *Windsor* park, *Oatlands* park, and severall other places; also, the Examination and confession of the said Mr. *Everard* before his Excellency, the manner of his deportment with his Hat on, and his severall speeches and expressions, when he was commanded to put it off. Together with a List of the severall Regiments of Horse and Foot that have cast Lots to go for *Ireland*.

Imprinted at *London*, for *G. Laurenson*, *Aprill* 23. 1649.

Figure 14.3 ***The True Levelers Standard Advanced*** **(1649) woodcut from a Diggers document by William Everard**

The institution of slavery was originally not associated with race. Challenges to the practice of slavery by the radicals in the English revolution produced the racialization of slavery such that Africans became identified as slaves, while Englishmen were increasingly understood to have rights that precluded involuntary servitude. Resistance to the impressment of men for service in the Royal Navy became quite intense, especially in the colonies where the boats of press gangs were regularly hauled up on shore and burned. The law of habeas corpus eventually emerged to protect citizens against imprisonment and seizure without due process. Related demands for radical egalitarianism have recurred in all of the subsequent world revolutions.

The Cromwellian phase of the English revolution suppressed the radicals and established a new, more commodified form of the legal protection of large-scale private property and slavery.

During a period of rivalry between Britain and France for European hegemony in the eighteenth century, slaves, peasants, the urban poor, and sailors began to systematically resist and to challenge the power of core states and business elites, and the American, French, and Haitian revolutions were important outcomes of these forms of transnational resistance from below (Linebaugh and Rediker 2000). The Haitian revolution, in which slaves came to power in the French sugar colony of St. Dominique, had a large impact on slave revolts and abolition movements elsewhere, and on the outcome of the struggle between France and England. The eighteenth-century movements from below had powerful effects on the outcomes of competition and conflict among global elites. Local and regional social movements (e.g., slave rebellions, indigenous revolts, pirates) affected the structures of global governance and the rise and fall of competing hegemonic core states. The Haitian revolution, itself a spin-off of the American and French revolutions, played an important role in Britain's defeat of Napoleonic France and thus in ushering in the nineteenth-century British hegemony, the decolonization of Latin America, and a new wave of capitalist globalization. Reports of the actions of the rebels fired resistance across the "Revolutionary Atlantic," but there was little in the way of coordinated action across great distances. Rather, the rebellions had their effects on the powerful mainly by clustering many local activities during the same decades (Santiago-Valles 2005).

Hegemonic Rivalry in the Eighteenth Century

After the decline of the Dutch hegemony, there was a long period of struggle between France and England for preeminence in the Central PMN. Recall that the Anglo-Dutch alliance had foundered in the seventeenth century. Both England and France followed the example of the Portuguese, the Spanish, and the Dutch in acquiring colonial empires in Asia and the Americas and further expanding the Central PMN. During periods of warfare among the European powers, the overseas colonies would change hands, and so wars took on a global aspect as the whole world came to be divided up by the colonial imperialism of the European states.

This was the period of the expansion of what Philip Curtin (1990) has called "the plantation complex," in which African slaves were forced to grow cash crops, especially sugar cane but also tobacco, indigo, and rice, on the islands of the West Indies and in North and South America. The first wave of exploitation of mineral raw materials evolved into an expansion in many regions of **latifundia**, large tracts of agricultural land that were used to produce cash crops for export to the European core. Indigenous peoples were often culturally unsuited to the kinds of labor mobilization required for the plantation complex, and they soon died of diseases. Africans had known a form of slavery and could survive the kind of labor required to grow, harvest, and process sugar, so the Europeans raided African societies for captives and purchased African slaves from states such as Dahomey. Sidney Mintz's (1974) important study of the Caribbean sugar islands notes the close connections between developing industrial production technology and organization in Europe and in the plantation complex, which he calls "factories in the field" because of the increasingly systematic organization of sugar production. Mintz (1985) also points out the importance of the consumption of jam, sugar, and tea by the English middle and working classes for incorporating them into the imperial project.

The competition between England and France had, of course, been ongoing for centuries. The Norman Conquest and a series of wars in which England and France had endeavored to take over each other's home territories had evolved into a competition for predominance in the larger interstate system and for profit-making opportunities in the world market. The successful integration of the French state with its capital in Paris had brought a very large territory under the jurisdiction of a single monarchy. Defending the borders and trying to find policies that could fit the interests of very different regions required great resources and difficult compromises. England's process of state formation and nation building was also long and difficult, involving the conquest and integration of the "Celtic fringe" (Wales, Scotland, and Ireland) into the United Kingdom of Great Britain, but the geographic situation was different. Because it was an island, the center did not have to spend as much to defend the borders against attacking armies, and it also encouraged investment in seagoing trade and naval power. These activities encouraged the pursuit of the trading nation niche and the exploitation of distant colonies.

At first, the English mainly focused on raiding Spanish galleons and claiming uncharted lands for the Crown. English nation building in the sixteenth century involved a crackdown on "foreigners" in London. The government of Queen Elizabeth acted to exclude the German Hanse merchants and Jewish traders[13] who had been important businessmen in London involved in the export of English wool to the textile

[13] Why do Shakespeare's plays display such aggressive anti-Semitism (e.g., Shylock in *The Merchant of Venice*)? The playwright reflected the spirit of his time, in which English nationalism was on the rise and foreigners were subjected to legal and social discrimination.

industries of the Netherlands and Belgium. The presence of a large bale of wool in Parliament is mute testimony to the early market and export orientation of English landholders. Domestic producers were encouraged by Elizabethan tariffs on the importation of textiles to use the raw English wool to produce yarn and cloth in an example of import substitution. The English Merchant Adventurers was formed, and the English East India Company began its business in India and the East Indies. These enterprises were spurred both by competition with the Dutch and by Dutch encouragement. The empowerment of a domestic class of merchants and manufacturers and the integration of some of them into the governing class of England during the time of Queen Elizabeth and the later English civil wars played an important part in the shift of the English state away from a tributary orientation toward the role of the developmental state.

This process of domestic business-class formation had an interesting counterpoint in peripheralizing Poland, where large Polish landowners were encouraging the immigration of Jewish merchants just as they were being kicked out of London. This retarded the emergence of an indigenous Polish capitalist class that might have challenged the landed aristocrats for political power[14] and created what has been called a "middle-man minority" of Jewish merchants and moneylenders in Polish cities and rural towns. This, and the expansion of capitalist serfdom in Poland, constituted a core/periphery differentiation between Northwestern and Eastern Europe that was to last for centuries.

This was England's first sustained bid to move up in the emerging core/periphery division of labor from a semiperipheral exporter of raw materials to a producer of manufactured goods for export. English state power was also used to expand the role of private property and production for the market by means of the enclosures of the commons. Feudal custom had provided use rights to landless peasants on large tracts of rural lands. The enclosures privatized these tracts and encouraged investments in the production of agricultural commodities. The commercialization of the English countryside drove peasants to the cities or motivated their participation in the rural "cottage industry," in which they spun yarn and wove cloth in their rural homes (Kriedte, Medick, and Schlumbohm 1981). The English state also legislated poor laws and debtor's prisons and expanded urban police forces to deal with the "dangerous classes" that economic reorganization had produced (Polanyi 2001).

The seventeenth-century English revolutions, like those of the Dutch, exhibited relative egalitarianism, pluralism, and the firm incorporation of diverse capitalist interests into a flexible state capable of mobilizing immense resources for international war while maintaining a somewhat sparse and inexpensive peacetime bureaucracy. It was Protestant Roundhead Oliver Cromwell who conquered Ireland. The unity of the coalition of different elite groups in Great Britain was not without contention, but the agrarian capitalist landowners were much more integrated into successful production for the world market and involvement in overseas colonial ventures than were the aristocrats of France.

The English depleted their own forests for fuel and building timber for cities and ships and were prodigious importers of wood from the Baltic and from the American colonies. The rising cost of wood was an important element in the expansion of the use of coal for heating, and England had its own large supply of coal mines in Wales and Newcastle. The shift to coal was the beginning of a transition from the wood and water power energy regime to the regime of coal that was to follow (Podobnik 2006). Pomeranz (2000) contends that it was the need to pump water out of the coal mines that was the most important stimulus behind the invention of the steam engine in England, a development that had enormous consequences for the expansion of the use of fossil fuel to power industry and transportation.

The French monarchy played an important great power role at several crucial junctures in the history of the European interstate system. Paris was not only the uncontested center of France, but also a great world city of cultural refinement, learning, science, and philosophy. The styles of

[14] The Jews were also invited to help challenge the power of German merchants in Danzig (Gdansk), an important port city in Poland that had long been dominated by the Hanseatic League of German merchants.

France's urbane elite were emulated from St. Petersburg to London, and the French language became the European language of diplomacy.

The French colonial empire spread to all the continents as the French and English states sought to emulate and outcompete the earlier European colonial empires. French Canada and Louisiana and the penetration of French explorers and trappers into the North American wilderness pushed the frontier outward. The French sugar plantation colony of St. Dominique was one of the largest sugar producers in the West Indies. The French set up a trading enclave at Pondicherry in South Asia to contend with the English expansion on that subcontinent as the Mughal Empire built by Akbar began to decline.

Capitalism developed in France along with its expansion in other European core areas, but the French landed aristocracy remained strong and disinclined to support capitalistic ventures at home or abroad. France was a case of too large a nation-state in which the formation of the Absolute Monarchy was necessitated by the divergent interests of economic regions (Braudel 1984, 315–351). The cities of the western coast (e.g., Nantes) were anxious to participate in the expanding Atlantic economy, while the older Mediterranean-oriented Occitania (Wallerstein 1974b, 262–269; 1980) displayed the tendencies of downward mobility characteristic of other areas that were becoming semiperipheral to the emerging core region of Europe. The mercantilist and industrializing policies of Jean Baptiste Colbert were undercut by the renewed focus on continental diplomacy and political-military aggrandizement (Lane 1966). The "bourgeois revolution" was delayed until 1789, by which time England had stolen the march on the newly emerging core industries. Paris remained the cultural and diplomatic center of Europe, while London became the hegemonic world city of the global economy.

The eighteenth century was a century of world wars between France and Britain for primacy of place in the Central PMN. The Seven Years' War (1756–1763) was both a global struggle between England and France and a continental struggle among contenders for upward mobility in Europe. Hinsley (1967, 176) emphasizes the relative degree of equality that characterized the leading states in the eighteenth century. Similarly, Ralph Davis (1973, 288) contends that the British economic hegemony achieved in the nineteenth century could not have been predicted a century earlier. The hierarchical structure of the core was fluid, and wars like the Seven Years' War facilitated the rise to prominence of expanding states like Prussia and Russia. The Seven Years' War linked the conflict among Prussia, Austria, and Russia for core status with the struggles between Britain and France for control of the resources of the periphery.

In US history books, the Seven Years' War is called the French and Indian Wars because the French colonists of North America allied with several powerful Native American tribes in their struggles with the British. Other tribes allied with the British (e.g., the Cherokee), and these alliances were important factors in the struggle for survival among Native American groups (Dunaway 1996). The British victories in key battles in North America reduced the power position of the French in North America and reduced the dependence of the English colonists on the support of the British army and navy, thereby facilitating the possibility of independence from the mother country. The American Independence was the first salvo of another world revolution that extended national sovereignty to much of the American periphery, the first wave of decolonization discussed in Chapter 13. The symbolic year chosen to represent this world revolution is 1789, the year of the French Revolution, but this world revolution included the American Independence, the Haitian Revolution, and the revolt of the Spanish colonies of Latin America led by Simon Bolivar that extended into the 1820s.

The expenses of the Seven Years' War, the victory of British over French forces on many fronts, and the subsequent costs of supporting the American colonial revolution weakened the French monarchy at home. The French Revolution of 1789 was made in the name of the ideals of the European Enlightenment—liberty, equality, and fraternity.[15] This was both the late

[15] Chou Enlai, Mao Zedong's foreign minister, was asked in the 1950s what he thought about the consequences of the French Revolution. He replied that it was "too soon to tell."

coming of the "bourgeois revolution" in France and the continuation of another challenge to the institutions of the geoculture. The French Revolution brought an end to the monarchy and evolved into another effort to establish a core-wide empire in the Napoleonic Wars. Though the British economy was more industrialized and urbanized than the French economy at the beginning of the nineteenth century, the outcome of the Napoleonic Wars was by no means a certain thing. Great Britain's ability to mobilize allies against Napoleon was good but not great. The French citizen armies won many victories, and Napoleon's navy was also formidable. But Napoleon committed the classical mistake of imperial overstretch in his march on Russia, and in the end the British were victorious, ushering in the hegemony of the nineteenth century that will be a main topic of the next chapter.

Tributary States in the Early Modern Period

The early modern story is not only the story of Europe, though some of the focus on Europe is due to more than Eurocentrism. It is true that Europe was unique with regard to the extent to which capitalism developed and was able to become institutionalized. The use of state power in the service of capitalist accumulation in certain key states, especially the Netherlands and the United Kingdom of Great Britain, did not completely eliminate the tributary mode of production in Europe. Indeed, many of the policies of even the most capitalist states are quite similar to tributary accumulation, especially in peripheral colonies. Marx called this "primitive accumulation," implying that coercion is necessary for setting up the institutional bases of capitalist accumulation, but that once set up, the institutions of capitalism can dispense with coercive power. But latter-day Marxists have increasingly come to realize that primitive accumulation is not just a stage at the beginning but rather an option that is repeatedly employed within the real world of capitalist accumulation even into the present. David Harvey (2003) uses the term "primary accumulation" to designate this recognition. While the most successful European states were also the most capitalist states, they have been repeatedly challenged by powers that were much more reliant on state-based coercion (e.g., Napoleonic France, Germany in the twentieth century). And so even though we call the modern world-system capitalist, the tributary mode of production is still with us.

The story in South, East, and West Asia is similarly complicated. The shorthand version is that the tributary mode remained predominant, which is the main reason why Europe was eventually able to get the upper hand. But the early modern Asian tributary states—the "gunpowder empires" mentioned above—became quite commercialized. Production for the market, contractually based labor relations, commodified property, and monetized exchange were highly developed. The ability of the Asian tributary states to maintain centralized state power (and to prevent the emergence of capitalist political power) was at least partly due to their successful adaptation to the market processes that were emerging within them.

In 1644 the Ming dynasty fell to another semiperipheral marcher state, this time from the forest zone to the north. The Jurchen (Jin) dynasty had emerged from Manchuria in the twelfth century to conquer northern China. It was an important precursor of the Manchu conquest and an indication that the tribal forest dwellers of the north were undergoing state formation. Like the earlier semiperipheral marcher states, the Manchus produced a powerful military machine that was able to defeat the Ming armies and conquer China. The resulting Qing dynasty substituted itself for the Han Chinese elite but compromised with the Han by incorporating them into all the levels of the Qing bureaucracy.

China had experienced waves of marketization of the economy since the Sung dynasty, when paper money was invented and a formidable iron industry flourished. But the rise and fall of Chinese dynasties, with peripheral and semiperipheral conquests and nativist restorations, reproduced, albeit at intervals, a strong centralized tributary state that was able to keep merchants, finance capitalists, and industrialists from taking state power themselves. The Columbian exchange with the Americas brought several new crops to East Asia that enabled more intensive exploitation of the land and the production of far more food. This facilitated the growth of large cities and rapid population growth. The marketized economy grew fast, and the Qing dynasty organized effective responses to floods and famines that protected peasants to some extent from exploitation by grain merchants and local gentry. The establishment of local public granaries and the storage of grain surpluses were effective institutions for preventing market-based exploitation and famine (M. Davis 2003). But population growth outstripped the growth of the economy, producing large numbers of landless peasants and unemployed workers.

A series of peasant movements, based on egalitarian ideologies and vegetarianism (such as the White Lotus movements), recruited supporters from these marginal groups (Hung 2005). These radical movements sometimes favored the expulsion of the Manchus as well as the redistribution of land, and so the Qing dynasty repressed them. In order to maintain a centralized state, the Qing dynasty embraced neo-Confucianism, a conservative hierarchical ideology of obedience to the patriarchs. But the Qing also made a great show of paternal responsibility toward the peasantry, which provided good excuses for cracking down on regional gentry and rich merchants whenever they sought to challenge the power and policies of the Manchu government in Beijing. Nascent regional trading states in the south occasionally challenged Qing control, but they were successfully subdued by the centralized tributary state in Beijing. Thus was the emergence of a capitalist state in China prevented.

The early modern world-systems were developing commodified relations and contractual law, but only in Europe did capitalists take state power in the core. The transition from Venice to Amsterdam represented the rise of the logic of capitalist accumulation to state power in a regional system. This had huge consequences for Europe and for the world.

Suggested Readings

Arrighi, Giovanni. 1994. *The Long Twentieth Century*. London: Verso.

Batten, Bruce L. 2003. *To the Ends of Japan*. Honolulu: University of Hawaii Press.

Braudel, Fernand. 1984. *The Perspective of the World*. Vol. 3 of *Civilization and Capitalism*. Berkeley: University of California Press.

Crosby, Alfred W. Jr. 1972. *The Columbian Exchange: Biological and Cultural Consequences of 1492*. Westport, CT: Greenwood Press.

Curtin, Philip D. 1990. *The Rise and Fall of the Plantation Complex*. Cambridge: Cambridge University Press.

Frank, Andre Gunder. 1997. *Reorient*. Berkeley: University of California Press.

Kennedy, Paul. 1988. *The Rise and Fall of the Great Powers: Economic Change and Military Conflict from 1500–2000*. New York: Random House.

Linebaugh, Peter, and Marcus Rediker. 2000. *The Many-Headed Hydra: Sailors, Slaves, Commoners and the Hidden History of the Revolutionary Atlantic*. Boston: Beacon.

Rediker, Marcus. 2007. *The Slave Ship: A Human History*. New York: Viking.

Schurz, W. L. 1959. *The Manila Galleon*. New York: E. P. Dutton.

Wallerstein, Immanuel. 1974. *The Modern World-System: Capitalist Agriculture and the Origins of the European World-Economy in the Sixteenth Century*. New York: Academic Press.

15

The Global Nineteenth Century

This chapter tells the story of the great wave of globalization in the nineteenth century. The rise and fall of British hegemony, the world revolution of 1848, the merger of the East Asian system into the Central System, and the rise of the United States are important parts of this story. The British hegemony was based on a second industrial revolution that began in England in the middle of the eighteenth century and spread to the other core and upwardly mobile semiperipheral areas. European interlopers surrounded China, and Japan leapt onto the global stage. The United States rose from the periphery to the core in the nineteenth century. And another world revolution emerged in the middle of the century. International trade and investment rose to a high peak in 1880, and the spread of the Industrial Revolution and the intensification of global markets allowed other core and semiperipheral states to challenge the economic and political hegemony of the United Kingdom. The British resisted the changing structure of economic power, and a new period of hegemonic rivalry emerged at the end of the nineteenth century.

The eighteenth-century struggle between Britain and France for global hegemony ended in 1815 with Napoleon's defeat. British forces tried to reconquer their lost colonies in North America in 1812. The new capitol building in Washington, DC, was burned to the ground, but US forces held in New Orleans and at Fort McHenry in Baltimore Harbor. Frances Scott Key wrote the poem that would become the US national anthem while watching British ships bombard Fort McHenry to no avail. The flag was still there. The story of the long rise of the United States is below, but first let us look at the British hegemony.

Modern hegemony is based on a complicated combination of economic comparative advantage, military superiority, and political consensus. It is both leadership and domination. British resolve had vanquished Napoleon and saved Europe from another marcher state conquest, but this did not completely resolve the issues that had been posed in the world revolution of 1789. Demands for democracy did not end with the defeat of Napoleon. The decolonized US republic survived, and the Haitian Revolution created a new state run by former slaves in the Caribbean. The ideals of the French and American revolutions had spread widely in Europe, the European colonies, and the uncolonized regions.

British industrialization was going great guns, and the Industrial Revolution was spreading to the European continent and to North America. The nature of business organization was evolving from the more corporate, centralized,

Brooklyn Bridge: A wood engraving by Rudolph Rusicka
Source: Wikipedia Commons.

and formally regulated structures typified by the English East India Company to the decentralized, informally regulated, and flexibly organized networks of firms that emerged in the late eighteenth and early nineteenth centuries in Britain (Barr 1999). In the English Midlands, the new industrial cities of Manchester and Birmingham were using steam engines to power huge spinning and weaving machines to produce cotton cloth in large factories. The demand for labor to supply, tend, and maintain the machines created and expanded a new class of urban industrial workers. Vast amounts of raw cotton were imported to feed the machines, and vast amounts of cloth for sails and apparel were produced. This product could be profitably sold both in the home market and abroad for a low price, and so the English manufacturers had a substantial comparative advantage with which to penetrate the home markets of other countries.

In this first phase of British hegemony, economic comparative advantage was combined with both political conservatism and some selected progressive international policies that were substantially congruent with the economic interests of the British elites. Conservatism was revealed in the repression of Chartism (an early trade union movement) at home, and in Britain's strong support of the organization of the Concert of Europe in the international arena. The suppression of the Chartists was accomplished by outlawing unions (so-called combinations). The Concert of Europe was a formally organized supernational alliance of European governments, the purpose of which was to prevent future French revolutions and Napoleonic escapades by sustaining traditional elites and resisting demands for popular sovereignty. The Concert of Europe was also intended to reproduce the interstate system, and yet it was itself a supernational political organization. In this respect it was a precursor to the League of Nations and the UN of the twentieth century.

Two other British international policies that emerged in the wake of the Napoleonic Wars were suppression of the international slave trade and covert support for the decolonization of Spanish colonies in the Americas. Both of these policies were progressive efforts to occupy the moral high ground with respect to the European Enlightenment ideas of equality and national self-determination. Support for Latin American decolonization was an easy option because decolonized states were much more likely to become trade partners with the British and to be open to diplomatic influence. This had to be done covertly because Spain had been an important ally of the British in the struggle against Napoleon. The suppression of the international slave trade was more politically complicated. The British navy went about intercepting slave ships traveling from Africa to the New World, effectively suppressing this booming business in coerced labor.

This unilateral British intervention into the international slave trade was opposed in Parliament by West Indian plantation owners, but their opposition was overcome, and the effective implementation of the policy of preventing further depredations on the peoples of Africa allowed the British government to regard itself as a leader in humane global governance and an upholder of Christian civilization (Hochschild 1998). As a consequence, the price of slaves in the New World went up to the benefit of those regions within countries that could produce slave children for sale (e.g., Virginia). The suppression of the slave trade and the abolition of slavery in the British colonies in 1834 provided validation for Haiti and for the abolition movements in other colonies and states.

One of the most important consequences of industrialization was urbanization, a large increase in the percentage of the total population living in big cities. The nineteenth century saw an upward sweep in the growth of cities. Britain led this trend, which then spread across Europe and to the other industrializing regions of the world. Another consequence of the British hegemony was that London became the most populous city in the world, surpassing Constantinople (the capital of the Ottoman Empire) and Beijing (the capital of the Qing dynasty) by 1825.

In the 1840s there arose in Britain a movement for international free trade that focused first on British tariffs (taxes on imports) on grain. The "Anti-Corn Law League" sought to abolish the Corn Law—a high tariff on imported grain ("corn"). This tariff protected British growers of wheat and barley against foreign competition and kept the price of bread artificially high. Thus the slogan of the Anti-Corn Law League was, "Down with infamous bread tax."

This was a successful use of the economic theory of Adam Smith, the father of modern economics, who published his famous book defending free trade, *The Wealth of Nations*, in 1776. Not only was the British Corn Law repealed, but the British government went on to campaign for international free trade in Europe and the Americas, and this campaign was rather successful in convincing other governments to reduce tariffs and to adopt the gold standard, in which their national currencies were valued in gold. The world economy was increasingly organized by world markets for money and commodities in the second half of the nineteenth century, and international trade as a proportion of all exchange peaked around 1880. This was the nineteenth-century wave of economic globalization (O'Rourke and Williamson 2000).

At the middle of the nineteenth century, London was the host of the Crystal Palace Exhibition, a huge "world's fair" at which the countries that were seeking a place in the arena of technical competition displayed their high-tech products and inventions. But already by the 1840s, Britain was losing its comparative advantage in textile manufactures to competitors abroad. British capitalists had begun making money by exporting textile machinery rather than cloth. They also began building railroads abroad and sold the steel tracks and the "rolling stock" (engines and cars). And soon would come the boom in the production of steamships and their sale to buyers all over the world. This was the capital goods phase of British hegemony described by Eric Hobsbawm (1969) in his book *Industry and Empire*. Railroads and steamships were lowering transportation costs across the world economy, and this expanded and intensified the markets for long-distance trade.

In the 1860s both England and France had to decide what to do about the "war for Southern Independence" in the United States. The war disrupted the export of cotton from the American South, which created a "cotton famine" in the English Midlands. Despite entreaties from the Southern Confederacy for support based on the principle of self-determination, both the English and the French governments decided not to support the secession of the American South. The English cotton textile manufacturers sought new sources of supply, and so cotton growing in Egypt was stimulated.

In the Crimean War (1854–1856), in which Russia tried to seize territory from the declining Ottoman Empire, the British allied with the Ottoman Empire to prevent the Russian advance. This is usually depicted as a crucial defeat for the Russian effort to keep its place among the "Great Powers" of Europe. But in Victorian England,[1] despite the eventual defeat of Russia, it revealed that the British navy had become moribund during the long period of relative peace since the Napoleonic Wars (Briggs 1964).

The Rise of Germany

The rising power of Prussia and the economic and political integration of Germany accelerated the emergence of German industrial prowess. Friedrich List, a German economist, had argued in favor of the "developmental state," in which government would ally with industrial business interests in order to promote national industrialization. This model was executed successfully in Germany, and many other states tried to emulate it.

The story of the rise of Germany needs to be told in order to understand how the Great War (World War I) could have happened. The lands in which the German language was spoken were divided into the Austro-Hungarian Empire, the remnant of the Hapsburg Empire (discussed in Chapter 14), and a large number of small independent states. The age of the Hanseatic capitalist city-states had passed, though the long history of successful German merchant capitalism demonstrated a strong cultural capability for successful business entrepreneurship and craftsmanship. The question after the Napoleonic Wars was whether Hapsburg Austria or some other center would lead an emergent German nation. The notion of the sovereignty of nations that was part of the political heritage of the French Revolution challenged the basic premise of the Austro-Hungarian Empire as well as the Ottoman Empire, because these were multicultural states held together by a small elite. A strong nationalist movement had emerged in Hungary during the world revolution of 1848, but it had been suppressed by the Hapsburgs. Though they would have preferred to lead the new Germany, their main energies were spent trying to hold together the empire. Prince Metternich of Austria and Lord Castlereigh of Britain had been the main architects of the Concert of Europe. But the British were enlightened conservatives who saw that the nationalist movements would need to be accommodated, while the Austrians could not afford to compromise. This difference of approach became visible in the different policies toward the emerging national movement of integration in Italy. The British supported Italian unification, while Austria-Hungary opposed it.

A German customs union, the Zollverein, was organized to allow for free trade among the thirty-eight independent principalities of the German Confederation in 1834 and a common external tariff border, and then the Prussians emerged victorious in the Franco-Prussian War with France. The Franco-Prussian War demonstrated that the Germans were a serious military power. It was the Prussian Junker elite of landed aristocrats with a strong military tradition that provided the core of the new German governing class that would lead the emergent nation. The idea of Germany as a nation of people who were related by blood and culture emerged in the nineteenth century and became the basis of the political unification of the principalities with Prussian leadership.

The Prussians supported the policy ideas of Friedrich List and accommodated the emerging industrial capitalists. It was the success of German industrialization and railroad building that provided the economic power that was the mainstay of German military capability, but the aristocratic military culture of the Prussians was also a big advantage in crafting the geopolitical policies of a world player and social policies of enlightened conservatism. The German state responded to a strong and organized labor movement by developing nationalism and by extending public education to the working class. Some

[1] Queen Victoria (reign 1837–1901) presided over the classical years of the British hegemony.

find it ironic that capitalist industrialization and modern nation building were led by an elite with deep roots in the tributary mode of production, landed aristocrats. But from another point of view, the German challenge to declining British hegemony had the look of an old strategy, the semiperipheral marcher state, and in that light the Prussians fit the bill perfectly. They were able to be nationalists without having to give up an existing empire, while their conationals in Vienna tried in vain to maintain an empire.

German successes in industrialization created international "lateral pressure"—the growing need for access to foreign markets and raw materials in a world that was already structured around British hegemony (Choucri and North 1975). In an attempt to accommodate this, the British participated in the Berlin Conference on Africa in 1884–1885, in which the European nations agreed on a division of Africa among themselves. The Germans were allocated Tanganyika, Southwest Africa (now Namibia), and the Kamerouns. This constituted an extension of the European system of colonial empires to Africa. Thus was Africa converted from a region of pure predation to a region of exploitation in which the imperial powers came to have an interest in the reproduction of the labor force and the development of the colonial economy. This was the further incorporation of the African land and the people into the Europe-centered world economy, and a transition from an external source of the "reserve army of labor" to an internal source of peripheral production (Wallerstein 1976; Rodney 1974).

As mentioned above, the Berlin Conference was partly an effort by the British to incorporate Germany into the club of European core states. But this effort was not enough. After agreeing to hold the conference in Berlin and granting Germany three colonies in Africa, the British hardened their attitude toward accommodating German expansionism.

The victory of the North in the American Civil War firmly set the United States on a path toward core status. While some in Britain continued to resent the upstart colonials, others saw opportunities for profitable investments and geopolitical partnership. The financial houses of New York and London became increasingly linked, and upper-class English gentlemen began increasingly to marry wealthy American women, tightening the links between the English and American elites.

The process of economic development in England was anything but a smooth upward trend. Ten-year business cycles of boom and bust were a prominent noted feature of the British economy, and larger forty- to sixty-year business cycles (later called Kondratieff waves after the Russian economist who observed and theorized them) were noticeable in price series that began in the 1790s (Goldstein 1988). The success of the Anti-Corn Law League at home encouraged free trade proselytizers to carry their message of economic liberalization abroad, and these ideas were also promoted by British legations in countries all over the world. In 1846 the US federal government lowered tariffs, and the governments of most European powers followed suit in the next two decades (Krasner 1976). Widespread adoption of the gold standard made national currencies tradable and encouraged international trade and foreign investment, because an investor could be assured that holdings in a foreign currency could be converted into gold at a predictable rate. The British pound sterling become the de facto currency of global trade. The great nineteenth-century wave of economic globalization can be seen in Figure 15.1, which shows the ratio of international trade to the size of the whole world economy.

There was an unusually large economic depression in 1873 and another big one in 1896. British hegemony in the world market for capital goods was in relative decline already by the 1870s as serious competition emerged abroad, especially in Germany and the United States. British capital was increasingly invested overseas, and the last phase of British hegemony was based on centrality in the world of finance capital. The City of London (the financial district of London) was truly the global center of high finance. Banking, currency exchange, stock and bond markets, and insurance were concentrated in London. This was quite similar to the global economic role that had been played by Amsterdam in the declining years of the Dutch hegemony. Though London was the most important center, there was a network of other world cities that included Paris, New York, and Berlin. These cities competed with one another, but they also complemented one another with regard to regional specialization.

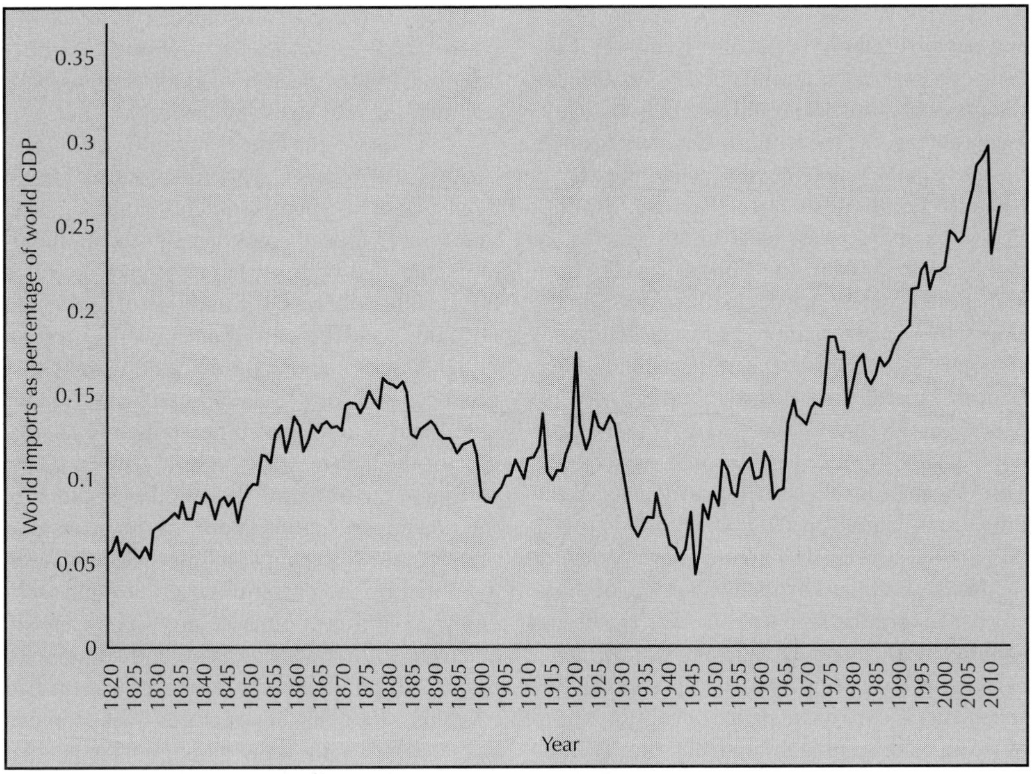

Figure 15.1 Waves of trade globalization, 1820–2010

As British hegemony in manufacturing declined, jobs were exported. Many urban and rural workers in England could no longer find jobs, and so they emigrated to the Americas and to Australia and New Zealand. Irish victims of the potato famine crowded into the East End of London, adding to the casualization of labor and the expansion of the "informal sector" in construction and petty services (Jones 1971). This "peripheralization of the core" and growing inequalities in the urban economy were similar in many ways to those studied by Saskia Sassen (2001) during the more recent rise of global cities such as New York during the most recent wave of globalization in the last decades of the twentieth century. As with contemporary globalization, the nineteenth-century wave saw growing inequalities within many of the countries that were involved in expanded international trade and investment (O'Rourke and Williamson 2000; M. Davis 2003).

One reason why trade globalization declined after 1880 (see Figure 15.1) is that many of the countries that had lowered tariffs and adopted the gold standard in the middle decades of the nineteenth century reversed these policies in later decades. The United States reasserted its policy of tariff protectionism during the Civil War and did not return to free trade until after World War II. In Germany, Friedrich List advocated that the national state should support national industrialization by using monetary and tariff policies to help found new industries. List advocated a strong national bank that would make credit available to strategically chosen industries. List's ideas were taken up by the newly integrated German state under the Kaiser Wilhelm and were influential in many other countries that wanted to catch up with the British.

The Edwardian reign[2] has been called the "Indian summer" of British hegemony, the last

[2] After Queen Victoria's death in 1901, King Edward served as the British monarch during the belle epoque of the declining years of British hegemony.

warm days before the winter of hegemonic rivalry and deglobalization. It has also been called the belle epoque, the "beautiful epoch," because life was good for those who could benefit from investments abroad. But the working class was again on the move in the union movement and in national politics. The English were the first to adopt free trade and the last to abandon this policy. Joseph Chamberlain, the political leader from Manchester, increasingly focused attention on the empire in the name of improving social conditions at home—so-called social imperialism. Cecil Rhodes expanded the British Empire in South Africa, but the Dutch colonists (Afrikaners) were not happy with the expansion of British control. The Afrikaners rebelled in the Boer Wars, and the British army carried on a long and bloody struggle that finally succeeded in saving South Africa for the British Empire. For many students of modern hegemony, the second Boer War represents an instance of "imperial overstretch," in which a hegemon that is losing its economic comparative advantages tries to maintain its global supremacy by using its remaining military superiority (e.g., Modelski 2005).

1848: Another World Revolution

Toward the middle of the nineteenth century, another world revolution was brewing. This time the volatile mixture was composed of reactions to capitalist exploitation of workers (slaves, serfs, and wage workers), resistance to rapidly expanding global markets, and demands for national sovereignty, especially in the remaining multicultural tributary empires—Austria-Hungary and the Ottoman Empire. Steamships and railroads brought distant regions into the sway of world market forces. Food was now exported to lands that had the ability to pay, and this often caused local shortages and increased prices. The workers' movement in Europe recovered from its earlier repression, and states that sought to mobilize citizens for war increasingly extended citizenship rights that enabled workers to play a greater role in national politics. In the 1830s new religious sects emerged in regions that were exposed to rapid social changes (in technology, migration, and marketization). Migration and economic reorganization disrupted older forms of community, and many new movements emerged to reestablish or to build new collective identities. Identity politics is another feature of globalization that is not unique to the twentieth century.

It is called the world revolution of 1848 because that is when workers' movements and demands for popular sovereignty came to a head in several European countries. But the mobilizations included both secular humanist demands for equality (following the tradition of the French Revolution and the leftist branch of the European Enlightenment) and radical religious sects that produced new forms of community with creative new interpretations of older religious ideologies. In the United States, several new Christian sects emerged during the middle decades of the nineteenth century. Both the prophets and the recruits were people whose lives had been disrupted by the powerful forces of rapid technological and economic change. These newly emergent forms of cooperation and community challenged traditional moral orders, established religions, and political structures. Not everyone had fared well in the rapid economic changes that occurred during the nineteenth-century expansion of capitalism, and people were needy for a reassertion of moral values and revitalized bases for generalized trust.

The new religious sects adopted many of the radical ideals and reforms of the European secular movements. Joseph Smith, the prophet of the Latter-Day Saints (Mormons), embraced communal ownership of property, obviously inspired by utopian socialist ideas emanating from Europe (Stegner 2003). The Mormons, who eventually established a large colony in Utah with pretensions of becoming an independently sovereign state, published newspapers in a radically simplified script for representing the English language. Linguistic reforms of this kind were intended to facilitate mass literacy, and they had been another prominent feature of the radical social movements in Europe.

Population pressures encouraged migration, and some of the lands to which people moved were environmentally marginal. In Northeastern Brazil, the sertao region receives enough rainfall in unusually wet years to support rain-watered agriculture. Thousands of immigrants and landless people from other areas of Brazil moved out to this region during years of unusually greater rainfall associated with the El Niño/La Niña climate oscillation in the nineteenth century (M. Davis 2003, 188–195). When the more usual low precipitation returned, the new crops failed and the pioneers faced starvation. Some left, but the others banded together into millenarian religious movements and established collectivistic communities that were seen as threatening by the newly independent Brazilian state and the large landowners. The city of Canudos, established by the followers of Antonio Conselhiero as a refuge from drought, was conquered and decimated by the Brazilian federal army in 1897.

In China the cycle of peasant rebellions discussed in Chapter 14 continued, but the rebellions came to be influenced ideologically and economically by strengthening interactions with Europe and the Americas. The Taiping Rebellion (1851–1864) was a huge movement that was joined by millions of landless peasants and unemployed workers. Like the earlier White Lotus peasant rebellions, the Taiping started off as a peaceful religious cult that stressed class and gender equality and vegetarianism. The leader was Hong Xiuquan, a member of an ethnic minority from South China called the Hakka. Hong had tried four times to pass the literary exams that were required to become an official in the Qing state. He came to be influenced by Issachar Roberts, an American Baptist missionary from Tennessee, who held to a very millenarian interpretation of Christianity. Hong came to think of himself as Jesus's younger brother. The Taipings turned to military action in order to expel the Manchus from China and to redistribute land to the poor. The Taipings recruited women as soldiers and proclaimed gender equality. They rejected private property and promoted a simplified language and mass literacy in order to overthrow the literary hierarchy of the Mandarins. The Taiping guerilla armies were formidable foes and it took decades and 30 million deaths for the Qing dynasty to crush the rebellion.

Was this connected to the world revolution of 1848? The Taiping Rebellion was certainly a continuation of the pattern of East Asian development described in Chapter 14, in which Chinese population growth enlarged the underclass, which then rebelled against that paternalistic neo-Confucianist political order using egalitarian and apocalyptic ideas. But the influence of Western millenarian ideas and the increasingly synchronous economic cycles linking China with the Central System in the nineteenth century constitute both ideological and structural links that justify considering the Taiping Rebellion to have been part of the world revolution of 1848.

Coordinated global party formation from below began in the world revolution of 1848. The movement to abolish slavery in the United States was inspired by the example of the Haitian revolution and led by an ex-slave from the Caribbean named Denmark Vesey. A large group of slaves in Charleston, South Carolina, plotted an uprising in 1822 that was discovered and crushed before the rebellion could emerge. Slaves who were able to escape to the free states played an important role, along with protestant ministers, in the development of the abolitionist movement in the United States. In England and France, abolitionist groups were emboldened by the suppression of the slave trade by the British navy. The radical abolitionist John Brown moved from Massachusetts to Kansas in order to try to prevent that state from adopting slavery. Frederick Douglass, a slave shipwright from Maryland's Eastern Shore, worked in a shipyard at Fell's Point in Baltimore before he moved to Boston, where he was a leading publicist in the rapidly growing abolitionist movement. The New England publisher and campaigner William Lloyd Garrison was a synergist who saw the potential for fruitful alliances among the several movements that were challenging the powers that be in the world revolution of 1848. The trade union movement was growing, and feminists were beginning to demand that women be able to vote. Garrison traveled to the World Antislavery Conference in London in 1840 with an American delegation that included women from New England and from the South. When the English majority refused to seat the women as American delegates, Garrison and several other male members of the American delegation sat with the women in the balcony as spectators (Keck and Sikkink 1998, 46).

The American Civil War was a battle between the peripheral capitalists of the South and the free farmers of the West over the extension of slavery (see below). In the midst of the war, under pressure from both England and France, the Union leadership embraced the abolition of slavery. This was an important moment in the global struggle to make slavery illegal.

In 1863 Czar Alexander II of Russia abolished serfdom in order to modernize Russia's economy and to improve its position in the international system. The abolition of serfdom failed to undermine the power of the Russian landed aristocracy, nor did it measurably improve the situation of the Russian peasants. But it did provide fuel for the next world revolution, which is often called the world revolution of 1917 because of the world-historical importance of the October Revolution in Russia.

One outcome of the world revolution of 1848 was the increasing popularity of the idea that the urban working class was going to be the main agent of the transformation of capitalism into a more collectively rational and egalitarian social order. Karl Marx, a German Jewish expatriate living in London in the middle years of the nineteenth century, wrote a brilliant analysis of industrial capitalism that assumed that the British path of development was the path that the whole world would take. Marx's analysis, mainly contained in Volume 1 of *Capital*, underestimated the continuing importance of the core/periphery hierarchy in the development of capitalism. Marx knew that European colonialism had been crucial for the emergence of capitalism in Europe, but he saw this as an early stage of "primitive accumulation" that would later be transcended. For Marx, capitalism was based mainly on wage labor, as it had come to be within the United Kingdom. Its spread to the rest of the world would create a global proletariat of wageworkers, which would then make socialist revolutions everywhere. Marx had no notion of peripheral capitalism, in which coerced labor would continue to be an important source of labor exploitation for producing commodities. And he only vaguely understood that the capitalist world economy is importantly and continually stratified into a global hierarchy of core and peripheral regions, with an important group of semiperipheral regions in between.

Marx was not entirely wrong, however. He saw that capitalism had internal contradictions that would eventually cause it to evolve into a qualitatively different kind of social system. His focus on class relations and the urban wageworkers as important players in the world-historical movements that are restructuring capitalism was a fundamental insight, but his failure to see the continuing significance of the core/periphery hierarchy was an unfortunate error because it blinded him to the phenomenon of semiperipheral development.

The First New Nation[3]

Before the Europeans discovered the Americas, regional indigenous world-systems were in the process of developing complexity and hierarchy, as discussed in Chapter 7 and the Web Chapter. The arrival of the Europeans incorporated these indigenous systems into the expanding Central System over a period of centuries. By the arrival of the nineteenth century, there were only a few pocket regions that had not been incorporated. These were in the western part of that portion of North America that became the United States, and during the nineteenth century, these too were brought within the Central web.

Though the Europeans had great technological and institutional advantages, the indigenous peoples were capable of mounting significant resistance to peripheralization (Dunaway 1996). But the fact that local indigenous elites had long been able to reinforce their power by means of goods obtained by trade—the prestige goods systems of the Mississippian culture—set the stage for the trade dependencies that formed the main basis for integration and peripheralization of the indigenous peoples. Once local societies grew dependent on the importation of European tools and weapons, they soon lost the craft skills

[3] In Chapter 2 we defined states, nations, and ethnic groups. A nation is simply a group of people who speak the same language and who identify with one another and see themselves as sharing a common history. *The First New Nation* is the title of a book by Seymour Martin Lipset (1963) in which he considers the history and character of the United States in comparative perspective. Lipset wrote the book in 1963 during the last wave of decolonization, in which the former colonies of European core powers were becoming sovereign states and were termed "new nations." Lipset alludes to the fact that the United States was the first of the new nations. The term "first nations" is now being used to designate indigenous peoples who have been subjected to colonialism or neocolonial domination.

necessary to produce traditional tools. And the old elites lost power when they could not protect the people from diseases. This led to their replacement by new leaders, many of whom were allies of the Europeans. A new political order emerged that was promoted by the Europeans as a means of controlling the indigenous peoples.

The very decentralized and localized political structure that the Europeans encountered among the Cherokees in the Southeast was the outcome of the devolution of former Mississippian complex chiefdoms. The decentralized polity was very difficult for the British colonists to deal with because treaties and trade agreements had to be made with each Cherokee town. Thus the British colonists successfully imposed a more centralized form of governance on the Cherokees (Dunaway 1996). It is interesting to wonder how the centralized political structure that emerged as a result of peripheralization was similar to, or different from, the earlier centralized Mississippian complex chiefdoms. Historically, Cherokee leadership was divided between two different organizational structures—the Red organization, led by a war chief (the Raven), and the White organization of elders, led by the peacetime White chief. The White chief was in charge during periods of peace, while the Red chief took over during war (Dunaway 1996). The British succeeded in consolidating the centralized Cherokee polity mainly around the warrior leaders. The White chiefs lost their power. This shift was partly due to the increased importance of warfare and slave raiding that accompanied incorporation in the Central System (Ferguson and Whitehead 1992). Trade was important in both the old and the new hierarchies, but in the old hierarchy trade fed into a theocratic system in which the sacred chiefs used imported prestige goods to reward subalterns. Trade with the Europeans was not a matter of symbolic goods used in religious rituals to glorify the sacredness of elites. Rather, the goods received were guns, ammunition, metal tools, and alcohol. While these sorts of goods have had (and do have) ritual importance in some societies, their effects on the Native Americans shifted power to the war chiefs and centralized that power.

The competing European states allied with different Indian groups and used these alliances to provide buffer zones of protection for colonies and to keep trade routes open. The Cherokee alliance with the British transformed the Cherokees from an autonomous and decentralized set of societies to a more centralized group that became a dependent and exploited periphery of the Central System. Their culture was corrupted and transformed, their lands were despoiled and appropriated, and their labor was exploited (Dunaway 1996). On the other hand, at least in the long run, the Cherokees picked the right bunch of invaders with which to ally. The Creeks and Choctaws had it much worse when their Spanish and French allies withdrew.

The Native Americans were thus peripheralized and exploited by the traders and colonists from Britain. The colonial economy was based at first on extracting valuables from the natives. But soon colonists began to produce agricultural cash crops (mainly rice and indigo) for export to the European core. This required massive amounts of labor. The Native Americans did not make good plantation slaves. But Africans, far from their homelands and able to survive lowland climes and hard labor, served the purpose well. On their backs the colonial economy took shape as a classical peripheral structure using coerced labor to produce agricultural goods for export to the core. Some have called the plantation economy noncapitalist because its use of coerced labor is similar to serfdom and slavery in tributary modes of accumulation. But the tight interdependence of manufacturing and industrial capitalism in the core with production based on labor coercion in the periphery of the modern world-system warrants the use of the term "peripheral capitalism" to designate the expansion of labor coercion that occurred in conjunction with the development of European capitalism.

In the emerging global capitalist world-system, "national development" is best understood as upward mobility in the hierarchical division of labor between the core and the periphery. Most areas that were incorporated into the expanding Central System became organized as peripheries and were unable to escape this position. The process of peripheralization—or as Andre Gunder Frank (1966) called it, the "development of underdevelopment"—reproduced the institutional structures that perpetuated peripheral capitalism and blocked the emergence of core capitalism. A few countries were able to overcome the forces of peripheralization, develop core activities, and move upward in the core/periphery hierarchy. By far the most successful was the United States.[4]

The developmental history of the United States, rather than being a replicable model of modern development for all countries, is an extremely unusual case of a region that went from being a colonial periphery to being a hegemonic core power, while the larger system remained a quite stable core/periphery hierarchy in which most countries did not change their positions. The American Revolution was an important first step in this trajectory. One interesting question that involves core/periphery relations is why the planter aristocrats of the South joined with the embryonic core merchants and producers of New England to drive the British out. Structurally, the Northerners had a shot at becoming another England and some of them knew it (e.g., Alexander Hamilton's *Report on Manufactures*), so they had a powerful reason to increase their autonomy from the mother country. But the Southerners were completely dependent on the British as customers and suppliers. The South was taking a big risk in joining up. Why did this happen? Several arguments have been suggested, including resentment at the reimposition of British taxes after a lax period of "benign neglect" and the indebtedness of Southern planters to English lenders. It has also been argued that the Southerners joined because they resented Crown efforts to keep them from expanding westward. Perhaps it is not such a mystery after all. Dominated peoples often rebel if they see a reasonable chance of success. After the threat of French dominion was settled in the Seven Years' War, the French became a valuable but unthreatening ally of the North American colonists. Thus, success was perceived to be possible enough for both Southerners and Northerners to take the risk.

Tariff politics in the nineteenth century provides a clear and wide window on how political power in the United States was in contention between the core and peripheral capitalists in the antebellum period (before the Civil War) (Chase-Dunn 1985). After the Revolutionary War, the different world-system positions of the North and the South engendered contrary attitudes toward tariff protectionism. As both exporters of raw materials to the European core and importers of manufactured goods, the Southerners were devoted to free trade. The manufacturers of New England and the Middle States came to embrace tariff protection of their "infant industries." The US trajectory over the nineteenth and twentieth centuries is reflected in its tariff history. The United States was a classical semiperiphery containing both core and peripheral regions—the North and the South. As with most peripheral countries, the South favored free trade because it depended on core markets. The North came to favor protectionism because it aspired to develop core industries and to rise in the value-added hierarchy that is the core/periphery division of labor.

Nascent core producers are likely to be driven out of business if they have to face competition from existing core producers, and so they need tariff protection to survive. Before the Civil War, the North and the South struggled over the question of tariffs. After the Civil War, the rising United States was firmly protectionist until after World War II, when, as a hegemonic power with a strong comparative advantage in core production, it shifted to free trade and went about the world trying to convince others to do the same. The English had followed the same trajectory. First they were dependent exporters of wool to the textile producers of the Low Countries. Then they engaged in protectionism to support their own domestic textile producers. When they had developed a global comparative advantage in the production of core commodities, they became champions of free trade. And when they lost their comparative advantage, they rediscovered the promise of protectionism. This was also the trajectory of the Dutch Republic in the seventeenth century.

The economy of the American South grew rapidly in concert with the English Midlands as the invention of the cotton gin made upland short-fiber cotton commercially viable. King

[4] Though we occasionally use the term "American" to refer to the residents of the United States, we are mindful that all the peoples of the Americas should be included in that term. The alternative, "United Statesian," is clumsy, and so we go along with common usage. The successful often see themselves as the center of the universe.

Cotton also exhausted the land quickly, and fresh western lands became an important need for the expanding South. The fight over tariffs began with the South Carolina nullification movement in the 1830s. Whereas the North was intellectually fortified with the protectionist economics of Henry Carey, the South had a pro–free trade economist in Dr. Thomas D. Cooper of the College of South Carolina. Though the South was a classical example of peripheral capitalism (producing cash crops with coerced labor), it was a dynamic peripheral economy. Indeed, by the time of the Civil War, the South was the ninth-largest economy in the Western world.

The Federal Congress adopted protectionist legislation in fits between 1816 and 1846. The farmers of the West supported free trade when the world market price of grain was high. But when the external demand was glutted, they supported the "American System" of Kentucky's Henry Clay—a program of tariff protection of domestic industry and the building of transportation infrastructure to connect agricultural and industrial regions. The North/South struggle over tariffs was largely over by the time of the Civil War, because by then the core capitalists of the North no longer needed tariff protection to prosper in the world market. The Civil War was primarily a fight between the plantocracy and Northern and Western workers and farmers. The Southerners' main reason for insisting on extending slavery to the west was that they needed to control the federal government in order to protect their "peculiar institution." The Republican Free Soilers brought the Eastern manufacturers into their coalition by committing to the ultra-protectionist Morrill Tariff of 1861, and the United States remained protectionist until after World War II. The plantocracy was brought to heel, and henceforth core capital ruled the federal state with substantial support from workers and farmers. In this light the political histories of most of the Latin American countries can be seen as anticolonial struggles that were followed by civil wars in which the local "Souths" won.

The first new nation was formed when thirteen of the English colonies in North America rebelled against King George of the United Kingdom and established their own sovereign government, a federation of former colonies that had become states. It is fairly easy to understand why the colonies of New England rebelled. A large-scale fishing industry, a boatbuilding industry, and a class of merchants who carried goods all around the Atlantic world had emerged by the middle of the eighteenth century. Shipbuilders and merchants of New England and the middle colonies in the eighteenth century were able to begin the process of capital accumulation in types of production that allowed them to compete with producers of core products in England. The later rise of the United States to core status and world hegemony stems from these developments.[5] The defeat of the French in the Seven Years' War meant that the New Englanders no longer needed the British army and navy to protect them from France. But why did the plantation owners of the Southern colonies join the rebellion? They were exporters of agricultural raw materials mainly to British markets, and so they were quite dependent on the goodwill of the British. Yet they joined the rebellion, and indeed the great general who led the rebel army was a plantation owner from Virginia, George Washington.

No doubt part of the explanation for the rebellion in the South was the popularity of republican ideas and the notion of national self-determination. The plantation class of Virginia is well known for the enthusiasm it had for Montesquieu and the ideals of liberty, as least insofar as these applied to landowning gentlemen. Another factor may have been the desire to expand toward the west. George Washington, in addition to inheriting a prodigious great plantation on the Potomac, was a surveyor who spent much of his young manhood establishing the official boundaries of properties in the relatively as yet undeveloped regions to the west. The Virginians wanted to expand their plantations into the west, but the British government was

[5] The establishment of shipbuilding firms and textile factories in New England did not inexorably lead to the rise and triumph of core capitalism, but rather the forces of peripheral capitalism and competing interests in England constantly challenged the very survival of these core producers until the issue was finally settled in the American Civil War.

standing by treaties that it had made with those Indian tribes that had supported the British against the French in the Seven Years' War. This was an immediate and material reason to be free of the Crown.

It was a long and difficult war, with the rebels resorting to tactics that would be labeled as terrorism or butchery if they had been carried out by individuals other than the totemic fathers of the nation. General Washington crossed the Delaware River at midnight on Christmas Eve to slaughter the holiday-inebriated Redcoats in their bunks. Then, as now, the distinction between terrorists and freedom fighters is not so simple.

At the crucial battle that turned the tide against King George, there were no Americans present. It was a naval encounter at the mouth of the Chesapeake Bay in which the French navy succeeded in repelling a British fleet that was headed to reinforce Lord Cornwallis at Yorktown. The French won, and the American Revolution was saved. As mentioned in Chapter 14, the expense of supporting the American rebels weakened the French monarchy's ability to deal with the challenges that emerged in the French Revolution of 1789. But French support had been crucial to the birth of the first new nation.

New England was a classical case of semiperipheral development. The involvement of its merchants in the "triangle trades" linking the Caribbean with Africa, the Mediterranean, and the ports of Northwestern Europe was tolerated by the benign neglect of the British authorities. But the rebellion was spurred by new efforts to enforce the Regulation Acts (mercantile laws that gave preferences to British merchants and shippers) and to collect taxes from the American colonies. The alliance between New England and the South was fitful because the two regions had rather different interests vis-à-vis the larger Atlantic economy. And Alexander Hamilton's 1791 *A Report on the Subject of Manufactures* was an original and innovative statement of the strategy of the developmental state. Hamilton's writings were an important inspiration for German economist Georg Friedrich List (1789–1846), who resided in the United States from 1825 to 1832. Hamilton advocated the establishment of a strong national bank that could use monetary policy and the allocation of credit to help establish and support industrial manufacturing. Hamilton also recommended a strong federal role in the development of transportation infrastructure that would link the new agricultural regions of the hinterland with the industrial ports of the coast.[6] The Southerners opposed these policies, which envisioned a strong and active central government. They wanted local autonomy and low taxes so that they could continue to export their agricultural commodities to the core areas of Europe. This regional conflict of interest was not fully resolved until the Civil War.

The anticolonial victory did not, in itself, guarantee the upward mobility of the United States in the world-system. After all, the Latin American republics successfully established formal political independence in the early nineteenth century, but economic neocolonialism continued to produce the development of underdevelopment and they remained in a peripheral position in the core/periphery hierarchy (Stein and Stein 1970). So how were the forces supporting the development of domestic core production in the United States able to win out over the interests that supported the maintenance of peripheral production for export to the established core in Europe?

The Americans did not declare war on Britain in alliance with Napoleon. Rather, they attempted to maintain neutrality so that their commerce could continue. It was British attacks on American shipping and the impressments of American sailors into the British navy by force that led to war. In the first encounters, fast and large American ships of the line roundly defeated the British navy to the great consternation of all who supported Britain and opposed Napoleon. But the long war with Napoleonic France was decided elsewhere, and during a lull the British decided that it was time to reconquer the upstart colonials, as recounted above. This time the colonials were able to hold their own without the help of the French in the War of 1812, though the new capitol building in

[6] Hamilton was killed in a duel with Aaron Burr. Dueling remained part of the code of male honor throughout the nineteenth century in all of the countries that were held to be "most civilized."

Washington was burned to the ground. The few Anglophiles left in the former thirteen colonies kept their feelings to themselves.

The politics of import duties reflects the struggle between classes that have different interests in the larger world economy. Thus the outlines of the struggle between core capitalists, peripheral capitalists, and the other classes that ally with or oppose them can be discerned in the tariff history of the United States.

During the Napoleonic Wars, imports to the United States from Britain and from other developed regions were severely curtailed because the war interfered with international trade. The resulting pent-up demand and rise in prices were a big incentive for "import substitution" of manufactured goods. Entrepreneurs from Providence, Rhode Island, traveled to Manchester and Birmingham to survey the latest technologies in cotton textile manufacturing. When these clever spies returned to Providence, they designed a new power loom that was a big improvement over the British technology. The cotton textile industry in Rhode Island was well under way when the war came to an end.

Lord Brougham gave a speech in Parliament recommending the export of vast quantities of British goods to be sold in New York at a price below their cost of production, thereby to drive out of business those industries that had emerged in the United States during the war so that the British manufacturers might retake the American market.[7] In 1816 the US Congress passed its first protective tariff in order to counteract the British dumping and to allow the new industries to survive.

Henry Clay of Kentucky proposed his "American System" to promote the alliance between agriculture and industry based on the protected development of a diversified national market. In Clay's scheme, the federal government would stimulate manufacturing by applying a protective (but not prohibitive) tariff. The revenues resulting from the tariff would enable the government to sell western land cheaply and to finance internal improvements in transportation between the agricultural West (and, presumably, the South) and the industrial East. Clay's program created a political alliance among core capitalists, farmers, and labor that supported increasing protectionism until Southern opposition reversed this trend in 1833. The program of internal improvements began in 1818 with the completion of the National Road, a federally built highway that connected Baltimore with the Ohio Valley. The General Survey bill of 1824 proposed an elaborate national transportation system of roads and canals, most of which were later built under the auspices of the separate states but with federal encouragement. The Erie Canal, connecting the Hudson River with the Great Lakes, was completed in 1825.

The shifts in US tariff policy between 1815 and World War II can be generally described as follows: The war duties during the Napoleonic Wars (which were intended to raise revenues for the federal government) were replaced in 1816 with a tariff that, although not high, was intended to be protective. The average rate in 1816 was 25 percent ad valorem, meaning that the import tax on an item was equal to one-quarter of the price of the item. This was increased in 1824 to 33 percent, and again in 1828 to 50 percent (Freehling 1968). In 1833, Southern planter and Northern merchant opposition forced the adoption of the Compromise Tariff, which slowly lowered rates until 1842. In 1842, protection was renewed until 1846 when the Walker Tariff, a victory for the free traders, was adopted. In 1857, tariffs were lowered even further. The Republicans, who gained much power with the election of Lincoln, passed the ultra-protectionist Morrill Tariff of 1861, and so protectionism reigned from then until after World War II.

This tariff history from 1816 to 1860 reflects the process of class formation in the antebellum period (before the Civil War). Core manufacturers expanded after the War of 1812 and, in alliance with farmers, succeeded in passing protectionist legislation. The peripheral capitalism of King Cotton in the South expanded even more rapidly, and the core and peripheral interests contended

[7] As Lord Brougham explained to Parliament in 1816, it was "well worth while to incur a loss upon the first exportation, in order, by the glut, to stifle in the cradle those rising manufactures in the United States, which war had forced into existence, contrary to the natural course of things" (Forsythe 1977, 69).

for power in the federal state by making alliances with other classes: merchants, workers, and yeoman farmers.

Peripheral capitalism in the South was by no means moribund. Indeed, it was a dynamic and differentiated economy based on commodity production with slave labor. By the 1840s the upper South had become a slave-breeding and semi-industrial region. But the mainstay of this slave-based peripheral economy remained the production of cotton for the English Midlands. The plantocracy of the South was able to dominate the federal state during most of the antebellum period by allying with Western farmers and Northern workers in the Democratic Party. This alliance, which ushered in the period of low tariffs in the 1840s and 1850s, eventually foundered on the issue of the legal status of slavery in the new territories of the West.

The shippers, merchants, and politicians of New England had opposed protectionism because they feared that it would interfere with their business, but New England eventually came over to protectionism. "In 1825, the great firm of W. and S. Lawrence of Boston turned its interest and capital from importing to domestic manufacturing, and the rest of State Street fell in behind it. So did Daniel Webster, who was now to become Congress's most eloquent supporter of protection" (Forsythe 1977, 79).

The advances made by the core industries in the 1820s and 1830s enabled them to survive and prosper in the period during the 1840s and 1850s when peripheral producers reestablished their control of the federal state. Zevin (1971) reports that between 1820 and 1830 American consumption of cotton cloth increased from 50 million to 175 million yards, while the share of that consumption supplied by New England increased from about 30 percent to about 80 percent. By 1825 even Hezekiah Niles, the ardent Baltimore protectionist, admitted that American coarse cotton textiles no longer needed protection. By 1832 these coarse cottons were competing with British products in the markets of the Far East. Thus further protection of cotton textiles was redundant.

There was considerable US support for the Latin American independence wars against Spain, especially from the Catholic enclave in Baltimore (Maryland), where Latin American colonial elites often sent their children to be educated in Jesuit colleges (Bornholdt 1949). In 1823 President Monroe refused a British proposal for a joint British-US declaration in support of Latin American independence and issued the precocious Monroe Doctrine, forbidding European interference in Pan-American affairs. The United States, itself still a noncore power, staked out the moral high ground on which its later hegemony would claim legitimation as "leader of the free world" and defender of national self-determination.[8]

The Rise of Opposition to Protection

The peripheralized colonial Southern economy, based on tobacco, rice, and indigo, seemed to have reached its zenith at the end of the eighteenth century. Contemporaries such as Thomas Jefferson predicted that slavery would wither away. Others thought that the South would turn toward maritime and industrial activities. But the invention of the cotton gin and the demand for cotton to feed the mills of the English Midlands gave plantation slavery a new lease on life. The cotton gin made cultivation of the upland short-fiber cotton commercially profitable with the application of slave labor.

The reorganization of the core/periphery division of labor between the South and England also affected the maritime and commercial interests of the North, particularly New York City. New York merchant shippers bought most of the cotton from the planters, at first transporting the cotton to New York for inspection before shipment to Liverpool. Later the New York merchants established factories in the port cities of the South that enabled them to ship directly. But they maintained financial control of most of the trade between the South and England. Specialized merchant-banker firms such as Baring Brothers

[8] Hegemony requires both power and legitimacy.

and George Peabody and Company established credit facilities in which American merchants could purchase English goods with drafts on London banks. Peabody, a Baltimore dry goods merchant, established a firm in London for this purpose and hired another dry goods importer, Junius Spencer Morgan of Boston. Through this connection the Morgan family entered the calling of high finance, founding a company that is still an important player on Wall Street.

Both Northern merchants and Southern planters came to fear that their British customers would retaliate against US protection by obtaining their raw materials from non-US producers. Also, Southern exporters were made aware that, as international economists have demonstrated, a tariff on imports is not only a tax on consumers of imports but also effectively a tax on exporters. Dr. Thomas Cooper, a disciple of Adam Smith and president of the College of South Carolina, suggested that the marriage between the states had become somewhat less than a transcendent relationship.

The Tariff of 1828 raised rates and extended protection to a large number of commodities not previously protected, including a number that angered New England. Antiprotectionist sentiment was growing, and free traders hoped that the election of Andrew Jackson would bring relief. But Jackson did not act to lower the duties. Southern planters organized an unsuccessful boycott of Northern products, and leading politicians appeared in public in homespun (clothing made from thread and cloth that had been produced at home) to dramatize their cause. The most rabid of the South Carolinians were talking of secession when their senator, John C. Calhoun, devised what he thought to be a compromise that would preserve the Union. Antitariff politicians had argued that tariff protection was unconstitutional. Calhoun (anonymously at first) proposed the doctrine that states have the right to nullify federal laws that they deem unconstitutional. Nullification received enthusiastic support in South Carolina but not in the other Southern states. In 1832 the South Carolina legislature called a convention and adopted nullification unilaterally, but President Jackson stood firm against this challenge to the sovereignty of the federal state and, after some saber-rattling, the South Carolinians backed down.

The controversy over the tariff is often portrayed as being based on sectionalism, and indeed the congressional voting record on the tariff acts from 1820 on shows that it was increasingly the Southern states that opposed protection. But the sectional aspect was due mainly to the conflict between core capitalists interested in creating a diversified and integrated national economy and peripheral capitalists specializing in the exchange of raw materials for European core products. These two groups contended throughout the antebellum period for the support of other politically important classes: merchants, farmers, and, increasingly, workers.

In the 1830s both farmers and plantation owners were increasingly dissatisfied with the tight money policies of Eastern bankers. And labor organizations emerged to oppose municipal monopolies and restrictive land-sale policies that were associated with Eastern financial and manufacturing interests. The Democratic Party chose Andrew Jackson, an Indian fighter from Tennessee, to symbolize the new coalition of farmers, laborers, and planters that led to the extension of suffrage to all white male citizens.[9] Jackson was not sympathetic to free trade, nor did he yield to nullification, but his election was the beginning of the coalition between the South and the West, which was to increasingly delimit the power of the domestic core capitalists in the federal state in the 1840s and 1850s.

Free Trade

In 1845 the potato famine in Ireland caused prices of American agricultural commodities to rise due to increased foreign demand. The recovery of the

[9] Formerly, property qualifications had limited voting to landowning white male citizens. Part of the Jacksonian coalition involved an agreement to expand at the expense of the American Indians. Jackson's fame as an Indian fighter and his toleration of the abrogation of treaties and removal of Indians from the lands of the South was an early example of the dark side of American democracy.

West from the crash of 1839 had been slow, but the new demand caused a renewal of expansion and brought the West back into the free trade coalition with the South.

Many industries in the United States no longer needed protection from imports. Cotton textiles were cheaper in New York than in Manchester. By 1839 the domestic market for many manufactures did not need tariff protection. Schumpeter (1939) points out that this period saw a long-term upswing in the pace of economic growth throughout the world. As mentioned above, tariffs were reduced all across Europe and the Atlantic economy as the benefits of trade came to outweigh the injuries done to domestic producers, and the British engaged in a globalization project that promoted free trade and the gold standard. The British economy shifted from the production of mass consumption goods toward the production of capital goods (Hobsbawm 1969), and the capitalists of other core states developed their own mass consumption industries by importing British machinery and railroad equipment.

The Crystal Palace Exhibition of 1851 (Figure 15.2) was a great promotional effort to expand the export of British technology, a reversal of the earlier attempt to monopolize production techniques (Landes 1969). The international division of labor between core producers became less autarkical and protectionist as a result. Richard Cobden and John Bright traveled widely, lecturing on the beneficial effects of a world free market. Their arguments were acted upon because the actual gains from free trade to consumers came to outweigh the costs to producers. And the producers, including core capitalists in the United States, had less to lose because the pace of growth was expanding and they wanted to import capital goods from England.

Protection Again: The Irrepressible Conflict

The Panic of 1857 came a few months after the passage of the tariff bill. It was similar to the depression of 1839 in that it followed a period of rapid inflation, economic expansion, foreign investment, importation, and westward movement. But the expansionary phase was based on the growth of manufactures and western free agriculture rather than slave-grown cotton as the growth of the 1830s had been. And, as before, the fall of grain prices (partly resulting from the end of the Crimean War, which allowed Russian wheat back onto the world market) and the fall of wages and employment renewed the spirit of protectionism.

The new growth of the labor movement (especially among immigrant German workers), the opposition to the extension of slavery to the western states, and the renewed enthusiasm for cheap land led to the birth of the Republican Party. The greatest issue of the new party was "free soil" and the passage of the Homestead Act (E. Foner 1970). The Republicans attracted Democratic voters with the slogan "Vote yourself a farm," and they supported prolabor legislation. Lincoln avowed the principle that labor is the source of all wealth and won the support of immigrant

Figure 15.2 Crystal Palace, London

workers by his opposition to an alliance between the Republicans and the Know-Nothings (P. Foner 1975). The Republicans were antagonistic to the "money power" of the East, but they eventually adopted protectionism in order to appeal to the manufacturers.

The success of the Republicans and the split between the Northern and Southern Democrats broke the alliance between the farmers of the West and the planters of the South that had allowed the Southerners to control the federal state through the Democratic Party. The crumbling of this alliance provoked the Civil War[10] even though the Republicans never advocated the abolition of slavery but only prevention of its extension to the west. Southern peripheral capitalism was expansionist because of its extensive nature and the quick exhaustion of the soil, but this was not the main reason why the South desired the extension of slavery to the west. The main issue for the South was control over the federal state. Planters opposed the creation of free states because the alliance with free farmers was tenuous and they felt they would have less and less power in the federal state. The result would be a direct attack on their "peculiar institution" and their subjugation to the North as an internal colony. Therefore, when the South-West coalition crumbled and Lincoln won the election in 1860, South Carolina did not even wait for him to take office. South Carolina seceded immediately, and most of the other slave states followed when it became clear that the North would make war in order to preserve the Union.

The argument that the conflict between the North and the South was due to the economic inefficiency of slavery has been sufficiently demolished. It should be noted, however, that plantation slavery remained highly profitable and the Southerners were well aware that emancipation in the British West Indies in 1834 had increased the cost of sugar production considerably. Slavery was not simply the basis of an aristocratic civilization; it was a profitable business. The plantocracy of King Cotton was probably the most successful peripheral capitalism in the whole history of the world-system because it was less encumbered by precapitalist institutions than the Hispanics, Germanics, and Slavs or even the British and French colonies had been. This was truly successful capitalist agriculture, and its very success led to dreams of a slave empire and the challenge to the Northern and Western interests (Genovese 1965). After all, the slaveholders started the Civil War. The core capitalists, workers, and farmers of the North only grudgingly made war to keep the Union intact.

The contention that capitalism and slavery were incompatible for political or cultural reasons simply does not fit with the historical facts. Barrington Moore's (1966) observation that the legal and political legitimation of slavery contradicted the more opaque form of exploitation that existed in the North is true, but insufficient to explain the violent conflict that developed. Similarly, Eugene Genovese's (1969) characterization of the divergence between the political culture of the aristocratic and precapitalist South and the fully developed capitalist mode of production based on wage labor in the North does not explain the Civil War. Regardless of cultural differences, both the North and the South were capitalist, only the North had become an area of core capitalism employing relatively high wage labor, while the South had remained an area of peripheral capitalism utilizing coerced low-cost slave labor (Wallerstein 1979a).

The evidence that supports the foregoing contention is to be seen in the political history that led to the Civil War. Northern manufacturers were not against slavery. In fact, in the face of increasing labor struggles they may have been envious of it. Their biggest conflict with the South had been over the tariff issue, and that was no longer crucial to them by 1860. A main cause of the Civil War was the opposition of the free workers and farmers to the extension of slavery to the west. These core workers and farmers were not abolitionists. The main issue for them was the threat of competition with slave labor and plantation owners for the lands of the West. Their unhappiness with the Compromise of 1850 was seen most vividly in the battle for Kansas and in the fight against Southern opposition to the Homestead Act.

The Lincoln administration did not contemplate emancipation until well after the Civil

[10] Northern sympathizers called it the Civil War. Southerners called it the War for Southern Independence.

War had begun, and then mainly to head off English and French support for the South (Case and Spencer 1970). Queen Victoria adopted a formally neutralist stance. The cotton famine caused by the blockade of Southern ports resulted in massive unemployment in the English Midlands. English support for Southern naval raiders allowed them to sink a large portion of the Northern merchant marine.[11] The Emancipation Proclamation generated enough support for the Northern cause in England and France to prevent further aid to the South.

It was not slavery that was the main issue, but the question of who would control the federal state. Free farmers and wageworkers found themselves at odds with the interests of the peripheral capitalists of the South on the issue of the frontier, and so they cast their lot with core capital. Thus was the plantocracy destroyed and a strong federal state was created that was firmly in the hands of core capital and supported by key sectors of core labor. This was the form that semiperipheral development took in the nineteenth century. The upward mobility of the United States was hereafter ensured. The regime crises of the antebellum period were over. Core capital had the state and was willing to invent the institutions needed to move onto the global stage as a core state. The alliance among the core capitalists, labor, and farmers would be tested at several points in the future, but the core capitalists would never again be challenged by domestic peripheral capitalists.

The history of the tariff issue is significant as a reflection of contradictory class interests as perceived by the actors and the changing political alliances of classes and interest groups. As mediators of the core/periphery trade, the merchants often sided with the peripheral capitalists, but when the imperial core state (Britain) became unusually hostile, or when manufacturing became more profitable than the maritime trade, the merchants and finance capitalists supported the politics of the domestic manufacturers.

The class alliances of the free farmers were a function of their changing position in the larger world economy. When the world market price of wheat was high, they went with the free-trading South. When the price was low, they supported protectionism and the American System.

A world-historical perspective sheds new light on the class position and alliances of American wageworkers, and implies a new interpretation of the problem of "American exceptionalism." In comparative perspective, the United States is held to be unusual (compared with European societies) because a labor party did not become an institutional part of the political system and the welfare state was only weakly institutionalized. The classic question of American exceptionalism is "Why no socialism in the United States?" As Aglietta (1978) has argued, the original reliance of the propertied classes on farmers and mechanics for support against the British in the War of Independence created a political constitution that allowed the early extension of citizenship and political rights to men of no property. The control that elites maintained over the law and the court system protected the concentration of private property and allowed for the incorporation of non-elite groups into the political process in a way that did not seriously threaten the propertied class. The competition and conflict between core and peripheral capitalists of the North and South caused both to try to mobilize the farmers and mechanics (workers) behind them. Both free traders and protectionists argued that adoption of their tariff policy would raise wages.

It was not the cultural incompatibility of slave society and wage-labor capitalism that led to the irrepressible conflict, but rather the diminishing amount of new territory in which to expand that exacerbated the confrontation between core capitalism and peripheral capitalism. And this was less a struggle between core capitalists and peripheral capitalists (as the earlier controversy over the tariff had been) than a fight between peripheral capital and core labor and farmers. The victory redounded to the favor of the manufacturers, but it was not primarily their interests that led to the conflict.

The conflict between core labor and peripheral capital over the "internal" policies of the state is not inconsistent with a sophisticated version of

[11] This injury and the emerging British superiority in ocean steamships caused the American maritime industry to go into a decline from which it did not recover until the end of the century.

the world-systems perspective. The examination of class conflict as it occurs in the context of the world political economy seeks to eliminate the internal-external distinction, which has confused much previous analysis. The confrontation was caused by "internal" scarcities only because the policy of annexation had come upon natural and political limits. The emergent relative harmony between core capital and an important sector of core labor can be seen in formation in the Civil War. This class coalition made possible the creation of a strong core state that could rise to hegemony in the world-system.

In addition, the dynamism of American economic growth was both a cause and a consequence of the interaction between capital and labor. The open frontier allowed expansion and, even with massive immigration, kept wages higher than they were in Europe. This encouraged capitalists to utilize laborsaving machinery and also provided demand from relatively well-paid workers for an expanding home market for manufactures and agricultural commodities. Thus the political constitution, the legal system, the class structure, and the rate of economic growth made possible a relative harmony between capital and labor in the first new nation, and the outcome of political struggles between core and peripheral capitalists favored the trajectory of upward mobility in the larger core/periphery hierarchy. The expanding frontier was an important factor in this success story. When later militant challenges emerged from the working class, the playing field was tilted in favor of compromise by the ability of the economy to incorporate and reward an expanding middle class and a large sector of labor.

By 1880 the United States had recovered from the Civil War. Industry was booming, and the United States was beginning to play the role of a core power in the newly global world-system. The intertwining of the finance capitalists of New York and London was getting very cozy and was spilling over into other sectors. The wounds of 1812 were healing over. The US economy was becoming more tightly linked by trade and investment with the great powers of Europe, and the West Coast was further developing its ties with the Pacific Rim. In 1898 the former champion of national sovereignty began to dabble in the "new imperialism" of the late nineteenth century by challenging Spain in Cuba and the Philippines. This was a new twist in the Monroe Doctrine in which the former first new nation was becoming the "colossus of the North" in the eyes of the Latin Americans. The British supported the United States against Spain, and the Anglo-American alliance was firmly on.

The indigenes of the American West whose cultures and lifeways had been overrun by the miners, farmers, rails, markets, and buffalo slaughterers developed millennial revitalization movements based on the idea that the white man would disappear and all the dead Indians would come back to life. Some of the enthusiasts of the Ghost Dance religion thought that their ghost shirts would repel bullets, and this belief contributed to some of the massacres of the 1870s and 1890s (Thornton 1986).

New York became the second-largest city on Earth in 1900, though London was still considerably larger (see Figure 15.3). New York did not surpass London in population size until 1925.

There was a strong and militant labor movement in the United States that produced important political institutions. Agrarian socialism emerged in the Granger movement, which opposed the power of big banks and railroads. Unions and parties carried on important struggles and won electoral political power in several midwestern states. The Socialist Party nearly won the presidency, and the Communist Party had 3 million members in the 1930s. So it is not true that there was no socialism in the United States. But the defeat of the radical Left and the incorporation of the labor movement into the Democratic Party does need explaining. The incredible two-hundred-year upward mobility of the United States in the world-system made it possible for the rewards of economic growth to be shared by a sizeable group of middle-class people and skilled workers. Waves of immigration undermined the power of labor organizations by pitting new arrivals against older working-class communities, as did the migration of sharecroppers from the South to the industrial cities of the North. In their book *Labor's Untold Story*, Boyer and Morais (1975) discuss how the relative harmony between capital and labor in the United States developed and what the implications of US hegemonic decline in the twenty-first century are for the future of class relations in the United States. The form of incorporation of the working

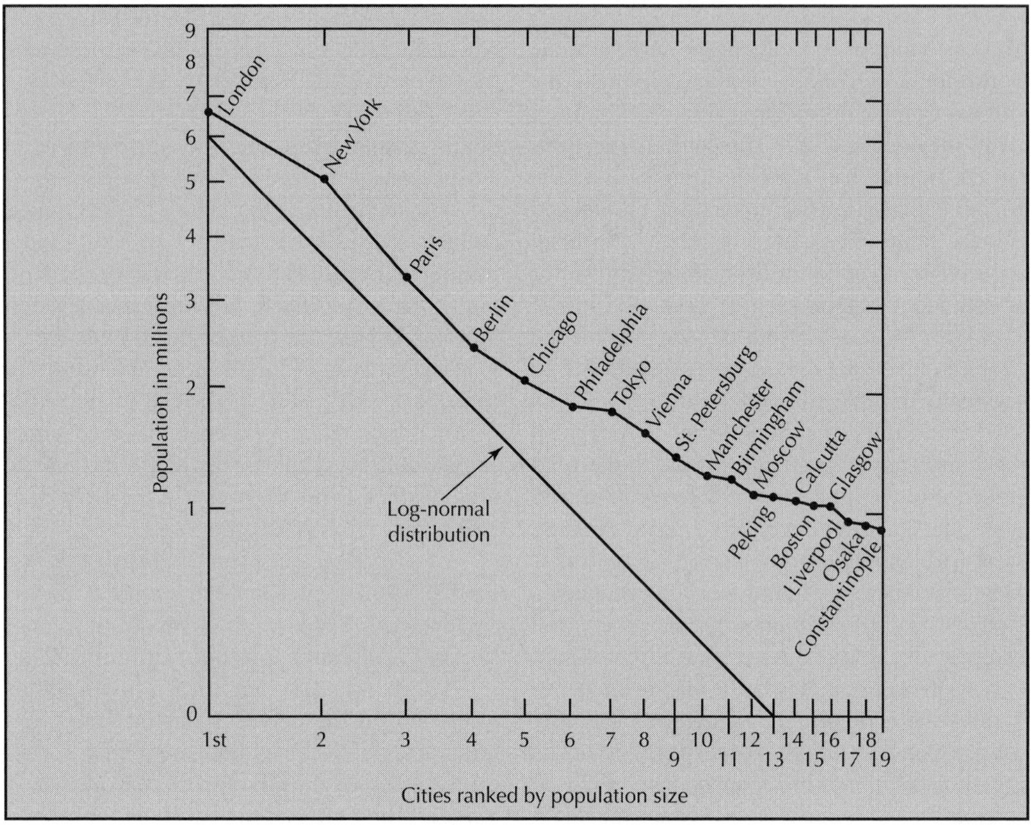

Figure 15.3 Population sizes of world cities in 1900
Source: Chandler 1987.

class in the United States was constructed around nationalism and military service. The first formal welfare institutions created at the time of the Civil War were for war veterans (Skocpol 1992). The citizen-soldier axis was the major institution for building federal welfare institutions in the United States, and this served to undercut the class consciousness of workers by strengthening nationalism. These elements will be traced in the next chapters.

The New Imperialism

Until the nineteenth century, the processes of contestation were substantially separate and autonomous in East Asia, where a trade-tribute system organized by China had long been the central institutional structure of an East Asian world order (Arrighi, Hamashita, and Selden 2003). East Asia had been indirectly linked with the Central (Western) state system by means of long-distance prestige goods trade since before the Roman and Han empires, and though this connection and interaction with intervening Central Asia steppe nomads had some effects on both Eastern and Western state systems, their world orders remained substantially independent until the nineteenth century. In the nineteenth century, the rising European preeminence incorporated the East Asian state system into a single global system of states with a strongly and directly connected set of core states. The increasingly Europe-centered Central System had become organized within its core as a system of spatially bounded and formally sovereign states, most of which claimed control over distant peripheral colonies.

Increasing interimperial rivalry in the late nineteenth century combined with nation building and pressures from emergent classes to produce another wave of European expansion. This can be seen in Figure 15.4, which shows the number of new colonies established from

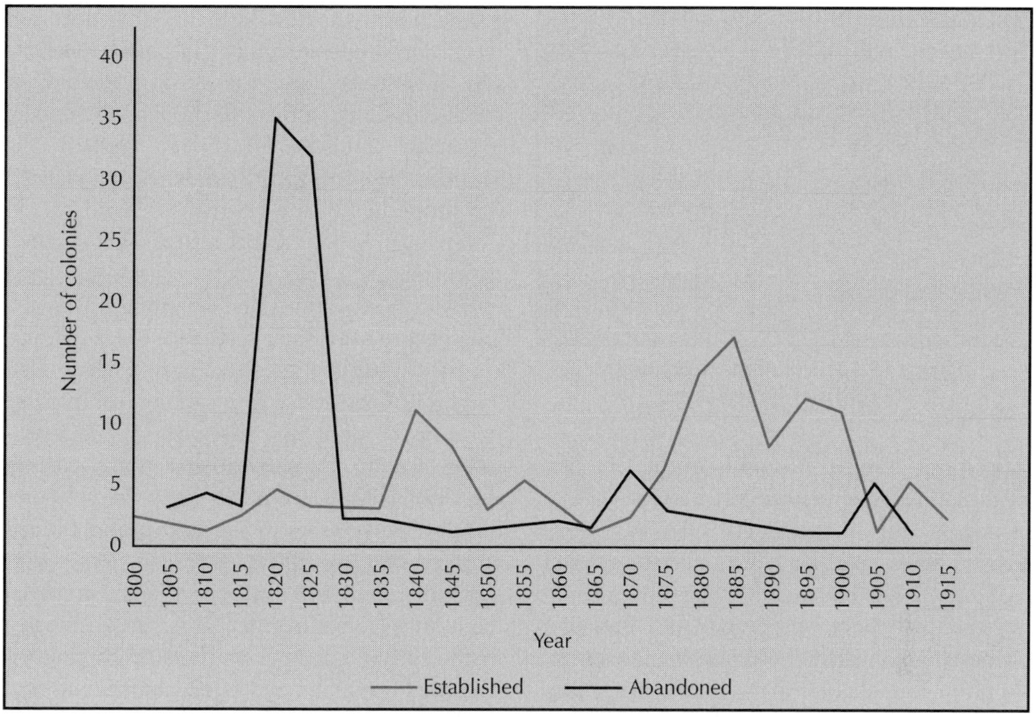

Figure 15.4 Colonial expansion and decolonization, 1800–1915
Source: Data from Henige 1970.

1800 to 1915. There was a wave of new colonies established from 1870 to 1905. This was called the "new imperialism," and the signal event was the Berlin Conference on Africa in 1884, in which the European powers gathered to divide Africa up among themselves.

Figure 15.4 also shows the number of colonies that were decolonized, which can mean that the colony gained sovereignty or that it was taken over by another core power. The vast majority of cases, especially in the first great wave of decolonization that occurred in the first decades of the nineteenth century, were instances of gaining sovereignty and joining the system of sovereign states. The world of sovereign European core states, each with its own colonial empire, was becoming a global interstate system because the former colonies demanded and gained entrance into the system of sovereign states.

These waves of colonization and decolonization had been going on for centuries, but the relations between core and periphery had also been evolving. The big pattern involved first an uneven and long-term transition from old-style tributary imperialism, in which a state would conquer its neighbors and extract tribute, to a new system of colonial empires, in which core states that were competing with one another economically would establish control over distant colonies as sources of raw materials or to help control shipping. The European colonial empires had somewhat different styles, and much of the comparative literature on colonialism focuses on these differences. For example, the British often preferred so-called indirect rule, in which they found a local leader to be their ally and to help them get access to raw materials and markets, while the French often tried to turn all their colonial subjects into French citizens. But in practice all the colonial empires used different mechanisms under different circumstances, and the long-run evolutionary processes can only be seen by more or less ignoring the complications of each case and period.

The second transformation, which is still under way, is from colonial empire to neocolonial dependency (see Figure 15.5). Some have argued that the attaining of formal political sovereignty by former colonies abolishes the core/periphery hierarchy and creates a world of equal states.

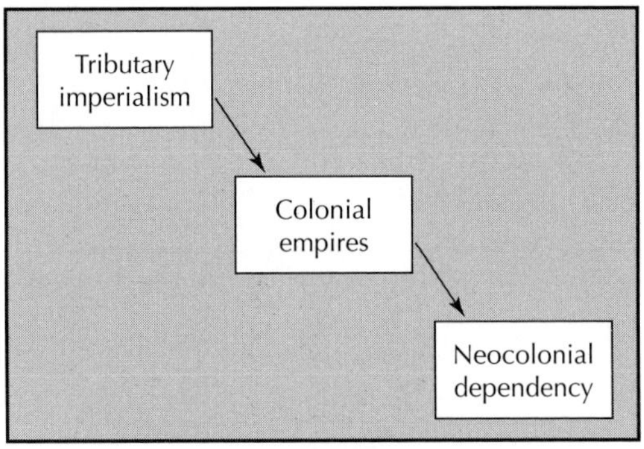

Figure 15.5 Evolutionary typology of forms of imperialism

Indeed, the General Assembly of the UN gives each national member one vote, so the votes of Honduras and of the United States have equal weight. But others point out that institutionalized international inequalities have continued to be structurally important despite the elimination of formal colonialism. What has happened is a shift from formal political mechanisms of control backed up by military power to a system based more on economic power. This shift has been occurring for centuries. Indeed, the prior transformation from tributary imperialism to colonial empires was also based on the rising importance of economic competition among core powers for shares of the world market in **generative sectors**. Semiperipheral capitalist city-states had had colonial empires for millennia before a whole regional system emerged in Europe in which all the core states adopted this type of imperialism. Both of the transitions were due to the increasing importance of capitalist accumulation in the processes of intersocietal competition.

Neocolonialism was one of the main structural innovations that became the basis of US global hegemony after World War II. Both Britain and the United States had perfected the mechanisms of controlling peripheral and semiperipheral countries in Latin America through policies that involved alliances with local elites and military forces, with occasional episodes of "gun boat diplomacy" when other methods failed to achieve the desired result (Go 2011). Control of access to international credit, direct foreign investment, and control over international financial institutions such as the IMF and the World Bank have resulted in de facto US hegemony over Latin America since the United States became a core power in the 1880s. But this does not mean that the United States has always had its way in Latin America. The Mexican Revolution produced a regime that was rather antagonistic toward the "colossus of the North." In the 1930s Mexican president Lazaro Cardenas nationalized the properties of the US-owned Standard Oil Company in Mexico. Other regimes that pursued an independent course have occasionally come to power, and Latin American countries have a long history of episodic resistance to US control.

It should be recalled that Britain also employed neocolonial forms of control in those parts of the periphery that were not incorporated into the formal British Empire. Just as the United States eventually supported decolonization movements in the British and French empires after World War II, Britain lent covert support to Simon Bolivar and the anti-imperial decolonization movements in Latin America in the early decades of the nineteenth century. This was the first wave of decolonization, and the British were quite happy to see the colonies of Spain and Portugal establish their freedom to trade with Britain. And their relations with these "new nations" employed the same mechanisms of financial manipulation, direct investment, and covert operations that would later be called neocolonial when they became the mainstays of US policy toward Latin America.

Though it is in the main correct to say that the United States, itself a former colonized region, never had a formal colonial empire, this is not entirely true (Go 2011). US expansion toward the Pacific Coast was a kind of internal colonialism that involved both buying territorial claims from other core states (France and Russia) and conquering territories claimed by other states. The Mexican-American War and the Treaty of Guadalupe-Hidalgo of 1848 gained a great expanse of western North America from Mexico. The treatment of indigenous peoples and of the Mexican residents of California was as brutal as anything that the other European core powers had done in their colonies, with perhaps a few exceptions.

In the wave of colonialism that was the "new imperialism" in the last quarter of the nineteenth century, the United States belatedly jumped on the bandwagon. Politicians from the American South had long had their eye on choice pieces of Central America and the Caribbean. In 1898 the United States took Cuba and the Philippines from Spain by force, thus participating in the "new imperialism" wave of expansion.

The new imperialism was also a response to pressure from working classes in the core that were agitating to either overthrow capitalism or be included in the capitalist development project. As nation building led to the incorporation of workers into political coalitions as citizens, politicians began to see the advantages of imperial expansion as a way of incorporating workers into their projects. This took different forms in different countries, but the overall pattern came to be known as "social imperialism."

The nineteenth-century wave of globalization was winding down and the winds of world war were blowing. Successful German development was pushing up against the glass ceiling of the world order structured around British hegemony. Hegemonic rivalry, new class struggles, ethnic conflicts, and challenges to the rule of capital were brewing. Anarchist terrorists were using dynamite in their "propaganda of the deed." Socialist parties and labor unions were proclaiming international solidarity of the world working class. Arms races were getting under way. The world revolution of 1917 and the Age of Extremes were peeking through the flowers in the garden of the beautiful epoch.

Suggested Readings

Arrighi, Giovanni. 1994. *The Long Twentieth Century.* London: Verso.

Boyer, Richard O., and Herbert M. Morais. 1975. *Labor's Untold Story*. 3rd. ed. New York: United Electrical, Radio & Machine Workers of America.

Davis, Mike. 2003. *Late Victorian Holocausts: El Niño Famines and the Making of the Third World*. London: Verso.

Dunaway, Wilma. 1996. *The First American Frontier: Transition to Capitalism in Southern Appalachia, 1700–1860*. Chapel Hill: University of North Carolina Press.

Go, Julian. 2011. *Patterns of Empire: The British and American Empires, 1688 to the Present.* Cambridge: Cambridge University Press.

Hobsbawm, Eric J. 1969. *Industry and Empire: An Economic History of Britain since 1750.* London: Weidenfeld and Nicolson.

Hochschild, Adam. 1998. *King Leopold's Ghost*. New York: Houghton Mifflin.

Hopkirk, Peter. 1994. *The Great Game: The Struggle for Empire in Central Asia.* New York: Kodansha International.

Mann, Michael. 1993. *The Rise of Classes and Nation-States, 1760–1914.* Vol. 2 of *The Sources of Social Power.* Cambridge: Cambridge University Press.

O'Rourke, Kevin, and Jeffrey Williamson. 2000. *Globalization and History.* Cambridge, MA: MIT Press.

Polanyi, Karl. 2001 [1944]. *The Great Transformation: The Political and Economic Origins of Our Time.* Boston: Beacon Press.

Ransom, Roger L. 2005. *The Confederate States of America: What Might Have Been.* New York: W. W. Norton.

Stegner, Wallace. 2003 [1942]. *Mormon Country.* Lincoln: University of Nebraska Press.

Thornton, Russell. 1986. *We Shall Live Again: The 1870 and 1890 Ghost Dance Movements as Demographic Revitalization*. Cambridge: Cambridge University Press.

Zinn, Howard. 1999. *A People's History of the United States.* New York: HarperCollins.

16

Public Spaces, Individualism, and Cognition in the Modern Age

The purpose of this chapter is to identify how changes in the technology, economy, and political systems of the core countries of the modern world-system influenced the construction of public and private places, the development of an individualist self, and the emergence of third order abstract thinking.

Public Spaces: The Rise of Secular Geography and Secular Architecture

In the early states we studied in Chapter 9, cities were thought of as a spiritual microcosm of the macrocosm of the stars. In his book *Conceptions of Space in Social Thought*, geographer Robert Sack (1980) argues that the center of the city is primarily a ceremonial center that is structured, if possible, near a sacred plant or tree. From there the four sacred directions radiate out through and beyond the city. Just as certain gods and goddesses were thought to inhabit different provinces in the stars, so did they on Earth occupy certain realms in the city. Sack shows that there is little secular orientation to city planning. In China the sites for the location of settlements were determined by attempting to study earth currents. Cities were square in shape, and the cardinal directions were enclosed by walls with twelve gates, one for each month of the year.

With the rise of agricultural capitalism, European cities began to lose their spiritual connection. Geographers and mapmakers started to lay out natural and social spaces as secularized quantities, infinitely open spaces emptied of their qualitative idiosyncrasies. Cartographers represented space as longitude and latitude, imagining the globe as a homogeneous surface ruled by a uniform grid. The abstract metrical time of the clock was joined by abstract metrical space. When space and time are quantified, they become separable and seem only contingently related. People, things, processes, and meaning became less anchored in space and developed their own autonomous meaning.

In the cities of the early states such as China, the psychic power of spaces was inseparable from the orientation of the bodies of the participants. "Left," "right," "up," "down," "front," and "back" all brought with them psychological experiences. "Up" is associated with superiority, light, purity, and optimism. "Down" came to be associated with inferiority, darkness, impurity, and depression. "Right" is considered full of value, normal, and representing order and spirituality. "Left" is considered depraved, abnormal, disordered, and material. Contrary to all this, the movement of city planners in the West increasingly ignored the psychic characteristics of bodily dimensions. Associations of psychic powers with buildings and directions became marginalized and rendered obscure curiosities.

In the industrial phase of capitalism, as the rate of trade and information sped up, the inseparability of time and the physical environment began to unravel in people's experience. The experiential meaning of space and time became separated from scientific and commercial understandings of geography and "clock" time. The physical environment lost its psychological connection with events and became a mere neutral container for them.

Social Psychology in Public Places: Seventeenth and Eighteenth Centuries

In his book *The Fall of Public Man*, Richard Sennett (1977) contrasts public life in the seventeenth century with public life during the Enlightenment. In the seventeenth century, public space was treated as if it were a stage on which roles are rigidly played, with people reacting to each other in stereotypical ways that go with their social class, and with little or no room for idiosyncratic interaction. For aristocrats, every minute of the day was accounted for, including what to attend, whom to be with, and how long to grow one's fingernails. For the aristocrats, taste was synonymous with good manners.

By the eighteenth century, things began to change. The men who built and sustained the European Enlightenment began to challenge aristocratic notions of civility as being inauthentic. In contrast to "civilization" of the court, the Enlightenment posed "culture," a unity that could be produced through discussion in the town square, where individual differences were at least somewhat addressed. Members of the Enlightenment wanted to demystify taste and art and put art and literature in the service of humanity. Culture was not something that a group "had or hadn't." Rather, culture was understood as a process, as cultivation, to grow what previously was a wild state.

Rise of the Public Sphere in the Eighteenth Century

According to Peter Burke and Asa Briggs (2008) in *A Social History of the Media*, the public sphere is a physical zone in class societies in which debate about political and religious controversies can take place among strangers and between different social classes in public. The public zone is larger than the family but smaller than the state or the church. It can take place through the medium of newspapers, coffeehouses, taverns, public baths, salons, and royal courts for debates in the arts and sciences. The arts through which these media are utilized include image-making/image-breaking (iconoclasm) plays, street theater, political oration, scientific lectures, sermons, writing, reading, and painting. Different social classes were predominant in different places. Taverns were places for artisans, and coffeehouses were for the merchants. The salons were more aristocratic and were organized by women.

Burke and Briggs tell us that there were incipient forms of the public sphere earlier than the modern period. In the Italian city-state of Florence in the thirteenth to fourteenth centuries, a large proportion of the population participated in political life. The squares of the city acted as a kind of public sphere in which speeches were given and politics discussed. This was also the case in Dutch and Swiss city-states including Antwerp, Nuremberg, and Basel.

Burke and Briggs argue that the public sphere had an important religious dimension beginning with the Reformation. The first religious disputes between Catholics and Protestants appealed to the people in Germany, France, and the Netherlands. There was simultaneous development of both propaganda and censorship.

In the early years of the Reformation, the use of propaganda was satirical. In the sixteenth century, Calvinists encouraged a wave of iconoclasm against stained-glass windows and statues. Between the Puritan revolution in 1640 and the Restoration in 1660, the clergy lost control of the public sphere and had to compete with lay preachers, some of them artisans and apprentices who were involved in politics on an almost daily basis. In 1640, a petition against the bishops was signed by 15,000 people. The first period of the public sphere was a *temporary* realm that was a reaction to a religious or political crisis.

Beginning in the seventeenth and eighteenth centuries, the public sphere was utilized in secular political fights between the king, nobility, and the merchants. A big part of the emergence of a public sphere was the emergence of newspapers and coffeehouses. Newspapers reported economic news, and currency rates were read aloud and discussed in coffeehouses. These two institutions turned an earlier temporary public sphere into a permanent institution, making politics a part of daily life for a larger section of the population.

The leading edge for newspaper circulation in the seventeenth century was Holland, with newspapers appearing one to three times per week in Amsterdam. In the United States, newspapers that sprung up in colonies advanced the revolutionary cause by describing atrocities committed by the British. Newspapers created a national political culture by spreading news of events beyond the local level and making it almost instantaneously available for deliberation. Though in France the development of newspapers lagged behind Holland, Britain, and Germany, just before the Revolution in 1789 there were 240 newspapers in circulation.

Some coffeehouses in the early eighteenth century began as appendages to coaching stations. Informal public discussion minimizing class differences was an important means of gaining information about conditions of the road or in the city or about capitalist currencies.

Commercialization Space in the Nineteenth Century

After the "century of revolutions" in the eighteenth century, planning of nineteenth-century cities aimed to create a crowd of freely moving *individuals* and to discourage movement of *organized groups* through the city. According to Sennett (1977), urban planner Georges-Eugène Haussmann created the greatest urban development scheme of modern times. Streets that carried heavy carriage traffic were straightened. Haussmann also separated communities of the working class and the poor with boulevards flowing with traffic. The width of streets permitted two army wagons to travel side by side, enabling the militia to fire into the communities lying beyond the sides of the street wall.

Public space becomes commercialized as roads and public squares are cleared of people in order to circulate raw materials and commodities for trade. Social gatherings and festivities lose their thick sprawl as roads and streets become limited to transporting people, raw materials, and finished products from one place to another. Social gatherings in the streets become thinned out and cleared.

Sennett points out how Harvey's (1999) description of the circulation of blood in the human body is used as a metaphor to describe the circulation of commodities throughout the social body under capitalism. Just as the heart pumps blood through the arteries of the body and receives blood to be pumped from the veins, and just as health was conceived of by Harvey as the free flow and movement of blood and nerve energies, so, too, Adam Smith argued that circulation of goods, labor, and money proved more profitable than fixed and stable possessions such as land. City planners imagined a city of flowing arteries and veins through which people streamed like healthy blood corpuscles. Just as the heart is the center of the body, the circulation of money, goods, and labor is the life of the social body. Just as air is like blood and must circulate through the body, so, too, must fresh air circulate through cities and sanitation conditions improve.

How much did changes in our mode of transportation affect how we experienced the world in the nineteenth century? How might we perceive the world differently when we are riding horses as compared to walking? How might riding in a stagecoach be different from traveling on the railroad? According to Wolfgang Schivelbusch (1986), the railroad profoundly changed our sense perception, our thinking, our emotions, and our expectations.

Unlike traffic on waterways, land traffic is the weakest link in a chain of capitalist evolution because animal power cannot be intensified above a certain fairly low level. Overland motion followed the natural irregularities of the landscape and the physical power of draft animals. During the Middle Ages, travel was limited to horseback or foot. In the sixteenth century, roads were improved, and the first carriages appeared.

There was mass propagation of coaches in the seventeenth century.

Eventually the concentrated power of the steam engine was put to use in the first locomotives. The first trains were used in coalfields, then in the manufacturing industry, and finally for human transport. The natural obstacles to be overcome by means of the rail are the friction between the wheel surface and the road surface and the irregularity of the terrain. A perfect road should be smooth, level, hard, and straight. The rail's primary function was to minimize the resistance caused by friction. Secondly, through cuttings, embankments, tunnels, and viaducts the terrain was leveled before laying the track. The joining of the rail and wheel was the decisive step that joined carriage and road into one machine. The steam engine provided uniform mechanical motion. Traveling time between the most important cities was reduced by four-fifths between 1750 and 1830.

Before the joining of the telegraph to the railroad, the train operators had to watch for obstacles. The telegraph relieved the operator from exercising his perception on the conditions that prevailed around him. He just had to follow the signals. He was the operator of a machine. According to Schivelbusch (1986), the telegraph gave the railway system a kind of central nervous system.

Before the railroad, the variables of riding in a stagecoach included the intractability of the horse, the mood swings of the driver, the driver's cruelty toward the horse, and the ruggedness of the roads. The animal's irregular movement raises and sinks the human body as one travels. There is a *direct experience of the ride being bound up with sensual perception of animal power and exhaustion*. Yet in coach travel, we heard our speed, we saw our speed, we felt it as thrilling.

Riding on a train drastically changed the experience of transportation. With the building of the railroads, the land is flattened and pathways are straightened. A locomotive has shock absorbers that contribute to the smoothness of the ride. The average traveling speed of early railways in England was twenty to thirty miles per hour, roughly three times the speed of stagecoaches. With the railroads, space was both diminished and expanded. It was diminished in the shrinking of transport time, and it was expanded by incorporating new areas into the transport network. The railroad takes you both above (into the mountains) and below (the earth's surface) and bypasses one's sense of touch, taste, and smell.

In part because the relationship between the wheel and the road is so smooth, the passenger loses a sense of the source of power that has been harnessed. There is a loss of sensorial perceptible animal power and fatigue. The railroad did not appear *embedded* in the space of the landscape the way the coach and the highway were. Speeding up travel makes passing towns seem like pictures on a wall. *Railroads transformed landscapes into vistas.* The hurtling railroad train and the endless telegraph poles act as a mediation force with which the new perception inscribes the panoramic landscape. The railroad mimics Newtonian space where size, shape, quantity, and motion are the only qualities that can be objectively perceived in the physical world.

The motion of the train shrank space and displayed in immediate succession objects and pieces of scenery that in their original spatiality seemed to belong to separate realms. That panoramic space is an evanescent landscape whose rapid motion made it possible to grasp the whole—*giving impressions, not details*. The pace of the train prevents the observation of natural objects, and it drives consciousness into subjective rumination for mental activity.

Before mass transit, people had rarely been obliged to sit together in silence for a long time, just staring. Travelers prior to the railroad formed small groups engaged in intensive conversation. Among the working class traveling on trains, this continued. But the railroad journey for the middle and upper classes was different. There were fewer conversations with strangers. The railroad carriage often turned all passenger seats to the "forward" position, leaving passengers to stare at one another's backs, rather than their faces. Both in the railway carriage and on the streets in the nineteenth century, people began to treat as their right not being spoken to by strangers. Reading became a substitute for conversation. The purchase of a train ticket became similar to that of a theater ticket. The more comfortable the moving body became, the more it withdrew socially, traveling alone and silently. In one sense the passenger ceases to be a traveler and becomes a parcel.

Before the railroad, the patchwork of varying local times was no problem as long as traffic between places was so slow that slight temporal differences really did not matter. But the temporal foreshortening of distances affected by trains forced the differing local times to confront each other. Regular traffic needs a standardized time. In 1889 the United States was divided into four time zones.

Twentieth-Century Space

By the twentieth century, public spaces are emptied of both their sacred and political content. Public squares are neither the microcosmic link between the city and the stars, nor the space for political discussion of the issues of the day. Public squares become a no-man's-land as people hover on the margins by themselves or in small parochial groups. There is no centralized public coherency.

Geographical planning divides up land into grids, and its plans project the movement of people, products, information, and raw materials to new areas. Capitalism makes practical the idea of repeatedly and efficiently filling, emptying, and moving things about within territories at all scales. Public space becomes runways for the production and delivery processes of commodities together with the filling of public places with commodities. Most other human activity that does not immediately serve commercial purposes is suspect, marginalized, or driven out by zoning laws or the police. From the point of view of the consumer, it is as if you have no business being in public unless you are buying something or are on the way to buying something.

In his book *Place, Modernity and the Consumer's World*, Robert Sack (1992) argues that in the twentieth century, the invention of automobiles helped to undermine the community life of cities. Streets were increasingly built for the use of autos and trucks, rather than for fairs, parades, and spontaneous gatherings. As the auto preserved and expanded individuality inside of these moving vehicles across space, the individual increasingly made encounters with people *voluntary*. Sadly, urban space today is measured in terms of the *ease with which we drive through it*. The sheer velocity makes it difficult to focus one's attention on the passing scene. Automobile engineers design ways to move through space without obstruction, effort, or engagement. Highway speed tends to neutralize and standardize the spaces through which a speeding vehicle travels. Illusionist parkways are built to present an experience of driving an automobile as a self-contained pleasure, free of resistance. Individuals moving through urban space gradually became detached from the space in which they were moving and from the people the space contained. As space became devalued through motion, individuals gradually lost a sense of sharing a fate with others.

The Evolution of the Private Realm

In his book *Segmented Worlds and Self*, geographer Yi-Fu Tuan (1982) points out that throughout most of the medieval period, private spaces were undifferentiated. A large, uncluttered, and unpartitioned hall served as a public area in which all people might meet, conduct business, and find temporary hospitality. Almost any traveler could make a claim on the hospitality of a manor. Some barons took pride in the openness of their house to all comers. Between the fifteenth and seventeenth centuries, a minor Parisian nobleman might have some twenty-five people living with him—his own family, protégés, clerics, clerks, servants, shopkeepers, and apprentices. People came at all hours, disrupting the routine of the household, but they were rarely shown the door. In the Middle Ages, sleeping was not thought to require a room apart. In a twelfth-century domestic household, retainers and servants slept in the hall, kitchen, or storeroom, anywhere it was warm, dry, and comfortable.

Until the end of the seventeenth century, interconnecting rooms made privacy difficult, if not impossible, to secure. Until the introduction of the corridor in the larger eighteenth-century houses, people could not move from one part of the house to another without passing through intervening rooms.

Multiple uses of space discourages privacy. The great chamber was no more specialized in its functions than the hall in its heyday. In addition to dining, it could also be used for music, dancing, games of cards, family prayers, and the performance of plays and masques. Retreat by the upper classes from these activities was frowned upon as effeminate and rude. Even kings had no privacy. Power and prestige required exposure. A lord who maintained his privilege and effectiveness must be seen, even in his own home. The late medieval house was both a producer of collectivist selves and a product of those selves.

The first room to be abandoned was the hall. In England, even as early as the second half of the fourteenth century, a great man no longer dined there except on special occasions. By 1500 in both royal palaces and private houses, the hall had become the dining room of the lower servants. Princes and nobles moved upstairs to feast in the great chamber, not in privacy, but ceremonially surrounded by people closer to their own status.

By the late Tudor period, servants, except for valets and personal maids, were pushed farther and farther away from the sight and consciousness of the family. In the eighteenth century, servants were isolated. Bell pulls were used to summon valets and maids from a distance. The aristocratic family bond among most relatives was gaining importance at the expense of the ideal feudal allegiance in a large heterogeneous household.

A process of withdrawal from the public use of the house for private purposes began some three hundred years ago, marked by withdrawal into the intimacy of the immediate family By the nineteenth century, rooms became differentiated so as to have specialized functions. The nineteenth-century bourgeois house was a family haven and symbolic embodiment of the psychic dimensions of the individual. During this three-hundred-year period, literate people used "I" in their writing with greater frequency. Words such as "self-knowledge," "self-pity," "ego," "character," "conscience," and "melancholy" emerged.

To retreat implies the existence of private quarters. An enclosed space contains, concentrates, and focuses the human psyche. Sitting by a fire alone or with friends inside a shelter, a person is likely to acquire a more intense awareness of self and of human reality than can occur in the midst of open and undifferentiated space. Within protecting walls, our capacity to attend, feel, or think is spared the distractive buffeting of events beyond our comprehension and control.

Yi-Fu Tuan's (1982) argument is that the emergence of differentiated, specialized places of work in the house is an expression of growing individualism. But Tuan also points to other indicators that went with the rise of individualism:

- The use of chairs rather than benches for eating
- The emergence of quality and discrimination in eating as opposed to quantity
- The use of specialized utensils for each individual rather than general utensils shared by everyone dining
- Table manners that make diners increasingly self-conscious as opposed to hearty gregariousness
- The presence of wall mirrors in the seventeenth century

Modern Individualism

A vertical collectivist identity is founded by living in one place more or less for one's entire life. Within this village or town, one's identity is constrained by loyalty to one's kin group and obedience to traditional authorities, whether lord, priest, or king. Social mobility across classes is low, and the pace of life is relatively slow (at least by twentieth-century standards). We will see how this way of life was weakened in the last five centuries. To review our earlier discussions on individualism, there have been individualist elements all the way back to pre-state societies in the person of a headman, big man, chief, and priest. Individualism grew stronger among upper-class philosophers and sages in the late Bronze Age. During the European Middle Ages and the Renaissance, those who occupied towns and cities, regardless of class, were more individualistic. Space does not permit us to narrate how the formations of the new social institutions impacted the growth of individualism, but we will list the institutions themselves and then provide a table of possible causal relationships (see Table 16.1).

- Agricultural capitalism
- Rise and proliferation of cities
- The absolutist state
- The printing press
- The Protestant Reformation
- The scientific revolution
- The constitutional state
- Representative democracy
- The nation-state
- Railroads, steamships, telegraph, and telephone
- Industrial capitalism
- Automobiles
- Computers and the Internet

Table 16.1 Institutions supporting the emergence of the individualist self

Institution	Description of support
Agricultural capitalism	Supports nontraditional work in towns. Supports the breakup of many local village economies.
Rise of cities	Supports relations with strangers and cosmopolitan influences from other societies.
The absolutist state	Provides new jobs in bureaucracies for intellectuals; new jobs in standing army for peasants.
The printing press	Makes knowledge acquisition private and portable; cultivates relationships with strangers through reading and writing together; undermines storytelling as collective knowledge.
Protestant Reformation	Undermines the priest-mediated basis for sacred experience; emphasizes Protestant work ethic as a divine calling and essential to self-identity.
Secular science	Creates a subculture for exploration into fields of astronomy, physics, chemistry, and biology; provides an alternative home from traditional religion.
The constitutional state	Rule under law is impersonal and free of the caprice of state authority and conformity to kin groups; separation of church and state brings religious freedom and toleration; separation of state from society makes criticism of the state possible; rights of man separate the individual from society via a social contract.
Representative democracy	Political parties are a channel for expressing political views (being a citizen, not a subject); civil society allows individuals social rights and freedom of assembly and of the press.
The nation-state	Creates an abstract, densensualized, expanded community to replace kin groups.
Railroads and steamships; telegraph and telephone	Expand accessible space and accelerate and standardize time; facilitate third order abstract thinking by making it easier to separate time and space from experience.
Industrial capitalism	Supports the accumulation of private property as a source of identity; reduces land to a price, undermining local community; reduces labor identity to a commodity (labor power) to be bought and sold at a price.
Automobiles	Compartmentalize individualist self in public life while expanding it across space in private life.
Computers and the Internet	Make individualized learning possible; increase mobility of learning through portability; instantaneous connection with a globalized network without state interference.

We do not claim that this list is exhaustive. Perspective painting, social contract theory, liberalism, the Enlightenment, and Romanticism could be added, along with colonial exploration and the rise of the novel in literature.

Characteristics of the Individualist Self

We are now in a position to examine how the individualist self experiences roles, situations, the generalized other, the biographical self, and "I-Me" dialogues in light of these sociohistorical changes. By the twentieth century, individualism in the core capitalist countries has spread to the middle class and sectors of the working class at least as an ideology, if not a practice. In other words, wealth buys privacy, time, and distance from other people. Those in working-class positions still have to live in smaller apartments or in multifunctional rooms and to rely on their neighbors for safety and support. We will begin with our modern individualist identity and how situations are constructed.

In routine situations, compared to the collectivist form and all previous forms of individualism, the modern individualist self images her relationship to society and nature in the form of a *contract*. The modern individualist might call into question her relationship with the kin group and with traditional authority figures more consistently. At the same time, she must find new group relationships based not on blood and tradition but on common interests. Examples include membership in clubs, political organizations, or nontraditional spiritual groups. Perhaps most important for our purposes, the individual is a buyer and seller of commodities and a member of a globalizing market, and this forms a substantial part of her identity, whether this identity is conscious or not. Further, all these new relations are perceived as instrumental, to be taken on or cast off depending on self-interest.

In part because the modern individualist selves have psyches clearly perceived to be inside their skin rather than diffused in nature or mixed with kin groups, individualists play roles but *identify* with them less. Because social relations are imagined to be contractual roles, they are instrumental and temporary. For the individualist self, their unique personality is what gives them definition. Since the rate of change is so much faster in the modern core countries, individualists are generally more comfortable with change and are better at *role-making* than role-taking. With rapid change, a greater number of situations cease to be routine, becoming either problematic or even crisis-driven. Compared to the collectivist self, the individualist self is far less loyal to traditional political or spiritual authorities and to their neighborhood. Individualists' loyalties are instead to their nation-state or sports teams.

In terms of the generalized other, the modern individualist will adapt to a multiplicity of roles because people in core countries in the modern world-system have many more roles to play than collectivists on average. They will understand these roles as detachable because of the increased rate at which they changed. Individualist selves understand roles as more global because the modern increase in world interdependence makes it clear that the roles they play are being played simultaneously on a global scale. Finally, this individualist has the potential to see roles as historical, because the emergence of the historical sciences such as anthropology and world history have exposed at least some roles as being relative and recent.

The individualist self also cultivates a sharper sense of *subjectivity*, an inner life that is a temporary retreat from the roles, rules, and expectations of family and kin, friends, workmates, and strangers. Because the individualist understands herself as separate from the group, the "story" (ontogenesis) of her biographical self is generally more important than her group history. In part because of this, she takes more responsibility for what becomes of her in her past, present, or future. The individualist allows the self-reflective part of her identity to have a separate life of its own. While most individualists believe in a monotheistic divinity, that source is seen by them as affording some autonomy to control their lives even as they are accountable to that deity for their choices. Individualists have an *internal* (rather than external) locus of control. Because of their cultivation of objectivity and subjectivity, the individualist self has greater potential to be a social reformer or a revolutionary than the collectivist self or previous forms of individualism.

By way of summary, here is a list of the skills and tendencies that go with the individualist self:

- Multiple sources of socialization
- Imagining the social and natural relations as a contract
- An internal locus of control of self
- A separation of self from roles
- More role-making as opposed to role-taking
- A more objective generalized other
- A greater capacity for situational transformation
- Preoccupation with their subjective states of consciousness
- Individual development conceived of as separate from group development
- "I-Me" dialogue weighted on the side of the "I"

However, all these skills require a higher "third order" form of abstract reasoning. It is to this we now turn.

Cognitive Evolution in the Modern Age: Third Order Abstraction

In Chapter 9 we argued that second order abstract reasoning began in the Bronze Age with the division of society into mental and physical workers. Some of the fruits of the work of mental laborers included the inventions of hieroglyphics and abstract counting systems. Three inventions in the Late Iron Age—the alphabet, standardized metal currency in Greece and India, and the political forum of the polis in Greece—consolidated second order abstraction. When artisans and peasants had to learn to use coined tokens, this expanded the power of second order abstraction. The question we want to address in this chapter is to what extent inventions in the *modern world-system* instigated a still higher level of abstraction.

Before proceeding, we want to make explicit the differences we see between second order and third order abstraction. Second order abstraction corresponds to the thinking processes of state bureaucrats and merchants of agricultural state societies. Third order abstraction corresponds to the activity of the middle and upper classes working in core and semiperipheral countries in science, education, political bodies, state organizations, and various forms of capitalist trade.

We've identified the following differences between the two forms of abstraction. In third order abstraction:

- *Symbols*, whether letters, math notations, or coins, become *more autonomous* from experiences and sense data of goods, people, and places.
- *Symbols are built upon symbols* and acquire a life of their own; they "square themselves."
- There is more powerful *manipulation of the objective world* (whether it be in the service of accumulating capital, in the study of nature, or in inventing tools).
- The manipulation of the world occurs across a *greater range of space and over a shorter period of time.* This has been called "space-time compression."
- There is an increase in the understanding of quantitative reasoning such as chance and probability.
- The mind becomes more *self-reflective and critical* of its own processes in studying epistemology.

Growth of Third Order Abstraction and the Scientific Revolution of the Seventeenth Century

Evidence and Explanation in the Middle Ages

According to Ian Hacking in his book *The Emergence of Probability* (1975), in the medieval world, at least for theologians, knowledge was based on certainty, or it wasn't considered knowledge at all. Understanding a problem by referring to probability was merely considered "opinion." For medieval theologians, knowledge, in contrast to opinion, was based on universal truths that are true of necessity, not probability. The basis of evidence in the Middle Ages was that it was approved by some authority or by the testimony of respected judges.

One way you showed a claim to be wrong was by *demonstration*. Since in order to have knowledge, evidence had to be 100 percent true, all you had to do was demonstrate one exception to the rule to prove it wrong. Another way of proving something wrong is through *verisimilitude*. Here evidence is weighed when an empirical example is compared to what the essence of something is supposed to be like. How do you know its essence? One knows essence by its definition. Both of these criteria are based on deductive logic.

Another category for weighing evidence was *signs*. But signs in the Middle Ages were different from how signs were understood during the scientific revolution. For Paracelsus, all signs were signatures. This means that every object in the world is connected to a set of correspondences at both the macrocosmic and microcosmic levels. So, for example, each of the planets had a sympathetic system of relationship with particular animals, plants, herbs, stones, incense, music, and the parts of the human body. A physician must learn these correspondences because the ailment of his client may have to do with the condition of the stars for the client. It was believed that God had left his signature in the stars, in nature, and in humanity and that they could be read and manipulated. In the Middle Ages there was little sense that anything of significance in the world could be due to chance. Everything was linked by a vast correspondence system of the very large (macrocosm) and the very small (microcosm). As the occult motto goes, "As above, so below." Summing up, we have evidence by demonstration, verisimilitude, and signs as signatures. The philosophical foundation for this was Aristotle.

Aristotelian science did not make a distinction that was made in seventeenth-century science between the primary characteristics of matter and the secondary characteristics of our senses. For Aristotle, matter could not be known independent of our senses. For Aristotle, the study of physics was the study of unrelated qualitative essences that could not be measured but could be known to some extent by our senses and partly through logical deduction. Evidence from demonstration, verisimilitude, and signs was a product of this deduction.

What was lacking in medieval science? *Inductive evidence*. What exactly does that mean? It means looking for physical evidence in the real world that could be publicly observed and verified independently of authorities, testimony, or definition. This evidence could indicate, contingently, the state of some other physical object. This meant that scientists had to interpret signs in new ways—not spiritually as part of a vast correspondence system but as either circumstantial evidence or chance occurrences. However, in order to be able to do this, an epistemological revolution was required in the relationship between the objective world and the subjective experience. The objective world had to be completely separated from the subjective world.

Epistemological Revolutions Set the Stage for Seventeenth-Century Science

The new science separated the objective properties of nature (primary qualities such as size, shape, motion, and weight) from our physiological states (secondary qualities such as taste, color, and sound). Further, primary qualities could be measured mathematically. Instead of physics as the study of unrelated categories of qualities, as in Aristotle, the new physics was the science of measurable qualities that could be related to one another by mathematics. Rather than Aristotelian forms, seventeenth-century science posed "laws of nature" that were about the interactive relationships of matter that could be measured. Where Aristotelian science tried to proceed by demonstration of effects from first causes, the new science identified efficient causes based on a new procedure: experiment. The process of scientific experimentation is the foundation for third order abstraction.

Roots of Scientific Experiment

In *The Emergence of Probability*, Hacking (1975) argues that different types of experimental methods converged in the seventeenth century. He distinguishes between four different types of experiments:

1. *The test*. This is a matter of deduction or hypothesis testing. One tests a hypothesis when the hypothesis predicts certain events will occur. If the event occurs, the hypothesis is proven right. If the event fails to occur, the hypothesis is disconfirmed.
2. *The adventure or dabbling*. This approach is not guided by a theory, and it is only exploratory. We make guesses as to what might happen. Any theory that develops happens after the "adventure" with reality. Hacking says that much of early alchemy operated this way.
3. *The diagnosis*. This consists of analyzing the character of an illness. You infer what is wrong by reading signs in the body of an animal.
4. *The dissection*. This is a matter of taking something apart to see what is inside. An anatomist dissects the dead.

Tests, adventures, diagnosis, and dissection all provide evidence, and the evidence in turn leads to different consequences. The test either demonstratively refutes or confirms a hypothesis. Dabbling at its best suggests a theory. A dissection shows the inner workings of an animal, and a diagnosis leads to a prognosis about what to do about a physical or mental problem.

Hacking argues that the Middle Ages had a concept of each kind of evidence, but there was a difference between the use of signs for making a diagnosis in the Middle Ages and the use of signs for making a diagnosis in the Renaissance. Table 16.2 is a summary of the different types of experiments.

In the Middle Ages, the distinction between signs as indicators of spiritual correspondences and signs as efficient causes was not made, because there was no inductive science. However, in medical textbooks of the Renaissance, there is a characteristic distinction between causes and signs. Causes are basically *efficient* causes or symptoms based on diagnosis or dissection. Signs are no longer just indicators of spiritual correspondences but could be *circumstantial evidence* that is present when something happens, for example, when planets are in conjunction or when a comet appears. This event could be interpreted as having to do with some *other* physical event, or it could be a chance occurrence. In the Renaissance, observation of signs was still interpreted as testimony from God or the authorities. However, alongside of it with the new science, evidence could be testimony *from nature*.

Table 16.2 Types of experiments

Type of evidence	Example	Consequences
Test—inner seeing that is deduction	Hypothesis testing	Demonstratively refutes a hypothesis or else corroborates it (proof—passing the test)
Adventure, dabbling—not guided by a theory and we may only guess what happens	Much early alchemy: you heated, mixed, and burned a substance to see what would happen	Suggests a theory
Diagnosis—from the character of the problem by reading signs	Physical or mental illness	Prognosis: what to do to relieve the illness
Dissection—taking something apart to see what is inside; visual motivation	A surgeon operates on the brain or an artist dissects the anatomy of a cadaver	Inner workings of man and beast

It is the transformation of signs into possible circumstantial evidences or chance events that is a landmark for induction. For the new science, looking for signs is not looking for formal, let alone final, causes. Signs are only indicators, possible efficient causes that must be analyzed and organized into an experiment with the hypothesis being falsifiable. Now the result of passing a test was to get *new inductive evidence* for the hypothesis. It is evidence of one thing that points to evidence somewhere else. There is a movement away from Aristotelian essences of nature to *laws of nature driven by the interaction of physical events independently of God, correspondences, or human volition*.

A new kind of evidence conferred *probability* on propositions, making them worthy of approval. This evidence could be assessed by the frequency with which these events made predictions come true. If they occurred frequently, they were significant in explaining what the scientist wanted to find out. If they did not appear frequently, they were chance events. A new kind of testimony was accepted, the testimony of *nature*. Nature could now confer evidence by law-like regularities and frequencies.

Induction is the method by which we reason about what is probably true and what is likely due to chance. Both are based on evidence that is contingent and that is not entailed on our claim. One of the products of the scientific revolution is our acceptance of probability based on induction rather than deductive certainty in coming to our conclusions about evidence. Reasoning deductively can be useful for structured games, math problems, or formal logic problems, but the real world is too complicated to know things for certain. Please see Table 16.3 for the transformation of signs.

In what fields was induction first developed? It was not in what has been characterized as the high sciences, such as astronomy, mechanics, or optics. Hacking (1975) claims scientists were still hoping for demonstrations. It was in the "low" sciences like alchemy, geology, astrology, and medicine that inductive evidence first took hold.

Early Modern Science Inseparable from Magic and Craft

There are serious limitations in the way the scientific revolution has been presented by Enlightenment historians. In this depiction we find heroic success stories of brilliant intellectuals who overcame religious superstitions to help give birth to an independent secular culture. From the Renaissance all the way into the eighteenth century, many of the greatest scientists of the period, including Copernicus, Kepler, and even Newton, saw themselves as part of a Neoplatonic, magical, and alchemical tradition, and this helped guide their discoveries, at least early on. For example, the alchemists produced how-to books on metallurgy, glassmaking, ceramics, dyeing, and painting. Astrology was used not just by ignorant peasants but by courts of kings hoping to predict the future. In the process of doing this, astrologers such as John Dee helped develop mathematics.

Two of the first disciplines to be impacted by the scientific revolution were astronomy and biology. But the tools that were necessary for both—the telescope and the microscope—were

Table 16.3 Transformation of signs to either circumstantial evidence or chance events

Category of comparison	Medieval science	Seventeenth-century science
How are signs interpreted?	Resemblances of macro-micro magical links	Conventional and arbitrary signs invented by humanity
Relationship between signs and causes	Signs and causes are inseparable	Signs and causes are separable
Place of chance	There are no coincidences; every sign has a meaning	Signs are circumstantial evidence for causes, or chance events have nothing to do with real causes
Type of cause of signs	Formal or final causes—an answer to the essence of something	Efficient causes—how physical objects interact
How is knowledge gained?	Demonstration, verisimilitude—signs as correspondences	Experiment
Are tests falsifiable?	Not falsifiable	Yes, can be proven wrong
Reasoning processes	Deduction	Induction
Why are signs valuable?	Comfort by confirmation of what one already believes	Judged by the frequency with which signs help make predictions; gaining new inductive evidence for a hypothesis or disconfirming evidence that allows for other exploration

provided by craftsmen who were lens grinders and spectacle makers. In his book *How We Got Here*, Hallpike (2008) points out that the development of experimental science in the West would not have fully blossomed until scientists engaged with craftsmen whose work necessitated accurate physical measurement. The expertise of these "artist-engineers" lay in the rational control of the materials themselves, the process of making them, and the practices of finding out what worked and what didn't work. These areas included clock making, navigation, surveying, printing, bronze casting, masonry, canal building, fortification, and gun powder.

Hallpike points out that one of the major differences between the science of Western Europe and the science of other great civilizations is that forums were developed where craftsmen, scientists, and artists worked on projects jointly. The merchant and artisan guilds were far more independent of the upper classes in Europe. By 1700 a number of colleges emerged to promote collaboration between craftsman and scientist. Hallpike (2008, 393) cites the activity of the Luna society in the late eighteenth century as just one example:

> Its members were a group of friends who met every month . . . and included James Watt and Matthew Boulton (steam power), William Murdock (gaslight), Joseph Priestley (chemistry), John Baskerville (printing), Josiah Wedgwood (pottery), Erasmus Darwin (botany and evolutionary theory), James Keir (chemistry and glassmaking), Richard Edgeworth (electricity and the telegraph).

Second Order versus Third Order Abstraction in Science

We are now ready to contrast the differences between second and third order abstraction. The foundation for these differences was, first, the revolution in cartography, astronomy, perspective painting, musical notation, and accounting that occurred between the twelfth and the sixteenth centuries (as discussed in Chapter 12). In addition, during the same period there were major changes in theatrical performances, in plot and character development. The third link is the scientific revolution of the seventeenth century and its new understanding of evidence. Later in this chapter we will discuss how capitalism invited third order abstraction.

Second order abstraction is used by most people in everyday life and was especially used in all of science prior to the twelfth to thirteenth centuries in Europe. Then things begin to change.

In second order abstraction, the mind abstracts from sense data and reorganizes (reverses) operations in a logical way, but it operates closer to the proximate space and time conditions in which it originated. Third order abstraction used by modern science operates in conditions far from the original context in which the problem was posed.

For example, Newton discovered gravity through the observations of the free fall of bodies, the orbits of the planets, and the ebb and flow of the tides. These were hardly processes that were happening right in front of his face at one time and in his local area. Further, not all the sense data immediately available to Newton were used. Only what Newton saw as *essential* about gravity was used. The rest were considered "accidents" and not worth attending to. Furthermore, these data were drawn from past times and other places and shaped into an idealized model. Finally, at its best, whatever the results of the experiment were, these results were systematically tested at different times and different places to see whether the experiment could be replicated. In second order abstraction, whatever is found to be true in the present is not systematically tested by varying the times and settings to try and replicate the findings. Second order abstraction, if the same procedure works in a new setting, continues to be used. If it doesn't, it is replaced by some other process in a trial-and-error way. What is missing in second order abstraction is the *systematic process of elimination* by which one hypothesis stands while another falls.

In second order abstraction, symbols are used for practical purposes in everyday life. There is no systematic attempt to make a study of the symbol system itself. While mathematical notations, paint marks, or literature are used to build architecture, make paintings, or write poetry, there isn't a separate study of trigonometry or calculus (the study of rational, irrational, or imaginary numbers), nor treatises on perspective theory or the study of language (linguistics) itself. In third order abstraction, from the seventeenth century on, the principle that emerges as true as a result of an experiment is incorporated into theories, and these theories are built into laws that are expressed mathematically and are hierarchically organized. These laws may not have any reference to local experienced conditions.

Another distinction between the two forms of abstraction is how they make sense of chance. In second order abstraction, a distinction is made between what can be predicted and what cannot be predicted. However, chance is understood in terms of accidents or things that were unintended. Chance is understood as lawless. There is no sense of the laws of large numbers, systematic combinations of possibilities that are independent of personal experience. It is only with third order abstraction that chance events are understood in terms of proportions and combinations that are independent of personal experience. This includes the law of large numbers and other laws that are learned today in courses on statistics and research methods.

While the study of probabilities is older than the seventeenth century, the study of chance takes off not just in the service of scientific investigation but in the policies of absolutist states when they attempt to take a census of the population, track taxes, and conscript subjects. It also occurs in the annuity policies of merchants, especially Dutch merchants, calculating the risks of trade.

In second order abstraction, the reasoning process closely follows what is called "informal logic." This means that a claim is tested on the basis of evidence in the real world with the understanding that the world is too complicated to know anything with absolute certainty. In addition, the distinction between the form of an argument and its content will be mixed together. For example, if we say:

> In the Outer Sunset District of
> San Francisco, all people are cold,
> even in the summertime.
> Jim lives in the Outer Sunset.
> Jim is cold.

This is a valid argument in formal logic, whether or not it is objectively true. However, in informal logic, you might say that the conclusion does not necessarily follow. Jim may dress extra warm, or his body may have adapted over many years of having lived in the Outer Sunset District. Formal logic by itself is not enough for third order abstraction. In the Late Iron Age, the upper-class people of Greece and India used deductive logic. A key addition of the scientific revolution was the systematic use of induction in experiments.

The Mind Reflects Critically on Its Own Processes

Let us turn to the ontological question of what the mind itself is. Ontological questions such as the place of human beings in the cosmos, the nature of sacred spirits, and the nature of the afterlife have been asked and answered by all societies all the way back. However, epistemological questions about the reliability and certainty of sources of knowledge were not explicitly studied until the Iron Age civilizations of Greece, China, and India. Tribal and early state civilizations understood the mind as part of either a spiritual substance or a physical substance such as smoke or breath. It was only with second order abstraction that the mind was understood not as a substance but as a process that mediates between the real world on the one hand and the body on the other.

In spite of this, second order abstraction is using the mind to operate on real things. A priest in an agricultural state might learn to think more abstractly by repeatedly coordinating the redistribution of agricultural products. Merchants in the same states may also learn to think more abstractly by repeatedly handling currency and bills of exchange. Yet the mind is still pointed at the objective activity of trading. In third order abstraction, the mind turns more inward, examining its typical predispositions, biases, and weaknesses.

In the early third order abstraction of the Greeks, the mind reflects on its own thinking process, not just on formal logic. The crafting of the science of rhetoric by Aristotle and Cicero also shows the mind reflecting on its own thinking processes. This time the mind is reflecting on the timing, setting, and kinds of evidence necessary to persuade audiences in speech making. Aristotle also developed his famous list of fallacies in rhetoric, and many others followed, including Francis Bacon in the early modern period with his idols of the cave, tribe, marketplace, and theater.

But the full consequences of the study of epistemology come in how scientists design, carry out, interpret, and defend experiments. It is here that the weaknesses and biases of the mind are clearly exposed to public scrutiny. In the case of interpreting statistics, typical fallacies such as base-rate neglect in estimating probabilities, inversion of conditional probabilities, small sampling, unrepresentative sampling, and gambler's fallacy are common knowledge in scientific communities.

The Possible and the Real

In second order abstraction, the starting point is the real problematic situation. What is possible are the realistic strategies the mind might employ to resolve the problem in an adequate way. What is *hypothetically* possible is a special case of reality that is taken as given. In an idealized third order abstraction, the starting point is not a particular situation in real life but a possible situation that the scientist constructs in setting up an experiment. In this case, the real is not a starting point, but only one of a number of possibilities.

In second order abstraction, not all the possibilities for a situation are considered before action is taken. The most obvious examples include jumping at the first job offer that is made without examining the entire field you want to work in, the different types of work within a field, and where the most promising work is located. Trial and error is used more often. People act before testing not just all *likely* outcomes but all *possible* outcomes. In third order abstraction, all possibilities are tested in a planned, systematic way. The scientist then tries to impose the best possibility on reality, rather than accepting reality as it is. In applied science, the results of an experiment are applied in the form of technology or energy-harnessing systems that can improve human life.

In second order abstraction, the mind develops a strategy to solve a problem and then tries the strategy out. But the conditions and reasons why the strategy works are limited in their rigor. Whatever strategy is used is not systematically compared with other strategies. The reasons for choosing the initial strategy include convenience, economy of cost, and habit. For example, you might use a lower form of abstraction if you possess average problem-solving skills and you are trying to fix a clogged pipe. You pick up and discard whatever tools you have accumulated over the years as they appear to become more or less helpful. Good plumbers think using third order abstraction. They have at their command all the possible tools they would use, and they have internalized when and where they might use them. Furthermore, they have prioritized their sequencing based on their assessment of the problem. While they might not be able to explain what they already know and do, third order abstraction is applied in practice. Further, the most serious test for the truth of a proposition is its ability to predict the future. People who think in a lower form of abstraction operation are not that ambitious. They just want the pipe fixed!

Falsifiability

The problem with attempting to predict the future with a hypothesis, as philosophers of science tell us, is that you cannot eliminate a number of other competing hypotheses that can just as easily fit the data. So as Karl Popper taught us, instead we state the conditions under which we would be willing to admit we are wrong—making claims falsifiable. In second order abstraction, claims are not presented in a falsifiable way. In second order abstraction, conditions of falsifiability are not stated. Sometimes their claim might be right and sometimes not, but right or wrong, without stating the conditions of falsifiability beforehand, it is hard for scientific knowledge as a whole to progress because no hypotheses can be *eliminated*.

A good hypothesis tries to state as clearly and as quantitatively as possible the conditions under which it could be proven wrong. This is done by operationalizing definitions of key terms. It makes predictions *before* rather than after whatever it has claimed to study. A good hypothesis acts efficiently, meaning it not only tries to show it is the best explanation but also disconfirms competing hypotheses. Disconfirming a competing hypothesis allows others to test the new hypothesis or test the hypothesis that has worked so far and test it in new realms. Being able to eliminate false hypotheses is an important and underrated scientific activity.

Further, modern science insists that solid new hypotheses not only explain new facts but also do not violate facts that have already been established. If a new hypothesis disrupts as much or more of an accumulated body of knowledge than it explains, it does not advance knowledge. It must conserve what already exists as well as expand on it.

In second order abstraction, types of evidence that are typically allowed are personal experiences (case studies), experiences of friends (testimonials), cultural myths, or expert authorities. In third order abstraction, these types of evidence are too unreliable. Cases may be atypical, the motives of friends or witnesses are always mixed, and there could be controversy between the sources of authority. The evidence of choice for third order abstraction is research based on statistics that are verifiable and replicated to ensure the results are not a fluke.

Lastly, in second order abstraction, a body of knowledge is often inseparable from a particular person who has the knowledge. When individuals die, the knowledge dies with them. Also, this knowledge is often hoarded, used, and released as it serves the self-interest of individuals, as was the case in early states. What feeds and enhances third order abstraction is a common pool of knowledge that can be built up and criticized publicly. This is not to say that the scientific community cannot be secretive and that better theories aren't developed for political or economic reasons. It just means that if third order abstraction is to be advanced, for better or worse, it is more likely to be found through this community. This lessens the chances of it being corrupted or derailed. A body of knowledge is manipulated and reorganized independent of who said it and when or where it was said. Furthermore, after an experiment is reported, peers criticize it. Before a finding reaches the public, it has been filtered through a specialized scientific body of practitioners that has self-correcting mechanisms built in. This means that *good science is a collective practice that evolves over time*.

The purpose of this entire section is not to review scientific methodology per se. Its purpose is not just to show what the differences between second and third order abstraction are, but how third order abstraction is something that developed over a five-hundred-year period in the West from the twelfth century to the seventeenth century. Table 16.4 is an overview of the differences between the orders of abstraction.

Reservations and Qualifications about Levels of Abstraction

So far we have presented third order abstraction in a way that might appear more rigid and unilinear than we think it is. In the spirit of being dialectical, we offer the following qualifications:

- *Third order abstraction is not more progressive or better than other forms of abstraction.* We follow the great cognitive psychologist Piaget in claiming that all human thinking processes as adaptations to an environment. In the case of human beings, that means adaptation to technology, political movements, and economic movements as they affect work, play, and home. The presence of second order or third order cognition simply means that people living in those societies have built up a complex social environment of institutions that requires more abstract thinking to work and live in them.
- *Third order abstraction is not automatically adaptative.* The fruits of the scientific revolution that was part of building third order abstraction were used to increase the scope and depth of war in the last three hundred years. Third order abstraction has presided over ecological degradation. As we will see in the section on third order cognition and capitalism, the wheeling and dealing of stock markets certainly demands third order abstraction, but it has become highly questionable whether those institutions and the people who run them are using long-term adaptation strategies. Neither does it mean that second order abstraction is not adaptative in social settings that require a more hands-on approach.
- *Earlier forms of abstraction do not disappear.* Just as coins and paper money do not disappear once checks and credit cards emerge, first and second order abstraction continue to exist among members of society when they switch to more hands-on problems.
- *The absence of a scientific revolution or the development of capitalism does not mean people on the margins of industrial capitalist societies do not use third order abstraction.* We are only suggesting that third order abstraction must be cultivated through practice in specific social institutions that demand it be learned. Without the necessity of learning it, there is nothing that is spontaneously pleasurable or that will serve natural selection. For example, how many people spontaneously teach themselves statistical laws of probability when they go to the racetrack or play the lottery? People will learn to think this way when social institutions demand it.
- *Not everyone in industrial capitalist societies uses third order abstraction.* Lastly, we are not suggesting that all or even most people use third order abstraction even if they live in industrial capitalist societies. At most, a minority of social classes—mostly middle and upper-middle classes—will use this, and even if they do, this does not mean they use this skill in settings outside of work. We are claiming that if, when, or whether third order abstraction emerges, science and capitalism are two social institutions that will invite its cultivation.

Capitalism and Third Order Abstraction

During and after the emergence of agricultural, industrial, and financial capitalism, the use of third order abstract thinking becomes a greater possibility for those classes that do mental work. Yet the development of capitalist exchange relations permeates social relations so that even those in the working class will be pulled into the maelstrom. Capitalist institutions such as banks and the stock exchange force everyone to cultivate some aspects of third order abstraction to some extent because we simultaneously handle coins, paper money, checks, and credit cards. To use any of these currencies, to put our faith in banks, the stock market, and the clerks, bank managers, and stock traders—strangers we will never meet—is no mean feat of abstraction. The events of September 2008 and their aftermath showed there is a steep price to be paid for this faith!

When coined money arose in the first millennium BCE, money was generally invested in

Table 16.4 Second order versus third order abstraction

Category of comparison	First or second order abstractions (pre-seventeenth-century science)	Third order abstraction (seventeenth century)
What is the relationship between symbols and reality? (Symbols include letters, math notions, music notions, painting, and coins)	Proximity in time and space from experience's sense data of goods, people	Greater distance from local space and present time from experience, sense data, goods, and people (Newton's experiment with gravity; experimental replication in different times and places attempted)
To what extent do symbols act on symbols?	Symbols are distinguished from objects (not magically enmeshed), but they are still used reactively in relationship to objects	Symbols "square" themselves; symbols are built on each other and take on a life of their own (algebra, trigonometry, calculus, music theory, theories of painting perspective)
What does the mind operate on?	Reversible operations on sense data and planned action	Reversible operations on systems of ideas
How are classification systems grouped?	Taxonomic: objects grouped into classes that have close spatial and temporal locations	Taxonomic: objects grouped into classes that have no spatial or temporal relations with each other (Linnaeus system)
Extent of manipulation of the objective world	Instrumental, episodic manipulation in local contexts	Systematic manipulation in inventing tools, study of nature
How are chance occurrences and likelihood understood?	Chance is the result of uncaused accidents, unintended results; likelihood estimations based on personal experience	Chance is the result of lawful combinations that have regularity whether they are intended or not; likelihood estimates may violate personal experience (Galileo, Pascal, Port Royal Logic; used by state for census collection, taxes, conscription, and annuity calculation by merchants)
Form of reasoning: By what process are conclusions drawn?	Informal logic: form (validity) of an argument is embedded in content (truth); truth derives from personal experience, and it cannot be counter to personal or human experience	Formal logic (deduction): separation between validity and truth; a proposition can be valid based on no experience as well as being empirically impossible (Euclidean geometry, Descartes, Spinoza) Induction—physical evidence independent of authorities and testimonies of others

commodities to sell. Profit was made by selling a good at a price that exceeded the costs at which it was bought. The important point is that money was used instrumentally, *as a means* to accumulate more goods. But with the rise of industrial capitalism in the nineteenth century, this process is joined by another process by which money is not just a mediator for the buying and selling of goods and services, but takes on a life of its own. Money is invested in commodities as a *means to make more money*. "Capital" is simply money made on money. In terms of third order abstraction, capitalists and all those who accumulate capital are moving from the use of symbols as a means (first or second order abstraction) to allowing symbols to build on themselves.

To be sure, in the case of industrial capitalism, profits are poured back and invested in the social infrastructure. This involves the transformation of roads, the building of railroads, investment in communications systems, investment in research and development, and investment in workers in the form of education and wages. However, this infrastructure is a means to accumulate more symbolic currency. The intention is less to produce more commodities or more social infrastructure and more to accumulate capital. This is the classic Marxian definition of capitalism—when

Table 16.4 Second order versus third order abstraction *(continued)*

Category of comparison	First or second order abstractions (pre-seventeenth-century science)	Third order abstraction (seventeenth century)
What is the mind for? (Solving everyday problems or studying the world objectively, along with reflecting on the thinking process itself?)	Mind in the service of reactions to the problems of the world and planning what to do	Studying the natural world; mind reflecting on itself, self-critical. In statistics, being sensitive to cognitive mistakes such as base rate neglect; small sample, unrepresentative sample, gambler's fallacy; experimental design in science.
What are sources of evidence?	Revelations of the authorities or personal experiences of a particular person; informal dialogue with friends	Truth through experiment and dialogue; authorities and personal experience less trusted
What is the starting point in thinking?	The real situation	The possible situation; applied to new technology, which improves productivity
Degree of foresight: trial and error, improvisation, or design?	Does not consider all possibilities before starting (trial and error, improvisation); acting before testing not just likely outcomes but all possible outcomes	Considers exhaustively all possibilities in a situation and forms a plan before acting; experimental design in science
What is the relationship between the real and the possible?	The possible is a special case of the real	The real is a special case of the possible; reality is a special subset within a totality of possible things that the data will admit as a hypothesis
What is the relationship between knowledge and thinker?	Ideas are embodied with individual thinker, particular time, place, and circumstance	Ideas are independent of any particular thinker, time, and place and are part of a scientific collective practice
Are predictions made?	Do not make claims falsifiable so they can never be proved true or false so theories cannot be eliminated	Makes findings falsifiable in scientific experiments so that some theories can be eliminated

money becomes unhinged from the circulation and production process and appears to develop an independent existence. In its extreme form, capital is invested in more capital with minimum investment in either goods or equipment. This has been called "financial" capitalism. The source of profit comes from investment in stocks, bonds, and other options. See Table 16.5 for an overview of the evolution of the forms of exchange.

Over the course of the last five hundred years, there has been an increase in the accumulation of industrial and financial capital the later in the history of capitalism we go. For our purposes, the point is that there is a definite movement of capital from a more "material" profit based on trade in commodities or investment in tools, equipment, and people to a more abstract investment in stocks, bonds, and so on. What we want to know is how the movement across these phases of capitalism affected how people think.

Table 16.5 Forms of exchange and societal types

Exchange relation	Type of society
Commodity A—commodity B	Primitive
Commodity A—coins—commodity B	Merchant capital
Coins—commodity A—capital	Industrial capitalism
Capital A—capital B	Finance capitalism

We are not claiming that once capitalism emerged all social classes were using these institutions equally. Certainly for the working classes, the primacy of the commodity–money–commodity relation is predominant. As producers the primary participation in the capital circuit for workers is in the commodity A–money–commodity B "circuit." Their labor is a commodity owned by the capitalist (commodity A); they receive a wage (money) from the capitalist, which these workers in turn use to buy subsistence commodities (commodity B). As consumers, the working classes are still in this circuit. Workers use money as an instrument to buy goods and services. They do not typically use goods and services to make more money.

Among the middle classes, the kind of work they do—supervising, planning—encourages the use of third order thinking on the job, and as the stock market opened up to the middle classes in the twentieth century, they had to learn to think like capitalists about their investments.

Just as in the Bronze Age it was the upper classes who first used hieroglyphics, and in the Iron Age it was the upper and middle classes who first used the alphabet and coined money, in the Modern Age it is the middle and upper classes who first invest in agriculture, industry, and stocks and bonds. However, in the industrial phase of capitalism, even working-class people (unlike peasants in ancient societies) had to grow accustomed to following more abstract, decontextualized taxonomic classifications of relations like the following:

- They did not own any portion of what they produced. Unlike the peasants, they could not claim any of the *product* of their labor (however small) as their own, whether it was food, clothing, or shelter.
- They did not own or make the *tools* they used; they "rented" them.
- The products and tools were available to them in the form of a *standardized price* (as opposed to bargaining and haggling). How did they acquire these products and tools?
- They paid for them with *wages*. Rather than being entitled to goods and services as part of either generalized reciprocity or a redistribution system, their labor itself became a commodity that was sold at a price.

Meanwhile, industrial and financial capitalist relations are engaged in primarily by the upper classes. These classes are far more likely to have capital to invest. In the industrial phases of the stock market, an investor is "investing liquid assets" in *companies* that produce commodities, construct machines, build roads, and set up communications and transport systems. This investment in the stock market is a more abstract investment in symbols because they are no longer investing directly in products and services but in the *institutions* that make them. These investors are betting that these companies will make a profit on these products in the future.

At some point moneylenders find it more convenient, more efficient, and ultimately more profitable to substitute their own bills of exchange for those of individual producers, forming institutions known as "banks." The rise of banks in the twentieth century is inseparable from the rise of credit. Banks are institutions to manage credit. Their job is to connect the various forms of credit to each other and lines of credit to real money—gold or legal tender. Banks use their own money to provide a centralized discounting function for many bills of exchange that originate and then circulate among individual commodity buyers and sellers. Bank notes replace bills of exchange. When banks issue their own notes or allow checks to be drawn from them, they substitute their own warranty for the particular capitalists who borrow from them. In exchange, banks derive a profit in part from the interest charged to capitalists for providing this service.

This stabilizing function that banks provide is only temporary, since banks also compete with each other. Competition between banks drives forward a still more ethereal symbolic abstraction in an attempt to stabilize the circulation of capital. This results in the creation of a central bank. The job of a central bank is to make the various forms of bank notes convertible with one another, and balance its accounts without the risk of shipping more concrete forms of currency, like gold, from bank to bank. A central bank guarantees the trustworthiness of private banks, just as private banks guarantee the trustworthiness of individual capitalists. Typically, central banks do not compete with each other, as they appear to be limited by the geographical boundary of the nation-state. With the current wave of globalization that occurred in the twentieth century, there was a need for a world bank to guarantee the quality of currency of central banks within nation-states.

To say that capital grows is an example of how the symbolic forms of exchange have become unhinged from the relations of production that underlie them. As David Harvey (1999) argues, capital increases by interest because capitalist enterprises have managed to produce enough surplus value within the banking period to cover their interest payment. Harvey identifies three functions of the credit system of banks:

1. *The mobilization of money as capital* through the credit system, which can convert the flow of monetary transactions into loan capital by bank drafts for cash. How can they do this? By counting on deposits to furnish a permanent balance that underwrites this loan capital.
2. *The reductions of the cost time of circulation.* Commodities that require extra long production periods are paid for on installments.
3. *Facilitating the quickening of the circulation of fixed capital.* For example, investments in the built environment have a much slower profit return than the more liquid forms. The liquid form means capitalists do not have to wait for the circulating and fixed capital flows to complete their cycles before accumulating more capital.

In an idealized capitalist world, the interest-bearing capital can best fulfill its function of coordination if it can be as flexible as possible and remain separate from a commitment to more concrete forms of investment—plants, tools, products, or workers. This is where capitalism runs into contradictions because without some investment in the real world, no profits can be made.

One temporary and very dangerous solution is for banks to issue fictitious capital—a flow of money that is not backed by any commodity transaction. For example, a capitalist receives credit on a commodity that hasn't even been sold yet. The bank holds the warranty that is backed by an unsold commodity. If these warrants begin to circulate, it is *fictitious* value that is circulating. A gap is opened up between capital accumulation based on already-sold commodities and capital based on commodities that have not been sold. Too much of the accumulation of fictitious capital, along with too much "betting ahead" by capitalists, is the stuff of depressions.

In short, with the rise in the power of banks in the twentieth century, profits are made less from concrete goods and services and more from making loans to capitalists. Profits are made with less and less return to the social body. Social abstractions of paper are piled on top of each other. Betting on the stock market and all the paper options offered is a feat of mind-boggling abstraction that most of us don't comprehend. Our suspicion is that most people invest in the stock market without understanding it and simply trust that their broker does understand.

Our point is that if you examine the characteristics of third order thinking in Table 16.4 and match them up against capitalist institutions like banks, the stock exchange, and all the various forms of currency, we think you'll agree that the use of third order abstraction is necessary in many of our categories, including at least the following:

- The relationship between symbols and reality
- The extent to which symbols act on symbols
- Extent of manipulation of the objective world
- Impact on space and time (Harvey's [1999] globalization and space-time compression)
- Understanding of chance (at least among stockbrokers)
- Reversible thinking operations between ideas (currency symbols)
- Epistemology—betting on fictitious capital
- Taxonomic classification—investment in wealth with no space-time referents
- Relationship between ideas (symbols) and thinker—commodities exchanged for a price independent of who the people are
- Starting point is the hypothetical, not the real (state of wealth)

The Dark Side of Third Order Abstraction under Capitalism

On the whole, the capitalist economic system falls far short of the discipline of the natural sciences and its capacity to use the powers of third order abstraction in practice. We will demonstrate this by comparing its performance against some of the categorical answers to third order abstraction. In terms of the sources of knowledge, there is no equivalent in capitalism to performing a scientific experiment to find out what is true. If a capitalist wants to find out whether people want his product, there is no social mechanism in place by which he could find out. On the contrary, capitalists compete with each other producing things that people don't want (they sit on the shelves), while not producing things that people say they want, because the rate of profit is too low to justify producing them.

Capitalists do not use the full power of science to build cars or clothes that are long-lasting. In fact, they have been known to repress or destroy technologies that undermine their resource base. Rockefeller's buying up and then destroying trolley cars as a means of public transportation to make way for buses and cars powered by oil is just one example. In the products they do make, capitalists plan for their products to wear out sooner rather than later. Whereas in a scientific experiment in which all possibilities are exhausted in the search for knowledge, capitalists do not exhaust all possibilities but pick selectively those investments that will maximize their profit.

Secondly, scientific communities try to work in conjunction with an overall plan in which the short-term and long-term consequences are considered. This means research and development programs, investing in new equipment, and repairing old equipment. As most of us are painfully aware, especially under finance capitalism, many capitalists neglect building infrastructure, refuse to repair bridges and sewer systems, refuse to pay health benefits to workers, will not invest seriously in education, pollute the biophysical environment, and don't want to pay the cost of cleanup.

When capitalists invest in prisons rather than schools they undermine their own resource base. Investing in prisons, which simply warehouse people rather than teaching them skills, leads to a loss of potential workers as long-term sources of profit both as producers and consumers. When capitalists invest in war they tear down the very buildings, transport systems, and communication systems that they helped to build. This is not a moral argument. We are trying to show how capitalists fail to see that infrastructure and workers are the foundation from which the capitalist makes a profit. Capitalists are the most powerful class in the world and have the most responsibility for determining how goods and services are exchanged. Not only is there no social plan beyond this generation, at least in the United States, there is no plan beyond a business quarter.

In science, mathematical systems create hypothetical scenarios that may not exist in nature. So science begins with the hypothetical and sees real life as a special case. But at the same time, science wants to use mathematics to go back into the real world with more powerful tools to solve social problems from their field of expertise. Mathematical symbol systems, in the long run, come back to reality. Capitalists, on the other hand, invent financial "instruments"—derivatives, stock options, credit swaps—that also have a basis in mathematics. But the application of these instruments loses its base in the real world. "Real" in this sense means making profits on goods and services. Capitalists draw sources of profit on hypothetical scenarios that have no basis in reality, because no real goods or services were created yet.

Lastly, in science there is an *accumulating* body of knowledge that includes not just what we know works but also what we know doesn't work. A new hypothesis must explain new facts while continuing to be grounded in what has already been proven. In other words, science is *self-reflective about its own process* and its history.

Under capitalism, do capitalists learn from past mistakes? Are they self-reflective on their own historical processes, including the depressions that have rocked the world, especially in the last 150 years? After the Great Depression in the 1930s, capitalists made some adjustments by introducing Keynesian economic policies. These policies have their own limits and do not solve capitalism's most basic problems, but they worked reasonably well, at least in the West, for about thirty-five years. Beginning in the middle of the 1970s when the Keynesian system ran into difficulties, capitalist strategists reverted to pre-Keynesian policies (what is now known as neoliberalism) as if the Depression of the 1930s never occurred.

In at least these four categories of third order abstraction—sources of knowledge, planning, use of symbol systems, self-reflective practice—capitalism *discourages* the use of third order abstraction at its institutional level. Furthermore, it discourages individuals and groups from thinking about social solutions to economic problems using full third order abstraction. To do that at an institutional level would require at least a social democratic economic system in which collective rationality was predominant.

Table 16.6 summarizes the application of third order abstraction categories to the two modern institutions we discussed: the scientific revolution and capitalism. Note that we've italicized the areas where capitalism as an economic system fails in operating with third order abstraction.

Theoretical Implications: The Sociohistorical Nature of Third Order Abstraction

As in Chapter 9 and part of Chapter 12, the purpose of these sections on cognitive evolution has been the following. We want to show that the power of reasoning is a social and historical process before it becomes psychological or internalized. Long before individuals are in a position to *internalize* second or third order abstraction, tools must be invented and housed in new social institutions, and individuals learn to think differently in the process of working in these institutions.

As in Chapter 9, we are arguing that new orders of abstraction emerge or are muffled based on the type of social formation they occur in, the point in world history, and the class location of the individual. In Chapter 12 we briefly showed how in the High Middle Ages and the Renaissance, the emergence of algebra, double-entry bookkeeping, mapmaking, musical scores, and linear perspective painting helped produce the beginnings of third order abstraction. In the case of this chapter, how well individuals do in learning third order cognition depends on:

- The emergence of a scientific community in which scientific research into new fields develops along with new methodology
- The emergence of capitalism along with its development of commodity production and multiple currencies

We are now ready to tackle our second purpose. Our aim is to show more precisely how these socializing institutions—the capitalist system, the scientific revolution—become imported inside the individual and then exported in the form of the work that people do. We do this through Vygotsky's threefold process of cooperative learning. To review our discussion in Chapter 9, according to the sociohistorical school of psychology, cooperative learning goes through three phases: (1) the local interpersonal learning is social, (2) the internalization of learning is psychological, and (3) "global" interpersonal interaction is social again. We also said in Chapter 9 that the process of abstraction itself—whether it is first order, second order, or third order abstraction—goes through three phases: extraction, deliberation, and generalization. So what is the relation between Vygotsky's three phases of cooperation and the three phases of abstraction?

The process of abstraction itself is first *social* before it becomes psychological. This means that when a new tool, means of exchanging goods and services, or political institution develops, *society as a whole* goes through Vygotsky's three phases:

1. Local interpersonal corresponds to the moment of *social* extraction
2. Internalization corresponds to *social* deliberation
3. Global interpersonal corresponds to *social* generalization

It is only as the individuals who do mental work in these fields develop expertise in their work that these social abstractions become internalized into their psychology. Then inside their minds they go through the process of individually abstracting—extraction, deliberation, generalization. At the end of this chapter we will show how abstraction goes from social to psychological. For now we will focus on how social abstraction occurs.

What we did in Chapter 9 was to show how second order cognition arises when a whole society has to learn new skills, usually in reaction to the rise of new technologies and forms of social organization. In Chapter 9 we traced how the invention of new writing systems, numbering systems, and coined money demanded new forms of cognition among priests, priestesses, and merchants. Table 9.5 shows how second order abstraction and its phases (extraction, deliberation, and generalization) were built up out of economic, technological, and political changes. Table 9.7 provides a closer look at how these processes might take place in the single generation moving between parents and children to when these children become adults.

What we will do now is narrate the three phases of abstraction as we did in Table 9.3 but with different historical institutions in operation. We will show how the phases of capitalism, from

Table 16.6 Application of third order categories to the evolution of modern science and capitalism

Categorical question addressed	Third order abstraction response	Scientific revolution	Industrial and finance capital
What is the relationship between symbols and reality? (Symbols include letters, math notations, music notations, painting, and coins)	Greater distance from local space and present time in experience, sense data, goods, and people	Newton's equations; Newton's experiment with gravity; experimental replication by other scientists in different times and places	The prices of commodities are unified into a price that is independent of the quality of the particular product, where it was made, or who the buyer or seller is From coins to paper money: Extracting the principle of social approval from material value of coin Greater trust in invisible relations between strangers and the state and the capitalists who stand beside them
To what extent do symbols act on symbols?	Symbols "square" themselves: Symbols are built on each other and take on a life of their own	Algebra, trigonometry, calculus	Extraction of self-expanding exchange value from circulation of commodities (time alone adds value); accumulation of financial capital process. Source of profit changes from money made on circulation and production to profit made on profit (interest, stocks, bonds, derivatives) Symbols of money "square themselves" into coins to paper money to checks to credit cards
What does the mind operate on?	Reversible operations but operates on systems of ideas	Development of epistemology, probability, falsifiability	Creation of systems of abstract currency
How are classification systems grouped?	Taxonomic: Objects are grouped into classes that have no spatial or temporal relationship to each other	Chemical, plant, and animal classification systems	Objects are grouped as commodities, independent of where or when they were produced
What is the extent of manipulation of the objective world?	Global systematic manipulation of the objective world	Harnessing of inanimate sources of energy; global study of nature (land, sea, air)	Penetration of capital into more areas of life within core countries and spreading to the periphery; "Everything's for sale"
What is the understanding of chance occurrences and likelihoods?	Chance is the result of lawful combinations that have regularity whether they are intended or not	Likelihood estimates may violate personal experience; work of Cardano, Galileo, Pascal, *Port Royal Logic*, Bernoulli	Annuities policies of merchants used by the state in the seventeenth century for census collection, taxes, conscription; insurance policies in the twentieth century; polling predictions for political elections. Financial "instruments"

Table 16.6 Application of third order categories to the evolution of modern science and capitalism *(continued)*

Categorical question addressed	Third order abstraction response	Scientific revolution	Industrial and finance capital
What is the mind for? Solving everyday problems or studying the world objectively and self-reflection?	Studying the world objectively and self-reflection on the thinking process itself	"Organized skepticism": peer review; statistical fallacies; reliability and validity tests	
What are the sources of evidence? Revelation of the authorities and personal experience, informal dialogue with friends, or truth through experiment?	Truth through experiment and dialogue	Scientific experiment; scientific community (Royal Society)	*Irrational: rate of profit. Makes things people don't want and does not make what people say they want*
What is the starting point in thinking?	The possible situation over the real situation	Starting point may be advanced mathematical theory possibilities, but eventually applied to solve problems and invent new technology that improves productivity	
What is the degree of foresight (trial and error and improvisation or design)?	Considers exhaustively all possibilities in a situation and formulates a plan	Extensive planning in research review of literature and setting up experiments; long-term planning in research grants	*Irrational: Will not systematically invest in building and repairing infrastructures; invests in institutions that destroy what it has built (prisons, wars)*
What is the relationship between the real and the possible?	Reality is a special subset within a totality of possible things that the data will admit as a hypothesis	The real is a special case of the possible; scientific theory starts with the real, invents a possible hypothesis, and then tests the hypothesis against the real	*Irrational: Derivative—betting on the future, which has not been earned yet*
What is the relationship between knowledge and the thinker?	Knowledge is independent of any particular thinker, time, or place		Capitalist system operates independently of any particular capitalist; "money talks" independently of who owns the money
Making predictions	Identifies conditions under which something could be proven wrong	Scientific community accumulates a body of knowledge that is public and independent of any thinker; scientific falsifiability	*Irrational: Capitalists do not learn from past panics and depressions; capitalists repress their own past and resume policies that have proven to be failures*

merchant to industrial to finance capital, are expressions of increasing social abstraction. In Table 16.7 we show how the forms of economic currency also reflect a movement of social abstraction as we moved from coined money, to bank notes, to paper money, checks, and credit cards.

How the Three Phases of Abstraction Manifest as the Circulation and Accumulation Processes of Merchant, Industrial, and Finance Capital

We will begin with the movement from mercantile to industrial capital. The *social extraction phase of abstraction* begins when the self-expanding exchange value of capital is separated from the circulation of commodities. The social deliberation phase is that capital is accumulated in a more *systematic* way than was done by mercantile capitalists. This can only be done with a more precise formulation of cost-benefit analysis. In other words, proto-industrialists apply a more rational analysis and plan in their investments over the long haul. In the case of Dutch capitalists, this involved the issuing of annuity policies and the calculation of the chances of piracy. The social generalization phase occurs in the nineteenth-century expansion of profits by investment in capital from circulation to *production*, that is, to the reorganization of land, labor, and capital. Let us elaborate on the social deliberation and generalization phases.

When mercantile capitalists weigh costs to benefits of buying and selling, they are subject to time and place contingencies. For example, a merchant's timing may be right as to when to sell a product, but the place he is delivering the goods to may have had a famine or an epidemic. So, too, the merchant may have delivered his goods to a society that wants them, but another merchant who got there first has cornered the market—the place was right, but the timing was wrong. In other words, the degree of control a merchant has over his accumulation of capital is significantly limited.

Of course, the industrial period also has its risks. When the industrial capitalist invests in a particular technology or energy source, his investment can be undermined if another invention or energy source is found that renders obsolete his investments. So, too, when the capitalist invests in upgrading the skills of the working and middle classes, providing them training and education, this is no guarantee that they won't oppose the interests of the capitalist by forming unions or opposing profitable wars. Still, because of the increase in concentration of capital and the intervention of the state in the industrial phase, new technologies, energy sources, and workers can now be more easily repressed, but only temporarily.

The movement from industrial to financial capital is even more extreme, but it can still be broken into Vygotsky's three phases. In the social extraction phase, exchange value is separated from *both the circulation and the production* phases of capitalism and becomes immediately expanded into more exchange value. In other words, it is not the investment in goods and services that adds value, but *the passage of time* alone that adds value. The social deliberation occurs with the collective intellectual work involved in the invention of credit systems, bank notes, the stock market, local banks, central banks, and world banks to abstract, concentrate, and coordinate institutions and practices that increase the rate of profit. The generalization phase occurs when banks and their paper currencies spread from nation-states of core countries to the entire globe. The basis for doing this is investing in unsecured lending: using bank notes and credit cards. Since there is less investment in concrete processes, capital is much freer to move across unsecured lending possibilities because the capitalist is not demanding that his debtors pay up immediately. He just keeps loaning and makes a profit off the interest.

How the Three Phases of Abstraction Manifest in Changes in the Forms of Economic Currency

The three phases of social abstraction not only can be applied to the historical phases of capitalist accumulation, but also can be used to track historical changes within the material forms of currency—from coins to notes to paper money to checks to credit cards (see Table 16.7).

The material value of coined money rests with long and trusted metal media—gold, silver,

Table 16.7 Building stages of third order abstraction applied to economic currencies in the history of capitalism

Economic exhange	Type of abstraction used	Stage of abstraction	Stage of abstraction	Stage of abstraction
Mercantile capital	Second order	Social extraction	Social deliberation	Social generalization
Industrial capital	Third order	Extraction of self-expanding exchange value from circulation of commodities	Systematic accumulation of capital by a more rational cost-benefit analysis	Expansion from circulation to production—reorganization of land, labor, infrastructure
Industrial capital to finance capital	Third order	Extraction of exchange value from either circulation or production; immediate expansion of exchange value (time alone adds value)	Rationalized system of increasing benefits' risk ratio. Minimize risk of techno-depreciation of fixed capital	Unsecured lending bank notes, credit cards, bonds; emergence of local, central, and world banks. Spreads from core countries (industry) to the semiperiphery and periphery
Coined money	Second order	Social extraction	Social deliberation	Social generalization
Bank notes	Third order	Extraction of "principle of approval" from the material value of the coin	Realizing that medium of currency can be any medium. Realizing it can be applied to other institutions besides the state	Application to private institutions (banks) of bank notes
Bank notes to paper money	Third order	Extraction of the principle of approval from a particular individual	Realizing the state can issue its own promissory notes	Issuing paper money by the state to groups, not just individuals
Paper money to checks	Third order	Extracting the principle of signification from denomination; extraction of the principle of trust from present time-space to the future	Seeing past problems with arbitrary fixed denomination; potential time-space bottlenecks; increased trust in invisible relations with strangers and institutions that stand behind them	Specified variable denomination; checks are issued and backed by banks
Checks to credit cards	Third order	Extraction of denomination variability from collateral not limited to present assets	Recognizing timeless availability of loans	Allows borrowing into the future from realm of assets to the realm of liability (credit cards)

and copper. This means the metal itself has value independent of whatever social agreements transpire to make it legal tender. In an economic crisis the metal content can be reconverted by smelting back into usable items such as tools or cups.

In the movement from coined money to bank notes we find the same three stages of social abstraction operating. The social extraction phase occurs when the principle of *social approval* is separated from the material value of the coin itself as a use-value. The social deliberation moment is the recognition that, at least in state societies, the medium of currency can be almost *any* material. Once this is recognized, whatever material the currency is made of can originate in private institutions besides the state (which was the case with coined money). The social generalization occurs when *banks* issue notes. This is a generalization because banks are institutions that, through centralization, can spread the use of bank notes across the land.

Once notes replace coins, there can no longer be a conversion back to some socially useful item the way metal can be converted. To be able to accept these notes requires complete faith in a more abstract, less visible social relationship than is required with coins. Peasants or working-class people may not have bank accounts or even enter a bank. Yet they accept that other social members will recognize the value that stands behind the bank notes even though it is "only paper." This act of faith requires some third order abstract thinking on the part of peasants and workers.

The movement from bank notes to paper money is not so much an intensification of abstraction as it is a converse movement at the same level. In the movement from bank notes to paper money, the principle of approval is separated from the particular individual. The moment of social deliberation occurs when the state operates with the collective understanding that *the state* can issue its own "bank notes" (promissory notes) just as the banks can. The social generalization occurs when the state issues paper money to everyone, not just to individuals and groups the way banks do. In other words, the state learns from the banks about bank notes and applies it to the issuing of currency the way it did with coined money *but at a higher level of abstraction*.

What happens when we move from paper money to checks? The social extraction movement occurs when the principle of signification is separated from any particular denomination. In other words, paper money is issued in denominations of one dollar, five dollars, ten dollars, twenty dollars, and so on. When we separate the principle of approval from fixed denominations, we allow both buyer and seller more freedom. How so?

The social deliberation movement occurs when the problems of fixed denominations are exposed to collective analysis. Operating with fixed denominations of paper causes some time-space problems that can reduce the circulation of goods and services. For example, let's say a consumer wants to buy an object but has only a hundred-dollar bill. The object is being sold for, say, sixty dollars. The buyer is not likely to part with a hundred-dollar bill and pay forty dollars more than the cost. If the seller does not have the right change, he might not make the sale at all. Conversely, if the buyer has only two twenty-dollar bills, the seller is not likely to sell the commodity for twenty dollars less. In other words, in some transactions involving fixed denominations, being in the wrong place or wrong time can slow down commercial exchange. Being able to write checks will correct for this.

The phase of social generalization involved in using checks occurs when the specific amount of the cost of a product can be written *exactly* by the buyer. With checks, the principle of signification (or approval) is preserved, while the check is not tied to the concrete constellation of paper that consumers have in their wallets at the time. A check can be written for an exact amount. Checks bypass the problem of making change and allow transactions to proceed more smoothly.

Now we will turn to how the *perception of time* changes with changes in currency. Like coins, paper money is liquid *on the spot*. No identification cards or driver's licenses are necessary to make a transaction. Furthermore, when you give someone paper money, you know that you are parting with something "real." From the point of view of the owner of the currency, checks begin the process of creating a distance between the present and the future. Although checks are not as "concrete" as paper money, you have to consider how much money you have in your checking account before you purchase something. Because checks, at least when they are first used, do not seem as "real" as a ten- or twenty-dollar bill, in one sense it appears that you can buy something for nothing, but in another sense you know your balance must cover the amount of the product you are buying.

If you know that the amount in your checking account will not cover what you are buying, you are now making a small gamble. You are betting that you will be able to get money that you may not have earned yet to cover the purchase by getting some money in your checking account before the check bounces. On the other hand, the seller is well aware of the increasing abstraction and trust that are necessary in accepting a check because some kind of collateral or security is expected. You cannot go into a store and say, "My checking account cannot cover this, but I'll put some cash into it right away. Give me the product and I'll come back soon with the check." But you can give the seller a check and buy something even if you have not yet earned the money, provided you make a quick adjustment in the *near* future. With the emergence of the credit card, economic exchanges become even more abstracted from present time. With a credit card you are buying many products even if you don't have the liquid assets to cover the price. When using a credit card, how much liquid savings you currently have on hand becomes even less relevant than when operating with checks. With credit cards you may buy large numbers of goods and bet that you will be able to produce income that has not been earned yet. You begin betting on your future labor to pay back not only the goods but also the accumulating interest. This of course requires you to develop a much more elaborate tracking system because the stakes are higher. Above and beyond the interest rates of credit cards, if you don't pay your bill at the end of the month, you may go into what seems to be permanent debt or even bankruptcy in part because you can't track and keep up with your present and projected future earnings against what you have actually spent.

We will close this section by applying the three stages of social abstraction to the movement from checks to credit cards. In the stage of social extraction, denominational variability (checks) is separated from collateral and not limited to present assets. The social deliberation stage is recognizing that the availability of loans can extend far into the future (from the point of view of the capitalist, so far into the future that long-term profit can be made by keeping people in more or less permanent debt). The social generalization occurs when borrowing into the future has moved from the realm of assets to the realm of liability.

Whether we discuss metal coins, bank notes, paper money, checks, or credit cards, these days, more and more, regardless of their class location, people are touched by the evolution of economic exchange media. This means the phases of capitalist accumulation, the currency used, and the changes in the perception of time are first housed in the "social mind" as the three phases of abstraction, deliberation, and generalization. Then this social mind cultivates the cognitive psychological thinking process known as third order abstraction. Therefore, there is a kind of "social" third order abstraction prior to its internalization as psychological third order abstraction. Once these cognitive skills are internalized and mastered on the job, they find their way into not just economic exchanges but political systems, religious traditions, child-rearing practices, and game playing.

Suggested Readings

Crosby, Alfred. 1997. *The Measure of Reality.* Cambridge: Cambridge University Press.

Mennell, Stephen. 1989. *Norbert Elias.* Dublin: University College Dublin Press.

Meyrowitz, Joshua. 1986. *No Sense of Place.* New York: Oxford University Press.

Murray, Alexander. 1978. *Reason and Society in the Middle Ages.* New York: Oxford University Press.

Olson, David. 1994. *The World on Paper.* Cambridge: Cambridge University Press.

Sennett, Richard. 1977. *The Fall of Public Man.* New York: Vintage.

Tuan, Yi-Fu. 1982. *Segmented Worlds and Self.* Minneapolis: University of Minnesota.

17

The Twentieth-Century Age of Extremes

The world history of the twentieth century includes three more world revolutions, two linked world wars, and two more waves of globalization that were separated by a period of deglobalization. All this was intertwined with the rise and decline of the hegemony of the United States. The human population of the earth increased from 1.65 billion in 1900 to over 6 billion people in 2000. More people were killed in twentieth-century interstate wars (about 32 million) than the total population of the earth in 1500 BCE.[1] The first half of the twentieth century was the "Age of Extremes," and

HMS *Audacious*, 1912
Source: Wikipedia Commons.

[1] Department of the Census, "Historical Estimates of World Population," http://www.census.gov/ipc/www/worldhis.html.

the second half was a relatively peaceful and prosperous round of globalization and the emergence of a world civilization based on continued contention over the values of the European Enlightenment. These stories are told in this chapter and the next.

The nineteenth century saw the emergence of geometrical growth in the number of people and the sizes of settlements. These trends continued in the twentieth century. The demographic transition also continued apace—the transition from large to small families spread from the core to the noncore. In core countries, natural population increase (not due to immigration) ceased as the birthrate came into balance with the declined mortality rate. People lived longer, and older people became a large proportion of the total population. But the total number of people in the world continued to increase rapidly because the noncore countries combine a decreasing death rate, due mainly to the spread of public health practices, with a birth rate that remains high and is declining only slowly. Where women gained political rights, increasing autonomy, and more education, the fertility rate came down, but these trends were slow in much of the noncore. The education and increasing autonomy of women gave them important work outside the family, and the movement of the majority of households from rural to urban settings also decreased the labor utility of having large numbers of children. By the end of the twentieth century, over half of the world's population lived in very large cities.

The chaotic first half of the twentieth century has been aptly characterized as the "Age of Extremes" by the eminent historian Eric Hobsbawm (1994). The British hegemony was in decline. The world of high finance remained centered on the City of London, but England had lost its comparative advantage in most of the generative sectors of the economy to Germany and the United States. The great nineteenth-century wave of global economic integration bottomed out in 1900 and was followed by a weak upturn that was in turn followed by a massive deglobalization after 1929. World War I was a classic global struggle for hegemony, but after the war, the United States, already an economic hegemon, refused to take up the mantle of political hegemony, and so the world remained without a stable leadership structure until after World War II.

The Belle Epoque

The Edwardian[2] Indian summer in the years after the end of the Boer War (1901) was like those days at the end of fall when the weather is still pleasant. Trade globalization had begun an upturn around 1900 after its decline since 1880 (see Figure 15.1 in Chapter 15). British foreign investment was flooding out from the City of London, and those able to get in on the returning profits were living well. The technological miracles of steamships, the Suez Canal, transoceanic telegraph communications, and railroads had brought the people of the world closer together (Hugill 1999). The network of international trade was becoming denser, but also less hierarchical, as England's centrality in world trade and industrial production had been in decline since the 1870s (Hobsbawm 1969). The British-centered world economy was being replaced by a system of contending centers of industry and trade. But the financial district in the City of London managed to stay on as the center of world banking, currency trading, stock trading, and insurance, and there was plenty of tea and jam for most of the residents of the British Isles, so they could feel that they too were sharing in the glories of the empire (Mintz 1985). Nationalism and the "new imperialism" evolved as a politics of reform and inclusion within core states that was coupled with expansion of colonial and neocolonial adventures abroad—so-called social imperialism.

Nazli Choucri and Robert North's (1975) careful and elaborate study of the great powers in the run-up to World War I is organized around the idea of **lateral pressure**—increasing competition for natural resources and markets as industrialization spread from Britain to other countries, especially the United States and Germany. This notion is related to the more general concepts of circumscription and population pressure, which we employed in our iteration model

[2] King Edward VII came to the throne following the death of his mother, Queen Victoria, on January 22, 1901.

of world-systems evolution (see Chapter 2). Circumscription refers to a situation in which an expanding system comes up against geographical and social limits to growth because all the adjacent low-hanging fruit has already been picked. The problems that had been solved by expansion increasingly required other solutions.

The rise of European hegemony was running up against global spatial limits. The United States had expanded to the Pacific Coast of North America and had integrated the natural resources of the West into the American development project. The European powers had conquered the Americas, the East Indies, South Asia, and Southeast Asia and had finally colonized Africa. Only China remained uncolonized, but it was surrounded by and subjected to the competitive incursions of the European core powers, the United States, and Japan. The incorporation of the East Asian PMN into the Europe-centered PMN meant that the whole globe was now integrated into a single closely wound system of states and colonies with a single interconnected set of core and semiperipheral states. No longer was there a Eurasian-wide PGN containing geographically separated and geopolitically independent PMNs in the West and the East. The now-global interstate system (with colonies) and the older global PGN had completely merged. Of course, the European powers had long been competing with one another over choice parts of the periphery, but now colonial imperialism was becoming an increasingly zero-sum game. This meant that one core power could expand only at the expense of another. This was global circumscription and lateral pressure.[3]

The core of the Europe-centered system was also expanding with the rise of Germany and the United States. This also increased the overall demand for natural raw materials and for opportunities to sell goods and to make profits, thus increasing the general level of competition in the system.

Imperial Overreach

By the end of the nineteenth century, Britain had lost its supremacy in trade and industrial production, but it still held first place in military power, financial centrality, and telecommunications. The British Empire was being challenged by nationalism in some of its colonies, and the labor movement was challenging elite rule at home. Economic nationalism among the contending core states had restored protective tariffs in the international economy, though Britain held out as the last bastion of free trade. British naval supremacy came into question during the Crimean War (1854–1856), as it became obvious that decrepit ships and corruption had taken their toll on a Royal Navy that had seen little serious action since dispatching Napoleon. A significant investment in new naval technology was made to remedy this situation (Briggs 1964).

The British elite had long been divided between the staunch conservatives who sought to perpetuate the role of the landed aristocracies and crowned heads of Europe (e.g., Queen Victoria) and a group of enlightened conservatives who realized that flexibility and creative reorganization were often more productive policies for dealing with the huge social changes that industrial capitalism and globalization had brought about. The enlightened conservatives had decided that a new emphasis on imperial expansion could be used to mollify challenges from an increasingly organized and vocal labor movement at home. This policy has been called "social imperialism" because it combines an awareness of the need for social reform and welfare at home with an expansive policy toward control and access to resources abroad, especially from the periphery. One of its main political protagonists at the end of the nineteenth century was Joseph Chamberlain, a Manchester industrialist who was appointed to the position of colonial secretary and later became the British prime minister. The British had long

[3] Rosa Luxemburg's (1951) theory of capitalist imperialism focused on the "realization problem"—the necessity of selling the produced commodities in order to realize profits. Capitalists try to cut labor costs and substitute machines for human labor, but they must eventually sell their products to workers who increasingly do not have the money to buy the goods. So, overproduction and underconsumption crises are a major contradiction that drives capitalism to expand into external systems to find new markets. Lenin and others put more emphasis on the competitive search for cheap raw materials.

championed free trade in the world economy, and they held to this position after most of the other core countries had gone back to tariff protectionism. Chamberlain favored a tariff reform that would give preference to products from British colonies or to members of the emerging British Commonwealth of English-speaking countries.

A group of British elite politicians, intellectuals, and journalists came together to form a set of intersecting networks of intermarried families and old-school ties—mainly from Balliol and All Souls colleges at Oxford (Quigley 1981). These men were originally inspired by Professor John Ruskin, a poet and historian of architecture who developed a philosophy of Christian Socialism that was sympathetic to the labor movement and the poor without posing a challenge to the rule of capital. Ruskin and other Oxford dons also favored the notion that the British way of life and the English language were the highest attainment of human civilization and that these features were the best possible bearers of true freedom for the rest of humanity. This high moral ground, rather than simply the desire for wealth and power, was used by certain members of the British upper class as justification for a new wave of imperialism, especially directed toward Africa, which was to bring the gifts of civilization to the less developed world. Some of these visionaries also favored the establishment of a strong federation of English-speaking countries that was to include the United States and the British Empire. This federation of English-speaking states was especially the vision of Cecil Rhodes, the organizer of the Royal African Company, and Alfred Milner, a journalist who took up the leadership of this cause after Rhodes died. Rhodes was linked with a group of intermarried nobles, which Quigley called "the Cecil bloc," that included Lord Salisbury. The confidants and agents of Alfred Milner included many important journalists. These groups were linked by a secret society organized by Rhodes, and this evolving network eventually became known as the "Round Table." This group pursued its goals by controlling newspapers, including the *Times* of London, engaging in what it itself termed "propaganda" and by speaking into the ears of the powerful, especially Queen Victoria and King Edward. They planned the Jameson raid, brought about the war against the Boers, and eventually were central players in the formation of the Union of South Africa and the League of Nations after World War I.

Rhodes and Milner envisioned a reorganization of the British Empire that was designed to sustain Britain's global preeminence and to help resolve class issues at home in favor of a national harmony that would preserve the rule of the propertied elites. The British Commonwealth was to be a strong federation of English-speaking countries that could jointly supply leadership to the world.[4] This federation was to be mainly composed of former British colonies in which English-speaking settlers were a majority—for example, Canada, Australia, New Zealand, and the United States. The Round Table group also desired that British control might hold sway over nearly the entire continent of Africa, and the key to this notion was control of South Africa.

The English had wrested control of the Cape Colony from the Dutch in 1806 and had taken over Natal by 1843. But the Dutch farmers (Boers) of the Cape had migrated to the interior to escape British authority. This was not a big issue until gold and diamonds were discovered in the Transvaal. British mining investors sunk their money into the Transvaal, and English-speaking miners migrated to the interior. Cecil Rhodes was the minister of the Cape Colony and head of the Royal Africa Company, which had large investments in railroads and mines in the Transvaal. The British mining and rail investors increasingly came to resent the taxes and restrictions placed

[4] Quigley (1981, 49) says of Milner and Rhodes, "Both sought to unite the world, and above all the English-speaking world, in a federal structure around Britain." Rhodes's first will, written in 1877, says, "The extension of British rule throughout the world, . . . the ultimate recovery of the United States of America as an integral part of a British Empire, the consolidation of the whole Empire, the inauguration of a system of Colonial Representation in the Imperial Parliament which may tend to weld together the disjointed members of the Empire, and finally the foundation of so great a power as to hereafter render wars impossible and promote the best interests of humanity" (33).

on them by the Boer Republics and sought to bring them down. The increasingly wealthy Boer Republics were also seen as a potential threat to British control of the Cape.

The Boer governments were accused of discriminating against the English-speaking Uitlander miners by not extending them the franchise. Rhodes, with initial support from Joseph Chamberlain, organized the Jameson raid, a failed effort to bring about a coup d'etat in the Transvaal. After this debacle the Boers were convinced that a war with Britain was inevitable, and they began to purchase the best modern armaments that the world market could supply (M. Evans 1999). In 1899 the Boers attacked and besieged some towns in Natal, initially defeating some of the small British forces that were present. The British mobilized a huge force to defeat the Boers in a war that went on and on because the Boers made effective use of guerilla tactics against the British army. The war was brutal on both sides, inviting comparison with more recent First World/Third World guerilla struggles.[5]

The eventual defeat of the Boers was sealed because none of the other powerful core states were willing to challenge Britain by supporting the Boers, despite that there was great public sympathy for the Boer cause in most of the countries of Europe and in the United States. In the Netherlands and in Germany, the old Boer leader "Uncle" Paul Kruger was very popular, and there was much sympathy for the pioneer farmers of the Boer Republics. But the German and Dutch governments prudently avoided a confrontation with the powerful British Empire over the issue of Boer independence. Kaiser Wilhelm of Germany was quite sympathetic to the Boers and considered supporting them militarily, but he was convinced to abandon the Boers by German foreign secretary Count Bernhard Von Bulow, who had made a secret pact with Britain to divide up the Portuguese colonies in Africa (Mommsen 2001, 4). The German government used the popular sympathy for the Boers to mobilize support for the expansion of the German navy, and a prominent officer in the German army wrote about the inevitability of future wars among industrial states (explicitly Britain and Germany) over control of global resources (Yasamee 2001). The Russian czar also had great sympathy for the Boers but was dissuaded from actively opposing the British campaign by the Russian finance minister Sergei Witte (Spring 2001).

The Boers were well armed with the best rifles and light artillery. They had been able to use the gold and diamonds mined in the Transvaal to purchase large stocks of the latest armaments and munitions on the international market. So the war was a true test of both British resolve and the military capabilities of the British army. The "plight of the Uitlanders" and the early Boer successes against the British army were successfully used by the Round Table politicians and journalists to garner significant public support in England for the war against the Boers. Many still know the campaign song "Marching to Pretoria," the capital of the Boer Transvaal.

Playing the military card was successful in bringing about the conquest of South Africa, and British armed forces proved that they could prevail over a serious challenge. But this unilateral policy of "might makes right" has been characterized as "imperial over-reach" by Paul Kennedy (1988) and as the "imperial detour" by George Modelski (2005). These scholars of hegemony and geopolitics see a repeated pattern in which a formerly powerful hegemon that has lost its economic preeminence tries to substitute unilaterally exercised military supremacy in place of its former ability to gain compliance based on economic comparative advantage and political legitimacy. The result is to mobilize significant resistance and counter-hegemony on the part of those who feel that power is being exercised illegitimately. The Round Table group failed to attain most of its most cherished goals. It did not create "so great a power as to hereafter render wars impossible and promote the best interests of humanity" (Quigley 1981, 33), though it did eventually play a key role in the emergence of the League of Nations, and its remnants were involved in the organization of the UN. It did not prevent the decline of British hegemony nor the dismemberment of the British Empire. The Commonwealth of Nations did not

[5] The 1979 movie *Breaker Morant* tells the true story of an Australian lieutenant serving in the British army who was tried, convicted, and executed before a British firing squad for killing Boer prisoners.

become the strong federal government that Rhodes and Milner envisioned. Rather, it became a trading bloc and a group of largely sovereign nations joined together by common ideals, culture, and language.

The So-Called Great War (World War I)

The Berlin Conference on Africa (1884) was a negotiation in which those European powers that were interested in obtaining colonies in Africa came to an agreement on the boundaries by which that continent would be partitioned. Britain had made an effort to incorporate Germany into the club of industrial core powers by agreeing to hold the conference in Berlin and by seeing that Germany got some of the pieces. But this did not do the trick. The Germans felt that Britain was going to continue to obstruct them, especially after the Boer War. And the British, for their part, had lost patience with the Germans, who were perceived as ungrateful and pushy challengers. The power vacuum created by the collapsing Ottoman Empire drew the powers in as it had in the Crimean War, but this time the Germans and their allies thought that they might win a quick victory while Britain's naval power was stretched across the globe.

During the Boer War there were public scares in both France and England that a Franco-British war might erupt at any moment over disagreements regarding control of Egypt and other issues. The fault line that was to develop into a chasm of conflict in the coming Great War (World War I) was as yet undefined. Britain still saw France and Russia as its main challengers. The contours of the world trade network in the decades before the war did not reveal the coming chasm that would emerge in the great conflict (Table 17.1). Germany and Austria-Hungary were deeply involved in commerce with Britain and the United States. There were old and strong dynastic ties between the royal elites of Germany and Britain (i.e., the House of Hanover). And the waves of migration in the nineteenth century had resulted in a large presence of Germans in the United States. German, English, Belgian, US, and French trade unionists and socialists had joined together in the Second International and had pledged not to go to war against one another (Haupt 1972).

Table 17.1 Factions in the Great War

Entente allies	Central powers	Neutral
Balkans	Austria-Hungary	Brazil
Belgium	Bulgaria	China
France	Germany	Denmark
Greece	Turkey	Mexico
Italy		Netherlands
Japan		Norway
Portugal		Spain
Romania		Sweden
Russia		Switzerland
United Kingdom		
United States		

Despite all the theories that predicted that trade among nations and other friendly ties should reduce the chances of conflict, and despite all the integration among elites and pacts of international solidarity among trade unions and socialist parties, the core split asunder and an estimated 8.5 million people were killed by the awesome power of industrialized warfare in World War I (Singer and Small 1972; Barbieri 2002).

The great mystery about World War I is why the Germans chose to fight on two fronts despite a long tradition of German statesmen who cautioned against such a risky move. Attacking both to the east and to the west, and making war against the British and eventually the Americans, while at the same time fighting Russia in the east seems in retrospect to have been suicidal. Peter Hugill (1999) has argued that there were really two Germanys: the aspiring industrialists centered in Hamburg and the military aristocrats of Prussia—the so-called coalition of Iron and Rye. The war was a compromise between these two groups, which explains the attack on two fronts. The western front was an effort to gain the upper hand in the world economy, while the eastern front was an effort to gain agricultural land by annexing adjacent territory. These are the two different strategies that have contended with one another within and between states for millennia. The Germans resolved an internal struggle by displacing it to foreign policy, and this is what led them to bite off far more than they could chew. The German leaders who led the charge also mistakenly adduced from their quick victory in the Franco-Prussian War of 1870 that they might be able to consolidate control before the conquered states and navies could mobilize their whole potential forces. The long stalemate in the trenches in France melted this fantasy.

The Anglo-American Alliance

A strong and important Anglo-American alliance emerged at the end of the nineteenth century. This development had to overcome large obstacles. The British had long felt that the Americans were colonial upstarts and hillbillies. On the US side, a strong Anglophobia and anger had been produced by the struggle for sovereignty from colonialism. The British had burned the new capitol building in Washington, DC, to the ground during the War of 1812. Overcoming these bad memories required new conditions and concerted action by those who sought to promote the new alliance.

The main structural changes in the relationship between Britain and the United States were:

1. The United States had risen from being a peripheralized region at the time of the American Revolution to a core power by the 1880s
2. Britain had lost its industrial hegemony and needed a strong ally to help it maintain its power and wealth in a world in which these were being challenged by other emergent national societies

Strong and symmetrical financial ties had emerged between London and New York. Recall from Chapter 15 that Junius Spencer Morgan of Boston got his start in high finance working in George Peabody's financial office in London. The house of Morgan became one of the world's largest banking concerns during the belle epoque. By the end of the century, British aristocrats whose fortunes had dwindled were increasingly marrying the daughters of rich Americans. Another factor was the intention of the British Round Table group to form a strong federation of English-speaking countries to help shore up and sustain the Pax Britannica.[6] The key move here was British support for the United States in its war with Spain in 1898. This welcome support was a key factor in convincing American politicians to ignore broad popular sympathy in the United States for the Boer farmers.

Developmental States and Also-Rans

The pattern of semiperipheral development that we have seen in earlier eras continued in the twentieth century. The United States, Germany, and Japan emerged from the semiperiphery to the core in the late nineteenth century. In the twentieth century, China and Russia were semiperipheral challengers to the hegemony of capitalism and the United States. The evolution of the world order continued to be a spiral of challenge and response.

Japan's developmental state success was strongly signaled to the rest of the world by its victory in the Russo-Japanese War of 1904–1905. Russia's defeat by Japan also trumpeted the failure of the Russian modernization effort and triggered an abortive but auspicious radical rebellion within Russia (1905) that was a prelude to the October Revolution of 1917. Japan had begun its modern colonial expansion in 1879 with the occupation of the Ryuku Islands (formerly ruled by China), and it took Formosa (Taiwan) from China in the Sino-Japanese War of 1894–1895. With the Russo-Japanese War (1905), Japan formalized its rule over Korea and added Kwantung Leased Territory on Southern Sakhalin Island to its empire (Henige 1970, 203–206).

The Chinese modernization effort had also failed. Several major factors conspired against the Chinese efforts to adapt Western technology to Asian conditions. China was a huge country with internal regions that had somewhat contradictory needs and interests vis-à-vis the larger world economy. The massive peasant rebellions of the nineteenth century (discussed in Chapter 14) took a huge toll on the energies of the Qing (Manchu) regime, which was also compromised by the fact that many of the Han Chinese continued to see Manchu rule as the illegitimate fruit of conquest by

[6] At one point Rhodes proposed that Britain should become a state within the federal structure of the United States (Quigley 1981, 38).

barbarians. To these factors was added the embarrassment of "treaty port" incursions by Western powers. All these factors, and the conviction held by many Chinese that China was still the center of the universe and that all foreigners were barbarians, undermined the efforts of some farsighted individuals to try to effectively respond to the external challenges posed by industrial technology and the aggressive actions of Europeans and the Japanese.

Empress Dowager of the Qing regime was so frustrated by European meddling that she vacillated when a new peasant and landless movement, the Boxer Rebellion, emerged in North China. The Boxers believed that martial arts could overcome the weapons of the Westerners, and they sought to expel the "foreign devils." This rebellion was strongest in those regions that had been penetrated by foreign-built railroads. The rail lines provided cheap transportation for the export of food grains, and this had the effect of creating local shortages and high prices. This is one of the cases analyzed by Mike Davis (2003) in his careful comparative study of famines. Davis contends that globalization, in the sense of international market integration, exacerbated famines and related disease epidemics, producing "late Victorian holocausts." The Qing empress shared the Boxers' anger, if not their hunger. But this did little to help organize an effective response to modernity of the kind that had emerged in Japan.

Globalization without a Hegemon

Karl Polanyi's (2001) analysis of waves of globalization as the "great transformation" points to the emergence of markets and high finance that become disembedded from politics and the moral order, which then produces a reactive "double movement" in which people resist commodification and try to reestablish communities and protect morality from commercialization. Some have interpreted the long-term world-historical interaction between expanding capitalism and socialist movements in these terms (e.g., Boswell and Chase-Dunn 2000), but the double movement also includes traditionalist, nationalist, and fundamentalist movements that are not considered to be progressive by the activists of the Left.

The Age of Extremes carried on in the postwar Roaring Twenties, when the spasmodic wave of globalization resumed and hot money flowed freely. But, though it was widely recognized that, despite winning, Britain was no longer hegemonic after the Great War, the United States, now the economic hegemon, refused to take up the political role of global leadership. US president Woodrow Wilson and the Round Table network strongly supported the formation of a global confederation that was eventually to include all the countries of the world—the League of Nations. But the senators from the American midwestern heartland were still heeding George Washington's warning about entangling alliances, and so the US Senate declined to ratify the membership of the United States in the League of Nations. Thus the world had no hegemon but money in the decades after World War I. Economic globalization rebounded, but without effective political globalization.

The Age of Extremes was composed of another world revolution, two linked world wars, and a nearly worldwide economic depression. People who had been left out of, displaced by, or immiserated by the great wave of capitalist globalization rebelled against authorities in all zones of the now fully global world-system. The first great depression began in 1873 and ended in 1896, and trade globalization (the ratio of international trade to the size of the whole world economy) bottomed out in 1900 (see Figure 15.1 in Chapter 15). Another short, shallow, and spasmodic wave of trade globalization started up in 1900, peaked in 1929, and then collapsed into a trough of deglobalization.

The World Revolution of 1917

The Chinese, Mexican, and Russian revolutions and World War I were linked and conjoint events in world history. Peasants and workers made revolution, and the great powers attacked one another in a violent spasm of industrial warfare. The strong economic ties that had been created by the nineteenth- and early twentieth-century waves of globalization did not prevent World War I. The British hegemonic decline was produced by the success of the spreading Industrial Revolution. Britain had managed to stay ahead of the curve through several phase changes by shifting its comparative advantage from mass-produced consumer goods to capital goods and then to financial services. But the spread of industrial success to Germany, the United States, Japan, and other European core powers increased competition for raw materials and for access to markets, driving profit rates down and creating conditions in which the use of military power by the German challenger appeared to be an attractive strategy.

Recall that world revolutions are based on popular movements that contest the existing institutions of governance. World revolutions have been assigned symbolic years. Thus we speak of the world revolutions of 1789, 1848, 1917, 1968, and 1989 as representational years in which especially dramatic events took place, but the world revolutions that clustered around these symbolic years often went on for several decades (Arrighi, Hopkins, and Wallerstein 1989; Boswell and Chase-Dunn 2000). **Transnational social movements** are those in which individuals and groups come together across national boundaries for political purposes but are not organized solely as representing their nations, whereas international organizations are mainly composed of nationally organized groups.

In 1864 Karl Marx and activists from labor unions and socialist, anarchist, and communist groups all over Europe and the United States organized the International Workingmen's Association (the First International). Samir Amin's (2008) recent discussion of the possibility of a "Fifth International" points out that the First International was very diverse in terms of the groups that participated, but that it nevertheless managed to achieve a high degree of democratic representation. This said, the First International eventually fell apart because of the intense disagreements between the Marxists and the anarchists over the goals and tactics of radical progressivism.

The Second International, formed in 1889, was an alliance of labor unions and socialist parties. It was explicitly an international federation of national parties representing unions and socialist parties, mainly from core states. The anarchists were left out, and the participants were representing nationally organized units of the labor movement. The Second International declared that the workers of the world should not go to war against one another at the behest of capitalists. That sworn alliance fell apart, and most of the workers of Germany, France, England, and the United States chose nationalism over international class solidarity by fighting one another in World War I. A large part of this failure was due to the rise of "social imperialism," in which politicians in core states symbolically incorporated workers and the labor movement into nationalist imperial ventures in the Third World. Despite the famous slogan "Workers of the world, unite!," core unions and socialist parties did not see that they had common interests with workers in the noncore countries. In practice, labor internationalism in the Second International meant solidarity among workers from different European countries or settler colonies with majorities of European descent. White racism played an important role in undermining the potential for Global North/South worker solidarity and worked in favor of nationalism in both the core and the periphery.[7]

A massive revolt by Russian workers, soldiers, and peasants made the Bolshevik Revolution after the czar's army had suffered large defeats in World War I. The revolutionary situation in Russia had been building for a long time. We have already mentioned the revolution of 1905 that occurred after the defeat in the Russo-Japanese War. The czarist government lost respect abroad and legitimacy at home when it was defeated by those developmental states (Germany and Japan) that had succeeded at the game of catch-up with Britain, a game that the czarist regime had failed at despite valiant efforts. But Russian industrialization had created only a small industrial working class, mainly in Moscow and St. Petersburg. The vast majority of people in Russia were peasants. The Bolshevik Party held that the industrial working class was the protagonist of history—the agent of the transformation from capitalism to socialism. The Bolsheviks acted out Marx's tendency to

[7] One of the most dramatic illustrations of this is a famous picture of South African trade unionists standing under a banner that proclaims "Workers of the world unite for an all-white South Africa."

identify peasants as a reactionary class, and so a party that saw a majority of the Russian people as reactionaries led the Russian Revolution. The Bolsheviks fully expected that there would be a communist-led revolutionary victory in Germany, the most advanced country with a strong labor movement. The Russian communists saw Russia as a backward and underdeveloped country, and they were greatly dismayed when their successful conquest of state power left them standing alone in a larger world in which the other powerful states were still under the control of capital.

But the Russian Revolution nevertheless gave heart to workers on every continent who believed that the labor movement could overthrow capitalism and create a more humane form of human society. The American journalist John Reed (1919) told the story of the heady days of October 1917 in his famous book, *Ten Days That Shook the World*.[8]

As mentioned above, the Mexican and Chinese revolutions were part of the world revolution of 1917. The Chinese situation has already been described above. The nationalist revolution of 1911, the collapse of the Qing regime, and regional differences led to a long period of strife in China from 1912 to 1949. The Chinese Communist Party was founded during a secret night meeting in a mattress factory in Shanghai in 1921. Marx's analysis of modern social change was based mainly on observations about the development of capitalism in Great Britain and the other industrializing countries in the middle of the nineteenth century. Marx saw the urban industrial proletariat as the leading group that would transform capitalism into a more humane socialist form of society. Like the Bolsheviks in Russia, the Chinese Communist Party was Marxist and held to the notion of the urban industrial proletariat as the revolutionary class. But, as in Russia, the urban proletariat in China was a minority of the population.

In 1934 the Communist Party, led by Mao Zedong, was forced to undertake the "long march" to rural Yenan Province because the communists were driven out of the cities by the nationalist (Kuomintang) army. Thus was Mao thrown into the arms of the peasantry, and the subsequent policies of the Chinese Communist Party were far less injurious to the agrarian sector of society than the policies of the Bolshevik Party had been in the Soviet Union. When the United States defeated Japan in World War II, Japan had to give up its colonies in Taiwan, Korea, and Manchuria. After further battles with the Kuomintang, the Communist Peoples Army forced the nationalists to retreat to Taiwan, and the communists formed a new state on the mainland in 1949.

Nineteenth-century Mexico gained independence from Spain, had a war with the United States (1848) in which California, Arizona, New Mexico, and Texas were lost, and endured a failed military campaign by France (during the American Civil War) to make it part of the French Empire under the Hapsburg emperor Maximilian. US support in driving out the French helped mend the badly broken fences left by the Mexican-American War of 1848 and explains why the Cinco de Mayo holiday celebrating a Mexican victory in 1862 is celebrated on both sides of the border. These momentous developments were followed by the regime of President Porfirio Diaz—the "Porfiriata." The Diaz government tried to modernize Mexico by privatizing and commodifying communal land titles and by inviting foreign investment in railroads, mining, and other natural resources. The radical ideas of the world revolution of 1848 and the emerging world revolution of 1917 encouraged popular resistance to appropriations of communally held land, especially in southern Mexico, where indigenous cultures and communities had not been completely erased by Spanish colonialism. The revolution of 1910 was led by Emiliano Zapata[9] in the south and by Pancho Villa in the north. When they met in the Zocalo, the great square in Mexico City, they rode their horses into the cathedral that the Spaniards had built over the ruins of the Aztec pyramid of Tenochtitlan. The Catholic Church was seen as implicated in the exploitation and domination that had occurred under Spanish colonialism and during the Porfiriata, and so the Mexican Revolution invoked the values of secular

[8] In the Hollywood movie *Reds* (1981), the role of John Reed is played by Warren Beatty.

[9] Marlon Brando starred as the revolutionary leader in the fictionalized 1952 movie *Viva Zapata*.

humanism against the powers and properties of the church and restored a dose of respect for the pre-Hispanic indigenous heritage of Mexico.

The Communist International: A World Party in the 1920s

Counter-hegemonic world party formation reached an apogee in the world revolution of 1917. The Communist International (Comintern or the Third International) was a vast and complex network of red labor unions, peasant associations, women's associations, youth organizations, and organizations of the unemployed that was constructed on an intercontinental scale. Called a "world party" and a "red network" by both its supporters and those who opposed it, the Comintern demonstrated that a popular alliance of workers, peasants, and other relatively powerless groups could exercise important political influence in core, peripheral, and semiperipheral countries and could have a serious and sustained impact on world politics. The Comintern networks competed not only with capitalist elites and hegemonic contenders but also with anarcho-syndicalists who successfully organized large numbers of peasants and workers in the late nineteenth and early twentieth centuries. The Comintern was organized explicitly to confront the issues of social imperialism and racism that were made evident by the failures of the Second International (Amin 2008). But rather than recognizing and trying to embrace diversity as the First International had tried to do, the Comintern tried to construct a single global workers' culture and political line, and this effort came increasingly to be dominated by the Communist Party of the Soviet Union.

The Comintern adopted V. I. Lenin's critique of the Second International and then tried to overcome the problems that Lenin had highlighted. Lenin thought that social democracy and the electoral road to socialist state power (reformism) was not a sufficiently strong challenge to capitalism. He blamed the success of this reformist tendency in the core labor movement on the emergence of a "labor aristocracy" in the core countries that was willing to form cooperative alliances with capital. This resulted in social imperialism based on capital-labor nationalist alliances and contributed to the interimperial rivalry that led to World War I. Though Lenin was critical of nationalism, he saw it as problematic mainly for the working-class movement in the core. Third World nationalism could be a progressive force. And so the Comintern was formed as a network of national organizations of Reds with attention to strong representation from the noncore countries.

The Comintern is often characterized as having been a puppet of the Soviet Union and as having had a hierarchical form of organization based on the principles and directions set forth in Lenin's book on revolutionary organization, *What Is to Be Done?* (1973).[10] But the Communist International was a very complicated creature, and it changed in important ways over its period of existence from March 1919 to June 1943 (Sworakowski 1965; McDermott and Agnew 1997).

The Comintern adopted its own statutes at its second congress in 1920. It was led by an executive committee and a presidium. These statutes mandated that congresses with representatives from all over the world were to meet "not less than once a year." The Comintern also organized and sponsored a number of other "front organizations"—the Red International of Labor Unions, the Communist Youth International, International Red Aid, the International Peasants' Council, the Workers' International Relief, and the Communist Women's Organization (Sworakowski 1965).

The Comintern was founded in the Soviet Union, the so-called fatherland of the proletariat, and so it is often depicted as having been mainly a tool of Soviet foreign policy. There is little doubt that this became true after the rise of Stalin. In perhaps the most blatant example, Stalin tried to

[10] A large part of *What Is to Be Done?*, written in 1901, is devoted to finding a middle path between the trade unionists who focused on narrowly defined issues of wages and working conditions and those who advocated acts of terrorism as a revolutionary tactic for bringing down the czarist regime. Lenin stressed the importance of developing an organized group of professional political agitators who were to serve as the revolutionary leadership of the workers' movement. This approach has come to be known as vanguardism.

use the Comintern to get communist parties all over the world to support the Hitler-Stalin pact of 1939. But during Lenin's time, the Comintern held large multinational congresses at which over forty languages were spoken. The largest of these congresses had as many as 1600 delegates attending. Sworakowski (1965, 9) says,

> After some attempts at restrictions in the beginning, delegates were permitted to use at the meetings any language they chose. Their speeches were translated into Russian, German, French and English, or digests in these languages were read to the congresses immediately following the speech in another language. Whether a speech was translated verbatim or digested to longer or shorter versions depended upon the importance of the speaker. Only by realizing these time-consuming translation and digesting procedures does it become understandable why some congresses last as long as forty-five days.

The Comintern was abolished in 1943, though the Soviet Union continued to pose as the protagonist of the world working class until its demise in 1989. In 1938 Trotskyists organized the Fourth International to replace the Comintern, which they saw as having been captured by Stalinism. The Fourth International suffered from a series of sectarian splits and the huge communist-led rebellions that emerged during and after World War II were led by either pro-Soviet or Maoist organizations that held the Fourth International to be illegitimate.

Wobblies and Reds in the United States

By the time of the Age of Extremes the labor movement in the United States already had a long and militant history. The great nineteenth-century waves of migration from Europe brought workers who had experience in the anarchist and Marxist revolutionary traditions in the Old World to the United States. But most of the labor leadership in the United States continued to represent the skilled craft workers in the American Federation of Labor (AFL), who had been able to improve their wages and working conditions in local struggles with employers. The new waves of immigrants, the growth of railroads, and large-scale industrial production in cities produced a situation in which less skilled workers could also be organized. In the United States, the world revolution of 1848 had mainly taken the form of the creation of new Christian sects and community revitalization movements (see Chapter 15). But later in the nineteenth century, the Socialist Party had mounted strong electoral challenges. The Granger movement had mobilized farmers to challenge the economic monopolies of the Eastern banks and railroads. And the anarcho-syndicalists, who believed that industrial workers could dispense with capitalists and could themselves operate large-scale industries, emerged to challenge the rule of capital, especially in the West.

The railroad and the telegraph were used by capital to expand and reorganize production and trade, and by politicians and military leaders to exercise power across the North American continent, but these new transportation and communications technologies also served as useful tools in the hands of those who challenged the rule of capital. Organizers could travel cheaply and communicate inexpensively across great distances. The strongest anarcho-syndicalist organization in the United States was the Industrial Workers of the World (IWW), also known as the Wobblies. Their slogan was "One big union of all the workers." The Wobblies sent organizers armed with pamphlets, songs, and dynamite into the mining camps and lumber towns of the West.[11] If the pot was ready to boil, two Wobblies could do the job—one at a late-night meeting with the workers, and the other beneath the closest rail-bridge to town. The IWW songbook contained popular ballads with lyrics that had been written by Joseph Hilstrom, a Swedish immigrant wordsmith, whose movement name was Joe Hill. In 1915 Joe Hill was executed in Salt Lake City for allegedly killing a grocery store owner in a robbery.

[11] It was easy to organize company towns because the power structure was composed of a single hierarchy. See the classic study by Kerr and Siegel (1954), "The Interindustry Propensity to Strike."

The Seattle general strike in February 1919 was part of the world revolution of 1917. A wage dispute that began with the dockworkers became a general strike of 65,000 workers when it appeared that the federal government was siding with the employers (see Figure 17.1). For several days, workers took control of the city of Seattle, organizing their own police force and an emergency food distribution system. Pamphlets were circulated that approved of the Russian Revolution with its organization of workers' councils (Soviets). Later, Seattle longshoremen refused to load arms destined to resupply the anti-Bolshevik White Army in Russia. The Seattle longshoremen attacked strikebreakers who were brought in to load the munitions. The AFL union leadership helped bring the general strike to an early end, and thirty-nine members of the IWW (Wobblies) were arrested despite the fact that they had not played a very central role in the general strike. This "first Soviet on American soil" was an important stimulus to the "Big Red Scare" and the crackdown on radicals and immigrants that emerged later in 1919.

The Big Red Scare was not the only reaction to the radical labor movement in the United States. The US ruling class was particularly incensed at the challenges that radicals posed to their control of big private property in the means of production (M. Mann 1993). When they felt that state and federal police agencies were not doing a good enough job, they hired private Pinkerton armed guards to attack strikers and defend property. It was in this period that the Federal Bureau of Investigation was created. And there was a major crackdown on and expulsion of immigrants who were believed to be radical "outside agitators." The famous anarchist Emma Goldman was deported, and the United States began an effort to regulate immigration. In Southern California the Los Angeles Diocese of the Catholic Church sent money to support the Cristeros, a conservative peasant movement in Mexico that opposed the anti-clericalism of the Mexican Revolution (M. Davis 1990). Some labor leaders also promulgated racist and xenophobic attitudes toward nonwhite workers.

The United States had been a crucial ally of Britain in the Great War and was victorious in that effort despite the huge human costs of the war. The economy boomed again in the Roaring Twenties, and the radicals were both repressed and ignored, though the American communists got their act together for the next round of counter-hegemonic struggles in the 1930s.

Germany and the other countries that had been defeated in World War II were made to pay

STRIKE CALLED

ALL UNIONS TO GO OUT

Seattle Union Record

DAILY EDITION

SIXTY THOUSAND TO RESPOND TO CALL

NO CONSTRUCTIVE LEGISLATION YET

ANNOUNCEMENT OF STRIKE

A general strike of all the union workmen in Seattle was decided upon definitely at a meeting held in the Labor Temple Sunday, February 2, 1919, when the date for the general strike was set for 10 a. m. Thursday, February 6, 1919.

Plans are perfected by the workers to feed the strikers and public at places which will be announced later by this committee. The plans, as outlined by a committee of the culinary trades, will insure the strikers and public in general no hardships or privations so far as having suitable places to eat are concerned.

A committee has been appointed to visit the Metal Trades and Central Labor Councils of Tacoma, who had decided to call a general strike for Tuesday, February 4, at 12 o'clock noon, to prevail upon them to postpone action until Thursday at 10 a. m., so as to act simultaneously with the Seattle Unions, thereby effecting a solid front, bolstering the metal tradesmen in their demands.

35,000 SILK MILL WORKERS STRIKE

Figure 17.1 The Seattle general strike: Front page of the *Seattle Union Record*, February 8, 1919

indemnities. German colonies in Africa were taken over by Britain and France after the war. Resentment and the failure of a new legitimate form of global governance to emerge, as well as strong challenges by labor, socialist, and communist parties, created fertile ground for the emergence of a new and virulent form of reactive supernationalism called fascism. Fascism glorified the state as the agent of the national community and stressed the duties of individuals to serve the national state. This was clearly a reaction to the radically individualized form of capitalism that had emerged in Europe, and to the disruptions that had been produced by marketization and international flows of volatile capital. Fascist movements took state power or were important in influencing politics in Germany, Italy, Japan, Spain, Portugal, China, Romania, Hungary, Austria, Slovakia, and Ukraine, and to a lesser extent in Brazil and Argentina as well (Goldfrank 1978).

It was in the context of the Age of Extremes that a transnational network of communist intellectuals claimed to lead the global proletariat in a world revolution that was intended to transform capitalism into socialism and then communism by abolishing large-scale private property in the means of production. Their actions were stimulated by, and contributed to, the chaotic nature of social change during the Age of Extremes. And the institutions that they created had large subsequent effects on the nature of the new US-led hegemony when it emerged after World War II. Procapitalist politicians, the new incarnation of the enlightened conservatives, needed to come up with a development project that had many of the same egalitarian goals as those espoused by the Soviet Union, while at the same time preserving private property in the means of production and the significant influence of privately owned capital within national states. This was a struggle over the definition of a good world order in which the Left and the Right versions of the European Enlightenment were contending with one another in a multicivilizational global context and thereby producing a new global culture.

Suggested Readings

Boyer, Richard O., and Herbert M. Morais. 1975. *Labor's Untold Story.* 3rd ed. New York: United Electrical, Radio & Machine Workers of America.

Choucri, Nazli, and Robert C. North. 1975. *Nations in Conflict: National Growth and International Violence.* San Francisco: Freeman.

Hobsbawm, Eric J. 1994. *The Age of Extremes: A History of the World, 1914–1991.* New York: Pantheon.

Hugill, Peter J. 1999. *Global Communications since 1844: Geopolitics and Technology.* Baltimore: Johns Hopkins University Press.

Martin, William G., Tuba Agartan, Caleb M. Bush, Woo-Young Choi, Tu Huynh, Foad Kalouche, Eric Mielants, and Rochelle Morris. 2008. *Making Waves: Worldwide Social Movements, 1750–2005.* Boulder, CO: Paradigm Publishers.

Mintz, Sydney. 1985. *Sweetness and Power: The Place of Sugar in Modern History.* New York: Viking.

Polanyi, Karl. 2001 [1944]. *The Great Transformation: The Political and Economic Origins of Our Time.* Boston: Beacon Press.

Quigley, Carroll. 1981. *The Anglo-American Establishment.* New York: Books in Focus.

Reed, John. 1919. *Ten Days That Shook the World.* New York: Boni and Liveright.

Silver, Beverly J. 2003. *Forces of Labor: Workers' Movements and Globalization since 1870.* Cambridge: Cambridge University Press.

Womack, John. 1970. *Zapata and the Mexican Revolution.* New York: Vintage.

18

The World-System since 1945: Another Wave of Globalization, Hegemony, and Revolutions

The second half of the twentieth century was a relatively peaceful era of economic development and the golden age of US hegemony. The Cold War between the United States and the Soviet Union provided justification for the United States to extend credits to other societies for national development and for the Soviet Union to sponsor urbanization, education, and industrialization in its Eastern European satellites. Another wave of national liberation movements in the remaining colonies brought independence and the trappings of national sovereignty to Africa and Asia. The demographic transition to lower birthrates continued to spread, but so did the transition to greater longevity and lower mortality rates, so the world population continued to rapidly increase, reaching more than 6 million by the end of the century. Cities continued to grow, and

Radical sociologist C. Wright Mills
Source: © Estate of C. Wright Mills.

in some areas this produced city-regions—dense concentrations of large cities with suburbs in between them. Countryfolk in noncore countries increasingly moved to dwell in large urban areas, and so by the end of the century over half of the human population of the earth lived in large cities. Another great wave of globalization and the falling costs of communication and transportation brought the peoples of the world into much greater contact with one another, and two more world revolutions (1968 and 1989) once again challenged and restructured the institutions of global and national governance.

America's Half Century

Those enlightened conservatives who wanted to take the rough edges off of capitalism in order to preserve it invented the New Deal and a global development project based on Keynesian economic policies. The intent was to overcome the perceived dangers of speculative capitalism and state communism that ran wild in the 1920s and the beggar-thy-neighbor economic nationalism that took hold during the deglobalization of the 1930s. The New Deal addressed the problems of overproduction and underconsumption by supporting the rights of workers to organize unions to collectively bargain with employers over wages and working conditions. In the United States, the Wagner Act of 1935 provided legal protections to union organizers. Henry J. Kaiser, a progressive industrialist based in California, encouraged the workers at his steel and shipbuilding plants to organize their own independent labor unions. Corporate businessmen and wealthy families in the older eastern industries and politicians from the American South opposed this enlightened conservatism. In order to get New Deal legislation passed, President Franklin Delano Roosevelt had to make compromises. Southern Dixiecrats (conservative Democrats) demanded that agriculture not be included in the New Deal labor legislation. The rising potential military challenge from Japan in the Pacific was a powerful argument for industrializing the American West. Eastern steel companies acquiesced in allowing new steel production in the West, but only under certain conditions. The Fontana steel mill in Southern California, built by Kaiser, had to be located far enough from water transportation to make its products too expensive to survive during peacetime (M. Davis 1990). Thus did the New Deal contain important aspects of the old deal.

The Congress of Industrial Organizations (CIO), with strong leadership provided by the American Communist Party, organized less-skilled workers and the unemployed and tried to overcome white racism in the labor movement by encouraging cooperation between black and white workers. In 1934 the American Communist Party had over a million members. That was the year of the San Francisco general strike, in which longshoremen and sailors led a successful organizing effort that resulted in radical unions taking control of hiring at all the West Coast ports of the United States. This victory and other important struggles signaled the growing power of the CIO.

World War II was a replay of World War I. But now the Japanese challenge and the German challenge came together in time and on the same side. This required the United States to fight wars in Europe and in the Pacific at the same time. Only a supersized superpower could pull this off. The war also ushered in the nuclear age. The "Manhattan Project" succeeded at detonating a plutonium implosion bomb near Alamagordo, New Mexico, in 1945 that physicist J. Robert Oppenheimer described as "brighter than a thousand suns." In August of the same year, the United States dropped two bombs that obliterated the Japanese cities of Hiroshima and Nagasaki, ostensibly to save lives by ending the fighting more quickly. But the US monopoly on nuclear weapons of mass destruction was short-lived. The United States and the Soviet Union had become allies in the fight against Nazi Germany in the war, but this evolved rapidly into the Cold War and a "balance of terror" arms race after the Soviet Union acquired nuclear weapons.

After World War II the United States actively took up the mantle of global multilateral hegemony. The establishment of the UN and the Bretton Woods institutions—the IMF and the World Bank—was a further move toward political globalization. The Marshall Plan facilitated the rebuilding of the Western European national economies by means of massive US lending. A similar approach was employed in East Asia, where developmental states were supported in Japan and later in Korea, and US corporations were prevented from buying up key domestic sectors of the Japanese and Korean economies. Getting support from conservatives in the United States for all these far-reaching global initiatives was not easy. And President Roosevelt, the great architect of the New Deal, died in April 1945. His vice president was Harry Truman, and Truman was elected president in a very close race with Henry Wallace, the candidate of the Progressive Party, in 1948. Truman was able to get the acquiescence of the heartland conservatives for the Marshall Plan and other international programs because he painted these as part of the effort to contain communism and to protect and develop "the free world." Thus did the Cold War, a global confrontation between different visions of the human future, serve as a powerful political justification for US hegemony and an important contributor to the further expansion of capitalist globalization.

The CIO and the US Communist Party (CP) emerged as powerful in certain unions and sectors in the United States after World War II. Many sympathizers with the radical labor movement had been badly put off by the CP's support for the Hitler-Stalin pact before World War II. But the CP played an important role in organizing workers in the steel and auto industries before and during World War II. Julius and Ethel Rosenberg were accused of passing the secret of the atomic bomb to the Soviet Union and were tried and executed for treason. Senator Joseph McCarthy from Wisconsin led a crusade to expose communists and fellow travelers in the federal government and higher education. And a battle took place within the labor movement between those radicals who wanted to fundamentally challenge the rule of capital and those other labor leaders who only wanted the workers that they represented to get a larger share of the pie.

McCarthy's methods were unscrupulous, and many innocents suffered until those who supported civil rights were able to prevail over the witch hunt.[1] But the "business unionists" prevailed over the Reds in most of the struggles within the labor movement in the United States. The prospect of an expanding US-led hegemonic project with a growing economy and an expanding middle class tilted in favor of class harmony rather than class struggle, at least within the core of the world-system. The business unionists won out in most of the labor movements because capitalism was able to incorporate a broad sector of the core working class into its developmental project as national citizens and consumers.

The wave of decolonization after World War II produced another spate of "new nations" in Asia and Africa. American leadership needed a development ideology that could compete with Soviet and Chinese communism. The experiences of the Age of Extremes and the demands of the Cold War produced a consensus on Keynesian national development as the main project of the American hegemony and the reformist alternative to communism. All these factors reduced the salience of world parties and transnational social movements and further increased the legitimacy of national societies as the totemic unit of world political and social organization. By constituting the world order as a set of separate national societies, each with its own allegedly unique history and culture, nationalism became an even stronger dimension of the institutional structure of the world-system than it had been in the nineteenth century. Transnational political organizations and non-national forms of solidarity based on class, religion, and ethnicity continued to operate, but they were upstaged by national states and international organizations such as the UN and the Bretton Woods international financial institutions (the World Bank and the IMF), in which national states were the main constituent members. The "new nations" of the periphery had a strong motive to support this institutional structure because they had only recently gained at least formal national sovereignty, and they had high hopes of using this new autonomy to modernize and develop their societies without the obstacles posed by colonialism.

The Bandung Conference (Asian-African Conference) of 1955 was organized by noncore

[1] The story of reporter Edward R. Murrow, who stood up to McCarthy, is dramatized in the 2005 movie *Good Night, and Good Luck*.

(so-called Third World) states, mainly former colonies, that wished to pursue policies that were nonaligned with either the Soviet Union or the West.[2] This nonaligned movement was an important development in the political representation of the noncore, and recent efforts to organize solidarity among peoples of the Global South owe a great debt to the legacy of the Bandung Conference. But even the nonaligned states did not encourage their citizens to directly participate in transnational political decision making. Global governance became increasingly defined as the representation of national societies.

Figure 18.1 shows changes in the distribution of shares of world GDP[3] among countries from 1820 to 2005 based on the estimates of national GDP produced by Angus Maddison (1995, 2001). Shares of world GDP are not an ideal indicator of hegemony, because they include simple economic size, which is an important but insufficient aspect of relative power among states. A large country with a lot of people will have a large GDP. But if we look at changes in the world shares over time, we can see the trajectories of hegemony that we have been discussing. Figure 13.3 in Chapter 13 showed the Dutch, British, and US hegemonies in a graph of the last five hundred years. Geopolitical hegemony is a relative, not an absolute, concept. The Dutch are no longer the fore-reachers of the capitalist world economy that they were in the seventeenth century, but the queen of the Netherlands still owns many of the stately mansions on embassy row (Massachusetts Avenue) in Washington, DC, renting them to countries that can afford this prestigious location. And Amsterdam is still an important center of world financial services nearly four centuries after the peak of Dutch hegemony in 1630. Figure 18.1 shows the trajectories of individual European countries, the United States, and Japan

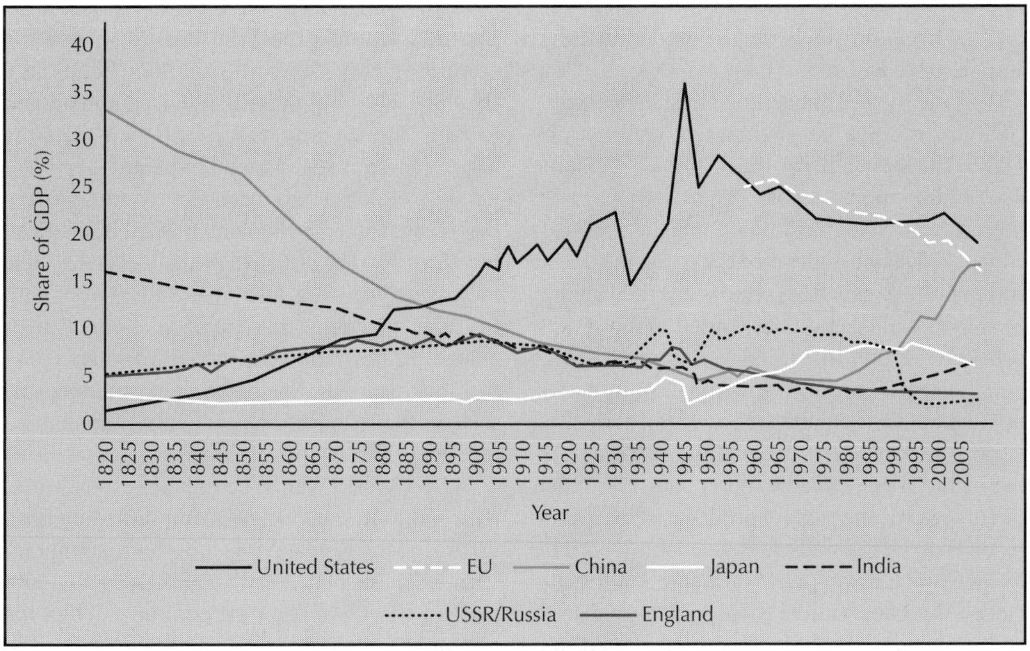

Figure 18.1 Shares of world GDP, 1820–2005

Sources: Data from Maddison 1995, 2001.

[2] A communist resistance movement led by Marshal Tito came to state power in Yugoslavia without much help from the Soviet Union. Tito championed the notion that non-Soviet-aligned leftist regimes should support one another and resist becoming agents of either the United States or Russia.

[3] The GDP of a country estimates the monetary value of all the goods and services that are sold within that country in a single year. The world GDP is the sum of all the country GDPs.

and lumps together those European countries that had joined the European Union (EU) by 1992.

The most striking feature of Figure 18.1 is the rapid ascent of the US economy in its size relationship with the world economy as a whole—from less than 2 percent in 1820 to a peak of 35 percent in 1944. The US share slumped precipitously from 1929 to 1933 and then rapidly ascended again to its highest point in 1944. A rapid post–World War II decline was followed by a slight recovery that began in 1949 and then, beginning in 1951, a decline until 1958, then a plateau until 1968, then another decline until 1982, followed by another plateau until 1998 at between 21 and 22 percent. The US GDP trajectory shown in Figure 18.1 strongly supports the contention that US economic hegemony rose and then declined in the twentieth century.[4] But some of the details of the timing contradict certain accounts of the US trajectory. By the measure of shares of world GDP, the US decline began in 1944, not in the late 1960s as some world-systems analysts have claimed. There were three steps of US decline, the first beginning in 1944, the second in 1951, and the third in 1968.

As mentioned above, the US share of world GDP had become larger than that of Britain by 1880. The stairstep nature of both hegemonic rise and hegemonic decline can be seen in the US trajectory in Figure 18.1. Economic hegemony is a matter of staying ahead of the game relative to competitors. Generative sectors are the key, and each modern hegemon has tended to move from consumer goods to capital goods and then to financial services (Wallerstein 1984). As discussed in Chapter 15, Britain's first wave of industrial leadership was in the production of cotton textiles, which then spread to other countries. Then Britain became the leading producer of machines, steam engines, railroads, and steamships, both for its own home market and for markets across the globe. As competition in these sectors increased, and profits declined, British capital shifted into financial services and making money on money. These areas, and a continuing predominance in global telecommunications, were the economic bases of the belle epoque.

For the United States the sequence was similar, though the particular industries were different, and the whole trajectory was somewhat modified because of the much greater size of the US economy relative to the sizes of other core powers and to the world economy as a whole. While Britain's home market was that of an island nation, the United States came to encompass a continent-sized home market, which was a big advantage in international competition.

US industrial hegemony emerged with the development of the oil industry and the production of automobiles. These were the **new lead industries** and generative sectors (Bunker and Ciccantell 2005) that further transformed the built environment of the North American continent and then the world.

Just as cotton textile manufacturing had spread in the British hegemonic rise, the automobile industry spread abroad and profits went down because of increased competition. The United States managed to stay ahead of the curve by developing electronic technology (the telephone, vacuum tubes, the transistor, and the computer chip) and information technology (Hugill 1999). But these also moved abroad and became more competitive, and new possible high-tech industries (e.g., biotechnology and nanotechnology) have been slow to move out of the research and development phase. So American investors, like the British in the belle epoque, have increasingly moved into financial services with the huge advantage that the US economy is such a large proportion of the whole world economy that making money on the US dollar and financial services is much less of a challenge than making money on the pound sterling had been.

After World War II, US military expenditures returned to peacetime levels, but they went back up during the Korean War, and after that military spending remained a very large proportion (nearly half) of the US federal expenditures. Thus the economic boom of the 1950s was stimulated in part by government spending—so-called military Keynesianism. US federal expenditures in the name of defense were used to subsidize key industries in the United States and to stimulate

[4] Gross national product (GNP) per capita measures also show a similar pattern (Chase-Dunn et al. 2005).

the development of new lead technologies, especially the transistor. The government also acted to prevent the phone company American Telephone and Telegraph (AT&T) (whose Bell Laboratory invented the transistor with federal grant support) from monopolizing and sitting on the new technology. As the world's biggest owner of traditional switching devices and vacuum tube amplifiers, AT&T had a lot of investment in the old technologies that solid-state electronics made obsolete. Despite the vaunted fecundity of private entrepreneurs, many of the techno-miracles of advanced capitalism were first developed with heavy financial support and organizational intervention from the US federal government—for example, nuclear energy, the transistor, and the Internet.

The most recent phase of **financialization** of the world economy has expanded the realm of virtual capital (based on securities that ostensibly represent future income streams) to a far greater extent than earlier financial expansions did. New instruments of financial property have multiplied, and information technology has facilitated the expansion of trading of securities in new venues located in the older financial cities and in the so-called emerging markets of the less developed countries (Arrighi 1994; Henwood 1997).

The post–World War II expansionary boom was based on new lead manufacturing industries in the United States, some of which spread to Japan and to Europe, especially Germany. In the 1970s Japan and Germany caught up with the United States in manufacturing, and the profit rate declined (Brenner 2002). This profit squeeze in core manufacturing encouraged an expansion of investment in financial services that was the beginning of the huge wave of financialization that has ballooned since the 1970s. Lending to noncore countries expanded rapidly, and there was a large debt crisis in the 1980s in which many noncore countries in Asia, Africa, and Latin America were unable to make the payments on external debt that they had committed to make (Suter 1992).

This development was not unusual. The capitalist world economy has experienced waves of debt crises since at least the 1830s when many states within the United States, as well as countries in Latin America, defaulted on foreign loans. Usually the house of cards collapses. The symbolic claims on future income are devalued, and the real economy of goods production, trade, and services starts up again with a reduced set of property claims and symbols of value. But this did not happen in the 1980s debt crisis. There was no collapse. Rather, the bankers of the core cooperated with one another and engineered a renegotiation of the terms of indebtedness of the noncore countries. This is an important indicator of the relatively high degree of cooperation achieved by the world's bankers by the time of the 1980s, and it supports the contentions of those who see the emergence of an increasingly integrated transnational capitalist class (Sklair 2001; Robinson 2004).

But one result of this new level of cooperation is that the huge mountain of "securities"—claims on future income streams—has continued to grow larger and larger such that it now dwarfs the real world economy of production, trade, and services. In the past, financial collapses periodically brought the domains of purely symbolic and material values back into balance with one another. The continuous rapid expansion of what some call "fictitious capital" since the 1970s appears to have altered some of the basic rules of the capitalist economy and has led many observers to claim that the old rules have been transcended by the new information economy. Whether that turns out to be the case in the long run remains to be seen.

The economy of the United States regained some of its lost share of world GDP in the 1990s. This was mainly due to financialization and a real estate investment boom based on a large inflow of capital investment from abroad. Though other national currencies have not been pegged to the US dollar since the 1970s, the United States continues to enjoy what historical sociologist Michael Mann (2006) calls "dollar seignorage."

The only use for surplus US dollars held abroad was now to invest them in the United States. Since most were held by central banks, they bought US Treasury notes in bulk, which lowered their interest rate. US adventures abroad could now be financed by foreigners, despite American current account deficits, and at a very low interest rate. The alternative, the foreigners felt, was worse: disruption of the world's monetary system, weakening US resolve to defend them, and a fall in the value of the dollar, making

US exports cheaper than their own. Hudson (2003, 20) concludes, "This unique ability of the US government to borrow from foreign central banks rather than from its own citizens is one of the economic miracles of modern times." This miracle of economic imperialism meant that the US government was now free of the balance-of-payments constraints faced by other states (Mann 2006).

The EU is shown in Figure 18.1 as if it already existed in 1950, though in reality it was not formally constituted until 1992. This is so we can see that those twelve European core countries that joined together in 1992 had a downward trajectory in terms of shares of world GDP that was similar to that of the United States. What was happening in this period was the rise of Japan (see Figure 18.1) and the rise of the newly industrializing countries in the semiperiphery (e.g., China, India, Korea, Taiwan, and Brazil). These rises partly account for the relative downward trend in shares of both the United States and the EU.

The Global Settlement System

The ancient volcano form of the city that emerged with the first cities in Mesopotamia 5,000 years ago had survived the Industrial Revolution and railroads, but it succumbed to the car-based multicentric suburban and edge-city settlement structure when residences and workplaces became organized around mass individual motor-car transportation (see Figures 18.2 and 18.3).

As mentioned in Chapter 17, the global population continued to move into cities in the twentieth century, and thus the proportion of the total population living in rural areas continued to fall and the sizes of cities continued to rise. But the world city size distribution flattened out after 1950. New York had been both the largest city and the biggest center of business in the world since it grew larger than London in 1925, but after World War II other cities began to catch up with New York in terms of population size. Tokyo-Yokohama became larger than greater

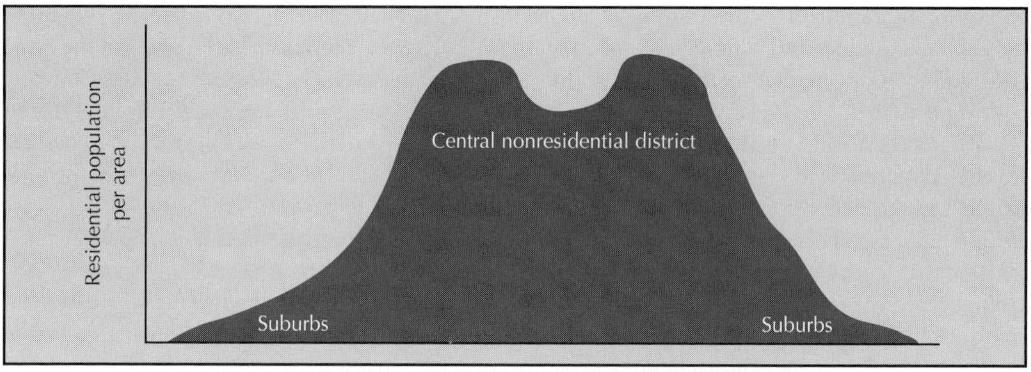

Figure 18.2 The volcano model of urban population density

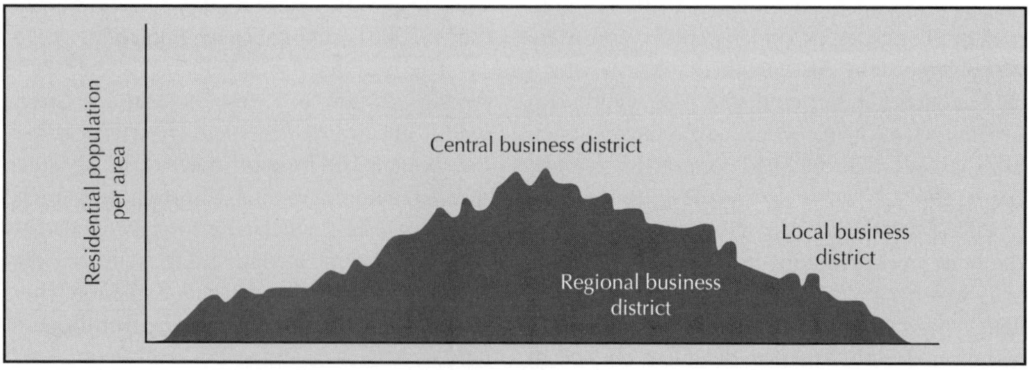

Figure 18.3 The multicentric pattern of automobile-based urban population density

metropolitan New York City between 1950 and 1970, and then other cities such as Sao Paolo, Mexico City, and Shanghai began to catch up (Chase-Dunn and Willard 1993, 1994). It seems that there is a contemporary growth ceiling on the population size of the largest cities that is around 20 million, and that cities in both the core and the semiperiphery are catching up to this ceiling. Some of the megacities of the noncore have become among the largest settlements on Earth.[5]

The other thing that is happening to the global settlement system is the formation of large city-regions. The whole eastern half of the United States is an urbanized region in which nearly contiguous suburbs have filled up the rural spaces between what were formerly separate cities. Europe is another city-region of this kind. The structure of the world settlement system can be seen in Figure 18.4, which shows city lights at night as recorded from satellites and in photographs taken by shuttle astronauts.

The Final Wave of Decolonization

Core countries mobilized soldiers from their colonies to fight in World War II, and when these soldiers returned home they demanded citizenship rights and sovereignty for their homelands. Movements for decolonization and sovereignty had been emerging since the earlier wave of late eighteenth-century and early nineteenth-century decolonizations (see Figure 15.4 in Chapter 15).

After World War II the United States was able to quickly build a global network of military bases by providing political and financial support to European powers to help them continue to control their colonial empires. Thus did the United States accomplish in a few years what it had taken the British Empire centuries to achieve—an intercontinental system of military power. This was made possible because the United States utilized the colonial structures that had been erected by the other European powers (Go 2008, 2011). In return for financial support, the United States gained locations for military bases as well as agreements to allow trade and investment.

But the postwar decolonization movements became increasingly militant, and in many cases they received encouragement from the Soviet Union. The principle of national self-determination had long been an important pillar of European civilization, and now the colonized peoples asserted that they too were citizens,

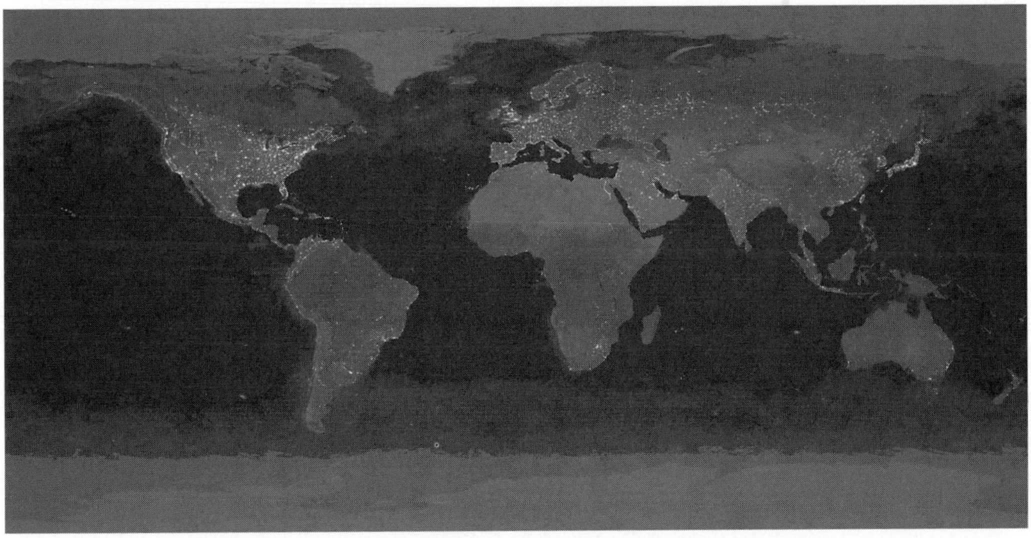

Figure 18.4 City lights from satellite and shuttle images
Source: Wikipedia Commons.

[5] Recall that we defined settlements as a contiguously built-up area. This definition allows for cross-cultural comparisons of settlement sizes because it does not rely on political boundaries or sociocultural attributes.

not subjects. And in this they found support not only from the Soviet Union but also from the UN Declaration of Human Rights. Eventually the United States also became a supporter of decolonization. Just as Britain had claimed the moral high ground by stopping the slave trade and supporting Latin American independence in the early nineteenth century, the United States proclaimed itself the leader of the "free world" and began to support (or did not oppose) most noncommunist independence movements in the colonies of the other core powers. The United States intervened covertly or overtly in countries in Latin America, Asia, and Africa where emerging nationalist or leftist movements appeared to be likely to align with the Soviet Union or to threaten the property rights of US companies (e.g., Nicaragua, Guatemala, the Dominican Republic, the Congo, and eventually Vietnam). But the wave of decolonization that began in the years after World War II was eventually successful in extending at least the formal trappings of national sovereignty to nearly the entire periphery, creating a global system of national states for the first time.

Figure 18.5 shows the number of colonies decolonized in each year for each of the core countries that had colonies. The great twentieth-century wave of decolonization occurred from 1940 to 1975. Some former German colonies became French and British "protectorates" for a while, but these too got their sovereignty after World War II. By the time Japan's colonies were taken from it at the end of World War II, it had become acceptable to go quickly to formal sovereignty, as did Korea and Taiwan, rather than having to pass through a long period in the status of protectorate. The white-lined triangle in Figure 18.5 represents Japan's former colonies—Korea, Manchuria, and Taiwan.

Figure 18.5 also shows that the timing of the dismantling of the French and British empires was somewhat different. The British experienced two big waves, while the French had a single wave. But from a world-historical point of view, these were minor variations, parts of an overall global phenomenon in which formal colonialism had ceased to be an acceptable practice of global governance. The enshrinement of the Universal Declaration of Human Rights as a foundational document of the UN, and the abolition of formal colonialism was as big a step toward global democracy as the abolition of large-scale slavery

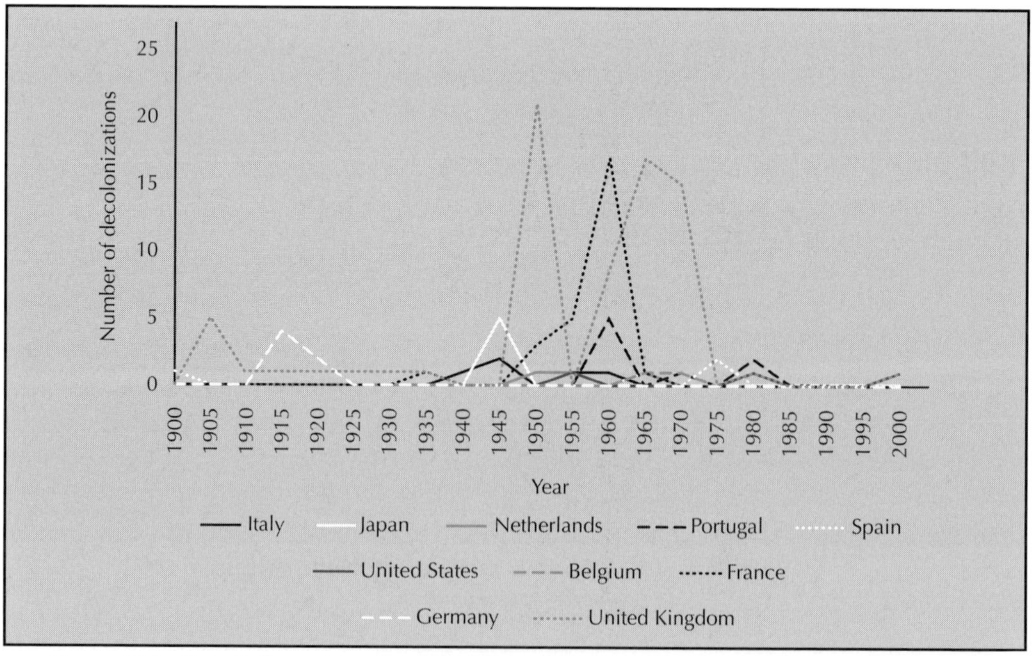

Figure 18.5 Twentieth-century decolonization—last year of colonial governors, 1900–2000
Source: Data from Henige 1970.

and serfdom had been in the nineteenth century. The very idea of empire in the formal sense was thrown into the dustbin of history, but huge global inequalities yet remained, and they were socially structured by the legacies of colonialism (Mahoney 2010) and by the continuing operation of the political and economic institutions of global governance.[6]

Rise and Demise of the Welfare State

Political incorporation generally meant gaining the right to vote in the election of representatives in governments that increasingly became legitimated *from below rather than from above*. Monarchies are usually based on the idea that the king represents a divinely sanctioned moral order—the so-called divine right of kings. This was an extension of the notion of the sacred chiefs, that some people—the elites—are closer to God or the ancestors or have great influence or control over the powers of the universe. Democracy is the idea that governance is legitimated from below. Polities have increasingly tended to be legitimated as existing to serve the people. It has become commonly asserted that government is based on a social contract in which the purpose of law is to serve the needs of the whole population of citizens, and in some states policies have increasingly been shaped by the will of average citizens (Tilly 2007).

Core states incorporated workers, and eventually women and students, by extending political, civil, and welfare rights. The capitalist welfare state emerged in somewhat different ways in each country and with different political configurations that depended on the nature of the economy and the kind of class structures that existed.

The shift from divine to demographic legitimacy enhanced the claims of "men of no property" to be allowed to participate as equals in political decision making. Democratic participation had formerly been constituted as the political right of aristocrats, and this had usually restricted voting rights to those who owned significant amounts of property. In the nineteenth century, many states extended the franchise to most adult males regardless of property qualifications, and eventually to adult females as well. In the twentieth century, the capitalist welfare state expanded further to take responsibility for the provision of mass public education, public health regulations (e.g., clean water), publicly provided health care, and retirement security. These expansions of the welfare state became strongly institutionalized in most of the European core states, especially after World War II, and a somewhat narrower version emerged in the United States as well.

The differences have to do with the ways in which welfare rights were constructed. In some states, especially those with ethnically homogeneous populations, rights became construed as applying to all citizens. In other states, the legal institutionalization of welfare rights was tied to soldier status or was connected with particular types of employment rather than being universal citizen rights.

In the United States the development of citizenship and welfare rights was complicated by the federal system and the way in which the party system was related to regional differences. The Democratic Party claimed to represent workers and urban populations in the North, but in the South it was the creature of conservative whites (Dixiecrats) who opposed the extension of citizenship to blacks and who managed to get agriculture excluded from the protections of the New Deal labor and welfare legislation. The rights of citizenship and federal welfare programs in the United States had been tied to service in the armed forces since the Civil War (Skocpol 1992). Even the post–World War II expansion of the welfare state in the United States was importantly tied to soldier status—the GI Bill of Rights that extended housing and education credits to veterans. Thus was national patriotism again linked to global order as the expansion of the US welfare state became an important source of support for the worldwide military network that was charged with protecting the "free world." This was the form that social imperialism took in the last half of the twentieth century.

The militarized welfare state in the United States was also linked to race relations. White

[6] Recall the discussion of neocolonialism in Chapter 13.

racism stood in the way of universal welfare programs that would benefit all citizens equally, because white working-class people could be mobilized against programs that would benefit the nonwhite poor. Racism was also an important factor when welfare programs were attacked and dismantled in the 1980s and 1990s (Reese 2005). Before and during World War II the armed services were racially segregated, and platoons of black soldiers and sailors were tasked with the unusually dangerous and dirty jobs. In 1948 President Truman ordered the desegregation of the armed forces. The actual desegregation of the US armed forces took quite a while to accomplish beyond the formal declaration, but its eventual success shows that racial inequalities can indeed be eliminated by strongly supported policies. Racial segregation was a huge embarrassment to the US federal government as it took up the mantle of leadership of the free world. Critics of the US hegemony and foreign policy both at home and abroad pointed to the public racism that was especially visible in the American South. And so federal policies began to turn against the most visible and formal aspects of institutional racism, adding a new twist to the racialized and militarized shape of the welfare state in the United States (Winant 2001)..

Bretton Woods and Keynesian National Development

In 1944 representatives of the forty-five countries that had been Allies against the Axis powers in World War II met in Bretton Woods, New Hampshire, to found a new set of international economic institutions that were designed to try to prevent the kinds of dysfunctional economic problems that had emerged in the 1920s and 1930s. The IMF was set up to help countries maintain stable currencies by creating a fund to make short-term loans. International currency speculation was curtailed by pegging currencies to the US dollar. The World Bank was set up as the International Bank for Reconstruction and Development to help countries recover from the disruption and destruction of the war and to help less developed countries industrialize.

These institutions, and the policies they were designed to support, were greatly shaped by the writings of the British economist John Maynard Keynes (1936). Keynes's studies of what had happened in the international economy in the 1920s and 1930s had strong implications for the ways in which national government policies should intervene in the economy in order to take the rough edges off the boom and bust cycles of capitalist development and to encourage full employment. Keynesian economics enjoins governments to use monetary adjustments in interest rates to even out the boom and bust cycles of capitalist development. In order to do this, states need to be able to control their money supplies by printing more money to keep interest rates low or by tightening the money supply to increase interest rates in order to slow inflation. The Bretton Woods institutions were originally designed to help each country develop industrial production that was owned by businessmen within the country. International investments were not discouraged, but global accounting systems were put in place in the IMF's *Balance of Payments Yearbook*, which allowed international investments and profit repatriations to be tracked.

Keynes also proposed the creation of an international clearing union that would help to even out international inequalities by creating incentives for countries with trade surpluses to invest in countries with trade deficits. This proposal was opposed by the leader of the US delegation at the Bretton Woods conference, Harry Dexter White, and the clearing union did not come to pass (Monbiot 2003, 159–169).

This was the international face of the New Deal. It was a global order that was designed to produce national development by expanding mass education and raising labor productivity in the noncore countries. The Roosevelt administration strongly supported both the founding of the Bretton Woods institutions and the UN.

The main purpose of the UN was to implement "collective security" by creating a mechanism that would allow countries to resolve their conflicts without resorting to warfare. This was also a reaction to the Age of Extremes, in which two devastating world wars had occurred. The founding conference of the UN was held in San Francisco in 1945. Franklin Delano Roosevelt seriously considered proposing that the headquarters of the UN should be located on Niihau, a small island off the coast of Kauai in the

Hawaiian archipelago. Roosevelt wanted the new protoworld government to strongly symbolize the incorporation of Asia into the new institutions of global governance. China, one of the Allied powers in World War II, became a founding member of the UN Security Council.

Roosevelt's global New Deal also involved a massive funding of reconstruction in Europe that became known as the Marshall Plan. And Roosevelt acted to prevent US corporations from gaining control of the conquered Japanese economy after World War II. Both Japan and Korea were protected from "Latin Americanization" by the US federal government's policies, thereby laying the foundation for the developmental states that emerged in these two countries (Arrighi 1994). The complicated deal allowed Japanese zaibatsu (family-based business conglomerates) to control the major industries of the Japanese economy, but proscribed them from competing in the aircraft industry. The purposes of these policies were not only to stimulate trade partners for American businesses but also to produce strong developmental states friendly to the United States that could help contain communism within the borders of China and the Soviet Union. Thus did semiperipheral state communism help to induce the expansion of core capitalism (Boswell and Chase-Dunn 2000).

This incorporation of Asia, and especially Japan, into the circle of core countries required confronting racism toward Asians within the United States. In California, where fears of the "yellow peril" had been inculcated since the gold rush, the requirement that the locals be polite to the Japanese was a hard sell, but a group of internationalists among the regional elites stepped forward to insist on equal treatment for Asians. This did not eliminate racism, but it did set a standard in which tolerance was expected and overt racist behavior was disapproved.

The Boom and the Bubble

The postwar boom was a further expansion of core capitalism that incorporated formal-sector workers in the core and expanded the size of the middle class in some of the noncore countries as well. In the United States it was a period of interstate highway construction, suburbanization, and the expansion of higher education. More families could afford to own their own homes, and this was supported by government-sponsored housing credits. Increasing sales buoyed the automobile industry, and automobile workers, now members of the United Auto Workers union, were earning good wages and working full-time. The lunch buckets were full.

Mass production of standardized goods that were affordable to the working class became known as Fordism, because this model was touted and implemented by Henry Ford in the early decades of the twentieth century. Ford opposed labor unions, but the Fordist model of industrial organization came to incorporate a more positive attitude toward unions that sought better wages and working conditions for their members in the period after World War II. This was part of the Keynesian effort to encourage full employment and to pay workers enough so that they could purchase the products produced by large capitalist firms. Manufacturing was also growing in Europe and Japan, and the US naval forces protected the seas so that oil from distant ports could be globally delivered in larger and larger tanker ships mentioned above.

Developmental states under the sponsorship of the United States emerged in Japan and in Korea (P. Evans 1995). Japan's reemergence as a strong and competitive economic power after World War II is shown in Figure 18.1. The Japanese developmental state combined a highly professional planning bureaucracy with strong links to zaibatsu and nationally coordinated higher education and research and development capabilities. The Japanese model developed business practices that were later adopted all over the world with the shift from Fordism to flexible specialization. Japan built the biggest ports and the biggest ships, and gained access to cheap energy and raw materials imported from distant continents. Korea, a Japanese colony from 1910 to the end of World War II, emulated the Japanese model with the help of both the United States and Japan. And Taiwan, another former Japanese colony, also joined the club of newly industrializing societies. The Chinese diaspora of the nineteenth century had spread migrants from China to Thailand, Singapore, and Indonesia as well as to the United States and the Caribbean. Giovanni Arrighi (2008) has contended that the East Asian regional system after World War II retained aspects of the earlier trade-tribute system that had existed before the Western states surrounded China in the nineteenth century. The United States took over the role that China played in the earlier system, a somewhat paternalistic power that acted to facilitate development by sustaining developmental states in Japan, Korea, and Taiwan. This stance by the United States was justified to the American public and Europe as containing Russian and Chinese communism (Cumings 1984, 1990). It also provided a context that allowed Japan to become an important economic center in East Asia despite having been defeated in World War II, and that subsequently allowed China to reemerge as a large and strong economy and a regional power after the Maoist era.

The World Revolution of 1968

But all was not happy, even during the great postwar boom. The middle class expanded, more people went further in school and had decent jobs, more people owned their own homes and had cars, and the homes had labor-saving appliances, making housework less onerous. The Frankfurt school had come to the conclusion that Marx had made a mistake in not analyzing more deeply the cultural processes of capitalism. Political scientists and sociologists wrote about the emergence of mass society in which middle-class consumers came under the sway of mass media that promoted social consensus and depolarized class struggle.

But not everyone was pleased. In the American South, black people were still kept from voting and were insulted every day by public segregation practices. The civil rights movement emerged to challenge racist institutions, and college students, now an expanded group that had not yet been fully incorporated into political life as citizens, brought the civil rights movement to the North. Radical sociologist C. Wright Mills wrote about the power elite, a governing class that manipulated the political process in order to have its way (Mills 1959; T. Hayden 2006). Mills and an important group of other US intellectuals—especially those associated with the independent Marxist journal, *Monthly Review*—were inspired by the Cuban Revolution that overthrew the rule of General Fulgencia Batista in 1959, and hoped that serious challenges to the rule of capital would reemerge within the United States.

The Vietnam War was a failed attempt by the United States to prevent the emergence of a communist regime in Southeast Asia. Perceived by radical students and some black leaders as a return to imperialism, the antiwar and civil rights movements brought forth the world revolution of 1968. In 1962 students who had been involved in the civil rights movement in the South returned to campuses in the North and came together to form Students for a Democratic Society (SDS). Tom Hayden (2006) wrote "the Port Huron Statement" for the founding conference of SDS in 1962. In 1964 students at the University of California in Berkeley found their political activities on campus restricted by a policy of in loco parentis that treated them as if they were children despite the fact that they had the right to vote and were seasoned political activists, some of whom had been on the front lines of the civil rights movement in the South. The Free Speech Movement at Berkeley mobilized students around their own interests and radicalized large numbers.

In 1966 Mao Zedong launched the Great Proletarian Cultural Revolution in China by mobilizing young "Red Guards" for the purpose of revitalizing the Chinese revolution. The news from China and Mao's philosophy spread widely across the globe as radicalized young people looked for critical alternatives to the mainstream mass media pabulum and circus. The People's Republic of China flooded the world with inexpensive translations of Mao's "Little Red Book" as well as other essays by Mao and classical Marxist texts. Radical students joined with militant workers in France and Italy in huge demonstrations. There were also important manifestations and violent government crackdowns in Argentina and Mexico, and the populist "liberation theology" of radical Latin American Catholic priests spread to both the core and the noncore.

In the United States, "the New Left" attacked electoral politics and the welfare state as counterrevolutionary and undemocratic fig leaves hiding the power of capital. As had happened in the past, radical social movements spun out of one another. Feminists criticized the macho Marxists leading the student movement and went on to form their own groups, thus revitalizing the movement for the equality of women that had emerged out of the abolitionist movement in the nineteenth century. The environmental movement was reborn as more people became aware of the massive ecological degradation produced by industrial capitalism. The youth movement produced a critique of the sexual mores of middle-class society, and proponents of alternative forms of sexual expression mobilized to assert their rights. Hallucinogenic drugs became popular as a way of protesting middle-class norms and added to the stew of resistance and revolution in the years around 1968.

The Neoliberal Counterrevolution

In the 1970s the Organization of Petroleum Exporting Countries (OPEC) organized a cartel and raised the price of crude oil. At the same time, Japanese and European manufacturing caught up with the United States, and the increasing competition caused a profit squeeze. The international monetary system erected at Bretton Woods had pegged national currencies to the US dollar and the dollar was denominated at a low "official" gold price that became more and more deviant from the market price of gold as time passed. In the 1970s the rise of other currencies in value relative to the dollar put financial pressures on the United States, and the Nixon administration unilaterally rescinded the Bretton Woods monetary agreement, allowing national currencies to trade against one another in a global market for money.

The profit squeeze and other pressures led to reneging on the New Deal social contract that had been established after World War II. In California a state referendum called Proposition 14 greatly constrained the use of property taxes for public education. Wealthier homeowners, most of whom no longer had children in school, were not willing to pay the educational costs of the children of renters, a group that was increasingly made up of nonwhite immigrants. The New Deal institutions were attacked as inefficient government interference in the market economy. Welfare programs were discredited as unfair taxation of workers to pay for "welfare queens," who were portrayed as fat and promiscuous black women (Reese 2005). Labor unions were attacked as "special interest groups" that obtained undeserved rents for their members by means of political muscle.

Politicians arose in the United States and Great Britain who championed the ability of markets to provide optimal production and distribution and vilified state interference. This set of political ideas has become known as **neoliberalism**. It championed the operation of free markets, justified attacks on organized labor, advocated the privatization of publicly owned or controlled resources, and supported "streamlining" business operations by replacing workers with technology. Governmental regulations were portrayed as inefficient relative to the private sector, which was alleged to be much more entrepreneurial, productive, and efficient. In the United States, California governor Ronald Reagan, who was later elected president of the United States, promulgated this neoliberal political ideology. In Britain, Prime Minister Margaret Thatcher championed a very similar approach.

The ideas were not new. They are basically some of the same moral and philosophical concepts espoused by some economists in the last few centuries. What was new was the vigorous promulgation of these concepts and policies by certain think tanks and politicians as replacements for the Keynesian policies that had been predominant in the West since World War II. The neoliberal political notions spread widely. Politicians in nearly all countries adapted neoliberalism to their local situations. Communist parties in Europe, Social Democrats in New Zealand, and the Chinese Communist Party all moved in the direction of market-based justifications for policy.

Neoliberalism was also adopted by international agencies, especially the IMF, under the banner of what came to be known as "the Washington Consensus." The IMF took it upon itself to try to enforce neoliberal policies by making them the condition for further loans—so-called structural adjustment programs that required governments to reduce or abolish subsidies for food, transportation, and so on. These policies were not popular, especially in poor countries in the Global South, and a large number of anti-IMF demonstrations and riots occurred in the 1980s (Walton and Seddon 1994). These and the Zapatista rebellion in 1994 in Southern Mexico were precursors of the so-called antiglobalization protests that gained greater attention in the late 1990s (Podobnik 2006).

In 1971 the World Economic Forum was founded by Swiss business professor Klaus Schwab. Annual invitation-only January meetings in Davos, Switzerland, are attended by leading global corporate executives, politicians, entertainers, and other celebrities. This institution is perhaps the most visible face of what Leslie Sklair (2001) and William I. Robinson (2004) have called the transnational capitalist class.

1989: Another World Revolution

The rise of information technology facilitated a shift in the organization of business away from mass production of standardized goods toward more flexible production of smaller customized batches. Businesses throughout the world adopted techniques that had been developed in Japan, such as "just in time" inventory deliveries from subcontracted firms. These changes in the organization of business practices also undermined the power of labor unions that had developed during the Fordist regime of mass production. And these changes were also incompatible with the "command economies" that had emerged in the Soviet Union and its satellites and in the People's Republic of China. Nationalist rebellion against Soviet dominance in Eastern Europe had been occurring since the Hungarian revolt of 1956. The clunky state-owned economy in the Soviet Union was also under great pressure because it was trying to keep up with the United States in a new arms race. President Ronald Reagan had undertaken another wave of huge military expenditures—the "Star Wars" program—that was to provide a shield against intercontinental ballistic missiles. These pressures led to a political crisis in the Soviet Union in which Mikhail Gorbachev proposed to dismantle party controls over communications and to open up political life. The resulting political upheaval led to the fall of the Soviet state and a series of major regime changes in Eastern Europe as well. This was the world revolution of 1989.

Gorbachev and the Solidarity Movement that emerged in Poland wanted individual political rights such as freedom of speech and freedom of the press, and more democratic political institutions, but they also wanted to preserve some of the progressive features of social life that had been achieved under state communism, such as protections for the rights of women, socialized health care, and public education. The transitions that ensued often did provide more political rights and individual freedoms, but the arrival of neoliberal consultants from the West advocating market-based "shock therapy," deregulation, and privatization dismantled most of the kinds of social equality that had been the legacy of the Soviet era.

The Great U-Turn of Inequality in the Core

In most premodern state-based world-systems, urbanized core societies in which a small elite ruled over a mass of urban poor and rural peasants had more internal inequality than noncore societies, where less social stratification was the norm. In the modern world-system, this pattern became reversed. In the modern system, noncore societies have a pyramid-shaped distribution of income and wealth, (△) with a small elite and a much larger number of poor urban and rural residents. Core societies, on the other hand, tend to have diamond-shaped distributions of income and wealth (◊) in which a large proportion of middle-class people compose a bulge in the middle of the distribution, with elites above and a smaller proportion of poorer people below. This simple fact about the modern world-system both reflects and causes other features of the system. Core countries have larger middle classes because their economies are more developed and they require larger numbers of educated and skilled workers (Lenski 1966). Representative democracy is more prevalent in the core because it is easier to establish and maintain the institutional prerequisites of electoral democracy when there is less inequality.

This situation has changed somewhat since the emergence of neoliberalism and the globalization project in the 1970s and 1980s. As described above, a number of things came together to produce the rise of neoliberalism: the profit squeeze produced by Japanese and German manufacturing catching up with US manufacturing, combined with the availability of new mass transportation technologies, communications technologies, and information processing. There was also a conservative reaction to the world revolution of 1968, especially in the United States, where evangelical Christians adapted some of the music styles of the 1960s (folk, rock and roll) to support a renewal of family and church-based community values. This development allowed neoliberal politicians to gain popular support while attacking the welfare state protections of the working class. And neoliberal businessmen also perceived threats to profit making from the emergent solidarities in the Global South such as OPEC and the initiative for the New International Economic Order (NIEO) that was pushed by noncore countries at the UN.

The shift to flexible specialization, the deindustrialization of the core produced by manufacturing businesses investing in the noncore, the attack on labor unions and the welfare state, deregulation, and privatization led to the phenomenon in some core countries that has been called "the shrinking middle class" (Rose 2007). Rose's research has shown that the size of the bulging middle of the US income distribution shrank as some households moved up while a much larger number moved down. A similar trend toward greater income inequality has also been demonstrated in many of the other core nations since the 1980s (Bornschier 2010).

Some analysts have overstated the significance of this trend by using terms such as "the peripheralization of the core," and others have declared that the world is flat (T. Friedman 2005), meaning that the earlier core/periphery hierarchy based on colonialism is a thing of the past. But these breathless celebrations (or condemnations) of the new global age are undoubtedly overstated. The United States, while its hegemony is obviously in decline, remains the most powerful national society on Earth. Inequalities at the global level have not diminished (Bornschier 2010). The core/periphery hierarchy is alive and well. It has always been a complicated and messy structure composed of nested local, regional, and international spatial inequalities, and that situation continues. But it has certainly not evaporated to produce a level playing field in the context of the latest wave of globalization. The economic rise of China and India is an important instance of the recurrent pattern of semiperipheral development, but the overall level of international inequality has not been reduced, at least so far (Bornschier 2010).

Nevertheless, the shrinking middle class in core societies is an important structural fact that has had huge consequences for social, political, and economic change in recent world history. In the United States, a new generation of extremely wealthy people are replaying the conspicuous consumption of the "robber barons" of the late nineteenth century, while the large majority of citizens work harder for less income and hope to win the lottery so that they, too, can live the life of the rich and famous.

Neoliberals and Neoconservatives

Neoliberalism was made possible in part by new transportation, communication, and information-processing technologies, but it was also spurred by a profit squeeze in core manufacturing and by conservative reactions to the world revolution of 1968. Another important motivating force was reaction to perceived threats to core profits posed by organized noncore resistance. OPEC, formed in the 1970s, was a cartel of noncore fossil fuel producers that demonstrated that states in the Global South could form powerful coalitions that could be major players in the global political economy. Research on the negative economic and inequality effects of dependence on foreign capital investment (Bornschier and Chase-Dunn 1985) and organized efforts to produce an NIEO, which would reduce core/periphery inequalities, also created a climate that provoked the neoliberal counterrevolution.

The neoliberal ideologues seized upon the fall of the Soviet Union and the world revolution of 1989 to proclaim the "end of history" and the final triumph of capitalism and parliamentary democracy (e.g., Fukuyama 1992). These developments helped to spread and support the emerging ideological hegemony of neoliberal policies. British prime minister Margaret Thatcher declared that there was no alternative to capitalist globalization.

But by the 1990s some of the neoliberals seemed to have lost their nerve. Some swung away from the radical notions of dismantling states and privatizing everything. Jeffrey Sachs, one of the most militant proponents of "shock therapy"—rapid marketization, deregulation, and privatization—in Eastern Europe and the Soviet Union, joined with Mary Robinson, former Irish prime minister and UN secretary of human rights, in a campaign to ameliorate the suffering of the poorest people in the periphery who have been left out of the wonders of capitalist globalization (Sachs 2005).

Others embraced a different approach that sought to prop up the declining US economic hegemony by means of the unilateral use of US military supremacy in a bid to obtain greater control over the global supply of fossil fuels. These **neoconservatives** proposed a plan entitled "A New American Century," in which strong military interventions by the United States would confront the growing disorder of the world-system. This approach made little headway until the terrorist attacks of September 11, 2001, propelled the administration of President George W. Bush to mount a "war on terrorism" by invading Afghanistan and Iraq.

Samir Amin (1997) suggested that the neoliberal policies were "crisis management" in the sense that they were motivated by the perception that the previous Keynesian policies were unlikely to be able to succeed in prolonging the hegemony of the United States and the stability of the global political economy. Crisis management is also an apt characterization of the rise of the neoconservatives who saw that neoliberalism could not succeed for long.

The neoconservative project was similar in many ways to the policies developed and pursued by an important element within the British ruling class during the decline of British hegemony at the end of the nineteenth century. The Boer Wars, discussed in Chapter 17, were the most obvious example. Unilateral military power was employed in an effort to sustain a world order under the sway of English-speaking peoples. This phenomenon has been called "imperial over-reach" by Paul Kennedy (1988) and "the imperial turn" by George Modelski (2005). Declining hegemonic core powers tend to try to shore up their global position by employing unilateral military coercion, playing the last card in which they still have a comparative advantage. These actions usually only exacerbate the problems of global disorder and help to usher in a period of hegemonic rivalry, resource wars, and rebellions.

The twentieth century ended and the new millennium began with a situation among humans that was similar in many ways to the end of the nineteenth century, except that the declining hegemon was far larger and even more tightly wound with the whole global political economy. The institutions of global governance beyond the interstate system and governance by hegemony were far more developed, but perhaps still not sufficiently evolved to be able to effectively deal with the new problems that our species had created for itself. Notably, the hugely enlarged human population, globalized industrial production, and the massive burning of fossil fuels had begun to degrade the biosphere on a global scale. Global warming would pose a huge problem, especially to the large numbers of very poor people living in areas that are particularly susceptible to disruption by rising sea levels, droughts, and violent storms. To this we can add the inevitable arrival of important resource shortages as nonrenewable fossil fuels bring about the end of cheap energy, and even renewable resources such as sources of fresh water become short because of the massive scale of human usage. Peak oil and peak water posed large challenges to the increasingly integrated single world society of humans, and these combined with the older challenges of huge inequalities and violent conflict to create the potential for a perfect storm of Malthusian corrections. But this is not the only possibility. The next chapter discusses several possible human futures for the twenty-first century.

Suggested Readings

Bornschier, Volker. 2010. "On the Evolution of Inequality in the World System." In *Inequality beyond Globalization*, edited by Christian Suter, 39–64. New Brunswick, NJ: Transaction Publishers.

Bornschier, Volker, and Christopher Chase-Dunn. 1985. *Transnational Corporations and Underdevelopment*. New York: Praeger.

Brenner, Robert. 2002. *The Boom and the Bubble: The U.S. in the World Economy*. London: Verso.

Bunker, Stephen, and Paul Ciccantell. 2005. *Globalization and the Race for Resources*. Baltimore: Johns Hopkins University Press.

Cumings, Bruce. 1990. *The Origins of the Korean War*. Princeton, NJ: Princeton University Press.

Glenn, Evelyn Nakano. 2002. *Unequal Freedom: How Race and Gender Shaped American Citizenship and Labor*. Cambridge, MA: Harvard University Press.

Harvey, David. 2003. *The New Imperialism*. New York: Oxford University Press.

———. 2005. *A Brief History of Neoliberalism*. New York: Oxford University Press.

Hayden, Tom. 2006. *Radical Nomad: C. Wright Mills and His Times*. Boulder, CO: Paradigm Publishers.

Kennedy, Paul. 1988. *The Rise and Fall of the Great Powers: Economic Change and Military Conflict from 1500–2000*. New York: Random House.

Mahoney, James. 2010. *Colonialism and Postcolonial Development: Spanish America in Comparative Perspective*. Cambridge: Cambridge University Press.

McCormick, Thomas J. 1989. *America's Half Century: United States Foreign Policy in the Cold War*. Baltimore: Johns Hopkins University Press.

Reese, Ellen. 2005. *The Backlash against Welfare Mothers*. Berkeley: University of California Press.

Robinson, William I. 2004. *A Theory of Global Capitalism*. Baltimore: Johns Hopkins University Press.

Rose, Stephen J. 2007. *The American Profile Poster*. New York: New Press.

Winant, Howard. 2001. *The World Is a Ghetto: Race and Democracy since World War II*. New York: Basic Books.

19

Late Globalization: The Early Twenty-First Century

This chapter discusses developments in the first decade of the twenty-first century, and Chapter 20 uses the comparative world-systems perspective to consider possible scenarios for the next several decades. This chapter considers major emergent challenges, another world revolution, the global class structure, and similarities and differences between the late nineteenth century and the early twenty-first century.

Major Challenges of the Twenty-First Century

There are three major crises that loom in the early decades of the twenty-first century:

- Global inequalities
- Ecological degradation
- A failed system of global governance in the wake of US hegemonic decline

The dark spots are large crowds on the Washington, DC, Mall on US Presidential Inauguration Day, January 20, 2009
Source: Reprinted with permission: Geoeye 1 satellite image.

Global Inequalities

Careful studies of trends in income inequality show that a huge global gap emerged during the nineteenth century between the average incomes of people living in the core countries and the average incomes of people in the noncore. That gap has not decreased despite all the efforts that have been made to develop the noncore societies (Bornschier 2010). The global income gap has not gotten worse during the period of neoliberal policies, but neither has it gotten better. There remains a huge, yawning chasm between the rich and the poor of the world that is not going away. Those who are concerned about inequality should be aware of, and focus on, this huge global gap. It is far larger than the inequalities that exist within most national societies.

This said, there has not been absolute immiseration, except in a few small regions, over the last century. Average incomes in most of the core and noncore countries have increased, but at different rates that have reproduced the huge gap. The number of the very poor has grown because the number of the total population has grown. There are now over a billion people going hungry and without clean water, medical care, or any hope of real employment. That is more people than the whole world had in 1900.

Trends in inequality within particular countries have varied. Some have increased and others have decreased. As discussed in Chapter 18, the United States and several other core countries have experienced an increase in within-country inequality since the 1970s, resulting in a shrinking middle class.

The causes of the emergence and reproduction of the global income gap in the nineteenth century include the uneven development of technologies and labor productivity, but also the operation of political and financial institutions. Wages went up in the core as industrialization increased the productivity of labor. But the core/noncore differences in income are much greater than the differences in labor productivity. Colonialism contributed to global inequality by allowing core countries to use the law as an instrument of exploitation and domination. Since decolonization, most countries of the noncore have experienced relative underdevelopment because of dependence on foreign investment and the operation of international financial institutions such as the IMF and the World Trade Organization (WTO).

Dependence on foreign investment means that foreigners own and control a relatively large part of a national economy. Cross-national comparative research has shown that investment dependence slows economic growth and increases within-country income inequality (Bornschier and Chase-Dunn 1985; Kentor and Boswell 2003). The operations of the IMF and the WTO have greatly favored core countries, especially since the rise of the neoliberal "Washington Consensus" in the 1980s. Structural adjustment programs (SAPs) imposed by the IMF have increased inequality in many countries. The WTO, despite its free trade ideology, has presided over a situation in which free trade has been imposed on noncore countries, while core countries have been allowed to maintain protective tariffs and trade quotas, especially on agricultural goods. Thus, global inequalities are partly a matter of uneven technological development and partly due to what Andre Gunder Frank (1966) called "the development of underdevelopment"—neocolonial global institutions that favor the core countries and reproduce low levels of economic development in most of the noncore.

But why is this a problem? Despite the continuation of the huge global gap in incomes, most noncore countries have experienced some growth of average incomes. Life expectancy has gone up, and most countries are beginning the demographic transition to lower birthrates. Should not these things make people happy?

Political scientists and sociologists have long understood that people's perceptions of a fair distribution of rewards—so-called distributive justice—are largely a function of "relative deprivation." Whether people are happy or not and whether or not they feel exploited are highly dependent on with what they compare their circumstances. If people in the noncore mainly compare their levels of consumption with those of their parents, most would perceive an improvement because life expectancies and average levels of living have increased, and so they should be content. But mass media (radio, television, cinema, etc.) and nearly instantaneous global communications have produced a situation in which people in poor countries increasingly compare their lives with those in rich countries. They see on television how people in core countries live. And they aspire to live that way.

Another contextual factor that makes continuing huge global inequalities a problem is the broad institutionalization of beliefs in the sanctity of equality. Equality is a value that is found in all the world religions and that was given powerful support by the European Enlightenment and the spread of secular humanism. The Universal Declaration of Human Rights is a foundational charter of global culture that is widely supported by the peoples of the world. Most local cultures have shifted toward individualized and merit-based ideologies of distributive justice and away from ideologies such as the caste system that justify inequalities based on categories that are inherited at birth (so-called ascriptive characteristics). Racism and gender inequality are held to be illegitimate nearly everywhere despite that strong currents of these old inequalities are still operating. In this cultural and political context, the existence of huge global inequalities appears to be unjust to broad segments of humanity in both the core and the noncore, and the frustrations of those who have unsuccessfully tried to better their condition has led to unhappiness with the existing systems of governance. International inequalities were masked when national societies were thought to be largely unconnected systems, each with its own unique history. But the increasing realization that national societies exist within, and are strongly affected by, a larger global system encourages people to compare themselves with those in other societies and to see the whole world as a single arena within which issues of fairness and inequity are judged.

The United States has been in decline in terms of economic production since at least the 1970s, and this has been similar in many respects to the decline of British hegemony in the late nineteenth century that was discussed in Chapter 15. The great post–World War II wave of financialization and capitalist globalization is faltering, and many now predict a coming period of chaotic deglobalization. The declining economic and political hegemony of the United States poses huge challenges for global governance (Chase-Dunn et al. 2011). Newly emergent economic powers such as India and China need to be fitted into the global structure of power. The unilateral use of US military force during the presidency of George W. Bush further delegitimated the institutions of global governance and has provoked resistance and challenges abroad. A similar bout of imperial overreach in the late nineteenth and early twentieth centuries on the part of Britain led to a period of hegemonic rivalry and world war. Such an outcome is less likely now, but not impossible, as we shall see.

These developments parallel to some extent what happened a century ago, but the likelihood of another Age of Extremes and a Malthusian correction like that which occurred in the first half of the twentieth century may also be exacerbated by some new twists. The number of people on Earth was only 1.65 billion when the twentieth century began, whereas at the beginning of the twenty-first century there were 6 billion. Moreover, fossil fuels were becoming less expensive as oil was replacing coal as the major source of energy (Podobnik 2006). It was this use of inexpensive, but nonrenewable, fossil energy that made the population expansion and industrialization of much of the world materially possible.

Ecological Degradation

Now we are facing global warming as a consequence of the spread and rapid expansion of industrial production and energy-intensive consumption, and energy is once again becoming more expensive. The low-hanging fruit of "ancient sunlight" in coal and oil has already been picked. "Peak oil"—the point in time when the maximum rate of petroleum extraction is reached—is rapidly approaching. Clean coal and nuclear fusion are still on the drawing board. The price of energy will almost certainly go up no matter how much is invested in new kinds of energy production (Heinberg 2004). None of the existing alternative technologies offer low-priced energy of the kind that has made the huge expansion possible. Many believe that overshoot has already occurred in terms of how many humans are alive and the amount of energy that is being used by those in the core countries. Adjusting to rising energy costs and dealing with the massive environmental degradation caused by industrial society will be difficult, and the longer it takes to shift to a sustainable economy, the harder it will be. Ecological problems are not new, but this time they are on a global scale. Peak oil and rising costs of other resources are already causing resource wars that are exacerbating the problems of global governance. The war in Iraq was both an instance of imperial overreach (of the kind that occurred during the British hegemonic decline) and a resource war because the US neoconservatives thought that they could prolong US hegemony by controlling the global oil supply. The competition for control of oil fields in Central Asia is strongly reminiscent of "the great game" in which European powers strove to control the Eurasian heartland in the nineteenth century (Hopkirk 1994).

The first decade of the twenty-first century has seen a continuation of many large-scale processes that were under way in the last half of the twentieth. Urbanization of the Global South continued as the policies of neoliberalism gave powerful support to the Livestock Revolution, in which animal husbandry on the family ranch was replaced by large-scale industrial production of eggs, milk, and meat. This, along with industrialized farming, was encouraged by the export expansion policies of the IMF-imposed SAPs. One consequence was the ejection of millions of small farmers from the land.

For most of these former rural residents, migration to the megacities meant moving to huge slums and gaining a precarious living in the "informal sector" of services and small-scale production (M. Davis 2006). These gigantic shantytowns lack adequate water or sewage infrastructure. The budget cuts mandated by the SAPs, required by the IMF as a condition for further loans, have often decimated public health systems. And so the slums have become breeding grounds for new forms of communicable diseases that pose huge health risks to the peoples of both the core and the noncore. These diseases are rapidly transmitted by intercontinental air travel. Many public health experts believe that a flu pandemic similar in scope and lethality to that of the infamous 1918 disaster is highly likely to occur in the near future (Crosby 2007). Most of the national governments have failed to adequately prepare for such an eventuality, and so a massive die-off is a possible outcome. Like most disasters, the lethality would be much greater among the poor, especially in the megacities of the Global South (M. Davis 2005).

Peter Taylor (1996) pointed to the important fact, which he called "world impasse," that it is an ecological impossibility for the global poor to catch up with the global rich. If the Chinese people ate as many eggs per person and drove as many cars as the Americans do, the global biosphere would be radically disrupted. Thus, global equalization will require that the rich go down to meet the poor, who are coming up. This is a huge problem that no one wants to discuss, especially in the core countries.[1]

Failed Global Governance and the Democratic Deficit

Institutions of global governance have been evolving for centuries. The system of sovereign states was extended to the noncore in waves of decolonization, and international organizations have emerged, grown in number and size, and taken on increasingly specialized and differentiated functions since the Napoleonic Wars. Democracy is still a contested concept, despite the triumphalism on the part of neoliberals after the demise of the Soviet Union. The old debates about economic and participatory democracy have been raised anew in the global justice movement, and there are new debates about non-Western forms of political participation and indigenous legal institutions. This said, the different notions of democracy are related to one another. All the forms involve legitimation from below, in which the human population rather than transcendent deities are understood to be the main constituency whose interests are to be represented and served by government. In this broad sense, democracy has become the predominant justification for governmental institutions across the world. The Universal Declaration of Human Rights states that "the will of the people shall be the basis of authority of government."

The existing institutions of global governance exhibit what many observers have called a "democratic deficit." This means that, by even the weakest standards, the institutions of power in the global system are not democratic. The world polity, despite the emergence and growth of international organizations, is still mainly operating according to the logic of the system of sovereign states, and global governance continues

[1] Mentioning this in polite conversation is usually considered to be in poor taste.

to mainly take the form of global power exercised by a single hegemonic national state—the United States—or by unelected bodies of powerful states such as the Group of 8 (G8).

The United States is the world's only superpower. It controls a massive global military apparatus that is formally under the control of the US commander in chief—the president. But the US president is not elected by the peoples of the world, but by the voting citizens of the United States. Thus the main system of global military force is not democratically controlled or legitimated. It remains a system of "might makes right," and dissenters outside the United States have no legitimate way to "throw the bums out." There has been growing popular sentiment against the policies of the US government in most countries of the world since 2001 (PEW Global Attitudes Project 2008). This constitutes a crisis in global governance in which the old mechanism of hegemonic leadership is being brought into question because of the decline of US economic hegemony and the widespread awareness that the whole world now constitutes a single global economy and polity.

Figure 19.1 Anti-global governance at the World Social Forum, Nairobi, January 2007

The main international organizations with general responsibilities for international and global governance are:

- The regional military apparatuses such as the North Atlantic Treaty Organization (NATO) and the South East Asian Treaty Organization (SEATO)
- The UN
- The international financial institutions (IFIs) such as the World Bank, the IMF, and the WTO

The regional treaty organizations are key institutions in the global system. They are intended to provide security and military cooperation.[2] They, and the other international institutions of global governance, lack what Jackie Smith (2008, 11) calls "external legitimacy," meaning that they are not at all subject to popular consent (see Figure 19.1). They also lack what Smith calls "internal legitimacy"—because their policies and actions do not represent the consensus of all the world's national governments. This is not just because they are regional organizations. They are primarily controlled by the great powers that are their members, mainly the United States.

The UN and the IFIs are increasingly seen both as incapable of dealing with challenges such as global warming and as primarily controlled by the United States or by the core powers, and thus the democratic deficit is a perception that applies to both the system of hegemony and the structure of global governance by international organizations.

The IFIs have been targeted by large social movement protests since the anti-IMF riots in the 1980s because of the unpopularity of the SAPs that they imposed on noncore countries after the rise of the neoliberal Washington consensus. The transnational "Twenty-five Years is Enough" coalition has advocated the abolition of the World Bank. And the WTO meeting in Seattle in 1999 became the occasion for a huge protest demonstration by labor unions, environmentalists, and others that has become known as the "Battle of Seattle," a totemic event in the growing global justice movement.

[2] Russia, in response to US plans to build a missile site in Poland, has repeatedly proposed the expansion of NATO into a Eurasian-wide treaty organization. If this were to happen it would constitute global state formation from a Weberian point of view (the state as the monopoly of legitimate violence).

Survey research shows that the UN is far less unpopular than the IFIs. But it is widely considered to be undemocratic even though the General Assembly of the UN makes decisions based on the principle of "one nation, one vote," which Jackie Smith (2008, 11) calls "internal legitimacy." Both large countries like China and small countries like Honduras have a single vote in the General Assembly. But the UN General Assembly has little real power. It is widely considered to be mainly a debating society with little real say over the implementation of its decisions. The important decisions about "collective security"—when and where to deploy UN peacekeeping forces—are the responsibility of the Security Council. The Security Council has five permanent members—the countries that won World War II. Germany and Japan are not permanent members. Proposals to restructure the Security Council to make it more representative have been advanced for decades. But the Security Council cannot legally be restructured except by a vote of the permanent members, and they have continued to obstruct reforms.

Neither the UN nor any other major international institution tries to directly represent the wishes of the world's peoples. The UN is constituted to represent national states. There is no global popular assembly or parliament. George Monbiot (2003) and others have proposed the formation of a global peoples' parliament, but such an institution is as yet only an idea.

The IFIs are even less democratic than the UN. The director of the World Bank is always from the United States. The director of the IMF is always a European. The formal structure of control of the WTO is more representative of the world's nations, but nearly all of the important decisions are reportedly made in the informal "Green Room" by the most powerful countries before they are brought to a formal vote. The IMF and the World Bank have their headquarters near each other in Washington, DC, while the UN is headquartered in New York City.

The World Revolution of 20xx

The world-system became more integrated than ever before during the latest wave of globalization. The current high degree of trade integration is somewhat higher than the high peak of the nineteenth century (see Figure 15.1 in Chapter 15). But waves of economic globalization have always been followed by periods of deglobalization in which long-distance interaction decreases, and this is likely to also be true of the future. As political globalization—the formation of a single global polity, the extension of the interstate system to the whole periphery, and the growing size of the hegemon compared to earlier hegemonies and the growth and elaboration of international political and financial organizations—has increased toward **global state formation**, world revolutions have become more frequent and have started to overlap one another.

As discussed in earlier chapters, the idea of world revolutions was originally formulated by Arrighi, Hopkins, and Wallerstein (1989; see also Boswell and Chase-Dunn 2000). World revolutions are composed of rebellions and resistance movements that are spread across the world-system. These rebellions and movements cluster together in time in ways that pose large challenges for the core powers and especially the hegemon. These clustered rebellions are an important cause of the evolution of global governance because enlightened conservatives consolidate new hegemonies by making compromises in which they adopt some of the demands of earlier world revolutions in order to preserve or extend their hegemony. The evolution of global governance by means of hegemony is the outcome of a struggle among competing elites in a context of waves of rebellions from "below," and below includes both subordinated classes within societies and popular movements from the periphery and the semiperiphery.

In earlier chapters we discussed the world revolutions that have occurred since the Protestant Reformation, as symbolized by key years in which signature events occurred—1789, 1848, 1917, 1968, and 1989. Another world revolution has emerged in the last fifteen years, but it is too soon to pick a signature year based on a key event that connotes its character (Chase-Dunn and Niemeyer 2009). Thus we call it the world revolution of 20xx (twenty dos equis). Like earlier world revolutions, it is a constellation of local, national, and transnational rebellions and protest movements that cluster together in time. These challenge the global powers-that-be simply because they all occur in the same period. The agents and institutions of global governance have to contend with rebellion on many fronts. This is analogous to a single national state getting into more than one war at the same time. But the world revolution of 20xx includes more transnational rebellions and movements than any of the earlier world revolutions had. This is a consequence of the saturation of the modern societies by mass media forms of communication, the very low cost of long-distance transportation and communications, and the Internet, which allows nearly instant communication among peoples and organizations all over the planet.

The phenomena of transnational social movements and global political parties that emerged in earlier centuries have grown to the point that there is now a vibrant global civil society of world citizens who consciously act in the arena of world politics (Smith and Wiest 2012).[3] No one knows how large this group of cosmopolitan world citizens is at present. Obviously the people who consciously think of themselves as acting in world politics remain a small minority of the global population. Most people continue to participate mainly at local or national levels. But this cosmopolitan minority of world citizens is undoubtedly larger than ever before, and it includes substantial numbers of farmers, workers, and students as well as the usual collection of scientists and intellectuals, artists, journalists, statesmen, and religious leaders who have acted in world politics for centuries.

The Core/Periphery Hierarchy and the Global Class Structure

Contemporary popular discourse about global inequalities and justice uses the terms "Global North" and "Global South." These replaced the earlier terminology of "Third World," which was often conceived as populated by backward peoples and underdeveloped countries. Our theoretical approach analyzes the contemporary world-system as a stratified structure—a multidimensional nested hierarchy of socially constructed inequalities that is analogous in some ways to the stratification systems within national societies. The core/periphery hierarchy is organized as a set of economic and military power differentials among national states and the peoples in different parts of the world. Some earlier world-systems also had core/periphery hierarchies, but in the modern Europe-centered system, the core/periphery hierarchy was originally constituted as a set of colonial empires in which most of the European core states had formal legal power over regions in the Americas, Africa, and Asia. As we have seen in earlier chapters, the colonial empires were abolished in two major waves of decolonization, but the core/periphery hierarchy became restructured as an unequal division of labor and a set of international economic institutions that have perpetuated neocolonial relations. The core/periphery hierarchy has evolved and there has been upward and downward mobility within it. It has been fundamental to the logic of development in the modern world-system (Wallerstein 1974b; Chase-Dunn 1998).

Jeffrey Kentor's (2000) quantitative measure of the position of national societies in the world-system remains the best operationalization of the core/periphery hierarchy because it includes GNP per capita, military capability, and indicators of economic dominance/dependence. We have trichotomized Kentor's combined continuous indicator of world-system position into core, periphery, and semiperiphery categories and added cases not included by Kentor in order to make a map of the core/periphery hierarchy (see Figure 19.2). The core category is nearly equivalent to the World Bank's "high income" classification and is what most people mean by the term "Global North." We divide the Global South into two categories: the semiperiphery and the periphery. The semiperiphery includes large countries (e.g., Indonesia, Mexico, Brazil, India, and China) and smaller countries with middle levels of GNP per capita (e.g., Taiwan, Turkey,

[3] The term "global civil society" is now widely used and is also criticized because it implies "civility" and an acceptance of the general rules of participation. It should be obvious that some of the participants in world politics contest the assumptions and legitimacy of the existing institutions of governance, and some also employ methods of contestation that others consider to be less than civil. Here we mean to include all those who consciously act on the world stage as participants in transnational politics.

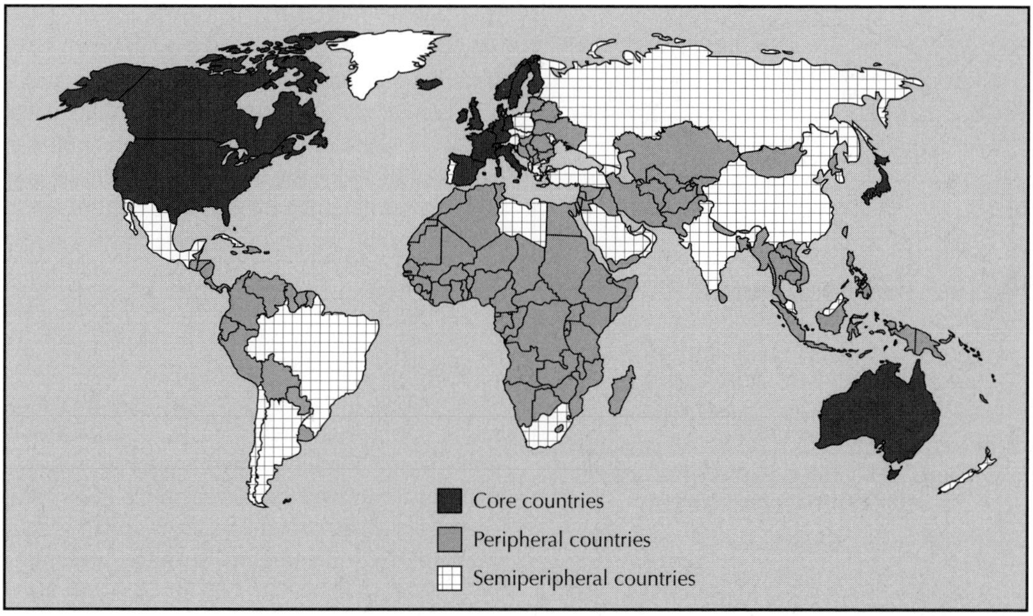

Figure 19.2 The global hierarchy of national societies: core, semiperiphery, and periphery

Iran, South Korea, South Africa, Israel, Libya, and Saudi Arabia).

Figure 19.2 depicts the global hierarchy of national societies divided into the three world-system zones. The core countries are in black, the peripheral countries are in gray, and the semiperipheral countries in the middle of the global hierarchy are in cross-hatch. The visually obvious thing is that North America and Europe are mostly core, Latin America is mostly semiperipheral, Africa is mostly peripheral, and Asia is a mix of core, periphery, and semiperiphery.

In its evolution, the core/periphery hierarchy has moved from a set of unequal relations among "mother countries" and their colonies, to unequal relations among formally sovereign national states, toward a set of global class relations. There has been a global class structure for centuries in the sense that the whole population of the earth can be assigned to membership in different social classes. But waves of globalization and resistance have increasingly formed intraclass links within and between social classes so that the global hierarchy has moved in the direction of a global class system in a global society of the kind described in the works of William I. Robinson (2004, 2008). Robinson contends that neoliberal capitalism has subjected both capitalists and workers to forces of restructuring, producing a transnational class structure that is increasingly the main form of inequality in world society. Robinson claims that this emergent global class structure has eliminated the old core/periphery hierarchy among national states.

The core/periphery hierarchy has always been a complicated nested system with core/periphery relations existing within countries as well as between them. But it has always been possible to assign national societies to the three zones of the core/periphery hierarchy: the core, the periphery, and the semiperiphery. And this is still possible today despite the move toward a global class system. There are still significant advantages to being a worker in the core and disadvantages to being a worker in the periphery despite the move in the direction of a global class system. The complicated reality is that the old core/periphery hierarchy of national societies continues to exist at the same time that globalized classes of the kind described by Robinson are emerging.

Figure 19.3 depicts the class structure of the world-system as a whole, and depicts transnational segments of all the classes. As mentioned above, William I. Robinson's (2004, 2008) theorization of the structure of global capitalism and world society contends that each country has a segment of elites who are members of what he calls the transnational capitalist class and that the

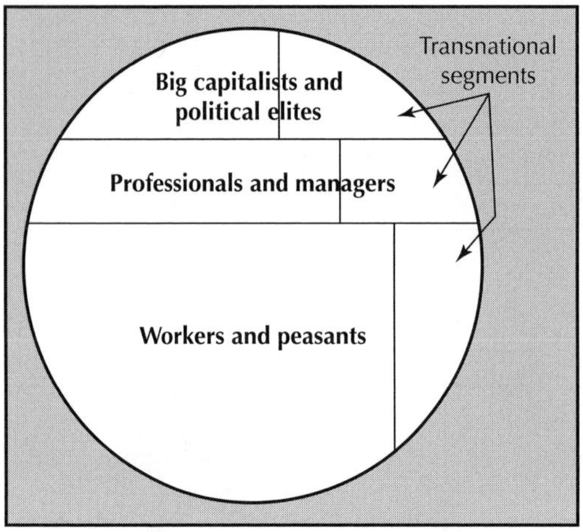

Figure 19.3 The global class structure with transnational segments

other classes also have transnational segments. William K. Carroll (2010) has studied the changes in the contours of the corporate board and policy interlocks among the transnational capitalist class since the 1970s.

The insight about the growing systemness of the world-system is helpful, but both the interstate system and national societies continue to be important socially structured institutions in the contemporary world (Sassen 2006). And despite the recent attacks on the welfare state in the core, it is still better to be a worker who is a citizen of a core state than a worker in the periphery. Overstating the completeness of transnationalization and world society formation becomes most obvious in the claim that the core/periphery hierarchy has been entirely replaced by "peripheralization of the core" and the emergence of clusters of monopoly privilege in parts of the noncore. Robinson himself reports that call-center workers in Argentina earn ten times less than call-center workers in the United States (2008, 127).

Despite the trends toward a more globalized world class structure, the core/periphery hierarchy remains an important reality of the world-system. On the average, it is still much better to be homeless in the core than in the periphery. The processes of capitalist globalization that Robinson (2008) discusses in his overview of recent developments in Latin America have undoubtedly produced more of a transnationally connected class structure than existed in earlier rounds of globalization. The political potential of a globally linked working class may be an important ingredient for the current world revolution and for future struggles, as suggested by Robinson.

No one knows how many people are now consciously participating in the global arena of politics, but it is obvious that the numbers have grown rapidly in recent decades as social movements have discovered that local and national political activities often cannot resolve problems that appear to have been created by global processes. Local and national social movements have been able to gain additional leverage by teaming up with allies abroad and by appealing to international institutions. This process, called "scale-shift" by scholars studying social movements, has produced a vibrant and diverse global civil society (e.g., Reitan 2007).

The world revolution of 20xx has primarily been a reaction against what we have called the neoliberal globalization project. Arguably, it began with the anti-IMF riots that broke out in the 1980s when the SAPs caused the prices of food and transportation to rise in many of the cities of the Global South. Comparative research has shown that it was the first round of SAPs that were devised and implemented in the 1980s that produced the largest increases in within-country inequality (Longhofer and Schofer 2013).

The World Social Forum (WSF) was established in 2001 as a counter-hegemonic popular project focusing on issues of global justice and democracy.[4] It was initially organized by European and Latin American NGOs that were miffed at being excluded from the World Economic Forum (WEF), which has met in Davos, Switzerland, since 1971. The WSF was organized as the popular and progressive alternative to the WEF. It was designed to be a forum for the participants in, and supporters of, grassroots movements and concerned citizens from all over the world rather than a conference of representatives of political

[4] *Wikipedia*, s.v. "World Social Forum," last modified March 29, 2013, http://en.wikipedia.org/wiki/World_Social_Forum.

parties or governments. The WSF has been supported by the Brazilian Workers Party and has been most frequently held in Porto Alegre, Brazil, a traditional stronghold of that party. Whereas the first meeting of the WSF in 2001 reportedly drew 5,000 registered participants from 117 countries, the 2005 meeting drew 155,000 registered participants from 135 countries. In opposition to Margaret Thatcher, who declared that "there is no alternative" to neoliberal globalization, WSF participants proclaim that "another world is possible." The WSF is both an institution—with its own leadership, mission, and structure—and an "open space" where a variety of social actors (activists, policy experts, students, intellectuals, journalists, and artists) from around the world can meet, exchange ideas, participate in multicultural events, and coordinate actions. The WSF is open to all those who are opposed to neoliberal globalization, but excludes groups that advocate armed struggle. The WSF has inspired the spread of hundreds of local, national, regional, and thematic social forums. The first US Social Forum was held in Atlanta in June 2007.

WSF participants are concerned about issues of justice for the Global South and seek to include movement activists from the Global South in the activities that take place in the meetings. But travel to the meetings is expensive and so poor people are at a disadvantage, and this is reflected in the actual participation rates from the different zones of the core/periphery hierarchy.

At the 2005 WSF in Porto Alegre, Brazil, the core was somewhat overrepresented in terms of proportion of the world population (20 percent at the meeting but 13 percent of the world population; see Table 19.1). The semiperiphery was overrepresented because Brazil, the site of the meeting, is a semiperipheral country and is adjacent to semiperipheral Argentina. The periphery, which contains 32 percent of the world's population, was seriously underrepresented at Porto Alegre (8 percent). This was an important part of the rationale for holding the 2007 WSF in Nairobi, Kenya. Table 19.1 also shows the distribution of attendees at the 2007 WSF in Nairobi across world-system zones. At the Nairobi meeting the periphery was overrepresented (56 percent), rather than underrepresented as it was in Porto Alegre, because Kenya and the surrounding countries in East Africa are in the world-system periphery. The core countries at the Nairobi meeting were ironically even more overrepresented (29 percent) than they had been in Porto Alegre (20 percent). The semiperiphery at the Nairobi meeting was seriously underrepresented. Only 15 percent of the attendees at the 2007 WSF were from the semiperiphery, which has 55 percent of the world's population. Efforts will continue to be made to facilitate participation from the Global South in future WSF meetings.

As discussed in earlier chapters, the comparative world-systems perspective has discovered that semiperipheral regions have been unusually fertile sources of innovations and have implemented social organizational forms that transformed the scale and logic of world-systems—the phenomenon of "semiperipheral development." This perspective suggests that attention should be paid to events and developments within the semiperiphery, both the emergence of social movements and the emergence of national regimes. The WSF process is global in intent, but its entry upon the stage of world politics has been primarily from semiperipheral Brazil and India. And the "Pink Tide" process in Latin America has seen the emergence of populist regimes in several Latin American countries in the last decade. We

Table 19.1 Surveyed WSF 2005 attendees by world-system zone

Zone	Number of respondents (2005)	Percentage of respondents (2005)	Percentage of 2005 world population (6,451,392,455)	Number of respondents (2007)	Percentage of respondents (2007)
Core	125	20	13	146	29
Semiperiphery	451	72	55	78	15
Periphery	49	8	32	283	56
Total	625			507	

will discuss these phenomena in Chapter 20 in connection with our consideration of the future of semiperipheral development.

Similarities and Differences between the Nineteenth- and Twentieth-Century Waves of Globalization

There are both important similarities and important differences between the nineteenth- and twentieth-century waves of globalization that need to be taken into account in order to understand the contemporary world-historical situation. Both were periods of increasing integration based on long-distance trade, increasing foreign investment, and the expansion and cheapening of global transportation and communications. In both periods, markets were deregulated and disembedded from political and sociocultural controls (Polanyi 2001). In both waves of globalization, a hegemonic core power rose to centrality in the global political economy and then declined, losing first its comparative advantages in the production of consumer goods and then capital goods. Both declining hegemons then used their centrality in global networks to make money on financial services. Indeed, much of the whole world economy became financially organized around the hegemon, whose currency served as world money (see Figure 19.4). The size of the symbolic economy of "securities"—financial instruments representing ostensible future income streams—grew far larger than the economy that was based on transactions of material goods and services. In both waves of globalization, capitalist industrialization spread to new areas and came to involve a far larger number of the world's people in global networks of production and exchange.

Figure 19.4 shows the trajectory of an indicator of global financialization from 1960 to 2008. The indicator is global domestic credit provided by the banking sector as a percentage of the global GDP. This indicator of financialization, which does not include credit that banks offered to borrowers abroad, rose dramatically over the last four and a half decades, indicating that the relationship between real goods and services and symbolic forms that may be used to pay a debt has changed. Financialization means that the symbolic economy and the activities of financial services have come to be much larger than the "real" economy of the production and exchange of goods and other services. It also indicates that finance capital has become a dominant player in

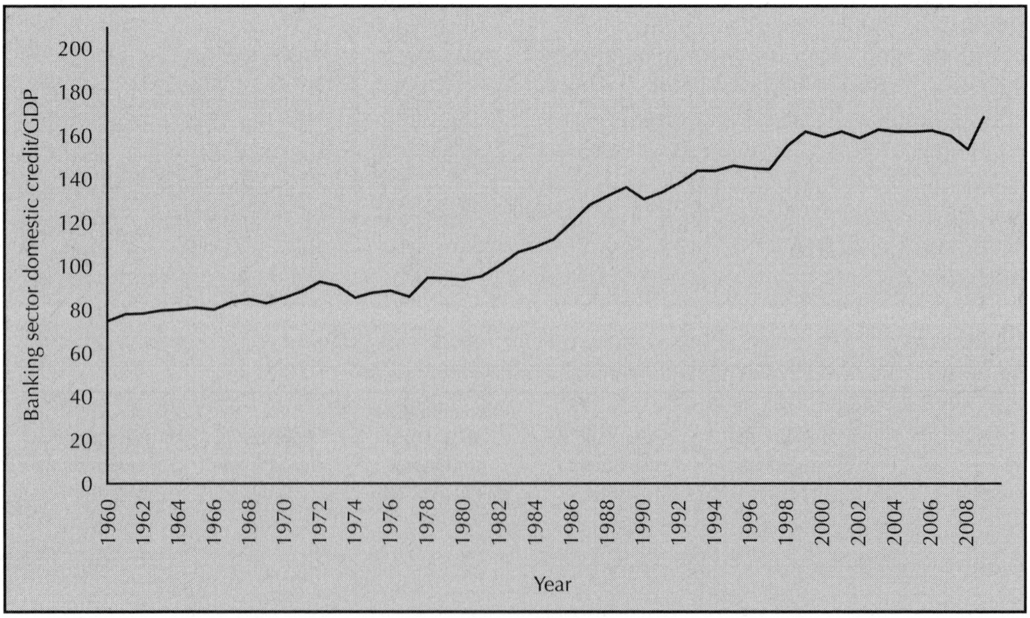

Figure 19.4 The expansion of credit as a percentage of global GDP, 1960–2008
Source: Data from World Bank 2011.

the whole world economy. Though we do not have comparable quantitative indicators for the nineteenth century to produce the kind of graph shown in Figure 19.4, it is well known that there was a somewhat similar expansion of finance capital during the period of British hegemonic decline in industrial production.

There were also important structural differences between the two waves of globalization. Formal colonialism was abolished from the global polity during the most recent great wave of globalization. The interstate system of legally sovereign states was extended to the noncore, and so core states could no longer extract tax revenues from their colonial empires. In the late nineteenth century and early twentieth century, the British were able to use their empire, especially its direct control over India, to finance the operations of the British state. And Britain also was able to mobilize large numbers of soldiers from its colonies to fight in the Boer Wars and in World War I. Both colonial revenue and cannon fodder were available to the hegemon as well as to many of the other contending core powers. That is a source of support that no longer exists because of the evolution of global governance. When the United States, like Britain, began to use its centrality in global military power to try to shore up its declining hegemony, it had to rely primarily on US citizens to perform soldierly duties. But unlike Britain, it could not directly tax a colonial empire to financially support its adventures.

Of course, there have been functional substitutes. The United States has tried to get its allies to pay more of the costs of the Gulf Wars and the war in Afghanistan by sending troops. Soldiers have been recruited disproportionately from noncitizen immigrants within the United States by holding out the promise of gaining formal citizenship. And the US government has increasingly privatized security by hiring companies of mercenaries to provide services in war zones. There have been huge efforts to rely on "smart warfare technologies" as a substitute for troops on the ground. None of these new factors have made the US foray into imperial overreach any more successful than was the British effort. The transition from hegemonic leadership to a policy that unilaterally employs military supremacy in what appears to be a self-serving way generates too much resistance from both the targets of coercion and erstwhile allies. The costs of empire were great in the nineteenth century, but they went up in the twentieth century because formal legal colonialism had been abolished. Rather than using colonial subjects as cannon fodder, the United States must use immigrants seeking citizenship and highly paid private mercenaries.[5]

The United States: "Too Large to Fail"

Probably the most important structural difference between the nineteenth- and twentieth-century waves of globalization is the far greater relative size of the hegemon. Figure 18.1 in Chapter 18 shows the proportions that the US and British home markets constituted in the total world GDP. At its peak in about 1900, Britain's share was less than 10 percent. At its peak in 1945, the US share was 35 percent, and though it has declined in a series of steps down since then, it is still about 21 percent. This is twice as large as the British economy was at its peak. Thus the relative size of the hegemon in the larger world economy has more than doubled. This simple fact has allowed the United States to play the financialization card much more effectively than the British were able to do. The British were capital investors in the rest of the world economy, and returning profits on foreign investment was an important factor sustaining the belle epoque of the Edwardian era before World War I.

The United States has obtained great returns on investment abroad, but it has also been sustained by huge flows of investment from abroad into the United States. This is a big difference between British and US hegemonic decline. The British mainly exported capital and got returns from investments abroad. The United States has done that too. The investments abroad of US multinational corporations grew rapidly in the decades after World War II. US companies established subsidiaries in many countries, branch offices and manufacturing operations as well as resource-extracting firms (mines, logging companies, fruit companies, etc.). This is called

[5] This may be construed as progress.

"direct" investment because the headquarters firm owns and controls the subsidiary. Other core countries and some noncore countries also greatly expanded the operations of their own multinational corporations. The core countries also expanded their purchases of bonds from foreign national and local governments, and eventually core capital flowed to newly emerging stock markets in noncore countries. This is called "portfolio" investment because the owner does not have control over the day-to-day operations of the entities whose securities are purchased. All this was similar to the export of capital by the British and other core countries in the great wave of nineteenth-century globalization.

But then something different emerged—huge inflows of foreign investment into the United States, first from other core countries, especially Japan and Britain, but later from noncore countries as well, especially China. It is these flows, which have taken the form of buying bonds as well as investment in real estate and stocks, that sustained the long US expansion during the 1990s and the first years of the twenty-first century. Michael Mann (2006) has called this "dollar seignorage." US federal government spending has been made possible without increasing taxes because governments and investors abroad have been willing to buy US government bonds. This massive influx of money has also allowed the United States to sustain a huge trade deficit in which imports of foreign goods and services have come to vastly exceed the amount of US goods that are exported, despite the outsourcing of jobs by US companies (see Figure 19.5). Because of its ability to sell bonds, the US government was able to keep interest rates low, and so developers built new housing and homeowners were able to sell their old houses and move into larger houses because the price of housing tended to go up. Residential mortgages were also subsidized as they had been since the GI Bill of Rights after World War II, but the mortgage industry kept expanding credit and lowering the requirements for obtaining a housing loan. Mortgages from the residential and commercial real estate markets were also repackaged by Wall Street financial entrepreneurs as global commodities and sold to institutional investors all over the world. Thus did the wave of financialization during the US hegemonic decline take on new dimensions that differentiate it from what happened at the

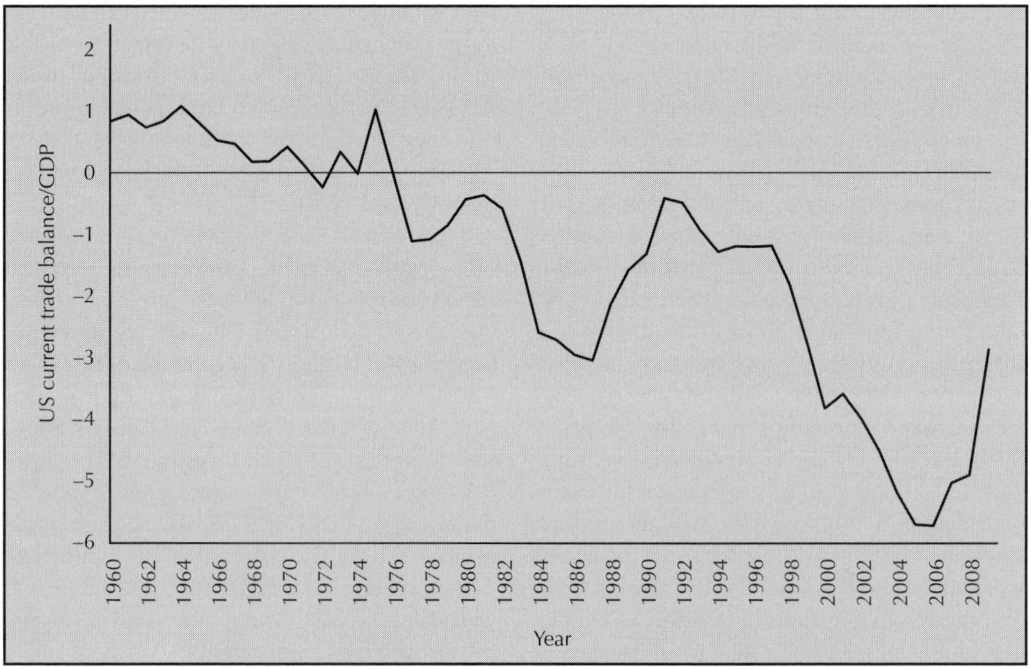

Figure 19.5 US trade balance (exports/imports), 1960–2008
Source: Data from World Bank 2011.

end of the nineteenth century. The US government was also able to finance overseas wars in Afghanistan and Iraq by selling bonds to foreign investors, including the Chinese, who came to have such a stake in the US-led financial bubble that they have become important supporters rather than challengers.

The dollar sector of the world economy is so large that there are no alternatives big enough to replace it even when foreign investors have become disenchanted about the prospects of future returns on their investments. The euro would seem a possibility, but the sheer size of the mountain of securities in dollar-denominated investments makes the euro sector look like a dwarf. The difference in relative size between Britain in the nineteenth century and the United States in the twentieth century means that the rest of the world is much more dependent on the economy of the hegemon now, and would-be competitors have come to have a huge stake in the ability of the United States to buy their products. As is sometimes said about gigantic corporations such as General Motors, the US economy is too large to fail.

The Global Policeman

The United States is also far more supreme in military terms than Britain ever was. The United States currently maintains 737 military bases abroad. By comparison, at the peak of its global power in 1898 Britain had 36 bases (C. Johnson 2006, 138–139).

Another important difference between the two waves of globalization is that alliances among core countries are much stronger now than they were at the end of the nineteenth century. Recall that during the Second Boer War there was great fear in both Britain and France that war might break out between them. After World War II the United States and the core countries of Europe organized a strong coalition based on international organizations and an international multilateral military command structure, NATO. The strongest economic challenges to US hegemony in manufacturing during the decades after World War II came from Germany and Japan, the countries that lost the war. During the long Cold War between the United States and the Soviet Union, the other core countries were content to let the United States be the superpower in military terms and so they did not develop their own military capabilities to any significant extent. After World War II both Germany and Japan renounced the use of military power and kept only small capabilities, relying on the United States for protection. The consequence, after the demise of the Soviet Union, is that serious global military power is a near monopoly of the hegemon. This is a very stable military structure compared with what existed in the world-system before World War I. No single country, and not even a coalition of countries, can militarily challenge the United States. But this structure had been legitimized by the Cold War and by a relatively multilateral approach to policy decisions employed by the United States in which major decisions were taken in consultation with the other core powers.

The Democratic Peace and Global Capitalism

International relations theorists have argued that conflict within the core is quite unlikely because all the major core powers have democratic regimes. The "democratic peace" idea is that sharing a set of political values makes conflict less likely, and that democratic regimes should be less likely than nondemocratic ones to initiate warfare. The relevance of this hypothesis for the future of the probability of war among powerful states is based on the assumption that the great powers remain democratic. This seems plausible enough if we could assume stable economic development, well-legitimized institutions of global governance, and fair access to a growing supply of natural resources. Environmental crises, population pressure, financial crises, and hegemonic decline might well provide challenges that the "democratic peace" factor is not strong enough to mitigate.

A similar argument applies in the case of those who contend that a global stage of capitalism has emerged or is emerging in which there is a single integrated transnational capitalist class (Sklair 2001) and an emerging transnational state (Robinson 2004, 2008). Globalization has indeed increased the degree of global coordination and integration, but will the institutions that have emerged be strong enough to prevent the return of conflict among the great powers during a new period of deglobalization, hegemonic decline, peak oil, resource wars, and strong challenges from social movements and counter-hegemonic regimes in the noncore? That is the question.

The United States has been in decline in terms of hegemony in economic production since at least the 1970s, and this has been similar in some respects to the decline of British hegemony in the late nineteenth century. The great post–World War II wave of globalization and financialization is faltering, and some analysts predict another trough of deglobalization. The declining economic and political hegemony of the United States poses huge challenges for global governance. Newly emergent national economies such as India and China need to be fitted into the global structure of power. The unilateral use of military force by the declining hegemon has further delegitimated the institutions of global governance and has provoked resistance and challenges. A similar bout of imperial overreach in the late nineteenth and early twentieth centuries on the part of Britain led to a period of hegemonic rivalry and world war. Such an outcome is less likely now, but not impossible, as we shall see in Chapter 20.

After the attacks of September 11, 2001, the United States adopted a more unilateral approach in which actions were taken despite the opposition of some of its most powerful allies. Germany and the UN Security Council did not support the invasion of Iraq in 2003. This unilateral approach was reminiscent of Britain's imperial overreach at the turn of the twentieth century, but the context is importantly different. In both cases, uneven economic development has led to the emergence of new challenges to the economic preeminence of the hegemon, but during the US hegemonic decline there have been no serious military challengers among the contending states. Armed resistance is mainly confined to those who employ "weapons of the weak" (e.g., suicide bombers) and a few low-intensity guerrilla forces in noncore countries. The United States has been encouraging Germany and Japan to expand their military capabilities in order to take up some of the expensive burden of policing the world. The US share of total global military power is so great that it is hard to imagine a situation any time soon in which the structure of military power among core states would become similar to the more even balance of military capabilities that existed before World War I.

The United States would have to greatly reduce its military capability, and potential challengers would have to dramatically increase theirs. Since military capability is highly dependent on economic wealth, the decline of US economic hegemony could eventually have such a result, a point that was made by Barack Obama during the presidential campaign of 2008. But it takes time to build up military capability. This could happen quickly if an arms race situation were to emerge, such as the one that existed before World War I between Germany and Britain. But in the current situation, who would play the role that Germany played before World War I—an economic challenger that morphs into a military challenger? No single country could do this, because the US supremacy is so great. But a coalition of countries (Japan and China, China and Russia, Germany and Russia, or the EU) could conceivably do it at some point in the future.

Suggested Readings

Arrighi, Giovanni. 2008. *Adam Smith in Beijing*. London: Verso.

Davis, Mike. 2006. *Planet of Slums*. London: Verso.

Johnson, Chalmers A. 2006. *Nemesis: The Last Days of the American Republic*. New York: Metropolitan Books.

Markoff, John. 1996. *Waves of Democracy*. Thousand Oaks, CA: Pine Forge Press.

Moghadam, Valentine. 2005. *Globalizing Women: Transnational Feminist Networks*. Baltimore: Johns Hopkins University Press.

Podobnik, Bruce. 2006. *Global Energy Shifts*. Philadelphia: Temple University Press.

Robinson, William I. 2008. *Latin American and Global Capitalism: A Critical Globalization Perspective*. Baltimore: Johns Hopkins University Press.

Smith, Jackie, and Dawn Wiest. 2012. *Social Movements in the World-System*. New York: Russell Sage.

Stiglitz, Joseph E. 2002. *Globalization and Its Discontents*. New York: Norton.

Wallerstein, Immanuel. 2003. *The Decline of American Power*. New York: New Press.

20

The Next Three Futures: Another Round of US Hegemony, Global Collapse, or Global Democracy?

Prediction is always a risky business, but some things are actually quite predictable, while others are less so. Natural cycles such as the seasons will continue, although human-caused global warming may be changing them to some extent. Human demographic processes are fairly predictable as well. Because of the spread of the demographic transition (to lower birthrates) in the Global South, demographers predict that the total population of the earth will peak around 2075. The steepness and duration of this continuing rise will determine how many people will eventually be on earth—estimates vary from 10 billion to 12 billion. The timing and height will be affected by the usual factors: food supply, diseases, and natural and human-caused disasters. The education of women and their employment in jobs outside the home are the main things that affect the demographic transition. Its rapidity or slowness and the consequent eventual size of the global population will have a huge impact on the effort to move toward a more sustainable global economy. The fewer humans that need to be accommodated, the easier the required adjustments will be.[1]

Cosmologists and astrophysicists observe that the sun is burning out, like a match. Eventually our solar system will turn very cold, and life will no longer be possible. But that will take another 4 billion years (Christian 2004, 487). On the scale that most humans reckon time, this is not very worrisome. Some observers think that the biosphere of the earth is seriously at risk as a result of human activities, such as from the ecological consequences of industrial capitalism (Foster 1994). But geological evidence shows that there have already been several huge species die-offs from natural causes and that the processes of biological evolution have always resumed along new paths and toward higher levels of complexity. Thus the biosphere would probably eventually recover in a few million years

[1] Some analysts think that the 6.5 billion humans alive now are already too many for a sustainable relationship with the biosphere (e.g., Heinberg 2004).

despite the possibility that humans might wreak unbelievable havoc on earth. It is rather we, the humans, who are primarily at risk. Because we are a large animal that requires a lot of food and energy, and because—unlike other populations of large animals (megafauna)—there are so many of us, both our civilizations and our very existence could conceivably be brought to an end by some human-caused cataclysm.

This chapter considers the likely future trends of the twenty-first century and three possible scenarios that might occur. Chapter 19 discussed three challenges that are likely to worsen in the twenty-first century: global North/South conflicts because of continuing global inequalities, environmental crises because of growing population and production, and a crisis of global governance because of the first two challenges and the declining hegemony of the United States. The timing and strength of these challenges and their interactions with each other will greatly influence how well the human species will be able to cope with them and how much disruption and tragedy they will cause. As in the past, large challenges are also opportunities for innovation and for reorganizing human institutions.

The point of this chapter is not to be scary. Nor will we simply assume that all problems can be easily resolved. As discussed in Chapter 19, the world-systems perspective allows us to see not only some disturbing similarities but also some important differences between what happened during the late nineteenth century and the first half of the twentieth century and what is happening in the twenty-first century. This chapter uses the analysis of similarities and differences between the nineteenth- and twentieth-century rounds of globalization and hegemony and the long-run processes of sociocultural evolution to imagine what is likely to happen in the twenty-first century. The point now is to try to avoid repeating something like the Age of Extremes and to make further progress.

Futurism

In world historian and futurist W. Warren Wagar's (1999) science fiction novel *A Short History of the Future*, the US hegemonic decline eventually leads to a political shift to the Left within the United States and the election of a Latina woman to the presidency. The US armed forces have become composed of the "internal Third World" of US immigrants and former minorities, mainly people of color. When the Latina is elected, disgruntled whites in the midwestern heartland attempt a military coup, but the newly elected regime puts down the rebellion quickly with the strong support of the military. The new US regime makes alliances with "rogue states" in the semiperiphery, so the protoworld government, now firmly in the hands of the largest capitalist corporations, decides that a military first strike is necessary to take out the wayward US regime. This launches a three-year global nuclear war in which two-thirds of the world's population, mainly in the Northern Hemisphere, is killed. This catastrophe allows the "World Party" to form a democratic socialist world government that cleans up the environment and greatly reduces global inequalities.

This is fiction. But is Wagar's scenario or something like it entirely impossible? It imagines the return of a military power configuration among states in which a world war among serious contenders could happen.

Heikki Patomäki (2008) has examined the macrohistorical patterns exhibited by the global political economy over the past two centuries and generated a set of possible scenarios that could happen in the twenty-first century. Patomäki focuses on the importance of competitive imperialism as the key process that produced the structural context that led to World War I. While Patomäki discusses and compares the rise and decline of both Britain and the United States, he does not see these as part of a long-run pattern of hegemonic rise and decline. As seen in earlier chapters, all hierarchical interpolity systems experience a sequence of the centralization and decentralization of power in which a powerful polity emerges and then declines. In the modern world-system, this has taken the form of the Dutch, British, and US hegemonies. Both Immanuel Wallerstein (1984) and George Modelski and William R. Thompson (1996) have outlined a sequence of stages that each hegemonic rise and fall passed through. Giovanni Arrighi (1994) depicted this as an evolutionary process of the development of the relationship between state power and finance capital in which more and more functions of the whole world-system have become internalized within the purview of the hegemonic state. This provides a centuries-long perspective on the evolution of global governance and implies future state formation, although Arrighi did not develop this implication of his model (but see Chase-Dunn et al. 2009).

Patomäki discusses the causes and effects of the revolution of 1848 in some detail, though he does not see the connections among the socialist forces in Europe, the new Christian sects in the United States,[2] and the Taiping Rebellion[3] in China that made it a world revolution. He also sees the importance (mainly negative) of the Bolshevik Revolution of 1917 but does not mention connections with the Mexican and Chinese revolutions in the same decade. He also discusses the student-led world revolution of 1968 to some extent, though he does not mention the links with the Cultural Revolution in China. A more systemic approach to world revolutions could serve to inform the project to construct a global democratic federation that Patomäki favors for the future. Patomäki has elsewhere discussed the world-historical emergence of global political parties since the nineteenth century (Patomäki and Teivainen 2008). And yet in his 2008 book, *The Political Economy of Global Security*, Patomäki claims that global civil society first emerged in the 1990s. In earlier chapters we discussed how elites have organized world parties at least since the Protestant Reformation (e.g., the Jesuits), and popular transnational social movements and parties became important players in world politics in the nineteenth and early twentieth centuries. Were these not earlier forms of global civil society?

Patomäki's possible future scenarios include (1) war among the core states and regions, (2) peaceful and democratic reforms of global governance, and (3) global warming or a catastrophe as a trigger for global reform. The trigger for all of the scenarios is the continued downslide of the global political economy that began in the mid-1970s. The first scenario, global military catastrophe, is spurred by a desperate United States and/or regional "superstates" such as the EU. It occurs because competing neo-imperialisms are marked by "reciprocal securitisation[4] and enemy construction" (2008, 159). The potential mechanisms for this scenario are uneven economic growth, global financial crises and the decline of the US dollar, the deleterious effects of neoliberalism that exacerbate inequality, competition over scarce resources, de-democratization, and an armaments race.

In Patomäki's second scenario, global governance is reformed by leaders of movements with new ideas for "regulatory innovation." Patomäki suggests that this could occur through collective learning from past and present failures of the global political economy, or, more likely, in response to the deepening economic crisis, failed states, and war.

His third scenario sees reform of the global political economy that occurs as a response to problems associated with global warming, including concerns over global injustice, or following the use of weapons of mass destruction by noncore states or other actors, or after the global military catastrophe of scenario one.

In his nicely written concluding chapter, Patomäki makes use of Marx's remark about history repeating itself, the first time as tragedy and the second time as farce, to begin a discussion of the ways in which his own future scenarios fit or do not fit into the standard categories of dramatic genres. In his analysis, the agents for construction of a future global democratic federation are cosmopolitan transnational social movements that help global citizens learn from emergent crises and disasters. Patomäki includes an interesting discussion about why individuals are moved to take political risks. But there is little about what can drive these movements or where they would get enough support to make the changes that need to be made. Patomäki's play looks like

[2] Joseph Smith, the original leader of the Mormons (Latter-Day Saints), was a communist.

[3] The leader of the Taiping Rebellion had been given millenarian pamphlets by a Baptist preacher from Tennessee and became convinced that he was Jesus's brother.

[4] As Patomäki (2008, 17) states: "The theory of securitisation is that actors can bring about securitisation by presenting something as an existential threat and by dramatising an issue as having absolute priority." For example, the concept of securitization in a geopolitical context has been reflected in the war on terror, in which political statements such as "You're either with us or against us" have prevailed.

Hamlet without the prince, or with only a thin prince composed of enlightened cosmopolitan individuals.

Recent Semiperipheral Development

Part of the cost of Patomäki's lack of focus on the process of the rise and fall of hegemonic core powers and the structural nature of the core/periphery hierarchy is missing the transformative role that has been played by semiperipheral states, movements, and parties in the past and the possible roles that such forces might play in the future. The idea of the semiperiphery[5] hardly appears in Patomäki's book, and this is partly due to his failure to see that the core/periphery relationship is a fundamental structure of the global system. He contends that imperialism is an important process because it causes world wars, but the exploitation of the periphery by the core and the actions of noncore actors are also fundamental causes of the main patterns of world history. The phenomenon of semiperipheral development becomes visible if one is consciously analyzing core/periphery relations and if one uses a comparative world-systems perspective to examine earlier regional world-systems.

Transformative innovations, both technological and organizational, have most often come from the semiperiphery, and it is from that intermediate position that changes in world-systems have most frequently emerged. Societies in the semiperiphery, relative to the core, have less of an investment in the current system and so they have more freedom to implement new technologies and forms of organization. They foster the development of generative sectors of the economy and they leapfrog over those competing societies that are stuck in the friction of an older infrastructure. Additionally, societies in the semiperiphery, relative to the periphery, may have enough resources to make the move into the core, to compete for hegemony, and to rewrite the rules of global order in their own favor. Semiperipheral societies can often protect their domestic resources from exploitation by core states and can garner additional resources by exploiting peripheral societies. Societies in the semiperiphery, then, are materially and structurally positioned to make the most radical changes in the system.

The pattern of semiperipheral development in the past implies that transnational social movements and progressive political regimes are likely to receive their greatest support from individuals, organizations, and states in the contemporary semiperiphery. The hegemon and the other core states are stuck in their old ways. Some individuals and organizations from the core will help, but the muscle and many of the ideas will come from the semiperiphery. This is the prince that was missing from Patomäki's analysis. If this is right, it has important implications for strategies of progressive transformation.

The Next Three Futures

We are going to posit three possible scenarios for the next several decades using the comparative world-systems perspective on sociocultural evolution and world-historical social change:

1. Another round of US economic centrality based on comparative advantage in generative sectors and another round of US political leadership (hegemony instead of supremacy).
2. Collapse: further US hegemonic decline and the emergence of hegemonic rivalry among core states and rising semiperipheral states. Deglobalization, financial collapse, economic collapse, ecological disaster, resource wars, and deadly epidemic diseases.
3. Capable, democratic, multilateral, and legitimate global governance strongly supported

[5] In the contemporary system, the semiperiphery consists of large noncore national societies such as Brazil, Mexico, Argentina, India, China, Indonesia, and Russia and smaller noncore societies that have significant sectors of industrialization such as South Korea, Taiwan, South Africa, Cuba, Poland, Hungary, the Czech Republic, Turkey, Iran, and Israel. These countries are in the middle of the core/periphery hierarchy either because of their size or because of important industrial sectors. The oil-exporting countries may also be understood as semiperipheral in some respects.

> by progressive transnational social movements, global parties, and semiperipheral democratic socialist regimes with the help of important movements and parties in the core and the periphery. This new global polity would democratize global governance, reduce global inequalities, and make the global human economy more sustainable.

We agree with Patomäki (2008) that, despite the structural logic of world-historical social change and long-term sociocultural evolution, world history has been, and remains, somewhat open-ended and conjunctural. Human agency makes a difference. Unpredictable things happen, such as the election of an African American president of the United States in 2008. And so our theoretical perspective will be used to posit three possible future paths.

Future Scenario #1: A Second Round of US Hegemony

Modelski and Thompson (1996) contend that there were two British hegemonies, one in the eighteenth century and another one in the nineteenth century. They believe that under some circumstances, a hegemon can succeed itself. The logic of sclerosis can be overcome if new internal interest groups that are partisans of new lead industries and generative sectors can overcome the power of the vested interests of the old declining industries. Normally this is not possible within the confines of a single national polity, and this explains why hegemony usually moves to a challenger. If states could easily overcome organizational sclerosis, those with an original comparative advantage might last for millennia rather than decades or centuries, and Mesopotamia (Iraq) might still be at the leading edge of human sociocultural evolution. Succeeding rounds of economic hegemony by the same state are obviously not typical. But even if something is unusual, it might happen under certain circumstances.

The most explicit argument for the likelihood of another round of US hegemony has been made by Joachim Rennstich (2001, 2004). Rennstich contends that the United States has developed a powerful capability by which newly rising industries can escape the clutches of old vested interests and flourish. He notes that high-tech firms that felt that they were being sidelined at the New York Stock Exchange were able to successfully form their own stock market, the NASDAQ. Part of this is due to the culture of the United States, which strongly supports innovation and independence, and an antimonopoly tradition in the US federal government that occasionally gets reinvigorated by political entrepreneurs who go after firms that appear to be too greedy at the expense of the consuming public, as exemplified in the recent prosecution of Microsoft for monopolistic behavior.

Rennstich also notes that US culture is quite open to social and economic change relative to other national cultures in both the core and the noncore. Europeans worry about genetically modified foods, whereas consumers in the United States apparently do not care enough to even require notification when they are having "frankenfoods" for breakfast. Rennstich's point is that this is a very flexible culture that is open to change, and that this characteristic is probably an advantage in future competition over emerging lead industries (especially biotechnology and nanotechnology). Hegemony requires a material basis. A country must be able to produce and sell products on the world market that are actually useful, and people in other countries must be willing to buy these products so that the producers can make some profit and the government can have tax revenues.

It is well known that the United States has a comparative advantage in higher education, especially in research universities that develop advances in both pure and applied sciences. This should lead to an advantage in the commercialization of new technological advances and, in principle, could be the basis of a restoration of US economic hegemony that is profitable enough to continue to support those aspects of hegemony that are less profitable. Information technology has probably already run the course of the **product cycle** from **technological rents** to competition over production costs. There will undoubtedly be a few new gadgets and profitable Internet services that will redound to US firms such as Apple, Google, and Facebook, but this is not likely to be the basis of a new growth sector in which profits and spin-offs are mainly concentrated within the United States.

Biotechnology and nanotechnology have greater possibilities. Green energy and materials technology that allow more efficient use of natural resources are also possibilities. A political regime with a strong industrial policy of renewal that was willing to husband resources and invest in education and product development, and that could overcome the internal resistance to new taxes by mobilizing a popular constituency to support these projects, might have a chance of success.

The restoration of US economic hegemony could provide resources for a revitalization of US political leadership and hegemony. Of course, the new regime would have to distance itself from the kind of unilateral adventurism displayed in the second Iraq war, and would have to respect the existing institutions of multilateral global governance that the United States championed after World War II. A new concern for global equality and effort to understand peoples who are culturally different might go a long way toward undoing the damage done by the neoconservatives during the Bush administration from 2000 to 2008.

One advantage of such a development that might find support from abroad is that the current unipolar structure of the global military apparatus could be maintained, thus obviating any likelihood of future war among powerful national states. This should relieve those who fear that another round of hegemonic rivalry might descend into world war, as it always has in the past. Such a unipolar structure of military power could also be made more legitimate by bringing it under the auspices of the UN or of NATO. And if this were combined with a larger disarmament of national forces, the size and expense of the global military apparatus could be reduced. Current multilateral efforts to prevent the proliferation of weapons of mass destruction would be made more legitimate if the institutions that control military power were themselves democratized, and if the most powerful states were more politically responsive to the majority of the world's people (see Scenario #3 below).

Future Scenario #2: Collapse—Rivalry, Ecocatastrophe, and Deglobalization

The second structural world-system scenario is that of continued US hegemonic decline, further disruption of the global financial system, an ecological train wreck, and a rapid decline in international trade. Here the scenario bears a strong likeness to what happened during the decline of British hegemony and the first half of the twentieth century, but with a few important differences. We have already seen that some of the recent developments are strongly reminiscent of the period of British hegemonic decline. As we saw in Chapter 18, the neoliberal globalization project was mainly a crisis-management response to a profit squeeze in manufacturing when Japan and Germany caught up with the United States after recovering from World War II. The rise of the neoconservatives and unilateral imperial overreach was again crisis management in response to the obviously untenable position of the US balance of trade that emerged after 1990. These and the rise of new economic competitors such as China and India are strongly similar to what happened during the earlier period of hegemonic decline. We have also mentioned the expansion of finance capital that was an important characteristic of the last phase of both the British and the US hegemonies.

Regarding differences, we have already mentioned that British decline and the interregnum between the British and US hegemonies occurred during a period of transition from the coal to the oil energy regime in which the cost of energy was falling. This time around, hegemony is declining during a period of generally rising costs of nonrenewable resources. Another difference already mentioned is the much greater size of the US economy and military supremacy compared with that of the British. And yet another difference is the disappearance of formal colonialism in the interim between the two hegemonic declines.

The energy cost difference probably slants the system toward chaos. It is well known that the rise of greater centralization and state formation over the long run of sociocultural evolution has been tied to the ability of complex systems to capture free energy (Morris 2010, 2013). Hierarchies and further differentiation are expensive in energy terms. Reductions in the availability of free energy have often been associated with the collapse of hierarchies and of complex divisions of labor (Tainter 1988). The coming peaks of renewable resources probably also raise the probability of future resource wars, especially in the absence of a strong and legitimate hegemon or a legitimate global state. The huge Global North/South inequalities in energy use also make it difficult to put together a cooperative global strategy for confronting global warming and other aspects of environmental degradation. In the past the biggest polluters have been the industrialized core countries, but now the semiperiphery is industrializing and large countries like China and India are becoming major producers of greenhouse gases. When global standards for reduction are proposed, the late industrializers point out that they are being punished for not having polluted the global atmosphere first. And the huge energy and resource usage levels of people in core countries are not sustainable, meaning that they need to reduce their usage of energy and materials. Thus do Global North/South inequalities exacerbate the problem of global collective action on the environment (Roberts and Parks 2007).

The size difference between Britain and the United States probably slants against a fast collapse. Even the economic challengers (China and India) have a vested interest in the current US-centered financial system and are unlikely to intentionally do anything that would seriously undermine it. They own too many US bonds and depend too much on the ability of buyers in the United States to purchase their products and services.

And though US military capability will undoubtedly decline as the ability of the US economy to support it continues to wane, this could take a long time, just as it will take time for new economic centers to develop their military capabilities and to change their attitudes toward offensive military power. Both Germany and Japan have developed constitutions and cultures that oppose the development of national military capability. The military and economic size factors do not preclude hegemonic decline, but they do slow it down and also delay the onset of strong hegemonic rivalries.

More environmental catastrophes are quite likely to happen because of industrialization and population growth overshoots and overconsumption in the core. Global warming may be slowed by reducing the production of greenhouse gases now that the United States has signaled support, though getting effective adoption and implementation should not be taken for granted even now. The pressure to use coal as oil prices rise is likely to overcome all the good intentions and international treaties. Environmental catastrophes will destabilize both the economy and the existing political arrangements. Fragile states will be challenged by internal resource wars (such as the "blood diamond" wars in Africa), and states will be increasingly tempted to use armed force to protect or gain access to natural resources. The continued collapse of fisheries; soil depletion; deforestation; pollution of streams, rivers, groundwater, and seas; and the arrival of peak fresh water, oil, and other natural resources[6] will add to economic problems and exacerbate population pressures. The environmental dimension of the current situation could conceivably make a positive contribution to global governance if the crisis encourages the formation of international institutions that can organize a cooperative approach to solving the problems. But they could also make such a solution less likely by increasing competition over increasingly scarce natural resources. In the collapse scenario, competition and conflict overwhelm cooperation and institution building.

Deglobalization means less international trade, less international investment, and the reemergence of greater local and national self-reliance for the production of goods and services. The rise of transportation costs because of rising energy prices is one factor that will reduce international trade. Efforts to reduce carbon emissions will also involve greater regulation of long-distance transportation by air, ship, and truck, and this will encourage a return to more local and regional circuits of production and consumption. International investment will decline if there is greater international conflict, because the risks associated with investments in distant locations will increase.

Greater local self-reliance will be good for manufacturing and for farmers in places where imports have been driving locals out of business.

---

[6] Recall that "peak oil" is the point in time when the maximum rate of petroleum extraction is reached. All finite resources have a similar peak.

But the costs of some goods will go up. Services may continue to be supplied internationally if the global communications grid is maintained. It is expensive to maintain the satellites and cables, but this may be a good investment because long-distance communication can increasingly substitute for long-distance transportation. International business and political meetings can be held in cyberspace rather than by flying people from continent to continent. The carbon footprint of transoceanic communication is considerably smaller than the carbon footprint of transportation because information is lighter than people. But the infrastructure of global communication also relies on international cooperation, and so the rise of conflict might make communications less reliable, or the big grid might even come down.

Future Scenario #3: A Global Democratic and Sustainable Commonwealth

Eventually the human species may escape from the spiral of population pressure and ecological degradation that has always driven human sociocultural evolution. If the demographic transition continues its march through the Global South, this could occur by the year 2100 or so. After the total human population ceases to rise, it will still take time to adjust to the economic, environmental, and political problems that will result from a global population of 10 billion or 12 billion people. And even then, history will not end, because human institutional structures and technology will continue to evolve and to generate new challenges.

But the main focus of this chapter is the next several decades. Many observers of human sociocultural evolution predict the eventual emergence of a single earth-wide state based on the long-term trend of polities to get larger. Robert Carneiro (2004) projects the decline in autonomous political units from 600,000 in 1500 BCE to a single global government by about 2300 CE.

The problem raised by the analysis above is that the existing institutions of global governance are in crisis, and a new structure that is both legitimate and capable needs to emerge soon to enable humans to deal with the problems that we have created for ourselves. But what could speed up global state formation such that an effective and democratic global government could be formed by the middle of the twenty-first century? This is the third scenario that we will imagine as a possible middle-term future.

Recall that in our understanding of the evolution of global governance, world state formation has been occurring since the end of the Napoleonic Wars in 1815. The Concert of Europe was a multilateral international organization with explicit political intent—the prevention of future revolutions of the type that emerged in France in 1789 and the prevention of future Napoleonic projects. The Concert of Europe was fragile and eventually foundered on the differences between the rigid conservatism of the Austro-Hungarian Empire, led by Prince Metternich, and the somewhat more enlightened conservatism of the British, led by Lord Castlereigh. But the emergence of a protoworld state was tried again in the guise of the League of Nations and once again as the UN. We can notice that the big efforts have followed world wars. And we should also mention that the UN is a very long way from being a true world state in the Weberian sense of a monopoly of legitimate violence.

All the previous advances in global state formation have taken place after a hegemon has declined and challengers have been defeated in a world war among hegemonic rivals. Recall that in Warren Wagar's (1999) future scenario discussed above, a global socialist state is able to emerge only after a huge war among core states in which two-thirds of the world's population is killed—a similar scenario is also suggested by Patomäki (2008). The idea here is that major organizational changes emerge after huge catastrophes when the existing global governance institutions are in disarray and need to be rebuilt. But using a global war as a deus ex machina in a science fiction novel is quite different from planning and implementing a real strategy that relies on a huge disaster in order to bring about change—"disaster socialism," to borrow a phrase suggested by Naomi Klein's (2007) examination of how neoliberal globalizers have been able to make hay out of tragedies. Obviously, political actors who seek to promote the emergence of an effective and democratic global state must also do all that they can to try to prevent another war among the great powers. Humanistic morality

UN headquarters, New York City

must trump whatever advantages might follow such a catastrophe.

That said, it is very likely that major calamities will occur in the coming decades regardless of the efforts of farsighted citizens and social movements. That is why we have imagined the collapse scenario above. And it would make both tactical and strategic sense to have plans for how to move forward if indeed a perfect storm of calamities were to come about.

But let us first imagine how an effective and democratic global government might emerge in the absence of a huge calamity. Instead, we will suppose that a series of moderate-sized ecological, economic, and political calamities that are somewhat spaced out in time can provide sufficient disruption of the existing world order and motivation for its reconstruction along more cooperative, effective, and democratic lines.

The New Global Left

The scenario we have in mind involves a network of alliances among progressive social movements and political regimes of countries in the Global South along with some allies in the Global North. We are especially sanguine about the possibility of relatively powerful semiperipheral states coming to be controlled by democratic socialist regimes that can provide resources to progressive global parties and movements.

Contemporary **global civil society** is composed of all the individuals and groups who knowingly orient their political participation toward issues that transcend local and national boundaries and who try to link up with those outside their own home countries in order to have an impact on local, national, and global issues. The New Global Left is that subgroup of global civil society that is critical of neoliberal and capitalist globalization, corporate capitalism, and the exploitative and undemocratic structures of global governance (Santos 2006). The larger global civil society also includes defenders of global capitalism and of the existing institutions of global governance as well as other challengers of the current global order. The New Global Left is the current incarnation of a constellation of popular forces, social movements, global political parties, and progressive national regimes that have contested with the powers-that-be in the world-system for centuries. The existing institutions of global governance have been shaped by the efforts of competing elites to increase their power and to defend their privileges, but also by the efforts of popular forces and progressive states to challenge the hierarchical institutions;

to defend workers' rights, access to the commons, the rights of women and minorities, and the sovereignty of indigenous peoples; and to democratize local, national, and global institutions of governance.

As we have seen in earlier chapters, the evolution of the modern world-system—its processes of economic development, the rise and fall of hegemonic core powers, and the waves of globalization and deglobalization—has been shaped by a series of world revolutions (congeries of local, national, and transnational struggles and rebellions that clump together in time) since the Protestant Reformation of the sixteenth century (Arrighi, Hopkins, and Wallerstein 1989; Boswell and Chase-Dunn 2000; Chase-Dunn and Niemeyer 2009). The contemporary world revolution is similar to earlier ones, but also different. The New Global Left needs to be understood in its world-historical context.[7] Our conceptualization of the New Global Left includes both civil society entities (individuals, social movement organizations, and NGOs) and political parties and progressive national regimes. The relationships among the movements and the progressive populist ("Pink Tide") regimes that have emerged in Latin America in the last decade are important for understanding the New Global Left. We understand these Pink Tide regimes to be an important part of the New Global Left, though it is well known that the relationships between the movements and the regimes are both supportive and contentious.

The boundaries of the progressive forces that have come together in the New Global Left are fuzzy, and the processes of inclusion and exclusion are ongoing. The rules of inclusion and exclusion that are contained in the charter of the WSF, though still debated, have not changed much since their formulation in 2001.[8]

The New Global Left has emerged as resistance to, and a critique of, global capitalism, especially those policies and political ideologies that have become known as neoliberalism. It is a coalition of social movements that includes old social movements that emerged in the nineteenth century (labor, anarchism, socialism, communism, feminism, environmentalism, peace, human rights), along with more recent incarnations of these and movements that emerged in the world revolutions of 1968 and 1989 (gay rights, anticorporate, fair trade, indigenous) and even more recent ones such as slow food/food rights, global justice/alterglobalization, antiglobalization, health/HIV, and alternative media. The explicit focus on the Global South and global justice is somewhat similar to some earlier incarnations of the Global Left, especially the Comintern, the Bandung Conference, and the anticolonial movements. The New Global Left contains remnants and reconfigured elements of earlier Global Lefts, but it is a qualitatively different constellation of forces because:

- There are new elements
- The old movements have been reshaped
- A new technology (the Internet) has been used to try to resolve Global North/South issues within movements and the contradictions among movements

There has also been a learning process in which the earlier successes and failures of the Global Left are being taken into account in order to not repeat the mistakes of the past. The relations within the family of antisystemic movements and among the populist regimes are both cooperative and competitive.

One scenario that could move the world-system in the direction of global democratic and sustainable development during the next few decades would involve a coalescent party-network of the New Global Left that would emerge from the existing "movement of

---

[7] Antonio Gramsci (1972) called the Italian Communist Party "the Modern Prince," acknowledging his debt to Niccolo Machiavelli's political how-to book, *The Prince*. Stephen Gill (2000) has used the term "post-modern prince" to characterize the New Global Left as it seemed to be incarnated in the coalitions of protesters confronting the WTO at the Battle of Seattle in 1999.

[8] The charter of the WSF does not permit participation by those who attend as representatives of organizations that are engaged in, or that advocate, armed struggle. Nor are governments, confessional institutions, or political parties supposed to send representatives to the WSF. The charter is presented as the first item of discussion in the Wikipedia article on the WSF.

movements" participating in the WSF process (Fisher and Ponniah 2003). Positive exemplars of what is possible have historically emerged as "globalizations from below" (della Porta et al. 2006). For example, direct participatory democracy emerged in the form of workers' councils that were formed during the Paris Commune of 1871, the Russian Revolution of 1917, the Seattle General Strike of 1919, the Spanish Revolution of 1936–1939, and the Chilean Revolution of 1970–1973. Similar formations have emerged recently as factory committees in Argentina and Venezuela and peasant councils in Brazil. Transnational social movements have expanded in recent decades, as discussed in Chapter 19. The hugely popular WSFs have been remarkable efforts to build the foundation for a just and democratic world society. The WSF international meetings have been held exclusively in countries of the Global South: Brazil, India, Pakistan, Mali, and Kenya.

The New Global Left has been theorized by **autonomists** such as Michael Hardt and Antonio Negri (2004) as a "multitude" of workers who have been casualized by the emergence of flexible specialization. As William I. Robinson's (2008) study of the effects of globalized capitalism on Latin America makes clear, flexible specialization and the casualization of labor are not confined to the Global North. The vastly expanded shantytowns of the cities of the Global South are the homes of the informal-sector workers, many of whom were formerly employed in the formal sector of large firms and public bureaucracies. Neoliberal schemes such as the North American Free Trade Agreement (NAFTA) and the SAPs promoted by the IMF and the World Bank have required the downsizing of public employment. So the informal sector has grown in most countries of the Global South.

But the formal-sector workers have not disappeared. As large-scale industrialization has moved from the core to the Global South, the formal-sector working class has grown along with trade unionism, labor unrest (strikes), and workers' parties (Silver 2003). President Luiz Inácio Lula da Silva of Brazil is a former auto worker, and the Brazilian Workers' Party (PT), which brought him into office, is mainly based on the formal-sector workers of Brazil. In other Latin American countries, domestic neoliberals allied with the neoliberalized IMF and the World Bank attacked the institutions of the welfare state, labor unions, and the political parties of the formal-sector workers. In many countries these attacks were successful. Downsizing, streamlining, and the destruction of welfare safety nets drove many formal-sector workers into the informal sector. In some of the countries where these things occurred, powerful social movements emerged from the informal sector, some of which were able to elect national governments—the populist Pink Tide regimes.

Thus the globalized working class of the Global South is a mix of formal-sector workers in mass production industries and informalized workers. The class basis of the other transnational social movements (feminists, environmentalists, farmers, peace/antiwar, alternative media, human rights, indigenous, and so on) is similarly complicated. Thus, Hardt and Negri's (2004) use of the term "multitude" is quite appropriate, though they seem to have missed the point shown clearly by the labor unrest research of Beverly Silver (2003) that the formal working class is still an important player in many countries.

Low-Energy Global Governance

A new energy regime will be a necessary component of the long-term sustainability of the human relationship with the biosphere and the geosphere. The best way to accomplish this would be the construction of a relatively low-energy global state. A reduction in the overall complexity of the world-system is needed. As we have seen in earlier chapters, the framework of a protoglobal state already exists as world-level institutions such as the UN, the World Health Organization (WHO), and the International Criminal Court. The global level of governance needs to be strengthened and made more capable in order for it to help humanity deal with the emergent challenges. This can be partly accomplished by eliminating redundancies. For example, transferring security responsibilities to a global institution could reduce the extensive military industrial complexes maintained by nation-states and regional security institutions such as NATO. A global democratic and collectively rational commonwealth with a unified authority and a program for reducing national military apparatuses (disarmament) could greatly reduce the vast expenditures on military weapons that are now being made. The global state's military capability does not need to be much larger than the forces that might be brought against it.

A global democratic government would at least have the support of the majority of the world's people. Legitimate and substantive democracy at the national level has been difficult to develop and to sustain, and has often been reversed (Tilly 2007). This will undoubtedly also be the case at the global level. Ulrich Beck (2005) claims that globalization has increased cosmopolitanism—the recognition and appreciation of cultural differences. This is important if nationalistic and xenophobic divisiveness is to be reduced. But relying mainly on this, as Patomäki (2008) seems to do, would be a mistake. Powerful social movements and progressive national regimes will be needed to overcome the resistance of the powerful forces that are vested in the existing realities of the world-system.

Strengthening the local level of governance will also be important for helping to confront the big problems of the twenty-first century, and this is not incompatible with a global strategy of democratic state formation. Richard Heinberg (2004) and Lester Brown (2008) have advocated the formation and strengthening of self-governing local communities as well as a move toward local energy and food production.[9] Global democratic institutions in which people from different continents work together to solve problems have been made much more feasible by the Internet (Florini 2005). The global peoples' parliament proposed by George Monbiot (2003) could be organized to take advantage of information technology and virtual worlds (interactive digital worlds such as "Second Life"), thus greatly reducing the costs of such an institution. Global meetings such as those held by the WSF involve intercontinental travel by large numbers of individuals to attend meetings. These meetings are expensive in both money and carbon terms. Internet meetings and wiki decision-making processes and manifesto writing are much cheaper and cleaner alternatives to flying humans from continent to continent.

The new democratic global governance structure would also try to organize a more equitable share in the costs and benefits of sharing the planet, including wealth distribution and resource use. Currently a third of the world's population does not have residential electricity at all (Smil 2008, 258–259). The rural poor need low-cost access to electricity and clean water. But there would need to be five Earths for everyone in the world to live like the average person in the United States. This would require a fivefold increase in global energy use (Smil 2008). There are real limits to growth, and one of the main ones is the extensive pollution that is a by-product of energy production (Meadows, Randers, and Meadows 2004). Finding ways to dispose of waste generated from energy production and transmission that do not foul the environment is one of the challenges of the new millennium. The expansion of global democracy needs to be strongly connected to ecological sustainability. Vandana Shiva (2005) calls this "Earth democracy."

The semiperiphery is structurally advantaged to take the lead in this endeavor. From an energy/ecology standpoint, there have already been impressive innovations. For example, Cuba has developed a massive organic farming and urban garden food system and has found ways to reduce its fuel use, particularly following the Special Period after the fall of the Soviet Union. Venezuela has used its oil wealth to try to implement "petro-socialism." Bolivia is struggling to return control over natural resources to the indigenous population. The cities of Curitiba and Porto Alegre in Brazil and the state of Kerala in India offer "islands of hope" for a sustainable and community-based political economy.

But the pathways taken by countries in the semiperiphery have been uneven. China is now the world's largest polluter, although it is still

[9] In Wagar's (1999) *Short History of the Future*, global state formation comes first but is followed by a very decentralized system once major issues have been resolved. The building of local communities is a value that is strongly supported by most of the participants in the WSF process. Heinberg's (2004) point is that both local communities and capable institutions of global governance are possible at the same time if the global institutions are truly democratic.

behind the United States on a per capita basis. Brazil leads the world in sugarcane-based ethanol production, followed by India, while Malaysia and Indonesia are major producers of palm oil. The production of biofuels, including switch grass, may have crippling impacts on the food system, and the net energy/ecological gain is low, or negative in some cases (Brown 2008). Countries such as Nicaragua and Russia have implemented SAPs as part of the increasing marketization of agriculture encouraged by the neoliberal policies of the IMF and the World Bank. Some of these programs have increased inequality and devastated small farmers. But agricultural marketization has been implemented differently in Cuba and China in ways that have encouraged more production for the market while protecting the viability of small farmers (Enriquez 2009).

Ann Florini (2005) acknowledges the need for democratic global governance processes to address global issues that simply cannot be dealt with by separate national states. Florini contends that global state formation is impossible, is undesirable, and would engender huge opposition from all quarters. Instead, she sees a great potential for democratizing global governance through use of the Internet for mobilizing global civil society.

George Monbiot's *Manifesto for a New World Order* (2003) is a reasoned and insightful call for radically democratizing the existing institutions of global governance and for establishing a global peoples' parliament that would be directly elected by the whole population of the earth. Ulrich Beck's (2005) call for "cosmopolitan realism" also ends up supporting the formation of global democratic institutions. Monbiot also proposes a radical reversal of the WTO regime, which currently imposes free trade on the Global South but allows the core countries to engage in agricultural protectionism. He describes a "fair trade organization" that would help to reduce global development inequalities. Monbiot also advocates abolishing the UN Security Council and shifting its power over peacekeeping to the General Assembly, in which representatives' votes would be weighted by the population sizes of their countries. The UN could also be structured as a system of checks and balances, with both population and territory represented in ways similar to the constitutions of many national states. If power were purely based on population, the world's largest states (China and India) would have great power. But if there were two houses—one like the current General Assembly, and the other a body elected by the world's peoples with representation based on population (like the US House of Representatives)—then both nations and demography could share power. The problem with UN reform is not a lack of good models (e.g., Schwartzberg 2003; J. A. Cook 2007) but the monopoly that the Security Council holds over the reform process.

George Monbiot (2003) also advocates global enforcement of a carbon tax and a carbon swap structure that would reduce environmental degradation and reward those that utilize green technologies. He also points out that the current level of indebtedness of noncore countries could be used as formidable leverage over the world's largest banks if all the debtors acted in concert. This could provide the muscle behind a significant wave of global democratization. But in order for this to happen, the global justice movement would have to organize a strong coalition of the noncore countries that could overcome the splits that tend to occur between the periphery and the semiperiphery. This is not just a utopian fantasy. It is a practical program for global democracy that could be implemented in the next few decades.

A Global Monopoly of Legitimate Violence

There is another grave deficit at the UN. It does not have the capacity to effectively help humanity meet the challenges of the twenty-first century. The UN peacekeeping forces would have to be superior to any combination of military forces that might choose to oppose it. It is more convenient to consider global governance without discussing Max Weber's (1978) definition of a state as most importantly "a monopoly of legitimate violence." But ignoring the issue of military power and security will not help us through the coming period of rivalry. The UN is not a state by Weber's definition. Rather, a near monopoly of global violent capability is held by the armed forces of the United States. This is a de facto world state but without legitimacy according to broadly accepted definitions of democratic control. The president of the United States is the commander in chief of the US armed forces. But the president is not elected by the peoples of the world. So US military power is not legitimate, especially when it is exercised unilaterally, as it has been since the Bush administration.

In order to have sufficient capability, the UN would need the legal ability to collect taxes, such as the proposed Tobin Tax on international financial transactions. With such capability, and with additional legitimacy produced by meaningful democratization, the UN would be in a position to effectively mediate the multipolar structure of interstate power that is emerging as a result of US hegemonic decline.

In order to effectively meet the challenges of the twenty-first century, the global military apparatus that has been erected by the United States, composed as it is of 865 facilities in 40 countries and overseas US territories (C. Johnson 2010, 183), should be sold to the UN and command should be transferred to a global multilateral agency similar in form to NATO but under the control of the democratized UN. The UN would also need to exercise greater and more democratic control over the international financial institutions—the World Bank, the IMF, and the WTO.

Conclusion

The world-system has been marked by waves of increasing democracy and global state formation over the past several centuries. These waves are likely to continue. The form that will best suit the future, as envisioned in this concluding chapter, is a global democratic and collectively rational commonwealth with a capable global state and empowered and self-reliant local communities. The sources of these sweeping changes are already emerging in the semiperiphery and the periphery of the global system. We expect that both the leadership and the resources will come mainly from the semiperiphery. The most powerful challenges to capitalism in the twentieth century came from semiperipheral Russia and China, and the strongest supporters of the contemporary global justice movement are semiperipheral countries such as Brazil, Mexico, India, and Venezuela. Earlier waves of democracy sprung from the semiperiphery. This observation would not be possible without the conceptual apparatus of the comparative world-systems perspective.

The transformative role of the semiperiphery is also expected to continue. The ways of the core are not sustainable. The semiperipheral way may not be either, but it is closer to where our species needs to go. We have argued for the desirability and feasibility of a collectively rational global democratic commonwealth that is built from the bottom up. We contend that such a system is possible within the next few decades. But our analyses and proposals are put forth with the hope that they will be considered and debated by those who seek to build a world-system that will be peaceful, equitable, and just, while sustaining and improving the biosphere.

Our schema of three possible futures has been intended to clarify the issues and provide a framework for futuristic analysis. But we also recognize that the real future is likely to combine features of the proposed three scenarios in ways that we have not supposed. Indeed, some of the positive changes seen as possible for the United States and its role in the coming decades would fit nicely with the establishment of a global democracy. Will the United States play mainly an obstructive role, or will it play a neutral or even supportive role? How will the various environmental and economic crises obstruct or facilitate the reorganization of global governance and political economy? A collapse of the global financial system would certainly be hard on a lot of people, and not just those who are directly employed in that industry. But it would also provide a strong incentive for people to build solidary and self-reliant local communities. The low-energy global state would be very reliant on the cheap communications made possible by the global grid of transmission towers and satellites that stand behind the cyberworld. If the big grid came down, or became much more expensive, organizing democratic global governance would be much more difficult.

This consideration of the future has focused on the middle term—the next few decades—though it has used a centuries-long perspective to analyze the contemporary world-historical situation. We also want to make more comments about the long term, though these are necessarily even more speculative. In our view the long-term tendencies toward the evolution of biological and sociocultural complexity are strong, and so if the humans should knock themselves back to a lower level as a result of a global Malthusian correction, it will only be a matter of time before a situation that is somewhat similar to the one we have now will come to exist again. In other words, this is probably not our last chance, and even if we succeed in completely destroying ourselves, intelligent life would probably evolve again, and that life-form would eventually be confronted with the issue of global-level societal cooperative organization.

If and when the humans solve the immediate problems, history will not end. Expansion to space stations and nearby moons and planets will pose new cultural and political issues. The problem of "transhumans" (genetic modification of ourselves) and the problem of what to do when the machines we invent become smarter than we are have been the subjects of science fiction. But if we solve our immediate problems, these new problems will likely be not too far down the road.

Regarding the future of social science, we are similarly optimistic. We think that social science will be reinvigorated by its interaction with biological and physical sciences. The study of the evolution of complexity will facilitate enlightening comparisons between physical, biological, and sociocultural evolution. The comparative world-systems perspective will be increasingly applied to the world of biology, as it already has been in biological geography, and the links between the human world-system and the biological and geological systems of the earth will be better understood. These advances in science will allow us to better comprehend ourselves, our relationships with others, and our relationships with the biological and physical worlds. And this knowledge will allow us to continue doing what we have been doing—moving into new environments, adapting ourselves to them, and adapting them to our needs. Let us get through the challenges of the twenty-first century so that we can get on with the exploration of the universe and ourselves.

Suggested Readings

Boswell, Terry, and Christopher Chase-Dunn. 2000. *The Spiral of Capitalism and Socialism: Toward Global Democracy.* Boulder, CO: Lynne Rienner.

Christian, David. 2004. *Maps of Time.* Berkeley: University of California Press.

Florini, Ann. 2005. *The Coming Democracy: New Rules for Running a New World Order.* Washington, DC: Brookings.

Heinberg, Richard. 2004. *Powerdown.* Gabriola Island, BC: Island Press.

Johnson, Chalmers A. 2010. *Dismantling the Empire: America's Last Best Hope.* New York: Metropolitan Books.

Monbiot, George. 2003. *Manifesto for a New World Order.* New York: New Press.

Patomäki, Heikki. 2008. *The Political Economy of Global Security.* London: Routledge.

Roberts, J. Timmons, and Bradley C. Parks. 2007. *A Climate of Injustice: Global Inequality, North-South Politics and Climate Policy.* Cambridge, MA: MIT Press.

Wagar, W. Warren. 1999. *A Short History of the Future.* 3rd ed. Chicago: University of Chicago Press.

Glossary

The chapter in the text where the term is first discussed is shown in square brackets.

administered trade: Exchange that is politically controlled by and at the behest of a centralized polity. [10]

asabiyah: Social solidarity "we-feeling" and trust among a group of people that facilitates collective action. [10]

band: A cluster of families who generally lived together and associated with other such groups that shared language and culture. Band membership is typically somewhat fluid. [5]

big man: A leader who operates by persuasion and prestige, and whose prestige is based on his ability to influence his followers to amass wealth for giveaway at ceremonies. A big man is more powerful than a headman but less powerful than a chief (Sahlins 1963). [6]

bulk goods network (BGN): The network of exchanges of "necessities," or low value to weight ratio goods; typically the smallest exchange network in a world-system. [2]

capital: Commodified wealth used to produce commodities. [2]

capitalism: Production of goods (commodities) for sale on a market. [2] See also **merchant capitalism**

capitalist mode of accumulation: Power and wealth are acquired by producing and selling commodities in a context in which land, labor, and goods are highly commodified. [2]

carrying capacity: The population that any natural environment can support within a specified region with a given production technology. [6]

chief: A leader with institutionalized access to substantial social resources, giving him coercive power. His resources are somewhat autonomous from the control of other lineage heads. The chief is typically, but not always, a hereditary office. [7]

chiefdom: A stratified polity that relies on generalized institutions for regional coordination and control, usually a hierarchical kinship structure that legitimates chiefly authority. [7]

circumscription: A situation in which emigration is blocked, either by physical barriers (environmental circumscription) or by social barriers such as a competing population (social circumscription) or both. [2]

collectivist self: A social identity that puts the perceived interest of the family, clan, or group ahead of the interest of the individual. [Preface]

colonial empire: A situation in which one or more core states dominate peripheral regions. [13]

commodification: The process or result of turning something into a commodity. Commodification is a matter of degree. [2]

commodity: A standardized good produced for sale on a price-setting market. [2]

commodity chains: Networks that link all the actors involved in the production and consumption of a commodity—from food producers to workers, raw material producers, transportation, final production, and final consumers. [14]

conical clan: An extensive common descent group, ranked and segmented along genealogical lines and patrilineal in ideological bias. [8]

conjuncture: An unlikely coming together of factors that make social change possible. [Preface]

core: Region of a world-system that dominates the system. Typically it consists of the most complex social groups in the system. [2]

core power: A powerful polity in the core region of a world-system. [2]

core/periphery differentiation: Societies at different levels of complexity and population density are in interaction with each other. [2]

core/periphery hierarchy: Intersocietal domination or exploitation. [2]

core/periphery relations: See **core/periphery differentiation**; **core/periphery hierarchy**

core-wide empire: A single state controls most of the territory within the core of a world-system. [10]

cultural globalization: The emergence over the tops of the civilizational and national cultures of a global culture in which assumptions about what exists (ontology) and what is good (ethics, morality, values) are coming to be shared across the whole earth. [13] See also **geoculture**.

desmesne: (pronounced "demain") That part of the tilled land of the manor from which all produce went to the castle and belonged to the lord. [12]

development of underdevelopment: The process in which developing countries extract capital from their economic and/or political colonies, which not only blocks colonial development but also systematically distorts development in harmful ways; that is, it is the relationship itself that causes "underdevelopment." [11]

doges: Merchant princes who governed Venice. [12]

down-the-line trade: A system of trade in which A trades with B, B trades with C, C trades with D, and so on. In this type of system, goods can travel a long way without the endpoints ever coming in contact. [2]

economic globalization: International trade and investment become large relative to the size of the whole economy. [13]

ecumene: Understanding and cooperation among different religions or cultures. [12]

empire: A state that has conquered other polities and peoples. [1] See also **core-wide empire**

ethnic group: People who identify with one another on the basis of language and shared history. [2]

external arena: An area outside a world-system. [14]

fall-off: The gradient of degradation of consequential effects over space. [2]

fealty: An important institution in feudal Europe involving a ritual swearing of loyalty by tenants and vassals to their lord, forming a voluntary bond among individuals who were not necessarily related by kinship. [12]

financialization: A phase in which symbolic claims on future income streams such as stocks, bonds, and other "securities" grow to become larger than the real economy of goods and services. [18]

flexible specialization: A form of labor organization in which workers are employed by small firms that produce for rapidly changing markets. [13]

generative sector: Emergent technological and organizational innovations that generate economic growth by stimulating forward and backward economic linkages. [15]

geoculture: A new, larger culture that emerges in a multicultural world-system. [13] See also **cultural globalization; ecumene**

global civil society: All the individuals and groups who knowingly orient their political participation toward issues that transcend local and national boundaries and who try to link up with those outside their own home countries in order to have an impact on local, national, and global issues. [20]

global governance: The patterned forms of political competition and cooperation that occur at the system level in a world-system. [13]

global state formation: The emergence of political globalization and regulation at the global level. [19]

globalization: Integration that occurs when long-distance interactions increase faster than local interactions. [2]

headman: A leader by virtue of personal charisma and respected abilities, typically in oratory, mediation, hunting, and fighting. He leads by influence. A headman is less powerful than a big man and much less powerful than a chief. [5]

hegemon: The one core state with an unusually large share of world economic and military power over other core states. [2]

hegemonic rivalry: A situation in which several core states within the same core region have similar amounts of economic and military power and are contending for hegemony. [2]

hegemonic sequence: The rise and fall of hegemons. [2]

hegemony (geopolitical): A situation in which one core state has an unusually large share of world economic and military power over other core states. This is often combined with an effort to represent "universal" interests and to provide global leadership. [Preface]

high level equilibrium trap: A situation in which labor is so cheap that producers have no incentive to invest in labor-saving technological change. [12]

horizontal collectivist self: A social identity in egalitarian society that puts the perceived interest of the family, clan, or group ahead of the interest of the individual. [Preface]

imperialism: The exercise of interpolity power—the domination and exploitation of a group of people by people from a different polity. [10]

information network (IN): The network of exchange of information in a variety of forms, including ideology, religion, technical information, and culture. [2]

institutions: Inventions that are made by people for solving problems. Hospitals, libraries, and schools are institutions, but so are language, writing, money, voting systems, the self, and states. Language is the original institution and is an important basis of all institutions. [1]

interaction networks: Regular and repeated interactions among individuals and groups. [2]

interchiefdom system: A set of chiefdoms that ally and make war with one another. [2]

interstate system: A set of interacting states that ally and make war with one another. [2]

kin-based mode of production: Social labor is mobilized and distribution is accomplished according to normative consensus about kinship obligations. [2]

Kondratieff wave: Forty- to sixty-year economic cycle of growth and stagnation discovered by the Soviet economist Nikolai Kondratieff. [13]

lateral pressure: Increasing international competition for natural resources and markets. [17]

latifundia: Large agricultural plantations or ranches, as opposed to "minifundia," which are small farms. [14]

law: Written rules that are legitimized by a state and backed up by state-organized rewards and punishments. [10]

manorial economy: A decentralized form of the tributary mode of accumulation based on the unit of the manor, which was under the legal jurisdiction of its lord, a warrior-knight. In principle, the manor was economically, politically, and religiously self-sufficient. Serfs contributed the labor power of the manor. The serfs were part of the property held by the landlord and contributed their labor in exchange for protection and access to a small parcel of land. [12]

merchant capitalism: Accumulation through exploiting price differentials across different regions. [11]

mode of accumulation: A *logic of development* in which the reproduction of social structures and cyclical processes occurs by means of certain typical forms of integration and control, a deep structural logic of production, distribution, exchange, and accumulation. Empirical indicators are forms of exchange and forms of control used to mobilize social labor and/or to extract surplus product. Different modes of accumulation may be present in the same system, and some forms of exchange and control have elements of more than one mode. Generally, one mode "predominates." [2]

nation: A group of people with a shared identity and sense of separate sovereignty. [2]

nation-state: A group of people with a shared identity who are citizens or subjects of the same state. [2]

neoconservatism: The idea that the United States should use its military power unilaterally to protect its interests and expand its influence in world politics. [18]

neoliberalism: A twentieth-century political ideology that glorifies markets and disparages state regulation; also called "Reaganism-Thatcherism," "the globalization project," and "the Washington Consensus." [18]

new lead industries: See **generative sector**

orientalism: East/West social distinctions that are understood in evaluative terms, although these evaluations are often buried under claims about objectivity. [12]

peripheral capitalism: Commodity production using coerced labor (slaves, serfs, and so on). [12]

peripheral marcher states: Confederations of peripheral nomadic tribes that try to conquer sedentary states. [10]

periphery: Region of a world-system that is dominated by the core and semiperiphery. Typically, it consists of the least complex social groups in the system. [2]

pochteca: Aztec agents of kings who combined religious, trade, and spying functions on their missions to distant lands. [10]

political globalization: International institutions grow over the tops of national societies. [13]

political-military network (PMN): The network of regular political or military "exchanges," including warfare and statecraft; typically a medium-sized network in a world-system. [2]

polity: A general term that means any organization with a single authority that claims sovereign control over a territory or a group of people. Polities include bands, tribes, and chiefdoms as well as states. [2]

population pressure: Population density (the number of people per unit of land area) rises to levels that degrade natural resources in a way that increases the costs of production. [2]

prestige goods: Symbolically important goods, typically exotic imports that are often of high value to weight ratio, whose ownership confers prestige on the owner. [2]

prestige goods network (PGN): The network of exchanges of "prestige" or luxury goods, or high value to weight ratio goods; typically the largest exchange network in a world-system. [2]

prestige goods system: Systemic exchange network in which local leaders monopolize the supply of symbolically important goods, typically exotic imports (prestige goods), which they use to reward subordinates. In many systems these goods are defined as necessary for important social rituals such as marriage. [7]

price-setting market: A market in which the competitive buying and selling of goods by actors operating to maximize their own returns largely determines the rates of exchange (prices) among traded goods. [2]

pristine state (primary state): A state that developed without contact with other existing states. [8]

product cycle: The developers of a new product can receive "technological rents" because they are the only producers, but eventually the product gets produced by competitors and competition drives the price down. [20]

protection rent: The differential returns received by merchants whose trading efforts are supported by a cost-efficient and protection-providing state; see Lane (1979). [8]

pulsation: Periodic spatial expansion and contraction of interaction networks. [5]

rise and fall: Cycles of intersocietal political centralization and decentralization, usually indicated by growth (or decline) of the largest core polity. [7]

secondary state: A state that developed in reaction to interactions with other, already-existing states. [8]

segmentary lineage: A form of kinship that can activate ties at various levels of relatedness. Support or opposition in any conflict is governed by degree of relatedness of two groups. This is encapsulated in the proverb "Me against my brother; my brother and I against the clan; my clan and us against the tribe; my tribe, my clan, my brother and I against the world." [12]

semiperipheral capitalist city-state: A state in a semiperipheral location that is under the control of those who accumulate trade profits. Most were maritime states specializing in shipping and naval power, but some were land based. [10]

semiperipheral development: Semiperipheries are fertile locations for innovations in techniques of power that enable upward mobility and the transformation of world-systems. [2]

semiperipheral marcher state: A state on the edge of a core region that attempts to conquer the other core states. [10]

semiperiphery: An intermediate location in an interpolity core/periphery structure. [2]

settlement size distribution: A list of the settlements in a region ranked by their population sizes. A flat distribution consists of settlements that are about the same size, and a primate size distribution has one settlement that is much larger than the others. [5]

state: A regionally organized society with specialized regional institutions—military and bureaucratic—that perform the tasks of control and management. [2]

state-administered trade: Exchange that is politically controlled redistribution organized by the state, often carried out by agents of the king. [8]

surplus product: The labor time and products of direct producers that are appropriated by the ruling class in a class society. [8]

techniques of power: Michael Mann's term for political and cultural institutions that facilitate the wielding of power. Mann (1986, 525) says: "They all have in common a capacity to improve the infrastructure of collective and distributive power, and they all have a proved survival capacity." [2]

technological rent: A high price that can be charged by the originators of a new product because they are the only producers. [20]

teleology: Explains an outcome in terms of final causes or ultimate purposes. [1]

trade diaspora: Philip Curtin's term (1984) for specialized trading ethnicity that occupies a scattering of settlements for conducting trade across cultural boundaries. [11]

trade ecumene: Philip Curtin's term (1984) for a region in which the norms of trade are widely understood and agreed upon among formerly separate and different cultural groups. A trade ecumene obviates the need for trade diaspora. [11]

transnational social movement: A social movement that includes activists from more than one country who are communicating with one another. [17]

tribelet: An autonomous polity usually consisting of a single village, but sometimes including two or three villages under the leadership of a single headman. [5]

tributary modes of accumulation: Labor is mobilized and distribution is carried out by means of coercive state-based institutions. [2]

vertical collectivist self: A social identity in a stratified society in which one puts the perceived interest of one's caste, class, or estate ahead of the interest of the individual, together with obedience and loyalty to higher stratified bodies. [Preface]

vertical individualist self: A social identity in a stratified class society in which the individual puts their own interests ahead of the perceived group interests of their class and family while offering begrudging obedience and loyalty to higher social classes. [Part IV]

world religion: A moral order not based on ethnic identity but rather on confessional action by the individual. [1]

world revolution: A widespread collection of local revolts, rebellions, and social movements that cluster together in time and that become increasingly linked with one another with the development of long-distance transportation and communications. [13]

world-system: Interpolity networks in which the interactions (trade, warfare, intermarriage, information, and so on) are important for the reproduction of the internal structures of the composite units and importantly affect changes that occur in these local structures. [2]

Bibliography

Abernethy, David B. 2000. *The Dynamics of Global Dominance: European Overseas Empires, 1415–1980*. New Haven, CT: Yale University Press.
Abram, David. 1996. *The Spell of the Sensuous*. New York: Pantheon.
Abu-Lughod, Janet L. 1987. "The Shape of the World-System in the Thirteenth Century." *Studies in Comparative International Development* 22:3–25.
———. 1989. *Before European Hegemony: The World System A.D. 1250–1350*. Oxford: Oxford University Press.
Adams, Robert McCormick. 1966. *The Evolution of Urban Society: Early Mesopotamia and Prehispanic Mexico*. Chicago: Aldine.
———. 1981. *Heartland of Cities: Surveys of Ancient Settlement and Land Use on the Central Floodplain of the Euphrates*. Chicago: University of Chicago Press.
———. 1984. "Mesopotamian Social Evolution: Old Outlooks, New Goals." In *On the Evolution of Complex Societies: Essays in Honor of Harry Hoijer*, edited by Timothy Earle, 79–129. Malibu, CA: Undena Publications.
Adams, Robert McCormick, and Hans J. Nissen. 1972. *The Uruk Countryside: The Natural Setting of Urban Societies*. Chicago: University of Chicago Press.
Adams, William Y. 1977. *Nubia: Corridor to Africa*. Princeton, NJ: Princeton University Press.
Aglietta, Michel. 1978. "Phases of U.S. Capitalist Expansion." *New Left Review* 110:17–28.
Ainsworth, Mary. 1979. *Patterns of Attachment*. Florence, KY: Psychology Press.
Algaze, Guillermo. 1989. "The Uruk Expansion: Cross-Cultural Exchange as a Factor in Early Mesopotamian Civilization." *Current Anthropology* 30 (5): 571–608.
———. 1993. *The Uruk World System: The Dynamics of Expansion of Early Mesopotamian Civilization*. Chicago: University of Chicago Press.
Allen, Mitchell. 1992. "The Mechanisms of Underdevelopment: An Ancient Mesopotamian Example." *Review* 15 (3): 453–476.
———. 1996. "Contested Peripheries: Philistia in the Neo-Assyrian World-System." PhD diss., UCLA Interdepartmental Archaeology Program.
———. 2005. "Power Is in the Details: Administrative Technology and the Growth of Ancient Near Eastern Cores." In *The Historical Evolution of World-Systems*, edited by C. Chase-Dunn and E. N. Anderson, 75–91. New York: Palgrave.
Ames, Kenneth M. 1991. "The Archaeology of the *Longue Duree*: Temporal and Spatial Scale in the Evolution of Social Complexity on the Southern Northwest Coast." *Antiquity* 65:935–945.
Amin, Samir. 1978. *The Arab Nation: Nationalism and Class Struggle*. London: Zed Press.
———. 1980. *Class and Nation, Historically and in the Current Crisis*. New York: Monthly Review Press.
———. 1989. *Eurocentrism*. New York: Monthly Review.
———. 1990. *Delinking: Towards a Polycentric World*. London: Zed Press.
———. 1991. "The Ancient World-Systems versus the Modern Capitalist World-System." *Review* 14 (3): 349–385.
———. 1997. *Capitalism in the Age of Globalization*. London: Zed Press.
———. 2008. "Towards the Fifth International?" In *Global Political Parties*, edited by Katarina Sehm-Patomäki and Marko Ulvila, 123–143. London: Zed Press.

Anderson, David G. 1994. *The Savannah River Chiefdoms: Political Change in the Late Prehistoric Southeast*. Tuscaloosa: University of Alabama Press.
Anderson, E. N. 2004. "Lamb, Rice and Mongol Hegemonic Decline." In *The Historical Evolution of World-Systems*, edited by C. Chase-Dunn and E. N. Anderson, 113–121. London: Palgrave.
Anderson, Perry. 1974a. *Passages from Antiquity to Feudalism*. London: New Left Books.
———. 1974b. *Lineages of the Absolutist State*. London: New Left Books.
———. 1979. "Peripheralization of Southern Africa, I: Changes in Production Processes." *Review* 3 (2): 161–191.
Anthony, David W. 2007. *The Horse, the Wheel, and Language*. Princeton, NJ: Princeton University Press.
Arrighi, Giovanni. 1994. *The Long Twentieth Century*. London: Verso.
———. 2008. *Adam Smith in Beijing*. London: Verso.
Arrighi, Giovanni, and Jessica Drangel. 1986. "Stratification of the World Economy: An Explanation of the Semi-peripheral Zone." *Review* 10 (1): 9–74.
Arrighi, Giovanni, Takeshi Hamashita, and Mark Selden. 2003. *The Resurgence of East Asia: 500, 150 and 50 Year Perspectives*. London: Routledge.
Arrighi, Giovanni, Terence K. Hopkins, and Immanuel Wallerstein. 1989. *Antisystemic Movements*. London: Verso.
Arrighi, Giovanni, and Beverly Silver. 1999. *Chaos and Governance in the Modern World System*. Minneapolis: University of Minnesota Press.
Baines, John, and Norman Yoffee. 1998. "Order, Legitimacy, and Wealth in Ancient Egypt and Mesopotamia." In *Archaic States*, edited by Gary M. Feinman and Joyce Marcus, 199–260. Santa Fe, NM: School of American Research.
Bairoch, Paul. 1975. *The Economic Development of the Third World Since 1900*. Berkeley: University of California Press.
———. 1986. "Historical Roots of Economic Underdevelopment: Myths and Realities." In *Imperialism after Empire: Continuities and Discontinuities*, edited by Wolfgang J. Mommsen and Jurgen Osterhammerl, 191–216. London: Allen and Unwin.
Balazs, Etienne. 1968. *Chinese Civilization and Bureaucracy*. New Haven, CT: Yale University Press.
Barbieri, Katherine. 2002. *The Liberal Illusion: Does Trade Promote Peace?* Ann Arbor: University of Michigan Press.
Barbour, Violet. 1963. *Capitalism in Amsterdam in the Seventeenth Century*. Ann Arbor: University of Michigan Press.
Barfield, Thomas J. 1989. *The Perilous Frontier: Nomadic Empires and China*. Cambridge, MA: Blackwell.
———. 1993. *The Nomadic Alternative*. Englewood Cliffs, NJ: Prentice Hall.
Barr, Kenneth James. 1999. "The Metamorphosis of Business Enterprise." PhD diss., Department of Sociology, Binghamton University.
Bartlett, C. J. 1993. *Defence and Diplomacy: Britain and the Great Powers, 1815–1914*. Manchester, UK; New York: Manchester University Press.
Bar-Yosef, Ofer, and Anna Belfer-Cohen. 1991. "From Sedentary Hunter-Gatherers to Territorial Farmers in the Levant." In *Between Bands and States*, edited by Susan A. Gregg, 181–202. Carbondale, IL: Center for Archaeological Investigations, Occasional Paper #9.
Batten, Bruce L. 2003. *To the Ends of Japan*. Honolulu: University of Hawaii Press.
Baugh, Timothy. 1984. "Southern Plains Societies and Eastern Frontier Pueblo Exchange during the Protohistoric Period." In *Papers of the Archaeological Society of New Mexico*, Vol. 9, 156–167. Albuquerque, NM: Archaeological Society Press.
———. 1991. "Ecology and Exchange: The Dynamics of Plains-Pueblo Interaction." In *Farmers, Hunters, and Colonists: Interaction between the Southwest and the Southern Plains*, edited by Katherine A. Spielmann, 102–107. Tucson: University of Arizona Press.
Baugh, Timothy G., and Jonathan E. Ericson, eds. 1994. *Prehistoric Exchange Systems in North America*. New York: Plenum Press.
Bean, Lowell John, and Harry Lawton. 1976. "Some Explanations for the Rise of Cultural Complexity in Native California with Comments on Proto-Agriculture and Agriculture." In *Native Californians: A Theoretical Retrospective*, edited by Lowell John Bean and Thomas C. Blackburn, 19–48. Socorro, NM: Ballena Press.
Beaujard, Philippe. 2005. "The Indian Ocean in Eurasian and African World-Systems before the Sixteenth Century." *Journal of World History* 16 (4): 411–465.
Beck, Ulrich. 2005. *Power in the Global Age*. Cambridge, UK: Polity Press.
Beckwith, I. Christopher. 1987. *The Tibetan Empire in Central Asia*. Bloomington: Indiana University Press.
———. 1991. "The Impact of the Horse and Silk Trade on the Economies of T'ang China and the Uighur Empire." *Journal of the Economic and Social History of the Orient* 34 (2): 183–198.
———. 2009. *Empires of the Silk Road*. Princeton, NJ: Princeton University Press.

Bennyhoff, James A., and Richard E. Hughes. 1987. "Shell Bead and Ornament Exchange Networks between California and the Western Great Basin." *Anthropological Papers of the American Museum of Natural History* 64 (2): 79–175.

Bentley, Jerry H. 1993. *Old World Encounters: Cross-Cultural Contacts and Exchanges in Pre-Modern Times*. Oxford: Oxford University Press.

Berdan, Frances F. 2005. *The Aztecs of Central Mexico: An Imperial Society*. Belmont, CA: Thomson Wadsworth.

Berger, Peter, and Thomas Luckmann. 1967. *The Social Construction of Reality.* New York: Anchor.

Berquist, Jon. 1995. "The Shifting Frontier: The Achaemenid Empire's Treatment of Western Colonies." *Journal of World-Systems Research* 1:17.

Bibby, Geoffrey. 1969. *Looking for Dilmun*. New York: Knopf.

Binford, Lewis. 1983. *In Pursuit of the Past*. Berkeley: University of California Press.

Blanton, Richard E., Stephen A. Kowalewski, and Gary Feinman. 1992. "The Mesoamerican World-System." *Review* 15 (3): 418–426.

Blanton, Richard E., Stephen Kowalewski, Gary Feinman, and Jill Appel. 1981. *Ancient Mesoamerica: A Comparison of Change in Three Regions*. Cambridge: Cambridge University Press.

Blanton, Richard, Stephen A. Kowalewski, Gary Feinman, and Laura M. Finsten. 1993. *Ancient Mesoamerica: A Comparison of Change in Three Regions.* 2nd ed. New York: Cambridge University Press.

Blumberg, Rae Lesser. 1978. *Stratification*. Dubuque, IA: William Brown Co.

Bocek, Barbara. 1991. "Prehistoric Settlement Pattern and Social Organization on the San Francisco Peninsula, California." In *Between Bands and States*, edited by Susan A. Gregg, 58–88. Center for Archaeological Investigations, Occasional paper no. 9. Carbondale: Southern Illinois University.

Bornholdt, Laura. 1949. *Baltimore and Early Pan-Americanism*. Smith College Studies in History 34. Northampton, MA.

Bornschier, Volker. 2010. "On the Evolution of Inequality in the World System." In *Inequality beyond Globalization*, edited by Christian Suter, 39–64. New Brunswick, NJ: Transaction Publishers.

Bornschier, Volker, and Christopher Chase-Dunn. 1985. *Transnational Corporations and Underdevelopment*. New York: Praeger.

Boserup, Esther. 1965. *The Conditions of Agricultural Growth*. Chicago: Aldine.

———. 1981. *Population and Technological Change*. Chicago: University of Chicago Press.

Boswell, Terry, and Christopher Chase-Dunn. 2000. *The Spiral of Capitalism and Socialism: Toward Global Democracy.* Boulder, CO: Lynne Rienner.

Bosworth, Andrew. 1995. "World Cities and World Economic Cycles." In *Civilizations and World-Systems: Two Approaches to the Study of World-Historical Change*, edited by Stephen K. Sanderson, 192–213. Walnut Creek, CA: Altamira Press.

Boxer, Charles R. 1969. *The Portuguese Seaborne Empire, 1415–1825.* New York: A. A. Knopf.

Bowlby, John. 1983. *Attachment*. New York: Basic Books.

Boyer, Pascal. 2001. *Religion Explained.* New York: Basic Books.

Boyer, Richard O., and Herbert M. Morais. 1975. *Labor's Untold Story.* 3rd ed. New York: United Electrical, Radio & Machine Workers of America.

Braudel, Fernand. 1972. *The Mediterranean and the Mediterranean World in the Age of Philip II*. 2 vols. New York: Harper and Row.

———. 1975. *Capitalism and Material Life, 1400–1800*. New York: Harper and Row.

———. 1984. *The Perspective of the World.* Vol. 3 of *Civilization and Capitalism*. Berkeley: University of California Press.

Brenner, Robert. 2002. *The Boom and the Bubble: The U.S. in the World Economy*. London: Verso.

Briggs, Asa. 1964. *Victorian Cities*. London: Odham Books.

Brown, James, and T. D. Price, eds. 1985. *Prehistoric Hunter-Gatherers: The Emergence of Cultural Complexity*. Orlando, FL: Academic Press.

Brown, Lester R. 2008. *Plan B 3.0: Mobilizing to Save Civilization.* New York: W. W. Norton.

Bunker, Stephen G. 1984. *Underdeveloping the Amazon: Extraction, Unequal Exchange, and the Failure of the Modern State*. Champaign: University of Illinois Press.

Bunker, Stephen, and Paul Ciccantell. 2005. *Globalization and the Race for Resources*. Baltimore: Johns Hopkins University Press.

Burke, Peter. 1974. *Venice and Amsterdam: A Study of Seventeenth Century Elites*. London: Temple Smith.

Burke, Peter, and Asa Briggs. 2008. *A Social History of the Media*. Cambridge, UK: Polity Press.

Buss, David. 1999. *Evolutionary Psychology*. Boston: Allyn and Bacon.

Buttel, Frederick H., and Kenneth A. Gould. 2006. "Environmentalism and the Trajectory of the Anti-corporate Globalization Movement." In *Global Social Change*, edited by C. Chase-Dunn and S. Babones, 269–288. Baltimore: Johns Hopkins University Press.

Caldwell, Joseph R. 1964. "Interaction Spheres in Prehistory." *Hopewellian Studies* 12 (6): 133–156.

Carneiro, Robert L. 1970. "A Theory of the Origin of the State." *Science* 169 (August): 733–738.

———. 1978. "Political Expansion as an Expression of the Principle of Competitive Exclusion." In *Origins of the State: The Anthropology of Political Evolution*, edited by Ronald Cohen and Elman R. Service, 205–223. Philadelphia: Institute for the Study of Human Issues.

———. 1981. "The Chiefdom: Precursor of the State." In *The Transition to Statehood in the New World*, edited by Grant D. Jones and Robert R. Kautz, 37–79. New York: Cambridge University Press.

———. 2004. "The Political Unification of the World: Whether, When, and How—Some Speculations." *Cross-Cultural Research* 38 (2): 162–177.

Carroll, William K. 2010. *The Making of a Transnational Capitalist Class: Corporate Power in the 21st Century*. London: Zed Books.

Carver, Charles, and Michael Scheier. 2004. *Perspectives on Personality.* Boston: Allyn and Bacon.

Case, Lynn M., and Warren F. Spencer. 1970. *The United States and France: Civil War Diplomacy*. Philadelphia: University of Pennsylvania Press.

Chafetz, Janet. 1984. *Sex and Advantage*. Los Angeles: Sage Publications.

Champion, Timothy C., ed. 1989a. *Centre and Periphery: Comparative Studies in Archaeology*. London: Unwin Hyman.

———. 1989b. "Introduction." In *Centre and Periphery: Comparative Studies in Archaeology*, edited by Timothy C. Champion, 1–21. London: Unwin Hyman.

Champion, Timothy, and S. Champion. 1986. "Peer Polity Interaction in the European Iron Age." In *Peer Polity Interaction and Socio-political Change*, edited by Colin Renfrew and J. F. Cherry, 59–68. Cambridge: Cambridge University Press.

Chandler, Tertius. 1987. *Four Thousand Years of Urban Growth: An Historical Census*. Lewiston, NY: Edwin Mellon Press.

Chandra, Meti. 1977. *Trade and Trade Routes in Ancient India*. New Delhi: Abhinav Publications.

Chang, Kwang-chih. 1980. *Shang Civilization*. New Haven, CT: Yale University Press.

———. 1983. *Art, Myth and Ritual: The Path to Political Authority in Ancient China.* Cambridge, MA: Harvard University Press.

Chapman, Anne C. 1957. "Port of Trade Enclaves in Aztec and Maya Civilizations." In *Trade and Market in the Early Empires*, edited by Karl Polanyi, Conrad M. Arensberg, and Harry W. Pearson, 114–153. Chicago: Gateway.

Charon, Joel. 1998. *Symbolic Interaction.* 6th ed. Upper Saddle River, NJ: Prentice Hall.

Chase-Dunn, Christopher. 1980. "The Development of Core Capitalism in the Antebellum United States: Tariff Politics and Class Struggle in an Upwardly Mobile Semiperiphery." In *Studies of the Modern World-System*, edited by Albert J. Bergesen, 189–230. New York: Academic Press.

———. 1985. "The System of World Cities: A.D. 800–1975." In *Urbanization in the World-Economy*, edited by Michael Timberlake, 269–292. New York: Academic Press.

———. 1988. "Comparing World-Systems: Toward a Theory of Semiperipheral Development." *Comparative Civilizations Review* 19 (Fall): 39–66.

———. 1990a. "Resistance to Imperialism: Semiperipheral Actors." *Review* 13 (1): 1–31.

———. 1990b. "World State Formation: Historical Processes and Emergent Necessity." *Political Geography Quarterly* 9 (2): 108–130.

———. 1992. "The Changing Role of Cities in World-Systems." In *Waves, Formations and Values in the World System*, edited by Volker Bornschier and Peter Lengyel, 51–88. World Society Studies, Vol. 2. New Brunswick, NJ: Transaction Publishers.

———. 1998. *Global Formation: Structures of the World-Economy*. 2nd ed. Lanham, MD: Rowman and Littlefield.

———. 2005. "Global Public Social Science." *American Sociologist* 36 (3–4): 121–132. Reprinted in *Public Sociology: The Contemporary Debate*, ed. Lawrence T. Nichols (New Brunswick, NJ: Transaction Press, 2007), 179–194.

Chase-Dunn, Christopher, and Salvatore Babones, eds. 2006. *Global Social Change.* Baltimore: Johns Hopkins University Press.

Chase-Dunn, Christopher, and Elena Ermolaeva. 1994. "The Ancient Hawaiian World-System: Research in Progress." Working paper no. 4, Institute for Research on World-Systems, University of California, Riverside. http://irows.ucr.edu/papers/irows4.txt.

Chase-Dunn, Christopher, and Peter Grimes. 1995. "World-Systems Analysis." *Annual Review of Sociology* 21:387–417.

Chase-Dunn, Christopher, and Thomas D. Hall, eds. 1991. *Core/Periphery Relations in Precapitalist Worlds*. Boulder, CO: Westview Press.

———. 1993. "Comparing World-Systems: Concepts and Working Hypotheses." *Social Forces* 71 (4): 851–886.

———. 1995. "Cross-World-System Comparisons: Similarities and Differences." In *Civilizations and World-Systems: Two Approaches to the Study of World-Historical Change*, edited by Stephen K. Sanderson, 95–121. Walnut Creek, CA: Altamira Press.

———. 1997. *Rise and Demise: Comparing World-Systems*. Boulder, CO: Westview Press.

———. 1998a. "Ecological Degradation and the Evolution of World-Systems." *Journal of World-Systems Research* 3:403–431.

———. 1998b. "World-Systems in North America: Networks, Rise and Fall and Pulsations of Trade in Stateless Systems." *American Indian Culture and Research Journal* 22 (1): 23–72.

Chase-Dunn, Christopher, Yukio Kawano, and Benjamin Brewer. 2000. "Trade Globalization since 1795: Waves of Integration in the World-System." *American Sociological Review* 65:77–95.

Chase-Dunn, Christopher, Roy Kwon, Kirk Lawrence, and Hiroko Inoue. 2011. "Last of the Hegemons: U.S. Decline and Global Governance." *International Review of Modern Sociology* 37 (1): 1–29.

Chase-Dunn, Christopher, and Kelly M. Mann. 1998. *The Wintu and Their Neighbors: A Very Small World-System in Northern California*. Tucson: University of Arizona Press.

Chase-Dunn, Christopher, and E. Susan Manning. 2002. "City Systems and World-Systems: Four Millennia of City Growth and Decline." *Cross-Cultural Research* 36 (4): 379–398.

Chase-Dunn, Christopher, Susan Manning, and Thomas D. Hall. 2000. "Rise and Fall: East-West Synchrony and Indic Exceptionalism Reexamined." *Social Science History* 24 (4): 727–754.

Chase-Dunn, Christopher, and R. E. Niemeyer. 2009. "The World Revolution of 20xx." In *Transnational Political Spaces*, edited by Mathias Albert, Gesa Bluhm, Han Helmig, Andreas Leutzsch, and Jochen Walter, 35–57. Frankfurt/New York: Campus Verlag.

Chase-Dunn, Christopher, Richard Niemeyer, Alexis Alvarez, and Hiroko Inoue. 2009. "Scale Transitions and the Evolution of Global Governance since the Bronze Age." In *Systemic Transitions*, edited by William R. Thompson, 261–284. New York: Palgrave MacMillan.

Chase-Dunn, Christopher, Christine Petit, Richard Niemeyer, Robert A. Hanneman, and Ellen Reese. 2007. "The Contours of Solidarity and Division among Global Movements." *International Journal of Peace Studies* 12 (2): 1–15.

Chase-Dunn, Christopher, and Bruce Podobnik. 1995. "The Next World War: World-System Cycles and Trends." *Journal of World-Systems Research* 1:6.

Chase-Dunn, Christopher, and Ellen Reese. 2007. "The World Social Forum—A Global Party in the Making?" In *Global Political Parties*, edited by Katarina Sehm-Patamaki and Marko Ulvila, 53–91. London: Zed Press.

Chase-Dunn, Christopher, Thomas Reifer, Andrew Jorgenson, and Shoon Lio. 2005. "The U.S. Trajectory: A Quantitative Reflection." *Sociological Perspectives* 48 (2): 233–254.

Chase-Dunn, Christopher, and Alice Willard. 1993. "Systems of Cities and World-Systems: Settlement Size Hierarchies and Cycles of Political Centralization, 2000 BC–1988 AD." Paper presented at the International Studies Association meeting, Acapulco, NM, March 24–27. http://www.irows.ucr.edu/papers/irows5/irows5.htm.

———. 1994. "Cities in the Central Political-Military Network Since CE 1200." *Comparative Civilizations Review* 30 (Spring): 104–132.

Chaudhuri, K. N. 1985. *Trade and Civilization in the Indian Ocean: An Economic History from the Rise of Islam to 1750*. Cambridge: Cambridge University Press.

Cheney, Dorothy L., and Robert M. Seyfarth. 1990. *How Monkeys See the World: Inside the Mind of Another Species*. Chicago: University of Chicago Press.

Chernykh, E. N. 1992. *Ancient Metallurgy in the USSR: The Early Metal Age*. Cambridge: Cambridge University Press.

Chew, Sing C. 2001. *World Ecological Degradation: Accumulation, Urbanization and Deforestation, 3000 BC–AD 2000*. Walnut Creek, CA: Altamira Press.

Chi, Ch'ao-ting. 1963 [1935]. *Key Economic Areas in Chinese History: As Revealed in the Development of Public Works for Water-Control*. New York: Paragon Books.

Choucri, Nazli, and Robert C. North. 1975. *Nations in Conflict: National Growth and International Violence*. San Francisco: Freeman.

Christian, David. 2004. *Maps of Time*. Berkeley: University of California Press.

Cioffi-Revilla, Claudio. 1996. "Origins and Evolution of War and Politics." *International Studies Quarterly* 40:1–22.

Clanchy, M. T. 1979. *From Memory to Written Record*. Cambridge, MA: Harvard University Press.

Clark, Wayne E., and Helen C. Rountree. 1993. "The Powhatans and the Maryland Mainland." In Rountree 1993a, 112–135.

Cochran, Gregory, and Henry Harpending. 2009. *The 10,000 Year Explosion: How Civilization Accelerated Human Evolution.* New York: Basic Books.

Cohen, Mark. 1977. *The Food Crisis in Prehistory*. New Haven, CT: Yale University Press.

Collins, Randall. 1978. "Some Principles of Long-Term Social Change: The Territorial Power of States." In *Research in Social Movements, Conflicts and Change*, Vol. 1, edited by Louis F. Kriesberg, 1–34. Greenwich, CT: JAI Press.

———. 1986. *Weberian Sociological Theory*. Cambridge: Cambridge University Press.

———. 1992. "The Geopolitical and Economic World Systems of Kinship-Based and Agrarian-Coercive Societies." *Review* 15 (3): 373–388.

———. 1999. *Macrohistory: Essays in Sociology of the Long Run.* Stanford, CA: Stanford University Press.

Cook, J. A. 2007. *Global Government under the U.S. Constitution*. Lanham, MD: University Press of America.

Cook, John M. 1983. *The Persian Empire*. New York: Shocken.

Cook, Sherburne F. 1955. *The Epidemic of 1830–33 in California and Oregon*. Berkeley: University of California Press.

———. 1960. "Colonial Expeditions to the Interior of California: Central Valley, 1800–1820." *University of California Anthropological Records* 16 (6): 239–292.

———. 1962. "Colonial Expeditions to the Interior of California: Central Valley, 1820–1840." *University of California Anthropological Records* 20 (5): 151–214.

———. 1976. *The Population of the California Indians, 1769–1970*. Berkeley: University of California Press.

Cooper, Jerrold S. 1983. *The Curse of Agade*. Baltimore: Johns Hopkins University Press.

Cox, Oliver C. 1959. *The Foundations of Capitalism*. New York: Philosophical Library.

Crosby, Alfred W. Jr. 1972. *The Columbian Exchange: Biological and Cultural Consequences of 1492*. Westport, CT: Greenwood Press.

———. 1997. *The Measure of Reality.* Cambridge: Cambridge University Press.

———. 2007. "Infectious Diseases as Ecological and Historical Phenomena, with Special Reference to the Influenza Pandemic of 1918–1919." In *The World System and the Earth System: Global Socioenvironmental Change and Sustainability since the Neolithic*, edited by A. Hornborg and C. Crumley, 280–287. Walnut Creek, CA: Left Coast Press.

Cumberland, K. B. 1962. "Moas and Men: New Zealand about AD 1250." *Geographical Review* 52:151–173.

Cumings, Bruce. 1984. "The Origins and Development of the Northeast Asia Political Economy: Industrial Sectors, Product Cycles, and Political Consequences." *International Organization* 38 (1): 1–40.

———. 1990. *The Origins of the Korean War*. Princeton, NJ: Princeton University Press.

Curtin, Philip D. 1984. *Cross-Cultural Trade in World History*. Cambridge: Cambridge University Press.

———. 1990. *The Rise and Fall of the Plantation Complex*. Cambridge: Cambridge University Press.

Custer, Jay F. 1984. *Delaware Prehistoric Archaeology: An Ecological Approach*. Newark: University of Delaware Press.

———. 1986. "Late Woodland Cultural Diversity in the Middle Atlantic: An Evolutionary Perspective." In *Late Woodland Cultures of the Middle Atlantic Region* edited by Jay F. Custer, 143–168. Newark: University of Delaware Press.

———. 1994. "Current Archaeological Research in the Middle Atlantic Region of the Eastern United States." *Journal of Archaeological Research* 2 (4): 329–360.

D'Altroy, Terrance, and Timothy K. Earle. 1985. "Staple Finance, Wealth Finance and Storage in the Inca Political Economy." *Current Anthropology* 26 (2): 187–206.

Danaher, Kevin, ed. 2001. *Democratizing the Global Economy: The Battle against the World Bank and the IMF*. Monroe, ME: Common Courage Press.

Davidson, Thomas E. 1993. "Relations between Powhatan and the Eastern Shore." In Rountree 1993a, 136–153.

Davis, James T. 1974. *Trade Routes and Economic Exchange among the Indians of California*. Ramona, CA: Ballena Press.

Davis, Mike. 1990. *City of Quartz*. New York: Verso.

———. 2003. *Late Victorian Holocausts: El Niño Famines and the Making of the Third World.* London: Verso.

———. 2005. *The Monster at Our Door: The Global Threat of Avian Flu*. New York: New Press.

———. 2006. *Planet of Slums*. London: Verso.

Davis, Ralph. 1973. *The Rise of the Atlantic Economies*. Ithaca, NY: Cornell University Press.

de Hatch, Marion Popenoe. 1997. Kaminaljuyú/San Jorge : evidencia arqueológica de la actividad económica en el Valle de Guatemala, 300 a.C. a 300 d.C . Guatemala : Universidad del Valle de Guatemala.

Dehio, Ludwig. 1962. *The Precarious Balance*. New York: Vintage.

della Porta, Donatella, Massimiliano Andretta, Lorenzo Mosca, and Herbert Reiter. 2006. *Globalization from Below: Transnational Activists and Protest Networks*. Minneapolis: University of Minnesota Press.

De Ste. Croix, G.E.M. 1972. *The Origins of the Peloponnesian War*. Ithaca, NY: Cornell University Press.
———. 1981. *The Class Struggle in the Ancient Greek World*. London: Duckworth.
de Waal, Frans. 1982. *Chimpanzee Politics: Power and Sex among Apes*. New York: Harper & Row.
Diakonoff, Igor M. 1954. "The Sale of Land in Pre-Sargonic Sumer." Paper presented by the Soviet delegation at the Twenty-Third International Congress of Orientalists, Assyriology Section. Moscow: USSR Academy of Sciences.
———. 1969. "Main Features of the Economy in the Monarchies of Ancient Western Asia." *École Practique des Hautes Études—Sorbonne, Congrès at Colloques* 10 (3): 13–32.
———. 1973. "The Rise of the Despotic State in Ancient Mesopotamia." In *Ancient Mesopotamia*, edited by I. M. Diakonoff, translated by G. M. Sergheyev, 173–203. Walluf bei Weisbaden: Dr. Martin Sandig.
———. 1974. *Structure of Society and State in Early Dynastic Sumer*. Monographs on the Ancient Near East 1, 3. Los Angeles: Udena Publications.
———. 1982. "The Structure of Near Eastern Society before the Middle of the 2nd Millennium B.C." *Oikumene* 3:7–100, Publishing House of the Hungarian Academy of Sciences.
———. 1991. "Early Despotisms in Mesopotamia." In *Early Antiquity*, volume editor I. M. Diakonoff, project editor Philip L. Kohl, translator Alexander Kirjanov, 85–97. Chicago: University of Chicago Press.
Diamond, Jared. 1997. *Guns, Germs and Steel: The Fates of Human Societies*. New York: Norton.
———. 2005. *Collapse*. New York: Viking.
Dincauze, Dena F., and Robert J. Hasenstab. 1989. "Explaining the Iroquois: Tribalization on Prehistoric Periphery." In *Centre and Periphery: Comparative Studies in Archaeology*, edited by Timothy C. Champion, 67–87. London: Unwin Hyman.
Di Peso, Charles. 1974. *The Gran Chichimeca: Casas Grandes and the People of the Southwest*. South Norwalk, CT: Reading Laboratory.
Dragoo, Don W. 1963. *Mounds for the Dead: An Analysis of the Adena Culture*. Pittsburgh: Annals of the Carnegie Museum Vol. 37.
Drennan, Robert D. 1984. "Long-Distance Transport Costs in Pre-Hispanic Mesoamerica." *American Anthropologist* 86 (1): 105–112.
DuBois, Cora. 1935. *Wintu Ethnography*. University of California Publications in American Archaeology and Ethnology 36 (1): 1–148. Berkeley: University of California Press.
Dunaway, Wilma. 1994. "The Southern Fur Trade and the Incorporation of Southern Appalachia into the World-Economy, 1690–1763." *Review* 18 (2): 215–242.
———. 1996. *The First American Frontier: Transition to Capitalism in Southern Appalachia, 1700–1860*. Chapel Hill: University of North Carolina Press.
Dunbar, Robin. 1996. *Grooming, Gossip and the Evolution of Language*. Cambridge, MA: Harvard University Press.
Durkheim, Emile. 1915. *The Elementary Forms of the Religious Life, a Study in Religious Sociology*. Translated by Joseph Ward Swain. New York: Macmillan.
Dyson, Stephen L. 1985. *The Creation of the Roman Frontier*. Princeton, NJ: Princeton University Press.
Earle, Timothy. 1977. "A Reappraisal of Redistribution: Complex Hawaiian Chiefdoms." In *Exchange Systems in Prehistory*, edited by T. Earle and J. Ericson, 213–229. New York: Academic Press.
———. 1991. "The Evolution of Chiefdoms." In *Chiefdoms: Power, Economy and Ideology*, edited by T. Earle, 1–15. Cambridge: Cambridge University Press.
———. 2002. *Bronze Age Economics*. Boulder, CO: Westview Press.
Edens, Christopher. 1992. "Dynamics of Trade in the Ancient Mesopotamian 'World System.' " *American Anthropologist* 94 (1): 118–139.
Egloff, Keith, and Deborah Woodward. 1992. *First People: The Early Indians of Virginia*. Charlottesville: University of Virginia Press.
Eisenstadt, S. N. 1963. *The Decline of Empires*. Englewood Cliffs, NJ: Prentice Hall.
———. 1969. *The Political Systems of Empires*. New York: Free Press.
Eitzen, Stanley, and Maxine Baca Zinn. 1995. *In Conflict and Order.* Boston: Allyn and Bacon.
Ekholm, Kasja, and Jonathan Friedman. 1980. "Toward a Global Anthropology." In *History and Underdevelopment*, edited by L. Blusse, H. L. Wesseling, and G. D. Winius, 61–76. Leiden, The Netherlands: Leiden Centre for the History of European Expansion.
———. 1982. " 'Capital' Imperialism and Exploitation in the Ancient World-Systems." *Review* 6 (1): 87–110. Originally published in *History and Underdevelopment*, ed. L. Blusse, H. L. Wesseling and G. D. Winius (Leiden, The Netherlands: Leiden Centre for the History of European Expansion, 1980), 61–76.
Ekholm-Friedman, Kasja. 2005. "Structure, Dynamics and the Final Collapse of Bronze Age Civilizations in the Second Millennium B.C." In *Hegemonic Declines*, edited by Jonathan Friedman and C. Chase-Dunn, 51–88. Boulder, CO: Paradigm Publishers.

Elvin, Mark. 1973. *The Pattern of the Chinese Past*. Stanford, CA: Stanford University Press.
Engels, Friedrich. 1953. *The Part Played by Labour in the Transition from Ape to Man*. Moscow: Foreign Language Pub. House.
Enriquez, Laura J. 2009. *Reacting to the Market: Small Farmers in the Economic Reshaping of Nicaragua, Cuba, Russia and China*. University Park: Pennsylvania State University Press.
Ericson, Jonathan E. 1977. "Egalitarian Exchange Systems in California: A Preliminary View." In *Exchange Systems in Prehistory*, edited by Timothy K. Earle and Jonathon E. Ericson, 109–126. New York: Academic Press.
Ericson, Jonathan, and Timothy Baugh, eds. 1993. *The American Southwest and Mesoamerica: Systems of Prehistoric Change*. New York: Plenum.
Ermolaeva, Elena. 1997. "Chiefdom to State: Cultural Resistance in the Ancient Hawaiian World-System." PhD diss. Department of Sociology, Johns Hopkins University.
Evans, Martin M. 1999. *The Boer War: South Africa 1899–1902*. Oxford, UK: Osprey.
Evans, Peter. 1995. *Embedded Autonomy: States and Industrial Transformation*. Princeton, NJ: Princeton University Press.
Fagan, Brian M. 1991. *Ancient North America*. London: Thames and Hudson.
———. 2003. *Before California*. Lanham, MD: Rowman and Littlefield.
Falkenstein, Adam. 1974. *The Sumerian Temple City*. Monographs on the Ancient Near East 1. Los Angeles: Udena Publications.
Feinman, Gary M., and Joyce Marcus, eds. 1998. *Archaic States*. Santa Fe, NM: School of American Research Press.
Feinman, Gary M., and Linda M. Nicholas. 1991a. "The Monte Albán State: A Diachronic Perspective on an Ancient Core and Its Periphery." In *Core/Periphery Relations in Precapitalist Worlds*, edited by Christopher Chase-Dunn and Thomas D. Hall, 240–276. Boulder, CO: Westview Press.
———. 1991b. "New Perspectives on Prehispanic Highland Mesoamerica: A Macroregional Approach." *Comparative Civilizations Review* 24 (Spring): 13–33.
———. 1992. "Pre-Hispanic Interregional Interaction in Southern Mexico: The Valley of Oaxaca and the Ejutla Valley." In *Resources, Power, and Interregional Interaction*, edited by Edward Schortman and Patricia Urban, 75–116. New York: Plenum Press.
———. 1996. "The Changing Structure of Macroregional Mesoamerica." *Journal of World-Systems Research* 2: x.
Ferguson, R. Brian, and Neil L. Whitehead, eds. 1992. *War in the Tribal Zone: Expanding States and Indigenous Warfare*. Santa Fe, NM: School of American Research Press.
Finley, Moses. 1973. *The Ancient Economy*. Berkeley: University of California Press.
Fisher, William F., and Thomas Ponniah, eds. 2003. *Another World Is Possible: Popular Alternatives to Globalization at the World Social Forum*. London: Zed Books.
Fitzpatrick, John. 1992. "The Middle Kingdom, the Middle Sea and the Geographical Pivot of History" *Review* 15 (3): 477–522.
Flannery, Kent V. 1971. "Archaeological Systems Theory and Early Mesoamerica." In *Prehistoric Agriculture*, edited by Stuart Struever, 80–100. Garden City, NY: Natural History Press.
———. 1999a. "Process and Agency in Early State Formation." *Cambridge Archaeological Journal* 9 (1): 3–21.
———. 1999b. "The Ground Plans of Archaic States." In *Archaic States*, edited by G. Feinman and J. Marcus, 15–57. Santa Fe, NM: School of American Research.
Flavell, John. 1963. *The Developmental Psychology of Jean Piaget*. Princeton, NJ: Nostrand Company.
Fletcher, Jesse B., Jakob Apkarian, Robert A. Hanneman, Hiroko Inoue, Kirk Lawrence, and Christopher Chase-Dunn. 2011. "Demographic Regulators in Small-Scale World-Systems." *Structure and Dynamics* 5, 1. http://escholarship.org/uc/item/6kb1k3zk.
Florini, Ann. 2005. *The Coming Democracy: New Rules for Running a New World Order*. Washington, DC: Brookings.
Flynn, Dennis O. 1996. *World Silver and Monetary History in the 16th and 17th Centuries*. Brookfield, VT: Variorum.
Foner, Eric. 1970. *Free Soil, Free Labor, Free Men: The Ideology of the Republican Party before the Civil War*. New York: Oxford University Press.
Foner, Philip. 1946. *Business and Slavery: The New York Merchants and Irrepressible Conflict*. Chapel Hill: University of North Carolina Press.
———. 1975 [1947]. *History of the Labor Movement in the United States*, Vol. 1. New York: International Publishers.
Foran, John. 1993. *Fragile Resistance: Social Transformation in Iran from 1500 to the Revolution*. Boulder, CO: Westview Press.
Ford, T. L. 1976. "Adena Sites on the Chesapeake Bay." *Archaeology of Eastern North America* 4:63–89.
Fornander, Abraham. 1880. *An Account of the Polynesian Race*. Vol. 2. London: Trubner.

Forsythe, Dall W. 1977. *Taxation and Political Change in the Young Nation, 1781–1833*. New York: Columbia University Press.

Forte, Angelo, Richard Oram, and Frederik Pedersen. 2005. *Viking Empires*. Cambridge: Cambridge University Press.

Foster, John Bellamy. 1994. *The Vulnerable Planet*. New York: Monthly Review Press.

———. 2000. *Marx's Ecology: Materialism and Nature*. New York: Monthly Review Press.

Fox, Edward W. 1971. *History in Geographic Perspective: The Other France*. New York: Norton.

———. 1991. *The Emergence of the Modern European World*. Oxford: Basil Blackwell.

Frank, Andre Gunder. 1966. "The Development of Underdevelopment." *Monthly Review* September: 17–31.

———. 1969. *Latin America: Underdevelopment or Revolution?* New York: Monthly Review Press.

———. 1978. *World Accumulation, 1492–1789*. New York: Monthly Review Press.

———. 1979a. *Dependent Accumulation and Underdevelopment*. New York: Monthly Review Press.

———. 1979b. *Mexican Agriculture 1521–1630: Transformation of the Mode of Production*. Cambridge: Cambridge University Press.

———. 1990. "The Thirteenth Century World System: A Review Essay." *Journal of World History* 1:249–256.

———. 1992. *The Centrality of Central Asia*. Comparative Asian Studies No. 8. Amsterdam: VU University Press for Center for Asian Studies Amsterdam (CASA).

———. 1993a. "Transitional Ideological Modes." In *The World System: Five Hundred Years or Five Thousand?*, edited by Andre Gunder Frank and Barry K. Gills, 200–220. London: Routledge.

———. 1993b. "The Bronze Age World System and Its Cycles." *Current Anthropology* 34 (4): 383–413.

———. 1997. *Reorient*. Berkeley: University of California Press.

———. 1998. *Reorient: Global Economy in the Asian Age*. Berkeley: University of California Press.

Frank, Andre Gunder, and Barry K. Gills, eds. 1993. *The World System: Five Hundred Years or Five Thousand?* London: Routledge.

———. 1995. "The Modern World-System Revisited: Re-reading Braudel and Wallerstein." In *Civilizations and World-Systems: Two Approaches to the Study of World-Historical Change*, edited by Stephen K. Sanderson, 163–194. Walnut Creek, CA: Altamira Press.

Frankenstein, Susan. 1979. "The Phoenicians in the Far West: A Function of Neo-Assyrian Imperialism." In *Power and Propaganda: A Symposium on Ancient Empires*, edited by Mogens T. Larsen, 263–294. Copenhagen: Akademisk Forlag.

Frankenstein, Susan, and Michael J. Rowlands. 1978. "The Internal Structure and Regional Context of Early Iron Age Society in South-Western Germany." *Institute of Archaeology Bulletin* 15:73–112.

Freehling, William W. 1968. *Prelude to War: The Nullification Controversy in South Carolina, 1816–1836*. New York: Harper and Row.

Fried, Morton. 1952. "Land Tenure, Geography and Ecology in the Contact of Cultures." *American Journal of Economics and Sociology* 11 (4): 391–412.

———. 1967. *The Evolution of Political Society: An Essay in Political Anthropology*. New York: Random House.

———. 1975. *The Notion of Tribe*. Menlo Park, CA: Cummings.

Friedman, Jonathan. 1982. "Catastrophe and Continuity in Social Evolution." In *Theory and Explanation in Archaeology: The Southampton Conference*, edited by Colin Renfrew, Michael J. Rowlands, and Barbara Abbott Segraves, 175–196. New York: Academic Press.

———. 1983. "Civilizational Cycles and the History of Primitivism." *Social Analysis: Journal of Cultural and Social Practice* 14 (December): 31–52.

———. 1992a. "General Historical and Culturally Specific Properties of Global Systems." *Review* 15 (3): 335–372.

———. 1992b. "Narcissism, Roots and Postmodernity: The Constitution of Selfhood in the Global Crisis." In *Modernity and Identity*, edited by Scott Lash and Jonathan Friedman, 331–366. Cambridge, MA: Blackwell.

———. 1994. *Cultural Identity and Global Process*. London: Sage.

———. 1998. *System, Structure and Contradiction: The Evolution of Asiatic Social Formations*. Walnut Creek, CA: Altamira Press.

Friedman, Jonathan, and C. Chase-Dunn. 2005. *Hegemonic Declines: Present and Past*. Boulder, CO: Paradigm Publishers.

Friedman, Jonathan, and Michael Rowlands. 1977. "Notes towards an Epigenetic Model of the Evolution of 'Civilization.' " In *The Evolution of Social Systems*, edited by J. Friedman and M. J. Rowlands, 201–278. London: Duckworth. Also published in same title and pages, University of Pittsburgh Press, Pittsburgh, 1978.

Friedman, Thomas L. 2005. *The World Is Flat*. New York: Farrar, Straus and Giroux.

Frymer-Kensky, T. 1992. *In the Wake of the Goddesses*. New York: Free Press.

Fukuyama, Francis. 1992. *The End of History and the Last Man*. New York: Free Press.

Gailey, Christine W. 1987. *Kinship to Kingship: Gender Hierarchy and State Formation in the Tongan Islands*. Austin: University of Texas Press.

Gailey, Christine W., and Thomas C. Patterson. 1987. "Power Relations and State Formation." In *Power Relations and State Formation*, edited by Christine W. Gailey and Thomas C. Patterson, 1–26. Washington, DC: American Anthropological Association.

Gallup, Gordon. 1970. "Chimpanzees: Self-Recognition." *Science*, January 2, 86–87.

Galtung, Johann. 1971. "A Structural Theory of Imperialism." *Journal of Peace Research* 8:81–117.

Gaulin, Steven, and Donald Mc Burney. 2001. *Psychology.* Upper Saddle River, NJ: Prentice Hall.

Gellner, Ernest. 1988. *Plough, Sword and Book*. 5th ed. Chicago: University of Chicago Press.

Genovese, Eugene D. 1965. *The Political Economy of Slavery*. New York: Random House.

———. 1969. *The World the Slaveholders Made*. New York: Random House.

———. 1976. *Roll, Jordan, Roll*. New York: Vintage.

Gereffi, Gary, and Miguel Korzeniewicz, eds. 1994. *Commodity Chains and Global Capitalism*. Westport, CT: Praeger.

Gershenkron, Alexander. 1962. *Economic Backwardness in Historical Perspective*. Cambridge, MA: Harvard University Press.

Gill, Stephen. 2000. "Toward a Post-Modern Prince? The Battle of Seattle as a Moment in the New Politics of Globalization." *Millennium* 29 (1): 131–140.

———. 2003. *Power and Resistance in the New World Order*. New York: Palgrave Macmillan.

Gills, Barry K., and Andre Gunder Frank. 1991. "5000 Years of World System History: The Cumulation of Accumulation." In *Core/Periphery Relations in Precapitalist Worlds*, edited by Christopher Chase-Dunn and Thomas D. Hall, 67–112. Boulder, CO: Westview Press.

———. 1992. "World System Cycles, Crises, and Hegemonial Shifts, 1700 BC to 1700 AD." *Review* 15 (4): 621–687.

Glenn, Evelyn Nakano. 2002. *Unequal Freedom: How Race and Gender Shaped American Citizenship and Labor.* Cambridge, MA: Harvard University Press.

Go, Julian. 2008. "Global Fields and Imperial Forms: Field Theory and the British and American Empires." *Sociological Theory* 26 (3): 201–229.

———. 2011. *Patterns of Empire: The British and American Empires, 1688 to the Present.* Cambridge: Cambridge University Press.

Godelier, Maurice. 1977. "Economy and Religion: An Evolutionary Optical Illusion." In *The Evolution of Social Systems*, edited by J. Friedman and M. J. Rowlands, 3–12. London: Duckworth.

Goffman, Erving. 1963. *Behavior in Public Places.* New York: Free Press.

Goldfrank, Walter L. 1977. "Who Rules the World? Class Formation at the International Level." *Quarterly Journal of Ideology* 1 (2): 32–37.

———. 1978. "Fascism and World-Economy." In *Social Change in the Capitalist World Economy*, edited by Barbara H. Kaplan, 75–120. Beverly Hills, CA: Sage.

———. 1981. "Silk and Steel: Italy and Japan between the Two World Wars." *Comparative Social Research* 4:297–315.

———. 2000. "Paradigm Regained? The Rules of Wallerstein's World-System Method." *Journal of World-System Research* 11, 2.

Goldstein, Joshua. 1988. *Long Cycles: Prosperity and War in the Modern Age*. New Haven, CT: Yale University Press.

Goldstone, Jack. 1991. *Revolution and Rebellion in the Early Modern World.* Berkeley: University of California Press.

Goody, Jack. 1977. *The Domestication of the Savage Mind.* London: Cambridge University Press.

———. 1986. *The Logic of Writing and the Organization of Society.* Cambridge: Cambridge University Press.

———. 1987. *The Interface between the Written and the Oral.* Cambridge: Cambridge University Press.

Gottmann, Jean, ed. 1980. *Centre and Periphery: Spatial Variation in Politics*. Beverly Hills, CA: Sage.

Gowan, Peter. 1999. *The Global Gamble*. London: Verso.

Gramsci, Antonio. 1971. *Selections from the Prison Notebooks.* Edited and translated by Quentin Hoare and Geoffrey Nowell Smith. New York: International Publishers.

———. 1972. *The Modern Prince and Other Writings*. New York: International Publishers.

Gregg, Susan A. 1988. *Foragers and Farmers: Population Interaction and Agricultural Expansion in Prehistoric Europe*. Chicago: University of Chicago Press.

———, ed. 1991. "Between Bands and States." Occasional Paper no. 9, Center for Archaeological Investigations, Southern Illinois University, Carbondale, IL.

Gurevich, Aaron. 1992. *Historical Anthropology of the Middle Ages.* Edited by Jana Howlett. Chicago: University of Chicago Press.

———. 1995. *The Origins of European Individualism.* Cambridge, MA: Blackwell.

Haas, Peter. 1992. "Introduction: Epistemic Communities and International Policy Coordination." *International Organization* 46 (1).
Hacking, Ian. 1975. *The Emergence of Probability.* Cambridge: Cambridge University Press.
Hall, Thomas D. 1989. *Social Change in the Southwest, 1350–1880.* Lawrence: University of Kansas Press.
———. 1991. "The Role of Nomads in Core/Periphery Relations." In *Core/Periphery Relations in Precapitalist Worlds*, edited by C. Chase-Dunn and T. D. Hall, 212–239. Boulder, CO: Westview Press.
———, ed. 2000. *The World-Systems Reader.* Lanham, MD: Rowman and Littlefield.
Hall, Thomas D., and Christopher Chase-Dunn. 1993. "The World-Systems Perspective and Archaeology: Forward into the Past." *Journal of Archaeological Research* 1 (2): 121–143.
———. 1996. "Comparing World-Systems: Concepts and Hypotheses." In *PreColumbian World-Systems*, edited by Peter N. Peregrine and Gary M. Feinman, 13–28. Monographs in World Archaeology, No. 26. Madison, WI: Prehistory Press.
Hall, Thomas D., and James V. Fenelon. 2009. *Indigenous Peoples and Globalization.* Boulder, CO: Paradigm Press.
Hallpike, C. R. 1979. *Foundations of Primitive Thought.* Oxford: Clarendon Press.
———. 1988. *The Principles of Social Evolution.* Oxford: Clarendon Press.
———. 2008. *How We Got Here.* Central Milton Keynes, UK: AuthorHouse.
Hantman, Jeffrey L. 1990. "Between Powhatan and Quirank: Reconstructing Monacan Culture and History in the Context of Jamestown." *American Anthropologist* 92 (3): 676–690.
———. 1993. "Powhatan's Relations with the Piedmont Monacans." In Rountree 1993a, 94–111.
Hardt, Michael, and Antonio Negri. 2004. *Multitude: War and Democracy in the Age of Empire.* New York: Penguin Press.
Harris, Marvin. 1977. *Cannibals and Kings: The Origins of Cultures.* New York: Random House.
———. 1979. *Cultural Materialism: The Struggle for a Science of Culture.* New York: Random House.
———. 1987. *Death, Sex and Fertility: Population Regulation in Preindustrial Societies.* New York: Columbia University Press.
———. 1988. *Culture, People, Nature.* 5th ed. Boston: Addison-Wesley.
Hartwell, Robert M. 1966. "Markets, Technology and the Structure of Enterprise in the Development of the Eleventh-Century Chinese Iron and Steel Industry." *Journal of Economic History* 26 (1): 29–58.
———. 1971. "Financial Expertise, Examinations and the Formulation of Economic Policy in Northern Sung China." *Journal of Asian Studies* 30 (3): 281–314.
Harvey, David. 1999. *The Limits of Capital.* London: Verso.
———. 2003. *The New Imperialism.* New York: Oxford University Press.
———. 2005. *A Brief History of Neoliberalism.* New York: Oxford University Press.
Hassig, Ross. 1985. *Trade, Tribute and Transportation: The Sixteenth-Century Political Economy of the Valley of Mexico.* Norman: University of Oklahoma Press.
———. 1988. *Aztec Warfare: Imperial Expansion and Political Control.* Norman: University of Oklahoma Press.
———. 1992. "Aztec and Spanish Conquest in Mesoamerica." In *War in the Tribal Zone: Expanding States and Indigenous Warfare*, edited by R. Brian Ferguson and Neil Whitehead, 83–102. Santa Fe, NM: School of American Research Press.
Haupt, Georges. 1972. *Socialism and the Great War: The Collapse of the Second International.* London: Oxford University Press.
Hauser, Marc. 2000. *Wild Minds.* New York: Henry Holt.
Havelock, Eric. 1963. *Preface to Plato.* Cambridge, MA: Belknap Press of Harvard University Press.
———. 1971. *The Greek Concept of Justice.* Cambridge, MA: Harvard University Press.
Hayden, Brian. 1981. "Research and Development in the Stone Age: Technological Transitions among Hunter-Gatherers." *Current Anthropology* 22 (5): 519–548.
Hayden, Tom. 2006. *Radical Nomad: C. Wright Mills and His Times.* Boulder, CO: Paradigm Publishers.
Heinberg, Richard. 2004. *Powerdown.* Gabriola Island, BC: Island Press.
Helms, Mary W. 1988. *Ulysses' Sail: An Ethnographic Odyssey of Power, Knowledge, and Geographical Distance.* Princeton, NJ: Princeton University Press.
———. 1992. "Long-Distance Contacts, Elite Aspirations, and the Age of Discovery in Cosmological Context." In *Resources, Power, and Interregional Interaction*, edited by Edward Schortman and Patricia Urban, 157–174. New York: Plenum Press.
Henige, David P. 1970. *Colonial Governors from the Fifteenth Century to the Present.* Madison: University of Wisconsin Press.

Henry, Donald O. 1985. "Preagricultural Sedentism: The Natufian Example." In *Prehistoric Hunter-Gatherers: The Emergence of Cultural Complexity*, edited by T. Douglas Price and James A. Brown, 365–384. New York: Academic Press.

Henwood, Doug. 1997. *Wall Street*. New York: Verso.

Herm, Gerhard. 1975. *The Phoenicians*. Translated by Carolina Hillier. New York: Morrow and Co.

Hewitt, John. 1991. *Self and Society*. 5th ed. Boston: Allyn and Bacon.

Hinsley, F. H. 1967. *Power and the Pursuit of Peace*. Cambridge: Cambridge University Press.

Hobsbawm, Eric J. 1969. *Industry and Empire: An Economic History of Britain since 1750*. London: Weidenfeld and Nicolson.

———. 1994. *The Age of Extremes: A History of the World, 1914–1991*. New York: Pantheon.

Hobson, J. A. 1988 [1902]. *Imperialism: A Study*. London: Unwin Hyman.

Hobson, John M. 2004. *The Eastern Origins of Western Civilization*. Cambridge: Cambridge University Press.

Hochschild, Adam. 1998. *King Leopold's Ghost*. New York: Houghton Mifflin.

Hodgson, Marshall G. S. 1974. *The Classical Age of Islam*. Vol. 1 of *The Venture of Islam: Conscience and History in a World Civilization*. Chicago: University of Chicago Press.

Hopkins, Keith. 1978. *Conquerors and Slaves*. Cambridge: Cambridge University Press.

Hopkins, Terence K. 1957. "Sociology and the Substantive View of the Economy." In *Trade and Market in the Early Empires*, edited by Karl Polanyi, Conrad M. Arensberg, and Harry W. Pearson, 270–306. Chicago: Regnery.

Hopkirk, Peter. 1994. *The Great Game: The Struggle for Empire in Central Asia*. New York: Kodansha International.

Hopper, Robert J. 1979. *Trade and Industry in Classical Greece*. London: Thames and Hudson.

Hornborg, Alf, and Carol L. Crumley, eds. 2007. *The World System and the Earth System*. Walnut Creek, CA: Left Coast Press.

Hoyos, Dexter. 2003. *Hannibal's Dynasty: Power and Politics in the Western Mediterranean, 247–183 B.C.* London: Routledge.

Hsu, Cho-yun. 1968. *Ancient China in Transition*. Palo Alto, CA: Stanford University Press.

Huber, Joan. 2007. *On the Origins of Gender Inequality*. Boulder, CO: Paradigm Publishers.

Hudson, Michael. 2003. *Super Imperialism: The Origins and Fundamentals of U.S. World Dominance*. 2nd ed. London: Pluto.

Hughes, Richard E. 1986. *Diachronic Variability in Obsidian Procurement Patterns in Northeastern California and Southcentral Oregon*. University of California Publications in Anthropology, Volume 17. Berkeley: University of California Press.

———, ed. 1989. *Current Directions in California Obsidian Studies*. Contributions of the University of California Archaeological Research Facility, No. 48 (December). Department of Anthropology, University of California, Berkeley.

———. 1994. "Mosaic Patterning in Prehistoric California-Great Basin Exchange." In Baugh and Ericson 1994, 363–384.

Hugill, Peter J. 1999. *Global Communications since 1844: Geopolitics and Technology*. Baltimore: Johns Hopkins University Press.

Hui, Victoria Tin-bor. 2005. *War and State Formation in Ancient China and Early Modern Europe*. Cambridge: Cambridge University Press.

Hung, Ho-Fung. 2005. "Rise and Demise of the Qing Empire: Neo-Confucianist State, Class Conflict and Arrested Transition to Capitalism in Early Modern China." Paper presented at the annual meetings of the American Sociological Association, Philadelphia, PA, August 15.

Innis, Harold A. 1972. *Empire and Communications*. Toronto: University of Toronto Press.

Inoue, Hiroko, Alexis Álvarez, Kirk Lawrence, Anthony Roberts, Eugene N. Anderson, and Christopher Chase-Dunn. 2012. "Polity Scale Shifts in World-Systems since the Bronze Age: A Comparative Inventory of Upsweeps and Collapses." *International Journal of Comparative Sociology* 53 (3): 210–229.

Jackson, Thomas L. 1986. "Late Prehistoric Obsidian Exchange in Central California." PhD diss., Anthropology, Stanford University.

———. 1989. "Reconstructing Migration in California Prehistory." *American Indian Quarterly* 13 (4): 359–368.

———. 1992. "Defining Small-Scale World Systems in California Prehistory." Paper presented at the annual meeting of the Society for American Archaeology, Pittsburgh, PA, April 8–12.

Jennings, Justin. 2010. *Globalizations and the Ancient World*. Cambridge: Cambridge University Press.

Johnson, Allan. 2001. *Privilege, Power and Difference*. Mountain View, CA: Mayfield Publishing Company.

Johnson, Allen W., and Timothy Earle. 1987. *The Evolution of Human Societies: From Foraging Group to Agrarian State*. Stanford, CA: Stanford University Press.

Johnson, Chalmers A. 2006. *Nemesis: The Last Days of the American Republic.* New York: Metropolitan Books.

———. 2010. *Dismantling the Empire: America's Last Best Hope*. New York: Metropolitan Books.

Jones, Gareth Stedman. 1971. *Outcaste London: A Study in the Relationship between Classes in Victorial Society.* Oxford: Clarendon.

Jorgenson, Andrew K. 2004. "Uneven Processes and Environmental Degradation in the World-Economy." *Human Ecology Review* 11:103–117.

Jorgenson, Andrew K., and Edward Kick, eds. 2006. *Globalization and the Environment*. Leiden, The Netherlands: Brill.

Jowett, Garth, and James Linton. 1989. *Movies as Mass Communication.* Newbury Park, CA: Sage.

Kaldor, Mary. 2003. *Global Civil Society: An Answer to War*. Cambridge, MA: Polity Press.

Kasaba, Resat. 1988. *The Ottoman Empire and the World Economy.* Albany: State University of New York Press.

Kavanagh, Maureen. 1982. *Archaeological Resources of the Monocacy River Region*. Maryland Geological Survey, Division of Archaeology, File Report No. 164.

Kea, Raymond. 2004. "Expansion and Contractions: World Historical Change and the Western Sudan World-System, 1200/1000 BC–1200/1250 AD." *Journal of World-Systems Research* 10 (3): 723–816.

Keck, Margaret, and Katherine Sikkink. 1998. *Activists beyond Borders: Advocacy Networks in International Politics*. Ithaca, NY: Cornell University Press.

Keenan, Julian. 2003. *The Face in the Mirror.* New York: HarperCollins.

Kelly, Raymond C. 1985. *The Nuer Conquest: The Structure and Development of an Expansionist System*. Ann Arbor: University of Michigan Press.

Kelly, Robert L. 1995. *The Foraging Spectrum: Diversity in Hunter-Gatherer Lifeways.* Washington, DC: Smithsonian.

Kemper, Theodore. 1990. *Social Structure and Testosterone*. New Brunswick, NJ: Rutgers University Press.

Kennedy, Paul. 1988. *The Rise and Fall of the Great Powers: Economic Change and Military Conflict from 1500–2000*. New York: Random House.

Kenoyer, Jonathan M. 1998. *Ancient Cities of the Indus Valley Civilization*. Karachi, Pakistan: Oxford University Press.

Kentor, Jeffrey. 2000. *Capital and Coercion: The Role of Economic and Military Power in the World-Economy 1800–1990*. New York: Garland.

Kentor, Jeffrey, and Terry Boswell. 2003. "Foreign Capital Dependence and Development: A New Direction." *American Sociological Review* 68:301–313.

Kepecs, Susan, and R. T. Alexander, eds. 2005. *The Postclassic to Spanish-Era Transition in Mesoamerica: Archaeological Perspectives*. Albuquerque: University of New Mexico Press.

Kepecs, Susan, Gary Feinman, and Sylviane Boucher. 1994. "Chichen Itza and Its Hinterland: A World-Systems Perspective." *Ancient Mesoamerica* 4:141–158.

Kerr, Clark, and A. Siegel. 1954. "The Interindustry Propensity to Strike: And International Comparison." In *Industrial Conflict*, edited by A. W. Kornhauser et al., 189–212. New York: McGraw-Hill.

Keynes, John Maynard. 1936. *The General Theory of Employment, Interest and Money.* London: Macmillan.

Khaldun, Ibn. 1958. *The Muqaddimah: An Introduction to History*. Translated by Franz Rosenthal. New York: Pantheon Books.

King, Chester. 1978. "Protohistoric and Historic Archaeology." In *Handbook of North American Indians*, edited by Robert F. Heizer, 58–68. Vol. 8 of *California.* Washington, DC: Smithsonian.

Kirch, Patrick V. 1984. *The Evolution of Polynesian Chiefdoms*. Cambridge: Cambridge University Press.

———. 1985. *Feathered Gods and Fishhooks: An Introduction to Hawaiian Archaeology and Prehistory.* Honolulu: University of Hawaii Press.

———. 1991. "Chiefship and Competitive Involution: The Marquesas Islands of Eastern Polynesia." In *Chiefdoms: Power, Economy and Ideology*, edited by Timothy Earle, 119–145. Cambridge: Cambridge University Press.

———. 2010. *How Chiefs Became Kings: Divine Kingship and the Rise of Archaic States in Ancient Hawaii*. Berkeley: University of California Press.

Klein, Naomi. 2007. *The Shock Doctrine: The Rise of Disaster Capitalism*. New York: Henry Holt and Company.

Klein, Richard G., with Blake Edgar. 2002. *The Dawn of Human Culture*. New York: John Wiley and Sons.

Knight, Chris. 1990. *Blood Relations*. New Haven, CT: Yale University Press.

Kohl, Phillip L. 1979. "The 'World Economy' in West Asia in the Third Millennium B.C." In *South Asian Archaeology 1977*, edited by M. Toddei, 55–85. Naples, Italy: Instituto Universitario Orientale.

———. 1987a. "The Use and Abuse of World Systems Theory: The Case of the 'Pristine' West Asian State." *Archaeological Advances in Method and Theory* 11:1–35.

———. 1987b. "The Ancient Economy, Transferable Technologies and the Bronze Age World-System: A View from the Northeastern Frontier of the Ancient Near East." In *Centre and Periphery in the Ancient World*, edited by Michael Rowlands, Mogens Larsen, and Kristian Kristiansen, 13–24. Cambridge: Cambridge University Press.

———. 1992. "The Transcaucasian 'Periphery' in the Bronze Age: A Preliminary Formulation." In *Resources, Power, and Interregional Interaction*, edited by Edward Schortman and Patricia Urban, 117–137. New York: Plenum Press.

———. 2007. *The Making of Bronze Age Eurasia*. Cambridge: Cambridge University Press.

Kowalewski, Stephen A. 1982. "The Evolution of Primate Regional Systems." *Comparative Urban Research* 9 (1): 60–78.

———. 1990. "The Evolution of Complexity in the Valley of Oaxaca." *Annual Review of Anthropology* 19:39–58.

———. 1995. "Large Scale Ecology in Aboriginal Eastern North America." In *Native American Interactions: Multiscalar Analyses and Interpretations in the Eastern Woodlands*, edited by Michael S. Nassaney and Kenneth E. Sassaman, 147–173. Knoxville: University of Tennessee Press.

———. 1996. "Corn, Clout, Copper, Core—Periphery, Culture Area." In *PreColumbian World-Systems*, edited by Peter N. Peregrine and Gary M. Feinman, 29–39. Monographs in World Archaeology, No. 26. Madison, WI: Prehistory Press.

Krasner, Stephen D. 1976. "State Power and the Structure of International Trade." *World Politics* 28 (3): 317–347.

Kriedte, Peter, Hans Medick, and Jurgen Schlumbohm. 1981. *Industrialization before Industrialization: Rural Industry in the Genesis of Capitalism*. Cambridge: Cambridge University Press.

Kristiansen, Kristian. 1982. "The Formation of Tribal Systems in Later European Prehistory: Northern Europe 4000–5000 B.C." In *Theory and Explanation in Archaeology*, edited by Colin Renfrew, Michael Rowlands, and B. Segraves, 241–280. New York: Academic.

———. 1987. "Centre and Periphery in Bronze Age Scandinavia." In *Centre and Periphery in the Ancient World*, edited by Michael Rowlands, Mogens Larsen, and Kristian Kristiansen, 74–86. Cambridge: Cambridge University Press.

———. 1991. "Chiefdoms, States and Systems of Social Evolution." In *Chiefdoms: Power, Economy and Ideology*, edited by Timothy Earle, 16–43. Cambridge: Cambridge University Press.

———. 1998. *Europe before History*. Cambridge: Cambridge University Press.

Kroeber, Alfred L. 1976 [1925]. *Handbook of the Indians of California*. New York: Dover Publications.

Lacina, Bethany, and Nils Petter Gleditsch. 2005. "Monitoring Trends in Global Combat: A New Dataset of Battle Deaths." *European Journal of Population* 21 (2–3): 145–166. http://www.prio.no/page/Project_detail/News_details/9244/45656.html.

Lakatos, Imre. 1978. *The Methodology of Scientific Research Programmes*. Vol. 1. Edited by John Worrall and Gregory Currie. Cambridge: Cambridge University Press.

La Lone, Darrell E. 1982. "The Inca as a Non-market Economy: Supply on Command versus Supply and Demand." In *Contexts for Prehistoric Exchange*, edited by J. E. Ericson and T. K. Earle, 292–316. New York: Academic Press.

———. 1993. "World-Systems and Transformations of Production in the Inca Empire." In *The Economic Anthropology of the State*, edited by Elizabeth Brumfiel, 17–41. Monographs in Economic Anthropology, No. 11. Lanham, MD: University Press of America.

Lamberg-Karlovsky, C. C. 1975. "Third Millennium Modes of Exchange and Modes of Production." In *Ancient Civilization and Trade*, edited by J. A. Sabloff and C. C. Lamberg-Karlovsky, 341–368. Albuquerque: University of New Mexico Press.

Landes, David. 1969. *The Unbound Prometheus*. Cambridge: Cambridge University Press.

Lane, Frederic C. 1966. *Venice and History: The Collected Papers of Frederic C. Lane*. Baltimore: Johns Hopkins University Press.

———. 1973. *Venice: A Maritime Republic*. Baltimore: Johns Hopkins University Press.

———. 1979. *Profits from Power: Readings in Protection Rent and Violence-Controlling Enterprises*. Albany, NY: SUNY Press.

Larsen, Mogens Trolle. 1976. *The Old Assyrian City-State and Its Colonies*. Copenhagen: Akadmisk Forlag.

———. 1987. "Commercial Networks in the Ancient Near East." In *Centre and Periphery in the Ancient World*, edited by Michael Rowlands, Mogens Larsen, and Kristian Kristiansen, 47–56. Cambridge: Cambridge University Press.

Lattimore, Owen. 1940. *Inner Asian Frontiers of China*. New York: American Geographical Society.

———. 1962. *Studies in Frontier History: Collected Papers, 1928–58*. London: Oxford University Press.

———. 1980. "The Periphery as Locus of Innovations." In *Centre and Periphery: Spatial Variation in Politics*, edited by Jean Gottmann, 205–208. Beverly Hills, CA: Sage.

Le Goff, Jacques Ed. 1997. *The Medieval World*. Great Britain: Parkgage Book Ltd.

Lekson, Stephen H. 1999. *The Chaco Meridian: Centers of Political Power in the Ancient Southwest*. Walnut Creek, CA: Altamira Press.
Lenin, Vladimir I. 1973. *What Is to Be Done?* Peking: Foreign Languages Press.
Lenski, Gerhard. 1966. *Power and Privilege*. New York: McGraw-Hill.
———. 1984. *Power and Privilege*. Chapel Hill: University of North Carolina Press.
———. 2005. *Ecological-Evolutionary Theory*. Boulder, CO: Paradigm Publishers.
Lenski, Gerhard, and Jean Lenski. 1987. *Human Societies*. 5th ed. New York: McGraw-Hill.
Lenski, Gerhard, Jean Lenski, and Patrick Nolan. 1995. *Human Societies: An Introduction to Macrosociology*. 7th ed. New York: McGraw-Hill.
LePan, Don. 1989. *The Cognitive Revolution in Western Culture*. London: MacMillan.
Lerro, Bruce. 2000. *From Earth Spirits to Sky Gods*. Lanham, MD: Lexington Press.
———. 2005. *Power in Eden*. Victoria, BC: Trafford Press.
Levathes, Louise. 1994. *When China Ruled the Seas: The Treasure Fleet of the Dragon Throne, 1405–33*. New York: Simon and Schuster.
Linebaugh, Peter, and Marcus Rediker. 2000. *The Many-Headed Hydra: Sailors, Slaves, Commoners and the Hidden History of the Revolutionary Atlantic*. Boston: Beacon Press.
Lintz, Christopher. 1991. "Texas Panhandle-Pueblo Interactions from the Thirteenth through the Sixteenth Century." In *Farmers, Hunters, and Colonists: Interaction between the Southwest and the Southern Plains*, edited by Katherine A. Spielmann, 89–106. Tucson: University of Arizona Press.
Lipset, Seymour Martin. 1963. *The First New Nation: The United States in Historical and Comparative Perspective*. New York: Basic Books.
Liu, Li, and Xingcan Chen. 2003. *State Formation in Early China*. London: Duckworth.
Liverani, Mario. 1987. "The Collapse of the Near Eastern Regional System at the End of the Bronze Age: The Case of Syria." In *Centre and Periphery in the Ancient World*, edited by Michael Rowlands, Mogens Larsen, and Kristian Kristiansen, 66–73. Cambridge: Cambridge University Press.
Livy. 2006. *Hannibal's War: Books Twenty-One to Thirty*. Oxford: Oxford University Press.
Lofland, Lyn. 1973. *World of Strangers*. New York: Basic Books.
———. 1998. *The Public Realm*. Hawthorne, NY: Aldine De Gruyter.
Logan, Robert. 1986. *The Alphabet Effect*. New York: William Morrow.
———. 1995. *The Fifth Language*. Toronto, Ontario: Stoddart.
Longhofer, Wesley, and Evan Schofer. 2013. "Structural Adjustment and National Income Inequality." Working paper, Goizueta Business School, Emory University.
Luria, Alexander. 1976. *Cognitive Development*. Cambridge, MA: Harvard University Press.
Luttwak, Edward N. 1976. *The Grand Strategy of the Roman Empire: From the First Century A.D. to the Third*. Baltimore: Johns Hopkins University Press.
Luxemburg, Rosa. 1951. *The Accumulation of Capital*. New Haven, CT: Yale University Press.
Maddison, Angus. 1982. *Phases of Capitalist Development*. New York: Oxford University Press.
———. 1995. *Monitoring the World Economy, 1820–1992*. Paris: Organization for Economic Cooperation and Development.
———. 2001. *The World Economy: A Millennial Perspective*. Paris: Organization of Economic Cooperation and Development.
Mahoney, James. 2010. *Colonialism and Postcolonial Development: Spanish America in Comparative Perspective*. Cambridge: Cambridge University Press.
Malowist, Marian. 1966. "The Problem of Inequality of Economic Development in Europe in the Later Middle Ages." *Economic History Review*, 2nd series, 19 (1): 15–28.
Mann, Charles C. 2005. *1491: New Revelations of the Americas before Columbus*. New York: Alfred A. Knopf.
———. 2011. *1493: Discovering the New World Columbus Created*. New York: Alfred A. Knopf.
Mann, Michael. 1986. *A History of Power from the Beginning to A.D. 1760*. Vol. 1 of *The Sources of Social Power*. Cambridge: Cambridge University Press.
———. 1993. *The Rise of Classes and Nation-States, 1760–1914*. Vol. 2 of *The Sources of Social Power*. Cambridge: Cambridge University Press.
———. 2003. *Incoherent Empire*. London: Verso.
———. 2006. "The Recent Intensification of American Economic and Military Imperialism: Are They Connected?" Paper presented at the annual meeting of the American Sociological Association, Montreal, August 11.
Marcus, Joyce. 1998. "The Peaks and Valleys of the Ancient State." In *Archaic States*, edited by G. Feinman and J. Marcus, 59–94. Santa Fe, NM: School of American Research Press.

Marfoe, Leon. 1987. "Cedar Forest and Silver Mountain: Social Change and the Development of Long-Distance Trade in Early Near Eastern Societies." In *Centre and Periphery in the Ancient World*, edited by Michael Rowlands, Mogens Larsen, and Kristian Kristiansen, 25–35. Cambridge: Cambridge University Press.

Markoe, Glenn E. 2000. *Phoenicians*. Berkeley: University of California Press.

Markoff, John. 1996. *Waves of Democracy*. Thousand Oaks, CA: Pine Forge Press.

Martin, William G. 1994. "The World-Systems Perspective in Perspective: Assessing the Attempt to Move Beyond Nineteenth Century Eurocentric Conceptions." *Review* 18 (2): 145–185.

———. 2005. "Global Movements before 'Globalization': Black Movements as World-Historical Movements." *Review* 28 (1): 7–28.

Martin, William G., Tuba Agartan, Caleb M. Bush, Woo-Young Choi, Tu Huynh, Foad Kalouche, Eric Mielants, and Rochelle Morris. 2008. *Making Waves: Worldwide Social Movements, 1750–2005*. Boulder, CO: Paradigm Publishers.

Marx, Karl. 1967 [1887]. "Genesis of Industrial Capital." Chapter 21 in *Capital*. Vol. 1. Edited by Frederic Engels, translated from the 3rd German edition by Samuel Moore and Edward Aveling. New York: International Publishers.

Maryanski, Alexandra, and Jonathan Turner. 1992. *The Social Cage*. Palo Alto, CA: Stanford University Press.

Mathien, Frances. 1986. "External Contacts and the Chaco Anasazi." In *Ripples in the Chichimec Sea: New Considerations of Southwestern-Mesoamerican Interactions*, edited by Frances Mathien and Randall McGuire, 220–242. Carbondale: Southern Illinois University Press.

Mathien, Frances Joan, and Randall McGuire, eds. 1986. *Ripples in the Chichimec Sea: New Considerations of Southwestern-Mesoamerican Interactions*. Carbondale: Southern Illinois University Press.

McCormick, Thomas J. 1989. *America's Half Century: United States Foreign Policy in the Cold War*. Baltimore: Johns Hopkins University Press.

McDermott, Kevin, and Jeremy Agnew. 1997. *The Comintern: A History of International Communism from Lenin to Stalin*. New York: St. Martin's Press.

Mc Elvaine, Robert. 2001. *Eve's Seed*. New York: McGraw-Hill.

McGrew, William C. 1992. *Chimpanzee Material Culture*. Cambridge: Cambridge University Press.

McGuire, Randall H. 1980. "The Mesoamerican Connection in the Southwest." *Kiva* 46 (1–2): 3–38.

———. 1986. "Economies and Modes of Production in the Prehistoric Southwestern Periphery." In *Ripples in the Chichimec Sea: New Considerations of Southwestern-Mesoamerican Interactions*, edited by Frances Mathien and Randall McGuire, 243–269. Carbondale: Southern Illinois University Press.

———. 1989. "The Greater Southwest as a Periphery of Mesoamerica." In *Centre and Periphery: Comparative Studies in Archaeology*, edited by Timothy Champion, 40–66. London: Unwin.

———. 1992. *A Marxist Archaeology*. New York: Academic.

———. 1996. "The Limits of World-Systems Theory for the Study of Prehistory." In *Pre-Columbian World-Systems*, edited by Peter N. Peregrine and Gary M. Feinman, 51–64. Monographs in World Archaeology, No. 26. Madison, WI: Prehistory Press.

McKillop, Heather I. 2005. *In Search of Maya Sea Traders*. College Station: Texas A&M University Press.

McLuhan, Marshall. 1969. *The Gutenberg Galaxy*. New York: Signet.

McNeill, John R., and William H. McNeill. 2003. *The Human Web*. New York: Norton.

McNeill, William H. 1963. *The Rise of the West: A History of the Human Community*. Chicago: University of Chicago Press.

———. 1964. *Europe's Steppe Frontier, 1500–1800*. Chicago: University of Chicago Press.

———. 1976. *Plagues and Peoples*. Garden City, NY: Doubleday.

———. 1982. *The Pursuit of Power*. Chicago: University of Chicago Press.

———. 1987. *Prehistory to 1500*. Vol. 1 of *A History of the Human Community*. 2nd ed. Englewood Cliffs, NJ: Prentice Hall.

———. 1990. "*The Rise of the West* after Twenty-Five Years." *Journal of World History* 1:1–21.

———. 1992. *The Global Condition: Conquerors, Catastrophes, and Community*. Princeton, NJ: Princeton University Press.

Mead, George. 1972. *Mind, Self and Society*. Chicago: University of Chicago Press.

Meadows, Donnela H., Jorgen Randers, and Dennis Meadows. 2004. *The Limits to Growth: The 30-Year Update*. White River Junction, VT: Chelsea Green Publishers.

Meilink-Roelofsz, M.A.P. 1962. *Asian Trade and European Influence in the Indonesian Archipelago between 1500 and about 1630*. The Hague: Martinus Nijhoff.

Meillassoux, Claude. 1981. *Maidens, Meal and Money: Capitalism and the Domestic Community*. Cambridge: Cambridge University Press.
Melko, Matthew. 1995. "The Nature of Civilizations." In *Civilizations and World-Systems: Two Approaches to the Study of World-Historical Change*, edited by Stephen K. Sanderson, 11–31. Walnut Creek, CA: Altamira Press.
Melko, Matthew, and Leighton R. Scott, eds. 1987. *The Boundaries of Civilizations in Space and Time*. Lanham, MD: University Press of America.
Mies, Maria. 1986. *Patriarchy and Accumulation on a World Scale*. London: Zed Books.
Mills, C. Wright. 1959. *The Power Elite*. New York: Oxford University Press.
Mintz, Sidney. 1974. *Caribbean Transformations*. Baltimore: Johns Hopkins University Press.
———. 1985. *Sweetness and Power: The Place of Sugar in Modern History*. New York: Viking.
Misra, Joya, and Terry Boswell. 1997. "Dutch Hegemony during the Age of Mercantilism." *Acta Politica: International Journal of Political Science* 32 (2): 174–209.
Mitchell, Donald, and Leland Donald. 1985. "Some Economic Aspects of Tlingit, Haida and Tsimshian Slavery." *Research in Economic Anthropology* 7:19–35.
Mithen, Steven. 1996. *Prehistory of the Mind*. London: Thames and Hudson.
Modelski, George. 1964. "Kautilya: Foreign Policy and International System in the Ancient Hindu World." *American Political Science Review* 58 (3): 549–560.
———. 2003. *World Cities: –3000 to 2000*. Washington, DC: Faros 2000.
———. 2005. "Long Term Trends in World Politics." *Journal of World-Systems Research* 11 (2): 195–206.
Modelski, George, and William R. Thompson. 1996. *Leading Sectors and World Powers: The Coevolution of Global Politics and Economics*. Columbia: University of South Carolina Press.
Moghadam, Valentine. 2005. *Globalizing Women: Transnational Feminist Networks*. Baltimore: Johns Hopkins University Press.
Mommsen, Wolfgang J. 2001. "Introduction." In *The International Impact of the Boer War*, edited by Keith Wilson, 1–7. New York: Palgrave.
Monbiot, George. 2003. *Manifesto for a New World Order*. New York: New Press.
Moore, Barrington. 1966. *Social Origins of Democracy and Dictatorship*. Boston: Beacon Press.
Morris, Colin. 2000. *Discovery of the Individual 1050–1200*. Toronto: University of Toronto Press.
Morris, Ian. 2010. *Why the West Rules—For Now*. New York: Farrar, Straus and Giroux.
———. 2013. *The Measure of Civilization*. Princeton, NJ: Princeton University Press.
Moseley, Katherine P. 1992. "Caravel and Caravan: West Africa and the World-Economies ca. 900–1900 A.D." *Review* 15 (3): 523–555.
Mouer, L. Daniel. 1986. "DMZ or Deer Park? Buffer Zones as Boundary Systems." Manuscript on file, Virginia Department of Historic Resources, Richmond.
Murphy, Craig. 1994. *International Organization and Industrial Change: Global Governance since 1850*. New York: Oxford University Press.
Murra, John Victor. 1980 [1955]. *The Economic Organization of the Inca State*. Research in Economic Anthropology, Supplement 1. Greenwich, CT: Jai Press.
Myrdal, Gunnar. 1971. *Economic Theory and Underdeveloped Regions*. New York: Harper and Row.
Nascimento-Rodriguez, Jorge, and Tessaleno Devezas. 2007. *Pioneers of Globalization: Why the Portuguese Surprised the World*. Lisbon, Portugal: Centro Atlantico.
Nassaney, Michael S., and Kenneth E. Sassaman, eds. 1995. *Native American Interactions: Multiscalar Analyses and Interpretations in the Eastern Woodlands*. Knoxville: University of Tennessee Press.
Needham, Joseph. 1959. *Mathematics and the Sciences of the Heavens and the Earth*. Vol. 3 of *Science and Civilization in China*. Cambridge: Cambridge University Press.
Nissen, Hans J. 1988. *The Early History of the Ancient Near East, 9000–2000 B.C.* Chicago: University of Chicago Press.
O'Brien, Patricia J. 1992. "The Routes and Subsystems of Cahokia's World-System." *Review* 15 (3): 389–417.
O'Conner, James. 1989. "Uneven and Combined Development and Ecological Crisis." *Race and Class* 30 (3): 1–11.
Oded, Bustenay. 1979. *Mass Deportations and Deportees in the Neo-Assyrian Empire*. Wiesbaden, Germany: Dr. Ludwig Reichert Verlag.
O'Kelly, Charlotte, and Larry Carney. 1986. *Women and Men in Society*. 2nd ed. Belmont, CA: Wadsworth.
Ong, Walter. 1988. *Orality and Literacy*. London: Routledge.
Oppenheim, A. Leo. 1957. "A Bird's-Eye View of Mesopotamian Economic History." In *Trade and Market in the Early Empires*, edited by K. Polanyi, C. M. Arensberg, and H. E. Pearson, 27–37. Chicago: Regnery.
———. 1969. "Comment on Diakonoff's 'Main Features of the Economy.' " *École Practique des Hautes Études—Sorbonne, Congrès at Colloques* 10 (3): 33–40.

———. 1974. *Essays on Mesopotamian Civilization: Selected Papers of A. Leo Oppenheim*. Edited by Erica Reiner and Johannes Renger. Chicago: University of Chicago Press.

O'Rourke, Kevin, and Jeffrey Williamson. 2000. *Globalization and History*. Cambridge, MA: MIT Press.

Padden, R. C. 1967. *The Hummingbird and the Hawk: Conquest and Sovereignty in the Valley of Mexico, 1503–1541*. Columbus: Ohio State University Press.

Pagden, Anthony. 2008. *Worlds at War*. New York: Random House.

Pailes, Richard A., and Joseph W. Whitecotton. 1979. "The Greater Southwest and Mesoamerican 'World' System: An Exploratory Model of Frontier Relationships." In *The Frontier: Comparative Studies*, Vol. 2, edited by W. W. Savage and S. I. Thompson, 105–121. Norman: University of Oklahoma Press.

Palat, Ravi Arvind, ed. 1993. *Pacific-Asia and the Future of the World-System*. Westport, CT: Greenwood Press.

Parenti, Michael. 1992. *Make Believe Media*. New York: St. Martin's Press.

Parry, J. H. 1966. *The Establishment of European Hegemony, 1415–1715*. New York: Harper and Row.

Parsons, Talcott. 1966. *Societies: Evolutionary and Comparative Perspectives*. Englewood Cliffs, NJ: Prentice Hall.

———. 1971. *The System of Modern Societies*. Englewood Cliffs, NJ: Prentice Hall.

Patomäki, Heikki. 2008. *The Political Economy of Global Security*. London: Routledge.

Patomäki, Heikki, and Teivo Teivainen. 2008. "Researching Global Political Parties." In *Global Party Formation*, edited by Katarina Sehm-Patomäki and Marko Ulvila, 92–113. London: Zed Press.

Patterson, Thomas C. 1990. "Processes in the Formation of Ancient World-Systems." *Dialectical Anthropology* 15 (1): 1–18.

———. 1997. *The Inca Empire: The Formation and Disintegration of a Pre-Capitalist State*. New York: Berg.

Pauketat, Timothy R. 2009. *Cahokia*. New York: Viking.

Pendergast, James F. 1991. "The Massawomeck: Raiders and Traders into the Chesapeake Bay in the Seventeenth Century." *Transactions of American Philosophical Society*, Vol. 81, Part 2. Philadelphia: The American Philosophical Society.

Peregrine, Peter N. 1991. "Prehistoric Chiefdoms on the American Mid-continent: A World-System Based on Prestige Goods." In *Core/Periphery Relations in Precapitalist Worlds*, edited by Christopher Chase-Dunn and Thomas D. Hall, 193–211. Boulder, CO: Westview Press.

———. 1992. *Mississippian Evolution: A World-System Perspective*. Monographs in World Archaeology, No. 9. Madison, WI: Prehistory Press.

———. 1995. "Networks of Power: The Mississippian World-System." In *Native American Interactions*, edited by M. Nassaney and K. Sassaman, 132–143. Knoxville: University of Tennessee Press.

Peregrine, Peter N., and Gary M. Feinman. 1996. *Pre-Columbian World-Systems*. Monographs in World Archaeology, No. 26. Madison, WI: Prehistory Press.

Perrson, Johnny. 2005. "Escaping a Closed Universe: World-System Crisis, Regional Dynamics and the Rise of Aegean Palatial Society." In *Hegemonic Declines*, edited by Jonathan Friedman and Christopher Chase-Dunn, 7–50. Boulder, CO: Paradigm Publishers.

PEW Global Attitudes Project. 2008. "Global Public Opinion in the Bush Years (2001–2008)." http://www.pewglobal.org/2008/12/18/global-public-opinion-in-the-bush-years-2001-2008/.

Pirenne, Henri. 1937. *Economic and Social History of Medieval Europe*. Translated by I. E. Clegg. New York: Harcourt, Brace, and Jovanovich (orig. 1933. *Histoire du Moyen Age*, Vol. 8, H. Pirenne, G. Cohen, and H. Focillon, eds.).

———. 1953. "Stages in the Social History of Capitalism." In *Class, Status and Power: A Reader in Social Stratification*, edited by R. Bendix and S. Lipset, 501–517. Glencoe, IL: Free Press.

———. 1980. *Mohammed and Charlemagne*. Totowa, NJ: Barnes & Noble (French original 1939).

Podobnik, Bruce. 2006. *Global Energy Shifts*. Philadelphia: Temple University Press.

Polanyi, Karl. 1957a. "Marketless Trading in Hammurabi's Time." In *Trade and Market in the Early Empires*, edited by Karl Polanyi, Conrad M. Arensberg, and Harry W. Pearson, 12–26. Chicago: Regnery.

———. 1957b. "Aristotle Discovers the Economy." In *Trade and Market in the Early Empires*, edited by Karl Polanyi, Conrad M. Arensberg, and Harry W. Pearson, 64–96. Chicago: Regnery.

———. 1977. *The Livelihood of Man*. Edited by Harry W. Pearson. New York: Academic Press.

———. 2001 [1944]. *The Great Transformation: The Political and Economic Origins of Our Time*. Boston: Beacon Press.

Polanyi, Karl, Conrad M. Arensberg, and Harry W. Pearson, eds. 1957. *Trade and Market in the Early Empires*. Chicago: Regnery.

Pomeranz, Kenneth. 2000. *The Great Divergence: Europe, China and the Making of the Modern World Economy*. Princeton, NJ: Princeton University Press.

Pomeranz, Kenneth, and Steven Topik. 2006. *The World That Trade Created*. New York: M. E. Sharpe.

Postgate, J. N. 1992. *Early Mesopotamia: Society and Economy at the Dawn of History*. London, New York: Routledge.

Potter, Stephen R. 1993. *Commoners, Tribute and Chiefs: The Development of Algonquian Culture in the Potomac Valley*. Charlottesville: University of Virginia Press.

Price, T. Douglas. 1991. "The Mesolithic of Northern Europe." *Annual Review of Anthropology* 20:211–233.

Price, T. Douglas, and James A. Brown, eds. 1985. *Prehistoric Hunter-Gatherers: The Emergence of Cultural Complexity*. New York: Academic Press.

Quigley, Carroll. 1979. *The Evolution of Civilizations*. Indianapolis, IN: Liberty Press.

———. 1981. *The Anglo-American Establishment*. New York: Books in Focus.

Radding, Charles. 1985. *A World Made by Men*. Chapel Hill: University of North Carolina Press.

Radin, Paul. 1959. *Primitive Religion*. New York: Dover.

Ransom, Roger L. 2005. *The Confederate States of America: What Might Have Been*. New York: W. W. Norton.

Rasler, Karen, and William R. Thompson. 1994. *The Great Powers and Global Struggle, 1490–1990*. Lexington: University of Kentucky Press.

Ratnagar, Shereen. 1981. *Encounters: The Westerly Trade of the Harappa Civilization*. Delhi: Oxford University Press.

Rediker, Marcus. 2007. *The Slave Ship: A Human History*. New York: Viking.

Redman, Charles L. 1978. *The Rise of Civilization*. New York: W. H. Freeman.

———. 1999. *Human Impact on Ancient Environments*. Tucson: University of Arizona Press.

Reed, John. 1919. *Ten Days That Shook the World*. New York: Boni and Liveright.

Reese, Ellen. 2005. *The Backlash against Welfare Mothers*. Berkeley: University of California Press.

Reese, Ellen, Mark Herkenrath, Chris Chase-Dunn, Rebecca Giem, Erika Guttierrez, Linda Kim, and Christine Petit. 2007. "North-South Contradictions and Convergences at the World Social Forum." In *Globalization, Conflict and Inequality: The Persisting Divergence of the Global North and South*, edited by Rafael Reuveny and William R. Thompson, 341–366. Malden, MA: Blackwell.

Reeves-Sanday, Peggy. 1981. *Female Power and Male Dominance*. Cambridge: Cambridge University Press.

Reifer, Thomas E. 2002. "Globalization and the National Security State Corporate Complex (NSSCC) in the Long Twentieth Century." In *The Modern/Colonial Capitalist World-System in the 20th Century*, edited by Ramon Grosfoguel and Margarita Rodriguez, 3–20. Westport, CT: Greenwood Press.

Reitan, Ruth. 2007. *Global Activism*. London: Routledge.

Renfrew, Colin R. 1975. "Trade as Action at a Distance: Questions of Integration and Communication." In *Ancient Civilization and Trade*, edited by J. A. Sabloff and C. C. Lamborg-Karlovsky, 3–59. Albuquerque: University of New Mexico Press.

———. 1977. "Alternative Models for Exchange and Spatial Distribution." In *Exchange Systems in Prehistory*, edited by T. J. Earle and T. Ericson, 71–90. New York: Academic Press.

———. 1986. "Introduction: Peer Polity Interaction and Socio-political Change." In *Peer Polity Interaction and Socio-political Change*, edited by C. Renfrew and John F. Cherry, 1–18. Cambridge: Cambridge University Press.

———. 1987. *Archaeology and Language: The Puzzle of Indo-European Origins*. London: Cape.

Renfrew, Colin, and Paul Bahn. 1991. *Archaeology: Theories, Methods and Practice*. New York: Thames and Hudson.

Renfrew, Colin, and John F. Cherry, eds. 1986. *Peer Polity Interaction and Socio-political Change*. Cambridge: Cambridge University Press.

———. 1987. *Archaeology and Language: The Puzzle of Indo-European Origins*. London: Cape.

Rennstich, Joachim K. 2001. "The Future of Great Power Rivalries." In *New Theoretical Directions for the 21st Century World-System*, edited by Wilma Dunaway. New York: Greenwood Press.

———. 2004. "The Phoenix Cycle: Global Leadership Transition in a Long-Wave Perspective." In *Hegemony, Globalization and Anti-systemic Movements*, edited by Thomas E. Reifer. Boulder, CO: Paradigm.

Revere, Robert B. 1957. "'No Man's Coast': Ports of Trade in the Eastern Mediterranean." In *Trade and Market in the Early Empires*, edited by Karl Polanyi, Conrad M. Arensberg, and Harry W. Pearson, 38–63. Chicago: Henry Regnery.

Rhee, Song Nai. 1981. "Sumerian City-States." In *The City-State in Five Cultures*, edited by Robert Griffeth and Carol G. Thomas, 1–30. Santa Barbara, CA: ABC-Clio.

Ringrose, David R. 2001. *Expansion and Global Interaction, 1200–1700*. New York: Longman.

Ritchie, W. A., and D. W. Dragoo. 1959. "The Eastern Dispersal of Adena." *American Antiquity* 25:43–50.

Ritter, Eric. 1991. "A Study of Glass Trade Beads from Some Protohistoric Wintu Villages in the Northern Sacramento Valley." In Sundahl and Clewitt 1991, Appendix 1.

Roberts, J. Timmons, and Bradley C. Parks. 2007. *A Climate of Injustice: Global Inequality, North-South Politics and Climate Policy*. Cambridge, MA: MIT Press.

Robinson, William I. 2004. *A Theory of Global Capitalism*. Baltimore: Johns Hopkins University Press.

———. 2008. *Latin American and Global Capitalism: A Critical Globalization Perspective*. Baltimore: Johns Hopkins University Press.
Rodinson, Maxime. 1981. *Islam and Capitalism*. Austin: University of Texas Press.
Rodney, Walter. 1974. *How Europe Underdeveloped Africa*. Washington, DC: Howard University Press.
Rose, Stephen J. 2007. *The American Profile Poster*. New York: New Press.
Rostovzeff, Mikhail. 1941. *Social and Economic History of the Hellenistic World*. 2 vols. London: Oxford University Press.
———. 1960 [1927]. *Rome*. New York: Oxford University Press.
Rountree, Helen C. 1989. *The Powhatan Indians of Virginia: Their Traditional Culture*. Norman: University of Oklahoma Press.
———. 1990. *Pocahontas's People: The Powhatan Indians of Virginia through Four Centuries*. Norman: University of Oklahoma Press.
———, ed. 1993a. *Powhatan Foreign Relations, 1500–1722*. Charlottesville: University of Virginia Press.
———. 1993b. "The Powhatans and Other Woodland Indians as Travelers." In Rountree 1993a, 21–52.
———. 1993c. "Summary and Implications." In Rountree 1993a, 206–228.
Rountree, Helen C., and Thomas E. Davidson. 1997. *Eastern Shore Indians of Virginia and Maryland*. Charlottesville: University of Virginia Press.
Rowlands, Michael, Mogens Larsen, and Kristian Kristiansen, eds. 1987. *Centre and Periphery in the Ancient World*. Cambridge: Cambridge University Press.
Rozman, Gilbert. 1973. *Urban Networks in Ching China and Tokugawa Japan*. Princeton, NJ: Princeton University Press.
Rueschmeyer, Dietrich, Evelyne Huber Stephens, and John D. Stephens. 1992. *Capitalist Development and Democracy*. Chicago: University of Chicago Press.
Sabloff, Jeremy, and William J. Rathje. 1975. *A Study of Changing Pre-Columbian Commercial Systems*. Cambridge: Peabody Museum of Archaeology and Ethnology, Harvard University.
Sachs, Jeffrey D. 2005. *The End of Poverty: Economic Possibilities for Our Time*. New York: Penguin Press.
Sack, Robert. 1980. *Conceptions of Space in Social Thought*. Minneapolis: University of Minnesota.
———. 1992. *Place, Modernity and the Consumer's World*. Baltimore: Johns Hopkins University Press.
Sahlins, Marshall. 1961. "The Segmentary Lineage: An Organization of Predatory Expansion." *American Anthropologist* 63 (2): 322–345.
———. 1963. "Poor Man, Rich Man, Big-Man, Chief: Political Types in Melanesia and Polynesia." *Comparative Studies in Society and History* 5 (3): 285–303.
———. 1968. *Tribesmen*. Englewood Cliffs, NJ: Prentice Hall.
———. 1972. *Stone Age Economics*. Chicago: Aldine.
———. 1985. *Islands of History*. Chicago: University of Chicago Press.
Sahlins, Marshall, and Elman R. Service, eds. 1960. *Evolution and Culture*. Ann Arbor: University of Michigan Press.
Sanderson, Stephen K. 1990. *Social Evolutionism: A Critical History*. Cambridge, MA: Blackwell.
———. 1994a. "Civilizations and World-Systems: An Introduction." *Comparative Civilizations Review* 30 (Spring): 2–7.
———. 1994b. "Expanding World Commercialization: The Link between World-Systems and Civilizations." *Comparative Civilizations Review* 30 (Spring): 91–103.
———. 1994c. "The Transition from Feudalism to Capitalism: The Theoretical Significance of the Japanese Case." *Review* 27 (1): 15–55.
———. 1995a. *Social Transformations*. London: Basil Blackwell.
———, ed. 1995b. *Civilizations and World Systems*. Walnut Creek, CA: Altamira Press.
———. 2001. *The Evolution of Human Sociality*. Lanham, MD: Rowman and Littlefield.
———. 2007. *Evolutionism and Its Critics*. Boulder, CO: Paradigm Publishers.
Santiago-Valles, Kelvin. 2005. "World-Historical Ties among 'Spontaneous' Slave Rebellions in the Atlantic." *Review* 28 (1): 51–84.
Santos, Boaventura de Sousa. 2006. *The Rise of the Global Left*. London: Zed Press.
Sassen, Saskia. 2001. *The Global City: New York, London, Tokyo*. Princeton, NJ: Princeton University Press.
———. 2006. *Territory, Authority, Rights: From Medieval to Global Assemblages*. Princeton, NJ: Princeton University Press.
Scheidel, Walter, and Ian Morris. 2009. *The Dynamics of Ancient Empires*. New York: Oxford University Press.
Schivelbusch, Wolfgang. 1986. *The Railway Journey*. Berkeley: University of California Press.
Schmandt-Besserat, Denise. 1992. *Before Writing*. Austin: University of Texas Press.

Schneider, Jane. 1977. "Was There a Pre-capitalist World-System?" *Peasant Studies* 6 (1): 20–29. Reprinted in *Core/Periphery Relations in Precapitalist Worlds*, ed. Christopher Chase-Dunn and Thomas D. Hall (Boulder, CO: Westview Press, 1991), 45–66.

Schortman, Edward M., and Patricia A. Urban. 1987. "Modeling Interregional Interaction in Prehistory." In *Advances in Archeological Method and Theory*, Vol. 11, 37–95. New York: Academic Press.

———, eds. 1992. *Resources, Power, and Interregional Interaction*. New York: Plenum.

Schulze, Hagan. 1998. *States, Nations and Nationalism*. Cambridge, MA: Blackwell.

Schumpeter, Joseph. 1939. *Business Cycles*. Vol. 1. New York: McGraw-Hill.

———. 1951. *Imperialism; Social Classes: Two Essays by Joseph Schumpeter*. New York: Meridian Books.

Schurz, W. L. 1959. *The Manila Galleon*. New York: E. P. Dutton.

Schwartzberg, Joseph E. 2003. "Entitlement Quotients as a Vehicle for United Nations Reform." *Global Governance* 9 (1): 81–115.

Scott, James. 1990. *Domination and the Arts of Resistance*. New Haven, CT: Yale University Press.

Seaman, Gary, ed. 1989. *Ecology and Empire: Nomads in the Cultural Evolution of the Old World*. Los Angeles: Ethnographics Press, Center for Visual Anthropology, University of Southern California.

Seaman, Gary, and Daniel Marks, eds. 1991. *Rulers from the Steppe: State Formation on the Eurasian Periphery*. Los Angeles: Ethnographics Press, Center for Visual Anthropology, University of Southern California.

Segall, Marshall, Pierre Dasen, John Berry, and Ype Poortinga. 1999. *Human Behavior in Global Perspective*. 2nd ed. Boston: Allyn and Bacon.

Sehm-Patomäki, Katarina, and Marko Ulvila, eds. 2008. *Global Party Formation*. London: Zed Press.

Sennett, Richard. 1977. *The Fall of Public Man*. New York: Vintage.

———. 1990. *Conscience of the Eye*. New York: Alfred A. Knopf.

Service, Elman R. 1971. *Cultural Evolutionism: Theory and Practice*. New York: Holt, Reinhart and Winston.

———. 1975. *The Origins of the State and Civilization*. New York: Norton.

Sever, Tom. 1998. "Chaco Canyon Prehistoric Roadways." May 12. http://www.ghcc.msfc.nasa.gov/archeology/chaco_compare.html.

Shannon, Thomas R. 1996. *An Introduction to the World-System Perspective*. 2nd ed. Boulder, CO: Westview Press.

Sherratt, Andrew G. 1993a. "What Would a Bronze-Age World System Look Like? Relations between Temperate Europe and the Mediterranean in Later Prehistory." *Journal of European Archaeology* 1 (2): 1–57.

———. 1993b. "Core, Periphery and Margin: Perspectives on the Bronze Age." In *Development and Decline in the Mediterranean Bronze Age*, edited by C. Mathers and S. Stoddart, 335–345. Sheffield: Sheffield Academic Press.

Shiba, Yoshinobu. 1970. *Commerce and Society in Sung China*. Ann Arbor: University of Michigan Center for Chinese Studies.

Shiva, Vandana. 2005. *Earth Democracy*. Boston: South End Press.

Shreeve, James. 1995. *Neanderthal Enigma*. New York: Avon.

Silver, Beverly J. 2003. *Forces of Labor: Workers' Movements and Globalization since 1870*. Cambridge: Cambridge University Press.

Silverberg, Robert. 1985. *Gilgamesh the King*. New York: Bantam.

Singer, J. David, and Melvin Small. 1972. *The Wages of War, 1816–1965: A Statistical Handbook*. New York: John Wiley.

Sjoberg, Gideon. 1960. *The Preindustrial City*. Glencoe, IL: Free Press.

Sklair, Leslie. 2001. *The Transnational Capitalist Class*. Malden, MA: Blackwell.

Skocpol, Theda. 1992. *Protecting Soldiers and Mothers: The Political Origins of Social Policy in the United States*. Cambridge, MA: Belknap Press of Harvard University Press.

Smelser, Neil. 1959. "A Comparative View of Exchange Systems." *Economic Development and Cultural Change* 7:173–182.

Smil, Vaclav. 2008. *Energy in Nature and Society: General Energetics of Complex Systems*. Cambridge, MA: MIT Press.

Smith, Bruce D. 1992. *Rivers of Change: Essays on Early Agriculture in Eastern North America*. Washington, DC: Smithsonian.

Smith, Jackie. 2008. *Social Movements for Global Democracy*. Baltimore: Johns Hopkins University Press.

Smith, Jackie, Marina Karides, Marc Becker, Dorval Brunelle, Christopher Chase-Dunn, Donatella della Porta, Rosalba Icaza Garza, Jeffrey S. Juris, Lorenzo Mosca, Ellen Reese, Peter (Jay) Smithy, and Rolando Vazquez. 2008. *Global Democracy and the World Social Forums*. Boulder, CO: Paradigm Publishers.

Smith, Jackie, and Dawn Wiest. 2012. *Social Movements in the World-System*. New York: Russell Sage.

Smith, Michael E. 2008. *Aztec City-State Capitals*. Gainesville: University Press of Florida.

Smith, Peter B., and Michael Harris Bond. 1998. *Social Psychology across Cultures*. 2nd ed. Boston: Allyn and Bacon.

So, Alvin. 1986. *The South China Silk District: Local Historical Transformation and World-System Theory*. New York: State University of New York Press.

———. 1990. *Social Change and Development: Modernization, Dependency, and World-System Theory*. Newbury Park, CA: Sage.

So, Alvin, and Stephen W. K. Chiu. 1995. *East Asia and the World Economy*. Thousand Oaks, CA: Sage.

Sohn-Rethel, Alfred. 1978. *Intellectual and Manual Labor.* Atlantic Highlands, NJ: Humanities Press.

Solecki, Rose L., and Ralph S. Solecki. 1982. "Late Pleistocene/Early Holocene Cultural Traditions in the Zagros." In Young, Smith, and Mortenson 1982, 123–140.

Spence, Michael W. 1982. "The Social Context of Production and Exchange." In *Contexts for Prehistoric Exchange*, edited by J. E. Ericson and T. K. Earle, 173–198. New York: Academic Press.

Spielmann, Katherine A. 1989. "Colonists, Hunters, Farmers: Plains-Pueblo Interaction the Seventeenth Century." In *Archaeological and Historical Perspectives on the Spanish Borderlands*, edited by David Hurst Thomas, 101–113. Vol. 1 of *Columbian Consequences*. Washington, DC: Smithsonian Institution Press.

———, ed. 1991. *Farmers, Hunters, and Colonists: Interaction between the Southwest and the Southern Plains*. Tucson: University of Arizona Press.

Spriggs, Matthew. 1988. "The Hawaiian Transformation of Ancestral Polynesian Society: Conceptualizing Chiefly States." In *State and Society*, edited by John Gledhill, Barbara Bender, and Mogens Trolle Larsen, 57–73. London: Unwin Hyman.

Spring, Derek. 2001. "Russian Foreign Policy and the Boer War." In *The International Impact of the Boer War*, edited by Keith Wilson, 43–64. New York: Palgrave.

Spufford, Peter. 2003. *Power and Profit: The Merchant in Medieval Europe*. London: Thames and Hudson.

Stanish, Charles. 2003. *Ancient Titicaca: The Evolution of Complex Society in Southern Peru and Northern Bolivia*. Berkeley: University of California Press.

Stanovich, Keith. 2001. *How to Think Straight about Psychology.* 6th ed. Boston: Allyn and Bacon.

Stark, Barbara. 1986. "Perspectives on the Peripheries of Mesoamerica." In *Ripples in the Chichimec Sea: New Considerations of Southwestern-Mesoamerican Interactions*, edited by Frances Mathien and Randall McGuire, 270–290. Carbondale: Southern Illinois University Press.

Starr, Amory. 2000. *Naming the Enemy: Anti-Corporate Movements Confront Globalization*. London: Zed Press.

Stegner, Wallace. 2003 [1942]. *Mormon Country.* Lincoln: University of Nebraska Press.

Stein, Gil J. 1999. *Rethinking World-Systems: Diasporas, Colonies and Interaction in Uruk Mesopotamia*. Tucson: University of Arizona Press.

Stein, Stanley J., and Barbara H. Stein. 1970. *The Colonial Heritage of Latin America*. New York: Oxford University Press.

Steponaitis, Laurie C. 1983. *An Archaeological Study of the Patuxent Drainage*. Vol. 1. Maryland Historical Trust Manuscript Series #34.

Stevis, Dmitris, and Terry Boswell. 2008. *Globalization and Labor: Democratizing Global Governance*. Lanham, MD: Rowman and Littlefield.

Steward, Julian. 1938. *Basin-Plateau Aboriginal Sociopolitical Groups*. Bureau of American Ethnology, Bulletin 120. Washington, DC: Smithsonian Institution.

———. 1955. *The Theory of Culture Change: The Methodology of Multilinear Evolution*. Urbana: University of Illinois Press.

Stewart, R. Michael. 1989. "Trade and Exchange in Middle Atlantic Region Prehistory." *Archaeology of Eastern North America* 17:47–78.

———. 1994. "Late Archaic through Late Woodland Exchange in the Middle Atlantic Region." In *Prehistoric Exchange Systems in North America*, edited by Timothy Baugh and Jonathan Ericson, 73–98. New York: Plenum Press.

———. 2004. "Changing Patterns of Native American Trade in the Middle Atlantic Region and Chesapeake Watershed: A World Systems Perspective." *North American Archaeologist* 25 (4): 337–356.

Stiglitz, Joseph E. 2002. *Globalization and Its Discontents*. New York: Norton.

Stokes, Doug, and Sam Raphael. 2010. *Global Energy Security and American Hegemony*. Baltimore: Johns Hopkins University Press.

Stringer, Christopher, and Clive Gamble. 1993. *In Search of the Neanderthals*. New York: Thames and Hudson.

Struve, V. V. 1973 [1933]. "The Problem of the Genesis, Development and Disintegration of the Slave Societies in the Ancient Orient." In *Ancient Mesopotamia*, translated by Inna Levit and edited by I. M. Diakonoff, 17–69. Walluf bei Wiesbaden: Dr. Martin Sandig.

Sundahl, Elaine, and S. Edward Clewett. 1991. "Archaeological Investigations in the Salt Creek Drainage, Shasta County, CA." Reports of the Shasta College Archaeological Laboratory, Shasta College, Redding, CA.

Suter, Christian. 1992. *Debt Cycles in the World-Economy.* Boulder, CO: Westview Press.

———, ed. 2010. *Inequality beyond Globalization*. New Brunswick, NJ: Transaction Publishers.

Sworakowski, Witold S. 1965. *The Communist International and Its Front Organizations*. Stanford, CA: Hoover Institution on War, Revolution, and Peace.
Taagepera, Rein. 1978a. "Size and Duration of Empires: Systematics of Size." *Social Science Research* 7 (1): 108–127.
———. 1978b. "Size and Duration of Empires: Growth-Decline Curves, 3000 to 600 B.C." *Social Science Research* 7 (2): 180–196.
———. 1979. "Size and Duration of Empires: Growth-Decline Curves, 600 B.C. to 600 A.D." *Social Science History* 3 (3–4): 115–138.
Tainter, Joseph A. 1988. *The Collapse of Complex Societies*. Cambridge: Cambridge University Press.
Taylor, Peter. 1996. *The Way the Modern World Works: Global Hegemony to Global Impasse*. New York: Wiley.
Teggart, Frederick J. 1939. *Rome and China: A Study of Correlations in Historical Events*. Berkeley: University of California Press.
Thapar, Romila. 1980. "State Formation in Early India." *International Social Science Journal* 32 (4): 655–669.
Thomas, Keith. 1973. *Religion and the Decline of Magic*. Victoria: Penguin.
Thompson, William R. 1988. *On Global War: Historical-Structural Approaches to World Politics*. Columbia: University of South Carolina Press.
———. 1990. "Long Waves, Technological Innovation and Relative Decline." *International Organization* 44 (2): 201–233.
———. 1995. "Comparing World Systems: Systemic Leadership Succession and the Peloponnesian War Case." In *The Historical Evolution of the International Political Economy,* Vol. 1, edited by Christopher Chase-Dunn, 271–286. Aldershot, UK: Edward Elgar.
———. 2006. "Climate, Water, and Crisis in the Southwest Asian Bronze Age." *Nature and Culture* 1 (1): 88–132.
Thornton, Russell. 1986. *We Shall Live Again: The 1870 and 1890 Ghost Dance Movements as Demographic Revitalization*. Cambridge: Cambridge University Press.
Tilly, Charles. 1984. *Big Structures, Large Processes, Huge Comparisons*. New York: Russell Sage.
———. 1986. *The Contentious French*. Cambridge, MA: Harvard University Press.
———. 1990. *Coercion, Capital, and European States, AD 990–1990*. Cambridge, MA: Blackwell.
———. 1993. *European Revolutions, 1492–1992*. Cambridge, MA: Blackwell.
———. 2007. *Democracy*. New York: Cambridge University Press.
Toynbee, Arnold. 1947. *A Study of History*. Abridgement of volumes I-[X] by D. C. Somervell. New York: Oxford University Press.
Triandis, Harry. 1995. *Individualism and Collectivism*. Boulder, CO: Westview Press.
Trigger, Bruce G. 1990. "Maintaining Economic Equality in Opposition to Complexity: An Iroquoian Case Study." In *The Evolution of Political Systems*, edited by Steadman Upham, 119–145. Cambridge: Cambridge University Press.
Tuan, Yi-Fu. 1982. *Segmented Worlds and Self*. Minneapolis: University of Minnesota.
Turchin, Peter. 2003. *Historical Dynamics: Why States Rise and Fall*. Princeton, NJ: Princeton University Press.
———. 2005. *War and Peace and War: The Life Cycles of Imperial Nations*. New York: Pi Press.
Turchin, Peter, and Sergey A. Nefadov. 2009. *Secular Cycles*. Princeton, NJ: Princeton University Press.
Turner, E. Randolph III. 1978. "An Intertribal Deer Exploitation Buffer Zone for the Virginia Coastal Plain-Piedmont Regions." Archeological Society of Virginia, *Quarterly Bulletin* 32 (3): 42–48.
———. 1993. "Native American Protohistoric Interactions in the Powhatan Core Area." In Rountree 1993a, 76–93.
Turner, Jonathan H. 1995. *Macrodynamics: Toward a Theory on the Organization of Human Populations*. New Brunswick, NJ: Rutgers University Press.
———. 2000. *On the Origins of Human Emotion*. Palo Alto, CA: Stanford University Press.
———. 2003. *Human Institutions: A Theory of Societal Evolution*. Lanham, MD: Rowman and Littlefield.
Turner, Jonathan H., and Alexandra Maranski. 2005. *Incest: Origins of the Taboo*. Boulder, CO: Paradigm Publishers.
———. 2008. *On the Origins of Human Societies by Means of Natural Selection*. Boulder, CO: Paradigm Publishers.
Upham, Steadman. 1982. *Polities and Power: An Economic and Political History of the Western Pueblo*. New York: Academic Press.
———. 1986. "Imperialists, Isolationists, World Systems and Political Realities: Perspectives on Mesoamerican-Southwestern Interaction." In *Ripples in the Chichimec Sea: New Considerations of Southwestern-Mesoamerican Interactions*, edited by Frances Mathien and Randall McGuire, 205–219. Carbondale: Southern Illinois University Press.
———. 1990. *The Evolution of Political Systems: Sociopolitics in Small-Scale Sedentary Societies*. Cambridge: Cambridge University Press.

———. 1992. "Interaction and Isolation: The Empty Spaces in Panregional Political and Economic Systems." In *Resources, Power, and Interregional Interaction*, edited by Edward Schortman and Patricia Urban, 139–152. New York: Plenum Press.

Upham, Steadman, Gary Feinman, and Linda Nicholas. 1992. "New Perspectives on the Southwest and Highland Mesoamerica: A Macroregional Approach." *Review* 15 (3): 427–451.

Upham, Steadman, Kent G. Lightfoot, and Roberta A. Jewett, eds. 1989. *The Sociopolitical Structure of Prehistoric Southwestern Societies*. Boulder, CO: Westview Press.

van de Mieroop, Marc. 1999. *The Ancient Mesopotamian City*. New York: Oxford University Press.

Van der Pijl, Kees. 1984. *The Making of an Atlantic Ruling Class*. London: Verso.

van der Veer, René, and Jaan Valsiner. 1991. *Understanding Vygotsky*. Cambridge, MA: Blackwell.

Veenhof, K. R. 1995. "Kanesh, an Assyrian Colony in Anatolia." In *Civilizations of the Ancient Near East*, edited by J. M. Sassen, 859–871. New York: Scribner.

Vehik, Susan C., and Timothy G. Baugh. 1994. "Prehistoric Plains Trade." In Baugh and Ericson 1994, 249–274.

Viraphol, Sarasin. 1977. *Tribute and Profit: Sino-Siamese Trade, 1652–1853*. Cambridge, MA: Harvard University Press.

Viviano, Frank. 2005. "China's Great Armada." *National Geographic*, July, 28–53.

Vygotsky, L. S. 1978. *Mind in Society: The Development of Higher Psychological Processes*. Edited by Michael Cole. Cambridge, MA: Harvard University Press.

Wade, Carole, and Carol Tarvis. 2004. *Invitation to Psychology*. Upper Saddle River, NJ: Prentice Hall.

Wagar, W. Warren. 1991. *The Next Three Futures: Paradigms of Things to Come*. New York: Praeger.

———. 1995. "Toward a Praxis of World Integration." *Journal of World-Systems Research* 2, 2.

———. 1999. *A Short History of the Future*. 3rd ed. Chicago: University of Chicago Press.

Wallerstein, Immanuel. 1972. "Three Paths of National Development in 16th Century Europe." *Studies in Comparative International Development* 7 (2): 95–101. http://www.springerlink.com/content/h57055663725107n/.

———. 1974a. "The Rise and Future Demise of the World Capitalist System: Concepts for Comparative Analysis." *Comparative Studies in Society and History* 16 (4): 387–415. Reprinted in Wallerstein, *The Capitalist World-Economy* (Cambridge: Cambridge University Press, 1979), chapter 1.

———. 1974b. *Capitalist Agriculture and the Origins of the European World-Economy in the Sixteenth Century*. Vol. 1 of *The Modern World-System*. New York: Academic. Republished 2011 by University of California Press.

———. 1976. "Three Stages of African Involvement into the World-Economy." In Peter C. W. Gutkind and Immanuel Wallerstein (eds.) Volume 1. Beverly Hills, CA: Sage.

———. 1979a. *The Capitalist World-Economy*. Cambridge: Cambridge University Press.

———. 1979b. "The Ottoman Empire and the Capitalist World-Economy." *Review* 2 (3): 389–400.

———. 1980. *Mercantilism and the Consolidation of the European World-Economy, 1600–1750*. Vol. 2 of *The Modern World-System*. New York: Academic Press. Republished 2011 by the University of California Press.

———. 1984. "The Three Instances of Hegemony in the History of the Capitalist World-Economy." In *Current Issues and Research in Macrosociology*, edited by Gerhard Lenski, 100–108. International Studies in Sociology and Social Anthropology, Vol. 37. Leiden: E. J. Brill.

———. 1989. *The Modern World-System III: The Second Era of Great Expansion of the Capitalist World-Economy, 1730–1840s*. New York: Academic Press. Republished 2011 by the University of California Press.

———. 1991. *Geopolitics and Geoculture*. Cambridge: Cambridge University Press.

———. 1995. "Hold the Tiller Firm: On Method and the Unit of Analysis." In *Civilizations and World-Systems: Two Approaches to the Study of World-Historical Change*, edited by Stephen K. Sanderson, 225–233. Walnut Creek, CA: Altamira Press.

———. 1998. *Utopistics: Or, Historical Choices of the Twenty-First Century*. New York: New Press.

———. 2000. *The Essential Wallerstein*. New York: New Press.

———. 2003. *The Decline of American Power*. New York: New Press.

———. 2004. *World-Systems Analysis*. Durham, NC: Duke University Press.

Wallerstein, Immanuel, and William G. Martin. 1979. "Peripheralization of Southern Africa, II: Changes in Household Structure and Labor-Force Formation." *Review* 3 (2): 193–207.

Walters, Pamela B. 1985. "Systems of Cities and Urban Primacy: Problems of Definition and Measurement." In *Urbanization in the World-Economy*, edited by Michael Timberlake, 63–120. New York: Academic Press.

Walton, John, and David Seddon. 1994. *Free Markets & Food Riots: The Politics of Global Adjustment*. Cambridge, MA: Blackwell.

Ward, Kathryn B., ed. 1990. *Women Workers and Global Restructuring*. Ithaca, NY: ILR Press.

———. 1993. "Reconceptualizing World-System Theory to Include Women." In *Theory on Gender/Feminism on Theory*, edited by Paula England, 43–68. New York: Aldine.

Webb, Malcolm C. 1975. "The Flag Follows Trade: An Essay on the Necessary Interaction of Military and Commercial Factors in State Formation." In *Ancient Civilization and Trade*, edited by Jeremy A. Sabloff and C. C. Lamberg-Karlovsky, 155–209. Albuquerque: University of New Mexico Press.

Weber, Max. 1958a. *The Protestant Ethic and the Spirit of Capitalism*. New York: Charles Scribner's Sons.

———. 1958b. *The City*. New York: Macmillan.

———. 1978. "Types of Legitimate Order: Convention and Law." In *Economy and Society*, Vol. 1, 33–36. Berkeley: University of California Press.

———. 1981. *General Economic History*. New Brunswick, NJ: Transaction Publishers.

Weigand, Phil C. 1992. "Central Mexico's Influences in Jalisco and Nayarit during the Classic Period." In *Resources, Power, and Interregional Interaction*, edited by Edward Schortman and Patricia Urban, 221–232. New York: Plenum Press.

Weigand, Phil C., and Garman Harbottle. 1993. "The Role of Turquoises in the Ancient Mesoamerican Trade Structure." In Ericson and Baugh 1993, 159–178.

Weigand, Phil C., Garman Harbottle, and Edward V. Sayre. 1977. "Turquoise Sources and Source Analysis: Mesoamerica and the Southwestern U.S.A." In *Exchange Systems in Prehistory*, edited by T. K. Earle and J. E. Ericson, 15–34. New York: Academic Press.

Weisler, Marshall, and Patrick Kirch. 1985. "The Structure of Settlement Space in a Polynesian Chiefdom: Kawela, Molokai, Hawaiian Islands." *New Zealand Journal of Archaeology* 7:129–158.

Wells, Peter S. 1980. *Culture Contact and Culture Change: Early Iron Age Central Europe and the Mediterranean World*. Cambridge: Cambridge University Press.

———. 1984. *Farms, Villages, and Cities: Commerce and Urban Origins in Late Prehistoric Europe*. Ithaca, NY: Cornell University Press.

———. 1992. "Tradition, Identity, and Change beyond the Roman Frontier." In *Resources, Power, and Interregional Interaction*, edited by Edward Schortman and Patricia Urban, 175–188. New York: Plenum Press.

Wertsch, H. 1985. *Vygotsky and the Social Formation of Mind*. Cambridge, MA: Harvard University Press.

Wheatley, Paul. 1975. "Satyanrta Suvarnadvipa: From Reciprocity to Redistribution in Ancient Southeast Asia." In *Ancient Civilization and Trade*, edited by J. A. Sabloff and C. C. Lamberg-Karlovski, 227–284. Albuquerque: University of New Mexico Press.

White, Tim D., Berhane Asfaw, Yonas Beyene, Yohannes Haile-Selassie, C. Owen Lovejoy, Gen Suwa, and Giday Wolde Gabriel. 2009. "*Ardipithecus ramidus* and the Paleobiology of Early Hominids." *Science*, October 2, 64, 75–86.

Whitecotton, Joseph W. 1992. "Culture and Exchange in Postclassic Oaxaca: A World-System Perspective." In *Resources, Power, and Interregional Interaction*, edited by Edward Schortman and Patricia Urban, 51–74. New York: Plenum Press.

Whitecotton, Joseph W., and Richard A. Pailes. 1986. "New World Precolumbian World Systems." In *Ripples in the Chichimec Sea: New Considerations of Southwestern-Mesoamerican Interactions*, edited by Frances Mathien and Randall McGuire, 183–204. Carbondale: Southern Illinois University Press.

Whiteneck, Daniel J. 1996. "The Industrial Revolution and Birth of the Anti-Mercantilist Idea: Epistemic Communities and Global Leadership." *Journal of World-Systems Research* 2 (1).

Whittaker, C. R. 1994. *Frontiers of the Roman Empire: A Social and Economic Study*. Baltimore: Johns Hopkins University Press.

Wilcox, David R. 1986a. "A Historical Analysis of the Problem of Southwestern-Mesoamerican Connections." In *Ripples in the Chichimec Sea: New Considerations of Southwestern-Mesoamerican Interactions*, edited by Frances Mathien and Randall McGuire, 9–44. Carbondale: Southern Illinois University Press.

———. 1986b. "The Tepiman Connection: A Model of Mesoamerican-Southwestern Interaction." In *Ripples in the Chichimec Sea: New Considerations of Southwestern-Mesoamerican Interactions*, edited by Frances Mathien and Randall McGuire, 135–154. Carbondale: Southern Illinois University Press.

———. 1991. "Changing Contexts of Pueblo Adaptations, A.D. 1250–1600." In *Farmers, Hunters, and Colonists: Interaction between the Southwest and the Southern Plains*, edited by Katherine A. Spielmann, 128–154. Tucson: University of Arizona Press.

Wilkinson, David O. 1987a. "The Connectedness Criterion and Central Civilization." In *The Boundaries of Civilizations in Space and Time*, edited by Matthew Melko and Leighton R. Scott, 25–29. Lanham, MD: University Press of America.

———. 1987b. "Central Civilization." *Comparative Civilizations Review* 17 (Fall): 31–59.

———. 1988. "Universal Empires: Pathos and Engineering." *Comparative Civilizations Review* 18 (Spring): 22–44.

———. 1991. "Cores, Peripheries and Civilizations." In *Core/Periphery Relations in Precapitalist Worlds*, edited by Christopher Chase-Dunn and Thomas D. Hall, 113–166. Boulder, CO: Westview Press.

———. 1992. "Cities, Civilizations and Oikumenes: I." *Comparative Civilizations Review* 27 (Fall): 51–87.
———. 1993a. "Cities, Civilizations and Oikumenes: II." *Comparative Civilizations Review* 28 (Spring): 41–72.
———. 1993b. "Civilizations, Cores, World-Economies and Oikumenes." In *The World System: 500 Years or 5000?*, edited by Andre Gunder Frank and Barry Gills, 221–246. London: Routledge.
———. 1995a. "Central Civilization." In *Civilizations and World-Systems: Two Approaches to the Study of World-Historical Change*, edited by Stephen K. Sanderson, 32–60. Walnut Creek, CA: Altamira Press.
———. 1995b. "Civilizations *are* World Systems!" In *Civilizations and World-Systems: Two Approaches to the Study of World-Historical Change*, edited by Stephen K. Sanderson, 234–246. Walnut Creek, CA: Altamira Press.
Wilkinson, Richard G. 1973. *Poverty and Progress: An Ecological Model of Economic Development*. London: Methuen.
Willard, Alice. 1993. "Gold, Islam and Camels: The Transformative Effects of Trade and Ideology." *Comparative Civilizations Review* 29 (Spring): 80–105.
Wilmer, Franke. 1993. *The Indigenous Voice in World Politics: Since Time Immemorial*. Newbury Park, CA: Sage.
Wilson, C. H. 1957. *Profit and Power: A Study of England and the Dutch Wars*. London: Longman.
Wilson, Keith, ed. 2001. *The International Impact of the Boer War*. New York: Palgrave.
Wilson, Peter. 1988. *The Domestication of the Human Species*. New Haven, CT: Yale University Press.
Winant, Howard. 2001. *The World Is a Ghetto: Race and Democracy since World War II*. New York: Basic Books.
Wissler, Clark. 1927. "The Culture Area Concept in Social Anthropology." *American Journal of Sociology* 32 (6): 881–891.
Wittfogel, Karl. 1957. *Oriental Despotism: A Comparative Study of Total Power*. New Haven, CT: Yale University Press.
Wolf, Eric R. 1959. *Sons of the Shaking Earth*. Chicago: University of Chicago.
———. 1969. *Peasant Wars of the 20th Century*. New York: Harper and Row.
———. 1982. *Europe and the People without History*. Berkeley: University of California Press.
Womack, John. 1970. *Zapata and the Mexican Revolution*. New York: Vintage.
Woolf, Greg. 1990. "World-Systems Analysis and the Roman Empire." *Journal of Roman Archaeology* 3:44–58.
World Bank. 2011. "World Development Indicators." http://data.worldbank.org/data-catalog/world-development-indicators.
Worthy, Edmund H. 1975. "Regional Control in the Southern Sung Salt Administration." In *Crisis and Prosperity in Sung China*, edited by John W. Haeger, 101–142. Tucson: University of Arizona Press.
Wright, Henry T. 1986. "The Evolution of Civilization." In *American Archaeology, Past and Future: A Celebration of the Society for American Archaeology, 1935–1985*, edited by David J. Meltzer, 323–365. Washington, DC: Smithsonian Institutional Press.
———. 1998. "Uruk States in Southwestern Iran." In *Archaic States*, edited by Gary Feinman and Joyce Marcus, 173–197. Santa Fe, NM: School of American Research.
———. 2006. "Atlas of Chiefdoms and Early States." *Structure and Dynamics* 1 (4). http://escholarship.org/uc/item/2r63702g#page-1.
Yasamee, Feroz. 2001. "Colmar Freiherr von der Goltz and the Boer War." In *The International Impact of the Boer War*, edited by Keith Wilson, 193–210. New York: Palgrave.
Yoffee, Norman. 1991. "The Collapse of Ancient Mesopotamian States and Civilization." In *The Collapse of Ancient States and Civilizations*, edited by Norman Yoffee and George Cowgill, 44–68. Tucson: University of Arizona Press.
———. 2005. *Myths of the Archaic State: Evolution of the Earliest Cities, States, and Civilizations*. Cambridge: Cambridge University Press.
Young, T. Cuyler, Jr., Philip E. L. Smith, and Peder Mortensen, eds. 1982. *The Hilly Flanks and Beyond: Essays in the Prehistory of Southwestern Asia*. Presented to Robert J. Braidwood. Studies in Ancient Oriental Civilization, Number 36. Chicago: Oriental Institute of the University of Chicago.
Yü, Ying-shih. 1967. *Trade and Expansion in Han China: A Study in the Structure of Sino-Barbarian Economic Relations*. Berkeley: University of California Press.
Zaccagnini, Carlo. 1987. "Aspects of Ceremonial Exchange in the Near East during the Late Second Millennium BC." In *Centre and Periphery in the Ancient World*, edited by Michael Rowlands, Mogens Larsen, and Kristian Kristiansen, 57–65. Cambridge: Cambridge University Press.
Zagarell, Allen. 1986. "Trade, Women, Class and Society in Ancient Western Asia." *Current Anthropology* 27 (5): 415–430.
Zelinsky, Wilbur. 1988. *Nation into State*. Chapel Hill: University of North Carolina Press.
Zevin, Robert B. 1971. "The Growth of Cotton Textile Production after 1815." In *The Reinterpretation of American Economic History*, edited by Robert W. Fogel and Stanley L. Engertnan. New York: Harper and Row.
Zinn, Howard. 1999. *A People's History of the United States*. New York: HarperCollins.
Zolberg, Aristide R. 1981. "Origins of the Modern World System: A Missing Link." *World Politics* 23 (2): 253–281.

Index

Note: f. indicates figure; t. indicates table.

About the Authors

Christopher Chase-Dunn is Distinguished Professor of Sociology and Director of the Institute for Research on World-Systems at the University of California–Riverside. His research considers cities and settlement systems in order to explain human sociocultural evolution. He also studies the relationship between the modern global political economy and earlier regional world-systems. Chase-Dunn is the founder and former editor of the *Journal of World-Systems Research*. Among many honors, in 2001 he was elected a Fellow of the American Association for the Advancement of Science.

Bruce Lerro has taught for 23 years as an adjunct professor of psychology at Dominican University, Golden Gate University, and Diablo Valley College. He is the author of two books about early human societies: *From Earthspirits to Sky-Gods: The Socio-Ecological Origins of Monotheism, Individualism, and Hyper-Abstract Reasoning* and *Power in Eden: The Emergence of Gender Hierarchies in the Ancient World*.